Fo

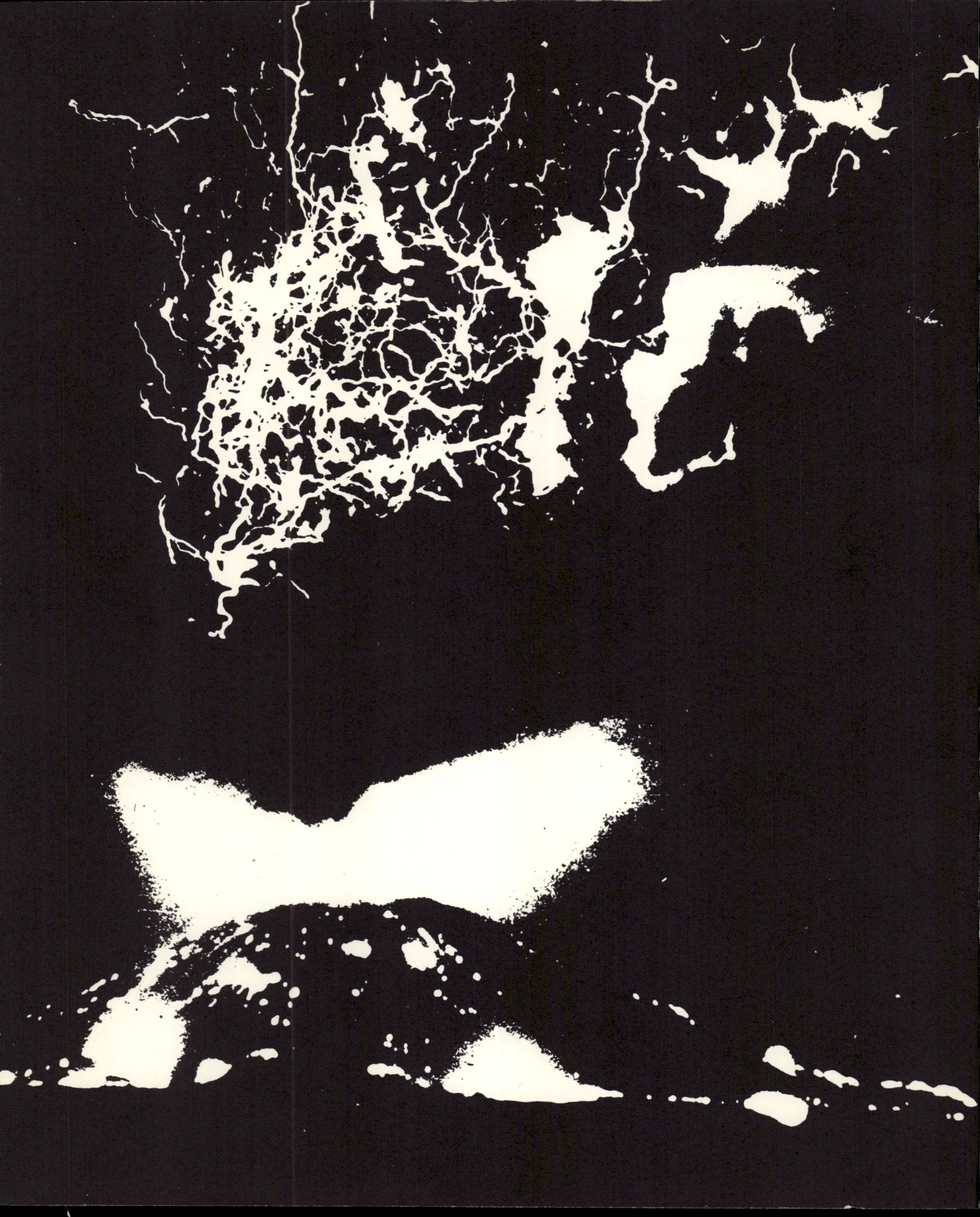

edited by Sir Vivian Fuchs

Forces of Nature

Martin Holdgate
P. J. Meade
John Latham
M. de Quervain
Valter Schytt
A. H. Bunting
J. Elston
Sir Norman Rowntree
E. A. Vincent
N. N. Ambraseys
W. J. Campbell

with 311 illustrations

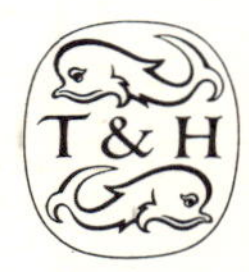

THAMES AND HUDSON · LONDON

Designed by Lawrence Edwards

Picture research by Sarah Waters

Filmset by Keyspools Limited, Golborne, Lancashire

Printed in Italy by Alfieri & Lacroix, Milan

Foreword by Sir Vivian Fuchs

The natural scene is compounded from the innumerable results of cause and effect; immutable, inevitable, in themselves unable to change. Only the complex interplay of countless factors obscures the sequence and confounds the human mind, understanding so little and left to wonder at so much. Since man appeared upon the earth he, like all living things, has been subject to the enormous and inexorable forces of nature which set the scene three thousand million years before life itself began. The successful rise of the human race during the last two million years has been due to the evolution of a brain which could increasingly anticipate events and plan to avoid untoward consequences. In this way man has achieved supremacy among living things and, indeed, survived many of nature's vicissitudes to which he would otherwise have succumbed. Yet in relation to the complex interplay of the physical forces which determine his environment, his capability is but puny. Many of these forces are now within his general understanding, but much remains to be learnt in almost every case. Perhaps the most we can say is that his knowledge, however incomplete, has removed the fears and superstitions with which primitive peoples invested the unknown.

In this book eleven authors, each an expert in his field, describe major physical forces which threaten or control our destiny. None is concerned with living matter, except to indicate the possible source of life itself from the action of natural energy – perhaps the flash of lightning – upon existing matter. The vagaries of the atmosphere in which we live, the extremes of climate and the sudden ferocity of natural events such as earthquakes or volcanic eruptions – these are the things with which we are concerned.

Some of them are sudden, brief and repetitive, others are long-term, insidious and fluctuating, producing changes which are less alarming, but in the end likely to have greater effect on the future of mankind. Everyone knows they should not shelter under a tree in a thunderstorm, but how many of us understand the implications of a small climatic change for the man who lives on a desert fringe? A volcano or an earthquake may destroy thousands within a few minutes, but the slow return to an ice age will only gradually displace or destroy nations.

Each author has sought to show the impact of his subject on the community of man, past and present, and to present an explanation of that particular natural force. In some cases it has been possible to demonstrate ways in which it can be put to use, in others only to explain how the potential effects can be avoided or ameliorated. Reading these chapters brings a realization of the often remarkable relationships between seemingly quite different events. The atmosphere is in delicate balance; continents and oceans, ice sheets and deserts, mountains, winds and solar radiation, all contribute their quota of control. A great volcanic eruption, itself perhaps heralded by earthquakes, can so cloud the skies with dust as to cut off part of the sun's radiation, changing the mean annual temperature, and thereby triggering other events. But the volcanoes and earthquakes are themselves only consequences of the earth's mobility. The internal heat derived from the breakdown of fissionable matter within the core causes convective currents to bring material to the surface, where it fractures the crust and slowly forces the continents apart, here and there releasing the pent forces from below.

Majestic in their age-long persistence through endless time, it is such forces which affect each generation of man as they are translated into sudden events, or result in creeping climatic variations. So the deserts and the polar ice caps expand or contract over thousands rather than millions of years, and result in local shorter alterations in temperature or rainfall in the marginal areas. It is these last which are so important, for they can be measured in tens or hundreds of years, and their effects on the ever-growing population can be directly seen in terms of crop failure, dying herds, famine and human misery.

Of all these forces, none can be controlled by human agency. Even if our growing knowledge was to make this possible, it is doubtful if we have, or could acquire, the wisdom to handle them for the general good. To precipitate artificially an earthquake to save one particular populated area could bring disaster to another; to alter the course of an ocean current, as by closing the Bering Strait, could also alter the climate of the Arctic regions, but with what unknown wider implications? Even inducing rain artificially to benefit one region means depriving another.

It may well be wiser to accept the broad interplay of natural forces, always learning better how to use them or to protect ourselves from them. To this end a new tool is already available in the form of man-made satellites. These we can use to monitor the changing pattern of events over the entire surface of the earth. Already, as we see in the last chapter, this is being done, and we may expect that ever-improving techniques will help to solve many of the problems which continue to afflict the peoples of the world.

One last word. The chapters that follow have been written by scientists – who use the metric system of measurement. For the benefit of English-speaking readers who may be unfamiliar with, or even repelled by, the metric system, a rudimentary conversion table is printed on p. 8, to supplement the more complete ones that can be found in many dictionaries and other works of reference.

Contents

Approximate conversions for the non-metric reader

Linear

Centimetres to inches: divide by 5, multiply by 2
Metres to yards: divide by 10, multiply by 11
Kilometres to miles: divide by 8, multiply by 5

Square

Sq. km to sq. miles: divide by 5, multiply by 2

Cubic

Cu. km to cu. miles: divide by 4

Weight

Kg to pounds: multiply by 11, divide by 5
Tonnes (1000 kg) to tons (2240 lb): ignore it, unless in very large amounts; the ton is 40 lb heavier

Temperature

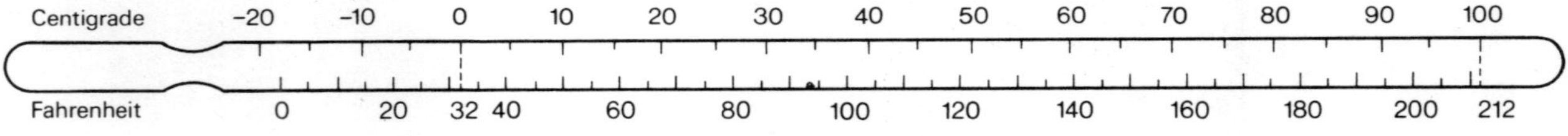

I

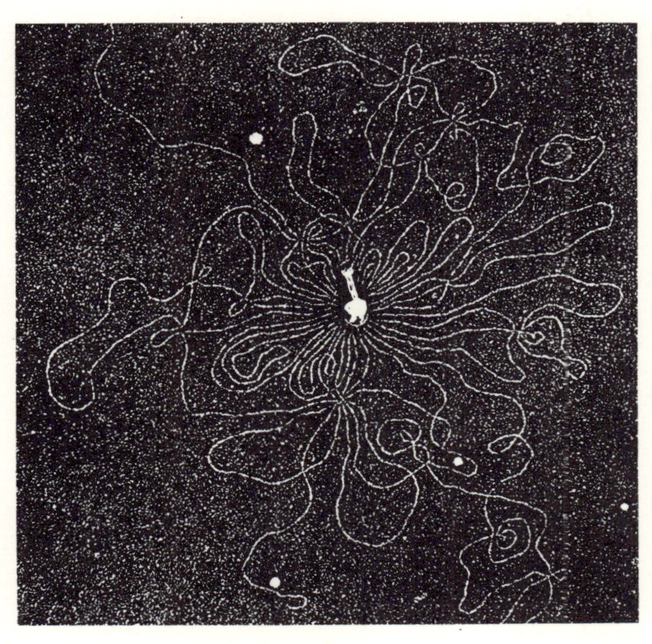

Life and the forces of nature

Martin Holdgate

THIS BOOK is about stability and instability, the forces which determine how far the seas, land and air of our planet exhibit the one or the other, and the consequences for life and human culture.

Change is universal. Even the sun, stars and galaxies have a term to their existence. The energy they pulse out, on which we and other living beings depend, is generated in the turbulence of mighty forces. Life itself is not still. Evolution develops new forms: new forms modify the patterns and processes of ecological systems: the spread, competition, success and extinction of species is enacted on the surface of a planet whose continents are adrift, oceans opening and closing, mountains rising and sinking, and air and water in ceaseless circulation.

Too violent an instability is inimical to life. Too unchanging a habitat may put a brake on evolution, by presenting less challenge to the processes of natural selection. On this Earth, for four thousand million years, conditions have remained in the middle range where life is possible – even though conditions have fluctuated widely and few places have been continuously favourable as habitats throughout this period.

In later chapters the authors describe the forces which control the most dramatic changes we can see around us in the natural world today. The movement of the great plates in the Earth's crust, which determines the pattern of continent and ocean, is explained in Chapter 9, which also explains the earthquakes that are an everyday consequence of these otherwise imperceptible motions. Chapter 8 explains how these same fundamental processes in the Earth's crust control volcanic outbursts. Changes in the distribution of land and sea, possibly linked to changes in the level of the sun's radiation, may account for the ice ages described in Chapter 5. Certainly the interplay of atmosphere and ocean, fundamentally affected by the sun's radiation, the Earth's rotation, and the division of the sea by land barriers, underlies the climatic patterns described in Chapter 2, the local but devastating manifestations of the power of avalanche snow explained in Chapter 4 and the advance and retreat of the deserts which is causing so much concern today and forms the theme of Chapter 6. Last, but by no means least, we are ourselves the children of the lightning, owing the molecules of our bodies to its interaction with the ancient atmosphere and the accumulation of the amino-acids thus formed in the waters of a primeval sea.

The forces of nature, discussed separately in this book, are not truly independent in their cause or operation. In this introduction it is pertinent to consider the wider setting in which we live, and some of the features of the living, evolutionary process which the forces of nature drive.

The cosmic background

On a cosmic scale, the dominant forces of nature are gravitational and electromagnetic. These govern the formation, interaction and breakdown of stars. Phenomena which impress us most with the power of nature – storms, lightning, volcanoes, earthquakes or the rare outbursts of new stars in the sky – are local manifestations of these dominant forces.

On a cosmic scale, hydrogen is by far the commonest element. The Earth and the other inner planets of our system are unusual in being rich in iron, nickel and other metals, and also in silica, carbon and similar medium-weight elements. There are grounds for believing that the sun and its associated planets are young compared with the universe as a whole – about five thousand million years old, whereas the origin of the universe can be placed twice as far back. There is also evidence that the heavier elements now present in the planets and the sun were formed in an earlier star, scattered in its explosion, and swept up along with large quantities of hydrogen in the formation of the present solar system. If this is so, the planets are not the first bodies to contain the matter that now composes them, and we are ourselves made of atoms that originated in a long-vanished star as it aged towards a supernova explosion.

Gravity controls the condensation of the hydrogen that forms a tenuous cloud in interstellar space. As condensations develop, pulling in whatever contaminating heavier materials the death of older stars may have scattered through that region of space, temperature rises. If the condensation is sufficiently massive, it becomes hot enough for the fusion of hydrogen atoms to form helium and a massive emission of radiation – it becomes a star. The process of contraction under gravity is balanced by the outward surge of radiation. In our sun such a balance has lasted about five thousand million years and is likely to last for as long again. The sun, like similar stars, is a massive self-sustaining hydrogen bomb! The gravitational forces which pulled its matter together and brought its temperature to radiation point also maintain the Earth and other planets in their stable orbits, the inward pull of the sun being balanced by the outward force of their angular momentum. The molecular processes of the sun, which have remained at a relatively constant level over thousands of millions of years, pour out the energy which lights and heats the surface of the planets and by constant bombardment blasts unshielded delicate molecules.

The Earth is a typical inner planet, too small for its condensation under gravity to raise the temperature to the point where nuclear processes could make it emit radiation, too small to retain significant amounts of lighter elements

Fig. 1 In the solar system only the Earth and Mars are within the narrow band, not too far from the sun and not too near, in which life as we know it is a possibility. Jupiter, though too cold on the exterior, may have in its interior conditions suitable for life.

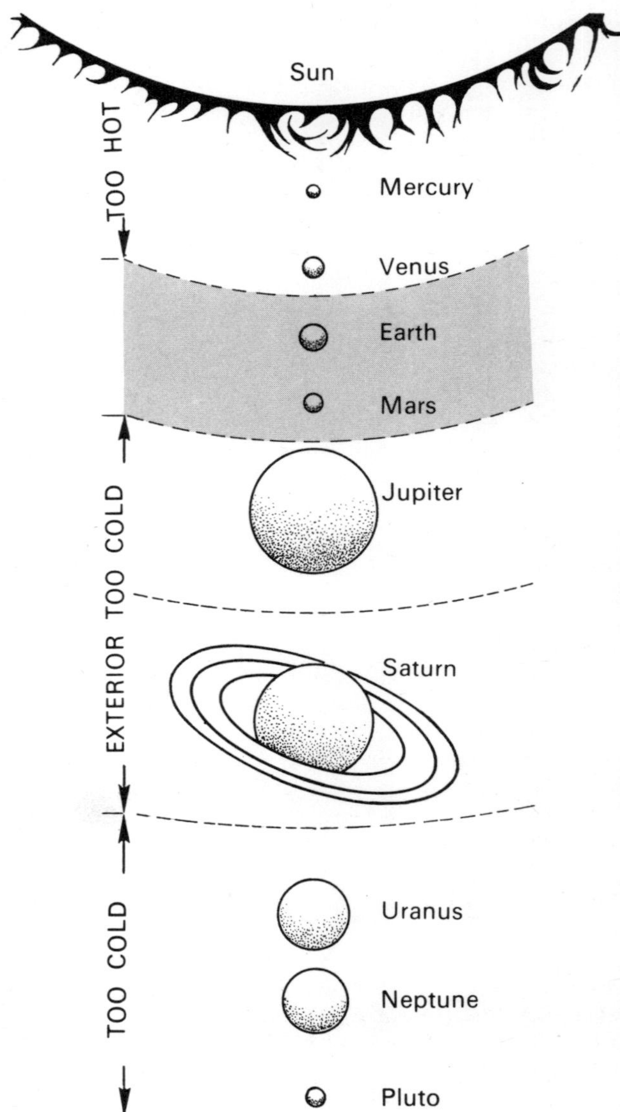

such as free hydrogen, but large enough to maintain a gaseous envelope of atmosphere. It is near enough to the sun for solar radiation to warm the surface several hundred degrees above the temperature of interstellar space. The rapid rotation distributes this radiation fairly evenly over the surface, while the atmosphere acts like a 'glasshouse', trapping much of the radiation for long enough to stop drastic cooling during the hours of darkness. The layers and circulation pattern of the atmosphere, described in Chapter 2, are the result of the size, composition and rotational period of the Earth and the impingement upon them of solar radiation: in turn they govern much of our way of life, and that of other animals and plants.

The properties of the Earth as we know it, and the existence and survival of life upon it, are entirely bound up with these facts of its origin, size, composition and location. It has been possible for life to develop as it has because the sun has remained relatively steady in its emission of radiation for so long, and hence the atmosphere and ocean have developed certain enduring features. A highly variable sun would have blasted air and water into space in periods of extreme heat and chilled the earth's surface to lifelessness in periods of cold. A more slowly spinning planet would have been exposed to extreme heat by day and chill by night, causing a turbulent flow of air from place to place. Whatever our impressions regarding the instability of the world today – and however dramatic the manifestations of natural forces described in this book – the fact is that the Earth has been remarkably stable as a habitat for many thousands of millions of years. If it had not been so, we would not be here.

The sun's radiation powers and drives the whole system of life. The energy we receive from the sun dwarfs into insignificance that which we generate in all the power stations of the world. Power stations burning coal or oil are not creating energy: they are simply releasing solar power fixed by plants long ago. Throughout this book, the dominance of Earth-sun interactions should not be forgotten.

The origins of life

Life on Earth is believed to have developed some four thousand million years ago – only about a thousand million years after the formation of the solar system. What is life? Basically, it is a capacity for self-perpetuation on the part of an organized molecular structure: a structure able to hold itself together and replicate itself in the face of those forces which all the time tend to degrade organization into randomness. On Earth, living organisms are mainly made

Fig. 2 The clock face of geological time. The grey circle indicates the time scale, in thousands of millions of years. On this clock man, even from his earliest state, occupies less than one minute.

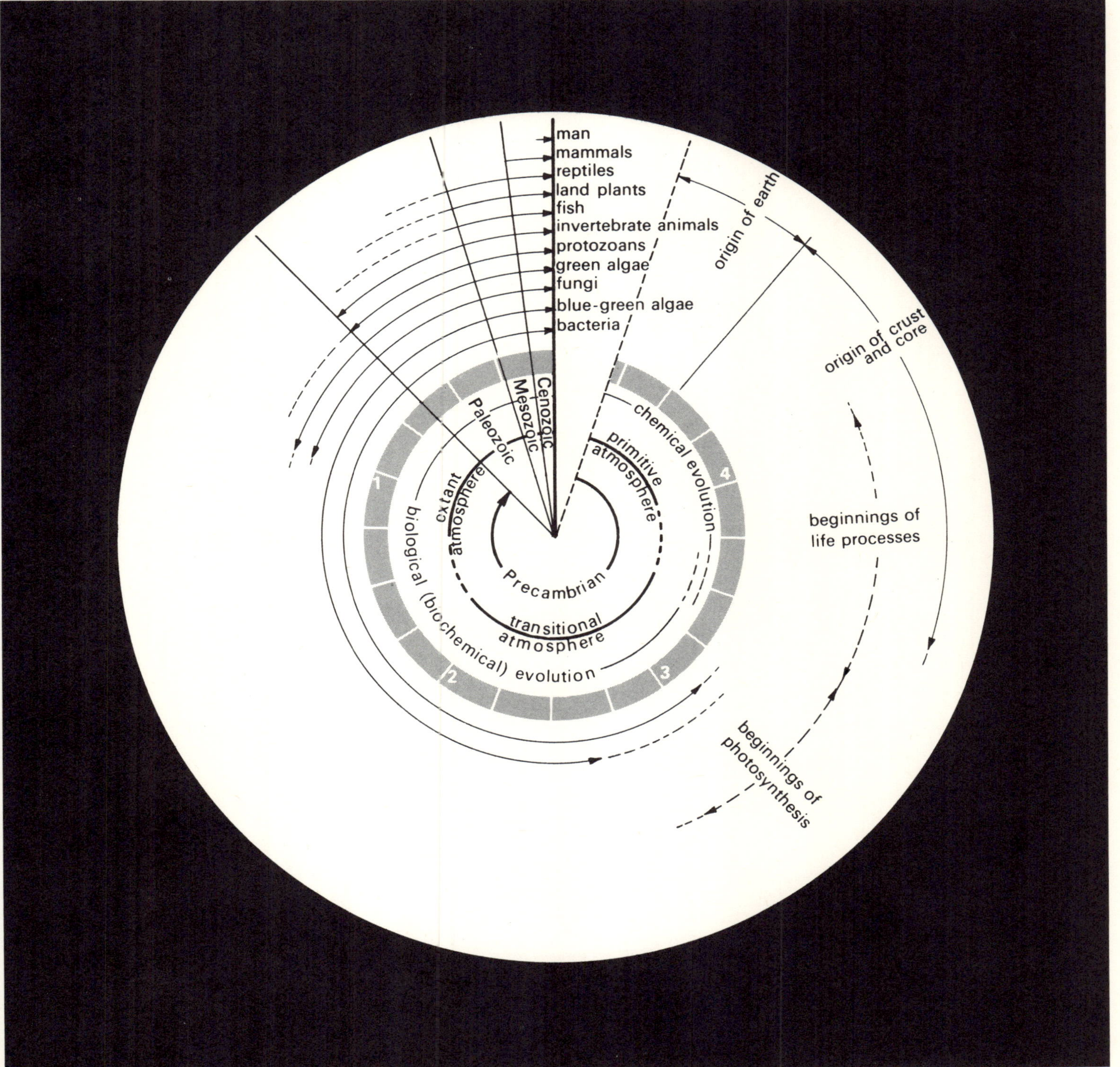

Fig. 3 Stanley Miller's 'origin of life' experiment, simulating the primeval atmosphere (see p. 26).

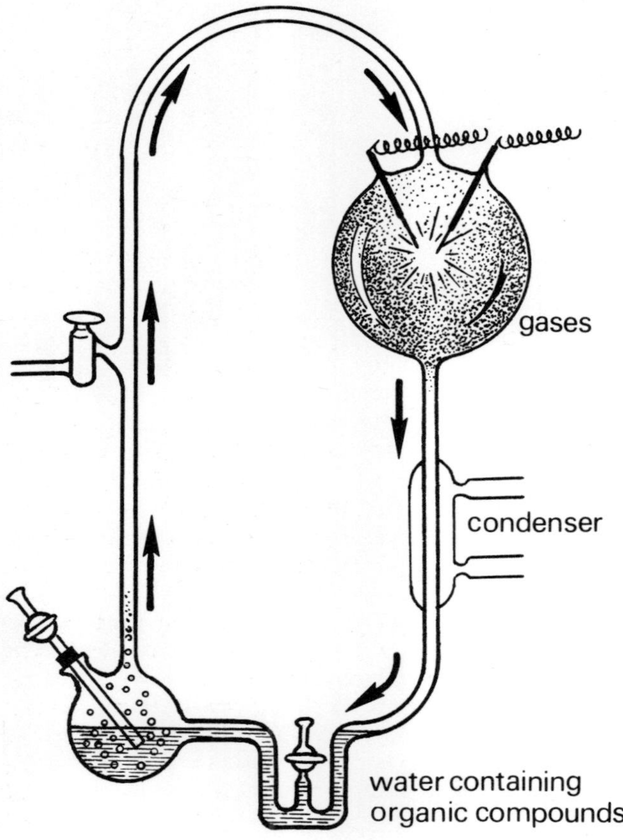

of proteins – chains of hydrogen, oxygen, carbon and nitrogen, variously branched and linked to other chains. Other types of living matter can be envisaged, but the predominance of this type on Earth indicates that it is the one best suited to our conditions of chemistry, temperature and radiation.

For life to appear there had to be conditions under which complex molecules potentially capable of aggregation into self-replicating structures could form. There is evidence (as Chapters 2 and 3 indicate) that combinations of carbon, nitrogen, oxygen and hydrogen into the chains we call amino-acids can be produced when electric discharges like lightning pass through an atmosphere rich in methane, ammonia and water vapour. We believe that this kind of atmosphere once prevailed on earth, formed (as Chapter 2 explains) through the volcanic exhalations from the earth's crust. Originally it contained no free oxygen or ozone: we owe these to the activities of green plants.

The origin of life thus depended on the properties of the early atmosphere and the ocean in which material synthesized by the lightning accumulated. In turn it led to the production of a new kind of atmosphere. But for the establishment of life it was not enough just for complex molecules to be produced. They had to accumulate and become organized into structures with a self-maintaining and self-reproducing potential. This demands certain other features in the environment.

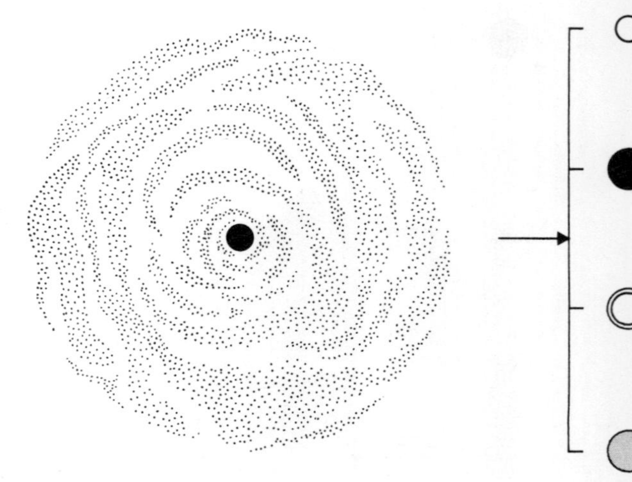

Fig. 4 The long, slow life-forming process can be pictured as a chain of cause and effect, from the birth of a star (left) and the formation of the elements, such as hydrogen, carbon, oxygen and nitrogen (reading downwards). These bond together in various combinations into the originating molecules of life, such as water, ammonia and methane. Under the influence of the star's radiation, these combine into the amino-acids, carbohydrates and the more complex proteins – the basic ingredients of life.

Stability is probably high among these. What radiation can create, it can destroy. Cosmic radiation from the sun bombarding the upper atmosphere is today potent in disintegrating even the durable products of modern chemistry like the chloro-fluoro compounds we use as aerosol propellants. Screening from such radiation is vital, even for the highly organized living organisms of today. It was probably even more important for the weakly structured aggregations of molecules from which our earliest ancestors sprang.

Many people look to the shallow sea for such stability. Damaging radiation is absorbed by the atmosphere long before it reaches the sea's surface. The water provides a support for tenuous structures – as witness the collapse of even the relatively highly evolved sea anemones or jellyfish when stranded by the tide. It equilibrates extremes of temperature. There are no cycles of frost and thaw to disrupt delicate structures by the intermittent formation of needles of ice. Life may well have formed from amino-acids and related hydrocarbons washed out by rain into shallow, tide-free basins in the primeval seas, and perhaps arranging themselves in a regular fashion on the natural lattices provided by crystals of clay or other minerals. Once such amino-acid chains developed an ability to attach simpler molecules to themselves in a regular arrangement which built up a duplicate amino-acid chain alongside – as a DNA spiral does now – life as we understand it was well on the way.

The persistent features of life

In this earliest stage when 'life' was no more than a collection of variously orientated amino-acid chains forming a kind of 'soup' in a shallow, salty sea, certain features which have persisted throughout evolution were apparent. First, the primitive chains of living molecules were supported in a watery solution of salts such as sodium, potassium and magnesium chlorides and sulphates. Ever since then the increasingly complex organic structures of life have carried within them fluids whose balance of salts differs from that of today's seas, but is thought by many to resemble more closely that in the ancient oceans – presumably because our tissues work best in that particular balance of salts. Secondly, in the very beginning there was some kind of ecological relationship between organism and habitat. Early life arose and persisted under favourable conditions, and its course of development must have been shaped by the development of the environment through the interplay of physical forces as well as by the inherent properties of the living molecules.

In the early millennia, new amino-acid material was presumably being formed continuously and added to the previous 'population'. Interactions between early life forms would be likely to produce new variants and new proto-organisms. Complexity undoubtedly increased. The development of lipid (fatty) outer layers as simple cell walls probably happened early. The permeability and electrical

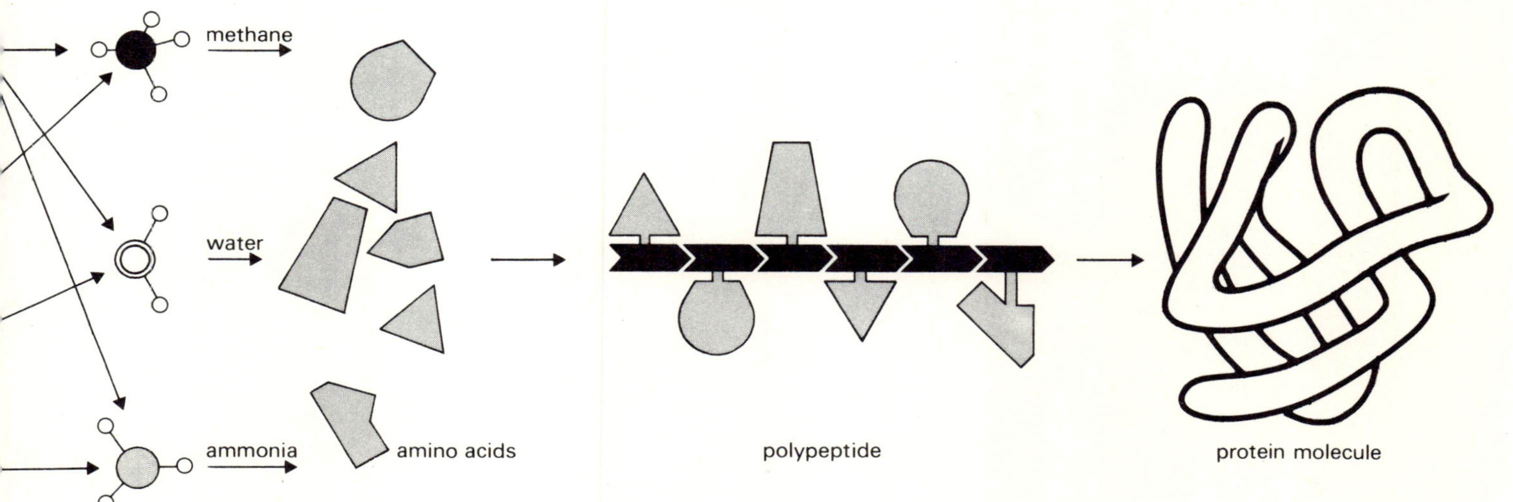

Fig. 5 Photosynthesis. In a green leaf in daylight, carbon dioxide from the air is combined with water drawn up by the roots to form sugar, using the sun's energy to drive the process. Oxygen is given off. In the dark the reaction is reversed, the sugars being 'burnt' with oxygen to release their stored energy.

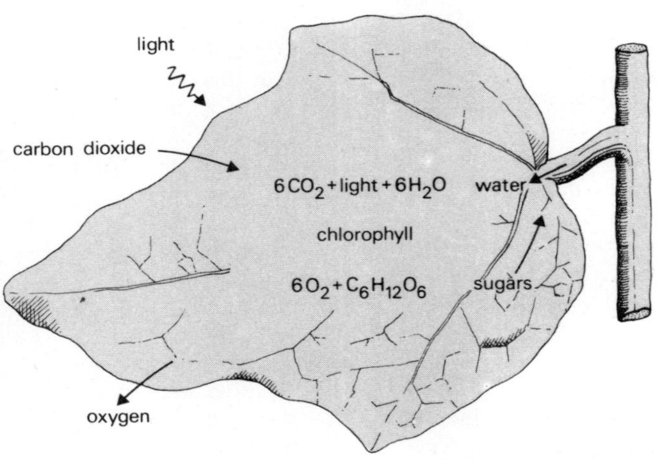

properties of these layers were to attain fundamental importance in the evolution of feeding and nervous systems. But the disintegrating, randomizing forces of nature would also have remained potent – and hence 'death' would continually have removed members of the population of proto-organisms, dispersing their material into the basic amino-acid 'soup'. The persistence of a population of proto-organisms must have depended critically on the balance of input of new material, its rate of agglomeration into whatever units it formed, and its dispersion under hostile environmental forces. This remains the essence of population ecology today.

This pattern established at the outset that the continuity of life depended on enough new individuals being produced to continue the life form over periods of environmental stress – for example, when the input of new molecules declined because the lightning was less vigorous or when the sea became less favourable as lagoons dried out or cooled or became more turbulent. So at this earliest stage natural selection, choosing among life forms and removing those least adapted to persist, would inevitably have made its appearance and begun to drive the evolutionary process.

The course of evolution

The whole trend of evolution has been towards the development of organisms that are increasingly independent of the vagaries of the environment. When stronger molecular chains appeared, they were more able to resist disintegration by radiation or physical buffeting. Cell walls protected the watery organic 'soup' within them from external stress and desiccation, and controlled the inflow and outflow of salts. Within the organism different parts of the structure became specialized for different functions, and one of the first developments is likely to have been the formation of a nucleus in which the basic code for the production of new organic structures resided.

Another vital early development must have been a capacity to trap materials needed for the formation of new organic structures – food. Initially this may just have involved means of absorbing selected substances from the surrounding sea, perhaps through the exposure at the proto-organismal surface of molecule groupings to which similar molecular arrangements in the medium attached themselves on a 'key and lock' principle. Later, areas of surface may have specialized as zones to which smaller proto-organisms became attached and were engulfed in the larger unit – an early step towards predation.

Some time early in the process, organisms developed the capacity to trap solar energy and use it to power the chemical transformations of inorganic material to more complex molecules which could in turn provide the chemical energy that drove the processes of living systems. This process of photosynthesis, using the green pigment chlorophyll, still drives the living world today. Solar radiation is used to combine carbon dioxide and water – both abundant constituents of the early atmosphere – to form carbohydrates such as sugars. In the process oxygen is released, and it is thought that the present high levels of free oxygen in the Earth's atmosphere – an anomaly, since one would expect this highly reactive element to be removed rapidly by chemical reactions to form a range of oxides – are due to the action of life. Organisms use their carbohydrate chemical energy store at a rate dependent on their own internal processes rather than on the visibility of the sun. In this process of respiration, oxygen is used and carbon dioxide re-created, and the energy released is equivalent to that part of the sun's power originally trapped in the photosynthetic formation of the carbohydrate. Photosynthesis in sunlight thus traps energy which can be released by respiration in darkness – at night or in internal parts of the organisms (or buried parts like roots) which the sun never reaches. It is an elegant example of how life can free itself from the fluctuations of the natural environment.

Large agglomerations of simple plants related to today's blue-green algae are among the earliest fossils. These formed what were probably slow-growing accumulations on the bed of shallow seas. Sunlight does not penetrate deeply into the ocean, and the presence of plants floating near the surface screens it even more, so that plant life today, as in the ancient seas, is restricted to the upper 'photic' or 'lit' zone, perhaps 100 to 200 metres in depth. It also demands water of suitable ionic balance and the presence of substances like phosphates, silicates and nitrates, released by the erosion of the rocks or the breakdown of organic matter. The cycling of such nutrients through the death and decomposition of living material and the absorption of the products into new organisms is likely to have been an early feature of the world's ecology.

Once plant forms were established they opened the way for two other ways of life: that of the decomposers and that of herbivores. Both derive energy secondhand from the photosynthetic activities of plants. The decomposers feed on dead plant or animal matter, breaking its structure down into simple inorganic compounds such as water, carbon dioxide, hydrogen sulphide, methane and metal salts. They probably evolved alongside plants very early in the evolutionary process. Some may soon have developed the capacity to invade living plant tissue and begin to break it down or divert its stored energy to their own reproduction, thereby producing the first parasites and 'diseases', for that is what a disease-causing virus or bacterium does.

Animals cannot trap solar energy by photosynthesis, but by eating plants they acquire their energy stores and turn them to their own use. Such interaction demands adaptation to overcome the physical structure of the plant tissues, to be able to break bits off, engulf them, and then degrade them by chemical processes into molecules the animal can use. This development of herbivorous animals must have had major evolutionary importance, and we can deduce some of the events that followed. First, the herbivore would gain advantage by developing mobility in order to move in search of food: mobility is a general animal characteristic, but rare in plants. Sense organs responding to light reflected from potential food or detecting its aroma would enhance the efficiency of a herbivore: sight and smell are almost universal animal attributes. Evolution has tended to concentrate such senses at one end of the body, the end which is foremost during movement, so that the animal 'looks where it is going'.

The difference in form between animals and plants can thus be explained by the requirements of each. Plants need first and foremost to trap sunlight and to absorb water, carbon dioxide and nutrients from the surrounding medium. Broad leaf surfaces, spreading and lying parallel to the surface of water or substratum are a logical development. But for an animal a head crowned with sense organs and a bilaterally symmetrical body with organs of

Fig. 6 The basic structure of an ecosystem. The plants, fixing energy through photosynthesis, stand at the base of a 'pyramid of numbers' sustaining lesser quantities of herbivore, and less still of carnivore. The decomposers (right) break down dead matter, returning minerals to the soil and gases to the air; in turn, these sustain special fungi and bacteria-consuming small animals.

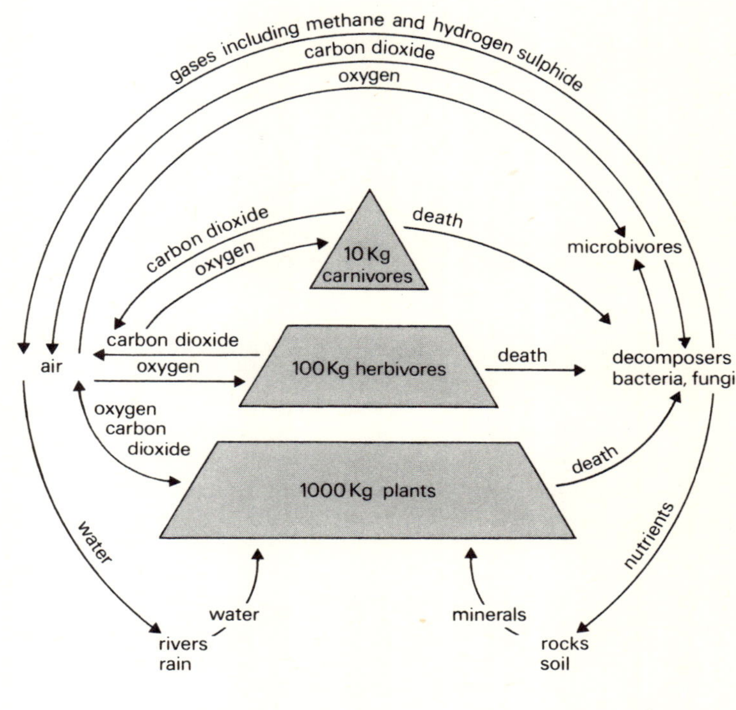

propulsion concentrated near centres of balance are equally sound principles. So is the development of a nervous system linking the sense organs to the muscles which control movement towards a food source.

Animal respiration is not a fully efficient process: energy is wasted as heat. Movement also consumes much of the energy animals get from plants. Even young and fast-growing animals need to eat from four to ten units of plant weight to make one unit of new body weight for themselves. It follows that there cannot be as much animal life as plant life in the world. Because there are similar losses in the conversion of animal food to the flesh of a predator like a lion, these in turn must be less numerous than the herbivores they eat. At an early stage in evolution what we now call a 'pyramid of numbers', with diminishing abundance of plants, herbivores and predators as one ascends the so-called 'trophic levels' or follows food through food chains, must have appeared. The evolution of herbivores must have intensified the pressure of natural selection on plants, just as the development of predation affected herbivores. Many plants have evolved substances which make them unpalatable or poisonous to animals. Others have tough or spiny cuticles; most can regenerate tissues lost in grazing. Many insect herbivores also taste nasty, and brilliant colours, especially yellows and blacks, protect because they warn predators.

The evolution of more complicated plant and animal forms prepared the way for successful colonization of the land, which is more hostile to life than the sea. Land plants and animals remain complexes of amino-acids entrapping a dilute salt solution, with a natural tendency to dry up when exposed to the air. They also need a skeletal system to replace the support which in the sea is derived from the water. But once land plants had evolved supporting cellulose cell walls or woody tissue, and became able to maintain a water balance, the land offered real advantages. The sun's radiation is more intense and not confined to a thin surface layer of water drifting with wind and currents. On land a plant can root firmly and spread its leaves to catch all the available sunlight. Both carbon dioxide and oxygen diffuse more rapidly in the gaseous medium of the air, and oxygen is more abundant than in the sea.

The land environment also has disadvantages. Temperatures range to greater extremes. Compare, for example, the almost constant temperature of the cold polar seas, where the water is always between -1° and $+1^\circ$C, with the annual fluctuation from $+5^\circ$ to -40°C on the adjacent Arctic and Antarctic coasts. There is a similar contrast in the tropical zones. On land drought is another problem, and there is less screening from solar radiation. To be successful, colonists of the land had to develop physiological controls to maintain their internal environment despite external variations. No doubt in the beginning they succeeded only in the most favourable places, such as wet lowlands and humid coastal zones. Their subsequent colonization of the extreme climatic zones of the world is a measure of the increasing capacity of life to sustain its essential features in the face of the disintegrating forces of nature.

For a long time this independence of the water was only partial – indeed it still is. Many plants and animals can only reproduce if the gametes (those tiny single-celled vehicles that carry the genes that combine to provide the blueprint for the new organism) are kept in a liquid phase. In lower plants they swim in a film of water over the surface. Many lower animals return to the water for reproduction and the development of early life stages. Even in man, fertilization takes place in fluid within the body. The same is true in all mammals, birds and reptiles. We have made ourselves reasonably independent of the threatening natural forces, but by a series of adaptations that almost seems to be haphazard.

It is a remarkable aspect of life's response to the threat of disintegration by natural forces that on Earth the solution chosen should have been one of death after a finite life span, and the generation of new individuals from very small and simple propagules. It would be possible to conceive of life forms with such efficient self-repair capabilities that they would be almost immortal, and it can be argued that this would be far more efficient. Every human body cell, for example, contains in its nucleus the genetic blueprint for the whole body of the individual. Why has not the physiological power been evolved for regeneration of substantial parts such as whole limbs? Many invertebrates and lower vertebrates have this power. Why should senescence lead to the ultimate breakdown and disintegration of bodies so laboriously built up with such expenditure of energy, and the loss of the associated experience, when it would seem more efficient for the complex physiologies that sustain them for a life span simply to go on doing so indefinitely?

One may speculate about the paradox of death, but it is so universal a feature of life systems on Earth that one can only conclude that the kind of chemical structures we and all other organisms are made of simply cannot be continued indefinitely. Periodically, we seem to need to revert to the basic genetic code and reconstitute a new framework from new materials. But whether the running down of the body we call senescence is due to intrinsic biological properties or external forces of nature we cannot yet say.

Life and the environment

Evolution took place on the foundation of a changing Earth. The chapters in this book demonstrate how these changes continue, with the movement of continents, the evolution of atmospheric processes, the waxing and waning of the ice sheets and the outbursts of volcanic eruptions and earthquakes. It was impelled by competition between life forms for the limited areas where photosynthesis was possible, where plant food could be found, or where animals could breed. It was also driven by environmental change. Because of the environmental variation and competition, the production of more offspring than were needed to replace the population clearly became a useful insurance, and the fact that the surplus must of necessity be excluded and die further fuelled the competitive process. It can indeed be argued that it was this competition that made death necessary: that organisms had to have the capacity to produce many offspring because of the vagaries of the forces of nature: that quick growth and rapid multiplication rather than longevity promoted evolutionary success because more genetic variants were produced and tested by competition.

In the sea there is a degree of continuity. In principle

Fig. 7 Rapid evolutionary change within one species was observed in 1835 by Charles Darwin in the isolated Galapagos Islands. Between the thick, heavy bill of the finch at top left, adapted for cracking hard-shelled seeds, to the thin beak of the insect-eater at No. 4, he noted 'no less than six species with insensibly graduated beaks'.

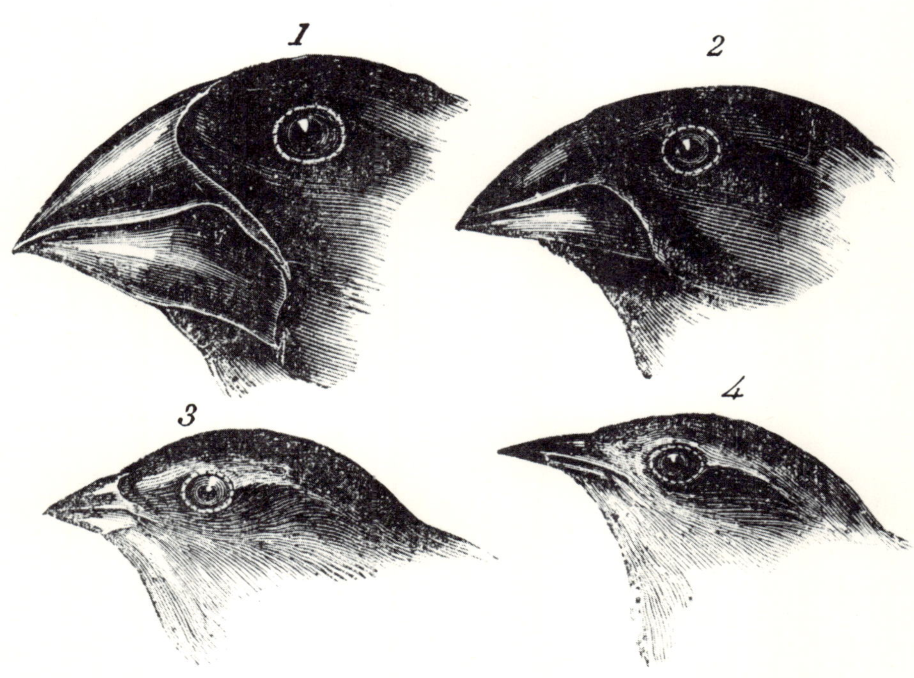

plants can drift and animals can swim or be carried anywhere within the continuous world ocean. There is certainly no incentive for marine organisms to develop means of dispersal across land barriers. It may not always have been so. Conversely, in the present age of fragmented land masses, moving as the tectonic plates shift and upwelling broadens the ocean floors, there is apparent value in a land plant or animal having the means of spreading across arms of the sea.

In fact this is an oversimplification, for the world is a mosaic of discontinuity. Neither all areas of sea nor all areas of land are alike as habitats. The deep ocean, with its intense pressures and low light level, can support only decomposers, detritus feeders and carnivores, sustained by the rain of dead material from the surface. How vast is the difference between this and the photic zone, where the concentration of green marine plants supports an entirely different community. Likewise, on land there are enormous contrasts between the humid tropics and hot deserts, and between these and the polar regions or high mountains. On a smaller scale, even in a temperate land, lakes, rivers, ponds, woods, sand dunes or cliffs provide a multiplicity of microhabitats. Even the surfaces of animals or plants, or their interiors, provide different potential habitats.

All life forms have evolved some dispersal capacity, but this is clearly a two-edged sword. If an organism is already in a favourable habitat, its progeny are most likely to perpetuate the species by remaining there. Too easy a dispersion, or an obligatory one, could spell disaster to organisms like date palms in the oases of a desert, or small winged insects or birds on islands in the midst of an ocean. This is Darwin's explanation of the fact that such insects and birds are commonly flightless. In practice most land plants and animals disperse over relatively short distances from one habitat to another, and few are adapted for long sea crossings. This has resulted in the genetic isolation of organisms as the continents have split and drifted apart, or even on a small scale as in the Hawaiian islands where forests have been dissected by new lava streams. Evolutionary change can be most rapid when it takes place in a small, isolated population, and the stocks of organisms in the fragmented habitats of Hawaii have displayed a remarkable local development of peculiar races. On the larger scale, the isolation of land masses over long periods has accounted for the distinctive differences we now find between the floras and faunas of regions with similar climates. The distinctive mammal faunas of Australia and South America result from the long isolation of those continents by water barriers. On the other hand, the similarity of forest and bog vegetation in Patagonia, New Zealand, temperate Australia and ancient Antarctica result from their former linkage in the great southern continent of Gondwanaland.

The forces of nature, shifting the lands and seas of the world, varying climates and habitats as deserts have expanded, ice waxed and waned or volcanic activity burst out, have affected evolution almost as much as the competition for limited resources of space, sunlight, water and food. Change in nature demands a response from life. It allows new forms to succeed at the expense of those previously successful. It divides genetic stocks and links them again, as when the raising of the isthmus of Panama linked the Americas only a few million years ago and brought about a new interplay between the mammal faunas of the two continents, leading to the extinction of many distinctive South American species.

These instabilities may also have had something to do with the paradox of mortality. Life on earth is so constituted that genetic change can occur only in the process of sexual reproduction, when genes from two individuals are reassorted to provide a new combination. If the world is changing rapidly, it is advantageous for this genetic reassortment to happen quickly, so that a population produces a wide range of variants within a short period. This may also explain one of the odd features of the fossil record: the sudden disappearance of forms which for millions of years had dominated the planet. The dinosaurs persisted for tens of millions of years and radiated into many successful species, but vanished relatively rapidly, at a time when the environment also seems to have changed. The flowering plants appeared and radiated suddenly at about the same time as the mammals, during the Cretaceous period around 115 million years ago. There were also many changes in the world's mammal fauna at the onset of the ice ages, some five million years ago. Perhaps dominant groups radiate to give a range of adapted species during periods of relative stability, but cannot change fast enough in later periods of rapid change, leaving the field open for smaller, more rapidly breeding competitors. In times of stability a high degree of specialized adaptation, long life and a low reproductive rate may be advantageous, because this reduces the inefficiency which a high wastage of surplus young must entail, while in times of change the opposite may be true.

All this is speculative. But it seems clear that the shifting surface of the Earth, impelled by physical forces and manifesting those forces in the ways described in later chapters of this book, has dominated and shaped the evolutionary course of life which has, in turn, altered the physical processes of the planet. Trees have bound soil, modifying the hydrological cycle, and have slowed the run-off of water: the result is to diminish floods and curb their erosive action. Ancient vegetation, beginning the process of photosynthesis, has altered the composition of the atmosphere, while accumulations of dead plant and animal matter in situations devoid of oxygen and so closed to the decomposers have formed coal and oil, giving us a source of energy and a means whereby to affect the properties of the atmosphere and possibly of the climate. The power of ice and snow is evident in Chapter 5 of this book: what is not so evident is the influence of glaciation in forming new soil. Over much of what is now the northern temperate zone, receding ice some 20,000 to 10,000 years ago left the land mantled in raw, churned debris. But these new soils are rich in minerals. Slow processes of solution by percolating rain tend to impoverish them, washing the minerals out into the rivers, and careless land clearance by man aggravates the process. Biological change follows both the uncovering of the new soil and its later depletion. Though the ice has gone, much of Europe and North America shows its imprint in vegetation and in the suitability of different areas for different crops.

Sometimes an organism may be 'pre-adapted' to environmental change. For example, in the southern oceans of the mid-Tertiary period there was a race of specialized sea-birds which had gained success as swimmers and divers through the increasing adaptation of the wings as flippers for undersea propulsion rather than flight. Even the temperate seas are cool relative to the temperature of a bird or mammal's body, and those birds that spend much of their time swimming and diving need insulation. Most have evolved thick, fatty layers under the skin, and close-set feathering which retains air when they dive and helps insulation further. Such birds, like seals, are 'pre-adapted' to even colder conditions, and it is not surprising that when the southern ice-caps extended, these swimming and diving birds persisted in the far southern lands as penguins.

The maintenance of a constant internal body temperature is one of the features of birds and mammals which we consider most advanced. The advantage is that it allows constant conditions for the chemical processes of the body whatever happens outside. Cold-blooded animals tend to move, and plants tend to grow, by fits and starts, increasing in activity as the sun warms them or the air temperature rises, and sinking into torpor as the environment cools. It is more efficient, and safer, to be able to keep going whatever the conditions, but it costs energy. A very small mammal or bird in a cool climate has to eat a lot to maintain itself, even though fur or feathers insulating the surface may cut heat loss. A mole or shrew eats more than its own body weight every day. Such very tiny animals have not been able to colonize the polar regions at all, and as one follows an animal form towards the poles its extremities – ears and limbs – tend to become more rounded, and hence have less surface per unit of volume. The larger and more spherical the animal, the lower its ratio of surface to volume, and the easier it is to maintain a constant temperature in the cold. Polar animals tend, therefore, to be relatively large and well rounded. Many have developed another adaptation to pass the winter when the land is snow-bound: hibernation. Time spent in an insulated shelter, with a lowered body temperature and a lower rate of energy consumption, ekes out the reserves of food stored as body fat. In the hot deserts, on the other hand (as Chapter 6 illustrates), quite different adaptations prevail – especially to conserve water, but also to avoid absorbing heat from the sun. Desert mammals have an adaptation exactly opposite to polar ones: fat reserves are stored within the animal rather than below the skin, so that there is minimal heat-retaining insulation.

Man and nature

All such adaptations speak eloquently of how, progressively down the millennia, animals and plants have evolved devices which free them from the forces of nature. Man, the most recently evolved of the dominant planetary life forms, has taken this development of independence of the environment a step further. He has learned to improve his scanty skin insulation by wearing the furs of other species or weaving artificial clothing. Thus we have gained the poles in borrowed or synthesized pelage. In the desert, we have developed clothing that minimizes the stress of excess heat. We have developed shelters, both static and mobile, with high insulation efficiency, and supplemented natural heat generation with fire or electricity. These artificial structures give protection from natural forces manifesting as hail, snow or torrential rain, before which our ancestors must often have moved in discomfort. We can ward off the lightning (as Chapter 3 explains). We have embanked rivers and controlled run-off to keep floods from our dwellings and farmsteads – even though we have from time to time miscalculated and built towns on flood plains that are still inundated once in a century or so. We have developed ways of ensuring a food supply more reliable and constant than our ancestors ever dreamed of. As a result, the numbers of people supported by each acre have mounted. In a natural rain forest where man lives as a hunter and gatherer, only about one person is supported by each square kilometre of land. In East Africa, grazing lands and simple cultivation together may support about 25 persons on the same area. In India, the more intensive farming of the monsoon belt supports about 230 people per square kilometre, and ships enough food from this area to sustain another 50 in the cities. All these systems receive about the same input of energy from the sun, and receive nothing from man other than the return to the soil of human or animal body wastes. But intensive western-style agriculture like that practised in the United States can support about 60 people per square kilometre on the land and 2,000 in the cities. Under such a system, nutrients flow from land to city and thence down the sewers to the sea. Artificial replenishment of those nutrients in the form of fertilizers has become essential. In addition, we have come to depend on mechanized cultivation and cropping, and on elaborate crop protection schemes involving artificial herbicides and pesticides. These technological products depend on energy additional to that supplied by the sun. The system is precarious in that less is left to natural checks and balances, and more depends on man's understanding, foresight and management.

In the developed countries we have won a partial independence from some of the forces of nature, but, as the chapter in this book on the atmosphere stresses, over most of the world even minor changes in climate – a drought here, a flood there – can bring disaster to millions. Even in the developed world we have no control over the vagaries of earthquakes (made the more damaging by the elaboration of our shelters) or volcanoes, and, as the chapter on snow and avalanches explains, our best way of dealing with the avalanche peril is to keep out of its way. We have no means of influencing the insidious long-term climatic changes that have shortened the growing season for certain crops in some northern temperate regions by two or three weeks in the last few decades. The Sahara marches southwards, and, as Chapter 2 states, we still do not know how far this advance is due to a natural climatic change and how far to human mis-management. Some people believe that the northern temperate zone was at a peak of warmth in the first half of the present century and may now be in a phase of cooling which will last for another fifty years. It may be that the advance of the Sahara is similarly linked to climatic oscillation, for we know that at about the time when the northern ice sheets were at their greatest extent there were cypress forests among the central Saharan mountains. In the caves of those remote hills early man, millennia nearer our own times, drew pictures of crocodiles, ostriches, elephants and antelopes. Indeed crocodiles still live there, in pools which are the last

Fig. 8 The evolution of the food supply. With a constant input of energy from the sun, we have advanced from the primitive rain-forest economy supporting one person per square kilometre to intensive western-style agriculture in which each cultivated square kilometre feeds 60 people on the land plus another 2,000 in the cities. But here the sun's free bounty has to be helped out by technology.

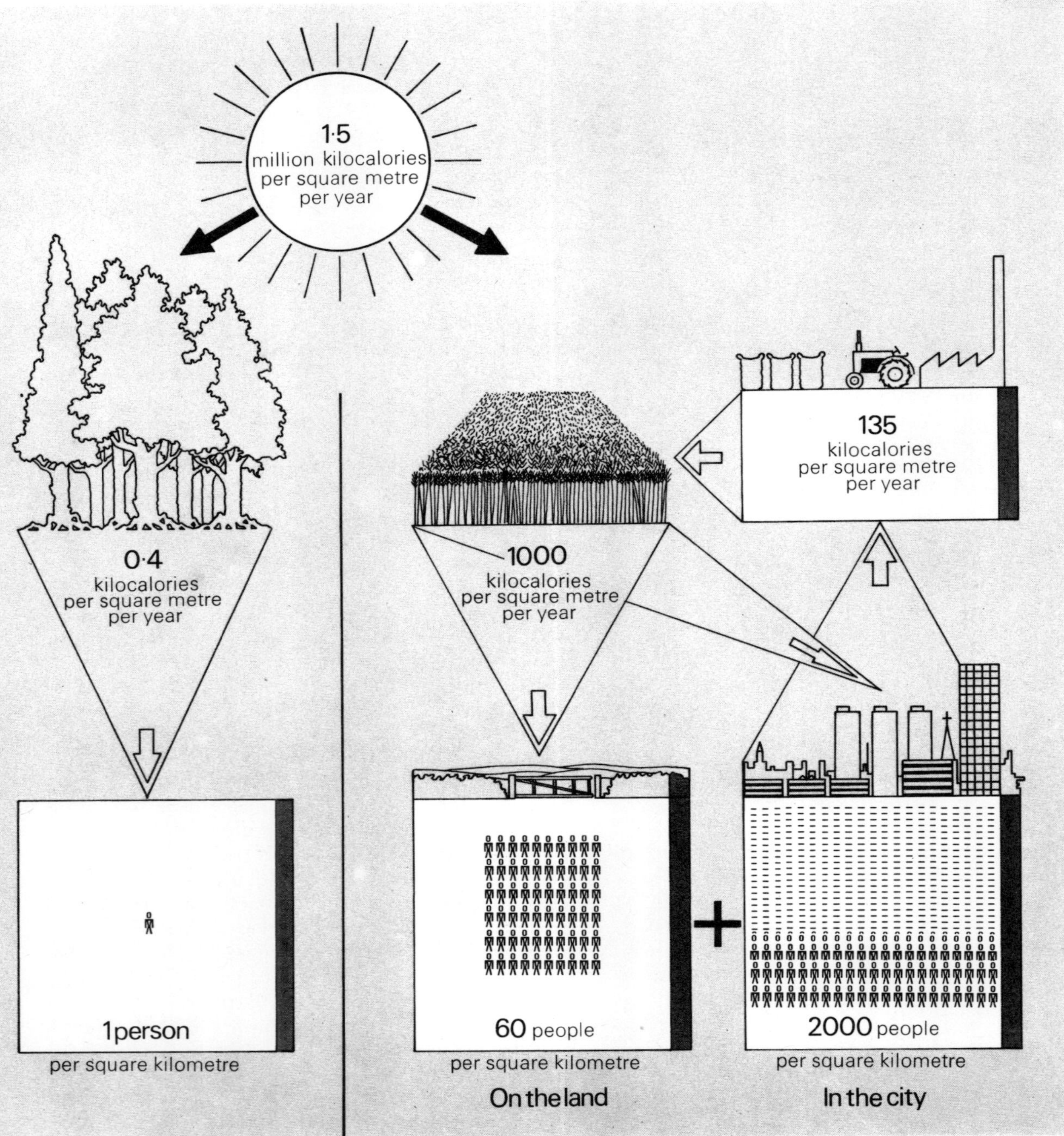

remnants of the headwaters of great rivers that once flowed northwards across what are now the dry Libyan sands. No technology has yet been devised to moderate such forces, or even reliably predict their trends.

Such prediction would be of great value. If we knew for certain that a century from now agriculture was doomed in Iceland and in Scotland north of Inverness, that the countries flanking the Sahara would inevitably become arid desert, that the central deserts of Australia would be increasingly moistened by rains, or that the Indian monsoon would fail utterly one year in five a decade from now, there would at least be a chance and a driving incentive for political and economic counter-measures. Such political action is not easy, as the chapter on deserts emphasizes, and it is foolish to assume that the countries of the world, with their present arbitrary boundaries, can expect anything like environmental equality; but through concerted action in regional and international organizations, something could undoubtedly be done to prevent massive famines and degrading poverty.

We need such foreknowledge also because there is a risk that the activities of our technologies may affect the climate of the world. As Chapter 2 says, the release of carbon dioxide into the air through the burning of fossil fuel may have a 'glasshouse' effect, retaining warmth and so raising world temperature. Conversely, dust and vapour at high altitudes can screen out sunlight. Sulphur oxides combining with ammonia can produce haze. Oxides of nitrogen from vehicles, fertilizer manufacture and even the use of fertilizers on a large scale, can possibly affect the ozone layer on which we depend for a screen against damaging ultraviolet radiation, and the chloro-fluoro compounds used as propellants for aerosol sprays may have a similar effect. We do not know enough about the subtle balances of the atmosphere, but if there is a prospect that we may perturb the world's climate to our detriment, we need to know how, how much, and on what time scale, while there is yet time to do something about it. The same applies to the possibility that the wastes of our cities and industries might affect the ecosystems of the oceans, fresh waters or broad tracts of land.

The first step towards combating a natural phenomenon is to understand its processes sufficiently to describe them in the form of a model and derive predictions we can test by experiment or observation. The second step, when the model has been validated, is to use it to predict crisis situations with enough time for the complex organizations of modern society to respond. The third step, which also depends on scientific understanding, is to develop means of controlling the phenomenon. To do that one needs to know the easiest way of altering it, with least input of energy, using the kinds of technology at our disposal. For example, we know that many earthquakes are due to slippage along particular fault lines, and that such slippage in some areas proceeds smoothly and continuously, with less serious earthquakes than where it is discontinuous and jerky. If we find that the second type can be converted to the first through lubricating the fault by injecting water into deep drill-holes, we are on our way to controlling earthquakes by releasing the tensions before they build up to danger level. This does not mean that we could stabilize the movements of the Earth's tectonic plates, but it does mean that we could prevent a minor, but to us devastating, consequence of such movement.

This book gives details of what we know about great and damaging natural forces, how far we can predict and how far we can control them. Great strides have been made in recent decades. By the end of the century we may well be able to predict serious volcanic eruptions, earthquakes and major climatic changes with enough 'lead time' to prevent massive devastation. Traditional methods of meteorological observation are being extended by satellite pictures and measurements, which are giving us a much more complete record of weather patterns and a much better chance of early warning of swift-moving atmospheric disturbances. Before long, we may learn how to disarm the hurricane before it strikes. We can already do something to batten down and safeguard places in its path – if the social organization is there to respond fast enough and efficiently enough when the warning comes. Chapter 2 explains how far we can now predict the weather and track cyclones, and hints at ways of predicting greater climatic changes.

There is room for much humility. Man is still an animal depending utterly upon green plants to trap the energy of the sun. We do not even cost this energy as a 'free good' in our economic systems. Yet it vastly outweighs all the energy we generate. Without photosynthesis, not only would our food supply dwindle to nothing, but the oxygen in our atmosphere would not be replenished and carbon dioxide would accumulate, making the earth hotter and veiling its surface in dense clouds. We also depend on natural processes to cycle nutrients. The decomposers in the soil and the sewage works, breaking down dead tissue and body wastes and making the inorganic products available to plant roots, are another massive 'free good' we take for granted. Although we have learned much about controlling them, our lives are still threatened by disease-causing pathogens invading our tissues and those of our crops and livestock. It seems unlikely that in any forseeable future we shall break out of this dependence upon plants, fuelled by the sun, to fuel our own organic processes. It seems unlikely that we, with our slow growth, long generation time and low reproductive rate, can do more than keep pace with the rapidly evolving bacteria, rushing through many generations each day and evolving resistant strains almost as fast as our medical technologists develop new drugs. In taking a few more steps towards control of a few of the forces of nature, we should always recall our vulnerability, as small organisms of saline solution within amino-acid and lipid lattices. We are tiny anomalies in the cosmic scale of things, and depend on processes we cannot hope to regulate.

Perhaps this dependence on nature is no bad thing. There are already cities in the world whose so-called planning cries out for the cleansing attention of an ice age. There are areas of soil whose fertility is so run down that centuries of natural replenishment are needed. The history of man's management of the environment is not one that should lead us to over-confidence. We would do well to try to understand the natural processes better, and interfere with them less until we have gained such understanding. The remarkable thing about the natural environment, and about the biological systems that live within it, is that fluctuation and change are everywhere characteristic but slow. It is the stability of the sun's output over four thousand million years that has made evolution possible. It is the resilience of living systems to short-term fluctuations that makes the planet stable as a human habitat and allows agriculture to plan now for next year's crops. By studying the forces of nature we see at work about us we may learn a little more wisdom in our conduct of affairs. Indeed, we may learn that 'managing nature' is not the right goal – but that we have everything to gain from managing ourselves so as to get the most out of our environment, in a stable and continuing way, on the easiest terms. The chapters of this book record how far we have come to understand some of those great forces that still hazard our planning and constrain our policies, but with which we have to learn to live.

Suggestions for further reading

D. Bergamini and the Editors of *Life: The Universe.*

Ruth Moore and the Editors of *Life: Evolution.* (Both published in 1969 in the '*Life* Nature Library' by Time-Life Books, New York.)

Cyril Ponnamperuma: *The Origins of Life.* Thames & Hudson, London, and Dutton, New York, 1972.

Z. Spinar and Zdenek Burian: *Life Before Man.* Thames & Hudson, London. 1972.

The Living World of Animals. Reader's Digest, London, 1971.

H. Gwynne Vevers (ed.): *Atlas of World Wildlife.* Mitchell Beazley, London, 1974.

F. W. Went and the Editors of *Life: The Planets* (in the '*Life* Nature Library'). Time-Life Books, New York, 1963.

C. S. Elton: *The Ecology of Invasions by Animals and Plants.* Methuen, London, 1958; Halsted Press, New York, 1966.

P. Farb and the Editors of *Life: Ecology* (in the '*Life* Nature Library'). Time-Life Books, New York, 1966.

Barbara Ward and René Dubois: *Only One Earth: the care and maintenance of a small planet.* André Deutsch, London, and Norton, New York, 1972.

The massive self-sustaining hydrogen bomb that is our Sun is the main source of all energy, and the physical support of all life, on this planet. Pouring $1\frac{1}{2}$ million kilocalories of energy per year on to every square metre of the Earth's surface, the sun far outweighs the power generated in all the power stations of the world – most of which, in any case, are spending, in the form of fossil fuel, solar energy invested aeons ago. Photographed in the narrow band of the hydrogen wavelength (*opposite*), vast jets of flaming hydrogen leaping from the sun's surface give a vivid impression of the most powerful force of nature that we know – the fusion of two atoms of hydrogen into one atom of helium. This reaction has been going on steadily at the rate of 564 million tons of hydrogen a second, for at least five thousand million years; it is this very steadiness, and the Earth's rate of rotation, which created the conditions in which, over millions of years, life could begin, develop, evolve, and colonize the sea and the land.

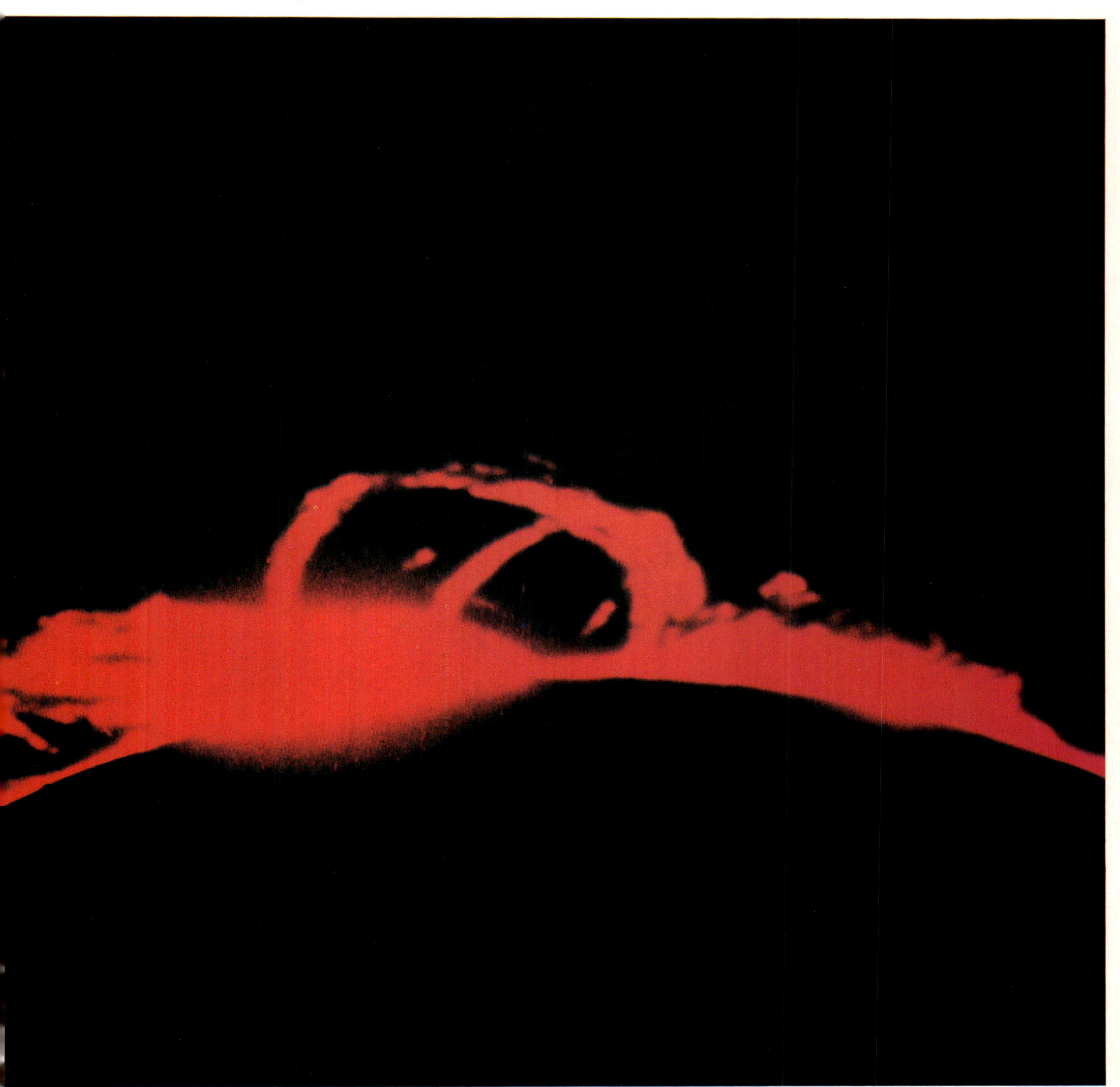

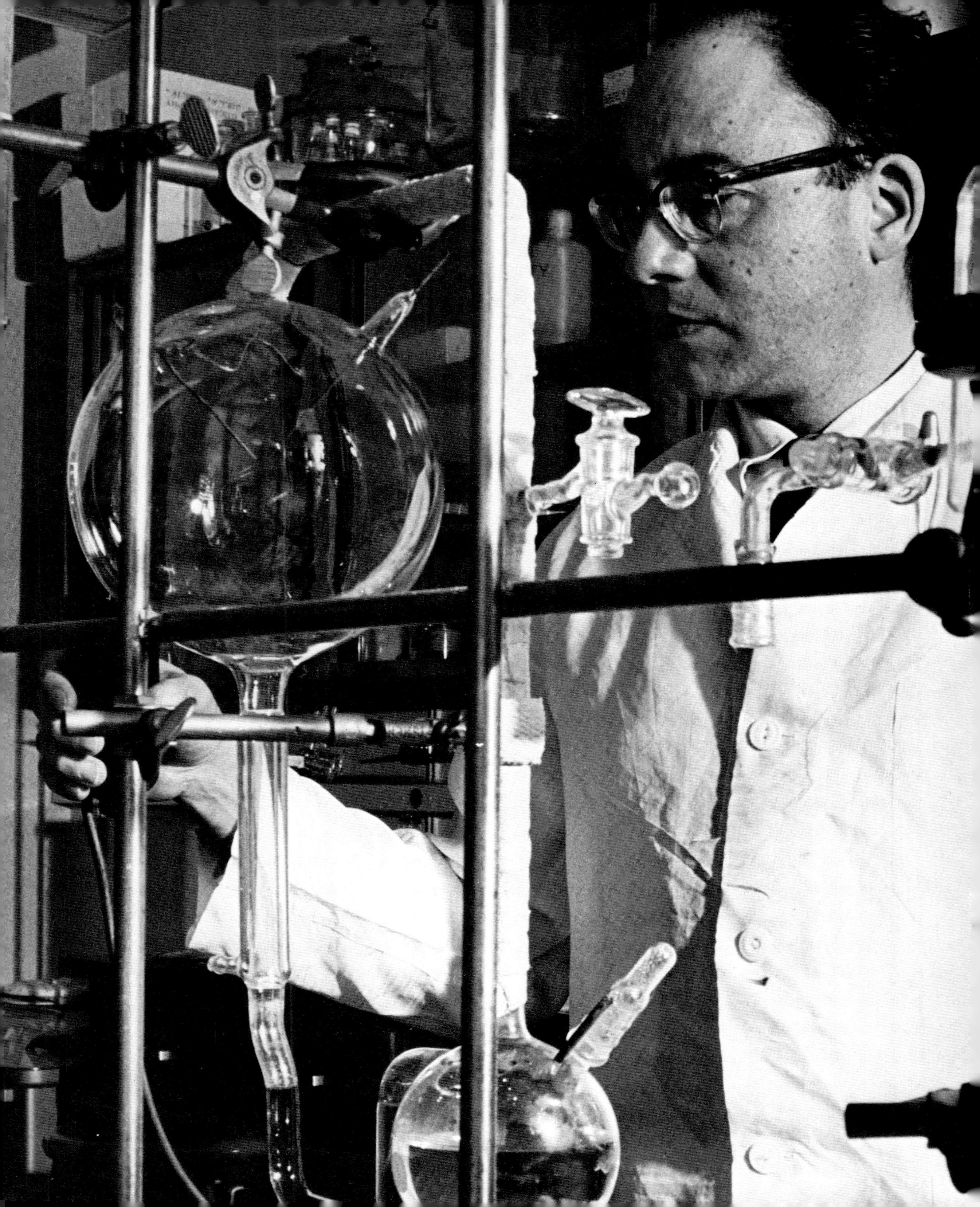

A seminal experiment in the search for the origins of life was performed in 1952 by Stanley L. Miller, an American graduate student. At the suggestion of his professor, Nobel prizewinner Harold Urey, he set up an apparatus (2) in which a mixture of ammonia (NH_3), methane (CH_4) and water vapour (H_2O), simulating the primeval atmosphere, was irradiated by a weak source of ultra-violet light provided by an electric arc. Only four elements were involved, but their actions, reactions and interactions span a broad field of organic chemistry. After a week, Miller analysed the condensate at the bottom of the apparatus, and found, in addition to formaldehyde (CH_2O), the two simplest amino-acids, glycine and alanine, with indications of others. The significance of this is that amino-acids link together to form proteins, and proteins are the basic building blocks of life. Such linking up to form protein-like chains can be made to happen in the laboratory under heat – such heat as would have been provided by the primitive Earth's volcanoes – and it is remarkable that when these long molecules are cooled in solution they tend to form minute spheres, about the size of bacteria. Under the microscope these look remarkably like cells, and can even give the appearance (3) of cell division. But this is still speculative. What is generally accepted is that somehow, after millions of years of trial and error, molecular sorting and re-sorting, under ceaseless electrical and ultra-violet bombardment, in the warm, salty 'broth' of the primeval oceans, life began.

3

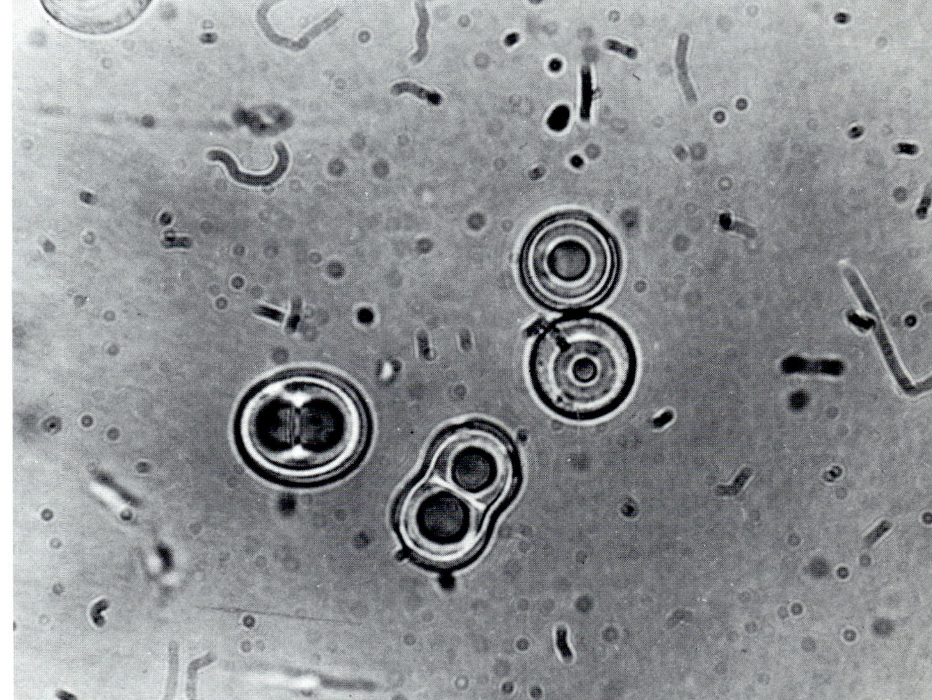

'In some warm little pond', Charles Darwin suggested in a letter to his friend Joseph Hooker, 'with all sorts of ammonia and phosphoric salts, light, heat, electricity, etc., present . . . a protein compound was chemically formed ready to undergo still more complex changes.' Many scientists still believe today that the first steps from the inert to the living – living in the sense of self-nourishing and self-replicating – could have been taken in shallow salty pools. Early in the process came the first organisms with the ability to trap the energy of sunlight and use it to drive the chemical processes of life – the first simple, single-celled plants. These were the algae. Their modern descendants still flourish in shallow saline pools along the world's shores (4).

4

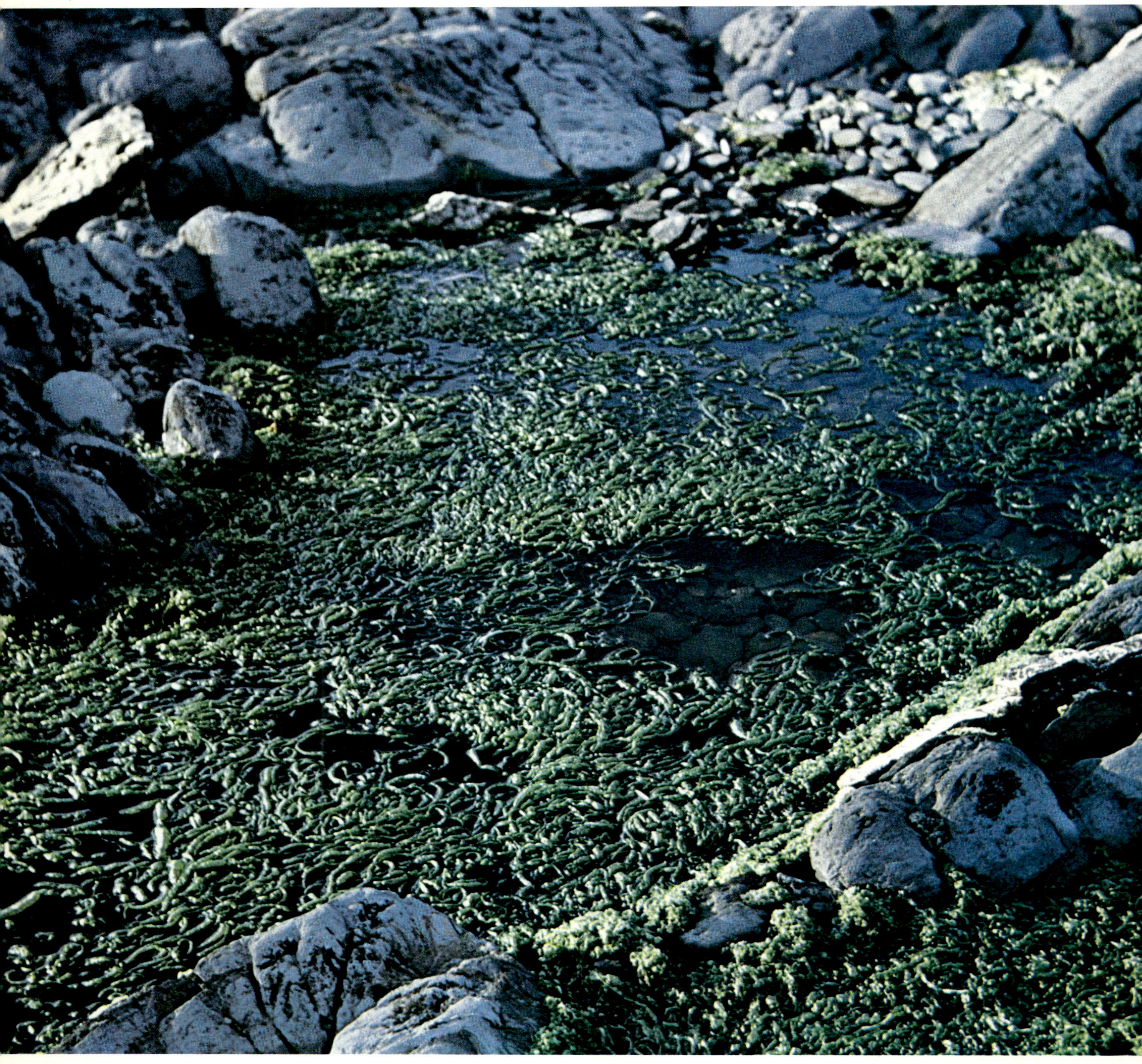

Among the oldest fossils ever found are these spore-like bodies and filaments of blue-green algae (5, magnification × 1820). They were found in some of the most ancient rocks on the surface of the Earth, on the shores of Lake Superior. Here too have been found fossil 'colonies' of such algae (6), slow-growing accumulations that formed in shallow seas. Colonial groupings of many shapes and arrangements are and always have been typical of algae. Both individually and in their groupings, living algae (7, 8) resemble their fossil ancestors, those progenitors of an immensely long evolutionary line, and providers, through photosynthesis, of the oxygen in the air we breathe.

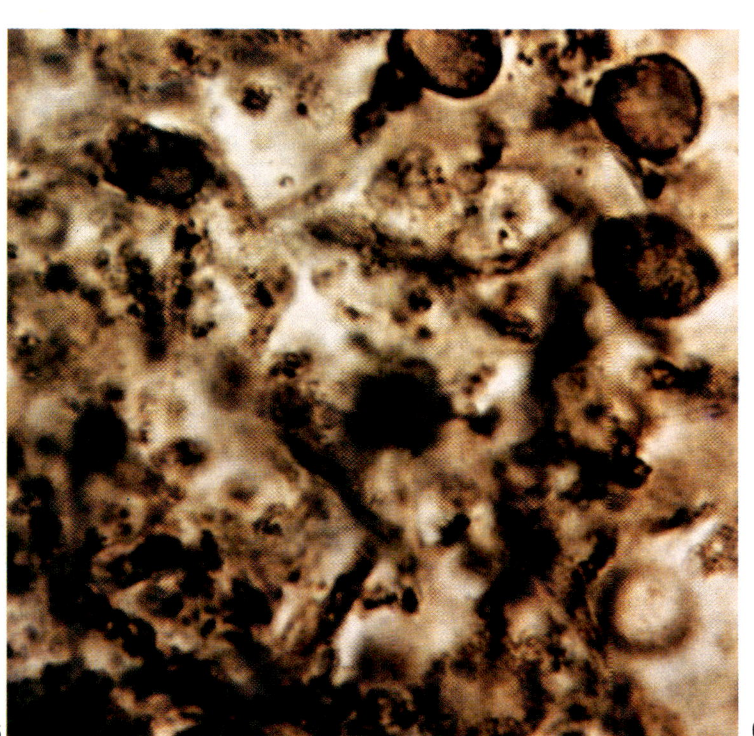
5

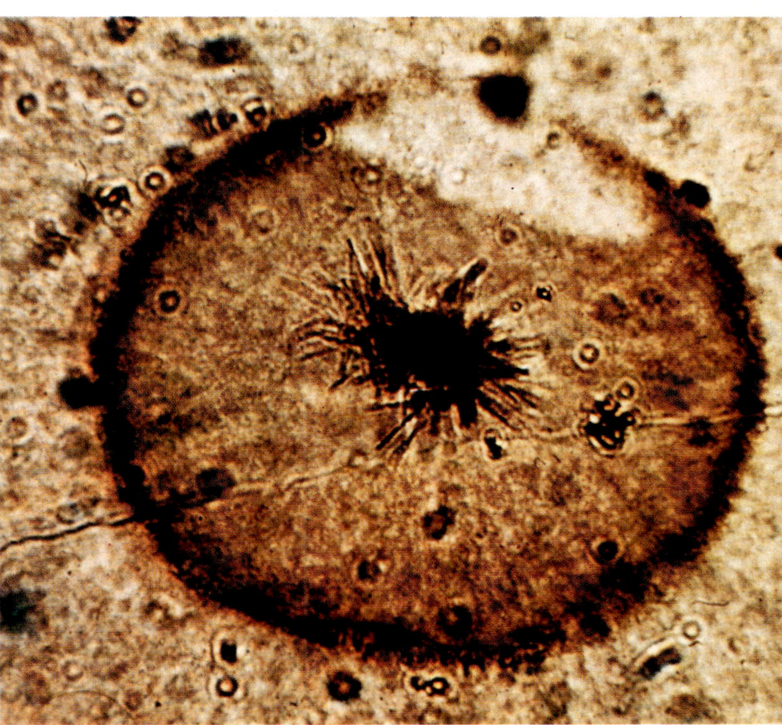
6

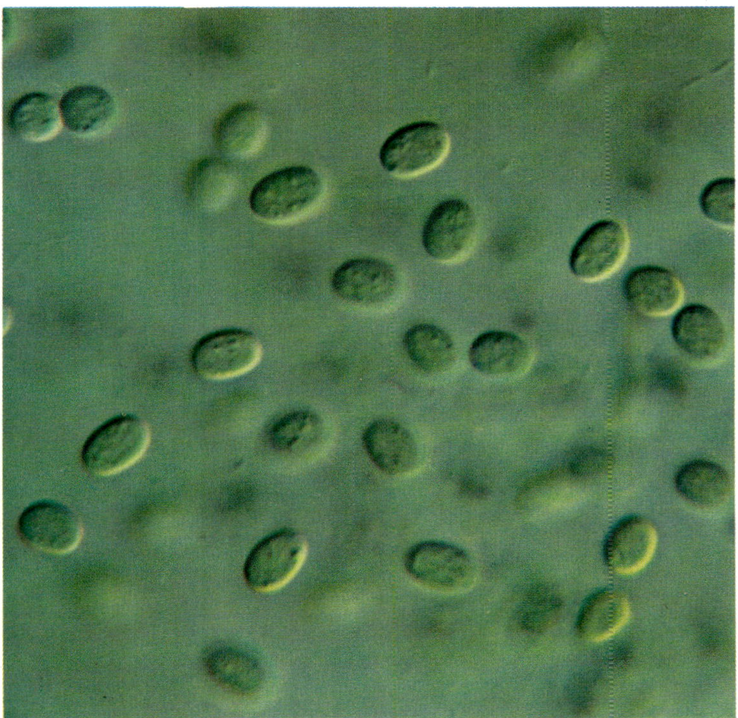
7

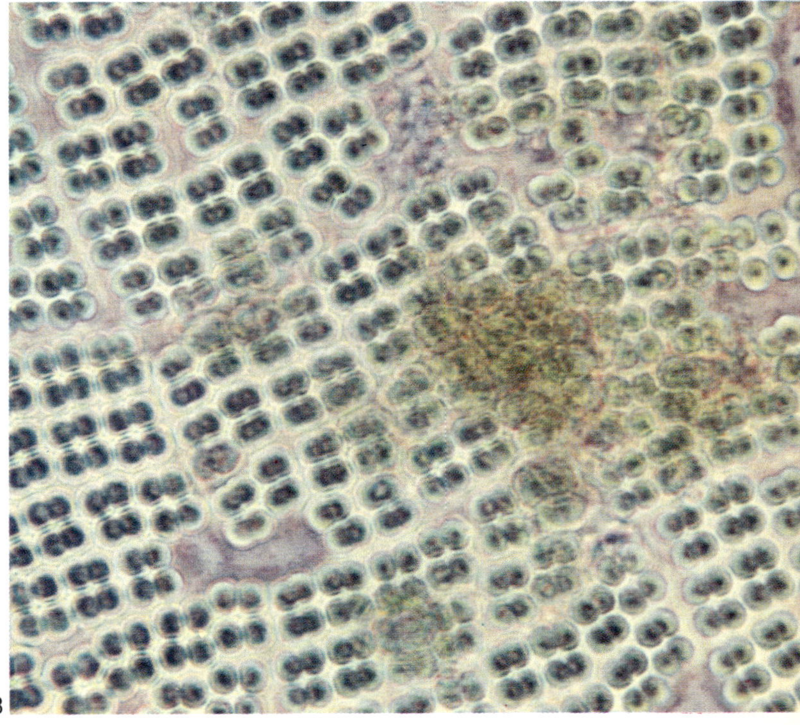
8

The lavishness of nature, in the production of far more offspring than are needed to replace the population, is an essential part of the evolutionary process. Part of an egg-rope of the common perch (9) shows over 200 eggs, each with an embryo fish clearly visible. Only a small percentage of these will survive to maturity. To even the very earliest organisms this over-productivity was a form of insurance, and the competition for survival was the fuel that powered the evolutionary machine.

9

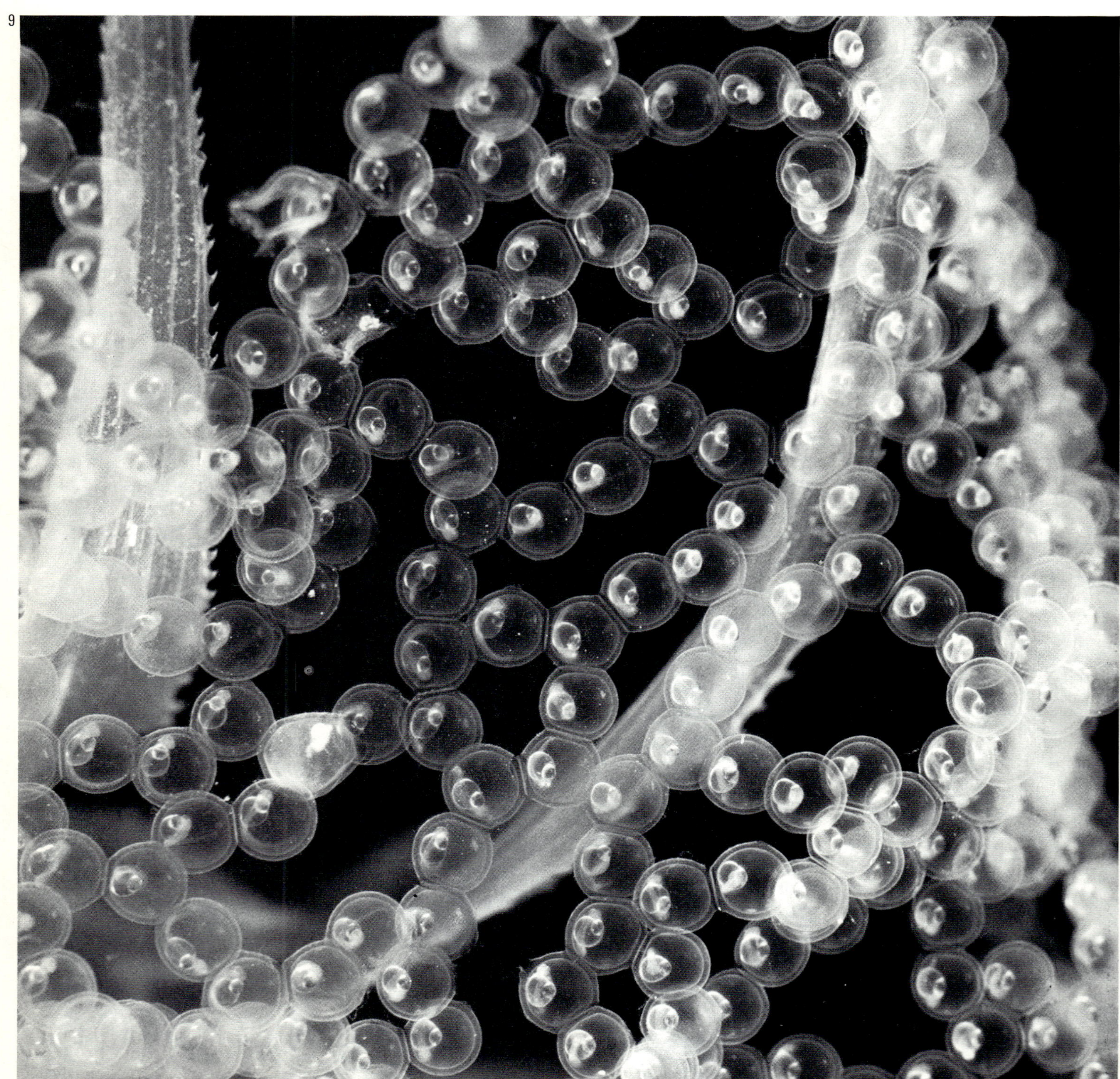

10

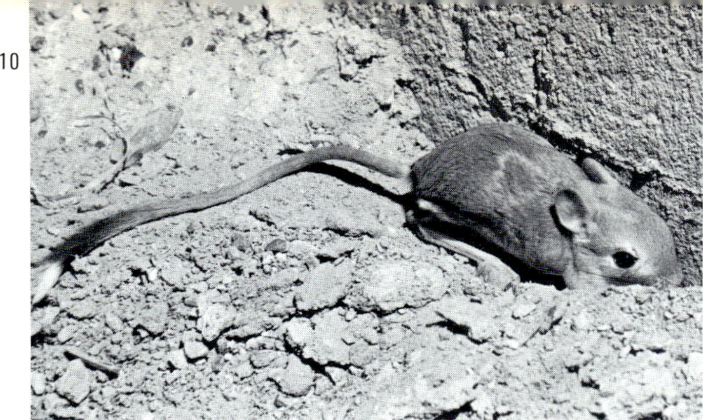

11

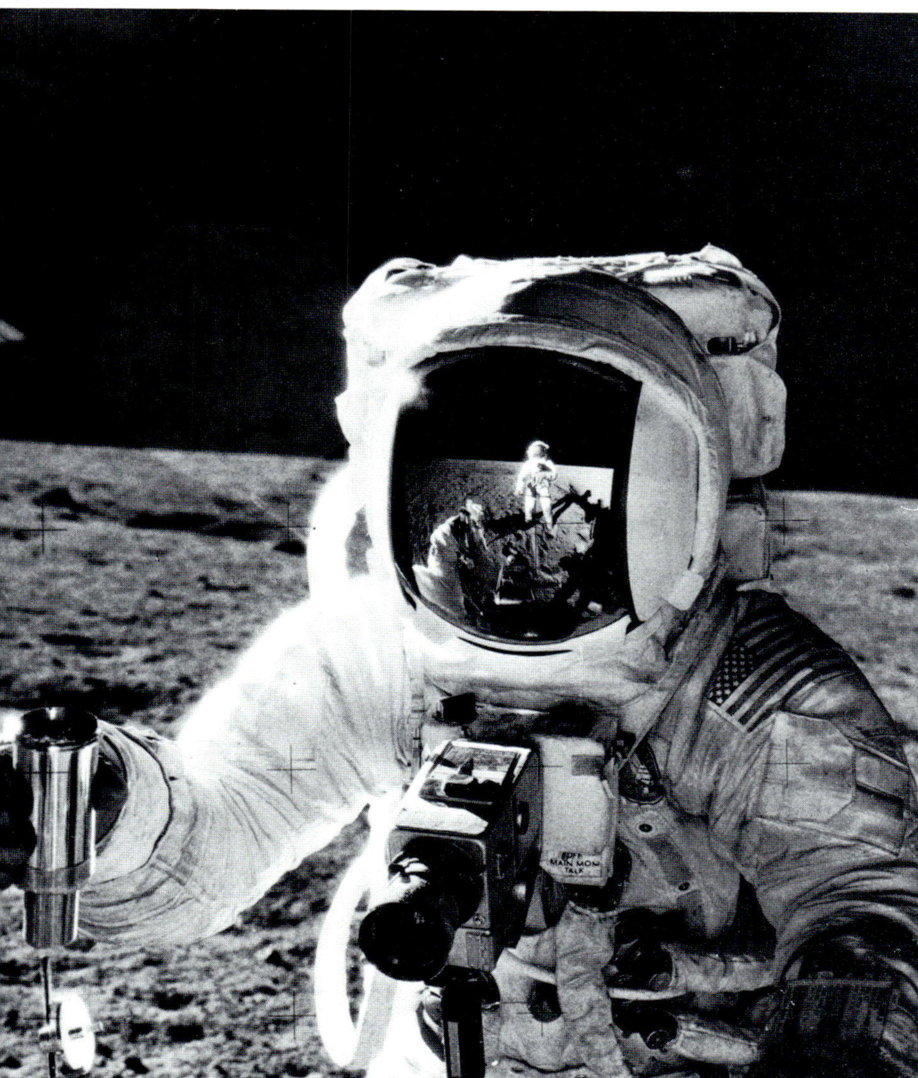

12

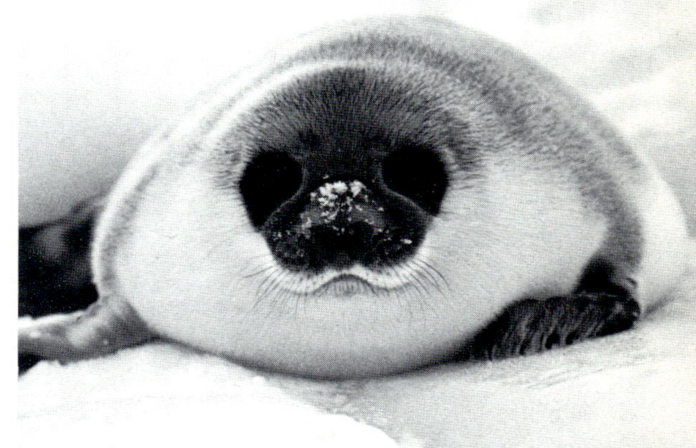

A constant internal temperature is essential for animal life, and its maintenance is one of the most advanced achievements of evolution. In hot desert country the jerboa (10), with its large ears, long tail and long, thin hind legs, has a high ratio of surface to volume and so avoids retaining the heat of the sun. The seal, on the other hand, with its well-rounded shape (12), has a low surface-to-volume ratio and retains as much heat as possible. In the most hostile environment of all (11), man adopts the same configuration.

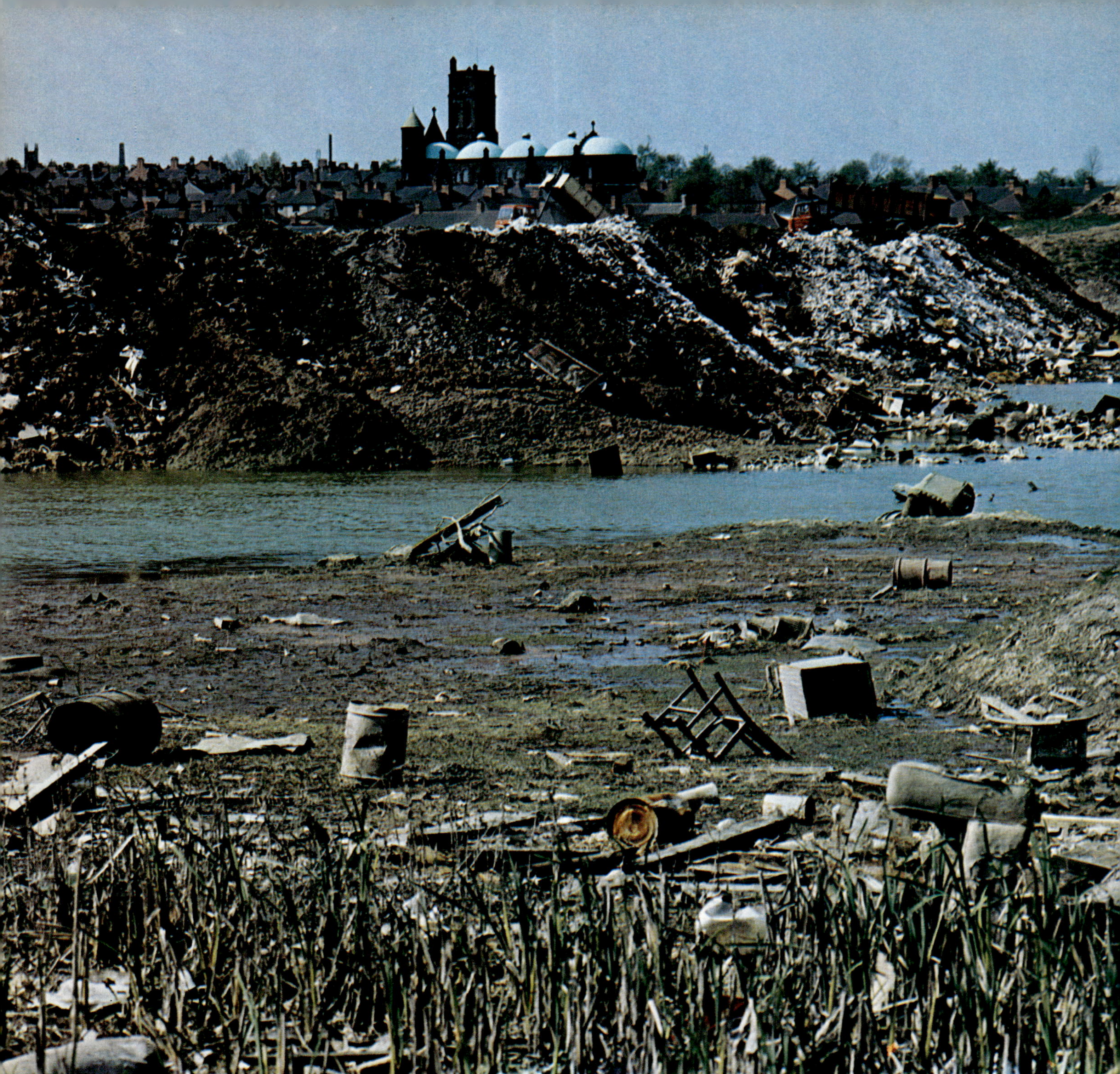

13
Man, the lord of creation and most recent dominant product of evolution, tends to maltreat his environment in a way that cries out for the cleansing attention of one of the great forces of nature – such as an ice age. This worked-out marl-pit on the outskirts of an industrial town, littered and contaminated by urban wastes, is both unproductive and dangerous. The scar can yield to plastic surgery: since this picture was taken the pit has been filled in, rehabilitated and landscaped. But too often the cruder and more blatant marks of unheeding past exploitation of the environment remain, because people cannot or will not afford to erase them. Former strip mining and shanty towns, exhausted and eroding soils and stinking rivers show that many communities have not yet learnt the prime lesson: that the world only remains productive, beautiful and healthy if people understand and work with nature.

2

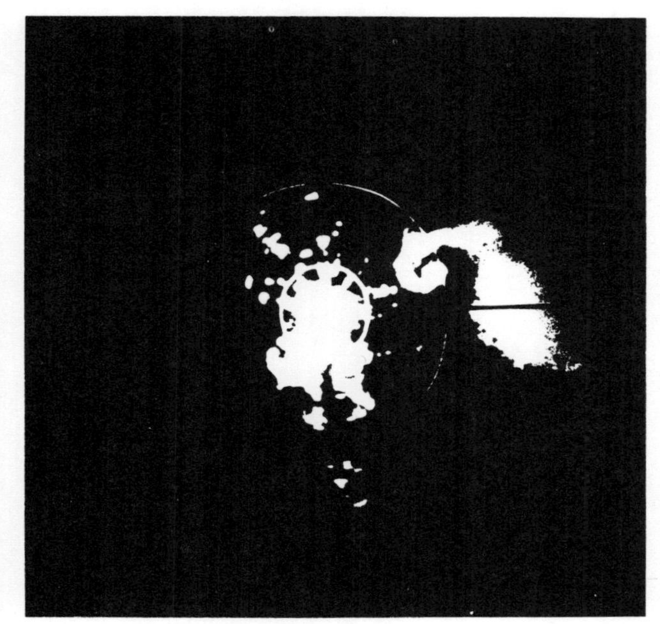

The air around us

P. J. Meade

P. J. Meade

The atmosphere is man's natural environment: the more he knows about it the better he is able to face its widely varying threats to his survival. By taking advantage of favourable conditions the quality of life can be improved. But if we fail to recognize the danger signs disaster on a local, regional, or perhaps even global scale can follow.

The spectrum of human life is wide. At one end there are those whose way of life is adapted to the average conditions in their natural surroundings, temperature and rainfall generally being the dominant elements. At the other end are the advanced populations in the highly industrialized countries who might appear to be insulated by technology from any severities that the environment might produce. But people at each end of this spectrum are vulnerable to short- and long-term changes in the atmosphere because their existence in relation to their surroundings is apt to be marginal, in the one case because of deficiencies, in the other because of unchecked demand. Those in the middle of the spectrum are also vulnerable to changes in weather and climate but to a lesser extent because their mode of life is more flexible.

For man, as for other living creatures, there are upper and lower limits to the atmospheric conditions in which he can thrive. If he finds himself outside these limits either through moving to an unfavourable locality or because the conditions change, difficulties are bound to arise. Therefore, the more that man can learn about the atmosphere and its ways, the better prepared he can be to anticipate and guard against any changes that might constitute a threat to the quality of life, or to life itself, whether in a small or large area of the globe.

The year 1972 may be used to illustrate these considerations. In that year abnormal weather, which may have been part of a climatic change already in progress or merely the warning signs of a change to come, produced such effects as regional droughts, floods, diversion of ocean currents and heavy pack-ice fields off Labrador. Many nations were affected in a variety of economic and social matters. In the Sahelian zone of West Africa 1972, which followed several dry years, had its lowest rainfall since 1913 and by early 1973 six million people were in danger of starvation, many died and thousands took refuge in towns to the south.

An event such as this poses many complex questions to meteorologists and climatologists. Is the reduced rainfall of recent years part of a long-term trend or a temporary phase in a cyclic phenomenon, or only a sample of random distribution? Are man's activities helping to create the desert? It has been calculated that the Sahara is currently expanding by 40,000 acres a year, not least because of man's misuse of the border regions. But how can man prevent desert encroachment or the creation of new desert areas and restore the vegetal cover of denuded soil surfaces before they are taken over by shifting sands?

Clearly meteorologists, climatologists and atmospheric physicists would not make much progress if they studied the atmosphere in isolation. The planet Earth is extremely complicated and its various aspects are interrelated, requiring for their description a variety of scientific disciplines – physics, geography, geology, biology and so on. The oceans occupy about 70 per cent of the Earth's surface and, because of their capacity to absorb and retain heat, they too are of great importance to an understanding of atmospheric processes. Meteorologists and oceanographers often describe their separate subjects as part of one over-all discipline, with numerous joint research projects to study the interactions between the oceans and the atmosphere, and to incorporate the influence of the oceans into medium-range weather forecasts and studies of climatic variability.

Our envelope of gas

The atmosphere, which most people call the air, is generally described as a gaseous envelope enclosing the earth and attached to it by the attraction of gravity. Stars and other planets also have their gaseous envelopes, and scientists whose main concern is the earth's atmosphere have found much to interest them in the atmospheres of such planets as Mars, Jupiter and Venus, knowledge of which has increased substantially in recent years.

It is convenient to describe the atmosphere according to its temperature distribution, because this provides a set pattern of stratification although the heights of the inter-surfaces or relatively shallow layers of separation may vary, sometimes widely. Figure 1 shows the average temperature structure of the atmosphere up to a height of about 120 km. The separate layers (troposphere, stratosphere, mesosphere and thermosphere) are determined by temperature lapse rates – the variation of temperature with height, characteristic of each layer – and the boundaries between adjacent layers are given special labels – tropopause, stratopause and mesopause.

The data for Figure 1 are taken from the 'standard' atmospheres adopted by the International Civil Aviation Organization (ICAO) from the surface to 32 km, and the extension from 32 km upwards to 700 km proposed by an official committee in the USA. These so-called 'standard atmospheres', which are based on the actual state of the atmosphere itself, serve very important practical purposes

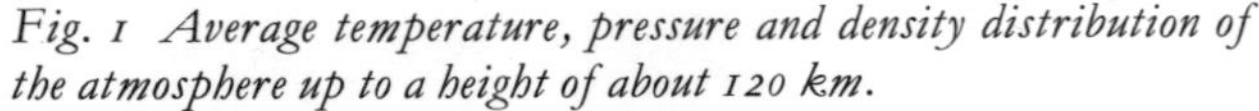

Fig. 1 Average temperature, pressure and density distribution of the atmosphere up to a height of about 120 km.

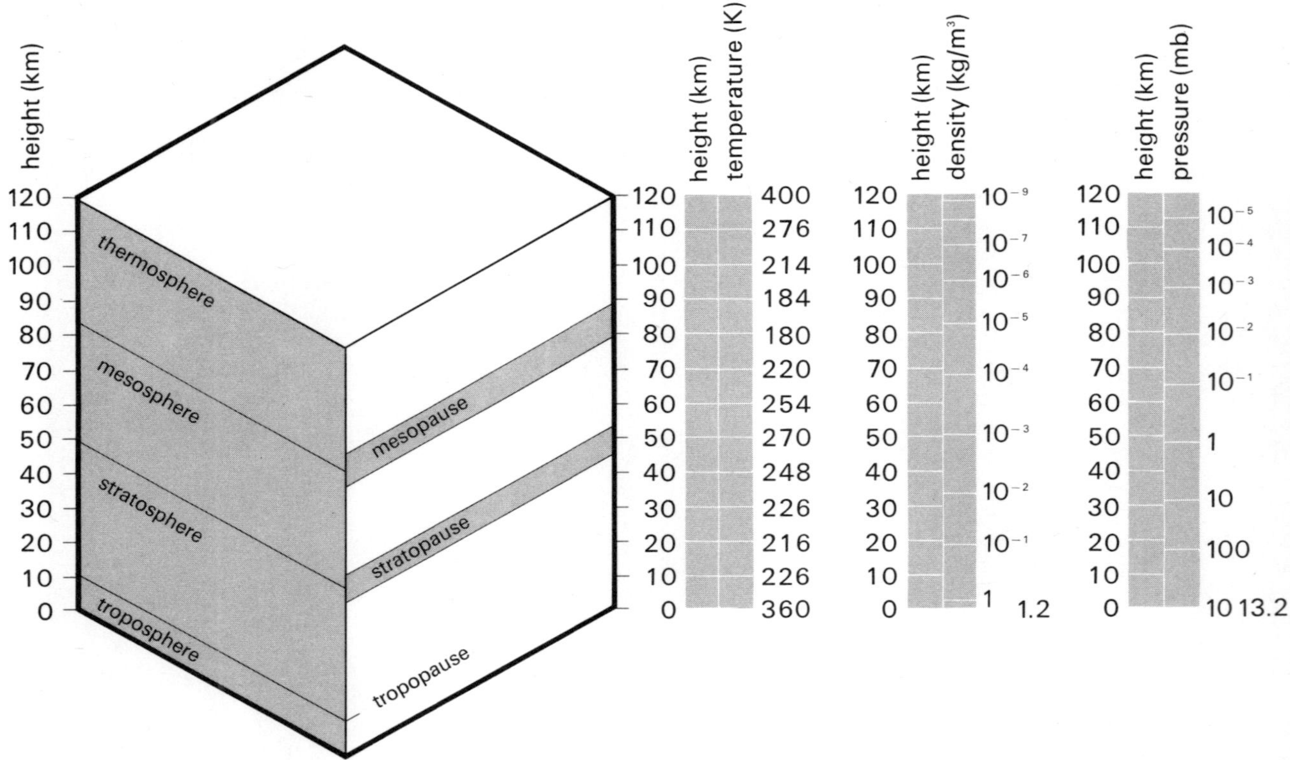

in comparisons of the performance of different aircraft and in the calibration of altimeters.

The layer nearest to the earth, the troposphere, is where the temperature tends to fall off with height and where clouds (except for the much higher mother-of-pearl clouds) and precipitation in the form of rain, sleet or snow are found. The limit of the troposphere, where the tropopause begins, is usually about 17 km at the equator and about 7 km at the poles. However, in the temperate latitudes the height of the tropopause can vary widely from about 13 km above certain anticyclones down to about 7 km above the deepest depressions; in the case of the latter, the structure of the tropopause itself can be exceedingly complex – it can be a layer rather than a surface, or even split into two or more tropopauses.

The stratosphere, the region between the troposphere and the mesosphere, has its upper boundary at about 50 km. In the stratosphere, in contrast to conditions above and below, the temperature either remains constant or increases with height. The stratosphere, which includes the ozone layer (see below) is extremely dry and therefore has no precipitation and few clouds. Modern jet airliners normally have their cruising altitudes in the stratosphere, which accounts for the expression 'flying above the weather'.

Figure 1 also indicates the average decrease of pressure and of density with height. Everywhere in the free air Boyle's well-known law applies: the pressure of a gas varies as the product of its temperature and its density. The pressure of the atmosphere is simply the weight of the vertical air column above a unit area centred at the point and is expressed as a force per unit area. The height of the column in a mercury barometer balances the weight of air above and this weight may be calculated from the density of mercury (13.6 gm/cm^3) and the height of the column, usually quite close to 76 cm for a barometer near sea-level.

A slight extension of the calculation would show that the weight of air above each square metre of the Earth's surface is about 10,000 kg or 10 tonnes. In meteorology pressures are universally expressed in millibars (mb), the average sea-level pressure over the globe being about 1013.2 mb, which is approximately equivalent to 76 cm of mercury.

Since the pressure is the weight of air above, it follows that the pressure must decrease with height in the atmosphere. For the average state of the atmosphere, the pressure is reduced to 500 mb at about 6 km above the surface. In other words, about half the mass of the atmosphere is concentrated in the first few kilometres next to the Earth, the other half being spread out over a height interval of some hundreds of kilometres. The rate of decrease of pressure with height is determined by the distribution of temperature in the vertical air column (Boyle's law again) and in a cold, and therefore dense, air column the pressure will naturally fall off more rapidly than it does in a warm column of air. Meteorologists, taking a three-dimensional view of the atmosphere, are therefore at pains to identify cold and warm air masses.

'Biosphere' is a term which has come into common use in recent years and denotes the boundary layer where physical processes within the surface layer of the Earth's crust (the lithosphere), the oceans (hydrosphere) and lower atmosphere interact with biological processes to form complex systems (ecosystems). The biosphere therefore constitutes the portion of the planet Earth occupied by human beings, animals, plants and other forms of life.

Ingredients and impurities

The atmosphere consists of mixtures of gases and layers of gases and also contains, mostly in the troposphere, water vapour, liquid water and ice particles. Both troposphere and stratosphere also contain aerosols, or minute solid particles which can remain in suspension because they have insufficient mass to be deposited by gravity. Apart from water vapour and particulate matter, the percentage concentrations of the different constituents of dry air are shown in the table. This proportionate distribution exists at least up to 25 km. Thus the air is well mixed and, of the gases mentioned in the table, only carbon dioxide and ozone have appreciable variations in concentration.

There are also present, particularly in the lower atmosphere, small quantities of sulphur dioxide, nitrous oxide, hydrogen chloride, some inert gases and others. Invariably the air is moist since it contains water vapour at a concentration of not more than 3 or 4 per cent in the lowest layers and usually decreasing with altitude. The maximum amount of water vapour that the air can hold, at saturation, is determined by the temperature: the warmer the air the more water vapour it can obtain without condensation.

Although the air is very nearly 100 per cent nitrogen and oxygen, various other constituents are of major importance. The relatively small amount of water vapour takes part in the hydrological cycle – evaporation from the oceans, lakes and rivers, condensation and return to the earth's surface – and provides clouds, rain, sleet, snow and hail.

Proportional composition of dry air

	By volume per cent	*By weight per cent*
Nitrogen	78.09	75.54
Oxygen	20.95	23.14
Argon	0.93	1.27
Carbon dioxide	0.03	0.05
Neon	1.8×10^{-3}	1.2×10^{-3}
Helium	5.2×10^{-4}	7.2×10^{-5}
Krypton	1.0×10^{-4}	3.0×10^{-4}
Hydrogen	5.0×10^{-5}	4.0×10^{-6}
Xenon	8.0×10^{-6}	3.6×10^{-5}
Ozone	1.0×10^{-6}	1.7×10^{-6}
Total dry air	100.0	100.0

Ozone (O_3) is a very important constituent of the atmosphere. It is formed at great heights by the action of the sun's radiation on oxygen molecules, breaking up the normal two-atom form and re-combining some as 'triplets'. Appreciable quantities of ozone are found at altitudes between 10 and 50 km, the maximum concentration occurring in the layer 20–25 km. Ozone prevents most of the ultraviolet radiation from the sun from penetrating the atmosphere and reaching the surface of the Earth, where it would present a serious threat to life. Some scientists express considerable anxiety lest man's activities should have the effect of reducing the ozone concentration and thus perhaps letting more of the sun's short-wave radiation through to the earth's surface.

Certain other constituents of the air are of special importance and most of these are included in the generic term 'pollution' since they are introduced into the atmosphere by external causes such as volcanic eruptions and man's industrial efforts. If a gas enters the atmosphere its residence time may be lengthy, perhaps a year or more, unless it is transformed by some chemical reaction with other gases into a substance that is readily removed from the air, for instance by rainfall. In the case of particulate matter in suspension, its probable residence time depends on whether it is in the troposphere or the stratosphere. In

Fig. 2 The components of the atmosphere–ice–land–biomass climatic system, and their interactions. The black arrows are examples of external processes and the open arrows are examples of internal processes in climatic change.

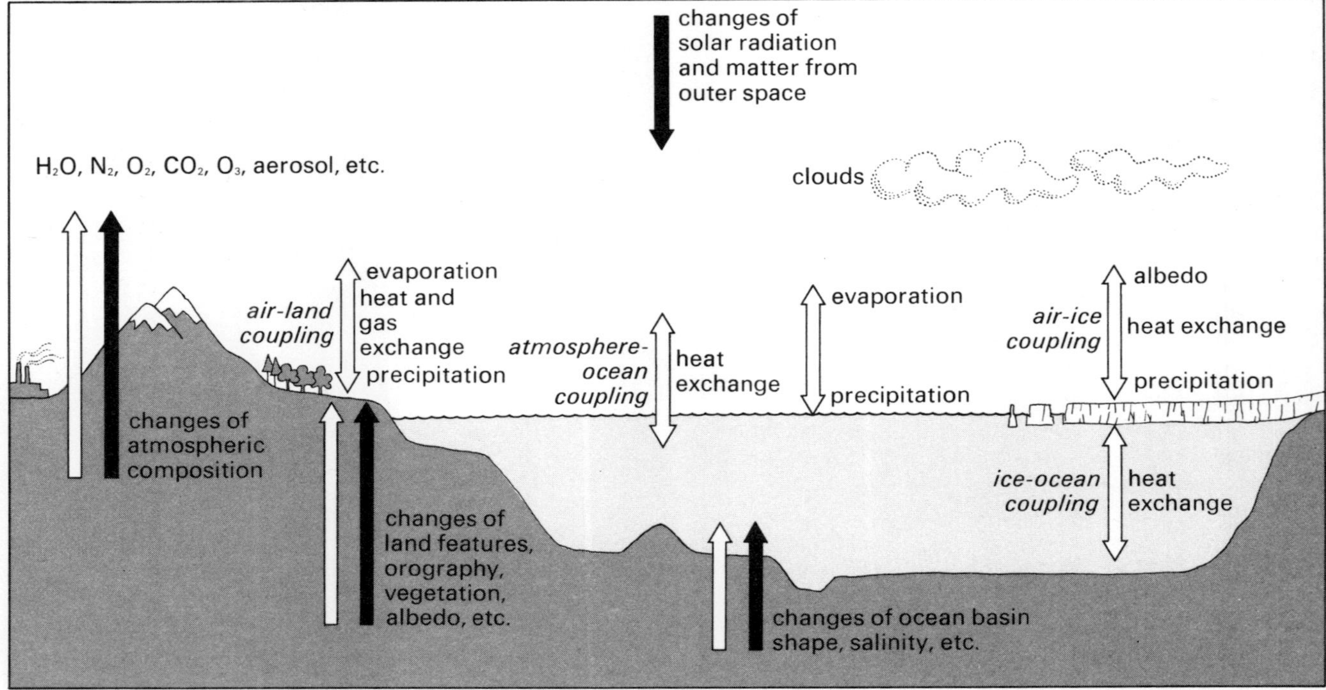

the troposphere it would be washed out by rain or, less likely, brought down to the surface by turbulence in the course of a week or two; in the stratosphere it might remain for months or even years, until it settled into the troposphere to return to earth relatively fast. Although the atmosphere is able to cleanse itself – and rainfall especially is a most efficient scavenger – it is worth remembering that the gases and aerosols which make up atmospheric pollution, certainly those resulting from industrial processes, are being fed almost continuously into the air. Are these infusions leading to a balance or a steady increase, and, if the latter, are any dangerous consequences likely?

Volcanic eruptions are the main source of widespread aerosols in the atmosphere, for although smoke and ash and the wind erosion of land contribute greater amounts, they are less widely distributed. A proportion of volcanic dust manages to penetrate into the stratosphere and is said to remain there for up to three years. It is possible that this dust, forming a widespread haze, may scatter solar radiation and as a result be the indirect cause of changes in the general circulation of the atmosphere which controls the distribution of weather over the globe. Particles of ash forced into the stratosphere by the eruption of Krakatoa, in the East Indies, in 1883, caused extraordinarily lurid sunsets all over the globe for several years. The explosion was followed by a series of unusually cold winters in Europe and North America, and various meteorologists – the late Harry Wexler in the USA and Hubert Lamb in Great Britain – have tried to establish a connection between major volcanic eruptions and cold spells and other weather phenomena.

As regards gases, carbon dioxide, which is released in the atmosphere through the combustion of oil, coal and other fossil fuels, also plays an important part in the radiation balance of the Earth's atmosphere. By 1960 the emission of carbon dioxide reached seven thousand million tons a year, and it is still sharply increasing. Carbon dioxide absorbs infra-red (heat) radiation from the Earth, and thus contributes to the 'greenhouse effect', whereby incoming sunlight is allowed in while outgoing radiation is trapped inside. If the amount of carbon dioxide present in the atmosphere were to increase substantially the radiation balance might be seriously disturbed. It is known that a carbon dioxide molecule has a probable residence time in the atmosphere of several years. Therefore, with fuel consumption increasing all the time, the amount of carbon dioxide in the atmosphere is becoming larger each year. The rate of increase is very slight, as it happens, but it leads to a highly important problem: at what stage does the total amount of carbon dioxide in the atmosphere raise the possibility of significant, adverse effects on world climate?

In view of this situation, the monitoring of the atmosphere to keep watch on the amount and distribution of its various constituent gases and particles is a compelling requirement. To this end the World Meteorological Organization has set in motion plans for establishing a world-wide network of stations to maintain continuous records of air pollution. A high proportion of the stations are already in operation.

Deteriorating conditions in the 'microclimates' where a majority of Westerners live – the big cities – have recently brought the problems of pollution into sharp focus. The most remarkable difference between city and country climates is the amount of fog or smog – 30 per cent greater in summer and 100 per cent in winter. On calm days the emissions of dust and fumes may hang over the city in a huge dome, and in certain conditions these particles will become nuclei for condensing water droplets, i.e. fog. In winter the sun may fail to break through the upper layers, with the result that an acrid smog will build up inside the dome, causing discomfort to everyone within, and premature death to many asthmatics and heart patients. In the USA there are regular 'air acceptability' reports, with grades ranging from 'good' through 'acceptable' to 'unacceptable' – a category mentioned all too frequently. In Los Angeles the yellowish smog layer overhanging the city is a feature unpleasantly familiar to all travellers touching down at the airport. In Tokyo smog masks are worn as a matter of course, and coin-operated machines provide oxygen for those overcome by fumes. In London there have been a number of dangerous smogs since the catastrophe of 1952, when thousands of people died prematurely.

How the atmosphere has evolved

Not many years ago atmospheric scientists with very few exceptions were only interested in the last century or two of the history of the atmosphere. The difficulties of going back even 50 or 100 years in trying to construct a continuous record of the world's weather did not seem of major importance. One well-kown meteorologist who used his spare time to browse into early literature up to the fifteenth century looking for any direct or indirect references to weather or climate was widely regarded as a genial eccentric when he published his accumulated jottings. He was, of course, a man of vision well ahead of most of his contemporaries in recognizing the mines where valuable data and inferences were waiting to be dug out.

However, in recent years there has been a strong upsurge of interest in climatology and climate variability, because it is now widely acknowledged that future climatic changes may have profound effects on mankind. Efforts have been made, to take the time-scale of climate back as far as possible, even to the origin of the atmosphere we live in.

The origin and early history of the atmosphere can only be inferred from the indirect evidence provided by geological discoveries. Some of the facts about the early history of the earth itself can be attributed to atmospheric causes, and these lead to deductions about some of the gases which must have been present in the atmosphere at the time.

The age of the earth has been estimated, partly through the presence of radioactive elements and a knowledge of their rate of decay, at some five or six thousand million years. The problem of how the original atmosphere evolved and ultimately settled to a fairly steady composition, depends on a variety of questions. What were the origins of the original gaseous components? How were their relative proportions modified by the influx of gases from the earth's interior and by losses of the lightest gases to outer space? How was equilibrium established between the amounts of carbon dioxide and oxygen, leaving sufficient excess of the latter to form a protective ozone layer, since this could only occur when plant life existed and photosynthesis could increase the rate of oxygen production.

An assessment of the rate at which gases, steam and lava are poured forth by volcanoes has led to the suggestion that the present atmosphere and oceans emerged from the interior of the earth as a result of volcanic activity. Their theory gains support when the data available lead to the rejection of other possibilities. For example, it appears that the present nitrogen content of the atmosphere can be explained, and can only be explained, by exhalations from the earth's crust, itself produced by volcanic and seismic activity.

The geological evidence provides facts and sound deductions which contribute greatly to the work of climatologists in trying to map the history of the earth's climate. The earliest ice ages form suitable reference points in the chronology and have been traced back to periods approximately 1,000 million, 500 million and 250 million years ago. These ice ages during which glaciers and ice sheets extended to latitudes as far south as 55°, were interspersed with inter-glacial phases of much longer duration. In the history of the last 100 million years, the major global fluctuations of climate have been traced. It is known that ice sheets were completely absent during the warm periods and that the global climate had to undergo substantial changes for ice sheets to develop. The earth today

Fig. 3 Main trends in global climate, viewed over periods of time ranging from 100 years (top) to 1 million years (bottom). Over 100 years, changes in the five-year running average of surface temperature in the northern hemisphere are measured in tenths of a degree centigrade but still had a noticeable effect. The figure points to the hot summers and mild winters of the 1940s. Next, the winter severity index for eastern Europe over the last 1000 years shows up the so-called 'Little Ice Age' (2), about 1400 to 1700. Here the range from minimum to maximum is no more than 1.5°C. Looking back over 20,000 years, the middle graph (based on such data as glacier fluctuations, changes in the tree line, etc.) puts the Little Ice Age in its proper perspective as a mere kink in the curve, which can now be seen to drop to 10°C below the present norm; the Younger Dryas cold interval (3) is a 5°C drop in a generally warmer trend, which is the present interglacial, or Holocene (4). We have to go back 125,000 years to the last comparable warm age, the Eemian interglacial (5). Finally, taking as the yardstick global ice volume, which can be worked out from changes in the oxygen isotope ratio in fossil plankton, the last million years show only three warm peaks approaching our favoured present. The scale shown represents a difference, maximum to minimum, of about 50 million cubic kilometres of ice, which corresponds to a fluctuation of about 12°C.

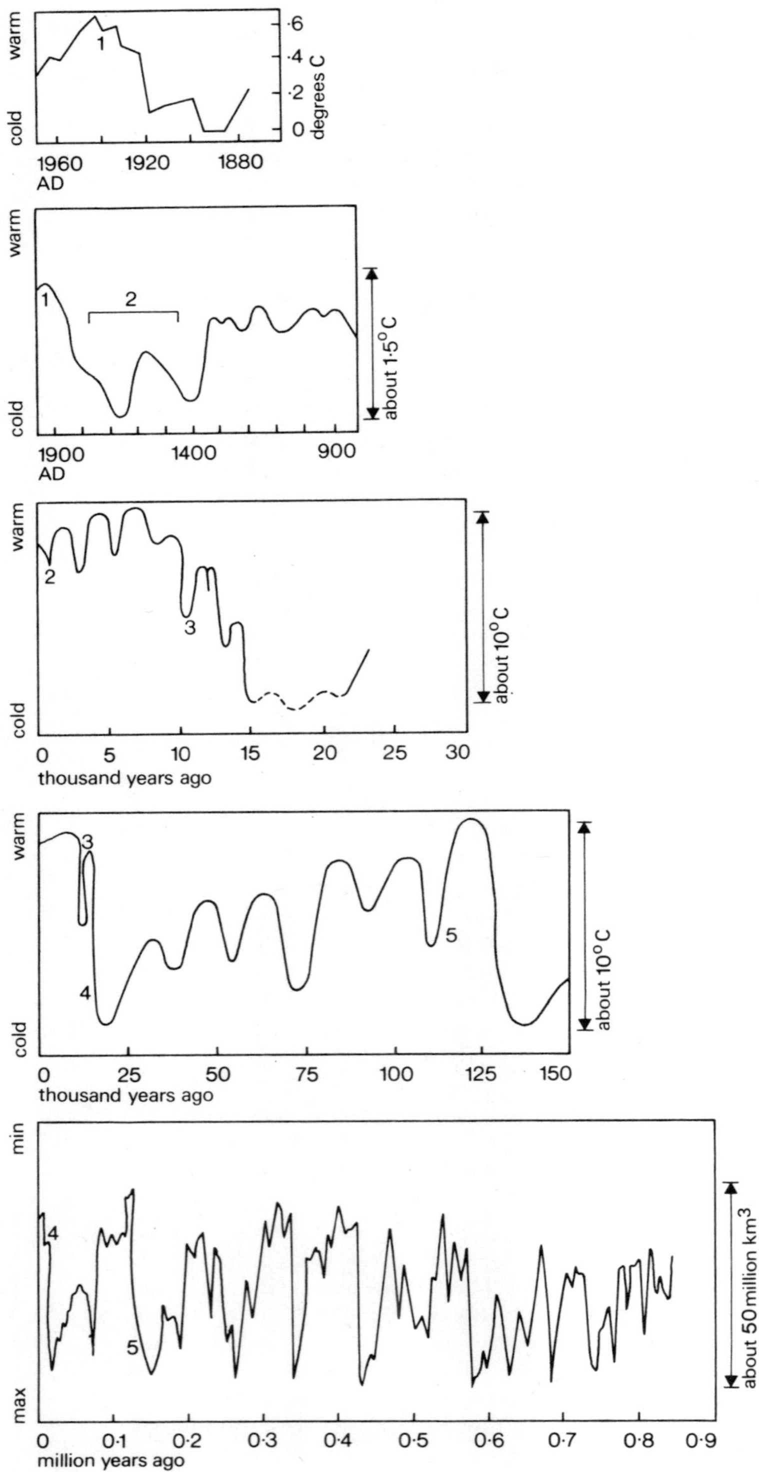

is in an inter-glacial period of the Quaternary ice age which began about one million years ago and in which four major glacial advances have so far taken place, the last about 8,000 to 10,000 years ago. The period extending from about 1550 to 1850 has been called a 'little ice age' and was noted for prolonged cold temperatures and the extension of glaciers, but these effects were not sufficient to justify the term 'glacial epoch'.

The main trends in global climate during the past million years are shown in Figure 3, which is taken from a report on climatic variation prepared in connection with the Global Atmospheric Research Programme of the World Meteorological Organization and the International Council of Scientific Unions. The intensive efforts of climatologists over the past few years have established the history of global climate for a million years in unprecedented detail and with greatly improved absolute dating.

Observing the atmosphere

Meteorology is primarily an observational science. As data accumulate, the physical processes which occur in the atmosphere may be explained partly by empirical or inductive methods and partly by using the data to test theoretical ideas. Long before adequate data became available, two of the outstanding figures in meteorology, V. Bjerknes of Norway and L. F. Richardson from Great Britain, the former at the beginning of the century and the latter some 20 years later, discussed mathematically the dynamics and thermodynamics of the atmosphere in ways that were so fertile in ideas that much of today's theoretical work can be traced back to the seeds which they sowed. Their theories perforce had to remain interesting academic exercises until the establishment of networks of upper air observing stations, which provided the extensive three-dimensional data for wind, temperature and humidity necessary to test theory and develop it further.

These procedures for assembling atmospheric data and evaluating theoretical and empirical methods must continue without end because it is a safe assumption that the available information will never be sufficient to solve all problems in the atmosphere. In any event the problems themselves are subject to change as a result of natural causes such as variations in solar activity, and of industrial processes which release heat, gases and particulate matter into the atmosphere on an ever-increasing scale. Nevertheless, in spite of the difficulties – the extreme complexity of the atmosphere and the inadequacy of the data – progress is being made, in the past 30 years or so quite remarkable progress, and theory and induction are providing new insights into the changes that take place, their causes and their mechanisms.

One of the special fascinations of studying the atmosphere is the continuing value of visual observations. The first meteorological instruments were not available until the seventeenth century, and before that time (and indeed for a considerable time afterwards) the science was visual and descriptive. Even today there remains a highly valuable role for careful observation and reporting of phenomena witnessed in the atmosphere. In 1918 a group of Norwegian meteorologists revolutionized the science of weather forecasting with a brilliant series of papers on the structure of depressions, introducing the concepts of air masses separated by fronts or discontinuities. But nearly a hundred years earlier Luke Howard, by observing the cloud systems associated with the approach and passage of rain belts, came to some broad conclusions about the physical processes that were taking place. These were largely confirmed by the research carried out in Norway. At the time Luke Howard did not have the data to support or disprove his speculations but early in the present century two British meteorologists, W. N. Shaw and R. G. K. Lempfert, making use of the information then becoming more plentiful, came very close to the flash point of the frontal theories which inspired their colleagues in Norway.

For many years meteorology has been regarded as the most international of sciences. This collaboration in observing the atmosphere and exchanging the data was acknowledged as essential when it was realized that the weather experienced in a small area on a particular day was not merely a local phenomenon but the end product of physical processes taking place on a much wider, perhaps regional or planetary scale. The seventeenth century saw a number of important advances like the formulation of Boyle's law and the invention of the barometer, and with these and other aids such as the thermometer it was possible to begin the quantitative study of the physics of the atmosphere. Meteorological observing stations came into existence and their numbers slowly expanded, and in a few areas rudimentary networks were set up for co-ordinated observations at specified times with standardized instruments. It seems remarkable that even before the invention of the telegraph in 1843 meteorologists were already drawing up plans for the atmosphere to be observed frequently, simultaneously and everywhere all over the globe. All these developments are seen today in the World Meteorological Organization's programme of World Weather Watch with its global networks of surface and upper air stations, supplemented by satellite observations, and a global telecommunications system for collecting data from individual countries and disseminating them all over the world.

With the collection and exchange of observations made at fixed times the practice of synoptic meteorology and the construction of weather maps developed rapidly. In the northern hemisphere, for example, thousands of ground stations and hundreds of merchant ships make observations of pressure, temperature, humidity, wind, cloud cover, visibility, rainfall etc. at regular intervals, every hour or every three hours or every six hours. About 600 upper air stations and a small number of ocean weather vessels launch radio-sonde instruments and radar reflectors to obtain measurements of pressure, temperature, humidity and wind up to 25 km once or twice each day.

Ever since cloud pictures were first transmitted by the American polar-orbiting satellite Tiros 1 in 1960, meteorologists have been provided with an almost uninterrupted flow of excellent photographs from successive American satellites. (Satellites are, of course, used to monitor other phenomena besides the weather, and a fuller and more detailed account of these and their contribution to meteorology is given in Chapter 10.) Cloud pictures taken from above give meteorologists an extra view of the different cloud types associated with the various pressure systems and the distribution of winds and temperatures in the atmosphere. The pictures have not only proved their worth in day-to-day weather forecasting, but have also given new and in some cases unsuspected information about the complex structure of the centre of a depression at various stages in its history.

Polar-orbiting satellites are able to photograph a large area at any one instant and a ground station can usually intercept the transmission from three successive orbits, one to the east, one overhead and one to the west, thus obtaining pictures of clouds and of snow on the ground over a very extensive area surrounding the receiving station.

The geosynchronous satellite, which is placed in orbit vertically above a point on the equator and synchronized with the rotation of the Earth, remains permanently in position relative to the point on the equator. The satellite is equipped to take pictures of the Earth every 20 minutes and satisfactorily photographs an area extending to about 45° N and S latitude, the pictures from higher latitudes becoming more and more distorted owing to the very oblique angle of viewing. Plate 1 shows a photograph taken from a geosynchronous satellite stationed over the Amazon which observes North and South America, most of the Atlantic Ocean and West Africa.

A more or less complete global coverage of cloud distribution would be obtained with two or three polar-orbiting and five geosynchronous satellites. A complete system on these lines set up by the USA, USSR, Japan and a group of European countries is planned to be in full operation towards the end of 1977.

Another satellite system, for the remote sensing of atmospheric temperatures, is now in an advanced state of development. These satellites would record the vertical distribution of temperature at a large number of points over the globe. When it reaches a reliable operational stage, the whole system of satellites together with the Earth-based surface and upper-air observing stations, including ocean station vessels and selected merchant ships, will account for a substantial portion of the observations for the World Weather Watch.

It might be wondered whether this would not provide too much data for forecasting services to assimilate several times each day. The answer is that there never is too much. A multiplicity of observing systems, satellite and ground-based, are supplementary to one another and are, in fact, mutually supporting since the data from one system are valuable in checking and calibrating others. This does not apply to the satellite cloud pictures which form a unique observing system but temperature- and, later, humidity-sounding satellites may not, at least for a very long time, rival in detail, accuracy and reliability the measurements made by the radio-sonde instruments launched from ground-based stations and ocean weather vessels. Comparison and calibration are therefore of extreme importance in improving the validity of a set of observations which would otherwise have to be rejected. The main advantage of the temperature-sounding satellites is that they promise global coverage with very good horizontal resolution, an objective that would be unattainable by a ground-based system because the number of stations required would present insuperable logistic problems.

The sheer quantity of meteorological data received each day in the larger forecasting centres raises a problem mainly of organizing the telecommunication and processing facilities. One of the most important tasks of the World Meteorological Organization is to ensure that global telecommunications function with the utmost efficiency in the collection and distribution of data from the world's national meteorological services. These must then organize their data-processing facilities – powerful computers with a range of peripheral equipment – so that the assimilation of data and the production of charts and forecasts can proceed smoothly within the inevitably exacting time schedules.

Is the climate getting worse?

The climate of an area is often defined as the synthesis of the weather that exists in that area, which may be small or large, so we may speak of a local, regional or global climate. To the layman the weather is interpreted in terms of sunshine, cloudiness, rain and so on, but since all meteorological, oceanic and other geophysical parameters contribute to climate, the main *meteorological* elements are pressure, temperature, humidity, precipitation and sunshine. In addition, records of such phenomena as thunder, frost, fog, soil temperature, sea surface temperature and many other factors are taken into account in a comprehensive study of climate. Observations from ground stations, made at fixed times by international agreement, enable realistic comparisons to be made between one region and another.

Like most subjects concerned with the atmosphere, climate is extremely complex, going much further than the calculation of averages for the hour, day, month, season or even year or longer. Two places may have the same average temperature but their climates could differ markedly in such matters as the difference between the maximum temperature during the day and the minimum at night, or between the rainfall, frost, fog etc. at each place. Averages are of course valuable as the first step in assessing climate, but other important derived quantities include extreme values, frequencies of values within specified ranges, combined summaries of two or more elements, and frequencies of weather types. There is also an essential qualitative or descriptive aspect in which the meteorological characteristics are related to such factors as geographical position.

Since the sun provides nearly all the energy that maintains the atmospheric processes, the latitude of a place must have a significant bearing on its climate. But latitude alone does not determine climate: the lowest recorded temperature in Tromsö, Norway, is $-18°$ C, while that at Omaha, Nebraska, almost 1700 miles nearer the equator, is $-35°$ C. Other important factors include the position relative to continents and oceans, local topographical features, and the incidence of pressure systems such as depressions and anticyclones. Consolidating the effects of all these relevant factors, various types of climate are recognized such as continental and maritime, the Mediterranean climate with its hot dry summers and cold wet winters, the desert climates of the subtropical zones and many others.

For the most part climate is taken for granted and people seldom realize that it is one of the most important factors in shaping civilizations and accounting for differences in way of life and culture from one part of the world to another. Nor is it fully realized how climatic changes have decisively affected the course of history. The Viking expansion, for instance, was probably due, at least in part, to the warmer weather which northern Europe enjoyed from AD 800 to 1000. In Norway and other Scandinavian countries this led to a substantial extension of the arable acreage, which in turn implied a larger and more vigorous population. The resulting overpopulation was almost certainly one reason for Viking invasion and settlement in England, France, Russia and elsewhere, as well as Viking penetration into the Mediterranean and exploration of north-west America. However, there is a general awareness that climate may change over very long periods – since everyone has heard of ice ages – but such changes are regarded as so slow as to be of no consequence in a normal lifetime. People do of course remember the good and bad summers and the mild and severe winters, but over a period they probably see these events as self-balancing, leaving in the aggregate little or no net change.

It is probably only in the present century that surface observations have been available on a sufficiently extensive scale for the climate of a country, a continent or the globe itself to be described with the authority conferred by physical measurements. For the climatology of the upper air the record is shorter, about 30 years. These time-scales are infinitesimal compared with the several thousand million years since the planet Earth was formed and so it is extremely difficult to assess whether any climatic variations, which may appear to be indicated by the instrumental record, are part of a systematic change or merely random fluctuations. The history of global climate in the past million years has been pieced together with remarkable skill and clearly shows a number of quasi-periodic components of long-term climatic change with wavelengths of about 100,000 years, 20,000 years and 2,500 years. There may have been others with wavelengths of the order 100–200 years. But these conclusions, extremely important as they are, do not give a complete picture of the variability of climate and certainly do not provide a basis for predicting changes.

In recent years there has been a lot of speculation among scientists, and considerable interest shown by the mass media, as to whether apparent trends revealed by atmospheric data for the past 70 years or so point to a worsening of global or regional climate, perhaps the approach of a new ice age during the next 50–100 years, or whether these apparent trends are merely random fluctuations which will be followed by similar variations in the opposite direction. There are two main areas of concern. Firstly there is the possibility, which some scientists assert has already revealed itself, that natural causes could have an adverse effect upon the world's climate. These might include one or more of: changes in the sun's radiation, volcanic eruptions polluting the stratosphere with dust, Antarctic ice surges and changes in sea-ice cover. Secondly there is the possibility that man's own activities may adversely affect the climate, for example, the release of heat to the atmosphere by energy production and consumption, increases in the amounts of carbon dioxide and of particulate matter in the atmosphere, agricultural operations which may alter the energy balance of the sun–atmosphere–earth system and perhaps change the hydrological cycle, in particular reducing the evaporation from the oceans, lakes and rivers. If both these possible causes, natural and man-made, were to operate adversely, then they would reinforce each other and mankind would be faced with a very serious problem.

To balance such pessimistic forebodings it should be said that other scientists of no less authority consider that the climatic fluctuations of recent years have been no greater than those experienced in the past few centuries and that there is as yet no significant evidence of a downward trend of temperature which might indicate the approach of a new ice age.

There can be no question that these problems and the possibilities they suggest should be matters of serious concern. The anxieties are real because even a small variation in climate with average temperatures falling by as little as 0.5° centigrade could have a serious impact upon agriculture with disastrous consequences since the total world food production is already said to be insufficient to feed the world population.

However, a doubt which must arise in connection with warnings about climatic change is that they imply an ability to predict climate, and such a claim is unacceptable at the present time. There is more than a hint of inconsistency when it is acknowledged that climate is controlled by the atmosphere–oceans–cryosphere–lithosphere system, yet predictions or warnings are issued as a result of studies confined very largely, if not entirely, to the atmospheric parameters. The problem of understanding the physical basis of climate is much more complex than the problem of analysing the general circulation of the atmosphere for short-term weather forecasting. It will be clear from Figure 2 that if climate prediction is ever to be a possibility, a host of exceedingly difficult problems must first be solved. These must be tackled with urgency because man's ever-increasing consumption of energy makes it essential to monitor and explain not only climate itself but man's impact upon it.

'Here is the weather forecast'

Atmospheric processes can be classified in many different ways but the most important for our purposes are the dynamic and thermodynamic processes concerned with the movement of air and with convection, condensation and precipitation. However, it must be emphasized that other processes like the radiation balance are also fundamental to an understanding of the atmosphere. The physical behaviour of the atmosphere conforms to well-known natural laws. It is therefore possible to write down in fairly precise terms a number of mathematical equations which can be used to analyse the state of the atmosphere at a particular time and then by integrating the equations to predict the behaviour of the atmosphere during the ensuing 24, 48, 72 hours and, on occasion, even further ahead. However, the factors in the equations are interrelated in space and time in such a complicated fashion that in practice the equations can only be integrated by resort to approximations. This is why the state of the atmosphere must be analysed at frequent intervals, every 6 or 12 hours, and fresh forecasts prepared.

Before the age of computers the forecaster solved the equations subjectively with the aid of weather charts for the dynamical processes and of aerological diagrams for the thermodynamic processes. In using these professional tools he would apply scientific knowledge, judgement and accumulated experience in what might be described as solving the mathematical equations by graphical methods. These methods remain valid and to a great extent indispensable even though computerized techniques have become standard practice in many national meteorological services throughout the world. The computer has emancipated weather forecasting. It has helped the forecaster to improve the accuracy and reliability of his forecasts beyond a period of about 24 hours and has opened up the prospect of predicting the weather for 5 days or even a week ahead. But the traditional methods must be maintained side by side with the computer products. Because the mathematical equations are so complex, the calculations performed by the computer must be constantly monitored so that any physically impossible or highly improbable developments can be detected and corrected. In an ideal world, analysis systems and forecasting models would be so advanced that the whole task, from analysing the raw data to the production of the forecast charts, would be left entirely to the computer. This is the ultimate aim and it is a realistic one. But for the time being forecasting models are very much in the research and development stage. Thus operational forecasting with the computer must be regarded as at least partly experimental.

One of the basic concepts in the dynamical aspect of weather forecasting is the approximate balance between the forces on a 'parcel' of air that are due to the pressure gradient and those caused by the Earth's rotation. Where a pressure gradient exists the tendency is for the air to move from high to low pressure in order to equalize pressures everywhere, but as soon as a particle is set in motion in the atmosphere it appears to be deflected by a force which acts to the right of the direction of motion in the northern hemisphere and to the left if the particle is in the southern hemisphere. This force, called the geostrophic or Coriolis force, has to be postulated because wind measurements are made relative to the Earth and an allowance has to be made for the fact that the Earth is not fixed in space but is rotating about its north-south axis. The Coriolis force is proportional to the sine of the latitude and is therefore zero at the equator. It becomes significant in latitudes greater than about 5°.

In the atmosphere the Coriolis force is approximately equal, but opposite in direction, to the force exerted by the pressure gradient. In consequence the air does not blow directly into areas of lower pressure but is constrained to move along the isobars, or lines of equal pressure. This was recognized by the Dutchman Buys Ballot in 1857 when he enunciated the law which bears his name: in the northern hemisphere an observer standing with his back to the wind would find that the pressure is lower to his left than to his right. The converse applies in the southern hemisphere.

The wind which expresses the balance between the pressure gradient and the Coriolis force is called the geostrophic wind. In the atmosphere the wind is only approximately geostrophic and one of the major problems is to identify the air movements which depart from the geostrophic balance. Vigorous deepening of a depression is a clear sign that this balance does not hold. The effects may be seen on a surface weather map where the air around the depression, instead of blowing along the isobars as it would of the balance were maintained, is inclined inwards, giving strong convergence of air towards the centre of the depression. On charts for levels above the surface this convergence is more than offset by divergence in the upper layers so that the net change of pressure would be negative.

In regions of high or low pressure, where the isobars have considerable curvature, a better approximation to the true wind is given by the gradient wind, which makes an allowance for the accelerations caused by the air moving in a curved path. The gradient wind is illustrated in Figure 4 for cyclonic and anticyclonic motion.

The geostrophic wind at the surface is usually measured at a height of about 500 m, above the layer in which other factors like surface friction play an important part. At greater altitudes, at 5 or 10 or 20 km or higher, it is found that the wind changes with height and this can be explained by the temperature structure of the atmosphere, obtained from radio-sonde data. In a vertical air column the pressure changes with height in accordance with the temperature in the air column. Pressure gradients, and therefore winds, would result between two places with the same sea-level

Fig. 4 The gradient wind in the northern hemisphere. The pointing figure illustrates Buys Ballot's law: his back is to the wind and the low pressure area is to his left.

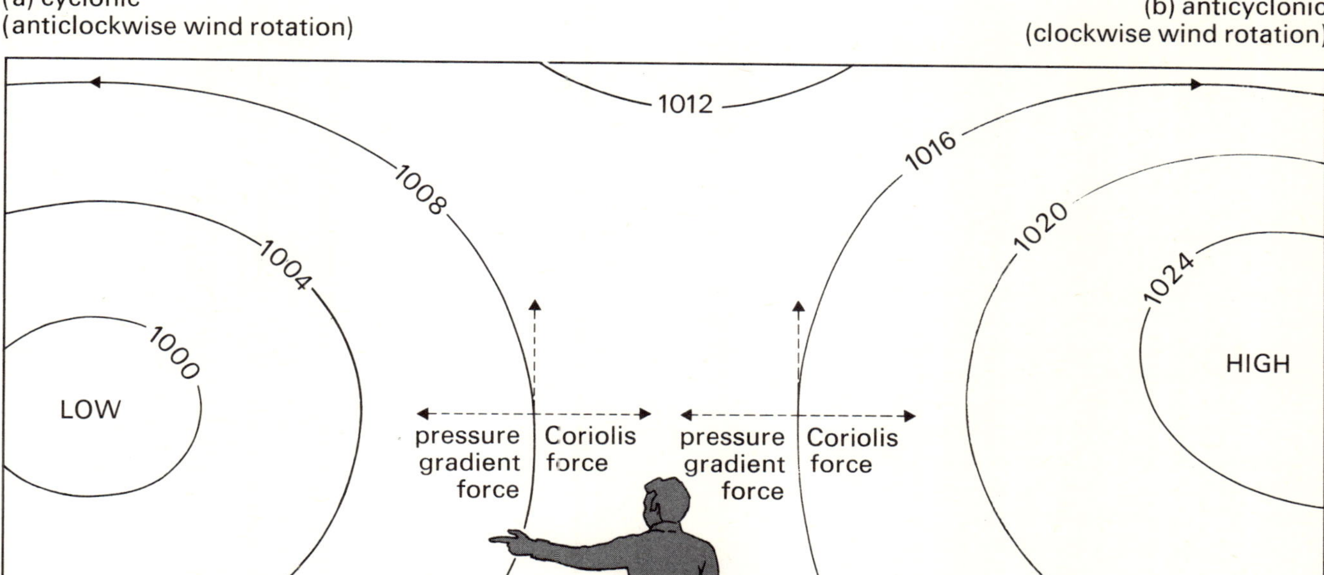

pressure but with air columns at different temperatures. Taking a layer of the atmosphere, the difference between the geostrophic winds at the top and bottom of the layer in the same vertical column of air is called the thermal wind. This wind and its variations are of the utmost importance at all stages of atmospheric processes.

Thermodynamic processes help to explain convection, condensation and the formation of clouds and rain, and these processes are most important in the troposphere. A 'parcel' of air possesses internal energy which is proportional to its absolute temperature. Now if such a parcel rises in the atmosphere it does so adiabatically, that is, there is no exchange of heat or energy across its boundary. On rising it moves into a region of lower pressure, expansion must occur and work has to be done against the external pressure. The parcel draws upon its own internal energy to perform this work and consequently its temperature must fall. If ascent continues, the parcel's store of internal energy will go on being reduced in the performance of work and its temperature will continue to fall. If the parcel of air were unsaturated at the start of the ascent, it may reach saturation when the temperature has fallen sufficiently. Further ascent would then be accompanied by condensation of water vapour and the release of latent heat which would slow down the rate of cooling. Thus a parcel of unsaturated air cools more rapidly than a parcel of saturated air when rising in the atmosphere. The reverse process, air descending in the atmosphere and undergoing compression, results in a rise in temperature, less marked if water drops are present because these would eventually evaporate and latent heat would have to be supplied.

The foregoing considerations must be set against the state of the environment in which the parcel of air is located. If at any level the environment is colder than the parcel, then the latter would be less dense and would be raised. If this condition applies over a substantial layer, then that portion of the atmosphere is said to be unstable. Aerological diagrams, on which are plotted the pressure, temperature and humidity data obtained from radio-sonde ascents, give valuable indications, almost at a glance, of the presence of stable or unstable layers in the atmosphere. Convection currents are characteristic of instability, and their strength or even their violence depends on the relative coldness and the depth of the unstable layer. Cumulonimbus clouds, showers and thunderstorms provide visual evidence of marked instability and an adequate supply of moisture over a considerable depth of the atmosphere.

The above remarks on a selection of atmospheric processes give a picture that is very far from complete. For example, while instability is an important cause of precipitation and is usually to be found behind the cold front of a depression, there are other causes which account for a substantial percentage of rainfall. The rain at a warm front is the result of warm air climbing slowly and steadily over a

Fig. 5 Cloud and rain structure of a typical hurricane. The concentric circles show distances from the eye, in miles.

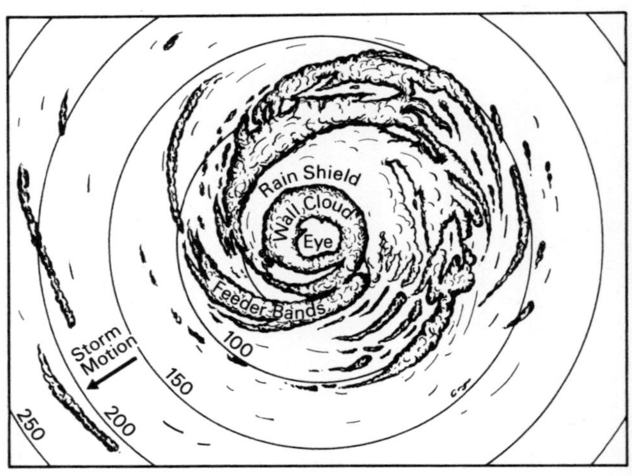

mass of cold air and the rain falls not from convection clouds but from stratus or layer-type clouds. Among all types of depressions, tropical cyclones, or hurricanes or typhoons as they are called in certain regions, provide the most striking examples of dynamic and thermodynamic processes.

Hurricanes and cyclones

Tropical cyclones are potentially the most devastating of all meteorological phenomena. Powered by the heat energy stored up in air passing over tropical seas, their impact on a country measured in terms of loss of life and material damage can be enormous. In November 1970 a tropical cyclone which formed in the Bay of Bengal moved into Bangladesh and more than 200,000 people lost their lives.

Cyclones or depressions may form anywhere but the more intense tropical cyclones occur in fairly well defined regions – the south-west Indian Ocean, the Bay of Bengal, the Arabian Sea, around the northern coast of Australia, in the West Indies and Gulf of Mexico, where they are called hurricanes, and in the north-west Pacific where they are called typhoons.

The following description of an encounter with a hurricane, by the single-handed sailor Weston Martyr, gives one a vivid idea of the overwhelming nature of the experience:

> Do you know that you cannot breathe with a hurricane blowing full in your face? You cannot see either; the impact on your eyeball of spray and rain flying at over 100 miles an hour makes seeing quite impossible. You hear nothing except the scream and booming of the wind, which drowns even the thunder of the breaking seas. And you cannot move except by dint of terrific exertions. To stand up on deck is to get blown away like a dead leaf. You cannot even crawl; you have to climb about, twisting your arms and legs around anything solid within reach.

While these intense tropical storms are over the sea, the strong winds and high waves are an obvious danger to shipping which, however, can usually take avoiding action provided an efficient warning service is in operation. If the cyclone reaches the coast and moves inland, damage is produced by the combined effects of wind, rain, flooding, storm surge and sea waves. Each of these factors separately can cause substantial destruction but in most of the major tropical cyclones, the greatest loss of life usually results from the flooding which follows the torrential rains. If, in addition to flooding, a storm surge funnels water from the sea into coastal inlets, bays and rivers as the cyclone crosses the coast, as happened in the case of the Bangladesh disaster of 1970, the death toll may be on a colossal scale.

An adequate warning service, enabling responsible authorities with the co-operation of the public to take all possible measures to prevent, or at least to mitigate, the disastrous effects of a cyclone, is essential for the saving of life. In areas of the USA which lie in the path of hurricanes a substantial decrease in the number of deaths is attributed to improved warning services and a comprehensive disaster organization which springs into action as soon as the weather bureau issues an alert. In certain other vulnerable countries the number of deaths caused by severe cyclones remains high and United Nations agencies have mounted urgent efforts with the governments concerned to develop in each country an organization for community preparedness and disaster prevention. The first essentials in such an organization are clearly the timely location of a tropical cyclone, forecasting its movement and estimating its effects in regard to wind strength, rainfall, flooding and the possibility of a storm surge.

Compared with the less violent depressions of temperate latitudes, a tropical cyclone is a small feature, about 300 km in radius and usually set in an area of quiet weather and light winds. The early detection and tracking of such a cyclone over large areas of ocean has been greatly helped in recent years by the use of high-power radar and by means of satellite cloud pictures which show the thick cloud system with the clear conditions in the centre or eye of the storm.

Forecasting the development and intensity of a tropical storm is one of the most difficult of all practical problems in meteorology. It is known that a tropical cyclone can form over an area of ocean where the surface temperature is

Fig. 6 One year's hurricane tracks (after G. W. Cry, 1965). The yearly average is about nine: this year (1961) had eleven. Some hurricanes (e.g. Betsy and Debbie) spend all their lives at sea: Esther described a complete loop, to add to the difficulties of forecasting. The dots mark 12-hour intervals.

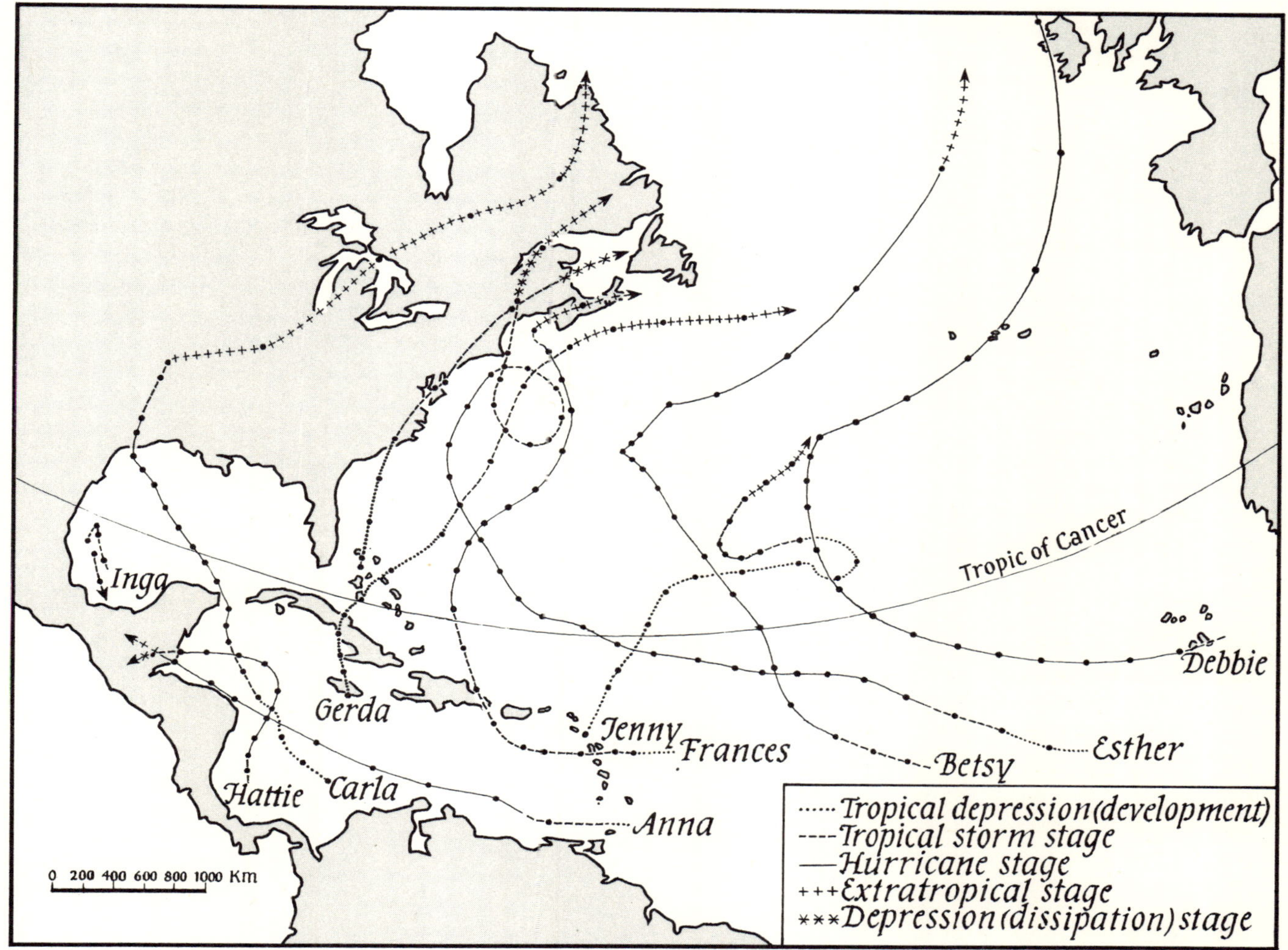

sufficiently high to warm the lowest layers of the atmosphere to such an extent that they will ascend with condensation of water vapour to heights of 12–15 km. A warm core thermal structure is then maintained by the latent heat of condensation but there are also other significant factors, still to be fully explained, such as strong divergence of air in the upper levels and the contribution of the Coriolis force. The latter must be larger than a certain minimum value since these cyclones do not form nearer to the equator than about 5°–8° north or south latitude.

The sea-level pressure at the centre of a tropical cyclone is extremely low, rising to a normal value on the outskirts at a radial distance of a few hundred kilometres, so the pressure gradients are steep. The central area, known as the 'eye of the storm', is a region of light winds but outside this the wind speed increases very rapidly and reaches a maximum, which may exceed 75 metres per second, about 30–50 km from the centre. The winds then fall off quite slowly as distance from the centre increases. The eye of the storm is usually quite free of clouds but is surrounded by a vertical cloud wall of great height. Within this wall the main ascent takes place, the ascending air being replaced by strong convergence near the surface.

Although it is possible to describe a tropical storm in considerable detail, a great deal of research is still needed in order to improve forecasting techniques and develop new ones. Numerical prediction models have so far shown little success, a sign that a deeper understanding of the dynamic and thermodynamic processes has to be acquired. The cost in human lives exacted by the more severe tropical cyclones makes it essential to give the highest possible priority to research which would contribute to the greater safety of people who live in countries which experience the dire effects of these storms.

Further outlook

The atmosphere will continue to present problems of extreme complexity to scientists in a variety of disciplines. There is every confidence that good progress will be made towards solving the most important practical problems but it would be unwise to underrate their difficulty. There will continue to be occasions when, in spite of the most up-to-date techniques, a weather forecast for a period as short as 12 hours ahead will go badly astray. On the other hand it seems realistic to look forward to the day when reliable forecasts of high quality, but subject to infrequent major errors, will be issued daily for periods of 5 days ahead, perhaps even a week ahead but probably not for longer periods.

If the possibility of climatic change represents a threat to mankind, the most potent contributor to such change may be man's own industrial activities. A global atmospheric monitoring programme is essential if any changes liable to lead to adverse effects are to be detected in time.

Increasing interest is now being shown in the possibilities of weather modification. In addition to the seeding of clouds to make rain, and the clearing of fog from busy airports, man has presumed with some success to take on nature's most violent phenomena. In 1969 Hurricane Debbie was seeded with silver iodide crystals to such effect that five hours later the wind force had fallen, albeit temporarily, by 31 per cent. In the USSR the bombardment of hail-producing clouds with silver iodide shells has considerably reduced hail damage. Both America and Russia have mounted large-scale projects for the regulation of rainfall. Computer-based simulation techniques have enormously extended the possibilities of intervention in natural atmospheric processes. But it should be recognized that if it becomes possible to control the weather of one area, others would inevitably be affected in unpredictable ways. It is to be hoped that governments will be alive to the political nature of many of the questions that will arise if ever weather modification becomes a practical proposition.

Suggestions for further reading

R. G. Barry and R. J. Chorley: *Atmosphere, Weather and Climate*. Methuen, London, 1971.

G. E. Dunn and B. I. Miller: *Atlantic Hurricanes*. Louisiana State University Press, 1964.

H. H. Lamb: *Climate: Past, Present and Future*. Methuen, London, 1972.

F. W. Lane: *The Elements Rage*. Chilton Books, New York, 1965; David & Charles, Newton Abbot, 1966.

D. H. McIntosh and A. S. Thom: *Essentials of Meteorology*. Wykeham Publications, London, 1969.

R. K. Pilsbury: *Clouds and Weather*. Batsford, London, 1969.

L. P. Smith: *Seasonable Weather*. Allen & Unwin, London, 1968.

O. G. Sutton: *Understanding Weather*. Penguin Books, Harmondsworth, 1960.

—— : *The Challenge of the Atmosphere*. Hutchinson, London, 1968.

P. G. Wickham: *The Practice of Weather Forecasting*. H.M. Stationery Office, London, 1970.

A weather eye on the world has become absolutely vital in view of our increasing power to affect the planet's perilous atmospheric equilibrium. The possibility of climatic change, with catastrophic results for mankind, demands a global atmospheric monitoring programme of the kind envisaged by the international World Meteorological Organization, which plans to have a complete satellite system operational by the end of 1977. This high-resolution satellite photograph, with the continental land masses outlined, provides a global view of drought conditions over the northern and western parts of Africa. Stirred by hot, dry winds blowing off the Sahara desert, the dust-laden air extends more than 1000 miles from Dakar out over the mid-Atlantic. The balloon-shaped dust pattern travelled west at 16 m.p.h. and reached Florida some eight days later.

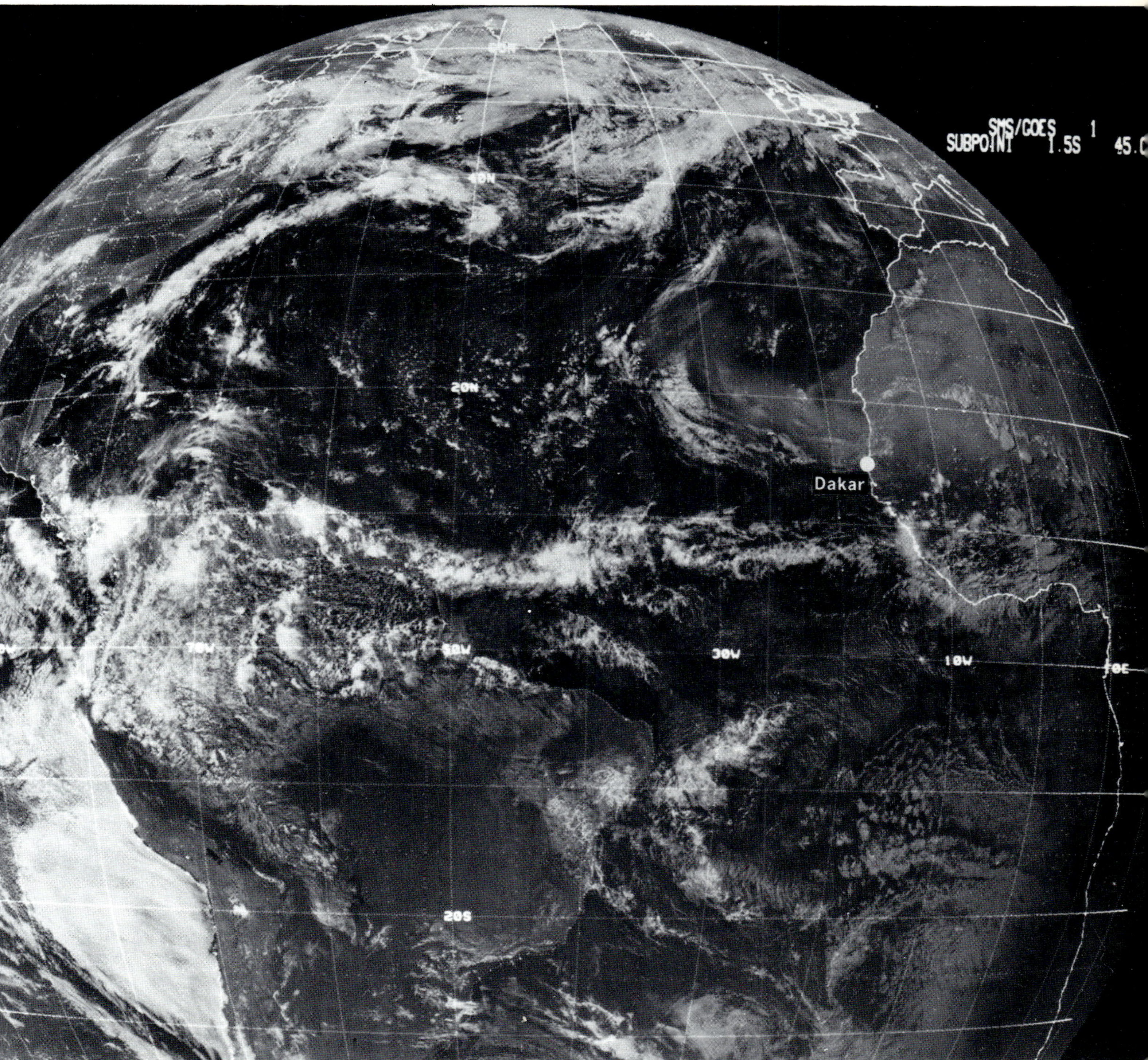
SMS/GOES 1
SUBPOINT 1.5S
40N
20N
Dakar
70W
50W
30W
10W
10E
20S

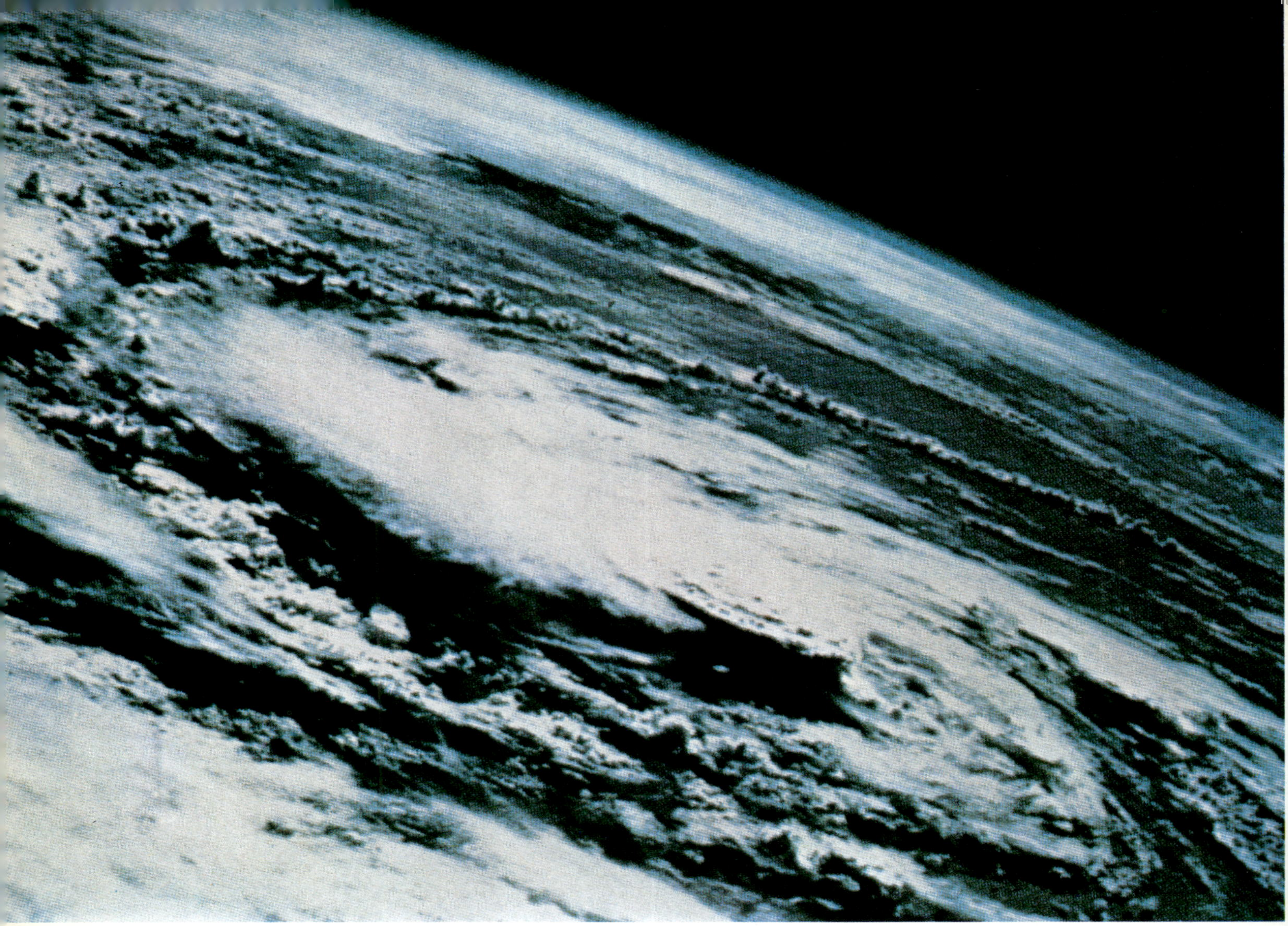

2

The coiled violence of Hurricane Gladys (2), seen from the manned satellite Apollo 7, is shown in the typical ragged spiral lines of cloud converging on a towering centre, eleven miles high, surrounding the eye of the storm. In the eye itself (3), here photographed from close to by a specially equipped aircraft, the winds are light and the cloud absent, but on its periphery they may reach a force of 150 m.p.h. The dark funnel of a tornado (4), seen crossing open land in Oklahoma, may be even more violent, with wind speeds at the vortex as high as 500 m.p.h. In America tornadoes cause more deaths than hurricanes.

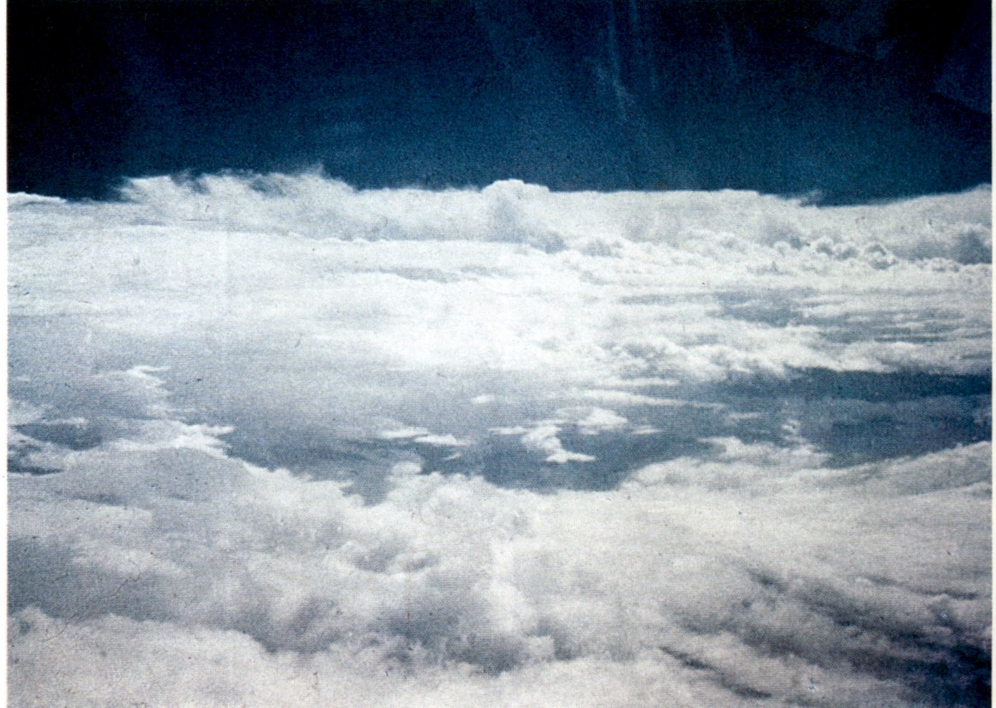

3

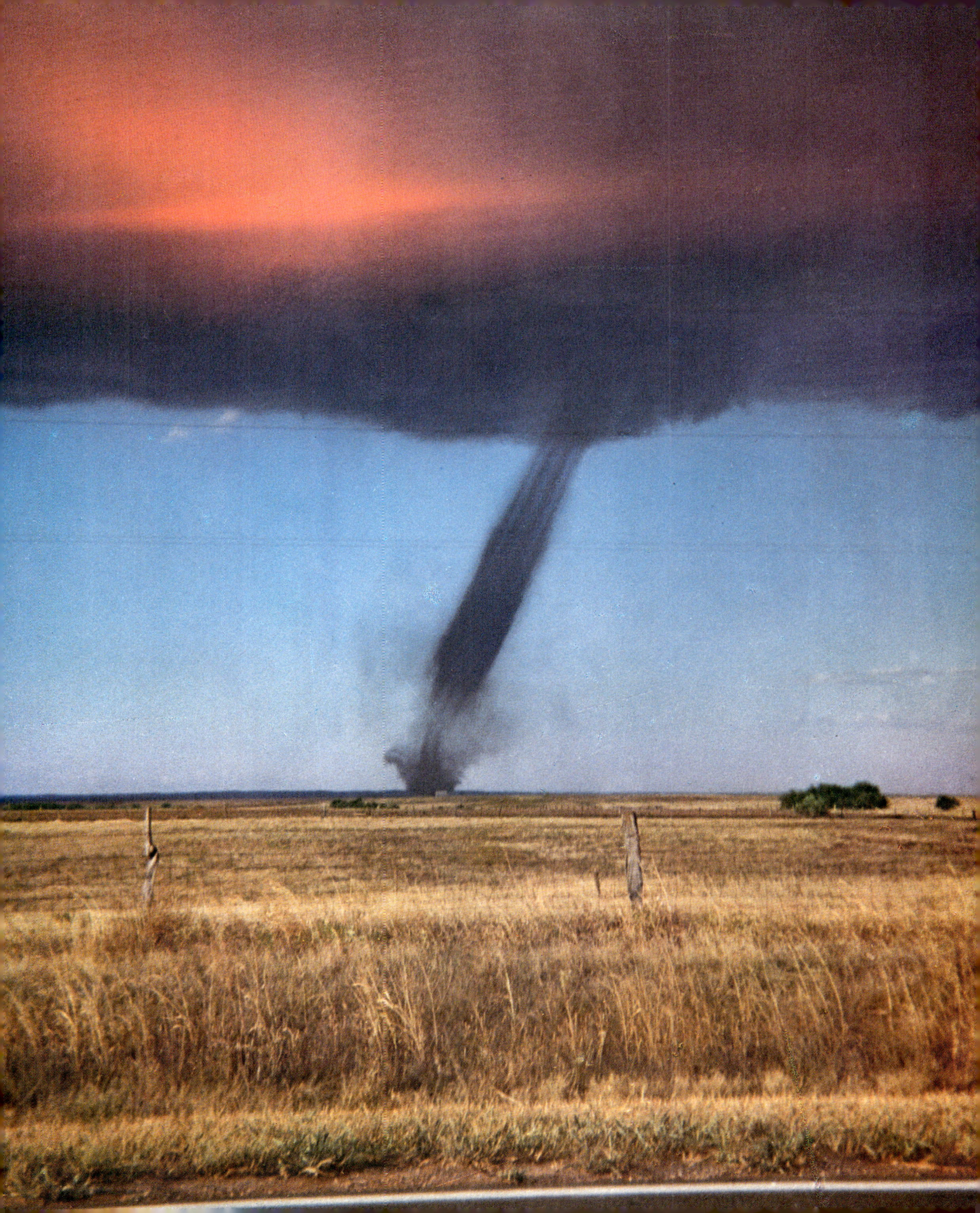

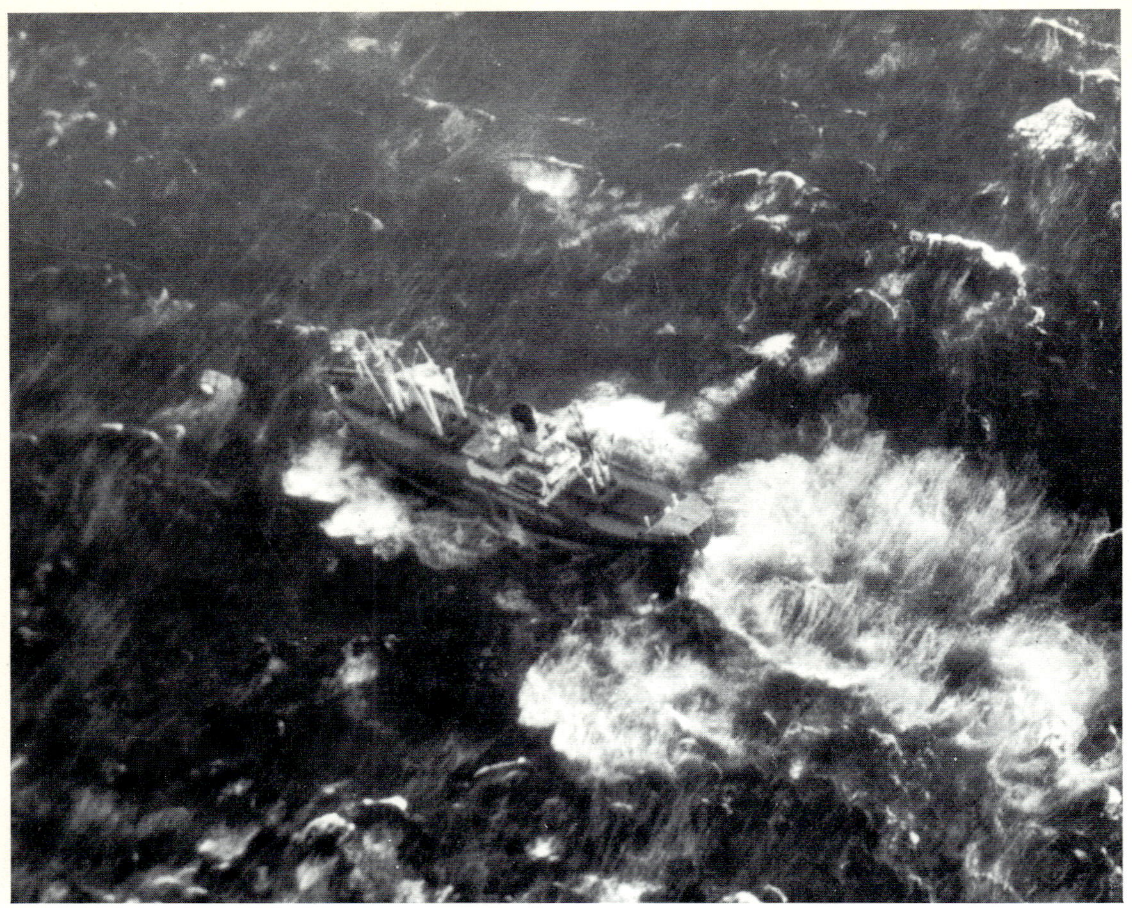

5/6

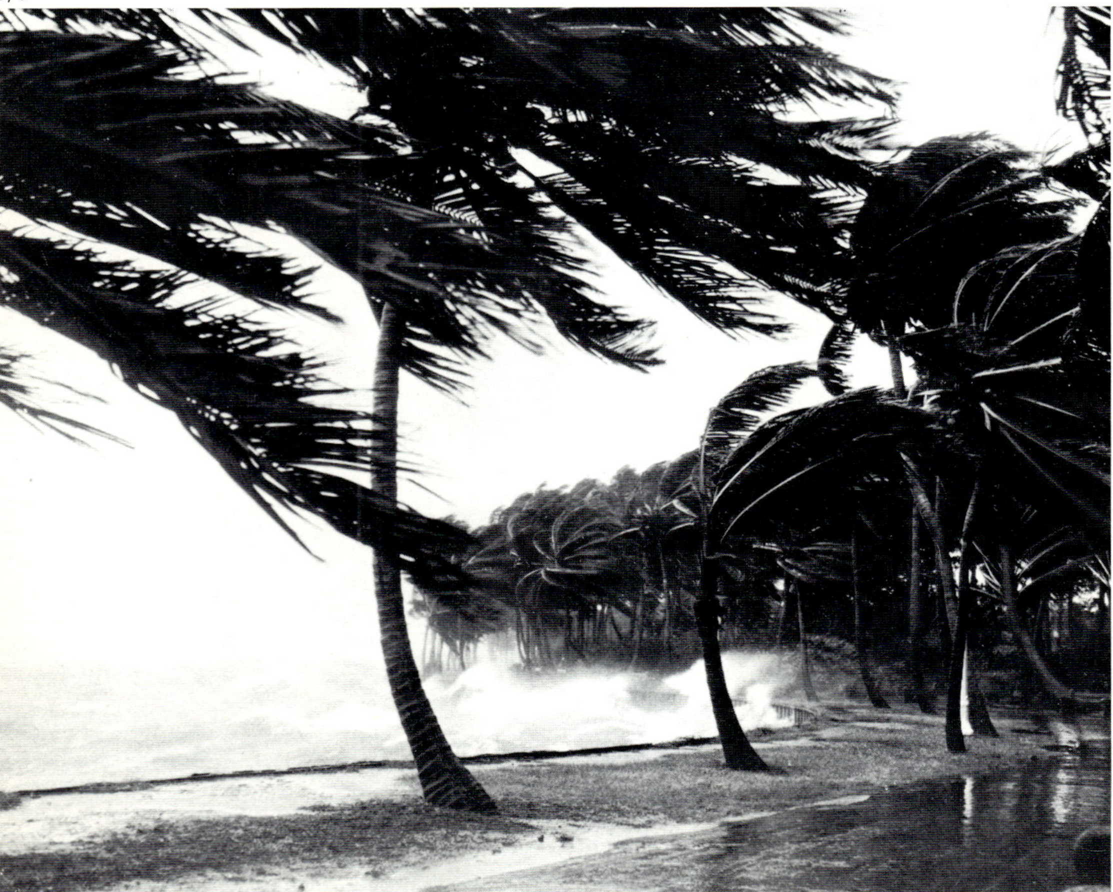

The destructive aspect of nature is manifested to the full in the shattering force of the hurricane and the tornado. Off the Florida coast a large ship (5) is caught and all but overwhelmed in mountainous seas, while palm trees along the coastline (6) are bent double before the violence of the wind Tornadoes (7 and 8), snaking down from dark banks of cumulonimbus, devour everything in their paths. Houses and other structures actually explode on contact, so low is the air pressure in the centre of the system.

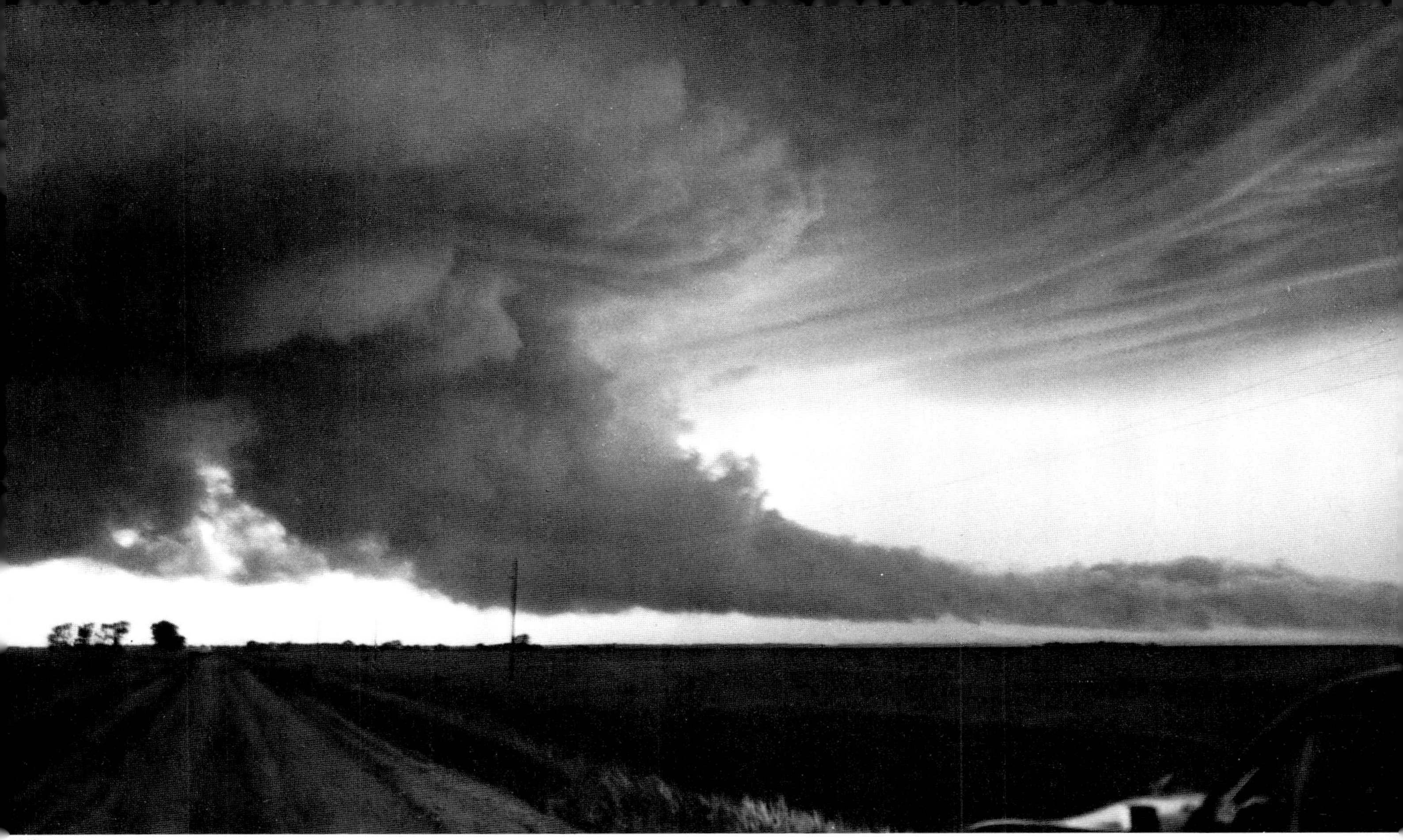

7/8

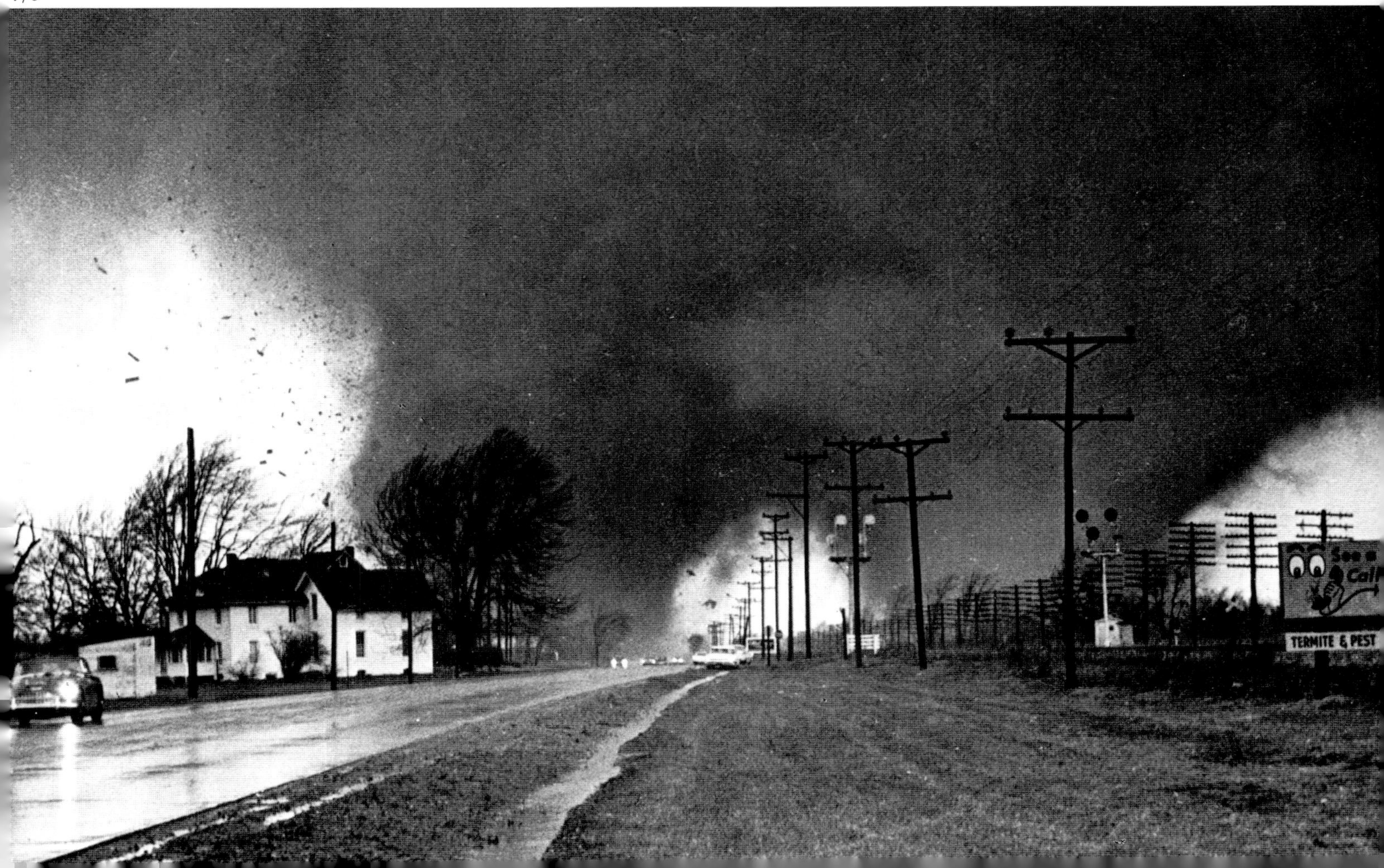

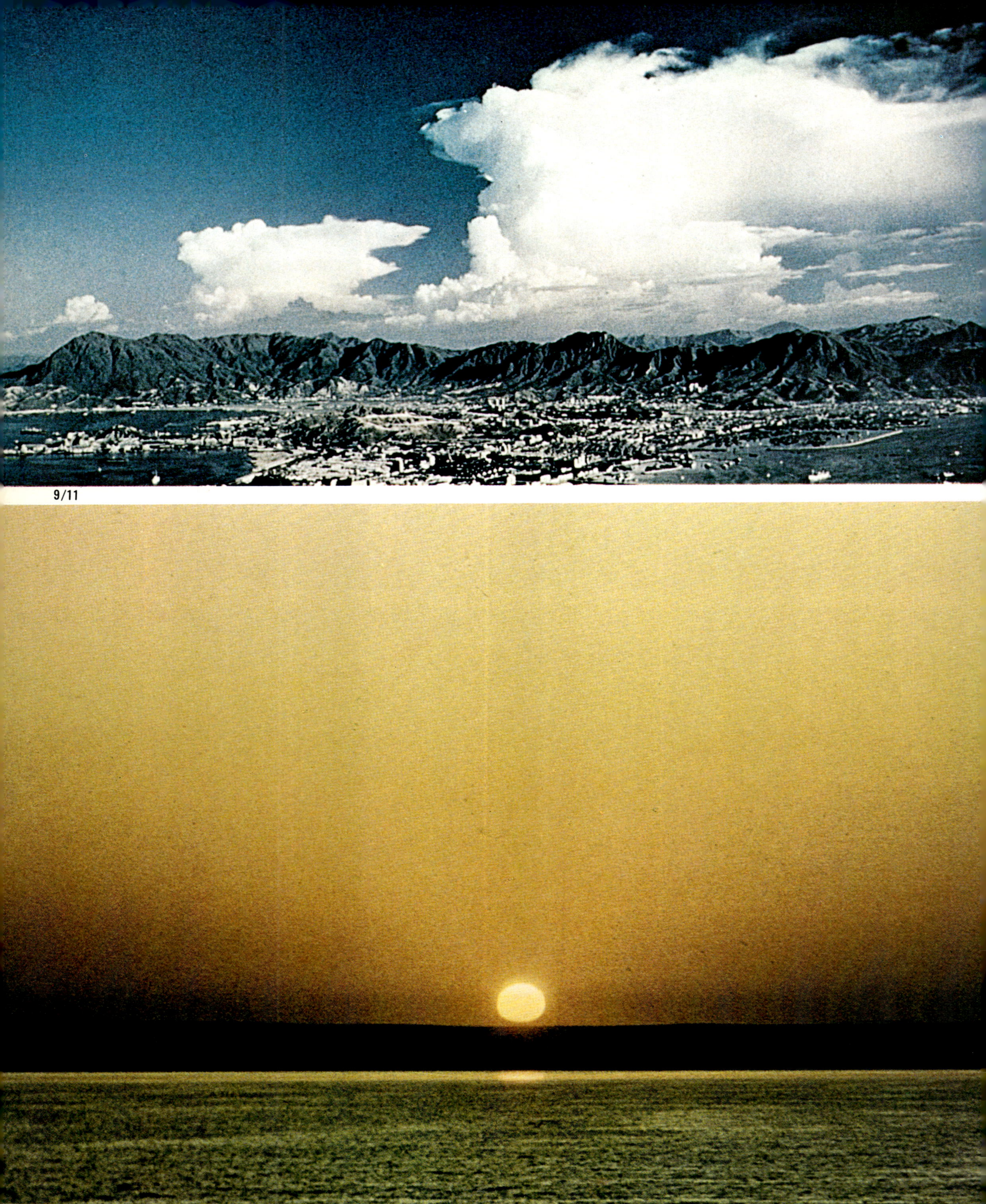

9/11

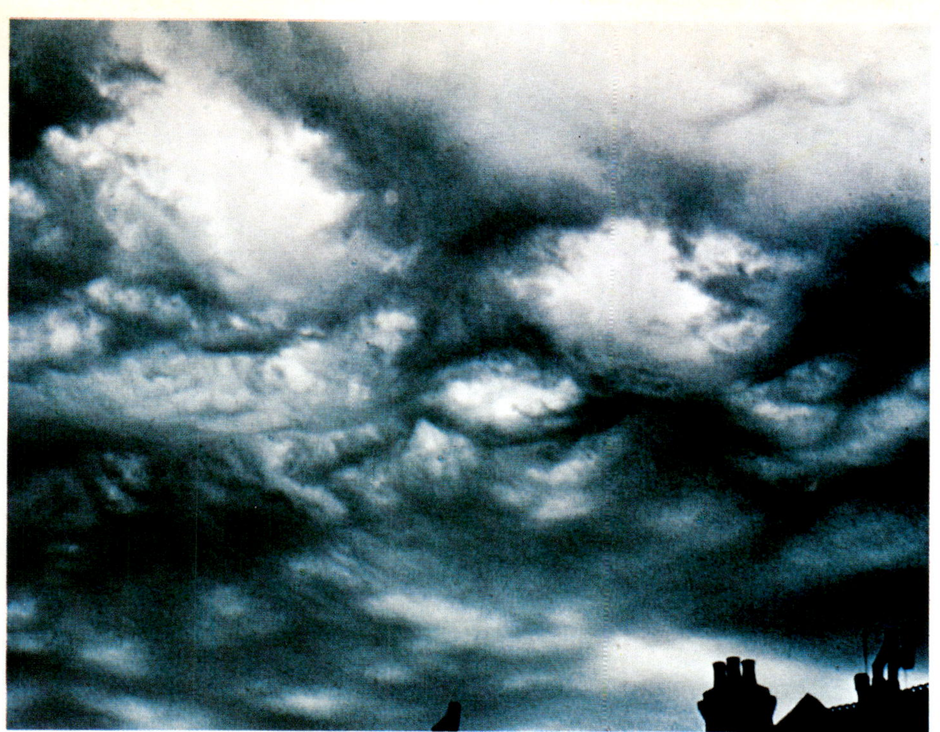

Cloud shapes have much to tell about air disturbance and the coming weather. A mighty cumulonimbus (9), showing the typical anvil-shaped head, builds up into a thunderstorm over the hills around Hong Kong. A layer of altostratus cloud (10) distorted by rapidly rising towers of cumulus shape shows a high degree of instability in the upper air; because of the turret-like shape, this formation is called 'castellanus'.

10/12

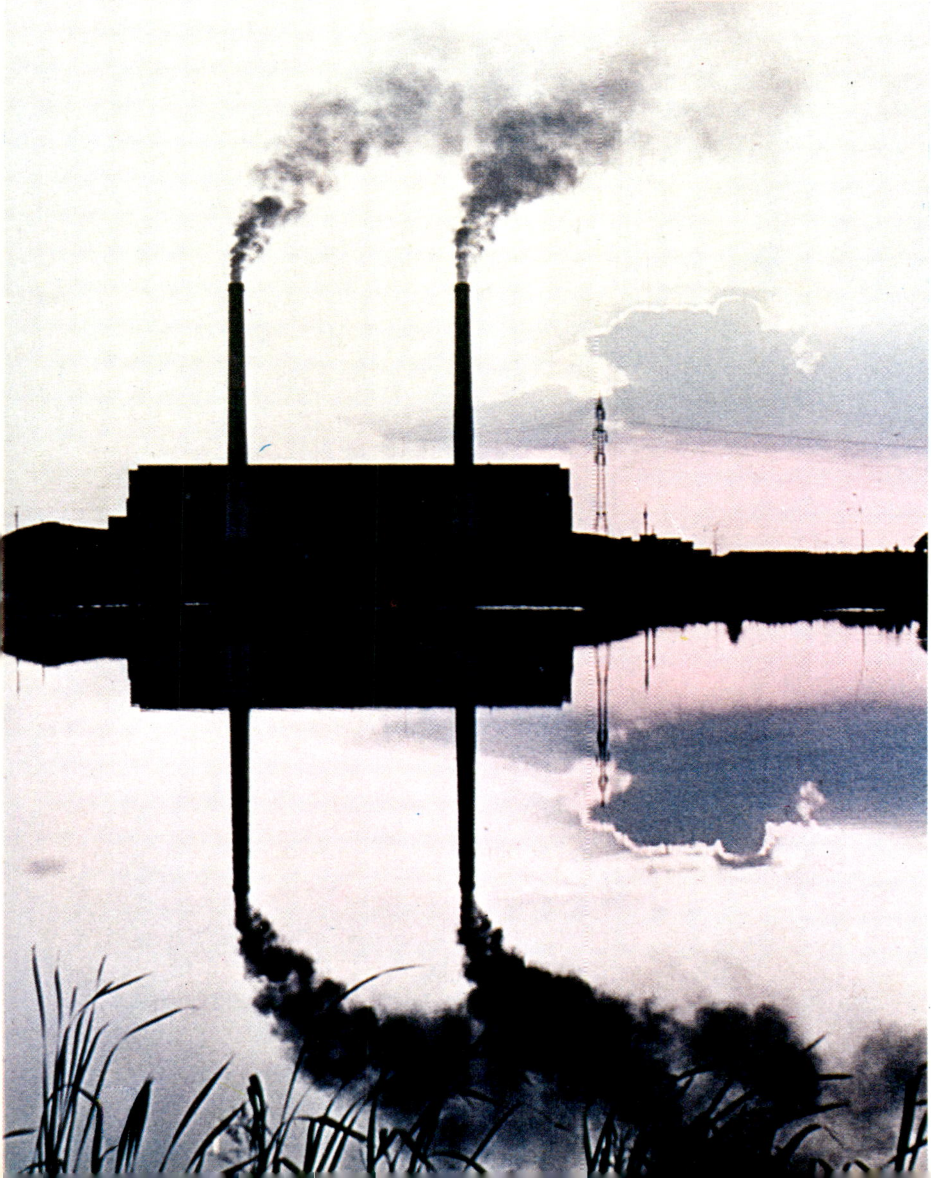

Pollution, natural or man-made, may present a beautiful aspect. Dust haze over the Aegean (11), carried by prevailing winds from the African deserts, forms a dark aura round the setting sun. Smoke plumes from a Czechoslovakian power station (12) are apparently dispersed efficiently in the atmosphere, but their polarized reflections in the water show up black and dense.

13

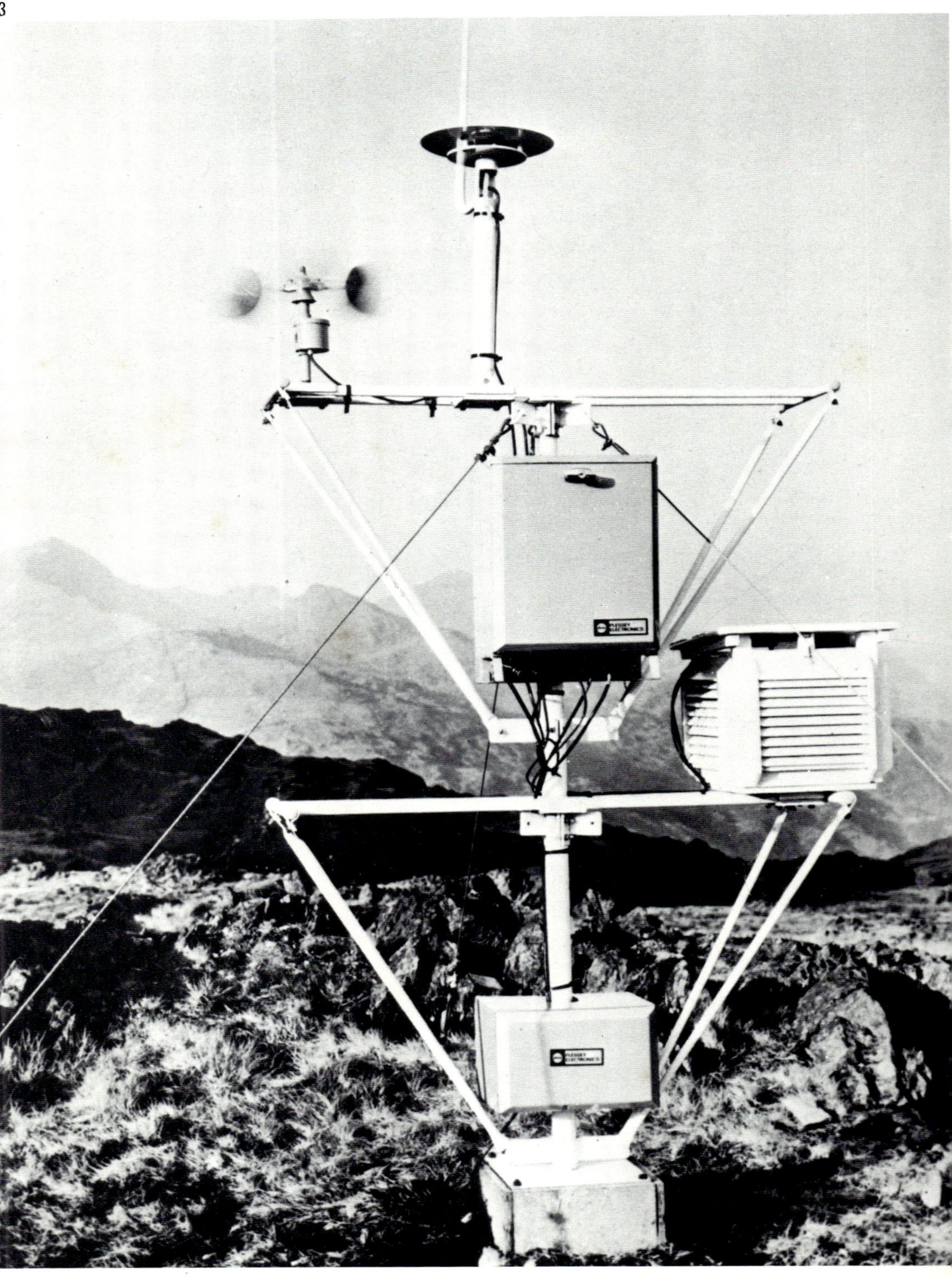

An outpost of technology in the wilderness, this automatic weather station includes a cup anemometer to measure the force of the wind, and a vane for direction. The box with louvred sides to let in the air contains thermometers for measuring temperature and humidity. Readings are recorded continuously on magnetic tape, and data are transmitted at regular intervals to forecasting centres. Automatic weather stations are also to be installed on ships, where their reports will be transmitted to major collecting centres by specially equipped communications satellites.

3

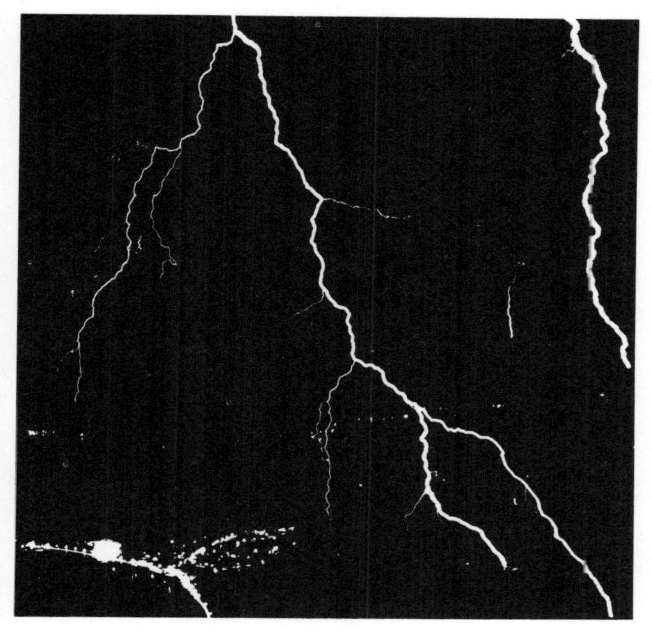

Thunder and lightning

John Latham

THROUGHOUT THE AGES man has regarded lightning with fear and often as the manifestation of something supernatural. The suddenness of the flash and the indeterminate pause before the thunder was heard were alarming to untutored minds incapable of finding an explanation. One can understand the rising sense of awe at the slow inexorable development of the conditions; violent winds aloft, the slow circling of birds in the ascending air, the deepening gloom and the stillness through which a few huge raindrops fell, then the nearby blinding flash followed by the almost immediate thunderclap. No wonder the gods were thought to be displeased.

The Norsemen believed that lightning was the sparks from Mjölnir, the magic hammer of the god Thor, as he hurtled across the heavens in his chariot. The hammer split the thunderclouds, causing them to fall as rain while the thunder was the sound of his rolling chariot wheels. This conviction was supported by the occasional finding of 'hammerheads', pieces of metal or stone foreign to the neighbourhood which were in fact meteorites, but this they could not know.

Similar beliefs in the divine origin of lightning are found in Indian, Greek, Roman, Egyptian, Japanese, Chinese, Tibetan and other mythologies, the differences being only in points of detail such as the shape of the thunderbolts and how they were launched. Indeed almost all tribal peoples have their own mystical explanations. Thus certain communities in South Africa believed that it was produced by a magical thunderbird called Umpundulo which dived from the clouds to earth. Thunder was the noise of its beating wings, lightning the reflection of the sun from its vivid plumage. Tangible evidence was to be seen in the scarified bark of damaged trees, which was attributed to Umpundulo's claws.

But two thousand years ago Lucretius wrote *The Nature of the Universe* with a powerful combination of objectivity, observational acuity and poetic expression. In it he disposed scathingly and convincingly of existing superstitions, asking why Jupiter and other gods should waste their thunderbolts upon the deserts, destroy the innocent and the guilty with equal impartiality, loose their weapons only from cloudy skies, warn foes of incipient attack by thundery muttering, evince a strong preference for striking high places and, particularly, destroy their own temples?

He concludes correctly from his observations and arguments that thunderstorms are more likely in unstable air conditions associated with seasonal changes; that high temperatures are associated with lightning; that a primary requisite of clouds which produce lightning is great vertical depth; that the dissipative stages of thunderclouds often produce lightning activity, of a less violent form; that lightning is the consequence of a sudden release of accumulated stress; and that thunder and lightning occur simultaneously within the cloud. Even his seemingly erroneous conclusion that the heating effect of lightning is due to friction – his analogy being concerned with the melting, in long flight, of a leaden sling shot – can be interpreted as an inspired guess at the production of heat by the resistance of the air to the passage of an enormous electrical current, which is of course the correct explanation. There is a strong parallel here with Newton's apparently unacceptable corpuscular theory of light, which later proved to be tenable in many aspects.

As an example of Lucretius' remarkable observations and deductive powers one may quote his reasons for believing that thunderclouds are deep:

> It must be supposed that thunderbolts originate from thick and high-piled clouds. They are never really hurled from the blue, nor from clouds of slight density. This is unmistakably shown by experience. Indeed, at such times the air is so crammed with a solid mass of cloud that we fancy all the darkness has forsaken Hell and come trooping from every side into the roomy vaults of Heaven. Such is the ominous night of cloudrack that gathers overhead, out of whose gloom the visage of black dread lours down upon us, when the storm is making ready to launch its bolts. Add to this that very often out at sea a black tornado falls upon the waves, like a river of pitch poured out of the sky, charged with far-shadowing gloom. With its heavy freight of fire and wind, it trails in its wake a murky tempest big with levin-bolt and blast. Even on shore men shudder at the sight and take cover under their roofs. From this we may infer what a depth of cloud is heaped above our heads. For surely the earth would not be overcast by such intensity of gloom were it not that clouds are piled on clouds up and up, till the sun is blotted out. And surely in their downfall they would not drench it in such a deluge of rain that rivers overflow and fields are drowned unless a great bulk of them were stacked up in the ether.

Franklin's experiment

The first systematic scientific investigation of lightning, culminating in the proof that it is an electric discharge or giant spark, was made by Benjamin Franklin, master-printer of Philadelphia, just over two hundred years ago. His researches began in 1746 when he was 40 years old, and concerned the manner in which sharp points of metal could discharge the electricity from electrified bodies. This work

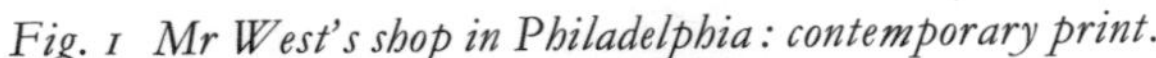
Fig. 1 Mr West's shop in Philadelphia: contemporary print.

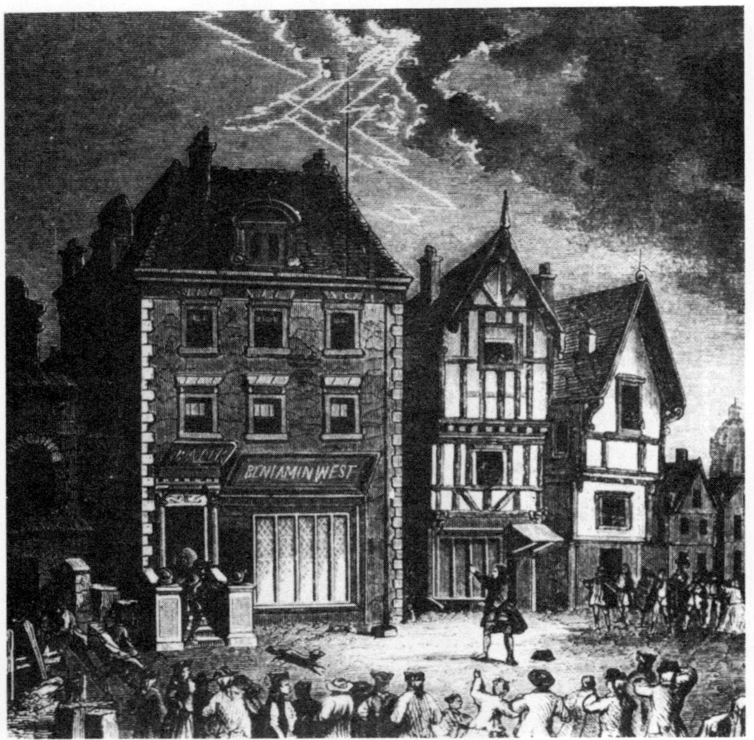

established the principle of the metal comb still used in many industrial applications of high-voltage electricity. It also led to the invention of the lightning rod.

Franklin listed several points of similarity between lightning and electric sparks generated by frictional electrical machines, which had just been invented. One of these was 'destroying animals' and Franklin confirmed this proposition with great ceremony at a picnic by electrocuting a turkey. He speculated that lightning, like the 'electric fluid', would be attracted by points, and delivered his famous exhortation 'Let the experiment be made'. His proposal for tackling the problem was made in a letter to the Royal Society in 1750:

> On the top of some high tower or steeple place a kind of sentry box . . . big enough to contain a man and an electrical stand (an insulating glass stool). From the middle of the stand let an iron rod rise and pass bending out of the door and then upright twenty or thirty feet, pointed very sharp at the end. If the electrical stand be kept clean and dry, a man standing on it when such clouds are passing low might be electrified and afford sparks, the rod drawing fire to him from a cloud. If any danger to the man should be apprehended (though I think there would be none), let him stand on the floor of his box and now and then bring near to the rod the loop of a wire that has one end fastened to the leads (earthed roof), he holding it by a wax handle; so the sparks, if the rod is electrified, will strike from the rod to the wire and not affect him.

The physical basis of Franklin's proposed experiment, and of the operation of a lightning rod, is as follows. When a charged object is in the vicinity of an electric conductor, such as a metal rod, it attracts charge of opposite sign to the near end of the rod and repels charge of the same sign to the far end, a process known as induction. If the electric field at the near end of the rod is sufficiently strong, the insulating properties of the air are destroyed, ionization of the air molecules occurs, and some of the charge will stream off the end of the rod towards the oppositely charged object. This discharging process is particularly effective if the rod is pointed, because the electric field is greatly intensified in regions of high curvature. Discharges from such pointed structures, giving a faint light visible in the dark, are known as 'corona discharges'. Since we now know that the lower regions of thunderclouds are usually negatively charged, we would expect Franklin's experiment to result in the loss of positive charge from the top of the iron rod.

In fact, the absence of a high steeple in Philadelphia deterred him from conducting his experiment immediately, and his idea was first tested by the French physicist Jean François Dalibard. He decided not to use a tower and employed a 40-foot-long iron rod insulated at its base with a glass bottle. This equipment was installed at Marly, near Paris, in the charge of an old soldier named Coiffier. On 10 May 1752, when a thundercloud was overhead, an earthed wire was brought near to the rod and a stream of sparks was observed. Franklin's arguments were vindicated.

A month later Franklin himself confirmed the electrical properties of thunderclouds by flying a kite in the vicinity of one and experiencing an electric shock when presenting his knuckle to a key hung from the end of the string. In some beautiful experiments he went on to establish that the bases of thunderclouds are negatively charged. With his superb eye for the application of fundamental discoveries, he had already made a practical suggestion in 1750:

> May not the knowledge of this power of points be of use to mankind in preserving houses, churches, ships, etc., from lightning, by directing us to fix on the highest parts of the edifices upright rods of iron, made sharp as a needle, and gilt to prevent rusting, and from the foot of these rods a wire down the outside of the building into the ground, or down the shrouds of a ship and down her

side, till it reaches the water? Would not these pointed rods probably draw the electrical fire silently out of a cloud before it came nigh enough to strike and thereby secure us from that most sudden and terrible mischief?

Two years later the first lightning rod was installed in Philadelphia; they then rapidly proliferated over the American colonies and were adopted in England at about the same time. Fittingly the first successful performance of these 'Franklin's Rods' occurred in Philadelphia, where the house of Mr West, a merchant, was saved from damage by a direct stroke. However, for several reasons the invention was not universally accepted as efficacious for a long time. The first was that the operation of the rod was not fully understood. Some people argued that it would attract lightning from thunderclouds, and others that it merely provided a safe conducting path to ground for lightning which occurred in the vicinity. We now know that the latter explanation is correct, but proponents of the former idea were afraid that the rods would increase the frequency of lightning striking vulnerable areas. A second reason was that lightning rods were often incorrectly earthed, either because of ignorance or violation of Franklin's instructions, or because they were so elaborate and delicate in construction that the conducting path was broken. In these situations of course the rod offered no protection, and the damaging stroke could be seen to have entered the building or ship through its tip. Finally, opposition arose from pure superstition, presumably through dread of tampering with a phenomenon as powerful and mysterious as lightning. In his book *The Thunder-storm*, published in 1877, Charles Tomlinson writes:

In Roman Catholic countries there was considerable difficulty in introducing lightning-rods, on account of the superstitions of the populace. About the year 1776, Morveau caused metallic conductors to be erected on the house of the Academy of Sciences at Dijon. He was violently attacked for his presumption, and a mob assembled to pull down the 'heretical conductors', as they were called, and much mischief would probably have been done but for the assurance of the secretary that the gilded points of the conductors had been purposely sent from Rome by the pope. A similar occurrence took place at Sienna. The cathedral church having been repeatedly damaged by lightning, a metallic rod was erected, but this was regarded with much terror by the inhabitants, who requested that the 'heretic rod' might be taken down. On 10 April 1777, however, a thunder-storm occurred, and a heavy discharge of lightning fell on the tower without doing the slightest damage. The people now began to regard the heretic rod with more confidence, and it is worthy of remark that, since its erection, the church has never suffered from lightning.

Fig. 2 The distribution of electric charge in a thundercloud.

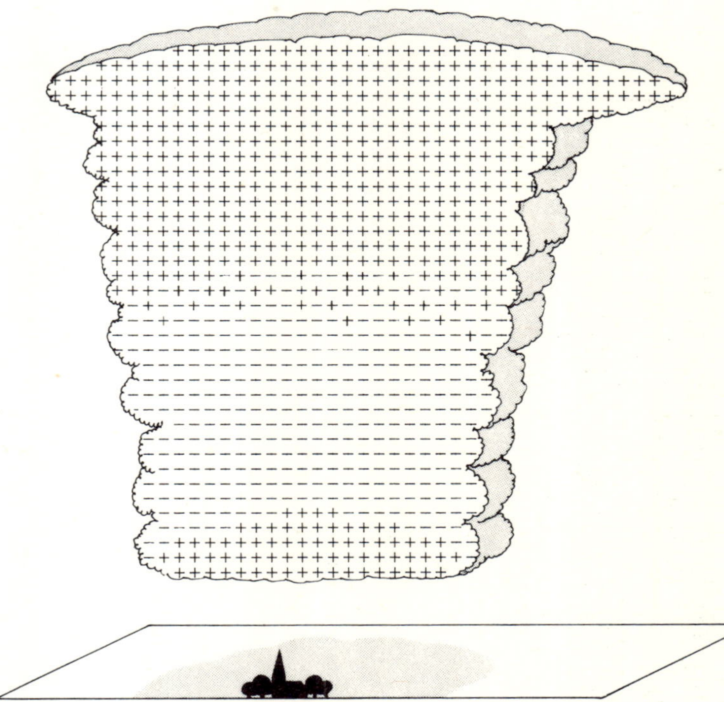

In this way statistics slowly accumulated which proved beyond doubt Franklin's contention that lightning rods were extremely efficacious protective devices. Many churches, with long histories of frequent lightning strikes and consequent damage, were found to be completely protected by the installation of rods. It became safe, albeit still unchristian, to store gunpowder in the vaults of churches and cathedrals. Sailing ships with wooden masts, which had formerly been particularly vulnerable, were now rendered safe.

The lightning discharge

Two forms of lightning are generally recognized – 'forked lightning' which passes between the cloud and the ground, and 'sheet lightning' which occurs completely within the cloud. If we could see the flash responsible for sheet lightning, it would look exactly the same as forked lightning, except that it passes between two regions of a thundercloud instead of to the ground. The different

Fig. 3 Initiation and propagation of a stepped leader. (a) Distribution of charge in the cloud. Note the small area of positive charge at the base: here the discharge starts (b). (c–f) Stepped leader moving towards the ground in 50-metre steps.

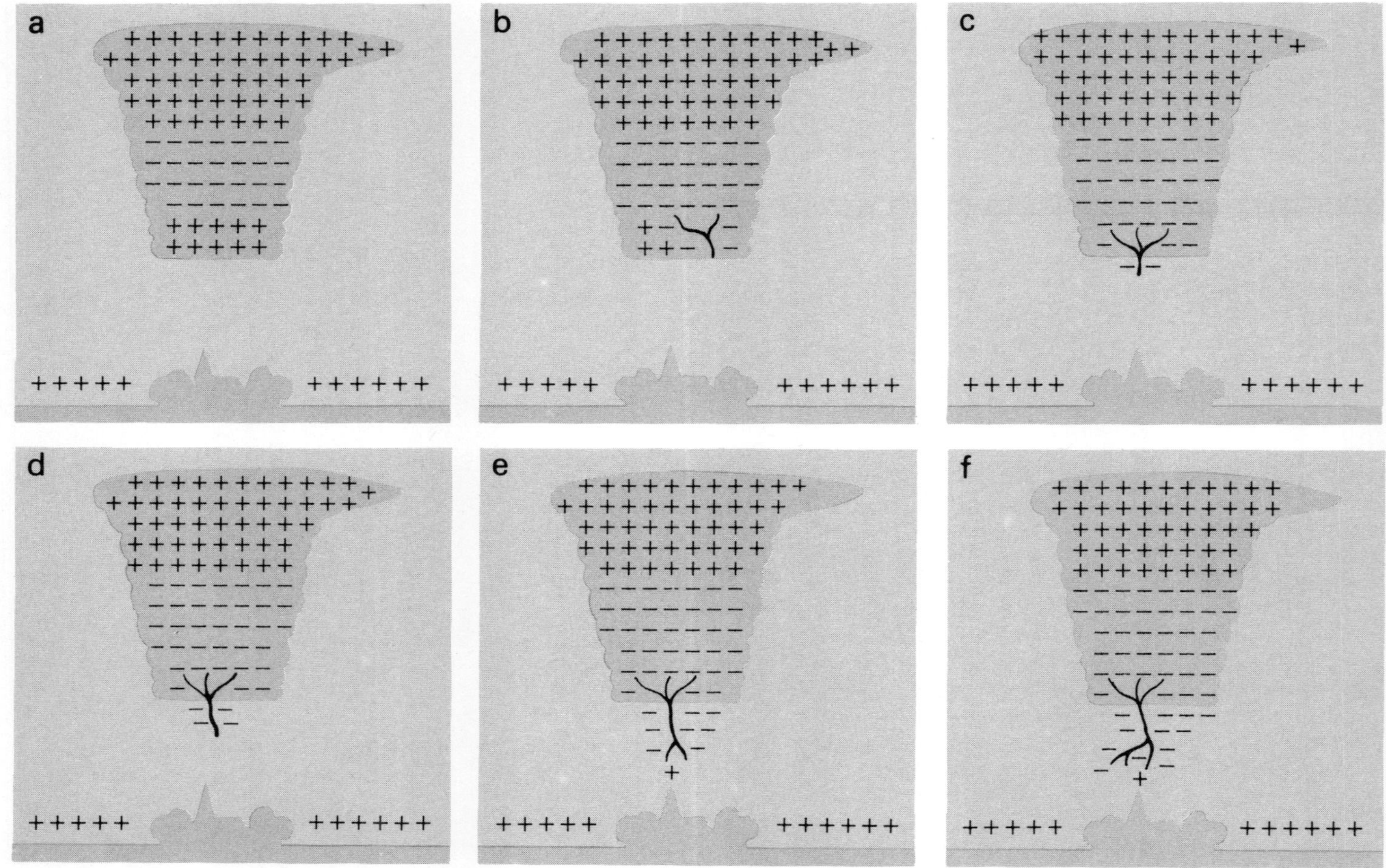

appearance is entirely due to the flash itself being obscured by the intervening cloud.

Both forms are due to a thundercloud being charged with positive electricity at the top and negative electricity at the bottom, though at the very base there is often another, but smaller, region of positive charge. On the ground below a moving carpet of positive electric charge is induced which follows beneath the drifting cloud. Over high points like buildings, masts or trees, its effects are greatly intensified. Thus the scene is set for the initiation of a lightning flash.

Although the proportion of flashes within clouds varies seasonally and in different parts of the world, over the Earth as a whole three-quarters of all flashes are internal. Forked lightning passing to the ground is much better understood and more easily explained, yet much of what will be said is equally applicable to internal strokes.

A discharge to the ground is initiated by the enormous differences of electrical potential between earth and cloud, which may reach something like 100 million volts. A total discharge, called a flash, lasts about 0.2 second and consists of one or more intermittent discharges, called strokes, having a faintly luminous phase lasting for several milliseconds at intervals of some tens of milliseconds. It is because the eye can just perceive the individual strokes that lightning appears to flicker.

It is believed that each lightning stroke to ground begins in the cloud as a local discharge between the negatively charged region and the small positive charge near its base. This frees electrons and forms a conductive channel along which they travel, neutralizing the small positive charge and continuing towards the ground as a *stepped leader*. The name indicates that it moves from cloud to ground in a succession of steps, each lasting less than a microsecond (millionth of a second), at intervals of about 50

Fig. 4 The return stroke. (a) Last stages of preceding figure. (b) Upward-moving discharge from a high point meets the descending leader. (c–e) Return stroke from ground to cloud: this is the visible flash, and the instantaneous heating of the air produces a shock wave, a 'sonic bang', which is the thunder.

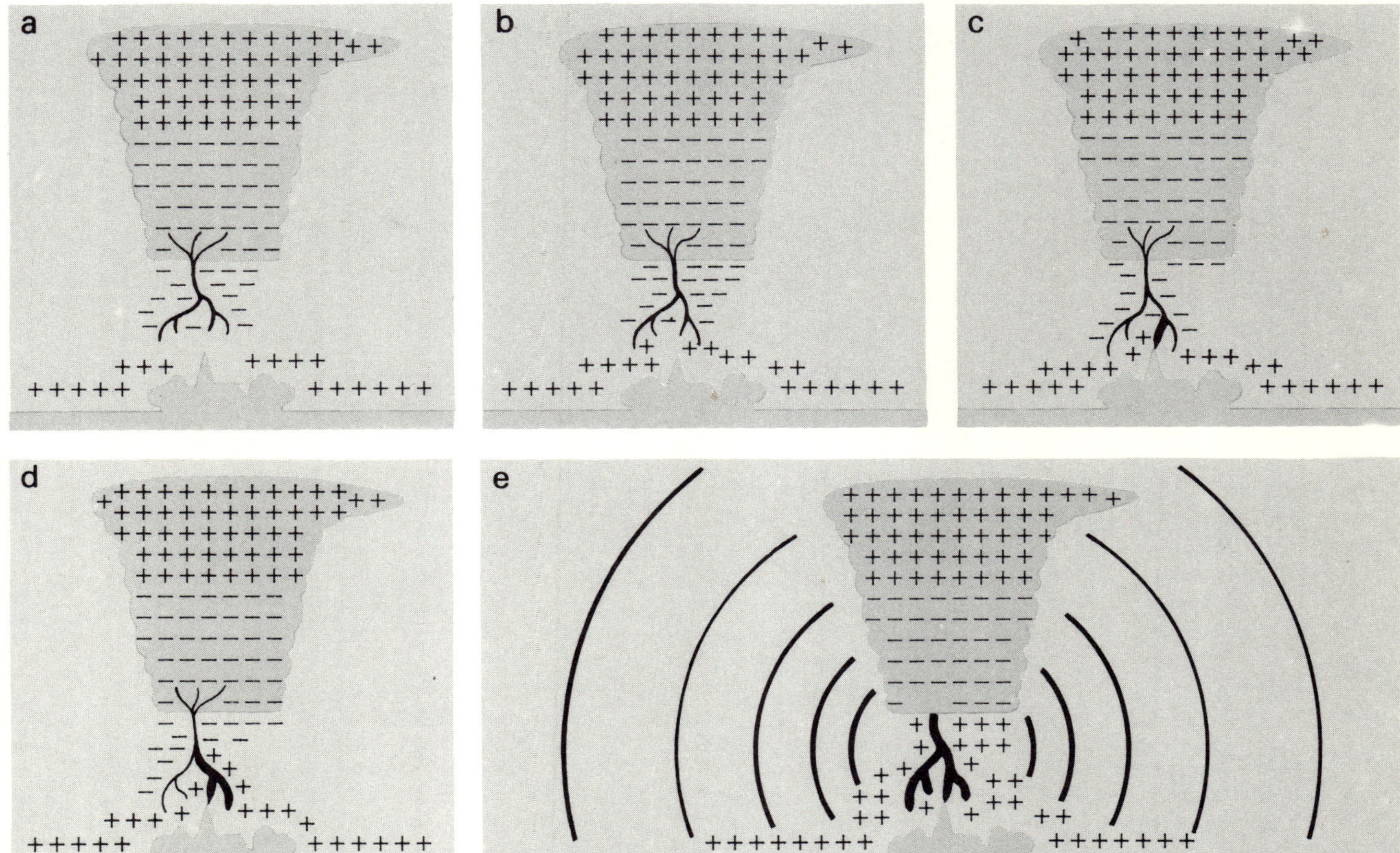

microseconds. It is these which give lightning its zig-zag appearance. In this way the negative charge from the cloud moves continuously towards the ground, rapidly extending an electrically conductive path through the non-conductive air along which the *return stroke* can flow. This is a discharge which leaps upwards from the earth, usually from a high point, for the stepped leader rapidly enhances the positive charge on the surface as it approaches the ground. When the two discharges meet, a conducting channel to earth is established, which becomes brilliantly luminous as the result of the return stroke, and it is this which we see as lightning as it moves upwards at one-tenth to half the speed of light. This is so fast that the entire channel appears to become bright instantaneously, obscuring the relatively weak luminosity of the stepped leader.

Sometimes a lightning flash ends after the return stroke current ceases to flow. More often flashes consist of three or four strokes separated by intervals of 40 to 50 milliseconds. These additional strokes are initiated by discharges which move upwards and outwards from the preceding stroke into the untapped negative charge within the cloud. When this happens a continuous leader, known as a *dart leader*, moves down the existing conductive channel, depositing negative charge and initiating another return stroke.

Thunder results from the passage of a return stroke, for the enormous surge of current through a channel of which the conducting core is believed to be only a few centimetres wide results in the production of great heat, the temperature being estimated to be about 30,000° Kelvin. This increases the pressure in the channel so that it expands with supersonic speed, and produces a shock wave that becomes the thunder we hear. Since sound waves travel at 1,090 feet per second, it is possible to find the distance of the lightning by counting seconds, five seconds to a mile.

Fig. 5 Relation between sunspot numbers and lightning strikes.

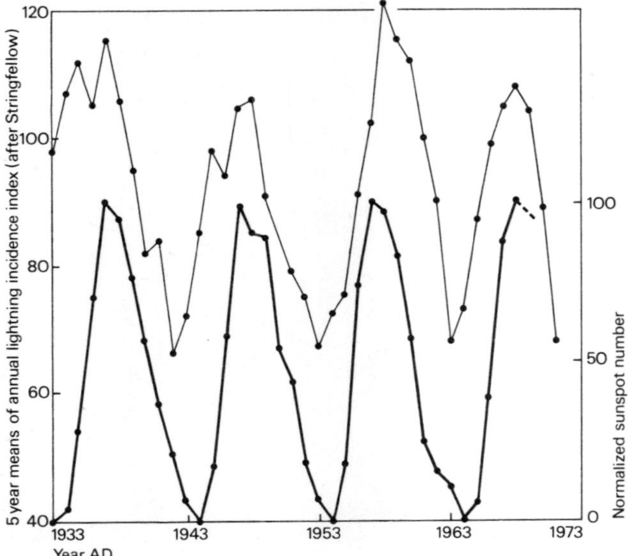

Sometimes no thunder is heard when lightning is observed. This is especially likely in the case of sheet lightning, for the strokes are not always strong enough to generate a shock wave audible at large distances upwind of the flash. On other occasions its absence may be the result of valleys or hills deflecting the sound above the observer; even the turbulent atmosphere can scatter it sufficiently for no sound to be heard. Rarely, in severe storms, lightning strokes may follow one another so quickly that there is continuous thunder for many minutes on end.

Relations between solar activity as shown by sunspot numbers and the occurrence of thunderstorms and lightning strikes have been reported from several countries. Fig. 5 shows such a relation for the United Kingdom. The upper curve shows the number of power failures per year due to lightning strikes on the power network, and the lower the normalized yearly average sunspot number. (The normalized sunspot number is that corresponding to a standard cycle range from 0 to 100.)

The initiation of lightning

In recent years much research has been conducted in an effort to establish the mechanism responsible for the initiation of a lightning discharge. It is known that to cause an electrical breakdown of dry air at ground-level pressure and temperature, an electrical field of about 3,000 volts per millimetre is necessary. The largest fields observed in a thundercloud have been around 400 volts per millimetre, suggesting that the breakdown must be due to the particles present in the cloud.

The most reliable measurements have been obtained by W. P. Winn in New Mexico, using a cylindrical rocket with vanes to make it spin in flight. This ingenious instrument uses its spinning motion to 'chop' the electrical field within the cloud, thereby producing an alternating current proportional to the field. Since the rocket's entire flight occupies only about two minutes, the computerized results provide a virtually instantaneous record of the electric field within the cloud. No reliable evidence for fields exceeding 400 volts per millimetre has been obtained. This is likely on theoretical grounds also, if the field is generated by particle separation. As the field increases, it exerts a mechanical force on the charged particles which opposes their separation.

One reason why discharges may occur in fields less than 3,000 volts per millimetre is that lightning strokes originate at altitudes of several kilometres, where the pressure is typically about two-thirds of normal ground-level values. Consequently the air density is lower, the mean spacing of the air molecules greater, and therefore the mean free path increased. It follows that ions will achieve more energy from the electric field before colliding with neutral air molecules. This means that they are more likely to ionize neutral air molecules and so initiate an 'electron avalanche' which can lead to a lightning stroke. The strength of the field at which breakdown will occur is lower at higher altitudes, and it has been estimated that at altitudes typical of the interiors of thunderclouds this must be about 2,000 volts per millimetre. This is still five times the known maximum field, and we must conclude that some process of local field enhancement exists.

A source of such intensification is charge separation on conducting ice or water particles. A spherical electrical conductor in an electric field can develop a field which is three times the strength of the ambient one at the poles of the sphere. The larger particles such as raindrops could thus produce a corona discharge which in turn could lead to lightning.

However, the maximum recorded ambient fields of about 400 volts per millimetre could only be raised in this way by a factor of three, which is well below the 2,000 volts per millimetre estimated for the initiation of lightning. Thus we must seek some way in which the field can be further increased.

It is possible that this could happen if the raindrop is elongated by electrical forces to produce a point, where the electrical field would become enormous and capable of initiating a corona discharge. Laboratory experiments have shown that this is possible, but even in the most favourable circumstances the onset field is never below 550 volts per millimetre.

The most likely source of corona leading to lightning appears to be the surface of a large ice particle or a pair of colliding raindrops. In the case of hailstones or snow crystals the onset of corona has been shown to be particularly dependent upon pressure, temperature, the shape of the particle and the presence of small-scale surface features upon it. In the particular case of melting hailstones the skin of water provides a deformable surface which the electric field can draw out into points and so produce corona, even if it is as low as 400 volts per millimetre.

In the case of colliding raindrops it has been shown that a long liquid filament may be drawn out between them as they separate, and that this could be several times the diameter of the larger drop. Since this filament is approximately parallel to the electric field, the shape of the drop-pair is particularly favourable to corona onset. In fact the lowest field in which corona occurs has been found by experiment to be 250 volts per millimetre, which is well within the possible limit for this mechanism.

So it appears that lightning may be triggered by corona from ice particles or colliding raindrops, processes which should probably be regarded as complementary and not exclusive of each other. In some clouds one or other of these mechanisms may predominate, and this will depend upon the height of the cloud base, the nature and concentration of precipitation present, and other factors.

Having established possible trigger mechanisms we still need to know how the necessary intense electric fields within thunderclouds are themselves produced. The studies which have been made during the last thirty years have resulted in a number of theories regarding their development. Unfortunately our knowledge of the meteorological and electrical properties of the clouds is so scanty that there is insufficient evidence on which to accept or reject most of these theories.

Aircraft and other means of sampling are unsatisfactory for a number of reasons, the greatest being the acquisition of truly representative data. A thundercloud has a volume of perhaps a hundred cubic kilometres and a lifetime of about an hour. Its properties vary enormously throughout its volume and lifetime, yet an aeroplane can only pass five or six times through the cloud during its life, and then only along a single line at a particular altitude. It is therefore impossible to be confident that the limited information obtained tells the full story.

Nevertheless, a pattern is beginning to emerge and there are now perhaps three or four possibly acceptable explanations of thundercloud electricity. Two of these theories associate the growth of the electric field with the

Fig. 6 The thermoelectric mechanism of cloud electrification. The falling hailstone grows while it falls, as the super-cooled droplets of the cloud freeze on to it, liberating latent heat on the surface of the hailstone in the process. This makes the hailstone slightly warmer than the ice crystals with which it collides, and the ice crystals pick up positive charge from the hailstone by the direct conversion of heat energy into electrical energy.

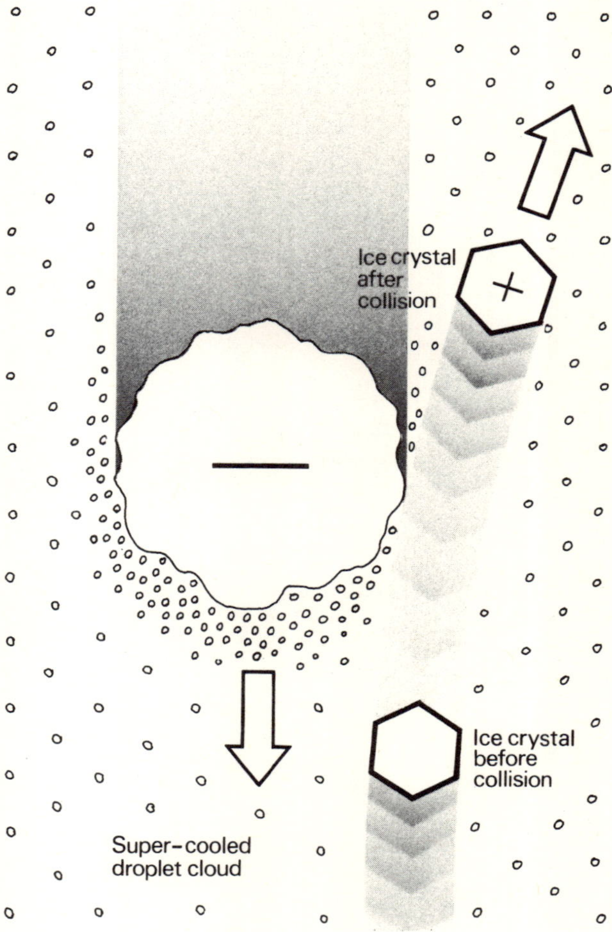

Fig. 7 The inductive mechanism of cloud electrification. The hailstone, falling faster than the lighter ice crystals, collides with them on the way down, and each time it does so, charge is transferred. This mechanism, or that proposed in Fig. 6, multiplied millions of times, would account for the observed charge distribution in a thundercloud (Fig. 2).

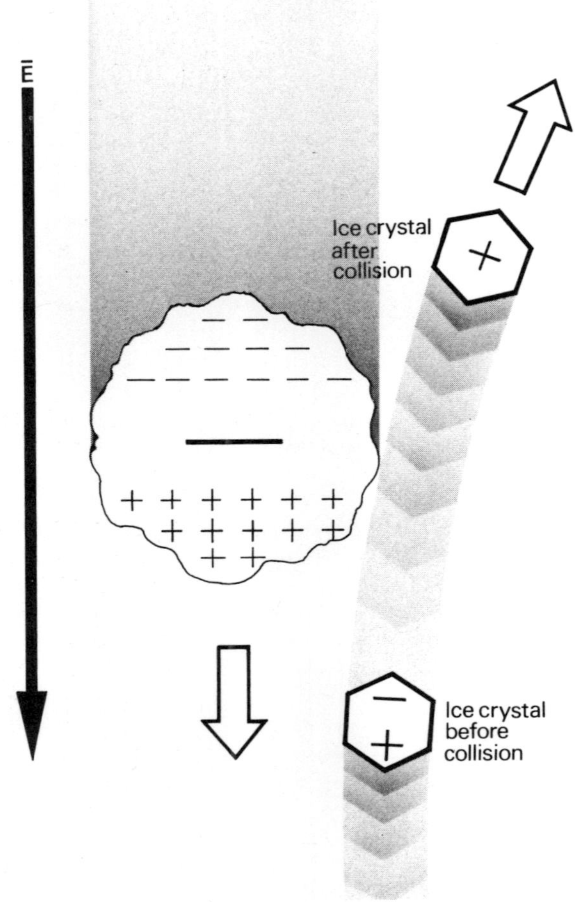

development of precipitation in the cloud. In either case it is assumed that collisions between large and small cloud particles result in the former acquiring negative charge and the latter positive charge. Separation of the large and small particles under gravity, coupled with the action of the updraught, result in the accumulation of positive charge at the top of the cloud and negative charge at its base. Thus the electric field grows.

In one theory, charge is separated because of the thermoelectric property of ice, and the fact that growing hailstones are warmer than the ice particles with which they collide. This is a consequence of the liberation of latent heat at the surface of a growing hailstone by the cloud droplets freezing on to it. The second theory is based on the fact that all cloud particles are polarized in the electric field. Thus, when a hail pellet overtakes and collides with an ice crystal some of the induced positive charge on its undersurface is carried away by the rebounding crystal.

Laboratory experiments have shown that both these theories could provide the necessary growth of a powerful electric field, but it is still far from certain that either mechanism is solely responsible for lightning. In any case, one or the other may predominate in a particular geographical region, or at a particular stage in the lifetime of a cloud. To illustrate this point we have only to note the beautiful lightning displays associated with volcanic eruptions, for neither theory can be applied to the electrical properties of volcanic material.

Strange forms of lightning

Besides forked and sheet lightning, there are other forms which may differ from them in fundamental or trivial ways, and some which are popularly regarded as lightning but are not strictly acceptable as such.

Ribbon lightning is a normal multi-stroke flash to earth, but occurring when a strong wind below the cloud moves the conducting channel sideways so that the camera can see the individual strokes.

In *beaded lightning* the channel appears to break up into luminous fragments. The flash starts as a continuous stroke, after which the luminosity gradually becomes fainter. As it fades the channel seems to break up into distinct beads, and these regions of high luminosity persist for some time after the parts of the channel between them have become invisible. This effect is due to the gradual decay of a continuing current which has followed the initial heavy discharge. The bright parts (beads) coincide with bends in the channel where the flash runs in the direction of the observer, thus providing an 'end-on' view of greater luminous depth. It is usually visible only through heavy rain, which prevents the initial bright stroke from temporarily blinding the eye.

Air discharges are frequently seen in dry countries. They emerge from the bottom of the cloud and branch profusely into the air below it without reaching the ground. Sometimes they make a very long, almost horizontal journey through the air below the cloud – one such meandering flash up to 30 km long has been reported. Usually they end in the clear air below the cloud or re-enter it perhaps 10 or 20 km from the point of emergence. In either case they must terminate at a positive charge. Occasionally these wandering air discharges turn earthwards and hit the ground far from their starting point. Such flashes must be responsible for the ancient belief that lightning sometimes appears from the clear sky as a 'bolt from the blue'.

Lightning does not always originate from thunderclouds. An example was the magnificent and extended display which occurred in 1963 when the island of Surtsey was born in the north Atlantic as a consequence of a volcanic eruption. In this case the electric charge separation was almost certainly due to the friction between particles of ashy material ejected from the volcano. It is well established that strong charging can result from rubbing materials in highly dispersed form, such as fine powders. Indeed, many explosions have occurred in such places as coal mines and sugar or flour mills as a result of discharges due to frictional electrification. Lightning has also been reported to occur occasionally in snow storms and sand storms, and frictional effects are again almost certain to be responsible.

The phenomenon of *ball lightning* would be classed by many as being about as reliably established as visitors from other worlds or abominable snowmen. Although accounts vary widely, a high proportion of reports about it mention one or more of the following characteristics: a spherical 'fireball' of diameter between about 1 cm and 2 m descending from, or in the vicinity of, a thunderstorm, occurring simultaneously with or following immediately after a lightning stroke to ground; a white, red, yellow or blue colour; a persistence time of some seconds during which it may pulsate or be quiescent; a sudden extinction, sometimes accompanied by an explosion or a popping noise and a sulphurous smell; a tendency to follow electrically conducting paths such as telegraph wires; a great propensity to enter rooms through chimneys and leave under doors or *vice-versa*; and a consistently perverse inclination to reveal themselves only to people without scientific training. Some reported observations of ball lightning are extremely vivid. The following account was provided by Herr Fasold, a postman who was walking near the small town of Bischofswerda in Saxony on 29 April 1925. He saw

> . . . a grayish-black cloud from which something dangled which looked like a trouser leg. Suddenly something fell from this dangling trouser leg which looked like a golden beer barrel. This body landed near a telephone pole with a loud crash, and I had the impression that it came apart, somewhat like emptying a basket of potatoes. From this heap real lightning jumped and one of the strokes hit the school. I was so surprised that I cannot say whether the crash was followed by real thunder or not, but I know that it was raining a bit before and that a little rain fell afterwards.

Fasold also stated that the trees looked for a short time like Christmas trees, as if they had candles at the tips of the twigs. This was probably an example of St Elmo's fire, which is discussed later.

Many explanations have been offered for ball lightning, some of them exceedingly erudite. One suggestion is that in the dry conditions prevailing during summer, a lightning stroke will select for its current flow to earth a stream or some other water surface. At certain points in this path the heating caused by the current will be extreme and large bubbles of gas, such as marsh gas or electrolytic hydrogen and oxygen, must be produced. The comparatively slow after-burning of these gases could explain their feeble continuing luminosity. The bubbles of gas would be electrified by the presence of large gaseous ions, and this could explain reports of fireballs sometimes being drawn to conductors such as wires. There are also a number of more exotic explanations, but until scientifically valid observations of the natural phenomenon have been made, the reality of ball lightning must be regarded as questionable, and complex theoretical analysis of this uncertain topic is unlikely to be profitable.

A luminous glow is often seen at night from the tops of ships' masts, the horns of cattle and even the upper extremities of people when electrified clouds are overhead. This ghostly apparition is commonly known as *St Elmo's fire* and has been erroneously reported as a form of lightning. In fact it is an extreme case of point discharge, and has already been mentioned in connection with Franklin's experiments. The 'flames' may be tens of centimetres in length and are often accompanied by audible crackling noises. The glow from the head takes the form of a halo. It has been suggested that the burning yet unconsumed bush encountered by Moses on Mount Sinai was due to a glow of this kind. Shakespeare describes St Elmo's fire in Act I, Scene 2 of *The Tempest*:

Fig. 8 St Elmo's fire on the masts and spars of a sailing ship.

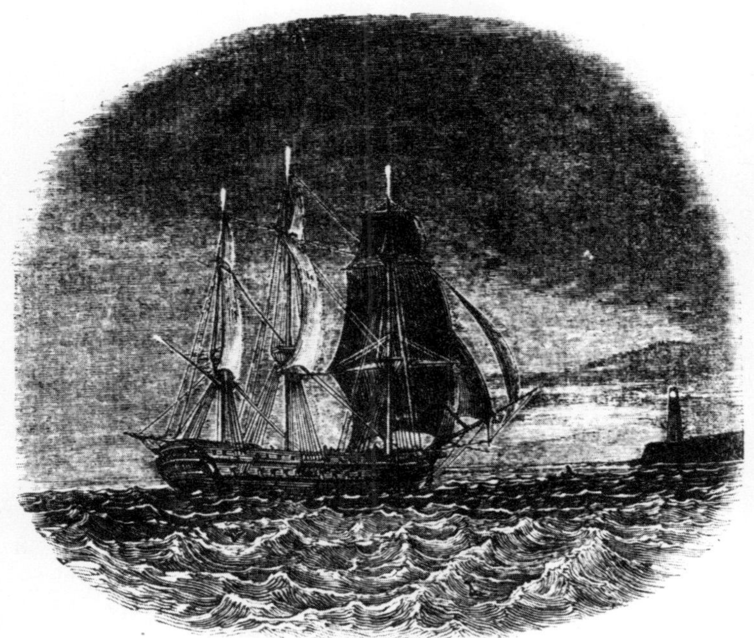

I boarded the King's ship; now in the beak,
Now in the waist, the deck, in every cabin,
I flamed amazement; sometime I'd divide
And burn in many places; on the topmast
The yards and bowsprit, would I flame distinctly
Then meet and join.

Sometimes radio emissions have been reported from electrified clouds at a time when they were not producing lightning. This is another form of electrical discharge which is not lightning, but is probably due to charged raindrops coming close together in an electrical field. When this occurs the local fields on their surfaces rise to immense values, which are eventually sufficient to promote spark discharges between the drops.

Lightning as a useful tool

Despite its potential dangers, there is one way in which lightning can be usefully employed. In recent years the radio signals from lightning flashes have been used to study the properties of the Earth's magnetosphere at great heights above the surface, up to about five Earth radii from the centre. The large electric current flowing in the flash generates radio signals over a wide range of frequencies. These give the well-known clicks which can be heard on radio receivers. The low-frequency parts of these signals can penetrate the ionosphere and are guided by the Earth's magnetic field into the opposite hemisphere. The lower frequencies travel more slowly than the higher by amounts which depend on the number of electrons present and the strength of the magnetic field. Thus it is possible to measure these quantities by studying the variation of delay with frequency. In practice small irregularities in the electron density between adjacent tubes of force cause some of the tubes to act as signal guides, similar to the well-known glass fibre guides for visible light. Thus most of the signal appears to come from a few particular tubes of force.

Movements in the magnetosphere cause these tubes of force to change position, and these changes can be studied by making direction-finding observations on the points at which the signals emerge from the tubes of force. Thus a lightning flash in the opposite hemisphere can be used to watch the movements of the high atmosphere between 16,000 and 10,000 km above the surface and to determine many of its properties.

The spark of life?

The primeval atmosphere contained methane, ammonia, nitrogen, water and hydrogen, but not significant quantities of the more complex organic compounds necessary for biogenesis. Experiments have shown that if a suitable source of energy is present, compounds such as amino-acids, nucleotides and hydrogen cyanide can be synthesized in a reducing atmosphere. In order for these compounds to accumulate and give rise to the even more complex ones involved in the formation of life they must have been transported into the primitive ocean or lakes.

The direct sources of energy available for organic synthesis on the primitive Earth were sunlight, thermal energy of volcanoes, cosmic rays, radioactivity, shock waves and electric discharges. On the basis of existing evidence it has been concluded that of these sources electric discharges are likely to have been of the greatest importance. Experiments have shown that discharges are particularly efficient in effecting organic synthesis, and since they occur in the lower atmosphere, transport of the products to the oceans would normally follow. These discharges could have been either lightning strokes or corona discharges from pointed objects in the vicinity of thunderstorms; the latter process being perhaps more likely, in view of the greater frequency and more widespread nature of its occurrence.

Clearly, corona occurring in the vicinity of the oceans would be of particular importance. Although land surfaces generally possess features of sufficient irregularity to permit corona emission in naturally occurring electric fields of moderate strength, it is not obvious that the ocean surface can be sufficiently rough. Yet recent experiments have

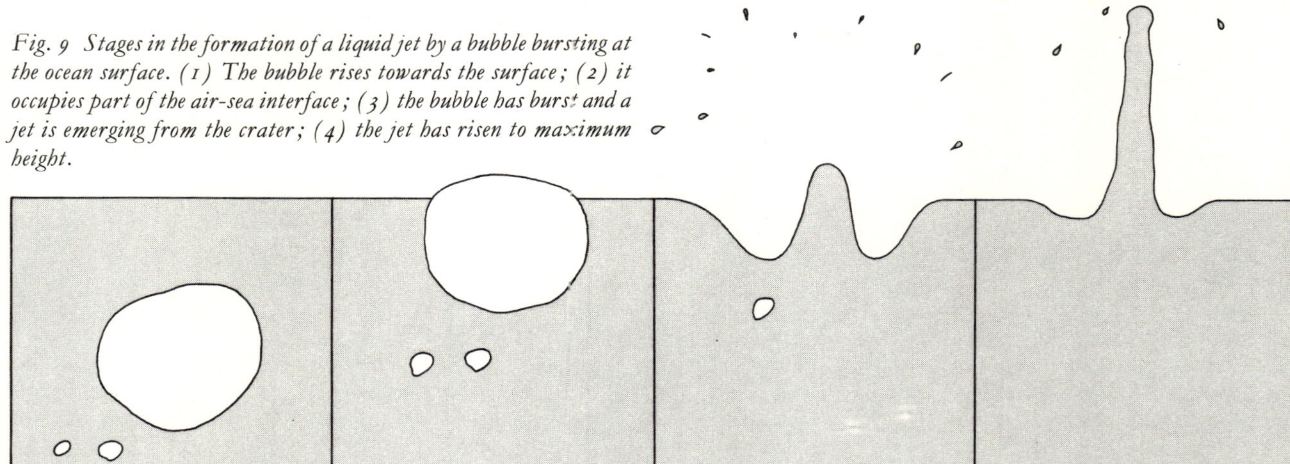

Fig. 9 Stages in the formation of a liquid jet by a bubble bursting at the ocean surface. (1) The bubble rises towards the surface; (2) it occupies part of the air-sea interface; (3) the bubble has burst and a jet is emerging from the crater; (4) the jet has risen to maximum height.

revealed three processes by which corona can be produced at or near to it.

In the first, corona is produced by colliding raindrops, as already mentioned in connection with the initiation of lightning, and experiments have shown that it can occur in electric fields down to 250 volts per millimetre.

The second involves the splashing of raindrops into water. The classic experiments of A. M. Worthington, conducted about a hundred years ago, showed that during the splashing process a jet of liquid is ejected vertically upwards. This has a diameter close to that of the drop and may rise several centimetres above the water surface. Clearly the tip of the jet could provide a favourable site for corona, and this possibility has been explored in recent experiments. Drops of radii between about 1 and 3 mm fell through a height of up to 2.5 m. A vertical electric field was applied in the region above the water surface, and corona was detected. The experiments showed that the jet was pulled out further by the field and when a critical value was reached the jet became pointed and corona was emitted. Using an image intensifier, beautiful photographs of positive and negative corona discharges were obtained. The lowest corona onset field occurred for the largest drops employed, and was about 180 volts per millimetre.

The third process which can give rise to corona emission is bubble-bursting at the ocean surface. Air forced into the oceans by wave motion or precipitation rises to the surface in the form of bubbles. When a bubble bursts, a jet of liquid rises at high velocity from the bottom of the bubble crater to achieve a height of several millimetres before ejecting a number of drops. The tip of such a jet is a likely source of corona in the presence of an electric field, and this possibility was recently investigated by the author, using apparatus similar to that employed in the drop-splashing experiments. It was found that corona discharges could be produced in fields down to about 260 volts per millimetre.

It therefore appears that all three processes can produce corona discharges in the vicinity of the ocean surface, and could perhaps have been responsible for the prebiotic synthesis of organic compounds in the primitive atmosphere of the Earth. All of them require the presence of strong fields associated with clouds which produce lightning. A full investigation of the corona resulting from raindrop collisions and bubble-bursting has yet to be made, but it seems likely that all three processes have corona threshold fields in the region of 200 volts per millimetre. Insufficient evidence exists at present to demonstrate which of them is likely to have been of the greatest importance to biogenesis. Nevertheless, it is fascinating to consider that in the beginning it may have been a force which has been a fear and a threat throughout the ages that gave rise to life itself.

Strange effects

Were it possible to harness all the energy in a lightning stroke, it would barely light a 300-watt electric bulb for a year; but because of the very high and concentrated currents in lightning, its discharge through various biological or inorganic materials can have curious effects.

Sometimes the surface rocks themselves provide particularly good conductors. H. A. Spencer, in his book *Lightning, Lightning Stroke and its Treatment*, tells how

> An elderly gentleman and his son were walking arm-in-arm one night outside their hotel on the outskirts of a village in the Transvaal, when a flash of lightning struck the ground about two hundred yards away from them, just as they were walking over an outcrop of ironstone. They received a shock which threw them to the ground locked in each other's embrace and rolled them about upon the ground for some minutes, unable to disentangle themselves or to call out. Finally, some people outside the hotel, thinking they were fighting, separated them and assisted them to their feet, still unable to explain what had occurred!

Later they were able to tell how their legs had suddenly given way and they found themselves rolling about with flexed limbs. Neither suffered burns or injury except that their muscles were cramped and sore. It was then found that a continuous outcrop of ironstone extended from where the lightning had struck to the point where the two had been standing. It seems that because they were arm-in-arm they straddled a length of the conducting rock, picking up an appreciable voltage between the right foot of one and the left foot of the other.

Lightning can produce both violent and seemingly innocuous effects on objects which it encounters in the last stages of its journey to earth. Particularly severe damage to wooden objects has been reported. For example, an eye-witness account of lightning striking the abbey of St Médard de Soissons in 1676 describes the effects on some of the roof rafters:

> They were found to be divided from top to bottom, to the depth of three feet, into the form of very thin laths; others of the same dimensions were broken up into long and fine matches; and some were divided into such delicate fibres that they almost resembled a worn-out broom.

In 1861 a lightning stroke entered a house in the Faubourg St Martin district of Paris and struck a large glass bottle containing cherry brandy. The bottle was cut by the lightning in a line as straight as if it had been done by a glass-cutter. The neck of the bottle was struck off, and driven through a window into the garden, a distance of more than thirty yards.

When lightning strikes dry rock or sand the heat of the discharge fuses the material and makes a hole surrounded by a glassy tube. In dry sand these very fine tubes, called fulgurites, may be up to about 3 metres in length. It has been estimated that in one sand-dune area of about 20 square kilometres on the south-eastern border of the Kalahari desert, there are not less than 2,000 fulgurites. Since lightning is locally very infrequent, at present at least, some of these fulgurites must have been formed by lightning flashes many thousands of years ago.

> The action of lightning upon the compass needle was ascertained for the first time in a curious manner. About the year 1675, two English convoys were proceeding to Barbadoes, and being arrived at the Bermudas, lightning fell upon one of them, destroyed the mast, and tore the sails; the other ship received no injury. The captain of the second ship having remarked that the injured ship had put about and appeared to be steering for England, inquired the cause of this sudden resolution, and was surprised to learn that his companion thought she was pursuing the previous track to the West Indies. A careful examination of the compass of the injured ship showed that the fleur-de-lis of the compass card, instead of pointing to the north, now pointed to the south, or, in other words, the polarity of the needle on board had been reversed, and remained so during the rest of the voyage.

Sometimes people have been killed outright by the direct effects of a lightning stroke. Occasionally, however, the victim has been almost unhurt, even though clothing has been torn off, set on fire, or, in the case of metallic ornaments, completely melted. Charles Tomlinson, from whose book *The Thunder-storm* I have already quoted, reports:

> The traveller Brydone relates a circumstance which happened to a lady of his acquaintance who was regarding a thunder-storm from her window. It lightened, and her bonnet, and her bonnet only, was reduced to ashes. According to Brydone, the lightning had been attracted to the metallic wire which maintained the shape of her bonnet and supported its softer materials. Hence he proposes that these wires should be abandoned, and protests against the prevailing fashion of maintaining the tresses and ornamenting the hair with gold and silver pins. And in the very natural apprehension that this caution would be disregarded, he offers this somewhat ridiculous advice: 'That every lady should wear a small chain or thread of brass wire, which she should hang, during the time of a thunder-storm, to the wires of her bonnet, by which the fulminating matter might pass to the earth, instead of traversing the head and other members.'

The *Dumfries Courier* presented the following account of the effects of a lightning stroke which devastated a farmhouse in Colvend, around 1870:

> On visiting it on the morrow, we found that the west gable-end had been thrown down, the bulk of the stones and rubbish falling inwards; that the walls, both back and front, were rent in several places; that the windows and doors were shattered to pieces; that the roof was forced over the front wall in one part and rendered dangerous even to pass under, not to say sleep beneath; and that the whole furniture of the family, with the

exception of a chest of drawers and a bed in the best room, was broken and torn in a manner truly distressing to behold; and yet, wonderful to relate, although there were four of the family sitting in different parts of the kitchen end at the time when the lightning struck the house, and although they were leaning on or standing by articles which were shattered around them, not one of them was killed – only a young woman had her left arm scorched, and a boy had a clog taken off his foot; another young woman had a letter which she was reading snatched out of her hand, and a steel hoop, which she had in her dress, completely torn out. The escape of the family amid all this wreck and ruin was truly marvellous. This is now the third cottage in Colvend which we remember to have been struck with lightning within the past few years, but never before did we witness such a ruin as may now be seen at Portling.

A curious phenomenon which at one time attracted a considerable amount of attention is known as a 'lightning figure'; it was first described by Benjamin Franklin in 1786. He stated that about twenty years earlier a man who was standing opposite a tree that had just been struck by a thunderbolt had an exact representation of the tree impressed upon his breast. The New York *Journal of Commerce* of 26 August 1853 contains the report:

> A little girl was standing at a window, before which was a young maple tree; after a brilliant flash of lightning a complete image of the tree was found imprinted on her body.

M. Raspail, in 1855, recounted an even more bizarre example of this phenomenon:

> A boy was climbing a tree for the purpose of robbing a bird's nest when the tree was struck by lightning and the boy was thrown upon the ground. On his breast the image of the tree with the bird and nest on one of its branches appeared very plainly.

Similar tree-like figures have been found on the bodies of people killed or seriously injured by lightning. The *Lancet* of 30 July 1864 contains an account of a straw-stack under which a man and two boys were sheltering when it was struck by lightning and set on fire. One was killed, the others injured.

> On taking off the clothes of one of the boys, a peculiar, sulphurous, singed odour was perceptible, and also several irregular but distinct red streaks of about a finger's breadth, running obliquely downwards and inwards on either side of the chest to a middle line in front of the abdomen, whence they converged. From this point they diverged again till they were lost in the perineum. The streaks were of a brighter red in the more vascular parts of the body. They disappeared in about four days, and the lad recovered.

The more exotic manifestations of lightning figures are almost certainly illusory figments of over-active imaginations. No mechanism is known by which lightning could cause a reduced image of an object to be imprinted on a body at a distance from it. However, when an intense electric current flows into a body it can follow simultaneously a multitude of paths, which may be revealed by the biological damage and may have some resemblance to the shape of a tree.

Finally, although we have concentrated on deleterious effects of lightning, it is possible that this most violent of phenomena may have some beneficial or therapeutic properties. In 1782 it was reported that the priest attached to the household of the Duke of Kent was cured of paralysis when struck by lightning. More recently my own eldest son was cured of a seemingly inveterate tendency to luxuriate in the hot water for at least two hours each time he took a bath. While he was performing his ablutions in a remote cottage high up in the hills of North Wales the chimney stack was struck by lightning which then passed to earth through the iron bath on the lip of which one foot was resting. This 'electric shock therapy' has produced a counter-reaction – an aversion to bathing which it is doubtful that lightning can remedy.

Today we must still regard lightning as a dangerous manifestation of natural forces, for in spite of our scientific knowledge we remain largely at risk. We may protect buildings with lightning conductors and take precautions for our own safety, avoiding such things as tall trees, electrical appliances, or even wire fences during thunderstorms. But we cannot protect every forest or building from fire, nor adequately reduce interference with telephones, radio communications and power lines. No longer is it seen as a supernatural force, but its power and its threat remain. Only by knowledge of its behaviour and sensible precautions can man ensure his survival when Thor's hammer strikes. However, there is no reason for over-anxiety, for most truly has it been said:

> If you heard the thunder, the lightning didn't strike you. If you saw the lightning, it missed you. And if it did hit, you're not likely to know it now.*

*Lane, F. W., *The Elements Rage* (1966).

Suggestions for further reading

Lucretius: *The Nature of the Universe*. Penguin, Harmondsworth and New York, 1958.

D. J. Malan: *Physics of Lightning*. English Universities Press, London, 1963.

B. J. Mason: 'The Physics of the Thunderstorm' in *Proceedings of the Royal Society* A, 327 (1971). Royal Society, London.

B. F. J. Schonland: *The Flight of Thunderbolts*. Oxford University Press, Oxford and New York, 1964.

C. Tomlinson: *The Thunder-storm: an account of the properties of lightning and of atmospheric electricity in various parts of the world*. London, 1859.

M. A. Uman: *Lightning*. McGraw-Hill, New York and Maidenhead, 1969.

—— : *Understanding Lightning*. BEK Technical Publications, Carnegie, Pennsylvania, 1971.

This is where it all begins. Within the towering mass of a 'thunderhead' violent, surging air currents, rising and falling raindrops and ice particles gradually build up an electrical field which can be measured in millions of volts. The mechanism of this build-up is not yet fully understood but the discharge to the ground in the form of a lightning flash and the accompanying thunder have impressed themselves on the mind of man since the remotest past, and are reflected in folklore and mythology. From this, one of the most dramatic and terrifying of the forces of nature, no protection was possible until the invention of the lightning conductor in 1753.

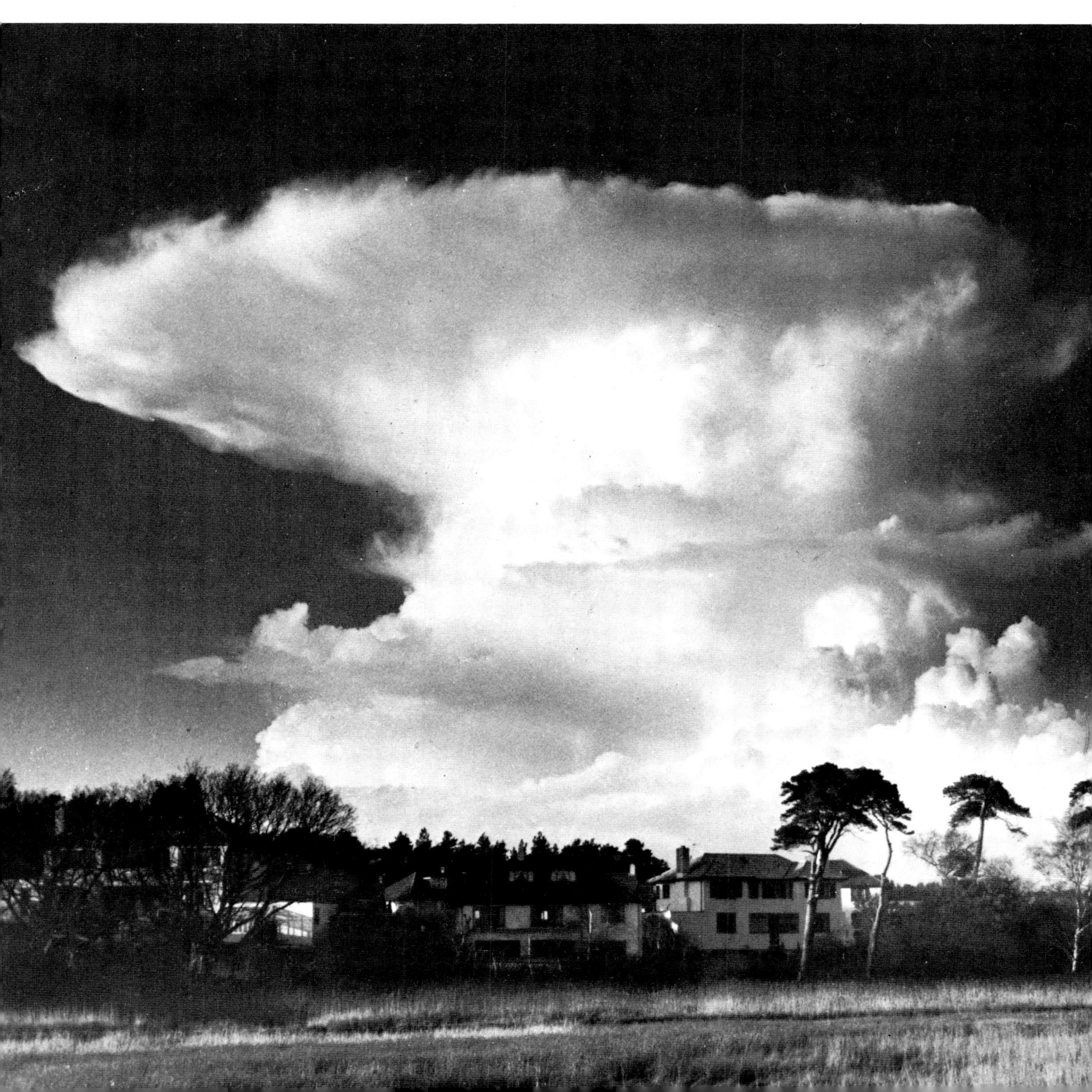

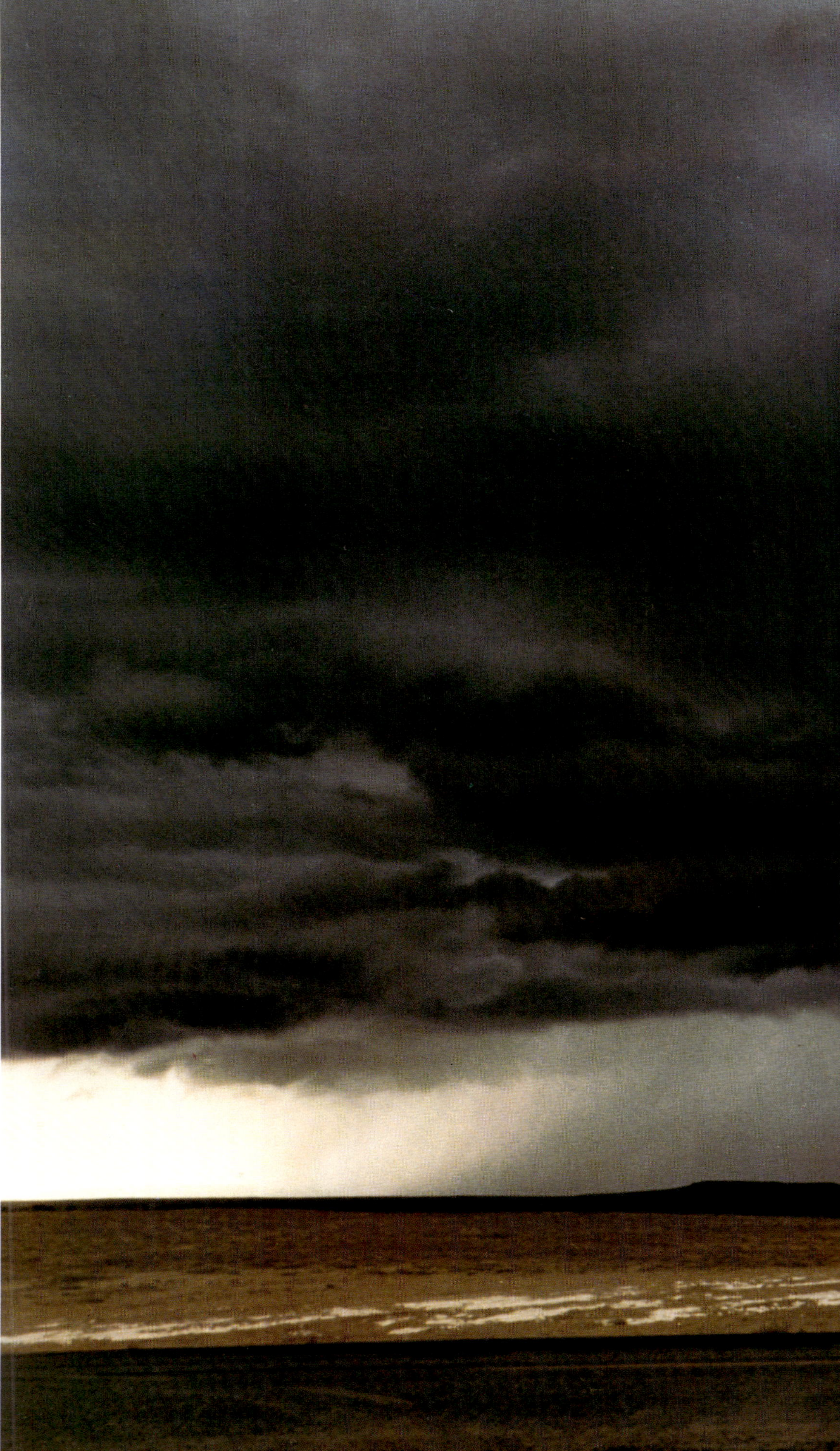

One single stroke, without fork or branch, is caught in this spectacular picture of a thunder cloud over the New Mexico desert, clearly associated with a torrential rainstorm. In that dark and menacing cloud base a vast volume of negative charge built up, followed on the ground by a moving carpet of positive charge. To release the tension of the multi-million-volt potential difference between cloud and ground, the negative charge from the cloud flashed down to the ground, stripping electrons from the air molecules and thus making a conducting channel for the return stroke from the ground. It is this return stroke, travelling through a channel only inches in diameter and heating the air to thousands of degrees, which is the visible flash.

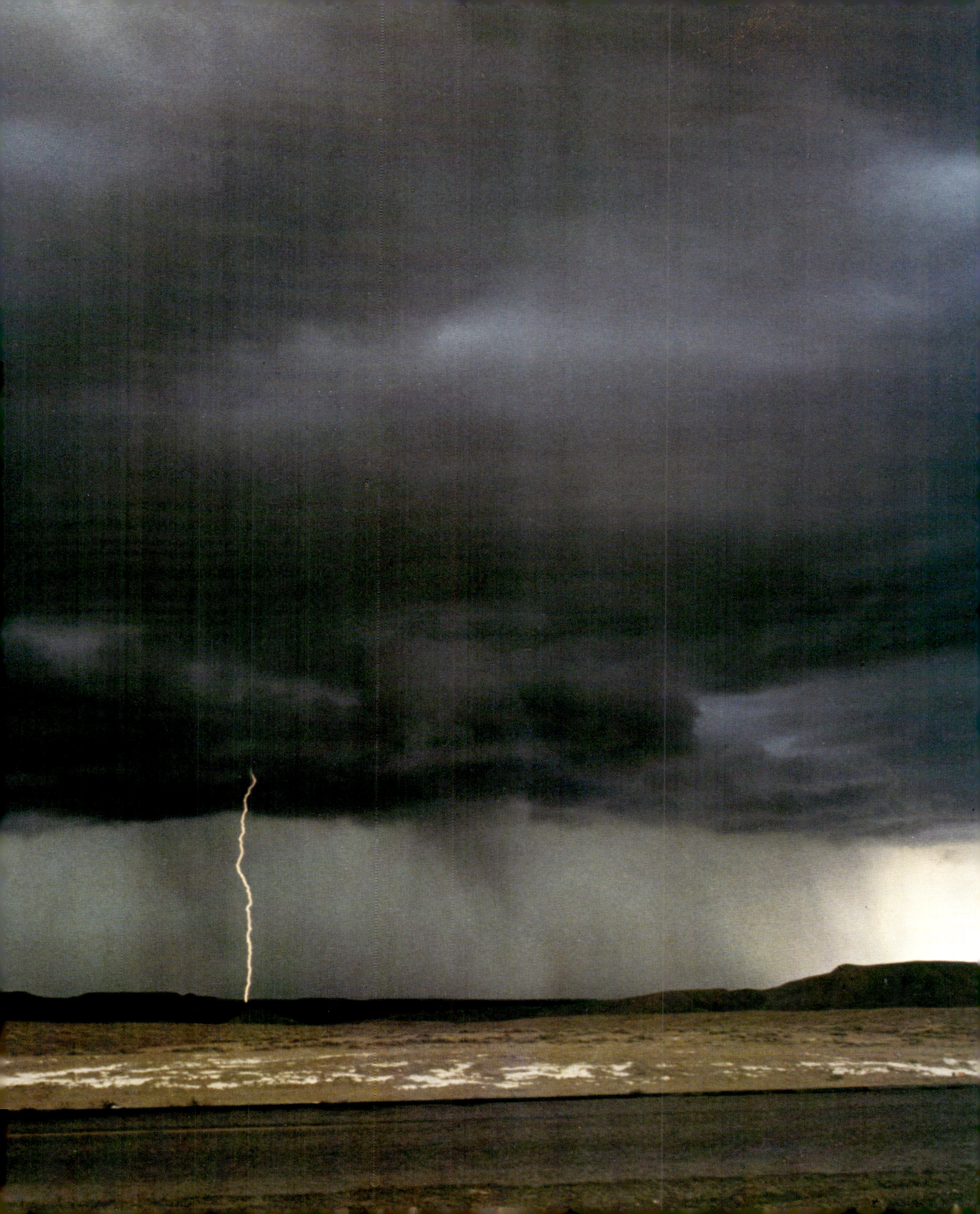

The savage violence of a lightning strike is caught in this rare sequence, taken on very high-speed cine film. From the first touch of the flash in the uppermost branches (3) to the beginning of the return stroke (5) that felled the tree was a few thousandths of a second. Split and shattered at the roots, the tree collapsed (6, 7).

3

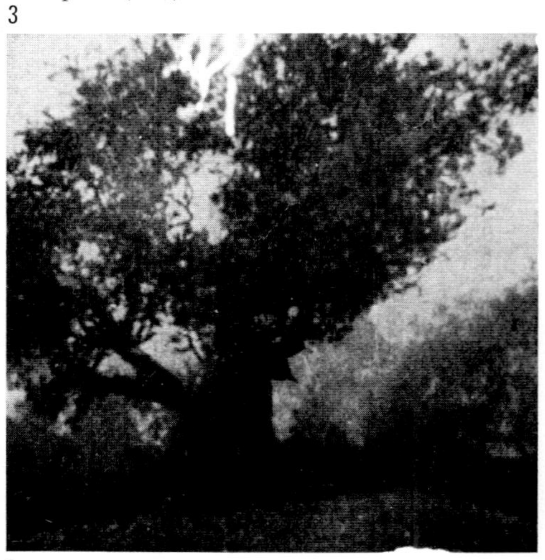

4

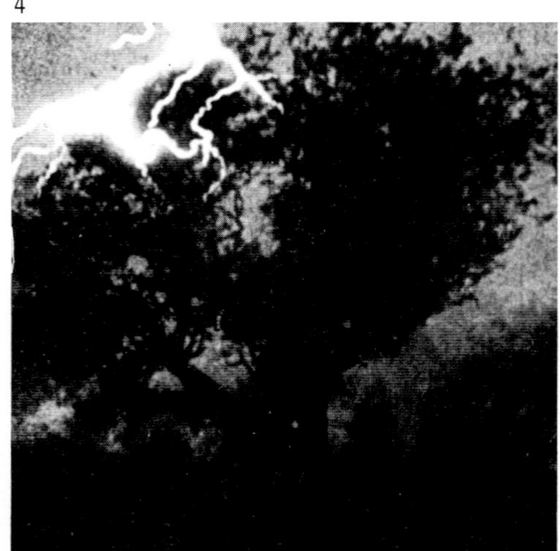

5

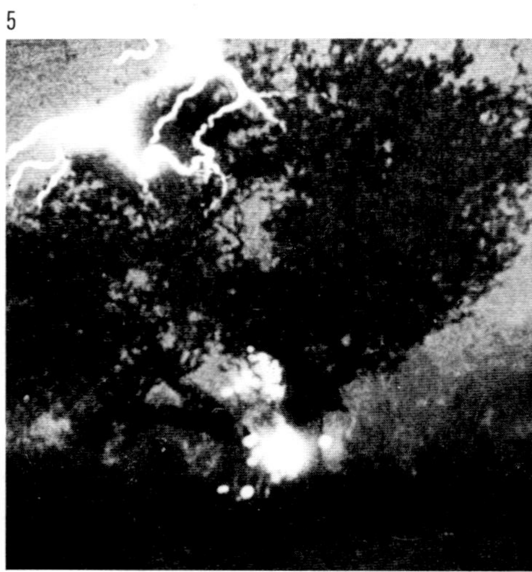

8

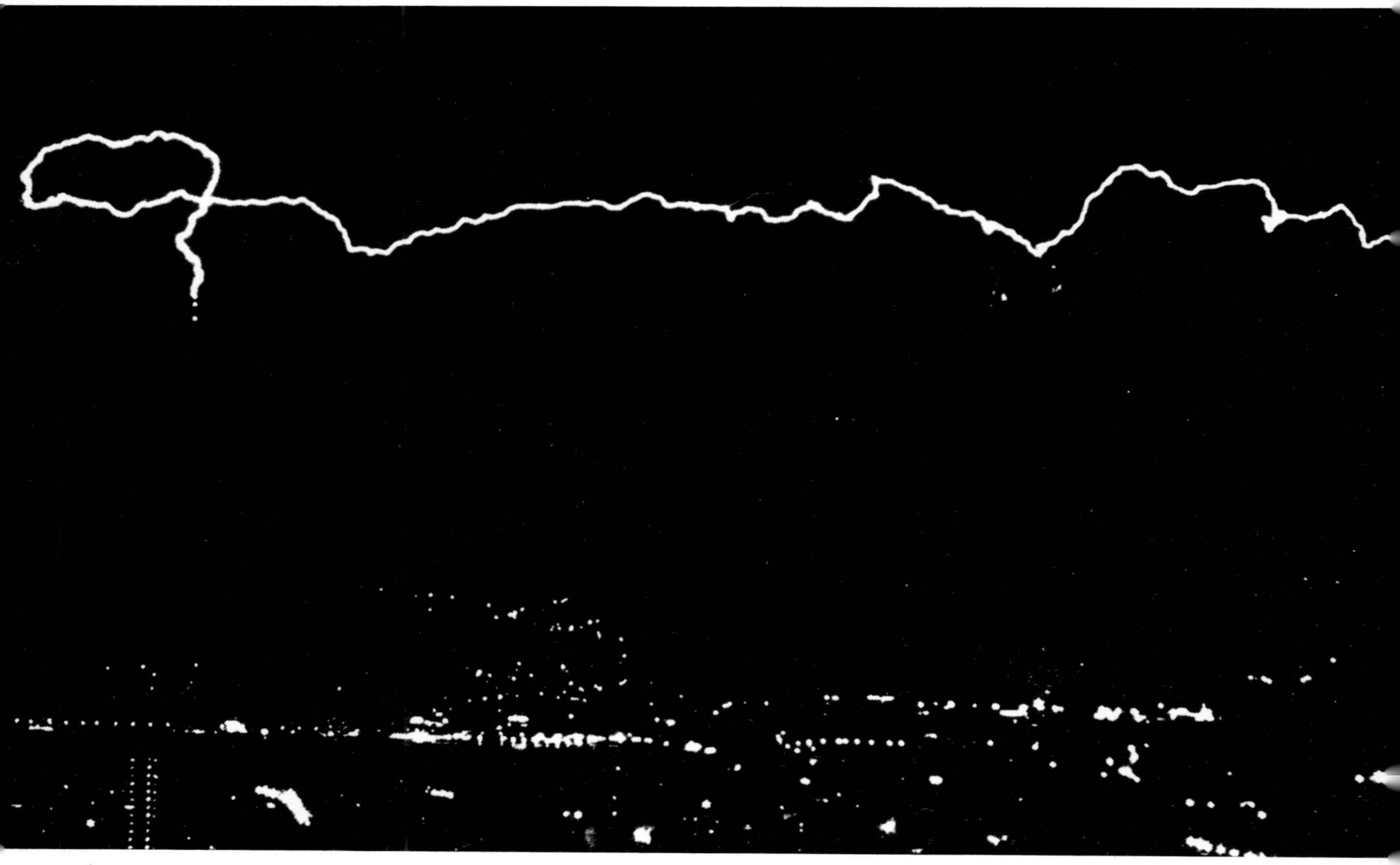

6

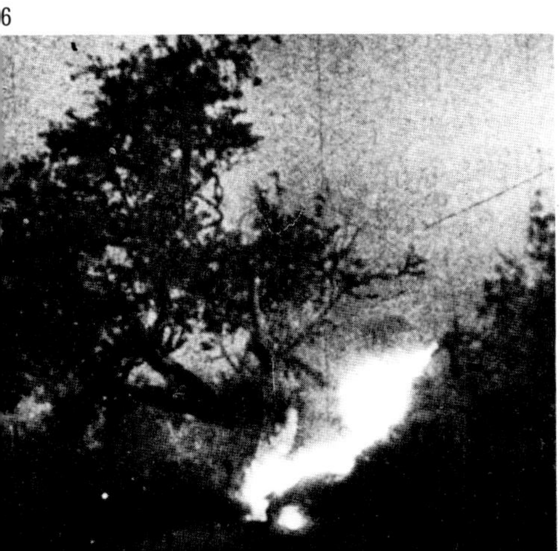

7

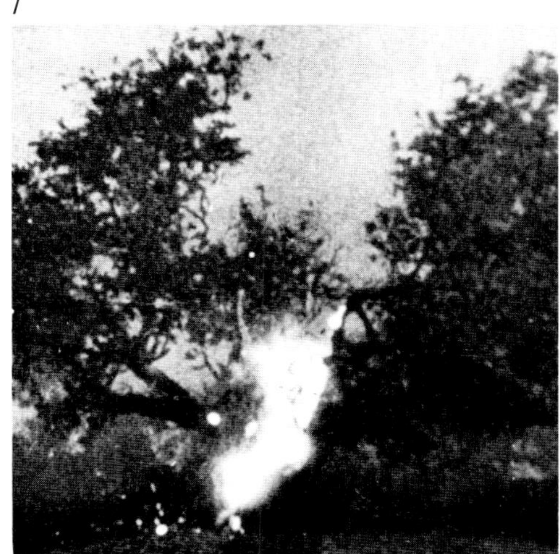

10

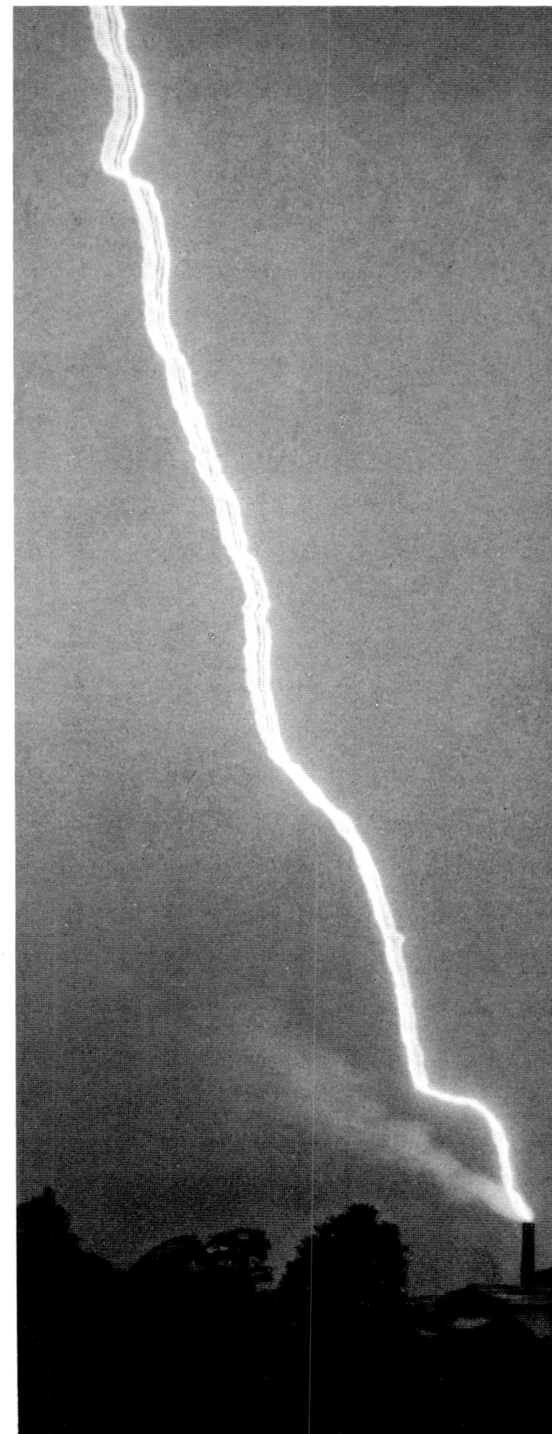

Lightning takes strange forms. A long horizontal stroke (8) can even be seen to 'loop the loop': these 'air discharges' sometimes, as here, terminate before reaching the ground, discharging into a mid-air pocket of positive charge. Spectacular displays of lightning over the erupting Icelandic volcano Surtsey (9) resulted from the charge set up by friction among the particles and ashes ejected from the crater. Ribbon lightning (10) is seen when a strong wind is blowing, so that the conducting channel of a normal multi-stroke flash moves bodily sideways.

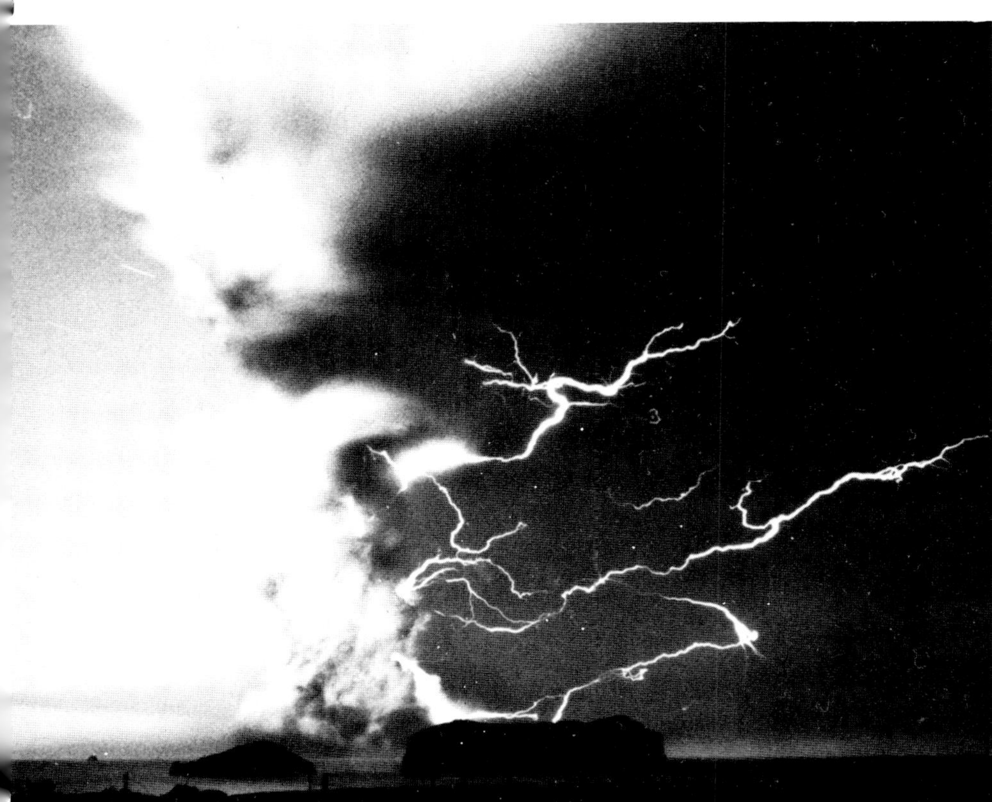

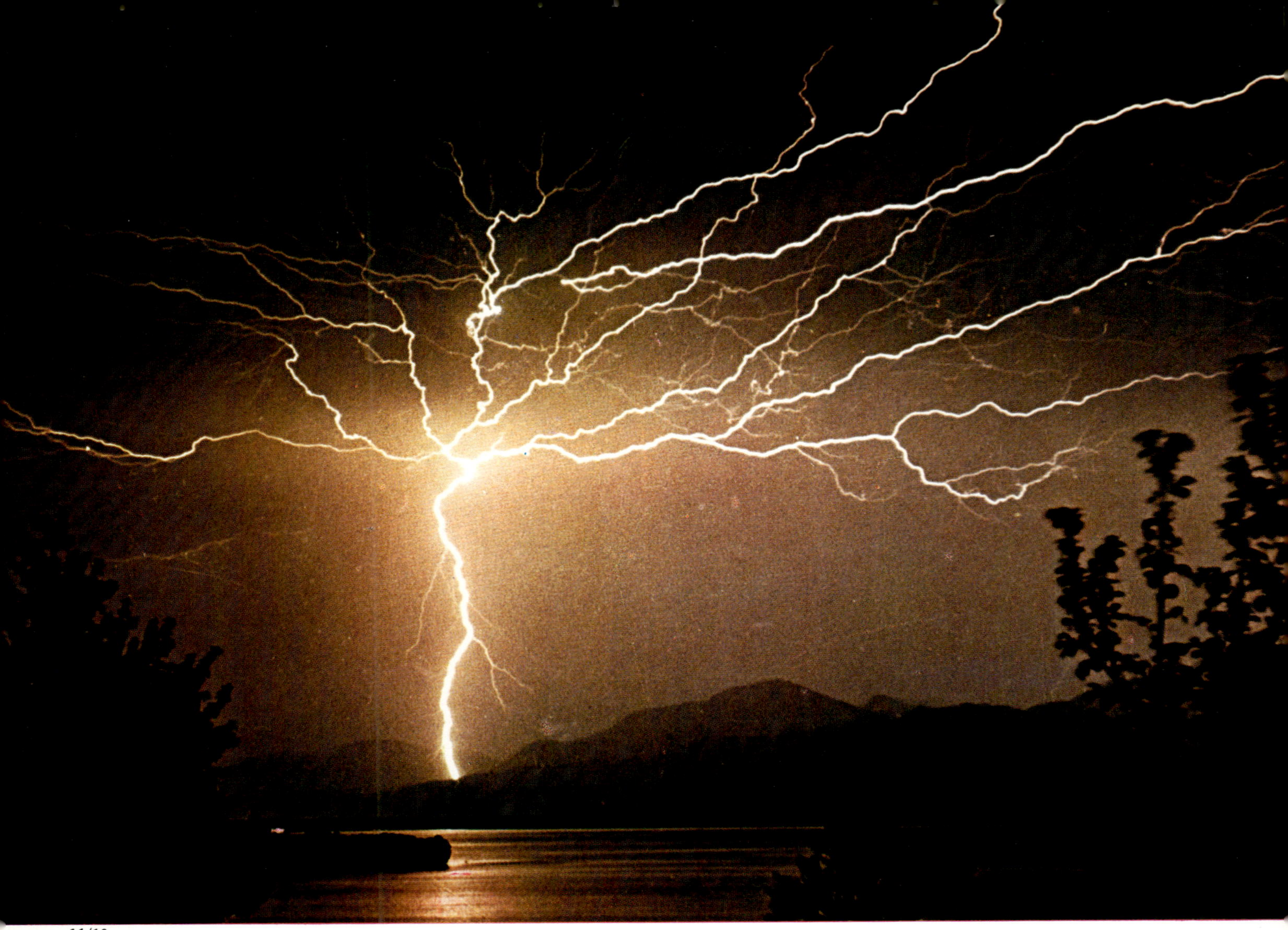

11/12

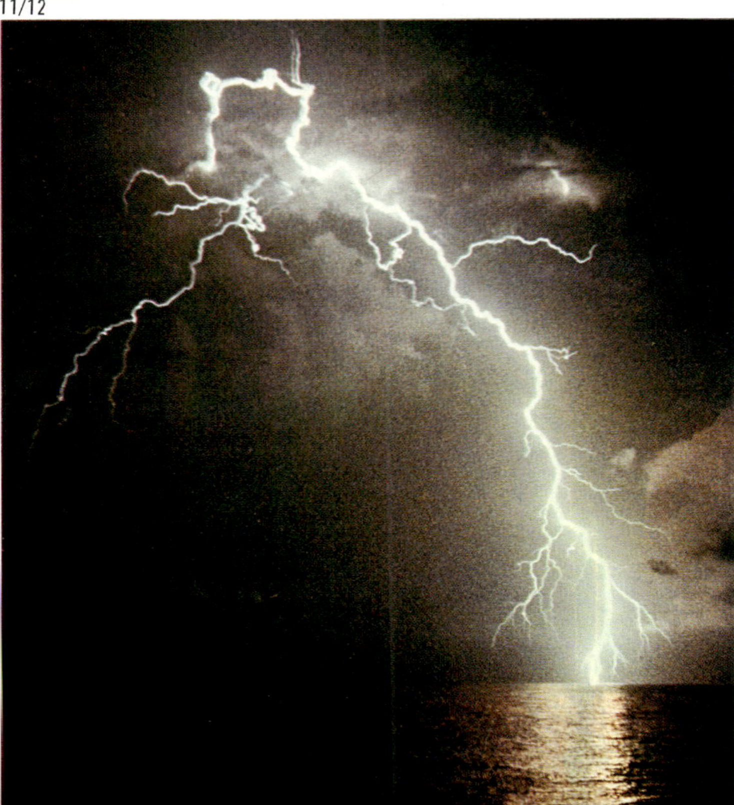

The blinding tracery of fork lightning over the Chiemsee, Bavaria (11), shows itself clearly as a return stroke – blazing strongly in the first flash up from the ground, and dying out at the end of each conducting channel. In a stroke of fork lightning photographed from a cruise ship in the Caribbean (12), loops and thickening in the upper part of the flash mark places where the channel pointed towards the camera. This end-on view can sometimes give rise to a 'beaded' effect. Where lightning flashes between positive and negative regions within a cloud (13), sheet lightning results – often combined, as here, with fork lightning in an impressive firework display.

13

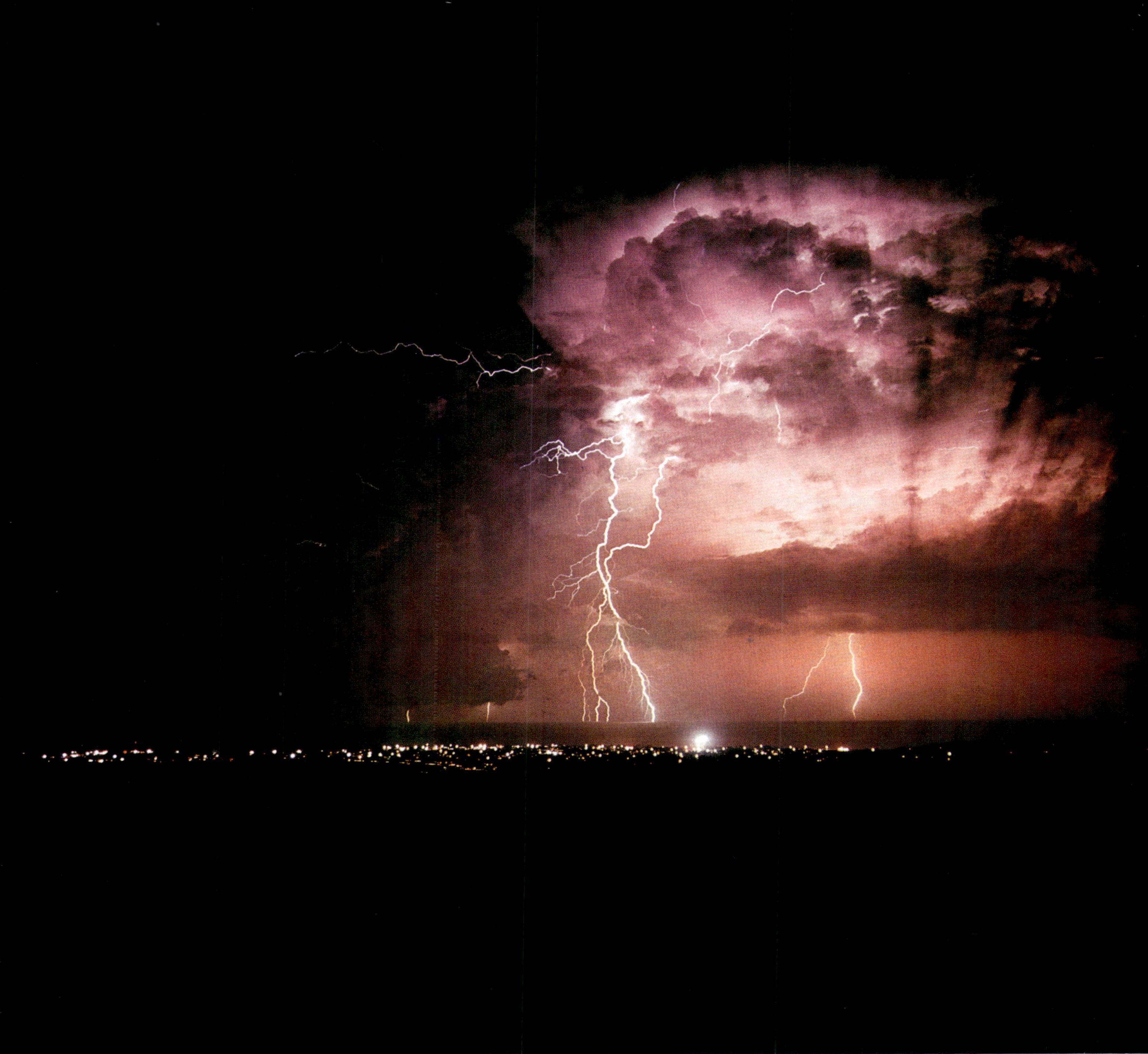

14

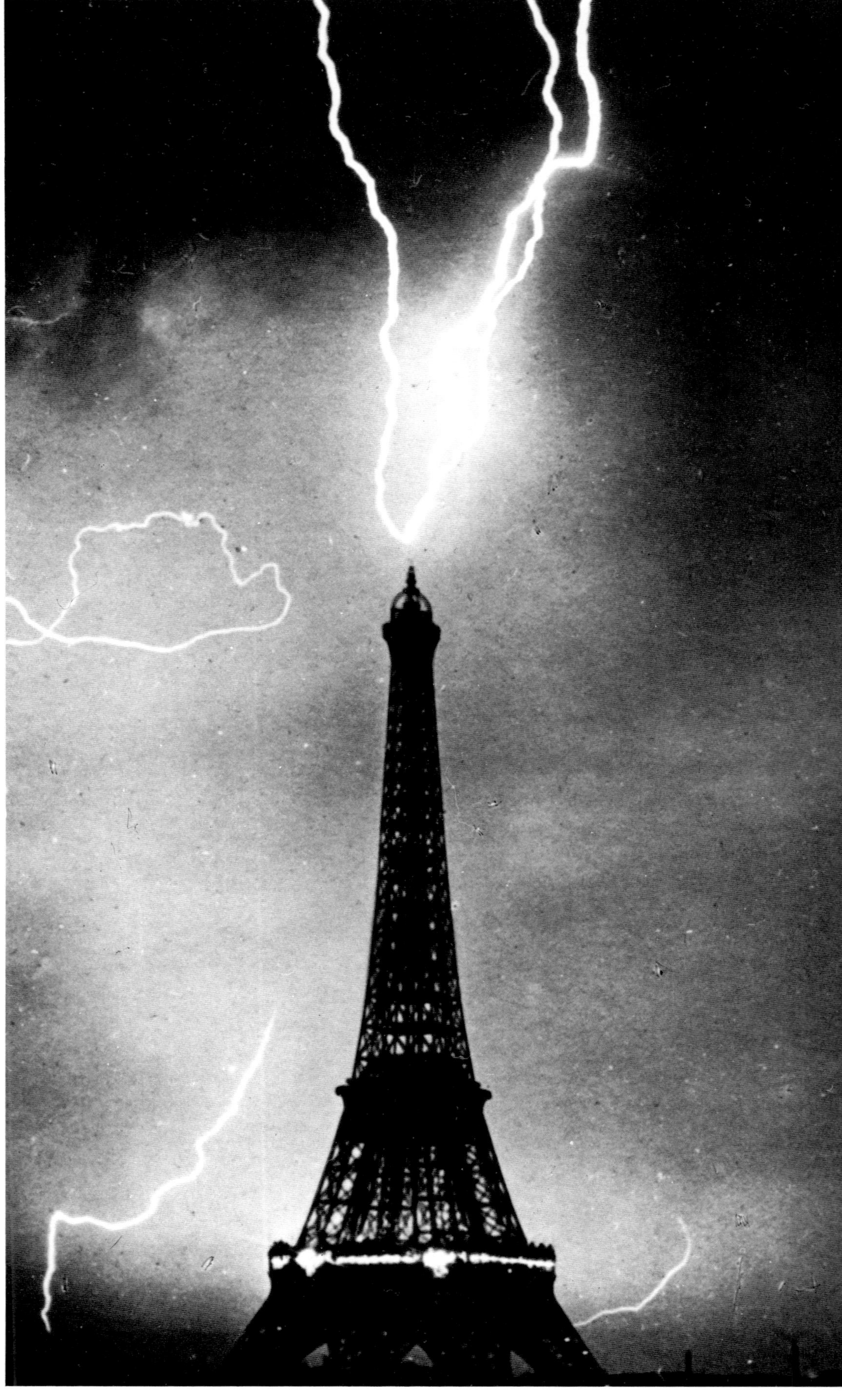

The tallest lightning conductor in Paris tops the 984-foot Eiffel Tower. Its effectiveness is demonstrated by the fiery horns of a return stroke flashing upwards in a thunderstorm. Benjamin Franklin (envoy from America to France a hundred years before the tower was built) wrote: 'Would not these pointed rods probably draw the electrical fire silently out of a cloud before it came nigh enough to strike and thereby secure us from that most sudden and terrible mischief?' More than two centuries after Franklin made his suggestion, the lightning conductor is still our only sure defence against 'that most sudden and terrible mischief'.

4

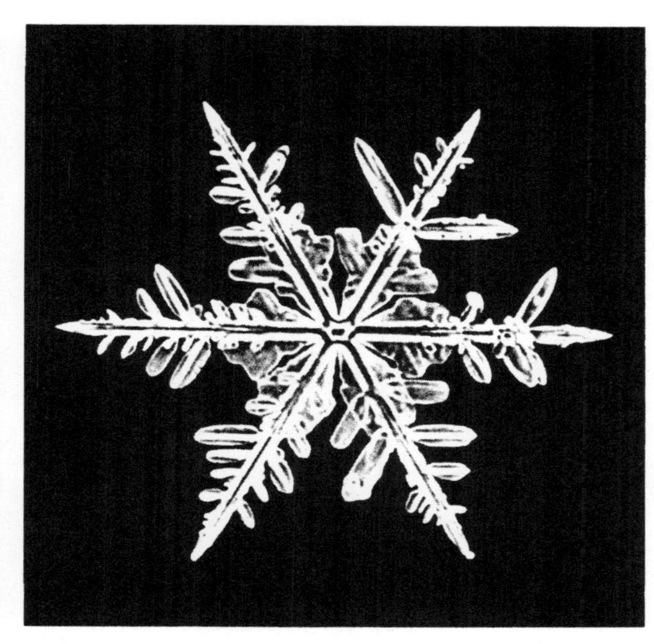

Snow and avalanches

M. de Quervain

Over large areas of our planet snow covers the ground in winter like a soft, white cloak, a bountiful gift of nature, a blanket and a water supply for plants and animals, a visual and physical delight for men, especially for the winter sportsman and the hotels and industries that serve him. In contrast, however, snow has some very negative and violent aspects, so that it must indeed be counted among the forces of nature. Above all there are the snowstorms, blizzards and avalanches. Although we remain liable to disturbance and damage by snow, modern technology has managed to devise a high measure of protection.

Within the framework of this book only the dramatic features of snow will be dealt with, with particular emphasis on avalanches; for it is these which, year by year, claim most victims and cause most destruction.

In the endless circulation of water over the globe the air absorbs moisture from the surface of the ocean and inland waters in the form of vapour, and the wind carries this to other parts of the Earth. When the air reaches colder regions, especially when it is carried to high altitudes, it becomes cooler and condenses into clouds of fine droplets. It would be wrong to assume that when the temperature is below freezing-point the droplets immediately turn into ice crystals. Actually the droplets can cool to well below 0°C without freezing. Only in the presence of what are called freezing nuclei (tiny mineral particles or, more rarely, organic particles) are ice crystals formed. This occurs in the temperature range between −8°C and −39°C. These particles are very few in relation to the large number of droplets, but, by vapour transfer and collision with the droplets, they grow, develop into snow crystals of many shapes, and sink to the ground. When the temperature of the lower air layers is well above melting-point, the beauty of the snow crystals is destroyed on their way to the ground and only rain falls.

The world's snow cover

From the equator to the poles, and with increasing altitude, the air temperature in general decreases. Temperatures sufficiently low for the formation of snow are found at ground level well into the temperate zones, and at high levels at the latitude of the equator. In practice, however, this general distribution of temperature is considerably modified by the distribution of land and water, by the result of air circulation and sea currents, and of course by the influence of the seasons. So it follows that within the great continental land masses – particularly Asia and North America – very low winter temperatures are prevalent, whereas the coastal regions in the same latitudes are appreciably milder. But even proximity to the coast does not guarantee the same kind of climate – compare the climates of New York and Naples, both around 40°N. Here, among other factors, it is the prevailing cold and warm sea currents which have a decisive effect.

Apart from a sufficiently low temperature, snowfall needs an adequate supply of moisture. In this respect the continental territories are insufficiently supplied. The moist sea winds lose their water content as they travel inland, and only a little rain falls as they cool. Hence the low precipitation in the continental heartlands. Quite apart from the relation between temperature and altitude, it is a general rule that the maritime countries have heavier, warmer snowfalls during a shorter season, whereas in the interior there is less but colder snow over a longer period.

The general decrease in air temperature with altitude of about 0.6°C per hundred metres in the lower free atmosphere affects the ground temperature and influences to a high degree the supply of snow in any area, if by 'supply of snow' we understand the annual precipitation which falls in the form of snow.

In climatic zones where it rains in the summer and snows in the winter, the snow season lasts longer at higher altitudes, and the snow cover reaches greater depths than in lower places, even if the period and intensity of precipitation are the same. To this basic phenomenon must be added the effect of a chain of mountains on the release of precipitation. Moist air masses approaching a mountain range are forced upwards on the windward side. They therefore cool (adiabatic cooling of an expanding gas), their moisture content condenses, and increased precipitation results. This so-called orographic effect can cause considerable variations in the deposit of snow even within a few kilometres.

The concerted action of the different factors is illustrated by the map of snow coverage on the North American continent and a snowfall profile along latitude 50°N through Canada. While the number of days of actual snow cover along the 50th parallel (apart from the immediate coastal zones) does not vary very much, areas of heavy snowfall are found in the west and the east, while in the central prairie between the Rocky Mountains and the Great Lakes the snowfall is light.

After a time (which may be a few hours or a thousand years) the deposited snow will re-enter the hydrological cycle through melting or evaporation. Both these processes need energy. Where in winter the available warmth and sunshine are not enough to melt the freshly fallen snow, there is an over-all seasonal snow cover which only disappears during spring and summer. What happens when these warmer seasons provide insufficient energy to melt

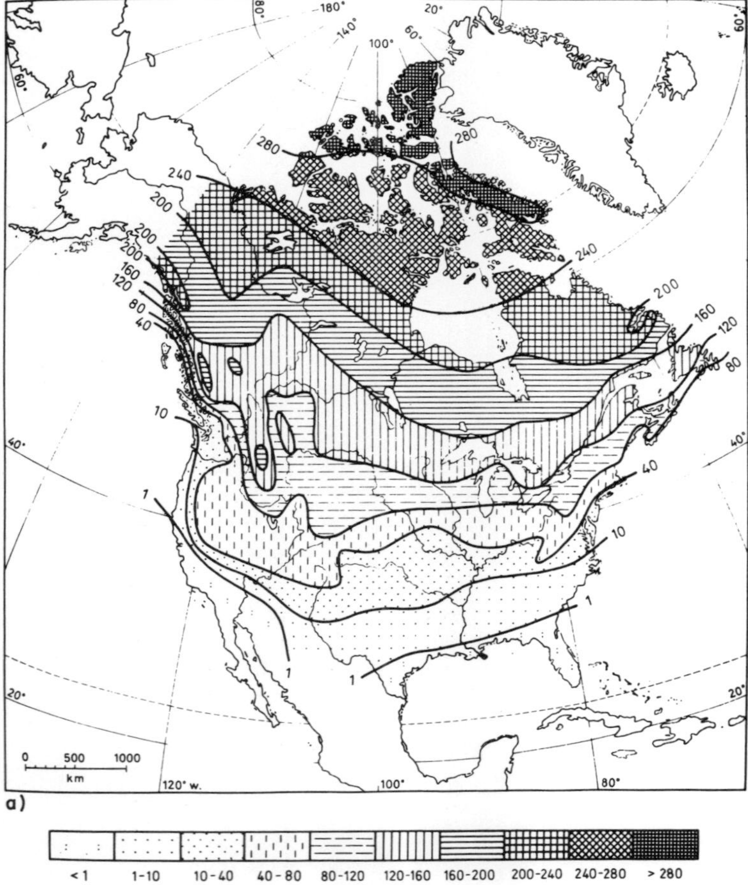

Fig. 1 Map of North America showing number of days per year with snow, ranging from one or less in California to over nine months in the Canadian Arctic. (From F. Wilhelm 1975 after S. S. Visher 1954).

the winter cover completely? Then part of the snow (in cold regions practically all of it) remains on the ground as 'firn' (old snow which has been transformed into denser material, literally, 'last year's') and will be covered by new snow layers the following winter.

This can be repeated for hundreds and thousands of years. In the polar regions, in the course of many millennia, ice sheets several thousand metres thick have been built up in Greenland and the Antarctic. Even in the temperate zones some of the mountain ranges have massive ice caps, and at the highest altitudes this phenomenon extends into equatorial latitudes, as on Chimborazo in Ecuador (6,267 m), Mount Kenya (5,200 m) and Ruwenzori in Uganda (5,120 m). But the snow cover is prevented from building up beyond certain limits; the firn becomes compacted into solid ice and flows as a viscous mass, spreading out wherever there is an outlet leading to a lower, warmer level or flowing directly into the sea.

The higher places with a permanent snow cover are divided from the regions with only seasonal snow cover by the firn line – the line which separates bare ice or old firn from last winter's snow at the end of the summer. The temporary boundary between unbroken snow cover and snow-free land is called a snow line, or a transient snow line. Both these lines trace a very complicated course across country, dictated by the irregularity of the snow deposition and, equally, through local differences in the energy balance (incoming and outgoing radiation, exchange of sensible and latent heat) which affects the degree of melting. While the snow line can move a considerable distance daily at the beginning and end of the winter, the firn line remains more nearly stationary. Its average position, however, can

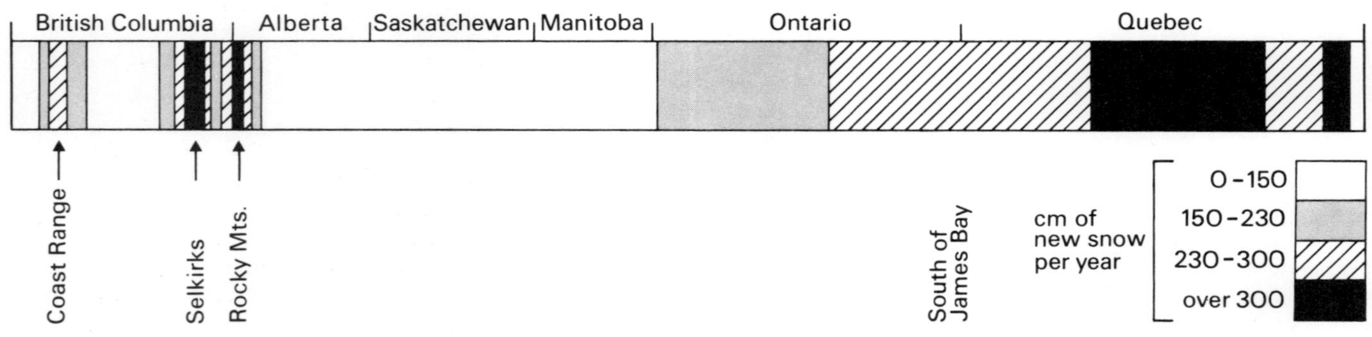

Fig. 2 Snowfall profile along the 50th parallel. Note how the heaviest snowfall occurs in the east and west, with little precipitation in the central prairie.

change during the course of years or even decades, indicating constant or fluctuating changes in climate. There are ice caps which once in an earlier colder period piled up to above the level of the firn line, and which remain in existence to this day simply because their tops are so high.

The processes which bring about the ablation* of the snow cover are individually very complex. Warmth from the wind and direct or indirect solar radiation compete with the radiation reflected from the snow and the infra-red radiation. Latent heat of evaporation or condensation is also involved in the interplay of received and transmitted energy. During the course of one day, melting can change to re-freezing and evaporation to condensation. Snowfall, together with compacting of snow through settling and ablation, results in temporal variations of snow depth within a given period, which for two neighbouring observation points at different altitudes will give the kind of picture shown in Fig. 3 for the Davos area in the Swiss Alps. From this one infers that in the early winter the two altitudes become snowed up on different dates. Before this date the precipitation falls in the form of rain, or possibly of snow which immediately melts again. As soon as snow is falling everywhere the snowfall at the different altitudes does not vary very much. Later the curves diverge as ablation sets in earlier in the higher temperatures of the lower regions. Thus by the time the snow has reached its winter maximum on the Weissfluhjoch (2,540 m) it has already almost disappeared in Davos (1,560 m).

Snow, wind and snowdrifts

When the wind blows at a speed of more than about 5 m a second over loose, dry snow, particles become caught up and whirled away. A more or less heavy flux of drifting snow develops, depending on the wind speed. Sometimes this snow transport takes place in a layer only a few centimetres deep. On open flat surfaces and on gentle slopes the to-and-fro movement of the whole surface, known as 'low snowdrift', offers a fascinating sight in fine weather. Where the snow comes from and where it goes is not immediately obvious. As the wind speed increases, so does the depth of the drifting layer, and the onlooker himself may be completely smothered; this is called 'high drift'. As the amount of snow that is blown away increases, the erosion effects on the surface become recognizable in the form of ridges and furrows known as *sastrugi*.

This carpet of drifting snow can extend over open prairie and tundra or on the polar ice sheets for hundreds of

Fig. 3 Average snow depth on the 1st and 15th day of each month over the last 30 years, at two places in Switzerland. Though they are only 4 km apart, there is 980 m difference in their altitude.

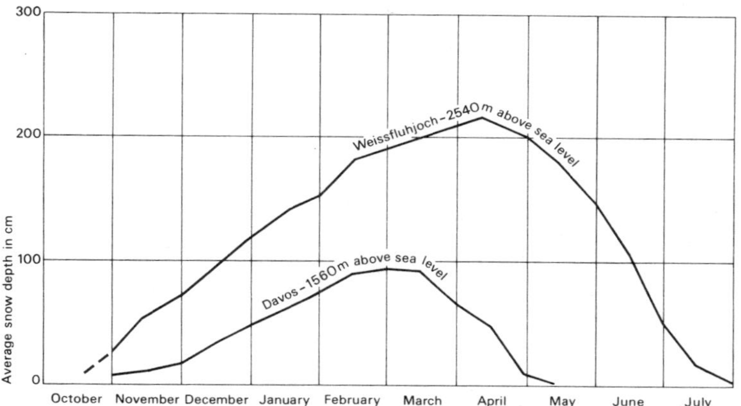

kilometres, and can cause considerable change in the snow cover through transportation from one area to another. Different types of terrain greatly affect the degree of erosion and deposition of drift snow; where the wind speed near the ground increases, as on the weather side of slopes and peaks, the snow is carried away to be dropped in places where the speed falls in the lee of crests and ridges or in clefts. This dispersal by the wind counteracts the great deposition on the weather side and can produce the opposite effect among the summits and crests, making for bare, windswept slopes on the upwind sides and deep drifts in the protected hollows.

On mountain crests, moreover, cornices are formed which often curl over and extend for metres to leeward like a breaking wave. It has been suggested that the shape of snowdrifts may be partly due to electrostatic forces set up by friction between the driving snowflakes. In any case individual projecting obstacles, houses, trees and hedges, quickly become enveloped in an aerodynamically shaped snowdrift.

The spectacle of low drift in the sunshine is by no means frightening to the suitably clad traveller; but when the increasing wind raises the drift above his head things become serious and the battle with the blizzard begins. To the squalls and gusts of the wind, which can throw a skier off his balance and make it difficult to walk straight, is added the chafing and cooling impact of ice crystals on unprotected parts of the body. Within a few minutes frostbite can set in. A curious effect of a blizzard is that people lose their sense of direction and are affected by feelings of giddiness. The power of thought becomes restricted; visions and hallucinations gain ground and produce irresponsible reactions; sometimes a skier can suddenly have the feeling that he is going uphill backwards, and so on.

* Ablation: all processes by which snow, ice or water in any form are lost from a glacier or snow cover.

Dramatic scenes are by no means restricted to high alpine regions and polar expeditions. One evening one of my neighbours, returning with his family in a jeep to his home on the outskirts of Davos, drove into a sudden blizzard. He could no longer recognize the road, the car became embedded in a snowdrift and he got out to see where he was, leaving the headlights on. His warm house, one of a group in a small housing development, could not be very far away. Yet after a few steps he was alone in the storm. After floundering about for a quarter of an hour in deep snow he stumbled accidentally upon my house, completely exhausted, with his fingers frozen and his face plastered with snow. The jeep was actually very close to his own house. That is only a small episode such as occurs somewhere or other in large numbers every winter, and sometimes such an encounter with a blizzard can lead to catastrophe.

Even after a blizzard, snowdrifts prevent people from getting about. The development of traffic technology has not made the problem any easier. The clearance of even normal snow deposits on streets, stations and airports delays the smooth running of traffic and swallows up large sums of money. Drifting snow is particularly frustrating for it continuously fills in again the clearings and cuttings made by snow ploughs. Cars, and even trains which run into snowdrifts can be completely trapped with no way out, forwards or backwards.

Snowdrifts can be dealt with in various ways. When roads are planned snowdrift zones can often be avoided by suitable routing. Cuttings at right-angles to the wind direction are avoided wherever possible, or else adapted to the wind conditions by following suitable angles of slope. Roads and railway lines built on embankments about two metres high are troubled less by snowdrifts. This principle was used successfully during the building of the Canadian Pacific Railway through the prairies in the 1880s.

If these fundamental preventive measures are not practicable, there is always the possibility of holding back drift from a road or railway line with snow fences placed at right-angles to the wind direction. These cause the snow to be deposited where it will do no harm and the places where it is not wanted are kept with a minimum snow covering.

Exhaustive experiments in many countries where this problem exists (Canada, Norway, USA, USSR and others) have established certain basic principles for the construction of fences and the best way of siting them. The surface of the fence must let the wind through – a ratio of about 60 per cent solid surface to 40 per cent gaps seems to be the most suitable. The distance of the screen from the screened area is also important. The minimum deposit of snow is often found at a distance from the fence of about eleven times its height (depending upon the wind velocity). As the usual height of the fence is about 1.8 to 2.7 metres, the optimum distance from the screened area is 20 to 30 metres (though this is naturally an approximation). Every problem must be solved individually in the light of local conditions. Where the roads to be protected run through cultivated land, snow fences will be removed in the spring. Thousands of kilometres of fences of different kinds are being used successfully, and a large number of them are erected and dismantled annually.

A natural form of protection against snowdrift, though it takes land permanently out of use, is the use of strips of woodland and hedges. Moreover they have the advantageous side-effects of improving the environment, providing maximum snow retention for water storage, and of enhancing the beauty of the landscape.

If we add up the time and energy expended in the struggle to keep lines of communication free from snow by the use of innumerable snow ploughs and snow sweepers, the erection of fences, and the many hundreds of millions of man-hours spent in clearing sidewalks each year we arrive at an astronomical sum. All this work has outwardly no lasting effect since the snow disappears on its own by the summer. This leads to the conclusion that people living in regions blessed with snow are the most deserving of pity;

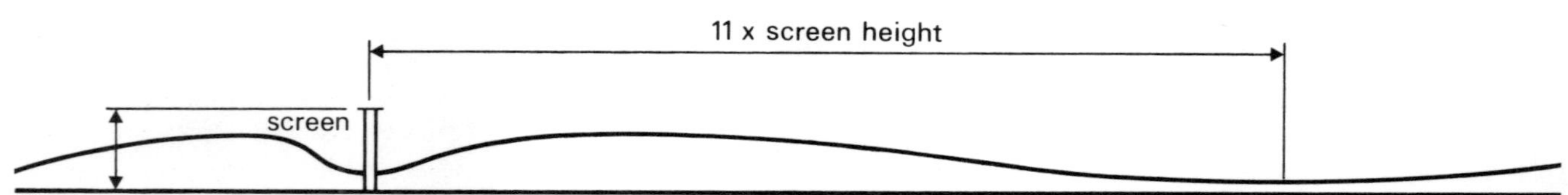

Fig. 4 When a snow screen is set up to protect a road or railway from drifting snow, it has been found that aerodynamics make the zone of minimum snow deposit about 11 times the screen height downwind from the screen.

but apparently this is not so, for everyone complains when the snow keeps them waiting too long, and all the more so when it does not come at all.

'Avalanche!'

In the steep-sided, thickly wooded and lowest part of the Engadine Valley on the Swiss-Austrian frontier lies the small hamlet of Vinadi, comprising a customs post, a restaurant and one house. At 11 o'clock in the morning of 18 February 1962 some frontier guards were standing in the forecourt of their post on the road leading to Austria. It was very cold and snowing lightly. Suddenly one of them shouted 'Avalanche!' Those outside ran for shelter in one of the buildings. The only exception was a holiday-maker who grabbed her camera and hurried to the balcony of the restaurant from where she witnessed an unparalleled drama.

In the woods high up on the northern horizon there was a movement among the spruce trees. Within a few seconds, with a splintering roar the whole forest plunged down towards the spectator, followed and overtaken by a great cloud of flying snow. The sky grew dark and when, after about a minute, silence fell once more, the whole previously wooded mountain slope lay bare while streams of tree-trunks, earth and roots flowed between the houses and right down into the River Inn. The buildings were considerably battered, but by a miracle still standing, and all the seventeen people in the village, including the daring witness, were unhurt. During the preceding three hours, further up the valley, two other avalanches just as big had fallen. A stretch of forest 2.7 kilometres long had been swept away and 25,000 cubic metres of felled timber lay on the banks of the Inn.

Another avalanche did not have such a happy ending. Vals, a farming village in the Swiss Canton of Grisons, lies on a small hill to the east of the stream, the Valser Rhein, which runs through the valley. The houses cluster round the church but the village has expanded more recently to the side of the valley. There were avalanches there 140 years ago, but since then, things have been quiet.

In the first half of January 1951 there were repeated snowfalls, and from the 15th snow fell daily with increasing intensity. On the evening of the 20th the leading men of the village met to consider the situation. The new snow was over one metre deep and avalanches had already smashed a few stables in the district. During the day the chairman of the village council had advised the evacuation of a number of houses on the outskirts but no one listened to him for they did not want to leave their warm houses in a blizzard.

At 10 o'clock that evening, while the elders were still deliberating, a sound of muffled thunder came from the western side of the valley followed by a sharp whistle and cracking, and simultaneously all the lights went out. It was soon clear what had happened; part of the village had been overwhelmed by an avalanche 200 metres wide. Four houses and various outbuildings were totally destroyed and several more buildings damaged. The population, alerted by the ringing of the church bells, searched all night for the buried members of seven families. Eleven people were rescued alive from the ruins, some of them injured. One woman was dead when she was dug out. There was no trace of the other victims. Outside help could not be expected as the village was completely isolated; even the telephone line had been cut. Four days later nineteen avalanche victims, including fourteen children, were laid to rest in the cemetery of Vals.

It is not possible to compile world-wide comparative avalanche statistics as, apart from their frequency, the nature and density of the population of mountainous regions have to be taken into consideration. For Switzerland the following list of disaster years, in which inhabited places were seriously affected, can be gleaned from old documents:

16th century	3 cases	over 178 victims
17th century	4 cases	over 164 victims
18th century	4 cases	over 285 victims
19th century	4 cases	over 157 victims
20th century up to 1975	5 cases	over 192 victims

However, we should not forget that compared with the disasters caused by glacier avalanches in Huascarán, Peru, which claimed over 4,000 victims on 10 January 1962, and almost in the same region over 25,000 victims on 31 May 1970, the Alpine avalanche disasters are insignificant. But these are outside our present scope.

Hardly any other line can have been hit so hard by avalanches as the Canadian Pacific Railway where it runs through the Rogers Pass in the snowy Selkirk Mountains. Even during the construction of this stretch from 1881 to 1886 there were avalanche victims among the labourers and engineers. On 5 March 1910, when the railway had already been in use for about 25 years, an avalanche suddenly buried the track immediately behind a trans-continental train approaching the Rogers Pass from the east. Immediately a snow-clearing team (snowsweeper, engine and rolling stock) with over sixty workers, mainly Italians and Japanese, was ordered to the spot to free the track from

Fig. 5 Avalanche destroying a village: engraving from Dürringer's 'Itinera Alpina', 1750.

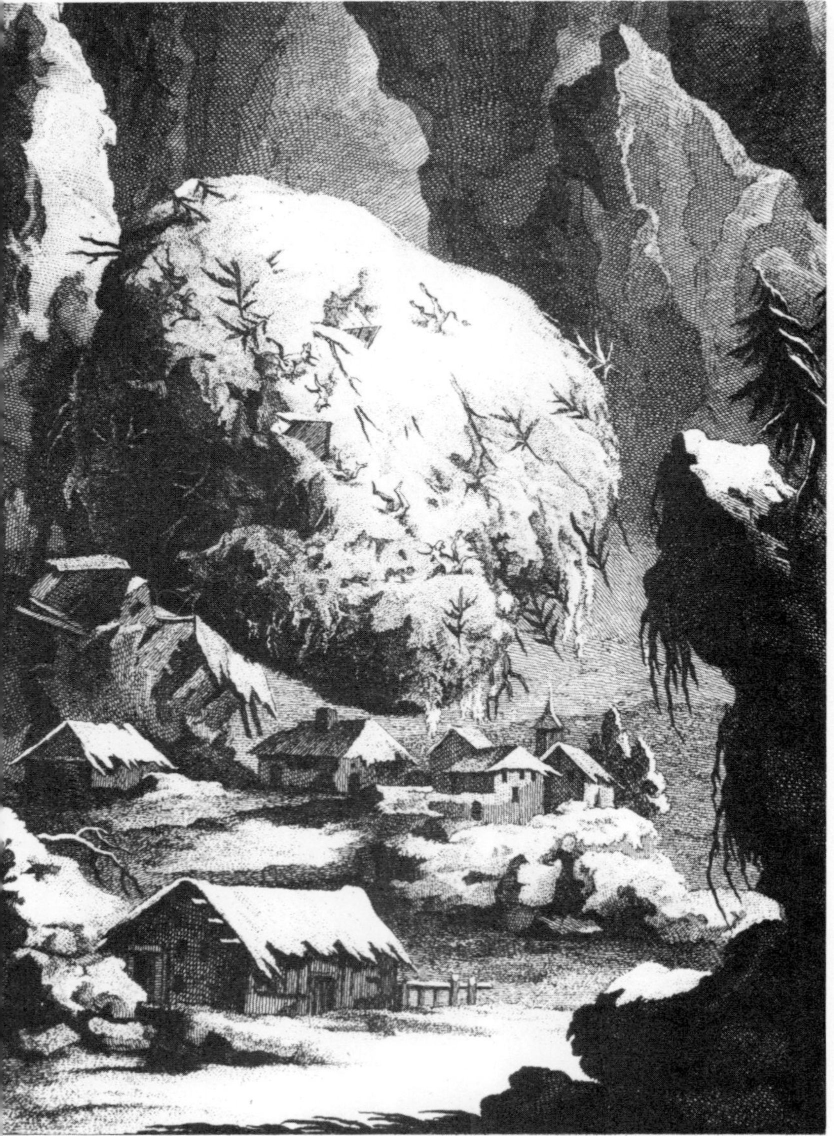

snow and debris. Late that evening just before the work was completed a second avalanche thundered down – at first a cloud of snow and behind it a flowing mass. The 100-ton snow-blower was lifted out of the cutting, turned over several times, and then smashed to pieces. The whole gang of workmen lost their lives in the mass of snow. Just one fireman was hurled through the air, landing safely in the snow beyond the path of the avalanche. Several years later the line through the pass was given up, to be replaced in 1916 by the 8-kilometre Connaught Tunnel; so at least the worst of the Company's avalanche problems was solved.

On a ridge above a steep incline falling away into a deep valley appears a group of skiers. They all stop and look at this snow slope sparkling in the April sun. Is it really in the superficially softened condition which is ideal for ski-ing? The one in front tries two short swings, waves to his friends, and at once the whole group is schussing elegantly downhill. They are all good skiers. Suddenly the group appears as if framed in the snow by a sharp outline. Above, the line quickly broadens into a crack and the snow cover breaks up into large lumps. A slab of snow is torn away and at first carries the skiers along with it like a big ship. The skiers struggle with their equilibrium and some try to escape by a daring burst of speed. But the avalanche overtakes them. One finds a way out towards the side, others fall and disappear. Apart from cries and a low, hissing roar, there is nothing at all to be heard. After about twenty seconds no further movement can be seen.

A few seconds of utter silence, then more cries – desperate cries. Figures rise up out of the snow in various places and tug at their skis. Here and there an arm is poked out and waves around. Those who are not buried scrabble frantically in the snow. Two who have been half buried are freed. Soon it is discovered that two friends are missing. Two members of the group still capable of ski-ing go to fetch help. The others stab with reversed sticks and the ends of skis into the snow where they think the missing people might be – but their efforts are unsuccessful.

An hour later an organized rescue team appears with an avalanche dog. Soon the missing are traced and dug out but, as was only to be expected, they are dead.

A small avalanche – one that did not have a long run and did not even raise the usual clouds of snow – has caught and partly buried a group of people who were seeking exercise and pleasure. This was no coincidence – the skiers themselves triggered the avalanche. In this instance man sought out the avalanche in its own environment, not the reverse.

These episodes illustrate four aspects of the snow avalanche and four orders of magnitude: the natural conflict between snow and forest; the disaster avalanche affecting inhabited areas; the 'surprise' avalanche blocking and threatening lines of communication; and the small, murderous slab avalanche involving skiers, which generally remains in its zone of origin. In the first three cases the run-out distance and the results of its force in the zone of propagation are highly important from a technical point of view. In the fourth case the mechanism of the rupture and triggering are basic features of interest.

How an avalanche is born

For an avalanche to develop it needs ground with an appropriate configuration and angle of slope, as well as a snow cover of low stability. Therefore there are only certain areas on a mountainside which are exposed to danger, and these only under certain snow conditions. Local and seasonal factors combine to give the avalanche its apparent unpredictability.

In considering terrain conditions we must distinguish between the zone of origin, the zone of propagation and the zone of deposition of an avalanche, bearing in mind that these cannot be rigidly demarcated. An avalanche starts in the zone of origin when the critical conditions for its generation exist. In the zone of propagation the movement of the snow accelerates or remains more or less constant, while in the zone of deposition it is slowed down until it comes to a standstill. So the danger extends over all three zones. In the zone of origin, and to a certain degree in the zone of propagation, avalanches may be released, whereas in the zone of deposition, except in abnormal cases, the danger lies only in their effects. The most important terrain characteristics are:

angle of slope: zone of origin, 25° to 50°.
zone of propagation, over approx. 21°.
zone of deposition, under approx. 20°.
orientation of the slope in relation to sun and wind
nature of the ground surface (including vegetation, rocks, pebbles, smooth ground, trees, scrub, grass).

In addition one has to consider the local topography – changes in the angle of slope, width of slopes, hollows, couloirs and ridges. All these characteristics of an area affect the distribution of snow, the likelihood of an avalanche occurring and its movement once it has started.

From the time that the fragile hexagonal crystals of snow fall on the surface they are liable to the effects of fluctuation in air temperature and radiation. There will also be differences of temperature within the different snow layers.

Fig. 6 Typical avalanche terrain: A, zone of origin; B, zone of propagation; C, zone of deposit.

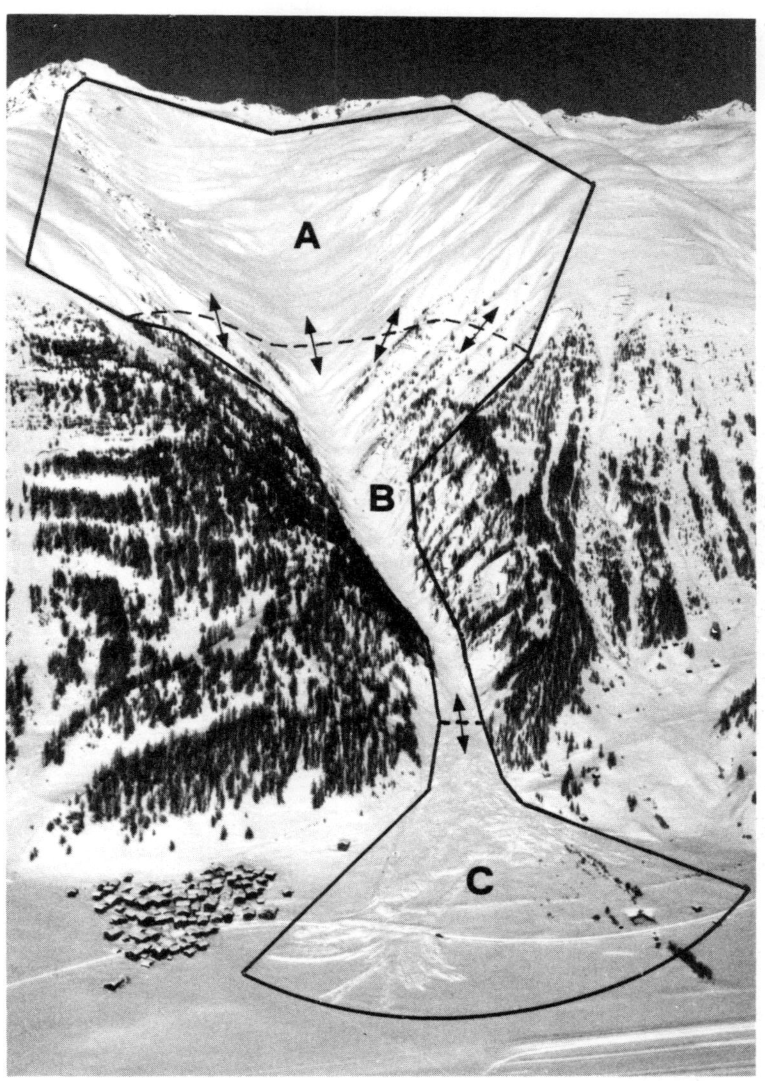

The original branched crystals gradually alter to form minute granules of ice. When warmer conditions prevail, this process is considerably accelerated, and where some of these crystals are colder than others they grow in size at the expense of the warmer ones by a process of vapour transfer. This often causes the formation of a stratum in which the rounded granules have grown to become larger faceted ice crystals, providing a fabric of which a high proportion is air space. Because of similarities to the formation of hoar frost on trees, such horizons in the snow are known as 'depth hoar'. These mechanically weak depth hoar layers are

Fig. 7 Two mechanisms of avalanche formation. At the upper end, tensile stress overcomes tensile strength and a step-like break occurs. At the lower end, a weak layer of hoar between new snow and compacted old snow shears, and the top layer slides. Either form of rupture can then initiate the other, and it is diffcult to establish which was the primary break.

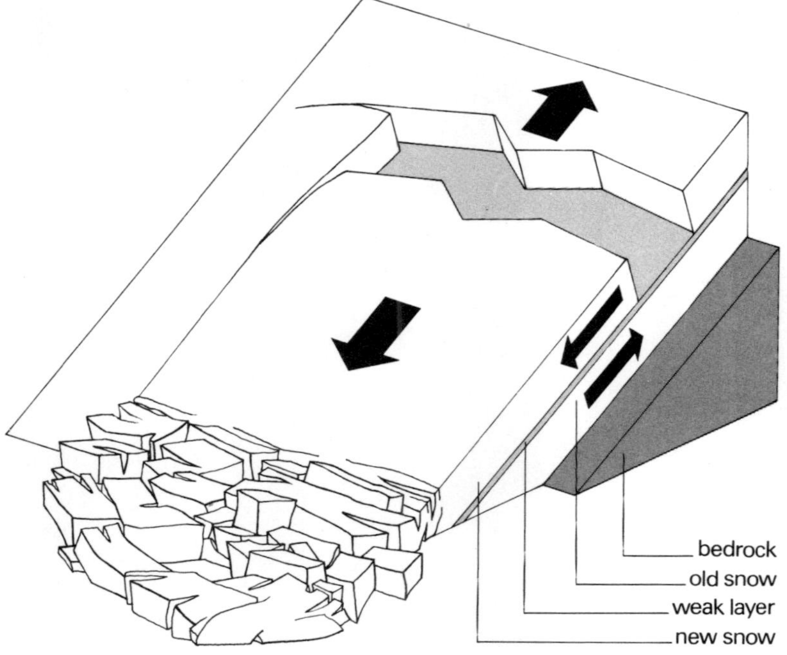

gradually buried by subsequent snowfalls, and may either collapse under the increasing load or remain as planes of weakness, capable of initiating an avalanche.

Such variations in the snow strata are particularly developed in the Alps, whereas colder areas like the Rocky Mountains or warmer ones such as central Japan are less liable to these differences in texture. From the point of view of its mechanics snow is one of the most difficult substances to understand, but its density and strength are fundamental in the generation of avalanches. Density of seasonal snow varies between 30 and 600 kilograms per cubic metre, and tensile strength from almost zero to 10 tonnes per square metre. Frequently, hardness is measured instead of strength, and this can be done with a simple instrument called a ramsonde.

One kind of avalanche often observed after a new snowfall starts from a point and is known as a loose-snow avalanche. It requires a steep slope, generally at an angle of 40° or more and, as the name suggests, a loose surface layer of snow. A small impetus – even as little as one single dislodged crystal – is sufficient to set other particles of snow in movement. The movement spreads and increases so long as the slope is steep enough to overcome the friction.

Loose-snow avalanches are either dry or wet. Because they seldom develop to a great width, and owing to their shallow depth and slow movement in the zone of origin, loose-snow avalanches are on the whole harmless, although sometimes large quantities of snow do become involved and descend over long distances.

Those lethal avalanches which crush villages, block roads and bury tourists are mostly slab avalanches, so called from the nature of their origin. A whole sheet of snow breaks away in a coherent piece, leaving behind it a sharp step-like fracture running more or less at right-angles to the slope. The snow plate or slab immediately breaks up into blocks of all sizes and by the time it has travelled about 50 metres may move at the speed of a skier in a fast schuss, so that if you are in the line of fall only luck will save you.

The mechanism of formation, highly complex in its details, can be described in a simplified form as follows. Inside the sloping snow cover is a layer parallel to the slope which is of particularly low resistance. The snow above it presses upon this weak layer and taxes it almost to the limits of its strength. Then when more weight is added, for example by a snowfall, the shear strength in the critical layer can be exceeded at some point by the shear stress and a rupture occurs which spreads rapidly in all directions. The snow-plate, so to speak, has the ground cut from under its feet and tries to set itself in motion. This results in tensile stresses parallel to the slope at the top of the slope where tensile stress is already in action. The break is completed along the sides and the slab avalanche is free to gather speed under gravity. In certain circumstances a rupture can extend to a width of several hundred metres, sometimes releasing a chain of avalanches far from the original break.

A rather different mechanism operates when the tensile break occurs at the upper end of the snow slab first. This is followed by a crack parallel to the slope in the underlying weak layer which extends downwards and, together with the tensile break, outwards. In practice it is hardly possible to decide which of the two mechanisms was in play in any particular case. At the same time the distinction is useful, for the first mechanism involving primary shear rupture shows that it is possible for a slab avalanche to be released by stress in the middle or even the lower part of a slope. In such a case the outwardly visible secondary tensile break might in some circumstances occur much higher up.

In describing snow slab rupture only two possible cases have been mentioned, but the basic theme has many variations. In place of the weak layer inside the snow cover the new snow itself can break away under its own weight. Alternatively the additional weight of a man applied to one place or a vibration (wind pressure, earth tremor or explosion) can quickly produce the critical tension. Again the fracture can equally well be caused by a decrease in the strength of the snow as a result of partial melting. So there are many possible explanations for a snow-slab avalanche and correspondingly many mathematical models.

In the first stage of the movement a snow-slab avalanche slides as a compact slab, but it soon crumbles into smaller slabs and lumps. At the same time the movement becomes increasingly turbulent and the rate of flow varies according to the locality. So long as the snow mass remains close to the ground one speaks of a 'flow avalanche'. If a torrent of dry snow reaches a surface speed of about 5 metres a second the snow is thrown up into the air. Then an ever-increasing cloud of powdered snow builds up and begins to run ahead of the flowing mass on the ground as a 'powder avalanche'. Unhindered by friction with the ground it reaches a hurricane-like speed. If the avalanche cascades over a steep declivity the groundborne flow becomes airborne, joins up with the dust cloud, and we get a pure powder avalanche.

If the speed and density of an avalanche are known, its pressure effect on an obstacle can be calculated. Unfortunately the density of the flow is not usually known, but with flow avalanches we can assume it to be approximately the same as that of the unbroken snow cover (200 to 400 kilograms a cubic metre); and with powder avalanches it will be in the area of 15 to 1.5 kg/m^3, decreasing from ground level to the upper limit of the avalanche. This gives us some idea of the pressures exerted by an avalanche on a large wall standing perpendicularly to its path.

Type of avalanche	*Density* kg/m^3	*Speed** *m/s*	*Pressure** t/m^2
Wet-flow	400	15	9
Dry-flow	200	30	18
Powder	3	70	1.5

* not maximum values

It is not the powder avalanche which is the most destructive, as is commonly supposed. Dry flow avalanches are much more violent, but even so powder avalanches can uproot standing timber and toss lightweight houses into the air. After all, neither trees nor most houses can be expected to withstand lateral forces of one tonne per square metre or more, and it has to be remembered that channelled avalanches are particularly powerful.

Two Soviet scientists, Otten and Goff, first measured avalanche forces in 1938. The measured values reach somewhere about 60 t/m^2 and are definitely no smaller than the calculated ones. In most cases of avalanches that take the lives of skiers or tourists it is not the mechanical damage which is important, but the burying action of the snow which causes the victims to sink down and usually suffocate to death.

Avalanches can break free spontaneously when the conditions develop steadily towards final instability; for example because of continual snowfall or a protracted warm spell. However, before this takes place the avalanche can be started through an outside impetus, and the nearer the snow is to a spontaneous break the smaller is the disturbance necessary. In legendary avalanche stories the chime of a bell, the crack of a whip, or the beating of a bird's wing are put forward as possible causes, but it would be foolish to take such weak influences into consideration since the continual variation of the wind provides a more intensive disturbance. On the other hand, a definitive triggering is caused when one or more people step on to a slope of low stability. The effect is unmistakable and probably most tourist victims have triggered their own avalanche. Still stronger is the effect of an explosion, which might include the bang of a supersonic aircraft.

The question whether a harmful avalanche began spontaneously or whether it was started by human action, and if so whether it would have happened anyway later on, even without this influence, has kept many lawyers busy. In many cases the question has had to remain open.

Is there any protection?

In the long history of human settlement in mountain country many different ways have been devised of averting the danger of avalanches, and yet there are deaths year after year right up to the present day. This is partly because the avalanche problem has changed with the opening up of mountain regions, partly because large avalanches reaching inhabited areas are rare. Indeed decades, if not centuries, can pass before a really heavy fall is repeated. Since unpleasant experiences are readily forgotten, the memory of a past catastrophe fades and the scene is set for an unexpected and unhappy repetition.

Avalanches are a danger to both tourists and those who live on the mountains, but the problems they face are different. The tourist enters the snowy landscape, where potential avalanches lurk, as an active partner and an avalanche factor. Much depends on his experience and behaviour. On the one hand there are those who unsuspectingly expose themselves to danger unburdened by any knowledge about how avalanches are started, or by any practical experience. On the other hand it is the 'experienced mountaineer' who, knowing the risks, becomes bolder and bolder until one day he gets caught.

The most elementary protection against danger of any

kind is a warning. The older generation warns the younger and the experienced warn the inexperienced, and there have always been such personal local warnings of avalanche dangers. But an organized warning system over a larger area has only become possible since the development of modern communications techniques and the beginning of systematic avalanche observation. In Switzerland such a warning system has been in operation since the end of the Second World War. Its object is to tell those who are actively or passively interested about the developing danger of avalanches by means of periodical announcements over the radio and television, through the press or by telephone. Among these interested people can be counted the inhabitants of mountain areas, those responsible for road and rail traffic, tourism and winter sports, and the rescue services, besides those living in the lowlands who are planning excursions into the mountains. The *Avalanche Bulletins* sent out at least once a week by the Snow and Avalanche Research Institute at Weissfluhjoch near Davos are based on daily observations collected from a network of about fifty stations covering every region of the Swiss Alps. Each morning about one thousand data on snow, weather and avalanches arrive at the Institute, and there is also a twice-monthly snow profile survey. On the basis of this material, and in the light of theoretical and practical experience, the avalanche situation for the various regions is summarized in a few sentences and broadcast in some such terms as this:

> A stormy north-west wind has brought an increase of snow of 50 to 100 cm in the past two days to the northern slopes of the Alps, the northern Valais Alps, the Gotthard region and northern Grisons. In these districts there is considerable and widespread danger of avalanches on the slopes which are sheltered from the wind. From catchment areas with large accumulated drifts, extensive avalanches reaching the valley floor are likely. Adequate safety measures in regard to threatened traffic routes and buildings are recommended, especially as there may be further snowfalls accompanied by storms. In the southern Valais Alps, in the Ticino Alps as well as in central and southern Grisons, there is a continued local snow slab danger above 2,200 metres, especially on slopes with northern and eastern exposure.

Obviously an avalanche bulletin only summarizes the general tendency. It cannot, and is not intended to, give a prognosis for the fall of any particular avalanche. The public should supplement them with their own observations and evaluations of local conditions.

Some time before an avalanche breaks spontaneously the snow cover is in a state of more or less low stability. In the last phase before the spontaneous fall the slightest vibration, even a gust of wind, is enough to cause the break. But already some time, possibly many hours, beforehand it is possible to trigger avalanches by a more forcible intervention.

The experienced tourist tests a slope that he is not quite sure of when he arrives at the top, by jumping or stamping to see whether it will hold. But even if this does not set off an avalanche there is no guarantee that the journey can be continued in safety. A more reliable test would be to cause an explosion on the snow surface. This method is used to initiate an avalanche at a particular moment so as to remove a threat, or to find out whether it is safe to traverse a slope. For this purpose it is essential for the blast to strike at the weakest part of the slope.

Furthermore, it is important to ensure that no one is in the danger zone of the avalanche when the shot is fired, that no material damage is caused by the triggered avalanche, and that there is no danger from the blast itself (badly placed explosion, duds etc.). It must also be remembered that blasting can set in motion not only the intended avalanche but occasionally other unwelcome neighbouring avalanches, sometimes of unexpected dimensions. For this reason blasting is usually not undertaken in the immediate vicinity of villages.

The explosion can be set off in various ways. The easiest and cheapest method is to take a charge (0.5 to 2 kg) with a pre-ignited fuse and throw it on to the snow from a safe position. A variation is for the charge to be dropped from a cable car or an aircraft (usually a helicopter). For repeated blasts in the same place cable-ways with charge carriers are used. A cable is installed in the summer, and along this the explosive is drawn by remote control over the place of blasting, lowered, and set off on the snow surface.

From the technical point of view the most suitable artificial means of starting an avalanche are military weapons such as mortars and bazookas. In most countries these can only be used by the military, which means that troops have to stand by the avalanche zones. In any case the use of military weapons in the service of a peaceful civilian task is not usually allowed. In Switzerland civilian agencies can borrow these weapons from the Army and buy the requisite munitions, provided there is expert approval and a trained operator. The method was first tested and practised as early as 1934 by E. Zimmermann, Director of the Bernina railway (between Pontresina, Switzerland, and Triano, Italy), who brought down a big unconfined avalanche by means of a mortar and so ensured the safety of the railway traffic. More than forty bazookas and mortars are at present being used successfully in this way. In America a civilian apparatus for the triggering of avalanches has been produced; this is the so-called 'avalauncher' – a projector operated by gas pressure.

The chance of an individual motorist driving along an avalanche-prone road, or even a lot of traffic on such a road triggering an avalanche and being caught by it is amazingly low. The same applies to a railway line. But roads and railway lines do become blocked by avalanches, vehicles are trapped and thus exposed to further danger. In one such case which happened in January 1970 on the road to Haraz in Iran thirty-eight people died, some of them frozen to death. Therefore, in avalanche country roads and railways need extensive winter protection, and the best permanent protection is the avalanche shed. The old Alpine roads, improved in the nineteenth century for horse-drawn vehicles, were even at that date being given the protection of sheds. Particularly famous was the Simplon road from Brig (Switzerland) to Domodossola (Italy), built by Napoleon Bonaparte in 1803. It was protected in various places by avalanche sheds, which have only recently been replaced. Modern examples of shed construction can be found on the Rogers Pass in Canada which, after the re-routing of the railway through a tunnel, was opened up again in 1962 as part of the Trans-Canada Highway.

Until about 1950, sheds were designed without taking the dynamic force of an avalanche into account, but now the vertical forces and those parallel to the slope which bear on the roofs are carefully calculated. These calculations also take into account the deflection forces which arise when the roof of the avalanche shed is not parallel to the general slope of the mountainside. The perpendicular load on a shed can be up to 10 tonnes a square metre, added to which are the frictional forces parallel to the roof of the shed, varying from one-third to one-half of the perpendicular load. This necessitates very heavy and expensive structures, and because of the high costs the sheds are built as short as possible – very often too short.

Sheds also have disadvantages quite apart from the cost. Those using them find that the view is blocked, which is a pity, especially in the summer, for if they are not completely closed in on the valley side drifting snow gets in and is difficult to clear. For all these reasons other kinds of protection for roads and railways are being used, including artificial avalanche triggering.

For hundreds of years a sensible choice of site was the only possible way of protecting villages from avalanches. The early mountain-dwellers are often thought to have had a sixth sense which enabled them to judge the safety of a site correctly. It is true that people who live among the mountains, being close to nature, are good observers, but their experience, as history shows, is also partly the cruel result of natural selection. Time and again single farmsteads or whole sections of villages were devastated, and even today buildings that have been standing for centuries occasionally fall victims to avalanches.

After centuries of reckless over-exploitation of the forests, which in the Alps extended well into the nineteenth century, people realized the protective value of timber. Certain forest zones were indeed put under a 'ban' in the Middle Ages and were not allowed to be touched; one of them still protects the centre of the village of Andermatt. No forest can give total protection, as shown by the disaster at Vinadi (p. 87) but timber, provided it is in good condition and thickly grown, still offers the best, most natural and cheapest protection.

The oldest man-made form of avalanche protection, suitable for single buildings, is a splitting-wedge erected above it. The church of Frauenkirch-Davos has an avalanche wedge dating from the seventeenth century. This saved the church as recently as 1968, but at the same time demonstrated the drawback of this method when the part of the avalanche that was diverted hit a house situated further down and buried one person inside it.

In order to protect a whole group of houses extensive guiding or deflecting structures are needed. The frontal braking of an avalanche by an embankment is only possible when the structure is high enough to ensure that the avalanche's kinetic energy will not be sufficient to carry it over the top. This is only possible in relatively flat areas, and even there the embankment has to be over 15 metres high.

The idea of preventing an avalanche from starting by means of structures in the zone of origin seems to have been tried as early as the fourteenth century, as can be seen in the traces of small terraces in the Valais. But the real technology of the present-day preventive structures only began to be developed towards the end of the nineteenth century. Evolved from the original terraces, walls were built, at first small ones in the belief that it was sufficient to increase the roughness of the ground. Later it was realized that the snow cover has to be supported right up to its surface if it is to be prevented from slipping. Today jointed structures based on calculations of snow mechanics are made of steel, light metal or pre-stressed concrete. Nets of steel cable or nylon bands are also suitable under certain conditions. Where only a temporary structure is needed until trees have grown again, impregnated wood is used.

Supporting structures are not intended to check fully developed avalanches for they would not be strong enough to withstand the forces involved. Nevertheless, they must be strong enough to withstand the pressure of the slowly creeping and sliding snow cover, and even this pressure can reach 2 tonnes a square metre. So it needs heavily built structures with deep foundations or rock anchors, mostly in steep and pathless areas, and this is very expensive. To make a comparison independent of monetary values, a structure the length of a car (about 4.5 metres), complete and erected, costs about half as much as the car. To cover a hectare would therefore cost the equivalent of 40 or 50 cars, and the area to be protected is often as much as 10 hectares. It is these high costs which limit the use of supporting structures.

The old method of simply avoiding avalanche areas when building houses cannot be given up, as it is impossible to hold back all destructive avalanches by means of supporting structures. In some countries it is accepted that the state should be responsible for the security of buildings. So as not to have to consider separately the avalanche threat in the case of every building project the danger zones are marked on a map and, according to the degree of the danger, new buildings may be banned or given special safety regulations.

Why should someone who wishes to build a home or a holiday house not have the responsibility for his own safety? Various reasons for public intervention are put forward. The builder of a house is often not competent to judge the danger objectively; the house can change hands and the unsuspecting buyer may be put at risk; tenants, visitors and public services will be imperilled, and an avalanche disaster does the reputation of a place no good.

Rescue routines

Let us consider the frequent cases where after the fall of a snow slab avalanche one or two members of a group of skiers stand at the edge of the avalanche area wanting to do something to help their companions who have disappeared without trace. What can they do, and what chance have those who are buried? First let us put ourselves in the place of one of these. So long as the avalanche is in motion he can still move his limbs, and occasionally he will succeed in working his way to the surface with swimming movements. Skis on the feet or ski sticks on the wrists can hinder these efforts or even make them completely ineffective. As soon as the avalanche comes to a standstill the snow settles more densely, often preventing any further body movement. So wherever possible one should make a hollow round the nose and mouth by cupping the hands in front of one's face before the avalanche stops.

Many different things can happen to someone buried by an avalanche, but in every case his life is in the greatest danger. Often at the moment he is buried he dies from shock, or snow fills the respiratory passages and in a short time the victim drowns. Packed snow cuts off the air, and even when the respiratory passages are free a man may lose consciousness, then die from suffocation. A few lucky ones may receive enough air through cracks or channels in the deposited snow to keep them alive for a longer period, only to be frozen to death by the creeping cold.

Fig. 8 Avalanche rescue: lithograph, 1830.

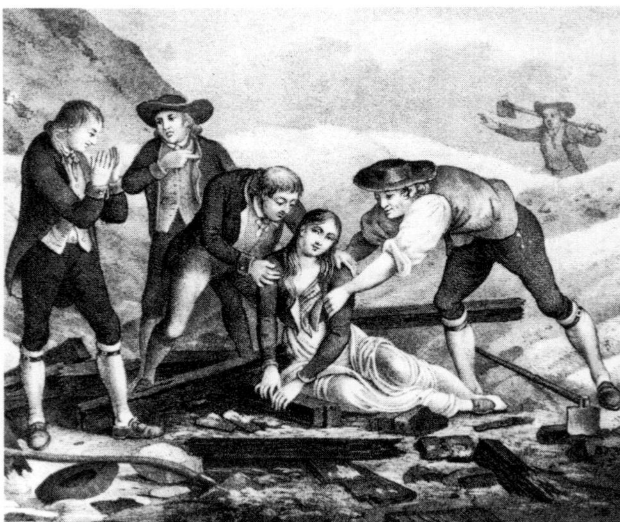

Experience shows that by the time an avalanche comes to a halt, about one in five of those buried is already dead. For the others the chance of survival rapidly diminishes and, after an hour, is perhaps only one in ten. It is therefore vital that anyone buried should be brought to the surface quickly, at most within an hour – an almost impossible undertaking if there are no clues as to their whereabouts.

First the survivors must search the avalanche area to see if arms or legs are visible, at the same time listening for faintly audible cries, and hastily probe the surface with skis or ski-sticks. If the search is unsuccessful the only remaining action is for the survivors to mark the position of the accident carefully and then, depending on the circumstances, send one or more for help.

The rescue party which arrives an hour or so later has the same problem of having to locate the bodies. Innumerable suggestions have been put forward as to how this can be made possible, some of them verging on science fiction. The methods discussed can be divided into two groups, those which presuppose that the buried person was carrying a specific marker, and those which apply when no such marker was carried. Unfortunately when there are no special markers, searching can begin only when a rescue party has arrived with suitable equipment, which usually means after the critical hour has passed.

In the latter case the search party must rely on special probes (supplemented if necessary by ski-sticks and skis) and on trained avalanche dogs. The former are a standard item in search equipment, and on principle every traveller over snow should carry one. Unfortunately probing is a desperately slow business, even a fast technique used by large numbers of widely spaced searchers; probing sticks usually find only dead bodies.

The avalanche dog has an astonishing ability to pick up the scent of a human through a considerable depth of snow, and is trained to indicate the spot. This takes years of training and an experienced partnership between dog and master. Often a dog is successful after only a few minutes on the scene, and many of those who have been buried by snow owe their lives to the dog that has rescued them from a white grave. However, there are limits even to the dog's achievements. If the bodies are more than two metres deep and the snow is too solidly packed, the dog may find the job impossible. Its performance also depends upon the weather, on atmospheric conditions, and on how tired it is. Other methods suggested, but so far not fully developed, include searching for metal such as ski edges with a modified mine detector, looking for the infra-red radiation given off by a human body, location by means of dielectric constants, and even radar.

The special markers which can be carried by the traveller are of two kinds, the avalanche cord and the pocket transceiver. Both have the fundamental advantage that the survivors can begin the search without delay. The avalanche cord, a strong red cord 15 to 25 metres long wound round the body, is uncoiled on entry into a danger zone and trails behind the man. The hope is that a piece of this rope will remain on the surface showing where the victim is buried. Unhappily experience has shown that this works in only 20 to 50 per cent of cases. Moreover, the cord, though light and cheap, is seldom worn and then only by people who are aware of the avalanche danger and are those who are most able to avoid it.

The battery-powered transmitter/receiver was first suggested when the miniature radio valve was developed in about 1940, and in those days the transmitter and the receiver were separate. With the development of the transistor the present-day compact style has become possible, and various models are on the market, such as the American Skilock and Skadi, the Austrian Pieps, the Swiss Barryvox and the Yugoslav Specht. Every member of a group which might be exposed to danger from avalanches carries a set, and the transmitter sends out intermittent short-wave signals continually. If someone is buried, the survivors switch to receive and listen to the victim's moment it should be possible to locate the buried person to within half a metre in a few minutes; either a change in signal volume or a direction-finder shows the way. These sets are especially suitable for organized groups away from crowded slopes – their only disadvantage is that they are expensive.

Other suggested forms of marker include a small portable magnet or ferrite stick and a resonance antenna ('bleeper'); both need the right location equipment brought to the spot, and neither can really compete with a trained dog.

The helicopter has greatly improved the chance of a successful rescue operation, though of course it depends on good flying weather and an efficient rescue organization.

To sum up, there is so far no system without markers which is as efficient as the dog's nose or the transceiver set, and which can be used by companions immediately after an accident. It is important to add that, even when the buried victim has been located, he has still to be dug out. Whatever happens he is not safe until a supply of air is ensured. A shovel, however small, should therefore be part of the equipment of every member of a search party.

Avalanche disasters in populated regions pose completely different rescue problems. Mechanical sounding with probes in snow mixed with debris is almost hopeless. Electronic methods are practically out of the question; only the dog has a chance, even though the site is pervaded with alien scents. The first aim must be to rescue survivors who are trapped in the ruins of their houses. Here only massive tools, bulldozers, and very many willing pairs of hands can help.

Wherever an avalanche may occur, whether among houses or out on the mountainside, the possibility of a further fall should be borne in mind until the rescue has been completed. All the unstable snow may not have fallen, or perhaps it has been snowing again and new masses are ready to crash down. During a rescue in the Ofen Pass, Switzerland, in 1951 six rescuers who had just succeeded in locating the one original victim were buried alive in two avalanches which followed the first. Still worse was the avalanche disaster of Blons, Austria, in 1954 in which a large number of injured who had been rescued, together with their rescuers, were killed by a further avalanche.

There can be no doubt that the available countermeasures have prevented many disasters. That there are still casualties in countries with highly developed avalanche protection is the result of greatly increased traffic in the mountains, and the influx of people who have forgotten all they ever knew about the forces of nature.

Suggestions for further reading

M. M. Atwater: *The Avalanche Hunters.* Macrae Smith, Philadelphia, 1968.

C. Fraser: *The Avalanche Enigma.* John Murray, London; Rand McNally, Chicago, 1966.

International Association of Hydrological Sciences: *International Symposium on Scientific Aspects of Snow and Ice Avalanches, Davos.* American Geophysical Union, Washington, D.C., 1965.

M. Mellor: *Avalanches.* Cold Regions Research and Engineering Laboratory, Hanover, N.H., 1968.

R. Perla: *The Slab Avalanche.* Alta Avalanche Center, Montana, 1971.

A. Scheidegger: *Physical Aspects of Natural Catastrophes.* Elsevier Science Publishing Co., Amsterdam, Oxford, New York, 1975.

G. Seligman: *Snow Structure and Ski Fields.* Macmillan, London and New York, 1936.

The pure, crystalline beauty of snow masks one of nature's most dangerous and dramatic forces. These climbers on the east ridge of the Doldenhorn, in the Swiss Alps, are probably experts, safe and sure-footed on snow. But even experience is not a certain guard against sudden disaster. In Switzerland alone, avalanches have claimed some two hundred lives in this century; snowstorms and blizzards, for which there are no casualty figures, are a perpetual risk in regions of heavy snowfall. Technology can do something to mitigate the danger – avalanche barriers and broadcast warning systems, snow sheds, screens and snow ploughs – but in the end it comes down to the fundamental contest, man against a force of nature.

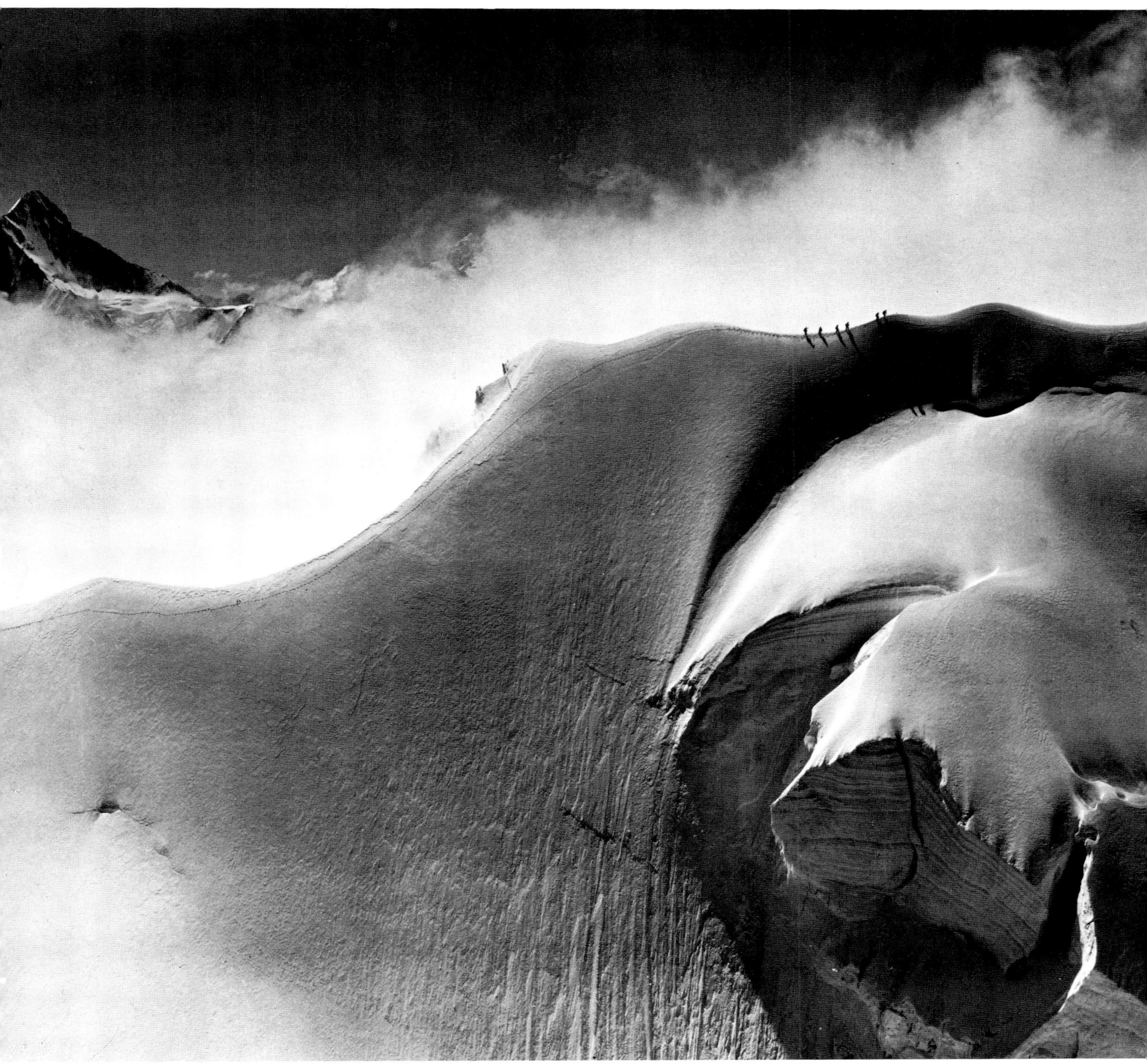

Snow on the move is capable of many strange effects, and some lethal ones. When wind speeds rise sufficiently, drifting snow may develop into a full-scale blizzard, blinding, smothering, depriving a traveller of all sense of direction. There is danger not only on an Arctic camp-site (2) but also in calmer and more civilized parts (3): the Swiss Volkswagen's 'beetle' shape is copied by the thick drift of snow that immobilized it. The ridges and furrows, 4 to 8 in. deep, called *sastrugi* (4) are carved out and eroded by wind-blown snow. A gentler movement is revealed in graceful folds and curves as a thick blanket of wet snow slides downhill under its own weight (5). This elegant wave conceals the enormous pressure and erosive power of the sliding snow.

2

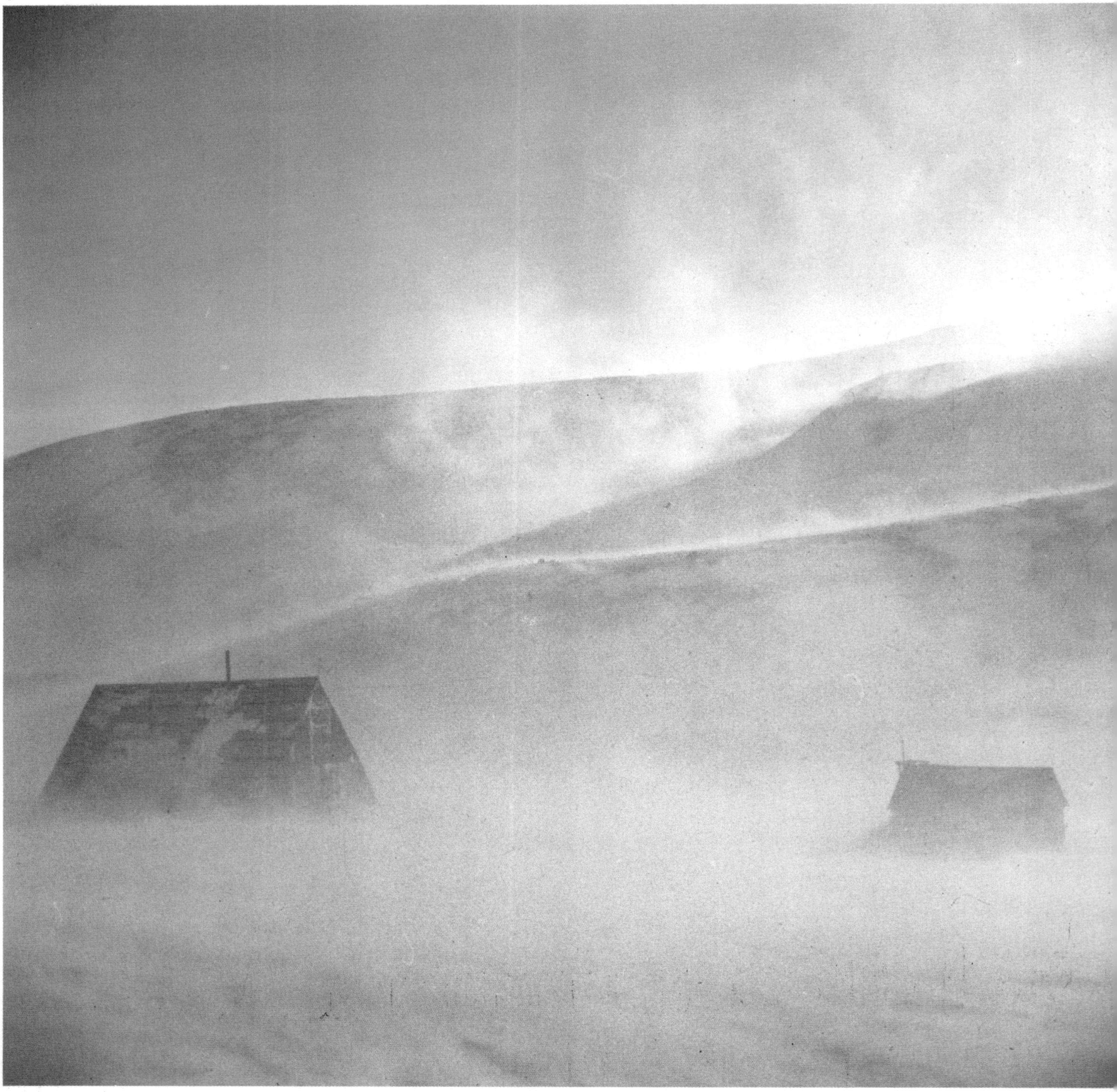

3

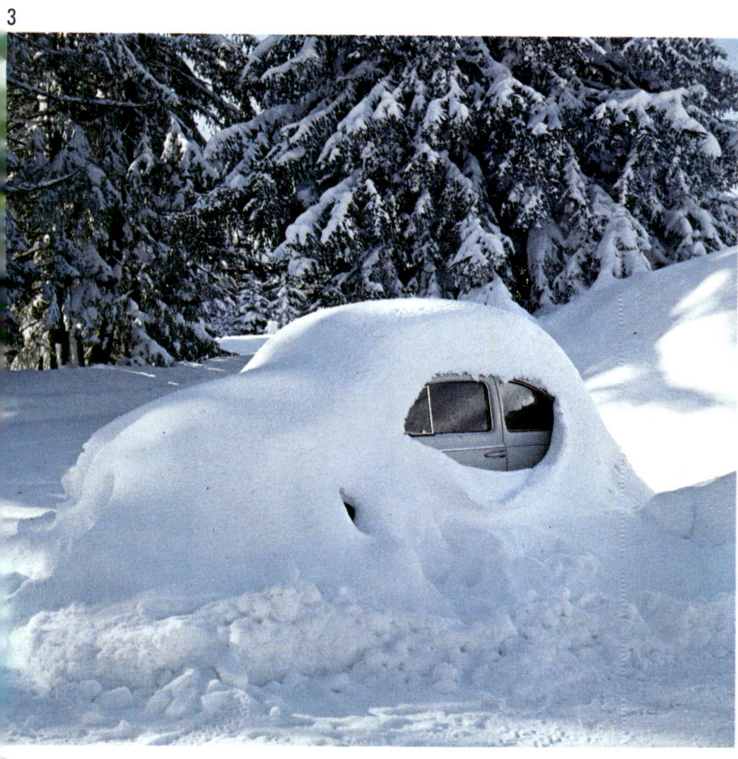

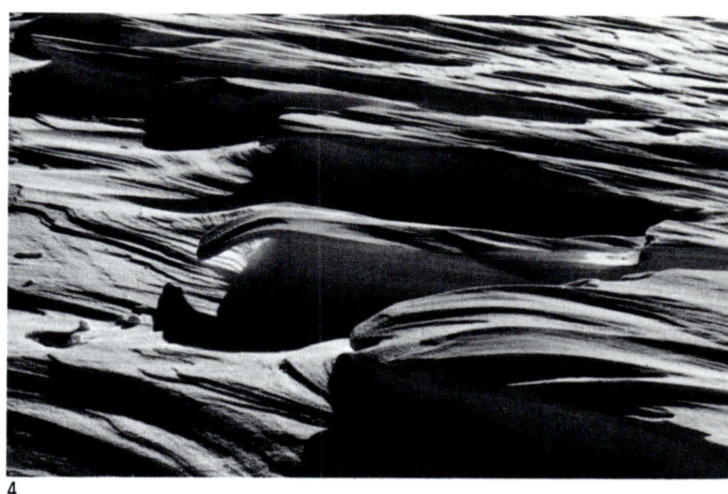

4

5

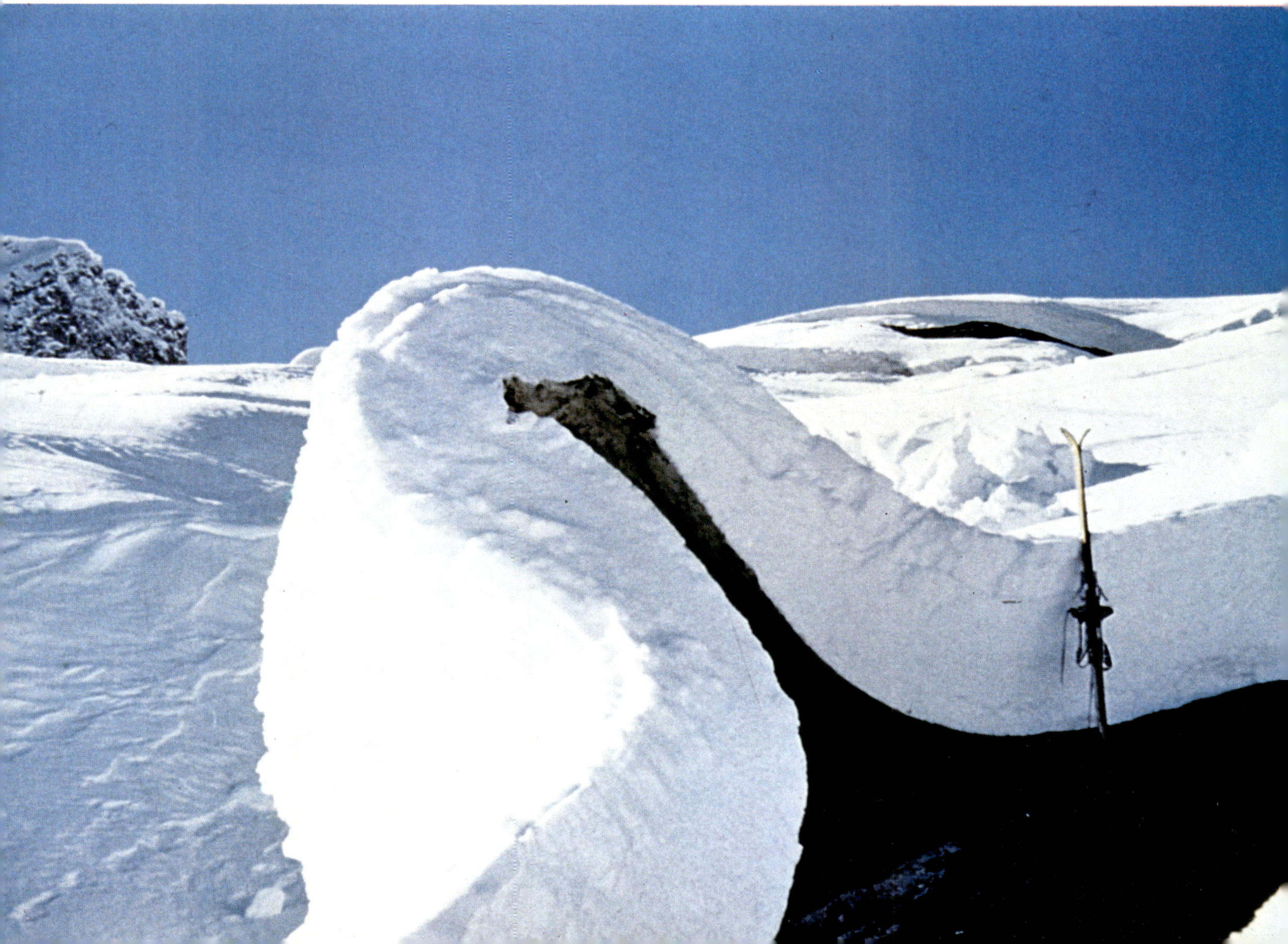

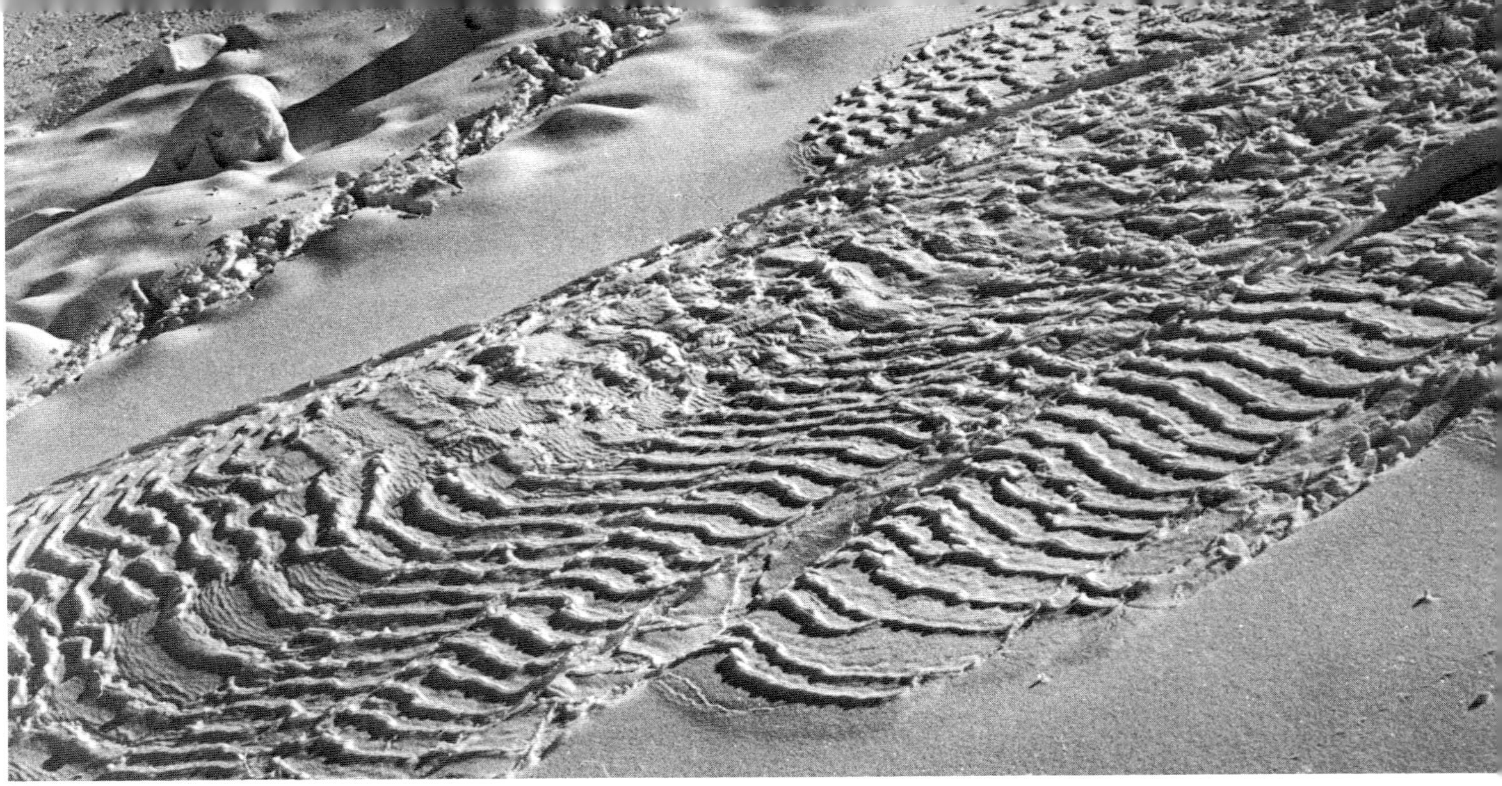

6/7

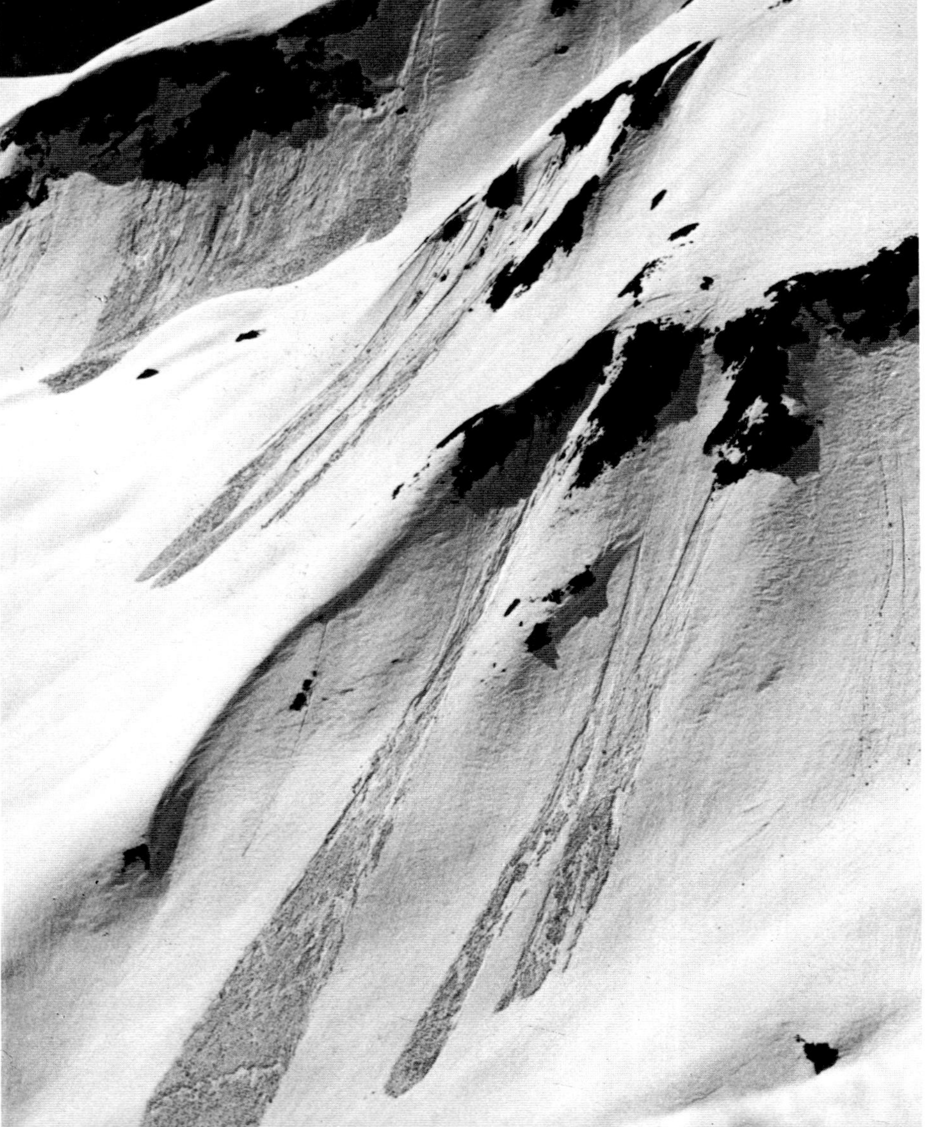

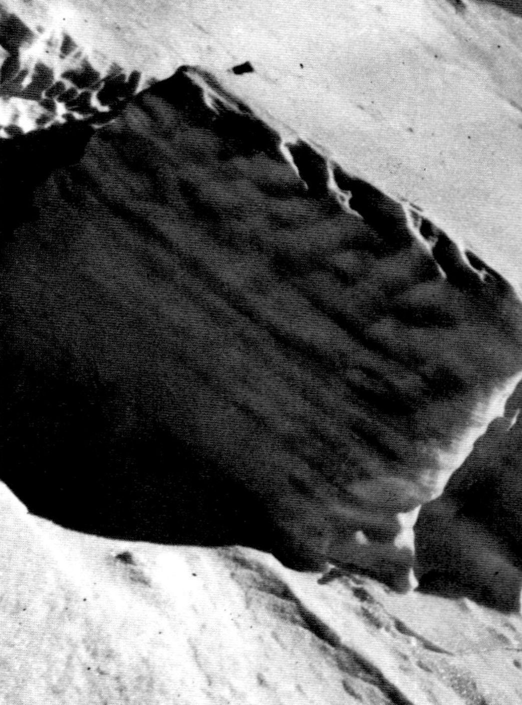

11

Some avalanches are killers, some are relatively harmless. Loose-snow avalanches are either wet (6) or dry (7); shallow and slow-moving, they are usually harmless. Three photographs of a powder avalanche near Adelboden, Switzerland (8, 9, 10), give a vivid impression of power and speed: though it is little but airborne powder snow, it can uproot trees and send houses flying. The most lethal type is the slab avalanche (12), which breaks away in a clean, step-like fracture (11) and slides downhill in a solid

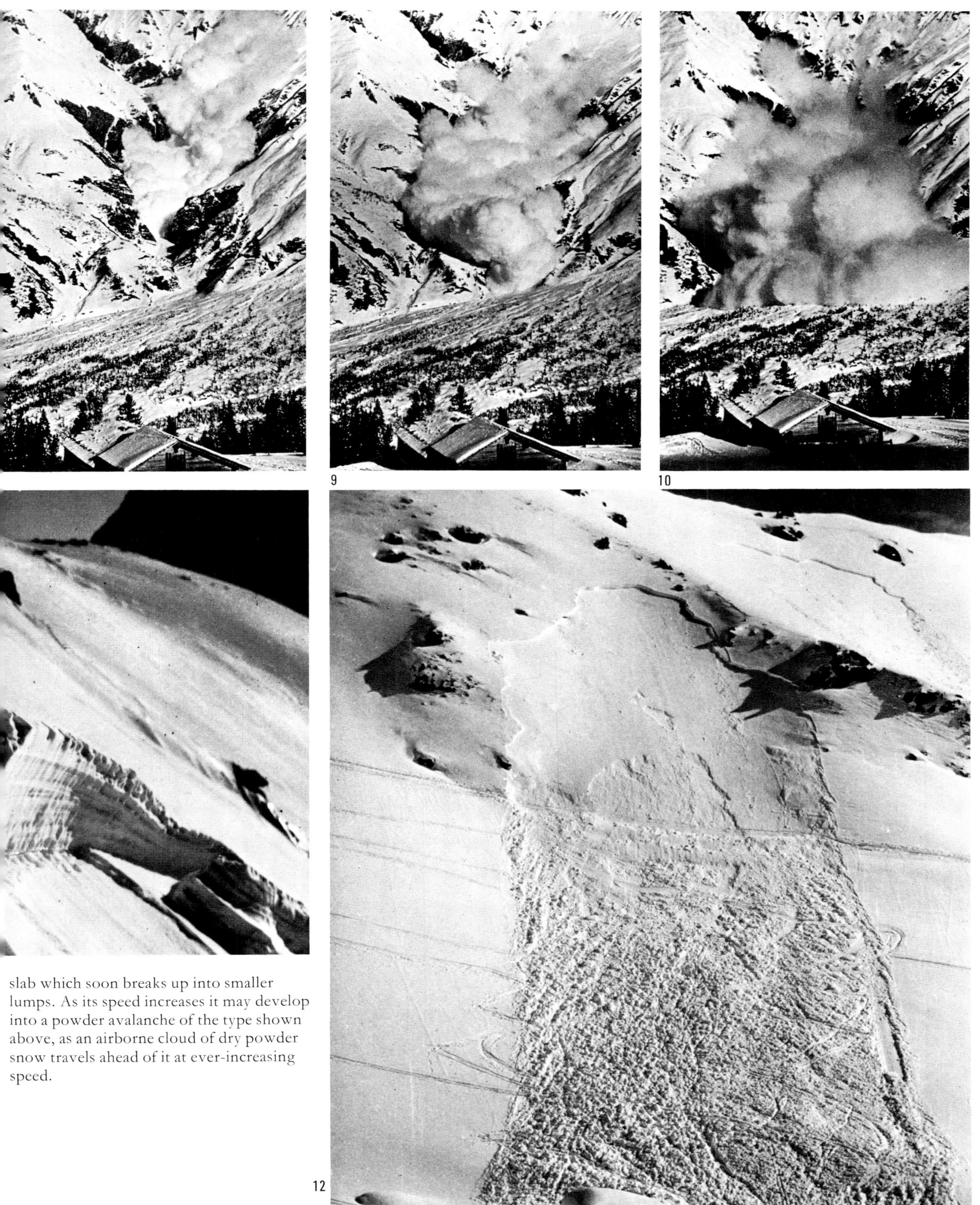

9

10

slab which soon breaks up into smaller lumps. As its speed increases it may develop into a powder avalanche of the type shown above, as an airborne cloud of dry powder snow travels ahead of it at ever-increasing speed.

12

Weapons of self-defence against avalanches have been tried for centuries. Snow sheds, built to withstand loads of over 10 tons a square yard, have been used since Napoleon's time to protect vulnerable sections of road or railway. A bus caught in a snow shed (13) escaped disaster, though exit was blocked at both ends. Above the church in Frauenkirch, Switzerland, is an avalanche-splitting wedge built in the seventeenth century (14). In many countries, mortars and bazookas are used, to trigger avalanches by firing explosive charges; the picture (15) shows an 81-mm mortar being fired by a Swiss civilian rescue service. Where roads are blocked by avalanches (16), powerful snow ploughs and snow blowers can cut a clear way through, but prevention is better than cure. In avalanche country, steel barriers in the zone of origin (17) pattern the mountain slopes to prevent the snow from breaking loose. Above the village of Andermatt, in the Swiss Alps, the effect of these barriers is reinforced with standing timber (18), none of which, by law, may be felled.

13

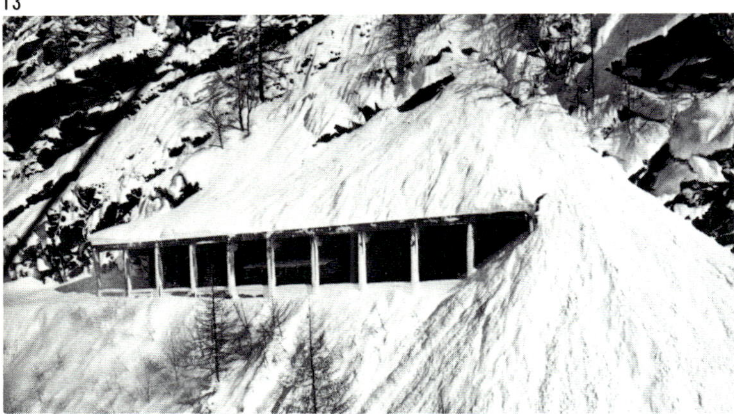

14

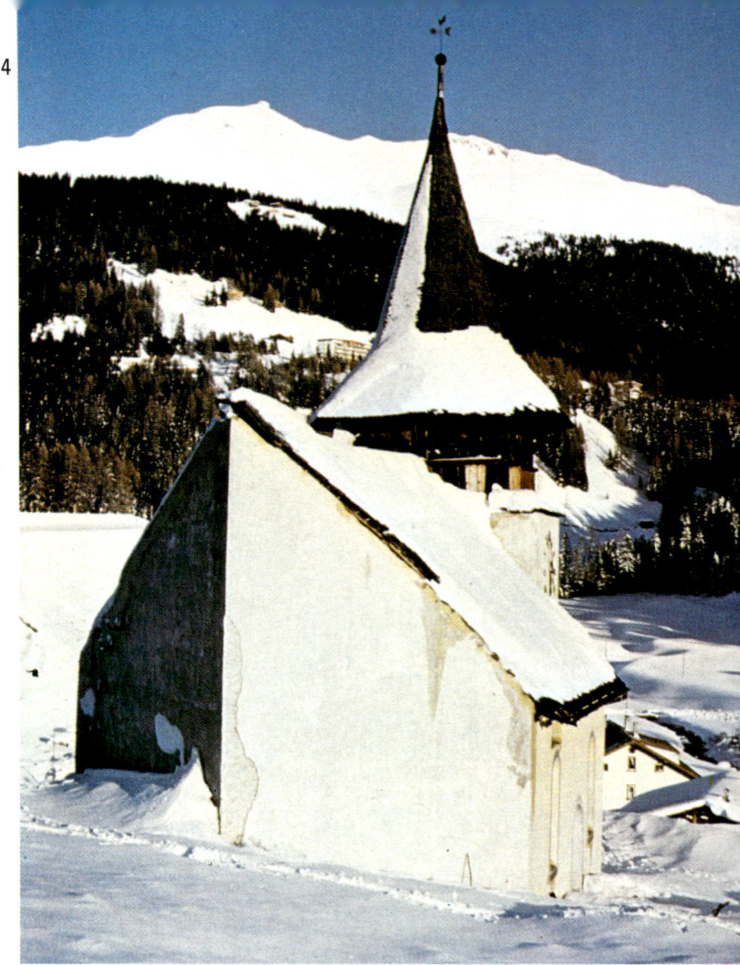

15

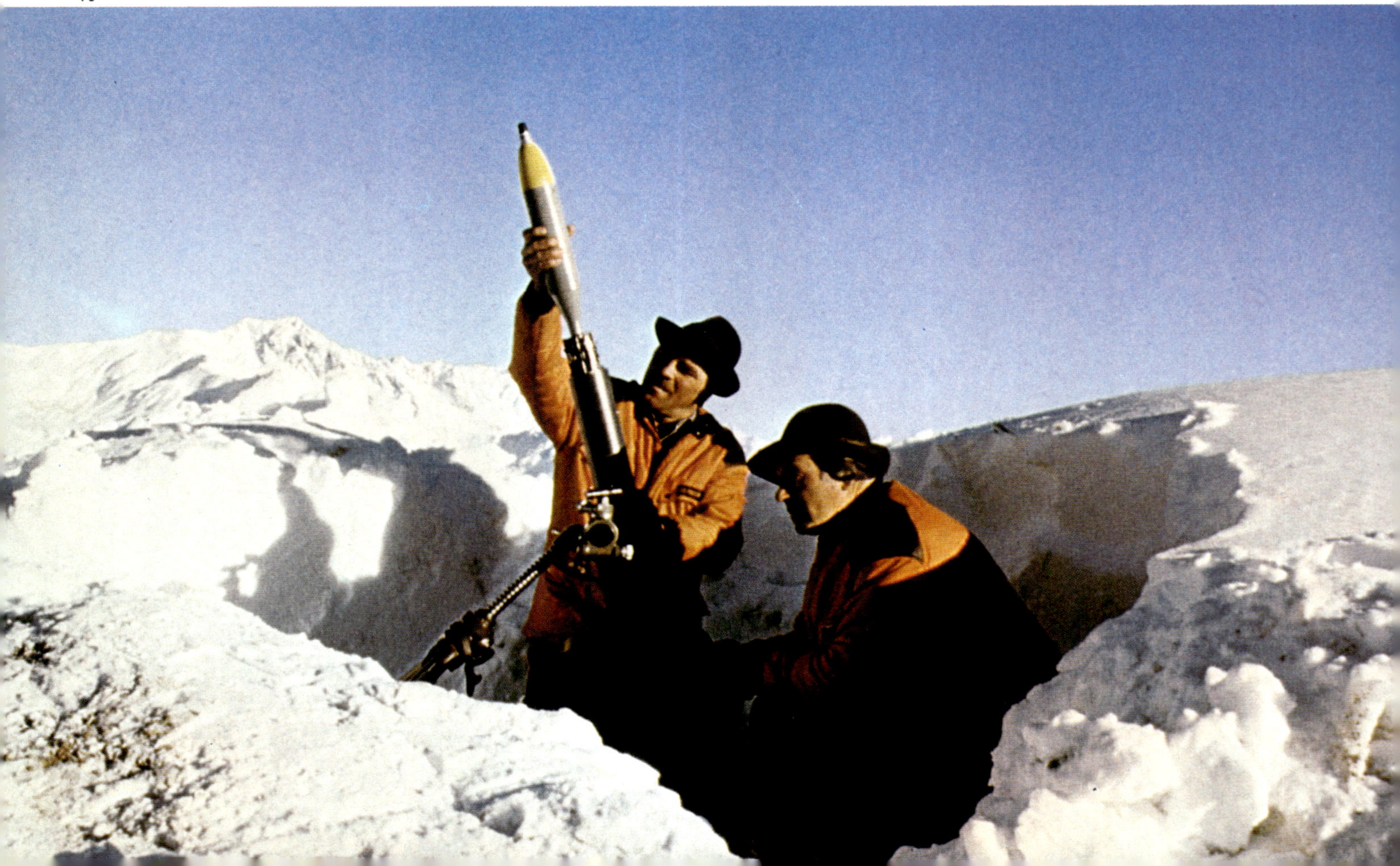

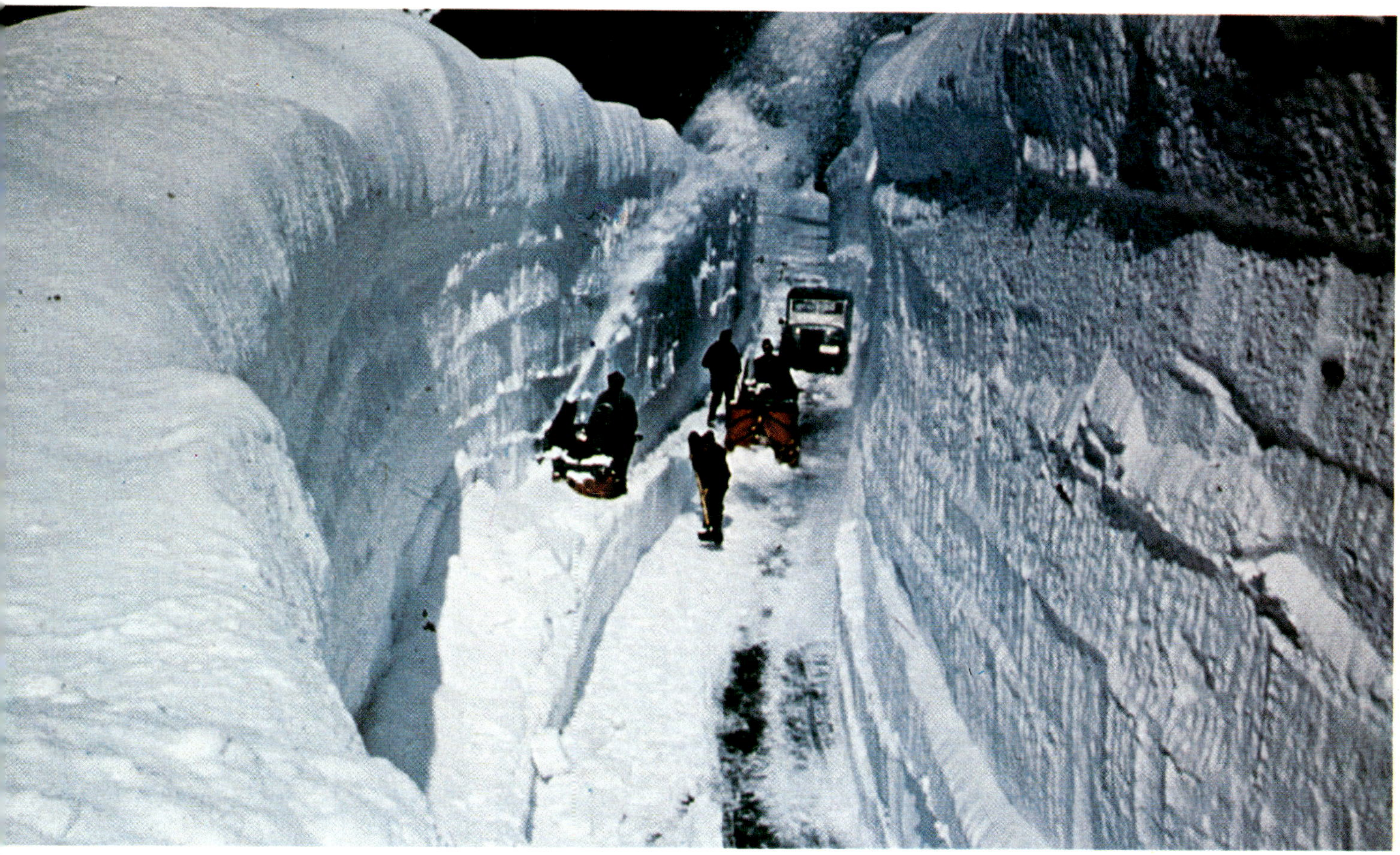

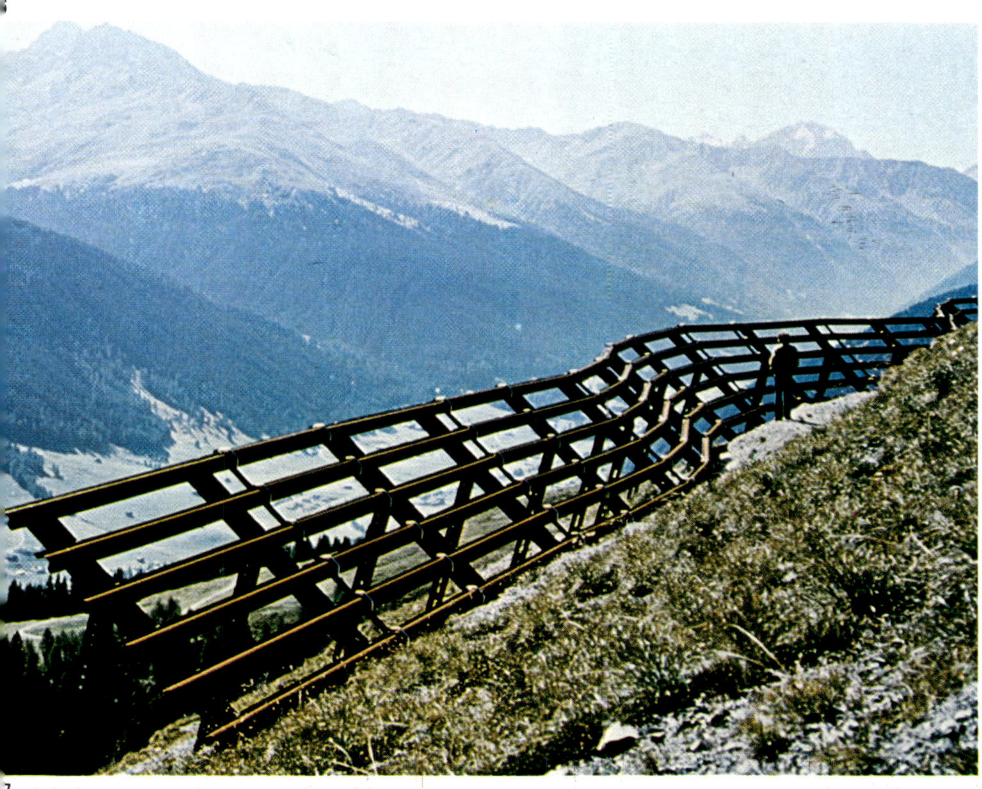

7

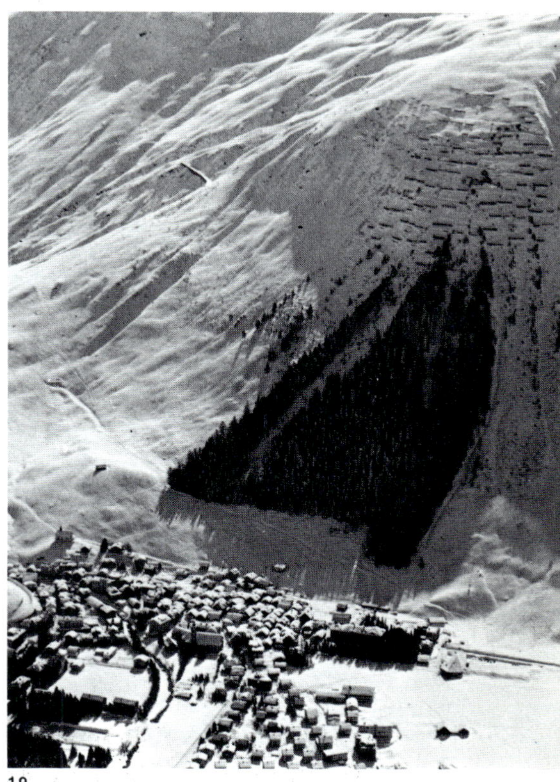

18

About one victim in five is dead by the time an avalanche comes to a halt. To recover survivors – and bodies in most cases – search and rescue routines have been worked out over many generations. Specially trained dogs (19) can pick up human scent through a considerable depth of snow, and 'point' to the spot where someone lies buried. Or a line of searchers (20) advance over the avalanche debris using long, thin probes in a systematic quartering of the snow. But this method is desperately slow, and usually too late. The chances are much better if victim and searcher are both equipped with the new electronic transceiver sets.

19

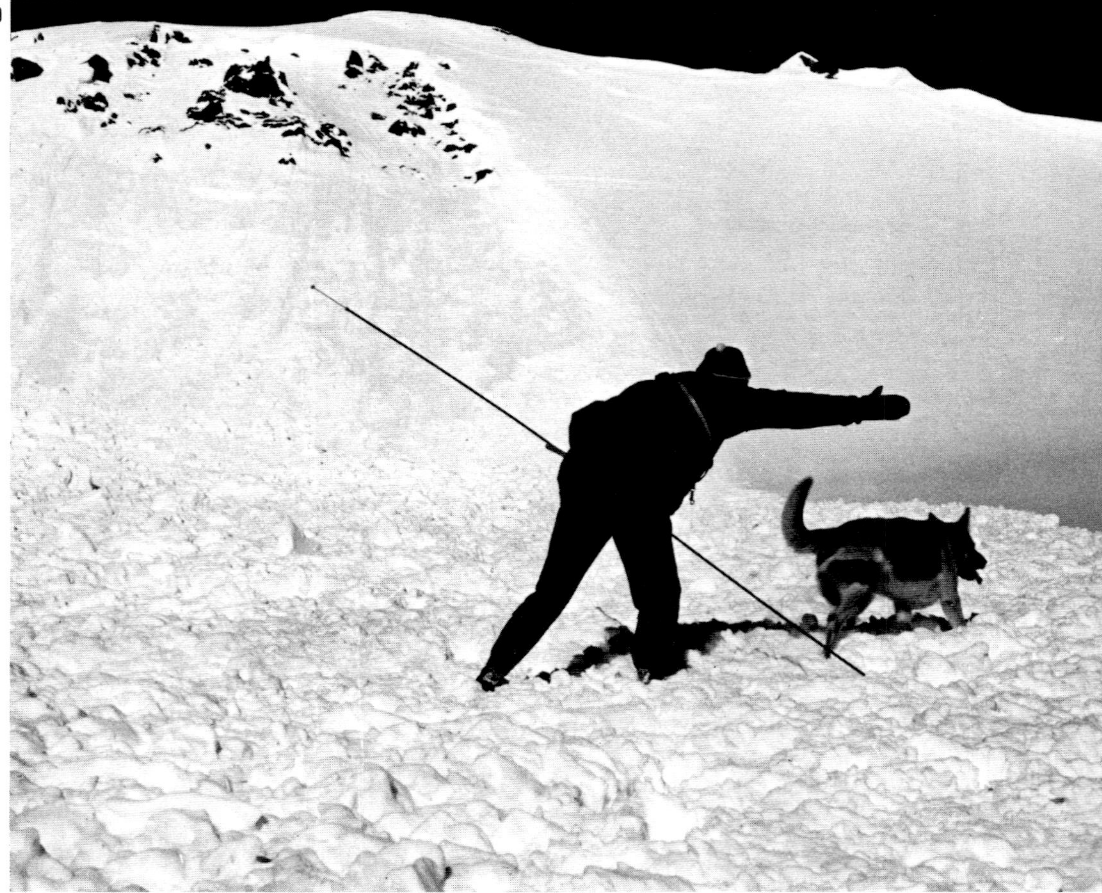

20

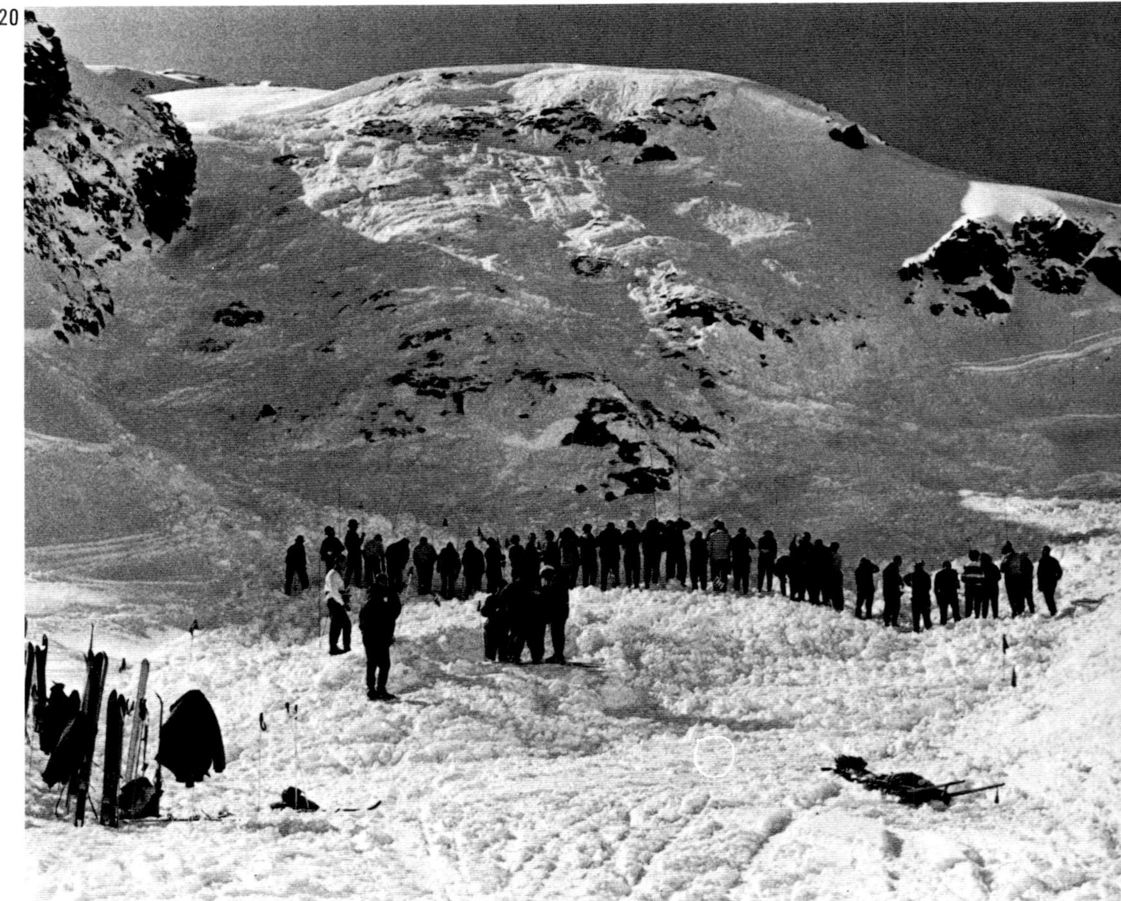

5

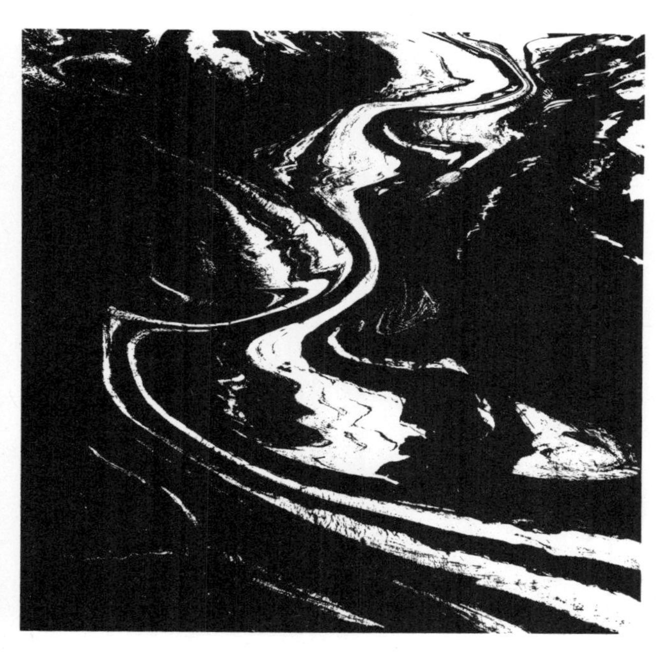

Glaciers and ice ages

Valter Schytt

Everyone who lives in cold or temperate regions knows that snow and ice affect their daily life from time to time; but few realize that these short-term episodes are no more than the fringe expressions of wider, long-term phenomena which, in these regions, control man's behaviour, indeed his very capability of existence.

The ice age which once encompassed northern parts of Europe, Canada and the Soviet Union has relaxed its grip on areas which it once made barren – today large parts of these regions are heavily populated. Yet Greenland and other Arctic lands are still within its influence, and the menace of its return waits only upon a change of climate.

Where and why?

Even though modern technology can affect man's environment – for better or for worse – to a considerable extent, its effects are still only marginal when compared with the weather and climate, and natural forces and phenomena that are conditioned by them. It is possible that our world-wide combustion of fossil fuel might increase the atmospheric carbon dioxide sufficiently to raise the mean temperature of the Earth by several degrees – but only as an extremely long-term effect. That certain summers are disastrously dry or very wet, that in some winters snow halts traffic in cities, where it is unwelcome, while winter sports areas report bare slopes – this is something we can do nothing about. For a very long time to come, we shall just have to accept the fact that climate and the weather are stronger than we are. For the same reason we have to accept that at some places the winter snowfall is greater than the summer thaw. Every year the snow cover becomes deeper and deeper, and the lowest levels re-crystallize into ice. When the ice has become thick enough it begins to flow downhill to warmer regions, and this mass of flowing ice is what we call a glacier.

Glaciers, therefore, are not simply a result of extremely cold winters or short, cold summers: the decisive factor is the balance between solid precipitation and melting. In cold regions, a winter snowfall of one metre is enough to keep a glacier going, whereas in a warmer area 8–10 m would be needed. Temperatures depend to a large extent on latitude and height above sea-level, precipitation on the distance from the sea and the prevailing wind. Thus the altitude below which glaciers cannot form (the glaciation level) is low in polar regions and high in the tropics, low in coastal areas and high in continental land masses. Down in the Antarctic, the glaciation level is at sea level. In Europe it rises from about 400 m in northern Spitsbergen to 900 m in the north of Norway; in the Alps it is 2,600 m in the west and as much as 3,200 m in the east (where it is drier and the increment of snow on the glaciers is therefore smaller). Similar conditions prevail in the south of Norway. On the west coast, where precipitation is high, glaciers can form at as little as 1,200 m above sea-level; 200 km farther east the climate is so dry that the glaciation level is 1,000 m higher. In this way, glaciation levels can be established for any mountainous area in the world.

Above the glaciation level, glaciers tend to form in the direction of the prevailing gales. Naturally, most of the precipitation falls on the windward side of a mountain, where moist air masses are driven upwards and their moisture content condenses; where glaciers are concerned, however, the important thing is not where the snow falls so much as where it lies. In gale conditions, great masses of snow are forced over mountain ridges by the wind and form drifts on the lee side. Of the 1,491 glaciers recorded in northern Scandinavia, about 80 per cent flow from snow basins on the eastern side of the mountains (between north and south-east), because the prevailing storm winds are westerly and south-westerly. This rule, that glaciers mostly form on the leeward side of mountains, is a general one, holding good for all climatic regions – if cold enough – and all epochs. Since glaciers carve out valleys on the slopes where they lie, it is actually possible to determine the direction of prevailing winds millions of years ago from the orientation of glacier valleys cut in remote geological epochs.

Where individual mountain peaks project above glaciation level, glaciers are few and small; in the case of a high mountain range or massif all the valleys can become filled with glaciers, so that the mountain tops stand out like islands in a sea of flowing ice. If the ice cover then increases the islands shrink as the ice grows thicker, until in the end the only sign of the original topography is some minor humps and hollows in an otherwise even layer of snow and ice. The original mountain glaciers have now evolved into an ice sheet. There are large areas of the Earth today which are completely covered by ice sheets, where the only activity open to man – supplied and supported from outside – is scientific research. About 15 million square kilometres – some ten per cent of the Earth's land surface – is ice-covered, and the total volume of ice is as much as 30–35 million cubic kilometres, a figure which most of us find difficult to grasp. But it is easier to understand, and more striking, if one says that this quantity comprises about 80 per cent of all the fresh water in the world. So there is no lack of fresh water; it is merely that it is in the wrong place and in the deep freeze.

Fig. 1 A glacier at the end of the summer melt, showing the accumulation area (where the snowfall is greater than the loss by melting) and the ablation area (where melting exceeds snowfall). The lower edge of the accumulation area is the equilibrium line, where loss and gain are in long-term balance.

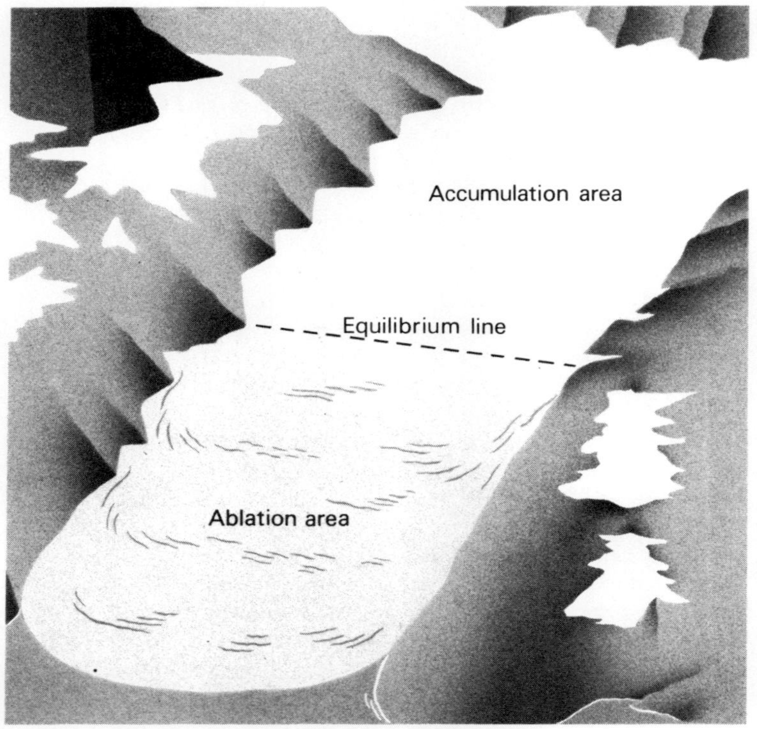

The glacier's economy

The whole existence of a glacier depends on the simple fact that in its birthplace snowfall is greater than thaw. If we take a normal valley glacier in a non-polar mountain area, a few metres of snow will accumulate during the winter in the lee of the high ridges – one or two metres in cold continental regions, ten metres or more in warmer coastal areas. During the summer, only part of this snow mass melts, and in the autumn and winter, new snow covers what is left. By now the old snow has become coarse-grained through thawing, freezing and re-crystallization, and this is called *firn*. (It must be admitted that not all glaciologists agree on this definition: for some, firn is synonymous with last year's snow, for others the deciding factor is grain size, for yet others a density of at least 0.55 g/cm^3 is the important thing. But for the purposes of the present discussion this is not crucial.)

Firn undergoes continuous re-crystallization, and during the first few years, before it is buried under too many new annual snowfalls, meltwater trickling down through it freezes into thicker and thicker layers of compact ice. A core taken from a mass like this would show the upper ten metres or so, of firn with included ice layers, gradually giving way to ice with layers of firn, which become thinner and thinner with increasing depth. The density increases very irregularly with the depth, finally reaching about 0.9 g/cm^3 – i.e. pure ice containing a few scattered air bubbles.

A mass of ice formed in this way is plastic and, when it has become thick enough, starts to flow down the valley to warmer levels until the melting rate is greater than the rate of supply. Thus a glacier has an accumulation area, where increase is greater than melting, and an ablation area, where melting predominates – in other words, a 'surplus area' and a 'deficit area'. If the glacier's shape does not change, the net surplus in the accumulation area must equal the net deficit in the ablation area. Furthermore, the same amount of ice has to be transferred from the one area to the other by ice flow. The line separating the accumulation area from the ablation area is called the 'equilibrium line' – the line where snowfall and melting are equal, at least as observed over a number of years. This means that on our simple, idealized glacier the equilibrium line agrees approximately with the lower edge of the remaining summer snow at the end of the melt season.

There are, however, glaciers that behave differently. In a polar environment snow can change to firn and to ice without any refreezing of meltwater, but by gradual re-crystallization alone. The material is then called firn as long as it is permeable to air, and since the air bubbles close at a density of about 0.82 g/cm^3, this density is normally accepted as separating firn from ice. Another great difference between our model glacier and a glacier in a polar region is the way in which snow and ice are removed from the glacier – how the ablation takes place. There are places where evaporation is the dominant factor, and there are other regions where calving of icebergs is responsible for most of the deficit. The main thing is that losses and gains must keep in balance, if the glacier is neither to advance nor retreat. The actual net balance, positive or negative, is the criterion of the glacier's 'state of health'.

Can one make any use of these processes of accumulation and ablation? Only in the most marginal situations can we hope to influence accumulation in high mountains or in the polar regions – if, that is to say, we do not resort to such drastic undertakings as, for example, closing off the Bering Strait or diverting the large Siberian rivers to the south. When it comes to ablation, however, there may be a greater potential for human initiative. Glacial meltwater is an important source of hydroelectric power, and in several countries sophisticated methods have been developed for forecasting and proper management of this valuable, and renewable, resource.

It is feasible to increase meltwater production from a glacier or snowfield by spreading dark dust on its surface. A thin cover of soot increases the absorption of radiation from sun and sky and accelerates the melting. This method has been used to provide water for irrigation in cultivated areas hit by severe droughts; the reports have not been entirely convincing, and even if an efficient method could be worked out, it would have to be used with extreme care. Any surplus water recovered in this way is taken from capital, and is not renewed.

Glacier comings and goings

Glaciers are part of the hydrological cycle; their life conditions depend on winter snowfall and summer melting, and their size reflects the present climate. Or rather, their variations in size reflect variations in the present climate.

We know from old reports, drawings and photographs that practically all glaciers in temperate regions were larger a hundred years ago than they are today. We also know that in the Alps there was a general advance of glacier fronts between 1915 and 1920, when more than 50 per cent of the observed glaciers advanced, whereas during the past 50 years the majority of Swiss glaciers have been steadily retreating. The Norwegian glaciers advanced between 1905 and 1910 and then again between 1925 and 1930, whereas in Sweden they reached their last maximum in 1915. In Alaska, glacier behaviour has been more heterogeneous than elsewhere. Most of its glaciers have certainly shrunk, and in Glacier Bay it is not a matter of hundreds of metres, as in most areas, but rather tens of kilometres. On the other hand there are some glaciers which have been very active – the Taku Glacier has advanced steadily for the past fifty years.

Most glacier variations are reported as fluctuations of the glacier front, i.e. variations in length. This frontal position depends on the balance between the loss of ice through melting and the gain through ice flow. If we start from an equilibrium condition and let the summer temperatures drop, the melting along the front will decrease and the ice will start to advance. But that is not all. If the winter snowfall stays constant the colder summer with its reduced melting will cause a positive mass balance and the glacier will grow in thickness, it will become steeper and therefore flow faster – and thus advance even more. The advance caused by reduced melting at the front acts immediately, whereas the advance caused by a positive mass balance may be delayed several years to permit the increase in steepness and velocity to reach the front. This is one reason why the long Alaskan glaciers do not always behave like their shorter relatives in the Alps.

It is, of course, the mass balance which is the ultimate cause of all glacier variations, and with the aim of relating glacier behaviour to climatic fluctuations, complete mass-balance studies have been carried out during the last 20–30 years on a number of glaciers in different parts of the world. All the gains and losses have been measured and related to winter snowfalls and average summer temperatures. On some glaciers micro-meteorological studies have revealed how the surface melting and evaporation depend upon wind speed, temperature, humidity and sunshine. Without going into details we can state that sunshine is the dominant factor in dry, continental areas, whereas warm, humid air causes most of the melting in maritime regions. Since high solar radiation is normally correlated with high temperature, one usually gets a good correlation between a summer's total melt and its mean temperature.

Let us take the studies on Storglaciären in northern Swedish Lapland as an example. Fig. 2 shows the total melting as a function of the mean temperature of June, July and August. This is a crude method, of course, but it shows quite well the effect of the temperature pattern on the glacier. Each degree corresponds to an average ablation of 41 cm. If we now look at the actual balance terms for Storglaciären, we know that the average accumulation (the total winter snowfall) over the period 1945–1974 has been 130 cm and the average ablation (summer melt) has been 183 cm. The summers have thus been so warm that they have caused a net loss of 53 cm. This could be balanced by a

Fig. 2 Storglaciären, northern Sweden: total summer melts plotted against mean summer temperature. Each degree rise in temperature is shown to correspond to a 41 cm increase in snow loss.

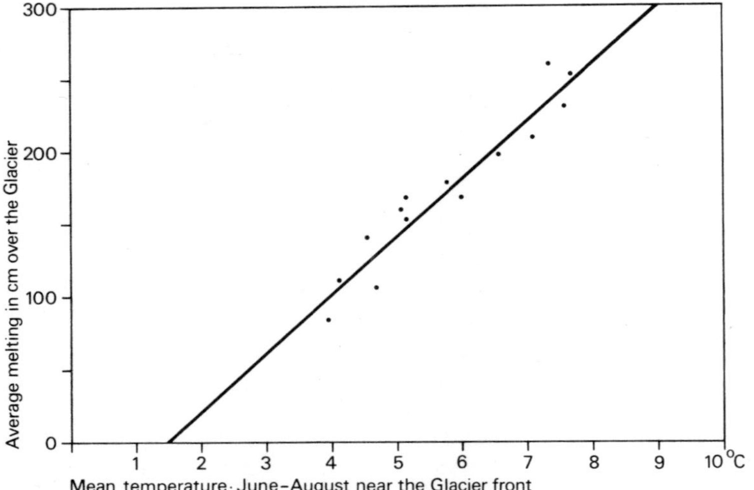

summer temperature drop of 1.2°C. And that is really not much. Greater changes were recorded at many meteorological stations in NW Europe during the early part of this century. Balance could also be achieved if the winter snowfall increased from an average of 130 cm to 183 cm. This, however, seems less likely to happen. During the 29 years of observation the accumulation has reached this high value only twice, whereas six summers have been cold enough to reduce the melting to the equilibrium level or even give a positive balance.

This little discussion is meant to show that the considerable retreat of the Scandinavian glaciers is a result of warmer summers. In fact, precipitation records from northern Lapland indicate a slight increase in snowfall, giving further support to this conclusion. Since we know from meteorological records that the general retreat of glaciers during this century was accompanied by a global change in temperature which probably culminated about 30 years ago, we can with good confidence apply our experience from Scandinavia to mountain areas in similar climatic environments, such as the Alps, the Caucasus, the Cascades etc. There are, however, Canadian glaciologists, who maintain that in the Canadian Arctic archipelago accumulation is the most important parameter for the state of health of the ice caps, and since by far the most of the melting on these glaciers is due to solar radiation (rather than heating from the air), they may very well be right.

If we turn to the large ice sheets, to Antarctica and to Greenland, we find that their reaction to climatic fluctuations can be the opposite of what we might at first expect. Most of the outlet glaciers reaching the coasts in the southern, populated parts of Greenland have retreated considerably, because of the warmer summers and the increased rate of melting at this low altitude. But what happens inland, at higher altitudes? In the interior the temperatures are so low that even if the summers become a couple of degrees warmer, there will not be any melting anyway. Warmer air can, however, carry more water vapour, and a warming trend may thus cause the ice sheet to grow. So the outlet glaciers may not tell the truth, and the volume of the ice sheet may have grown. There is some observational evidence of increased accumulation in the interior, and some of the outlet glaciers, particularly those at high altitudes, are in fact expanding.

The vast Antarctic continent is almost completely buried under a thick ice-cover. Since this ice sheet normally flows out into the sea, there are few places, if any, where one can get really representative observations of changes in extent, thickness or volume. Recent retreat has been recorded in certain ice-free coastal areas, most of which are situated outside the Antarctic Circle. Numerous studies have been carried out of the total mass balance of the Antarctic ice sheet, but the experts have come to very different results, from large net losses to large net gains. The truth may be that the ice sheet is fairly near to equilibrium, for if it was not, the ocean level would not be as stable as it is. An average thinning in Antarctica of only 30 metres, which of course is very little in comparison with changes in European glaciers, would raise the sea level a full metre.

Let us turn back to glaciers in temperate areas. The warming culminated around 1945; since then the summers have become colder, but not cold enough to change the situation completely as far as the glaciers are concerned. Most of them are still retreating, but the number of advancing glaciers is steadily increasing. In southern Norway glaciers with positive mass balance are no longer rare exceptions, and a 29-year record of mass balance data from Storglaciären in northern Sweden shows that the slightly cooler summers have not yet reversed the trend. Only 5 out of the 29 years could be called good years, and during the whole period the glacier lost nearly 15 per cent of its volume and became 330 m shorter.

Glacier advances and glacier retreats have alternated in 'glaciological history' and even if the changes during this century have been great, they have not been very exceptional, save in one respect: scientists have for the first time been able to study the glacier variations and the climatic fluctuations simultaneously. Most previous variations can be deduced only from such traces as they have left. If the front once built up a terminal moraine, which has not later been overridden, that moraine serves as reliable evidence of an early glacier advance. Or if the glacier invaded a forested or cultivated area, organic material buried under new glacier deposits can even be dated by the carbon-14 method and tell us when the advance took place. In Norway, in Iceland and in the Alps, where man has had to live close to the glaciers, one can find historical documents describing how the threatening ice has encroached upon good pasture lands and even destroyed farms and churches.

There is geological, palaeobotanical and historical evidence of a cold period about 2,500 years ago, and it can be shown that in front of several glaciers in Europe and America the outermost end moraines date from this period. We also know that about 1,000 years ago, during the Viking age, the climate was warmer, and the Norsemen colonized Iceland and southern Greenland, ultimately finding their way to the American continent. The glaciers were then as small as they are today, or even smaller, but started to grow again in about AD 1300. During the following centuries the glaciers grew large; in some areas they reached their maximum extent in the seventeenth century and in others a hundred years later; there are even glaciers which were larger sixty years ago than they have ever been.

One climatic fluctuation of global character does not have the same effect everywhere, and the glaciers in one climatic belt may not react in the same way as a glacier in another region. One has to expect a considerable variability when looking at details, but on the whole the glaciers in the temperate regions of the world react similarly to long-term variations in the global climate.

The moving ice

Ice is a peculiar material, brittle and plastic at the same time. If you hit a chunk of ice with a sharp object it will crack like a piece of brittle glass, whereas a horizontal bar of ice supported at one end only will deform plastically under its own weight – given enough time. And glacier ice has enough time. In an accumulated mass of snow, firn and ice the material will start to deform through the action of gravity on its mass. The rate of deformation will thus depend on the stresses involved, i.e. on the weight of the overlying ice column and on the slope of the upper ice surface. Applied to a real glacier it means that the rate of deformation increases with increasing ice thickness and increasing surface slope. There is yet another important parameter – ice temperature. Cold ice moves less readily than ice near melting point, just as oil is more viscous at low temperatures. A thick, steep glacier in a temperate region is therefore apt to flow fast, whereas a thin, flat ice cap in the Arctic is a slow-moving feature.

Ice movement has been a difficult problem for glaciologists for a long time. Different specialists used very different approaches to the problem, and not until the early 1950s did a group of English physicists manage to establish a set of physical and mathematical laws which laid the basis for a better understanding of ice physics and for a rapid development in the study of glaciers and inland ice sheets.

It has long been known that a glacier's surface velocity rises to a maximum near the centre line and diminishes towards the sides, where the friction against the rock wall brings the velocity to zero or close to it. This was found in the Alps about a hundred years ago. It was, in fact, in 1874 that four straight rows of rocks painted in different colours were laid out across the Rhonegletscher at various altitudes. The deformation of the red line, 2,550 m above sea-level, where the glacier was 1,100 m wide, was studied until 1880; it was found that 100 m from the rock wall the annual movement was 12.9 m, at 200 m it was 50.9 m, at 300 m 79.1 m, at 400 m 92.1 m, and at 500 m it was 98.2 m. This general result has been confirmed on glaciers all over the world;

Fig. 3. The Rhonegletscher experiment. The positions of the coloured stones, plotted yearly, showed how surface velocity increased to a maximum near the centre line.

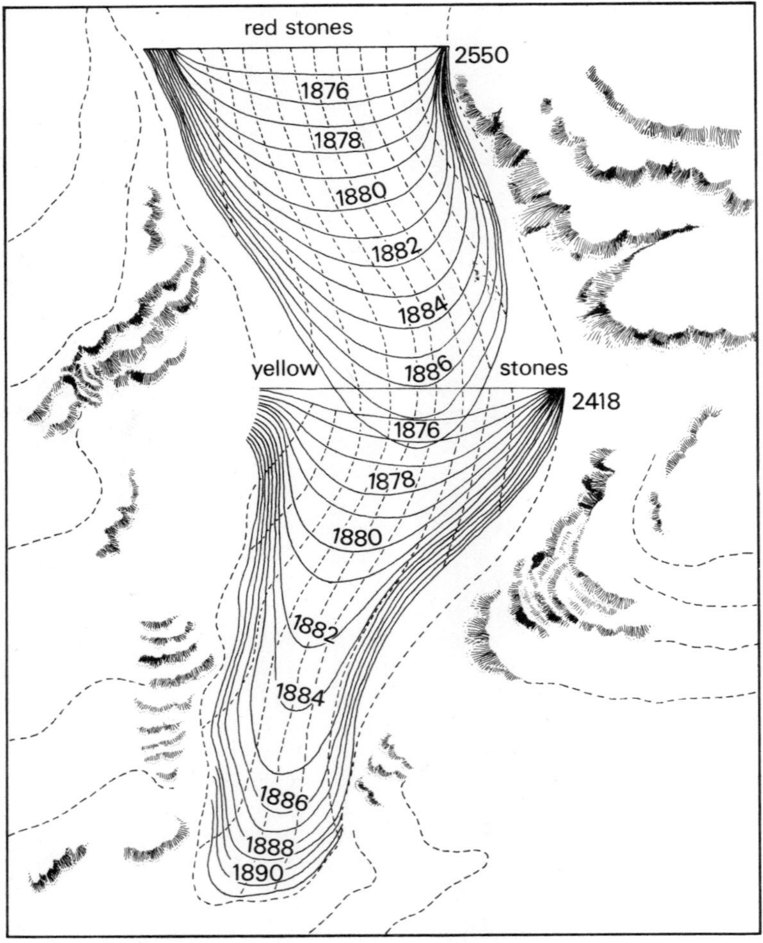

sometimes the velocity near the edges is rapid, sometimes moderate, but the maximum is always near the centre line.

It is through the ice movement that the balance is kept between accumulation and ablation. If we consider any cross-section in the ablation area, it is obvious that the volume of ice carried through this section must equal the total net loss over the glacier surface below this section. The higher we choose the section the more ice must pass through – until we reach a section through the equilibrium line, where all the surplus from the accumulation area has to pass. On an ideal glacier, lying on an even bed with the same surface slope and with parallel sides, the ice velocity will thus increase from the snout up to the equilibrium line and then drop again.

These velocities are all easy to measure, and there has for long been general agreement about this general, and very regular, geometry of the surface movement. When it comes to subsurface velocities, however, the agreement has not been so close. There was, in fact, a period when glaciologists were separated into two groups – for or against 'extrusion flow'. The idea was that the great hydrostatic pressure made the ice at depth more plastic, more easily deformed, than the ice near the surface. One would therefore expect a glacier to move faster at depth than at the surface, and the velocity maximum was believed to lie somewhere between the bottom and the middle. The discussion went on for years. Then in 1958 George Rigsby managed to prove by laboratory experiment that the deformation rate was independent of hydrostatic pressure as long as the difference between the ice temperature and the melting temperature at a particular pressure was kept constant. The concept of 'extrusion flow' was thus based on false assumptions.

The real blow to this theory, however, had been delivered six years before, when John Nye worked out how the ice in Greenland would behave if extrusion flow existed. An ice particle would move from the centre of the ice sheet out to the coast in two hours! 'Or, if the acceleration were sustained for 100 years, which is not long compared with the lifetime of a piece of ice in Greenland, the ice would reach nearly one-fifth the velocity of light.' After that statement 'extrusion flow' never recovered again, but in some peculiar way it still influences the thinking of many geologists and geomorphologists.

In order to study ice movement at depth, a number of holes have been drilled to the bottom of several glaciers and pipes filled with antifreeze have been planted in these holes and used for repeated surveys. The position of the top of the pipe in relation to fixed points outside the glacier is determined by triangulation, and the deformation of the pipe below the surface is accurately measured with an inclinometer lowered to known depths. It has been found that the velocity decreases with depth but, normally, very slowly in the upper half of the hole. Further down, velocity decreases at an increasing rate, but variations from one glacier to another are very great. On Athabasca Glacier, Canada, the bottom velocity was only 10 per cent of the surface velocity in one hole but 75 per cent in another – on the same glacier, at a distance of only 1.5 km. Velocity ratios of 45, 50, 65 per cent have been reported from other glaciers in temperate mountains.

The glaciers dealt with so far all consist of ice which is at or quite near its melting point. We have seen that 'warm' ice moves more readily than cold ice, and if we now move polewards, we may get a glacier which is 'cold' all the way from the surface to very near the bottom, where the constant geothermal heat flow brings the temperature up to pressure melting point and even causes some melting. Such a glacier is likely to show 100 per cent bottom sliding – or, if it is not all true sliding, very intense shearing in the layers near the bottom.

The third type of glacier is the one which is cold all the way from the top to the bottom. Such a glacier is not believed to slip at all on its bed, but to move through plastic flow only. It will move very slowly and since it does not slide over the bed it will not cause any erosion; we will come back to this type later.

The physics of glacier movement is now quite well established. Given the thickness, width, surface slope and internal temperature of a glacier, the glaciologist can work out an approximate value for the movement. There are, however, glaciers which do not follow the normal rules: all of a sudden they may start to expand with ten times the usual velocity.

On 21 March 1953 the natives of the Kutiah Valley, in the western Karakoram, saw the glaciers of three tributary valleys grow rapidly and bring great volumes of ice down into the main valley, where they flowed together into one big glacier, which advanced rapidly through the mature forests. One can easily imagine the terror spread by the advancing ice front. The peasants saw their woods and fields and villages disappearing under the ice, and there was no means of halting it. The front advanced with an average speed of 100 metres a day, or about 5 metres an hour. On 11 June the glacier's momentum ceased, the advance came to a halt, and the unfortunate people of Kutiah had to accept that their whole valley was filled by a new glacier 12 km long. The lower-lying Stak Valley had its upper part closed off from Kutiah by ice and the dam thus formed eventually created a large lake. It will take decades before all the ice has melted away from the Kutiah Valley, and more decades still before the forests are restored.

This kind of catastrophic advance is called a 'glacier surge', and, by definition, it is a surge when the glacier's velocity suddenly increases to 10 or even 100 times its normal value. Surges are not common, but since good air photography and satellite pictures have made studies of glaciers possible even in the most remote regions, over two hundred glaciers in western North America have been reported as surging more or less regularly; there is every reason to believe that there are at least as many more in the Himalaya, the Karakoram, the Caucasus and other mountain ranges.

The largest surge known so far took place from one of the large ice caps of North East Land, in the Spitsbergen archipelago, some time between 1936, when a British expedition passed the area with dog teams, and 1938 when it was photographed from the air. During this interval the southern part of the ice cap had made a sudden advance and formed a new glacier or ice-tongue, 20 km long and up to 30 km wide. The total area of this new glacier was 400–500 square kilometres and with an estimated mean thickness of 200 m, which is probably a fairly conservative figure, the volume of ice taking part in this surge must have been of the order of 100 cubic kilometres. Since all this ice had to come from somewhere, the upper parts of the ice cap must have become 70 to 100 m thinner.

This is the largest surge yet recorded. It came from a small ice cap, about 8,000 square kilometres. What would happen if the Antarctic ice sheet, over 12,500,000 square kilometres, started to surge? It would carry so much ice out into warmer areas that the world's climate would change, and we will therefore return to that when we deal with ice ages and climatic changes.

The glacier surface

The ice of a glacier tongue is not a completely homogeneous material. It was formed by snowfalls in the accumulation area, and some of it was exposed to sunshine, some to re-freezing of meltwater, some to pollution from airborne dust from neighbouring mountains or faraway deserts or steppes, so that the final product, the glacier ice, is a mixture of ice, air bubbles and dirt. The three ingredients are not actually mixed, but rather stratified, layers of clear ice alternating with bubbly layers and dirty layers. This original stratification can leave its marks far down in the glacier tongue and under favourable conditions annual accumulation layers may be identified, just like the annual rings in a tree. That is interesting for the glaciologist, but for the mountaineer it is important because it makes the glacier surface broken and rough. If the ice was completely homogeneous the whole surface would absorb the same amount of the sun's radiation, the rate of melting would be constant over large areas, and the surface would be smooth. But since dark ice does not reflect as much as white (bubbly) ice, it will melt faster, and all the bubble-rich layers will stand up as ridges. As long as these white ridges are low, they make walking easier; when they grow higher they become obstacles. If most of the melting is due to solar radiation, the surface tends to be rough, whereas on maritime glaciers, with little sunshine, the ice surface stays smooth. As a rule, a glacier surface is much easier to walk on after several days of sunny weather than after some overcast days with warm winds and rain.

Surface features of moderate importance to the traveller but of great scientific interest are the ogives, the regularly spaced arcs that appear below steep and narrow icefalls. They can consist either of dark and light bands or of actual waves in the ice. It has been shown on several glaciers that their wavelength corresponds to the annual movement, and the pattern may be due to the fact that some of the ice passes through an icefall in the summer, when melting is intense, and some comes through in the winter without any mass loss at all – perhaps even with the crevasses filled with winter snow. But the problem still awaits a solution.

Of all a glacier's surface features, the crevasses are the most striking – and the most dangerous too. They are formed by the tensions in the ice and are thus closely related to the glacier movement. We have seen that movement is greatest near the equilibrium line – at least in the ideal case. This means that an ice particle travelling down-glacier increases its velocity from the head-wall to the equilibrium line and then loses speed towards the ice front. There is *extending flow* above and *compressing flow* below the equilibrium line. Extending flow means surface tension – and crevasses are likely to appear. Compressing flow, on the other hand, closes already existing crevasses. The accumulation area is thus the most dangerous part of the glacier, and the fact that many crevasses are hidden under the previous winter's snow, which may form fragile bridges over deep chasms, makes life even more difficult for the mountaineer and the glaciologist. Extending flow also appears on slopes of increasing steepness, i.e. where the profile is convex. All such slopes are likely to be crevassed; this applies to the ablation area as well as the accumulation area, even though the latter is always the more dangerous.

These rules are general ones and easy to use in practice on any glacier. There are, however, still other reasons for the ice to fracture. For instance, marginal crevasses may appear in the 'shearing zone' near the sides, where the surface velocity decreases rapidly. They develop at an angle of about 45° up-glacier but are slowly rotated down-glacier since the inner ends move faster than the outer ones.

The depth of crevasses varies a lot. They are deeper in the accumulation area than in the ice on the tongue (and – dare one say? – they are deeper when estimated by a mountaineer than when measured by a glaciologist). On a temperate glacier, i.e. a glacier consisting of ice near its melting-point, measured depths have seldom exceeded 25 or 30 m, and the depths are often reduced considerably by old, fallen snow bridges. In the Arctic and Antarctic the low temperatures make the ice more brittle and crevasses some 40 m deep have been observed.

Moraines

When the glacier moves over its bed, and particularly when there is a high ratio of bottom sliding, the ice mass will act as a land-form sculptor. Large rocks, picked up from the underlying bedrock and incorporated in the basal ice, will act as powerful chisels and further increase the rate of erosion.

Attempts have been made to study the erosion experimentally by drilling accurately measured holes in bedrock just beyond advancing glaciers. After the glacier has moved over the rock face for some years and retreated again, one can measure how much shallower the holes have become. Such an experiment may take a few years or hundreds of years, depending upon the glacier's fluctuations, and as it is difficult to forecast the climate, only a few such series have been started. At Oberer Grindelwald Gletscher an erosion of 3.9 cm over a period of 10 years has been measured by this method. This sounds a high figure, but it was probably representative of only that particular rock in which the holes were drilled. Another method of measuring glacier erosion, or rather a proportion of it, is to record the amount of rock material carried out of the glacier by the meltwater streams. Several such studies have been made, leading to the conclusion that erosion under the average glacier amounts to 1 millimetre a year, or 1 m every 1,000 years. This is certainly a minimum value, since the measurements do not include all the eroded material, but mainly that which is carried downstream in suspension.

It is probably best to be careful and not try to give any average erosion values, for there are many examples of insignificant erosion on ground laid bare of ice during the present glacier retreat. It can be shown that glaciers in Iceland have advanced over peat bogs, and when the ice retreated, hundreds of years later, the peat was still there, although one would not expect peat to be particularly resistant. There are many similar examples. Recently a Polish Spitsbergen expedition recovered organic material,

Fig. 4 *The maximum extent of the last glaciation. The darker area represents sea ice.*

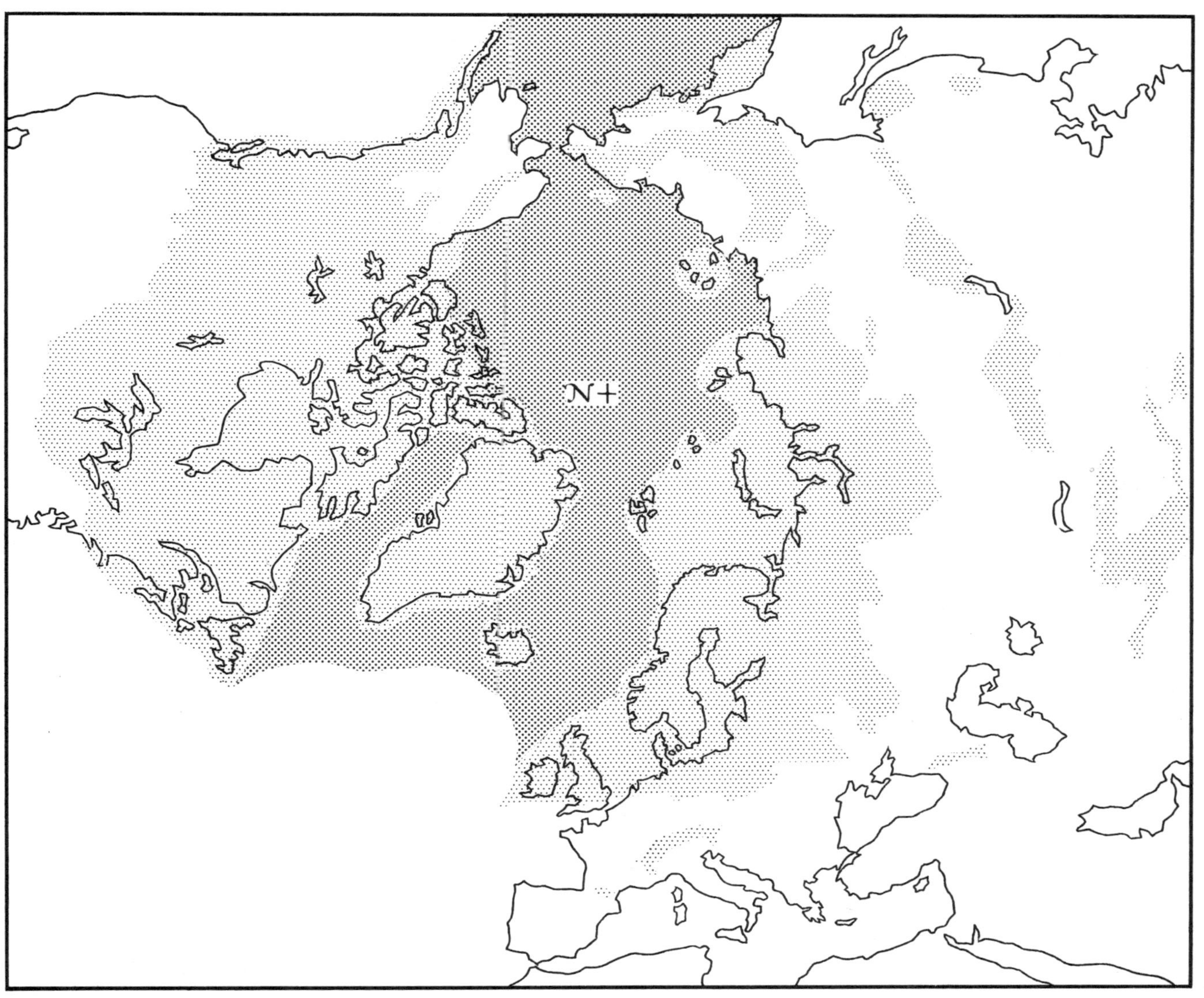

which had been buried by the ice during the Viking age, and had stood up to the glacier's erosion for a thousand years.

That was one extreme. The other extreme is best illustrated by the fiord topography. A fiord is part of a deep, glacially eroded valley that is submerged under the sea. A true fiord is shallower at the mouth than further in, and only the erosion of a glacier can bring about such a profile. A classical example is Sognefjord in Norway, which is 170 km long and reaches a maximum depth of 1,308 m though it is only 150 m deep at the entrance. The side walls are over 1,500 m high and it is very likely that a great deal of the total excavation has been done by streams through millions of years, but the streams do not erode below sea level. The extra depth of over 1,000 m, and the U-shaped cross-section, are due to glacier erosion, and must have taken a long time.

What we do see in the field is all the morainic material gathered on the surface of the glacier. Some, but not very much, has been brought up from the bottom – most of it has fallen down from the walls around the glacier. The material which falls down from the actual head wall will not re-appear until it reaches the front; it will take hundreds or even thousands of years because it will travel along the bottom. Rocks falling from side walls above the equilibrium line will be embedded in the ice and appear again at a corresponding distance below this line, forming lateral moraines. When two glaciers flow together and continue as one, the two coalescing lateral moraines will continue as a medial moraine, which will separate the two contributing glaciers and preserve their identities.

Lateral moraines are thus deposited along the sides of a glacier; the ridges built up outside the front are end moraines, sometimes called terminal moraines. In front of many present glaciers there are whole systems of end moraines, each ridge marking one stage in the history of the glacier's fluctuations. The old theory that end moraines are 'bulldozed' by an advancing glacier front have proved to be more dramatic than true. These so-called 'push moraines' are the exception rather than the rule, and the largest reported so far was only 9 metres in height. The majority of end moraines mark positions where the glacier front has stood in equilibrium for a long period of time, or it may perhaps have reached the same position several times. Even though many glaciers look very dirty and seem to work as efficient conveyor belts, the mass of rock carried every year to the front is very small compared with the enormous accumulations represented by the end moraines, which are often 25–50 m high and occasionally up to 200–300 m.

The end moraines help us to work out the chronology of glacier variations. The ridges can sometimes be dated historically from written reports or even photographs, but for the old ones other methods have to be used. Where old tree stumps are buried under the moraine, or a peat layer or any grass-covered soil, the time of original advance can be found by radiocarbon dating (^{14}C-dating). Lichenometry, which uses a correlation, fixed for the general region, between the diameter of a lichen and its age, has also been used successfully. The main disadvantage of end-moraine chronology is that, as a rule, it is only successively smaller advances or standstills that are apparent; earlier sequences may be completely erased by one single advance. It may also happen that a glacier simply overrides an end moraine without destroying it, advancing several hundred metres beyond it to build a younger end moraine further out.

The study of glacier erosion and of the transport and deposition of morainic material is, of course, not just of academic interest. The soils of all the land covered by ice sheets fifteen to twenty thousand years ago – and that means all north-west Europe, almost all of Canada and an important part of the USA – were to a great extent laid down by the ice or meltwater streams, and what we can learn about present-day processes can be applied to deposits from the Ice Age.

The water from a glacier

Some of the materials referred to in the last section were deposited by glacier streams, and since running water sorts material into particles of different sizes, some of the best gravel used for building houses, bridges or highways is quarried from such deposits. In an esker – the long, narrow ridge deposited in or just outside an ice tunnel carrying great quantities of meltwater – large, rounded boulders are most frequent near the inner core, while the very finest material, the clay, is washed out and carried in suspension over vast distances.

But how does the water pass over and through a glacier? Some of the meltwater runs off as surface streams, and this is particularly true on cold glaciers where it cannot penetrate the ice, for if it flows down into a crevasse the water refreezes and heals the fracture. However, on a temperate (warm) glacier most of the water finds its way down to the front through subglacial or englacial channels, i.e. along the bottom or through the ice itself. When it disappears from the surface into cracks, crevasses or drainage holes ('moulins') it is difficult to follow from there on. Exactly what this sewage system looks like is not known: does the water go straight down to the bottom, are there several large tunnels collecting all the water, or is there a thin water film along the very sole of the glacier? These and many other questions are still unanswered. There are, however, different hydrological systems in a glacier. Some water flows fast through wide channels, as subglacial rivers; a strong dye poured into a drainage hole one kilometre from the front may show up within less than an hour in the stream outside the glacier. But besides this discrete drainage there is also a kind of ground-water system through which water moves very slowly: it may take years for some of the meltwater from the accumulation area to reach the front. These two systems (if not more) are complementary, the fast drainage carrying the large quantities, the ground-water system helping to even out the discharge.

Glacier meltwater is of great economic value in many parts of the world, where melting reaches a maximum at the time of year when normal rivers start to dry out. In the Alps and in Norway the glacier meltwater is so important in the production of hydroelectric power that elaborate schemes have been developed for forecasting the discharge. Water is even artificially trapped in tunnels from beneath the glaciers. In semi-arid areas at the foot of glacier-bearing mountains the meltwater can be used for irrigation. As we have seen, it is even possible to speed up the rate of melting if glaciers are covered by a thin film of soot or some other dark material. Unfortunately, this is not an ecologically sound method and is only permissible in times of exceptional drought.

Glacier rivers are always naturally polluted. They carry in suspension all the silt, the rock flour, produced at the bed of the glacier by its sliding, and this discolours the rivers – though it is not, strictly speaking, pollution. The thousands of tons of rock material carried annually even by quite small glacier streams are deposited in lower valleys or lakes and add to the arable land. Naturally it is less popular with engineers developing dams and power plants. The rate of silt deposition in artificial reservoirs has to be taken into account, and the wear on turbines and duct systems in hydroelectric plants can become serious.

However, on the whole, glacier water is very valuable wherever man can find it. It is, of course, more valuable in the Alps than on the east coast of Greenland, but since the shortage of fresh water is becoming one of the most serious problems of our time, we may have to seek it even in less accessible places. And that search has started. We know that about 80 per cent of the world's total freshwater resources are locked up in the two large ice sheets – in Greenland and in Antarctica. Why not move the ice from where there is plenty of it to where the water is needed? The idea has been thoroughly studied and, to the surprise of the scientists who did so, W. F. Weeks, and W. J. Campbell, it proved to be a possibility – perhaps even a very attractive one from the economic point of view. One large, purpose-built tug of, say, 200,000 h.p. would be able to tow icebergs from the Antarctic to south-western Australia at the rate of 14 cubic km of ice per year. This would be enough to turn 16,000 square km of desert into productive land, without using a non-renewable resource. In the future, technology may find yet other means of bringing polar water to thirsty soils.

Ice ages

When we use the term 'ice age', we mean a period in the geological time scale when the world's glacier coverage was considerably larger than it is today; when now densely populated areas were hidden under thick masses of ice (and there were times when ice sheets even spread over areas now occupied by hot deserts). But we should realize that for the scientists working in Antarctica it is obviously an ice age now. The Antarctic ice sheet covers 12.6 million square kilometres; the whole continent is buried under ice with an average thickness of 2,200 m; the greatest thickness measured up to now is 4,450 m. The total volume, about 25 million cubic kilometres, is so large that if it all melted the sea-level would rise 60 m or a bit more. Fortunately we need not worry too much about that, for the ice sheet has

Fig. 5 Generalized sea-surface temperature curve for the last 400,000 years (after Emiliani, modified), as deduced from analysis of the ratio of oxygen isotopes in fossil foraminifera shells. Eight fairly regular low-temperature periods are apparent.

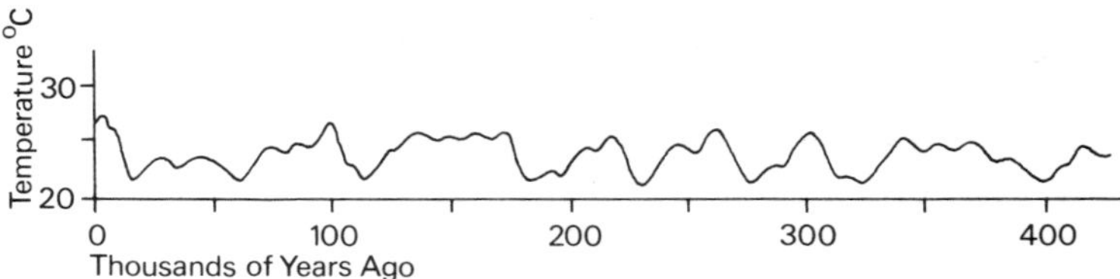

apparently been there for 10 million years or more.

It is nearly 150 years since Louis Agassiz, a young Swiss zoologist, presented so much evidence of a former, considerably larger, glaciation in the Alps that the concept of a 'glacial age' or an 'ice age' became widely accepted by scientists in Europe and North America. Stratigraphic studies soon showed that there have been four different ice ages: in the Alps called Günz, Mindel, Riss and Würm and in North America, Nebraskan, Kansan, Illinoian and Wisconsin. Four glacial periods and three interglacial periods – simple, clear-cut and easy for the students to learn.

However, soon after the Second World War new radioactive dating methods were developed as well as methods for measuring average temperatures in prehistory. This led to a complete revision of the old scheme, and the last ice age has now been broken down into at least three different stages. The three previous classical 'ice ages' proved to be no less complicated.

A wealth of information about climatic variations during several hundred thousand years comes from the studies of deep-sea sediments. If fossil shells are analysed for the ratio between the oxygen isotopes ^{18}O and ^{16}O, it is possible to draw conclusions, from variations in this ratio, about the surface temperature of the sea at the time when these shells were living. A look at Emiliani's paleotemperature curve, obtained with this method, shows very regular temperature variations during the last 450,000 years. There are eight pronounced minima during a time-span which covers only the last two classical ice ages. The curve shows such regular variations that it is tempting to use them to forecast future changes.

For the last 100,000 years we can see a more detailed picture. In the middle of the Greenland ice cap there is a continuous accumulation of snow, with no melting. Each snow layer's $^{18}O/^{16}O$ ratio is determined by the general temperature conditions at the time of snowfall, and this ratio stays as a characteristic of that particular snow for a very long time. One can calculate the age of the ice at various depths, and it is even possible to identify each annual layer for more than a thousand years back. Fig. 6 shows the result of a Danish-American project in NW. Greenland, where a hole was drilled through the 1,390 m

Fig. 6 Oxygen isotope record of ice (after Dansgaard, modified) from a 1387 m borehole in the Greenland ice sheet. All the climatic fluctuations known from other research in the Würm (Wisconsin) period are seen in the record, as are other known and unknown variations before the onset of that ice age.

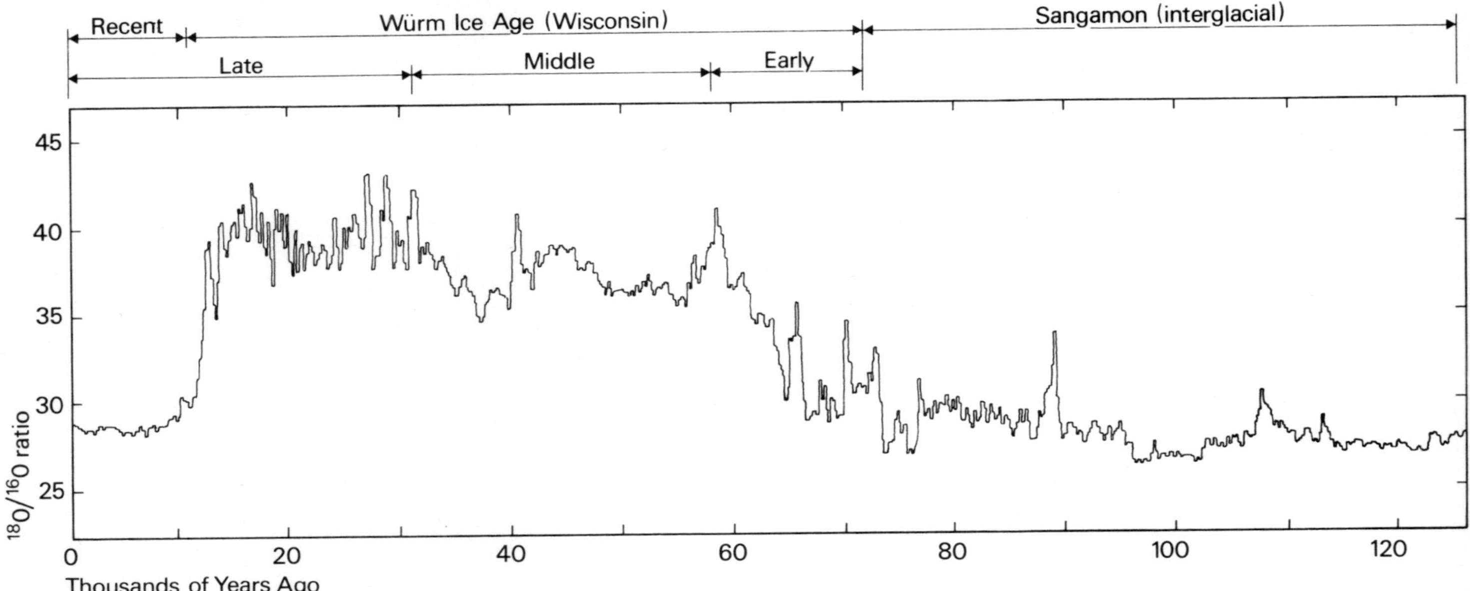

of ice and an almost complete core was recovered. Low ratios (δ-values) indicate low temperatures, and the curve tells us that 'the last ice age' started 73,000 years ago and finished 10,000 years ago. That is the classical Würm (or Wisconsin, as it is called in the USA), when some periods were very cold and other periods mild, so that the ice sheets in Europe were insignificant or had disappeared. These colder and warmer periods identified in the Greenland ice core can be correlated with corresponding cold and warm periods found by Quaternary geologists working with the climatic history of Middle Europe, where for example the peat bogs represent a valuable climatological archive. But what is the significance of the very rapid temperature drop 89,500 years ago? Apparently, within 100 years the climate changed from warmer than today to full glacial severity. After another thousand years the temperatures were back to normal again. This is very dramatic, but it is not understood.

If climate can change as fast as is demonstrated by this catastrophic temperature drop, one can imagine that an inland ice sheet can develop rapidly and, once formed, it will tend to perpetuate itself. The argument is, that if the sudden fall in temperature permits snow to survive the summers even in low-lying regions, the cold surface induces precipitation, allowing the ice sheet to grow immediately over an enormous area and this means that it does not have to start in the high mountains and flow outwards from there. However, that remains to be proved.

No one can yet give us a good explanation of why climate changes drastically and why inland ice sheets start to grow. There is no lack of theories; the trouble is that there are too many. Some of the most popular ideas are: (*a*) variations in solar activity, (*b*) variations in geometric relations of the Earth's orbit, (*c*) variations in dust content and composition of the atmosphere, (*d*) continental drift and vertical displacement of land masses. The world's climate is in such a delicate balance that very specific combinations of several causes may be necessary to produce a full glacial climate. A complicating factor is the interdependence of ice sheets and climate. Since the vast snow deserts reflect 80 to 90 per cent of the incoming radiation they make their own climate. A climatic deterioration, which would be short-lived in a less critical region, could thus initiate lasting snow accumulation over huge areas, causing the radiation balance to become increasingly unfavourable, and this in turn would promote a further fall in temperature, thereby preserving or even enhancing the change of climate.

An interesting example of this is the theory advanced by A. T. Wilson, a New Zealand scientist. He attributes the global climatic changes of ice-age dimensions to enormous surges of the Antarctic ice sheet. The idea is that the ice sheet grows so thick that its weight causes melting at the bottom. This would trigger glacier surges of continental proportions and the floating ice shelves would expand outwards across the ocean to the Antarctic Convergence, at about 50°S latitude, the point where the cold southern waters meet the warmer surface water of the north. Because of this expanded snow and ice area the radiation conditions would change so radically that the heat input of the whole Earth would decrease by 4 per cent. That would be enough to start an ice age in the northern hemisphere; the heat input would continue to decrease, by as much as 8 per cent, and the world's average temperature would drop by 6°C. Once the surge had come to an end the expanded ice shelves would break up quite quickly and the icebergs melting in the warmer seas would contribute to further cooling; but the main point is that Antarctica would then, within a fairly short time, return to its present extent, and the radiation balance become restored to its original value. The ice sheet would then be thinner, it would once more freeze to its bed, and tens of thousands of years would elapse before it grew to surging thickness again.

The theory is fascinating; it is simple and it explains the cyclicity. One can scarcely say that it has gained general acceptance, because glaciologists can hardly believe in a circumpolar Antarctic surge, nor do they think that ice shelves could extend as far as the Convergence without breaking up long before that. One drainage basin could perhaps surge, but not the ice sheet as a whole. If, on the other hand, someone can prove that each glacial period has started with a 12–15 m rise of sea level, then Wilson's theory certainly has to be taken seriously.

And what do we have to expect in the future? The answer is of course 'a new ice age'. But no one can say if the temperature drop will start in 1,000, in 10,000 or in 100,000 years. The geological history tells us that there have been periods of hundreds of millions of years without any known ice age. On the other hand, the climatic curve for the last 70,000 years shows that the warm intervals have been about 10,000 years long, and it is now 10,000 years since the last glacial period came to an end. This makes many scientists expect a new glacial period very soon.

Let us not worry too much. Statistical analysis of the variations of the $^{18}O/^{16}O$ ratio in the Greenland core shows a regular cyclicity with periods of 78, 180, 405 and 2,400 years. W. Dansgaard has extrapolated this set of mathematical functions into the near future, and he says 'the tentative prognosis suggests that the cooling within the recent decades may soon be replaced by a slight warming up till approximately 1990. Thereafter, the tentative prognosis suggests minor fluctuations with cold peaks around AD 2005 and 2060. The warm peaks foreseen for the coming century will hardly bring back the extremely warm conditions of the 1930s.' So it really does not look too bad for this or for the next few generations.

Suggestions for further reading

C. Embleton and C. A. M. King: *Glacial and periglacial geomorphology*. Edward Arnold, London, and St Martin's Press, New York, 1968.

R. F. Flint: *Glacial and Quaternary geology*. Wiley, New York, 1971.

Journal of Glaciology, Cambridge, 1947.

L. Lliboutry: *Traité de glaciologie*. Masson, Paris, 1964.

W. S. B. Paterson: *The Physics of Glaciers*. Pergamon Press, Oxford and Elmsford, N. Y., 1969.

R. J. Price: *Glacial and fluvioglacial landforms*. Oliver and Boyd, Edinburgh, and Hafner, Riverside, N. J., 1973.

R. R. P. Sharp: *Glaciers*. University of Oregon Press, Eugene, Oregon, 1960.

A. E. Wright and F. Moseley: *Ice Ages: Ancient and Modern. Geological Journal*. Special Issue No. 6, Seel House Press, Liverpool, 1965.

A tongue of plastic, flowing ice, Mount Thomlinson Glacier (British Columbia, Canada) creeps downhill from its birthplace on the heights. Where snowfall is greater than thaw – the accumulation area – the lowest levels of the snow cover very gradually recrystallize into a thick mass of ice, which flows down to warmer levels until it reaches a point where melting predominates – the ablation area. Loss through melting and gain through ice flow govern the fluctuations of glaciers, which shrink and advance accordingly. Here the amount of crevassing and the condition of the glacier's terminus or snout suggest that it has recently been quite active. The high lateral moraine to the left of the glacier probably represents its extent some 50 years ago.

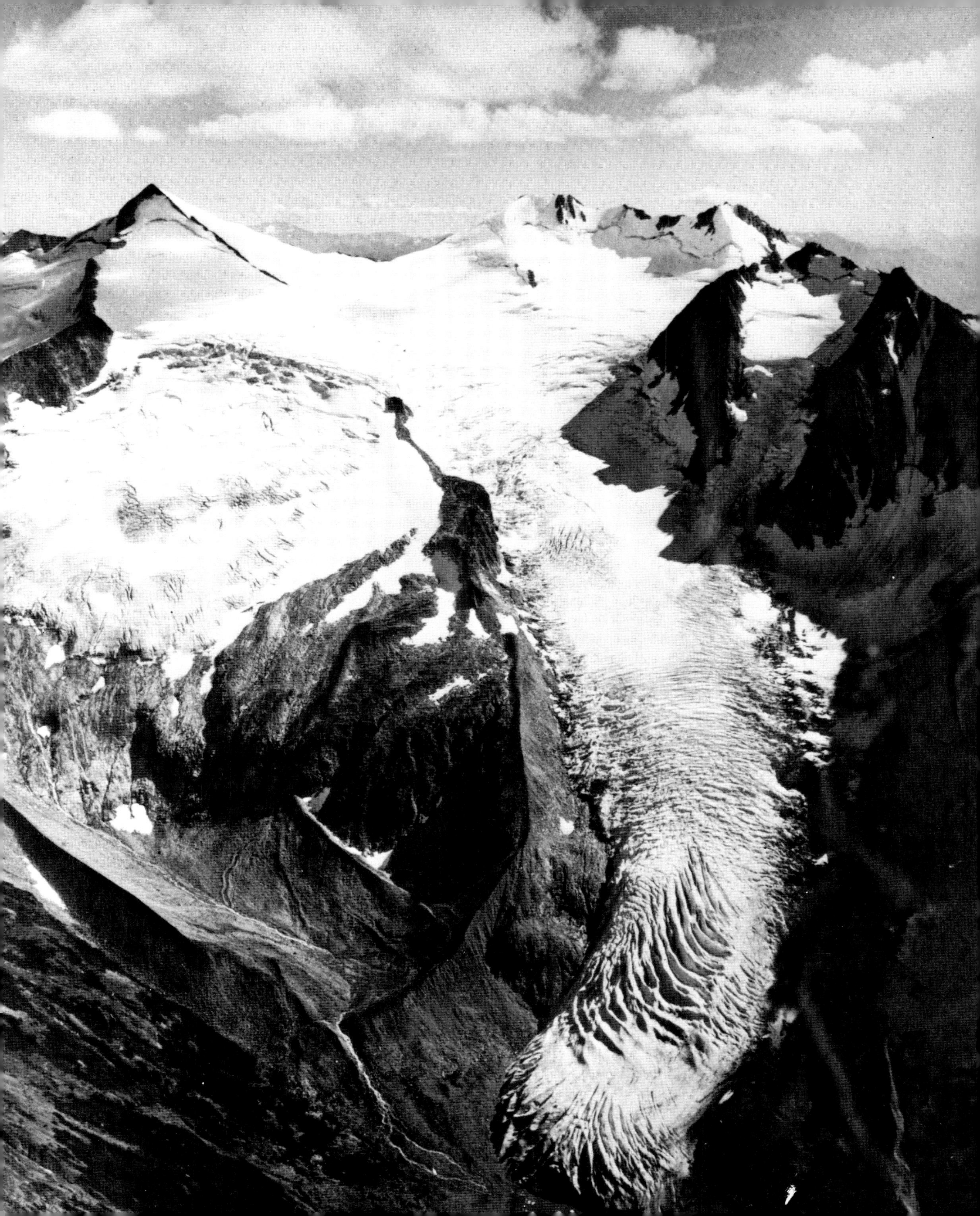

2

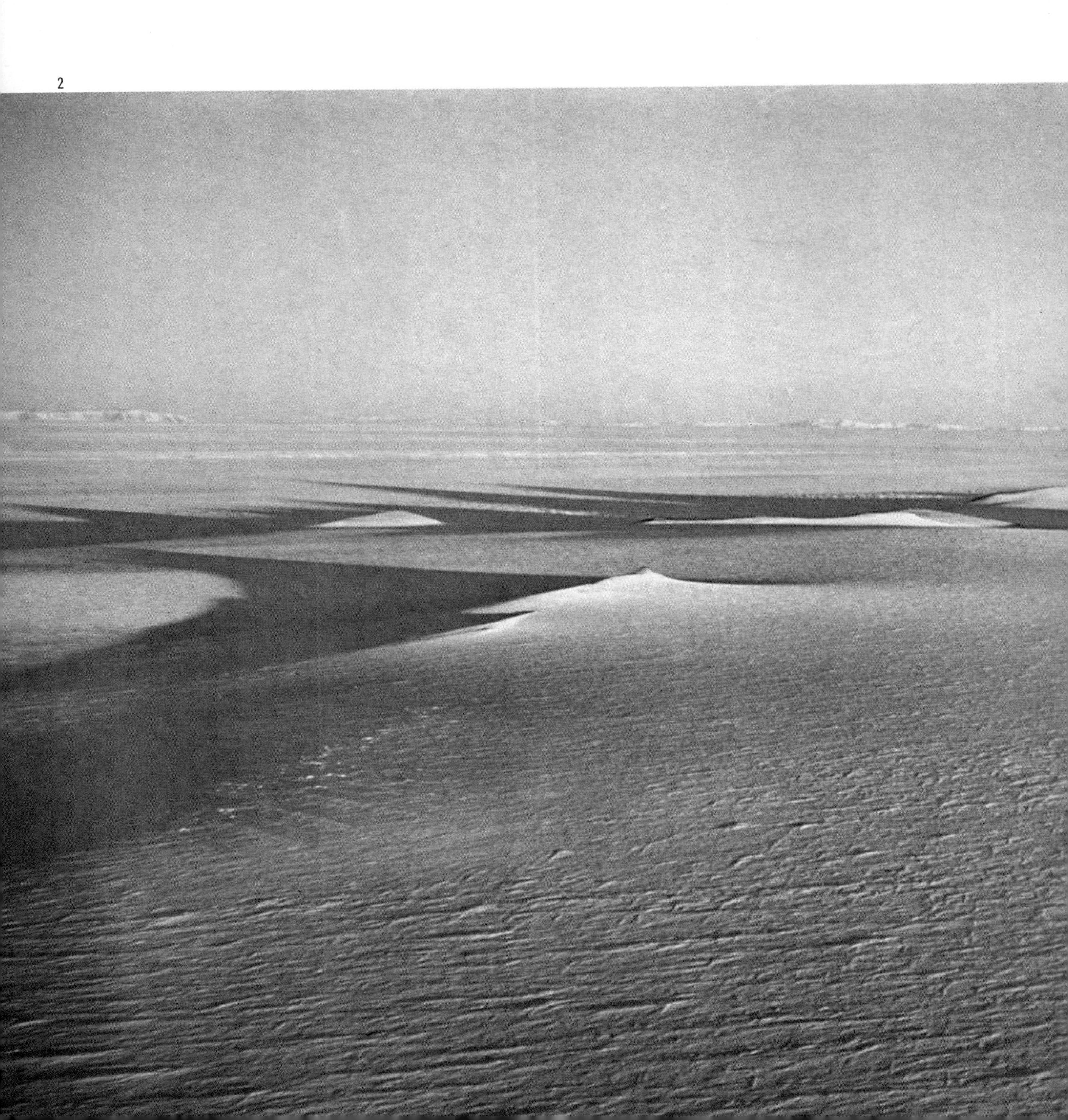

Rising from one to eight thousand feet above the underlying rock, the snow cover of the polar ice sheet, 700 miles from the South Pole (2), threatens to engulf the last of the nunataks (areas of bedrock completely surrounded by ice). Scientists, the only human inhabitants, use snocats (3) to traverse the continent from one side to the other. To take the mean temperature of the ice (4) a drill is turned by hand until it reaches a depth of 35–40 feet.

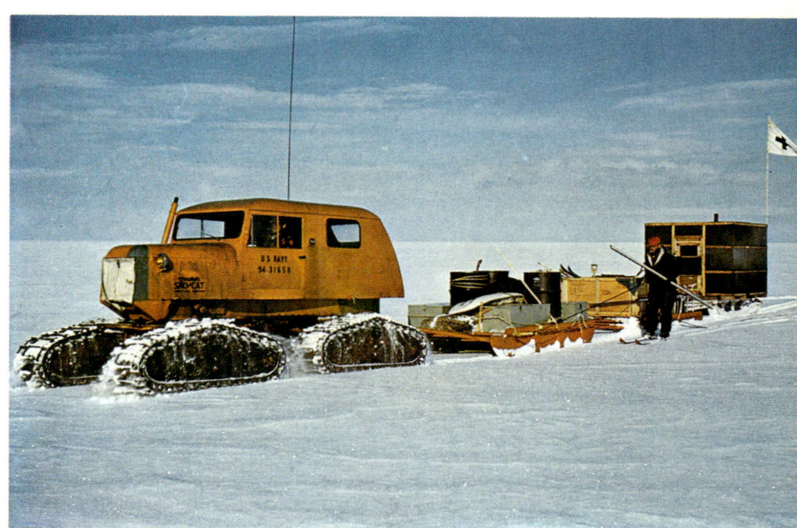

3/4

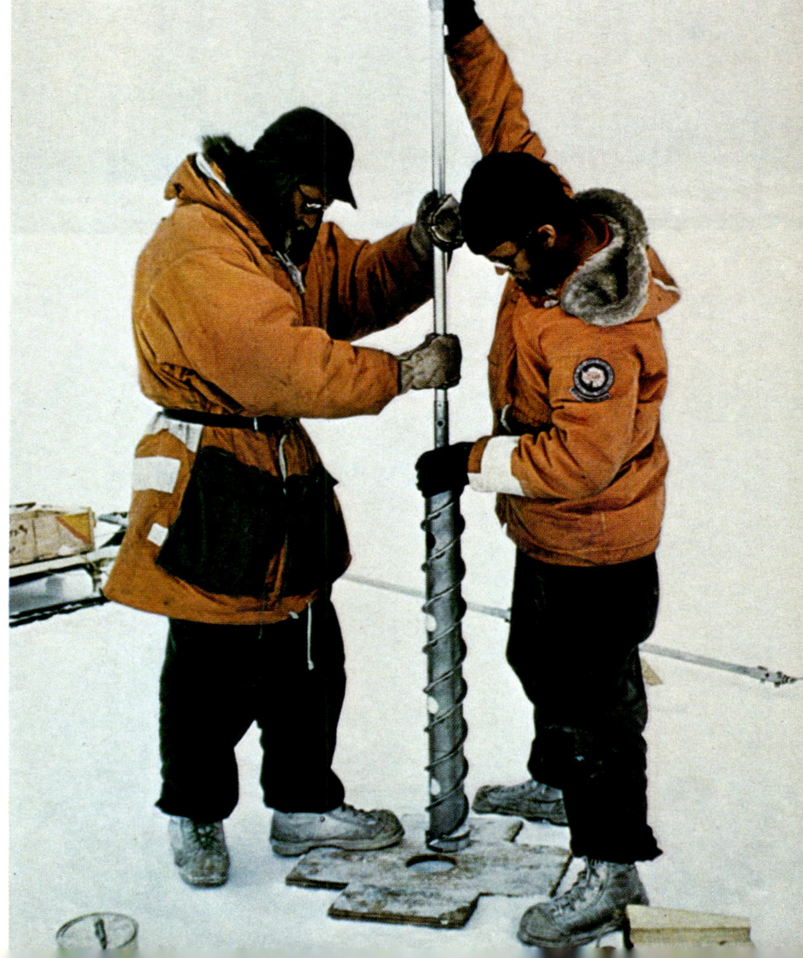

A landscape of stripes, miles long, is created by medial moraines – narrow ribbons of rock erosion debris carried down by ice streams, and formed when the ice tributaries converge. Each stripe in this aerial view of a large Alaskan glacier demarcates a different tributary.

5

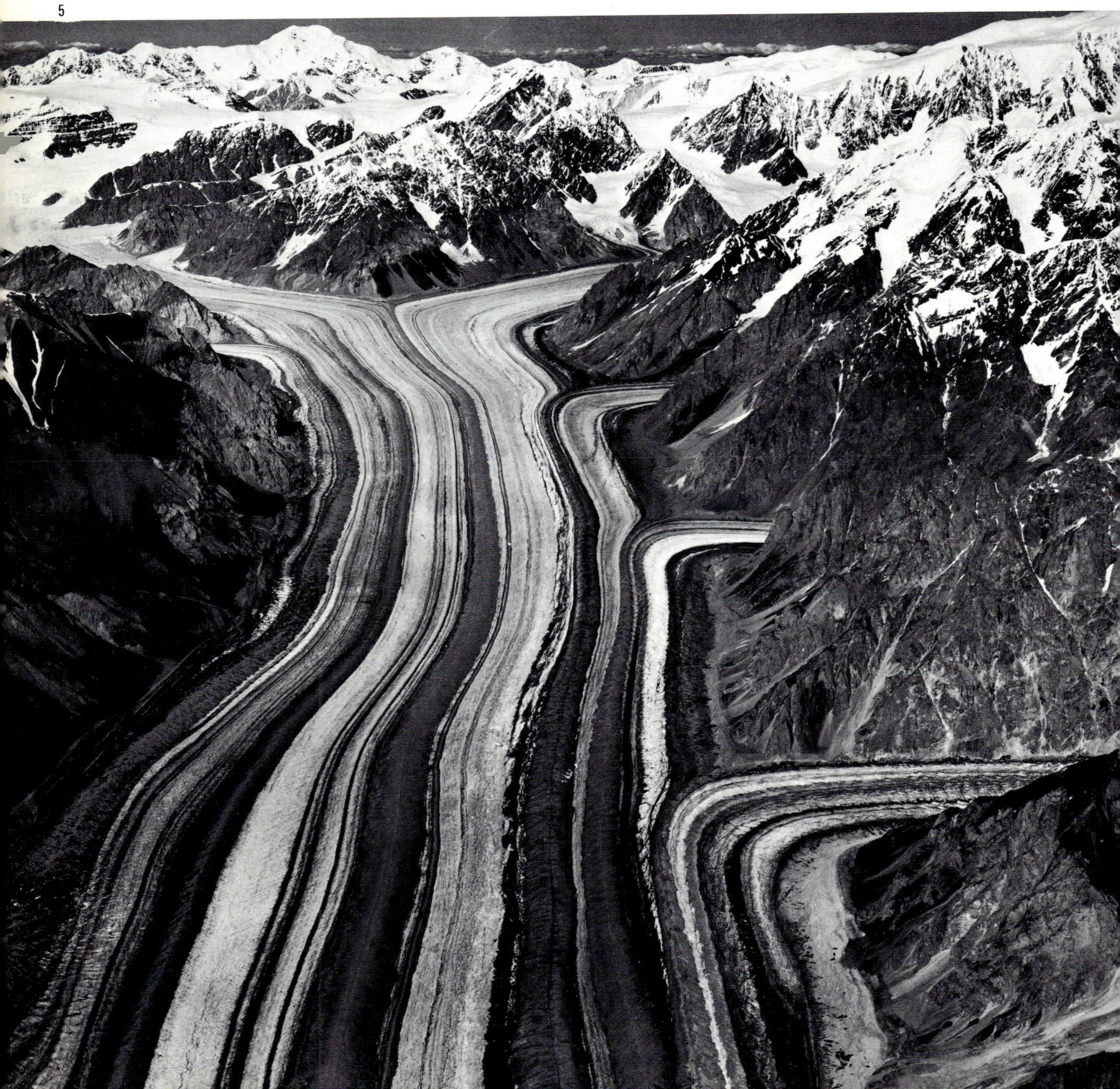

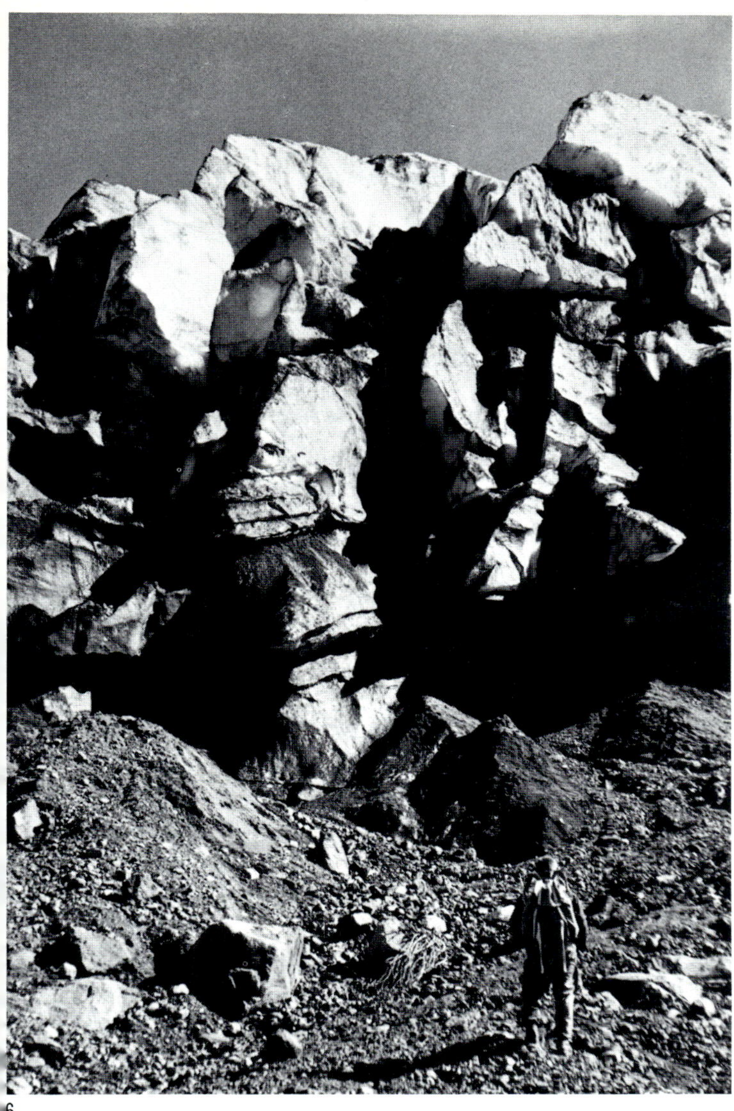

6

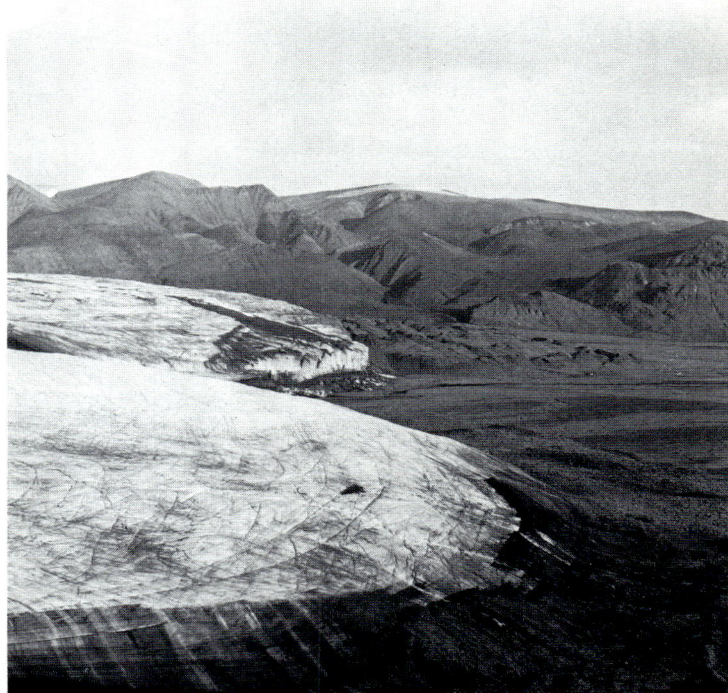

7

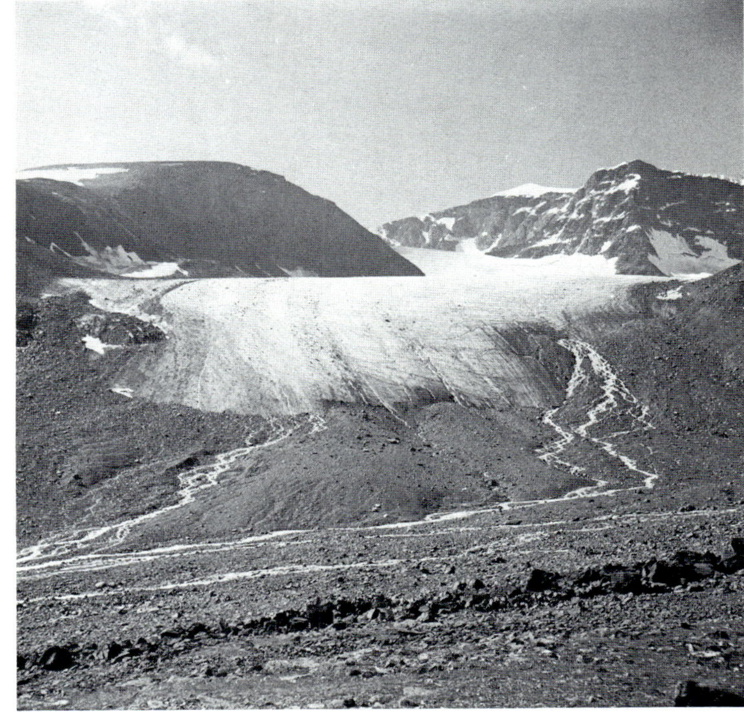

8

The advancing cliff of the terminus of Coleman Glacier, Mt Baker, Washington (6) indicates a preponderance of accumulation over ablation, with the clean ice of the upper levels overthrusting layers of dirty ice beneath. Adjacent glaciers can react in different ways, as shown by Canadian Arctic glaciers (7), where the smooth, convex snout of White Glacier in the foreground is in retreat, while the cliff-like terminus of Thompson Glacier beyond is advancing Storglaciären in Swedish Lapland (8), photographed in 1970, clearly shows its retreat from the line of rock in the foreground, almost reached by the glacier in 1915.

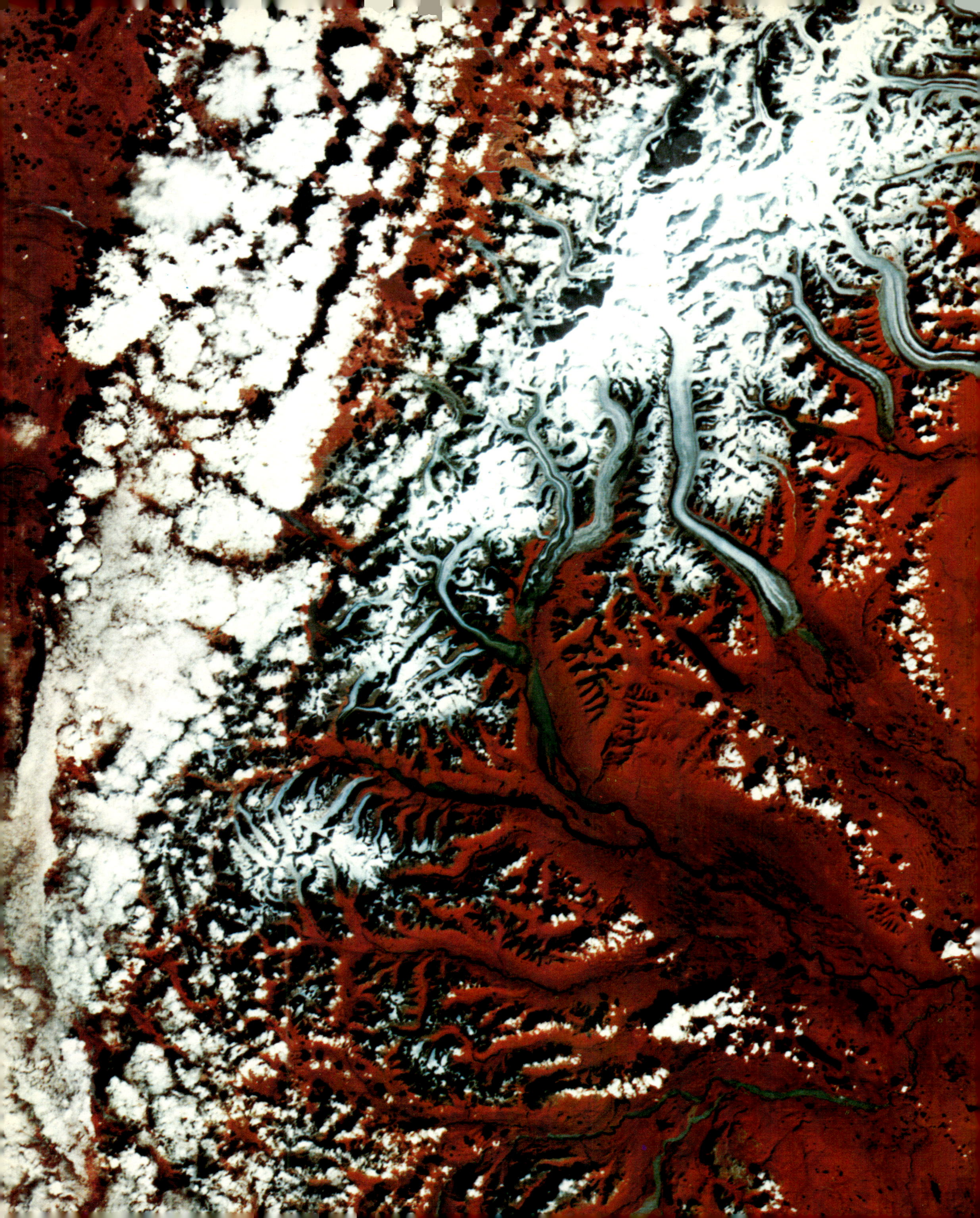

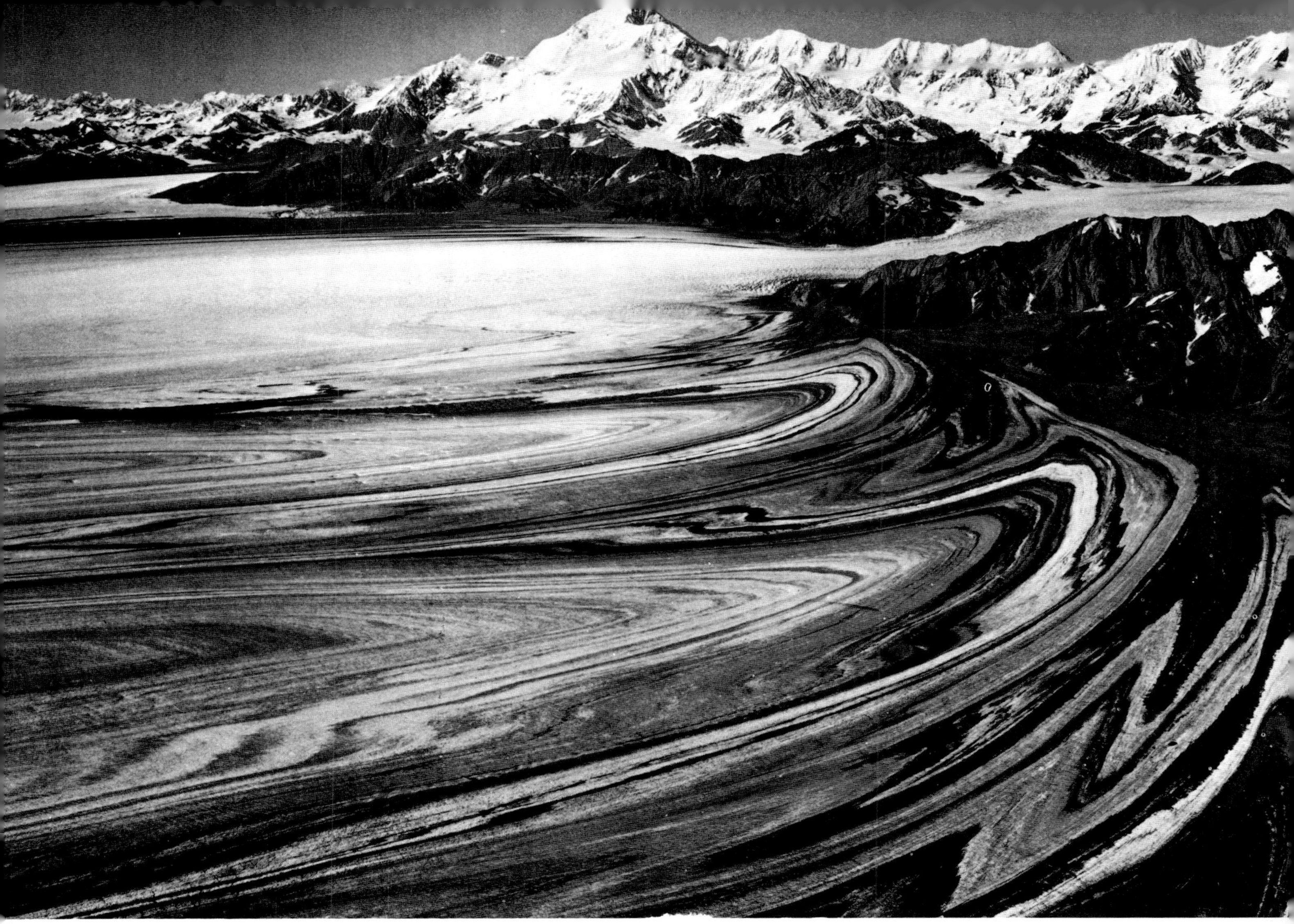

0

The mystery of glacier surge, when ice flow uddenly accelerates by 10 or even 100 times, is still not understood. In a satellite picture of glaciers flowing south from Mt McKinley, Alaska (9), the surges show up as serrations on he glaciers' paths. Seen from close to, the moraines of the Malaspina Glacier, Alaska (10) appear as giant loops, each representing a eparate surge. A glacier in mid-surge (11) demolishes everything in its path, but the trees may appear later in moraine, and thus provide material for Carbon 14 dates of past surges.

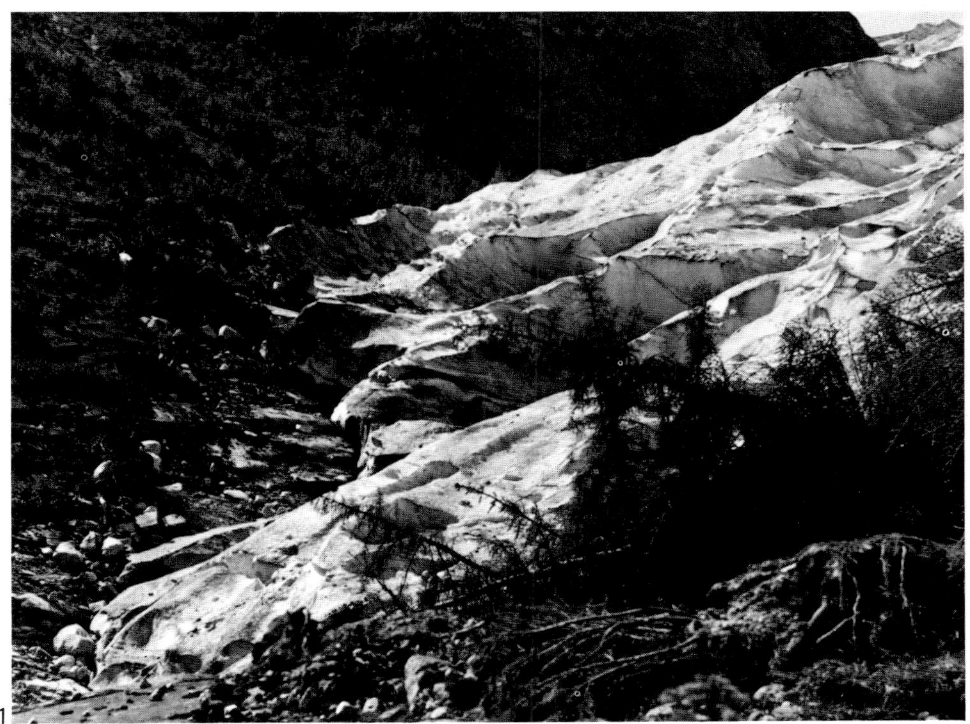

11

14

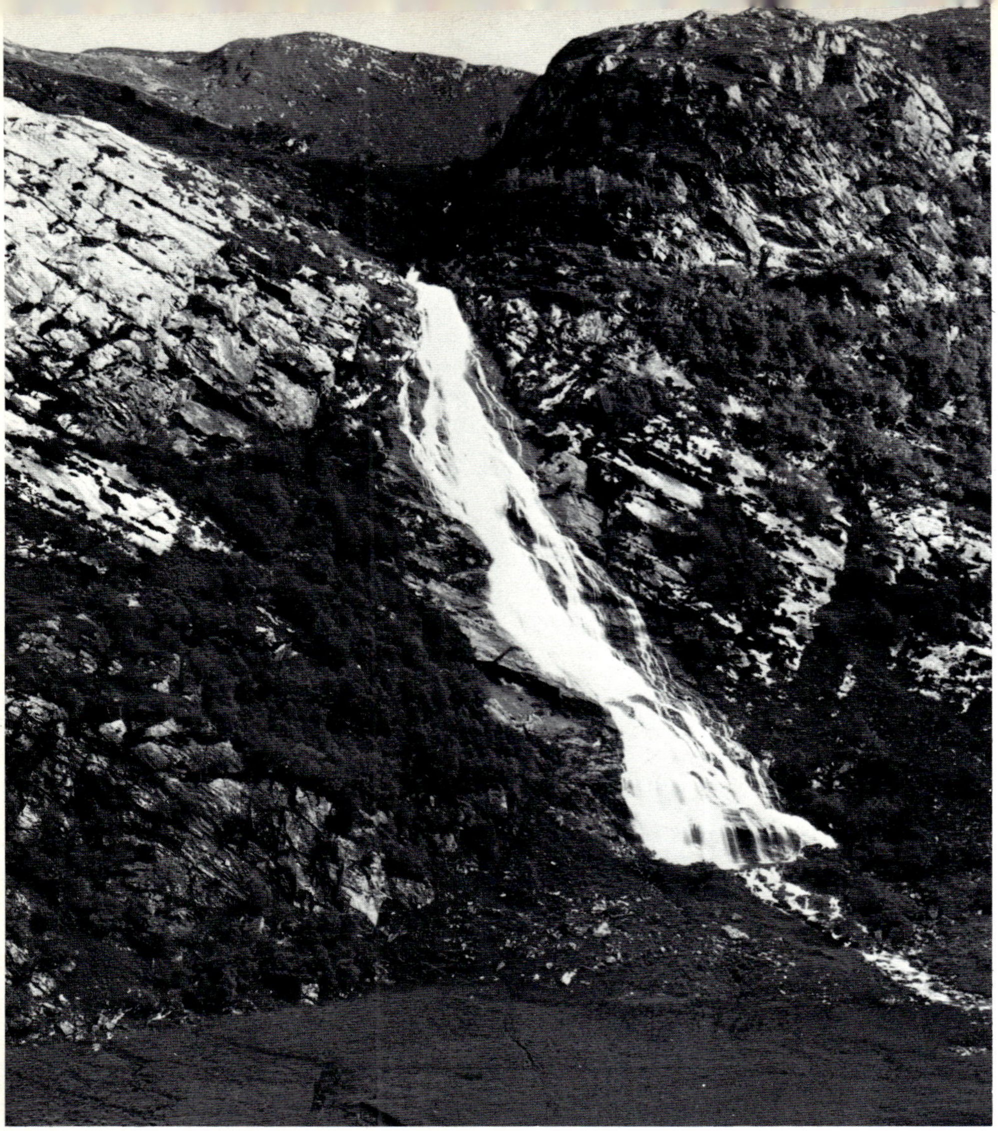

Potent land-form sculptors, glaciers of the past are responsible for many impressive landscape features. In the 'hanging valley' of Glen Nevis, Scotland (12), the foreground has been abruptly sheared away, while a large *roche moutonnée* (13), like a giant recumbent sheep, bears striations carved by glacier flow. And the fertile U-shaped valley of Dol-Goch, Merionethshire (14), now contains farmland where a glacier once flowed.

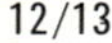

12/13

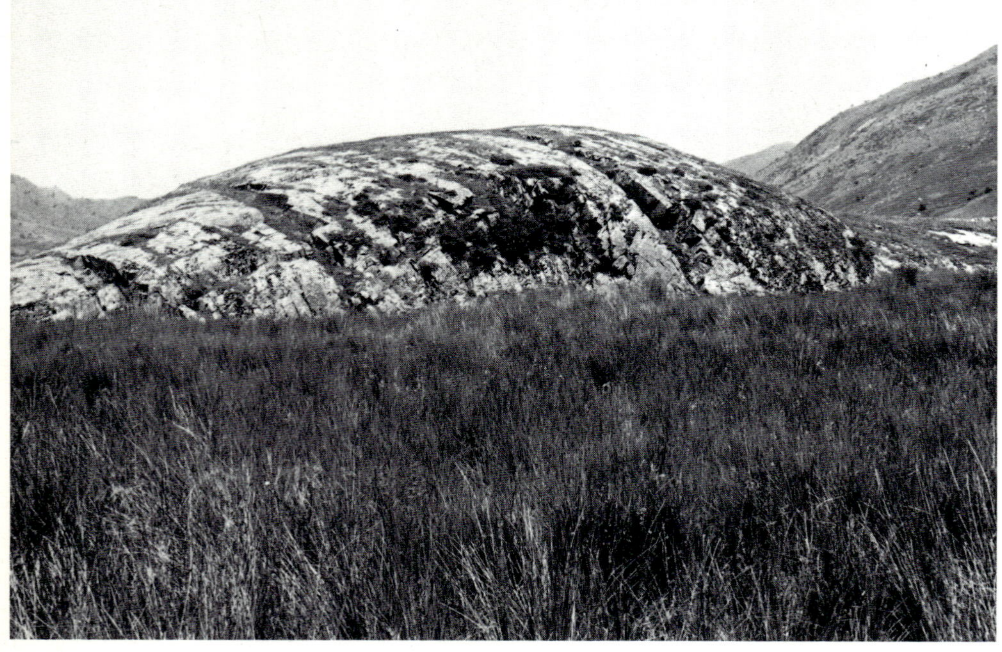

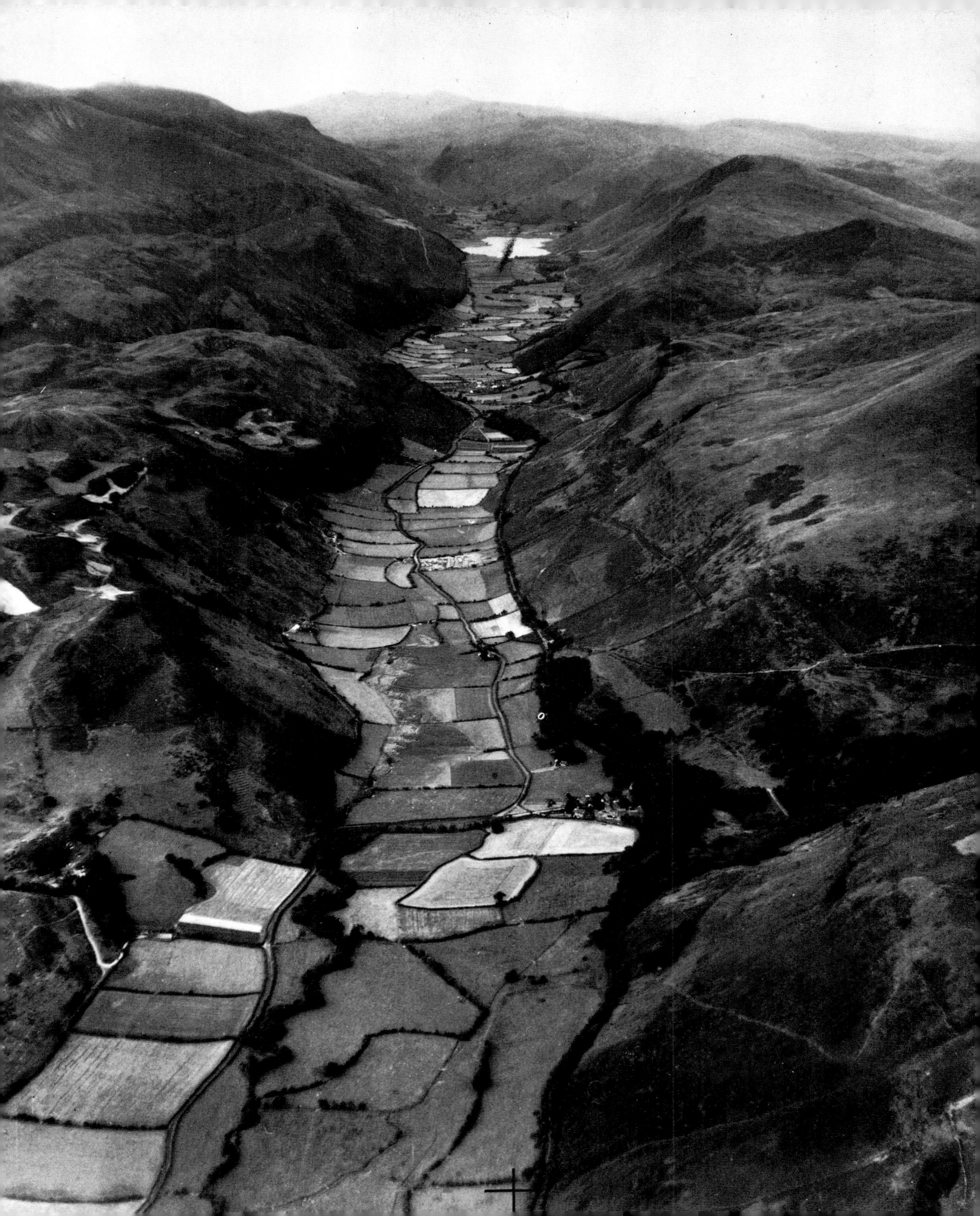

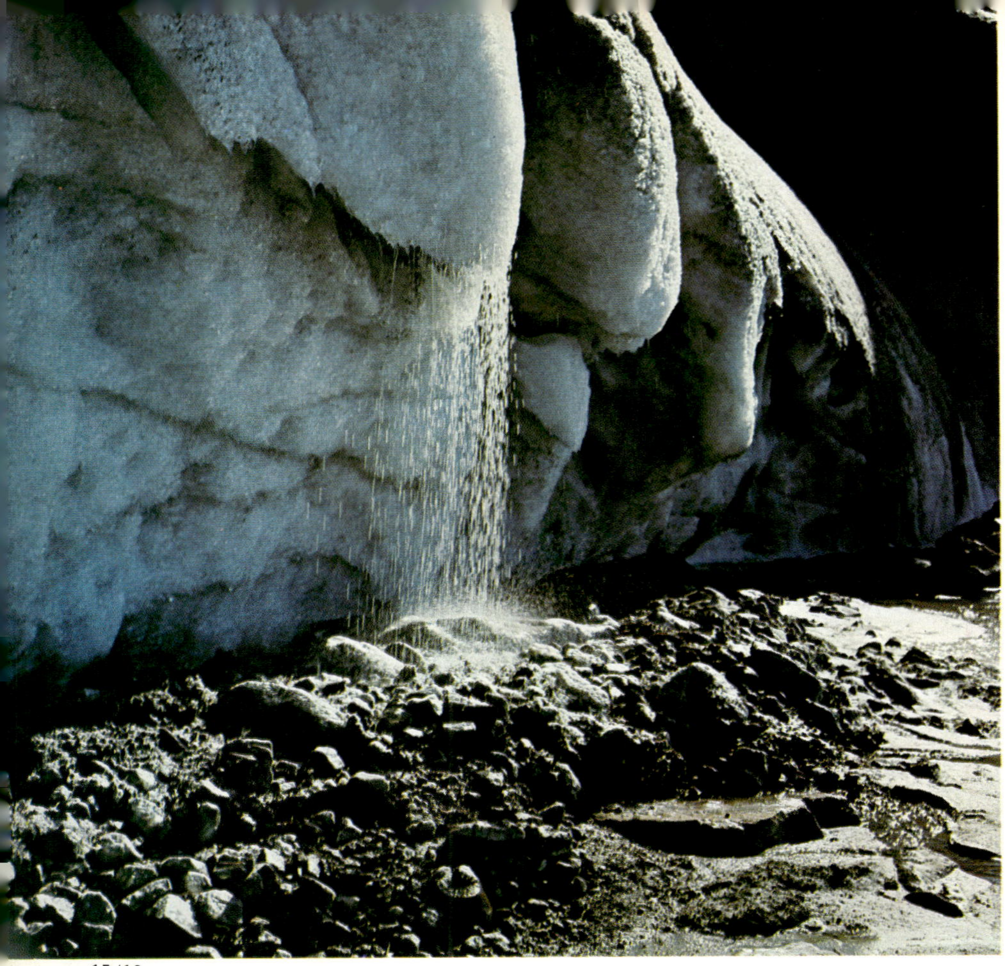

15/16

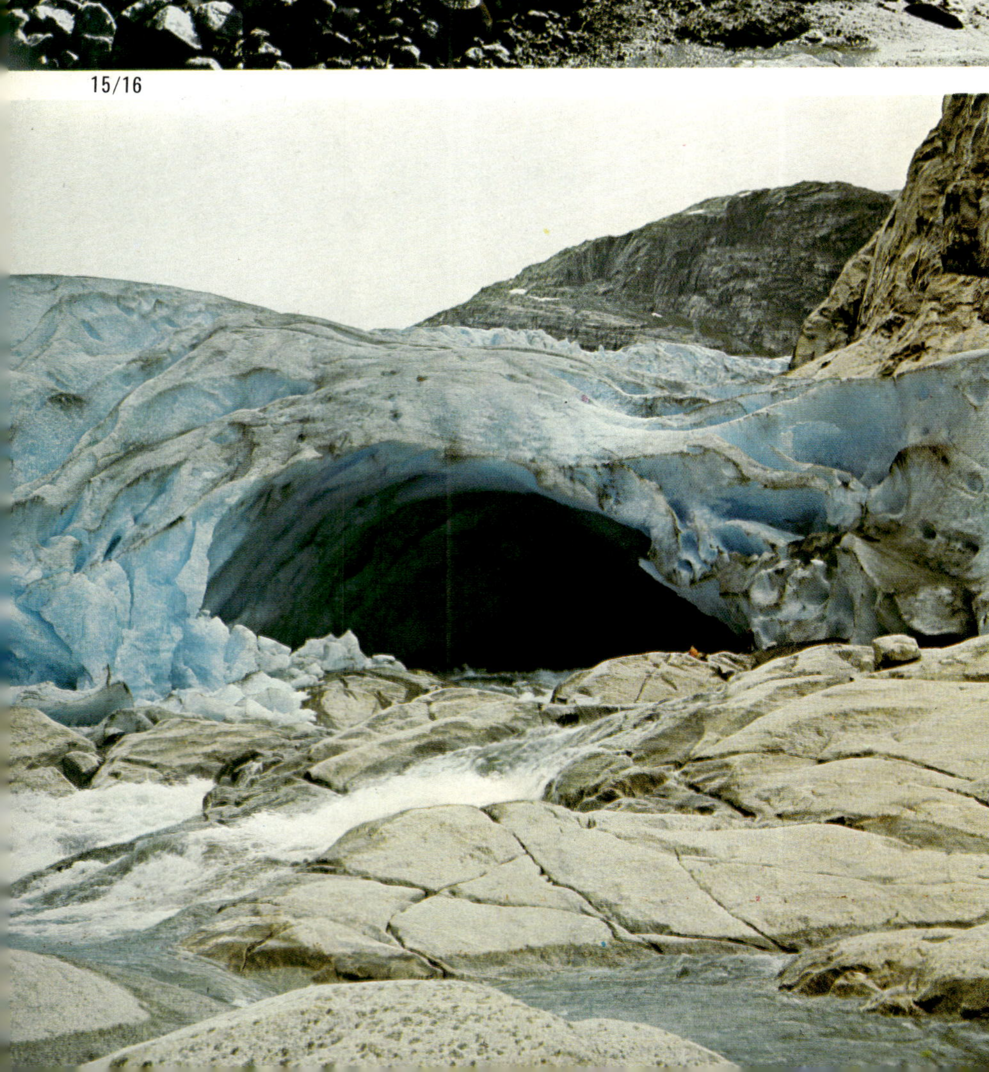

18

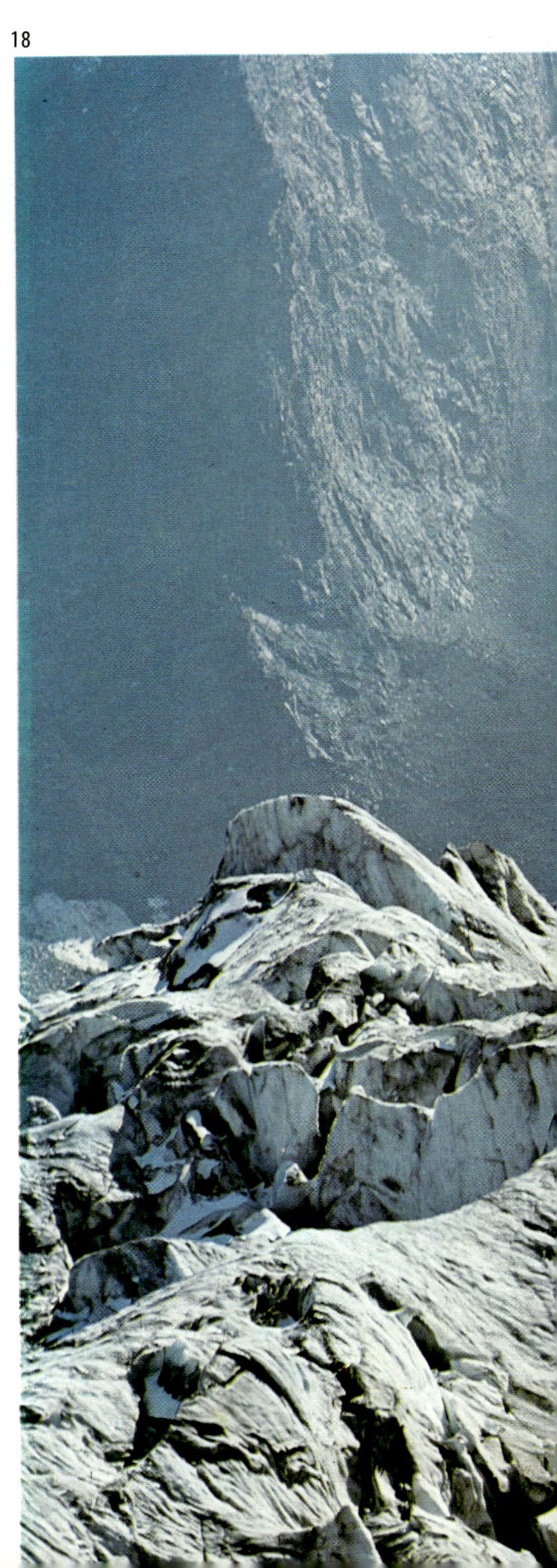

17

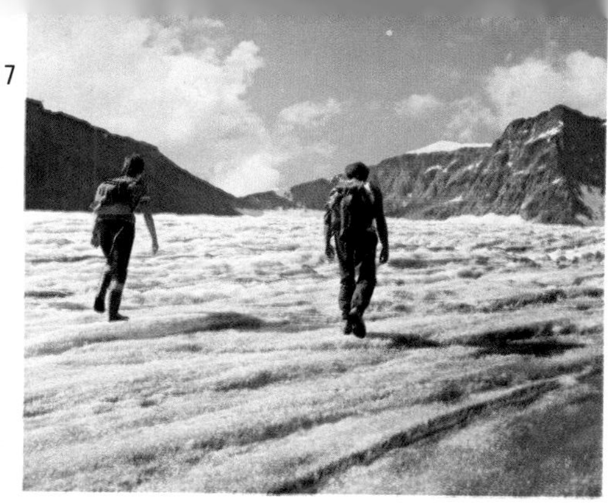

Composition, movement, and response to the climate are revealed in a glacier's surface. Under the sun's rays water cascades from the snout of an advancing Greenland glacier (15), while the cavern mouth of a sub-glacial stream in Norway (16) indicates a river of meltwater flowing beneath the surface. The streaked ice of Storglaciären (17) is caused by dirt blown from neighbouring mountains, with the darker ice tending to melt more rapidly, while the chaotic surface of an icefall on the Fee Glacier, Switzerland (18), caused by greatly increased flow velocity as the glacier descends a steep gradient, is made even rougher by the action of the sun.

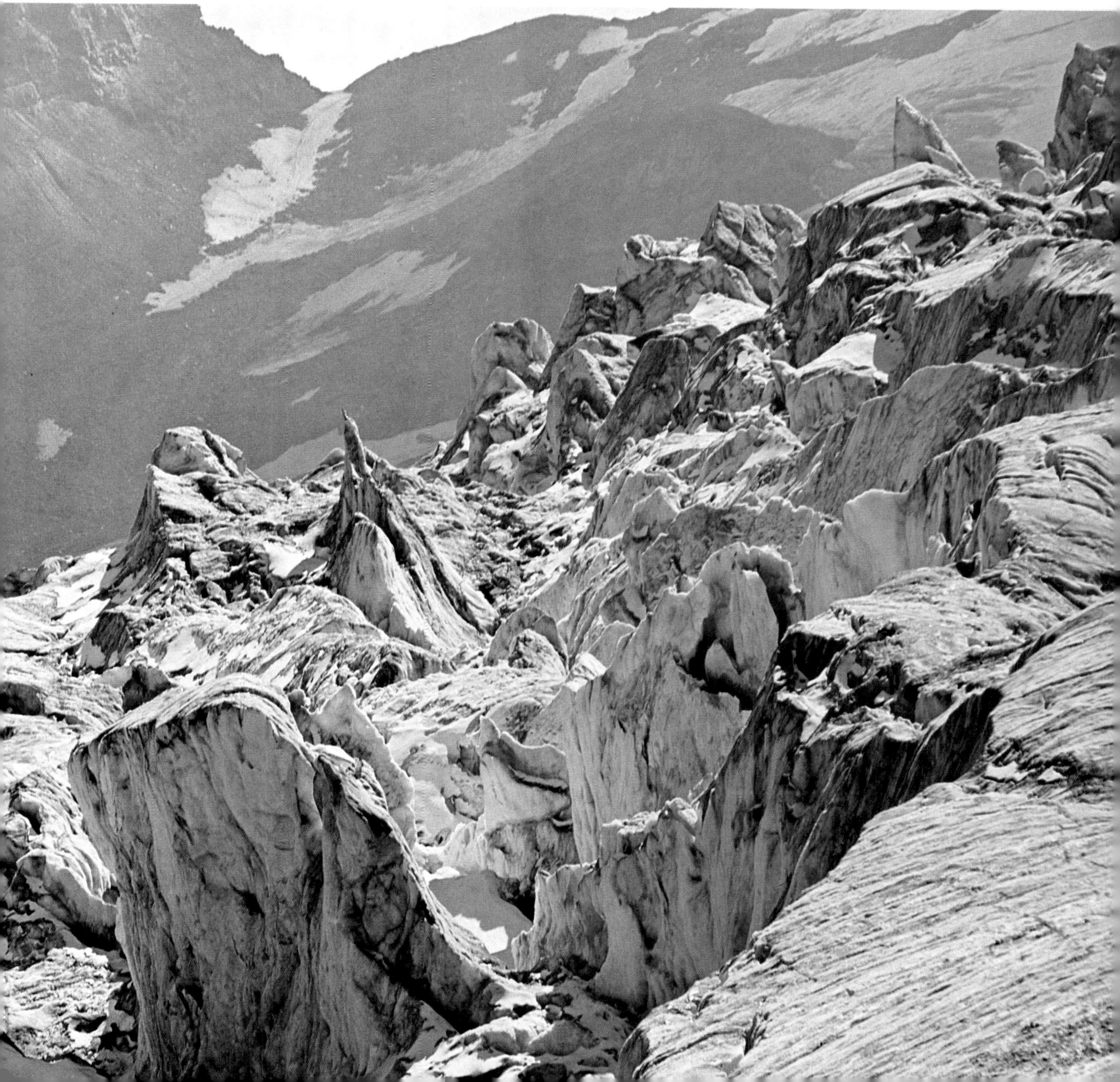

19

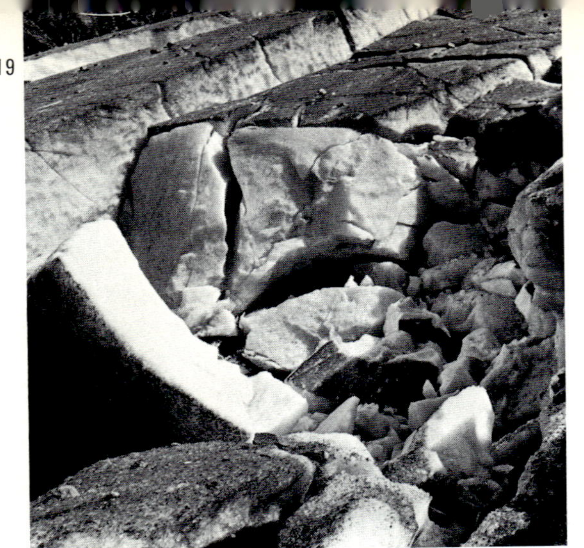

Sunshine splits the flowing ice of the glacier surface, creating a difficult landscape for the traveller. Dirty ice (19), absorbing radiation more quickly, melts first, and deep crevasses (20) present major obstacles. Fields of *nieve penitente* (21), so called because the pinnacle tips often droop like the heads of praying monks, can be hard on the feet though they are usually only a few centimetres high. Sun cups (22), caused by melt in the hollows and evaporation on the surface, look like shell craters in an Arctic battlefield. Antarctica's Lambert Glacier (23), the biggest in the world, runs every summer with huge slush rivers, tens of yards wide, ponding as they meet a higher surface.

20

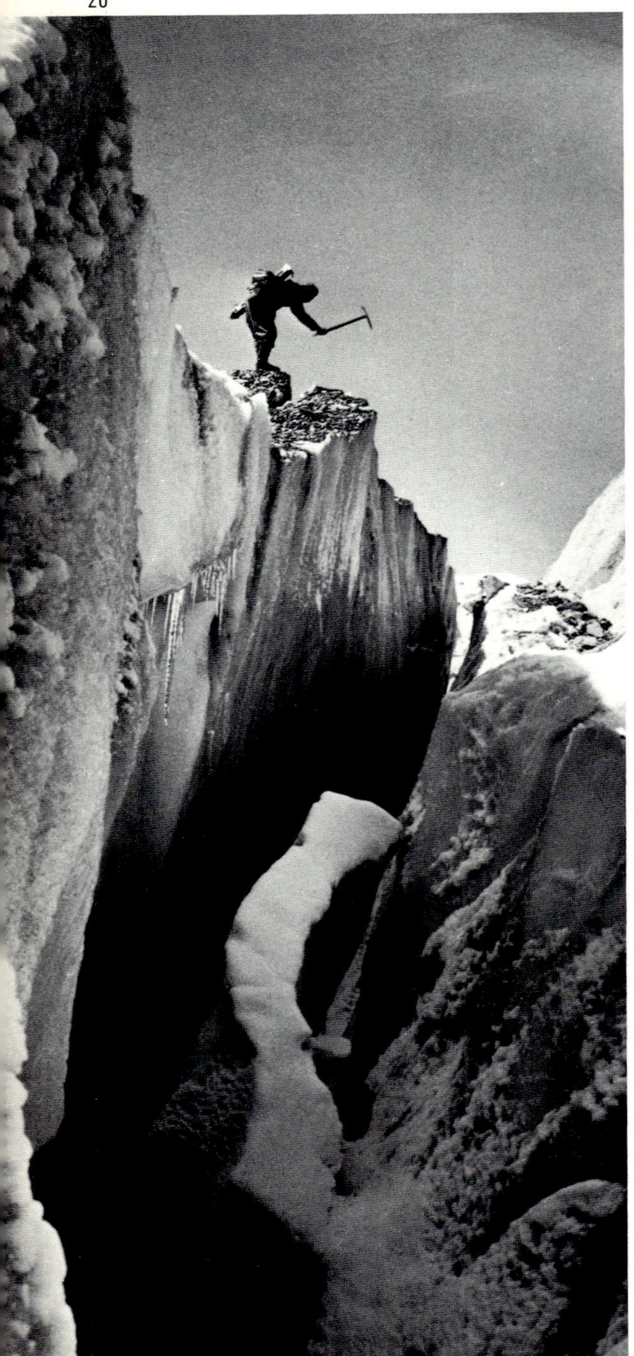

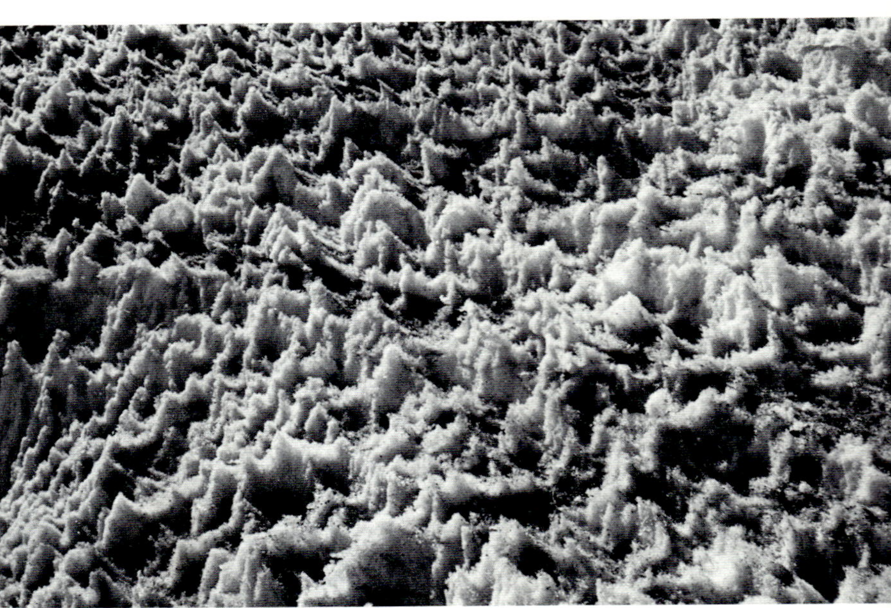

21/22

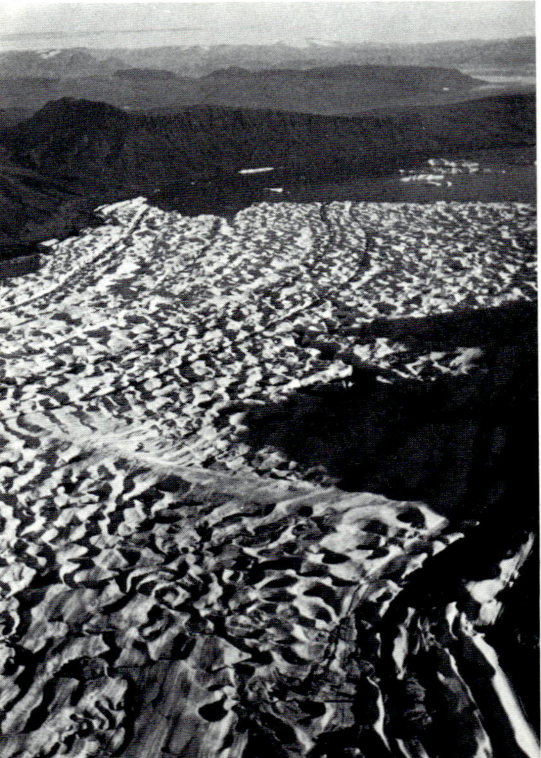

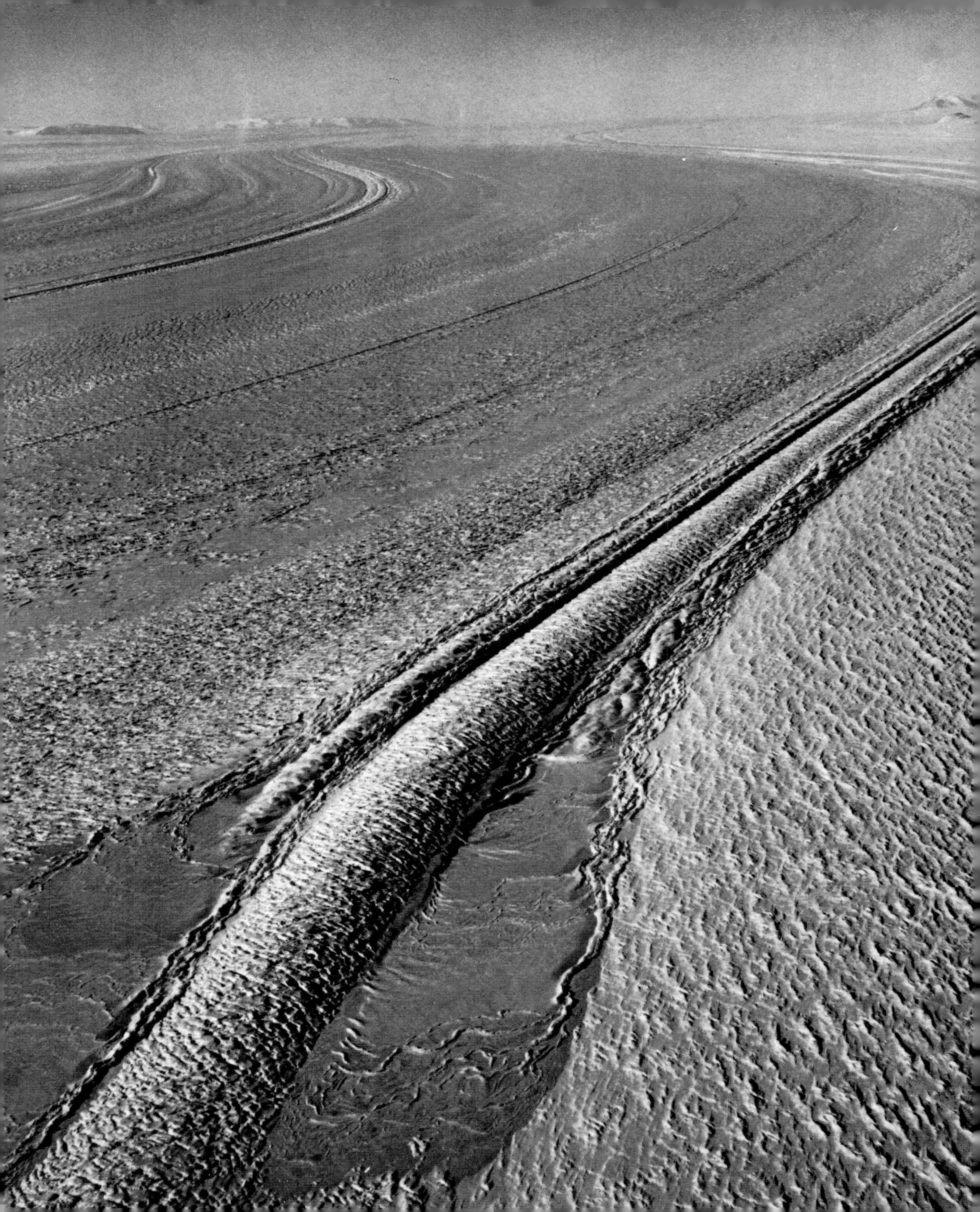

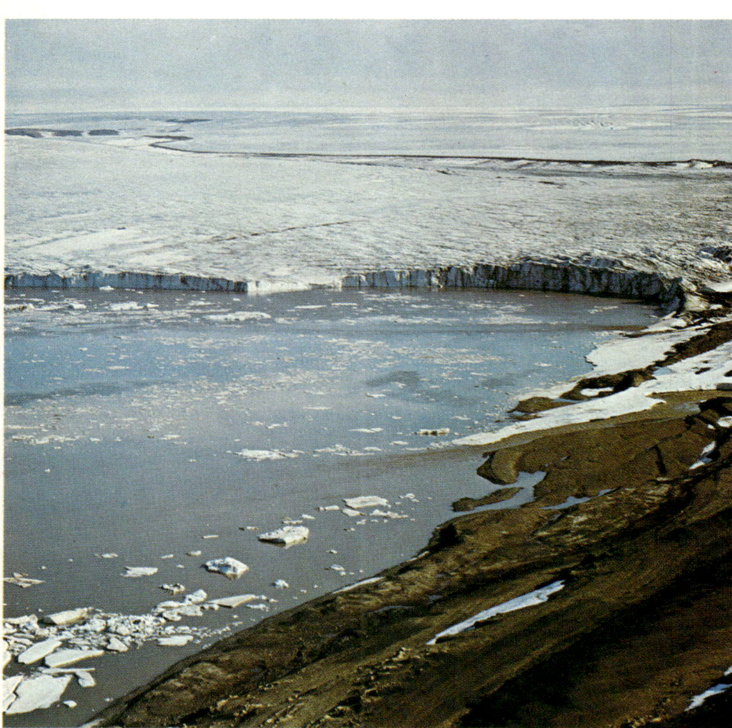

24

Glaciers give birth to icebergs when they reach the sea. A glacier at Spitsbergen (24) will 'calve' icebergs from its terminus as the ice extruded by glacier flow is eroded by water. The calving process releases huge bodies of ice, shown here actually falling from the Knik Glacier, Alaska (25, 26). Even vaster icebergs are caused by the crevassing of the Antarctic ice shelf (27), where the layers show the annual growth of the ice cap. The tabular iceberg thus formed (28) then floats out to sea. The largest, now being tracked by satellite, is about 45 × 20 miles in size and about 500,000 million tons in weight.

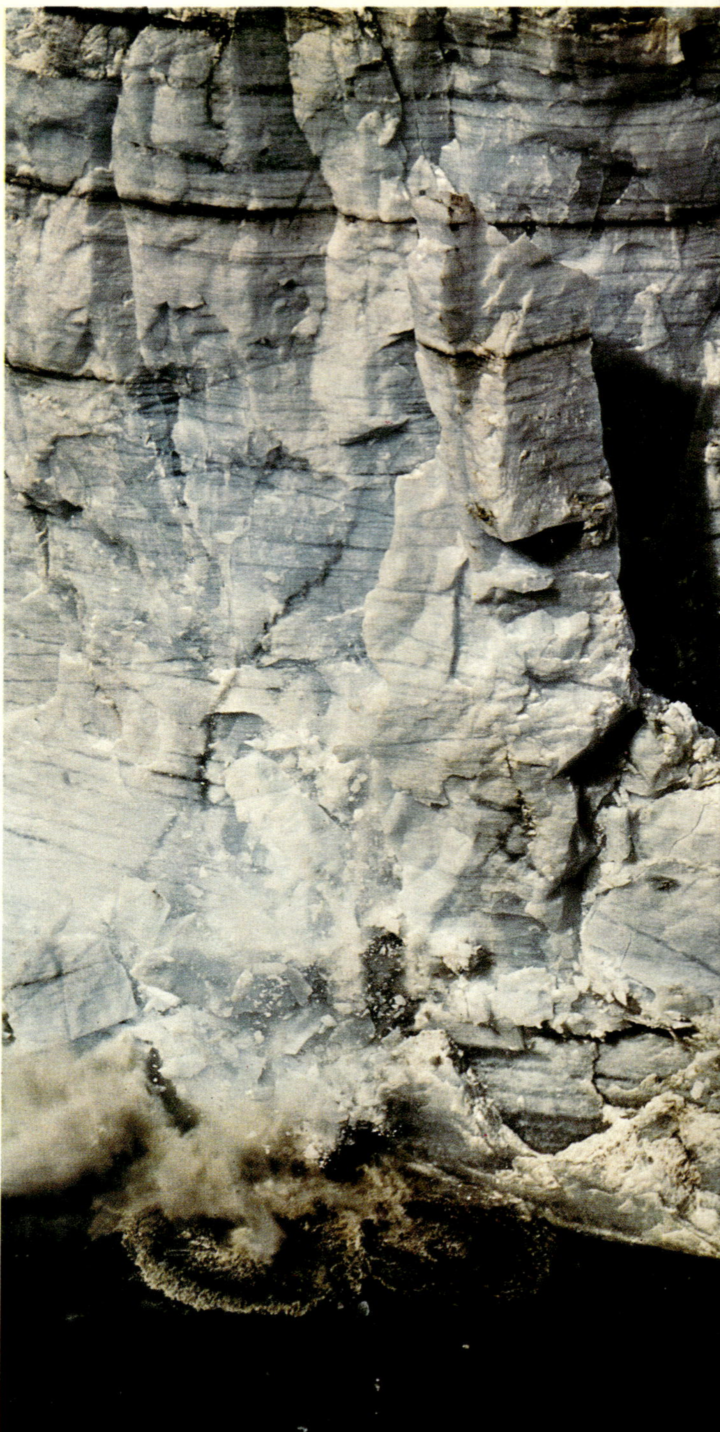

25

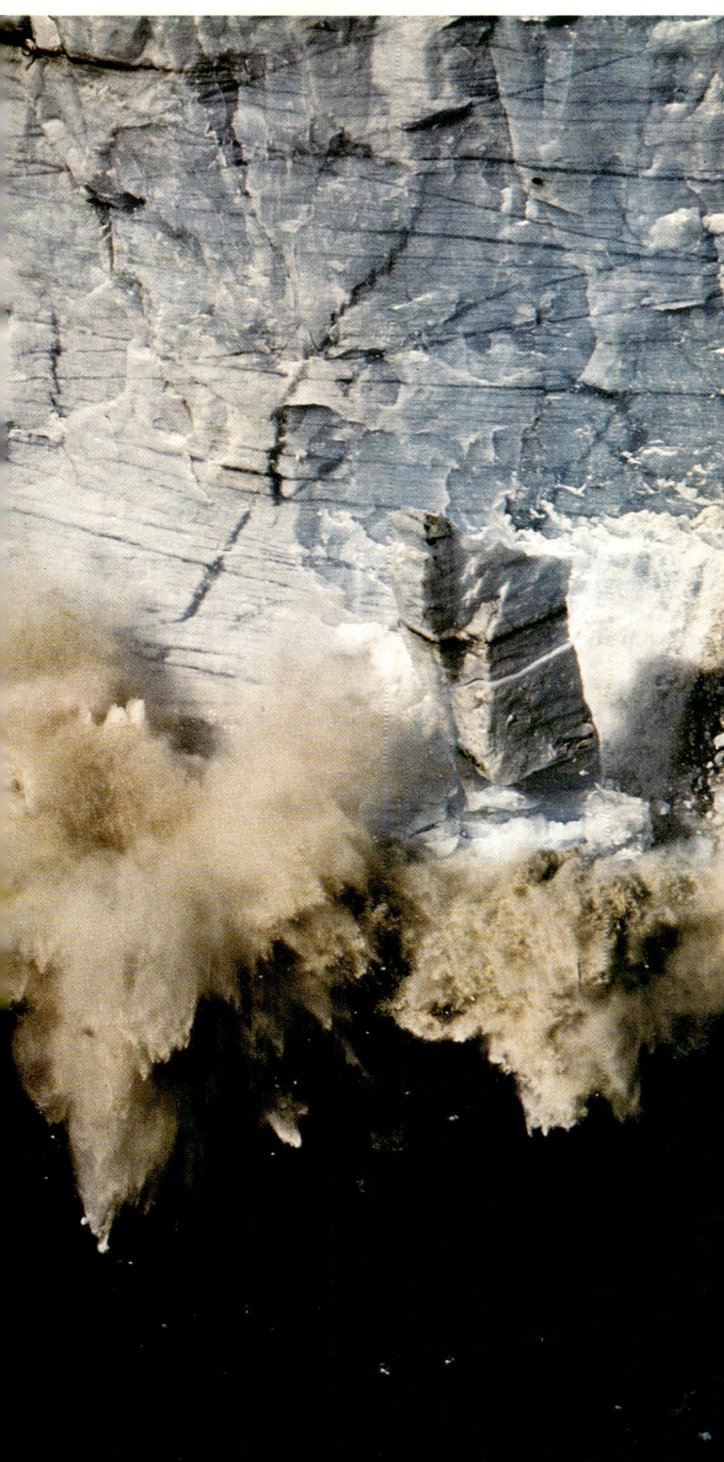

26

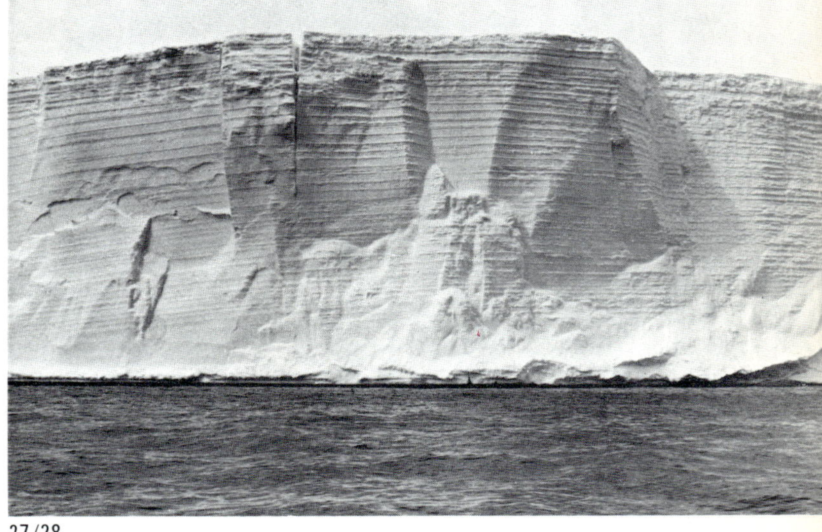

27/28

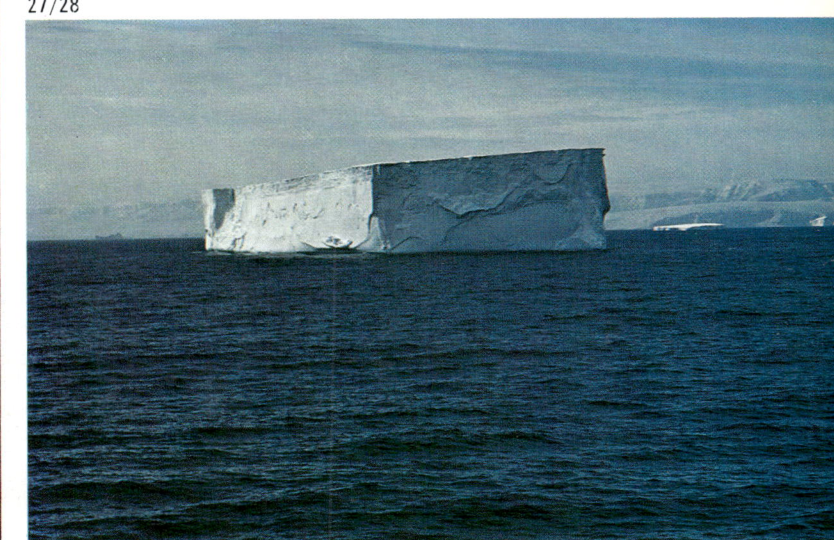

How to shift an iceberg. In December 1965 the approach route to the scientific station at McMurdo Sound, Antarctica, was blocked by a drifting iceberg $\frac{1}{4}$ mile long. This unusual picture shows three US icebreakers, *Burton Island*, *Atka* and *Glacier*, posted at 100-yard intervals, in the act of nudging the obstacle out of the way. But the redirecting of ice from the great polar ice sheets, where about 85 per cent of the world's fresh water resources are locked up, to places where there is chronic water shortage, is being seriously advocated by some experts. It is estimated that one purpose-built tug towing icebergs from Antarctica could turn 6,000 square miles of Australian desert into productive land – and keep it productive.

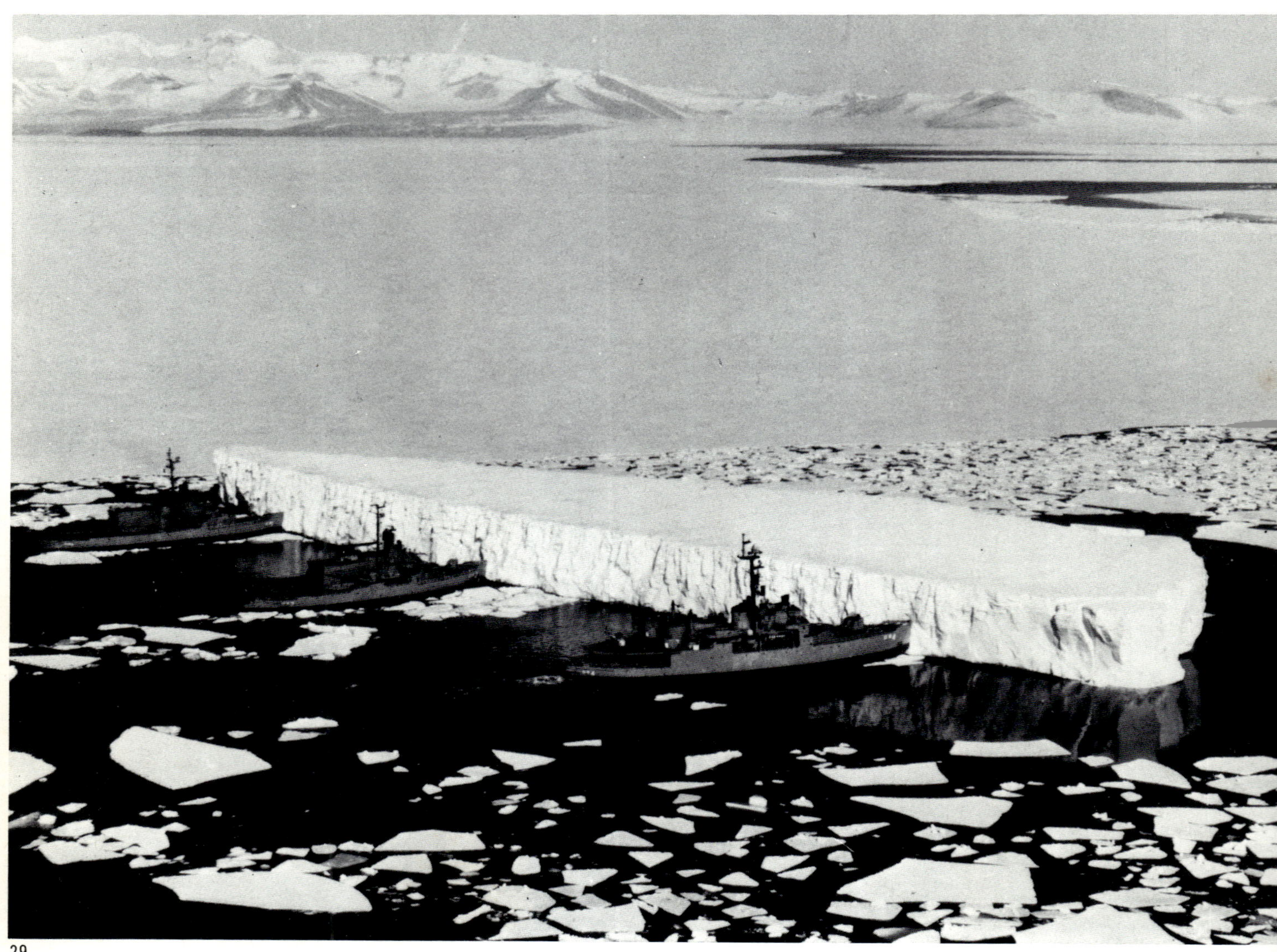

29

6

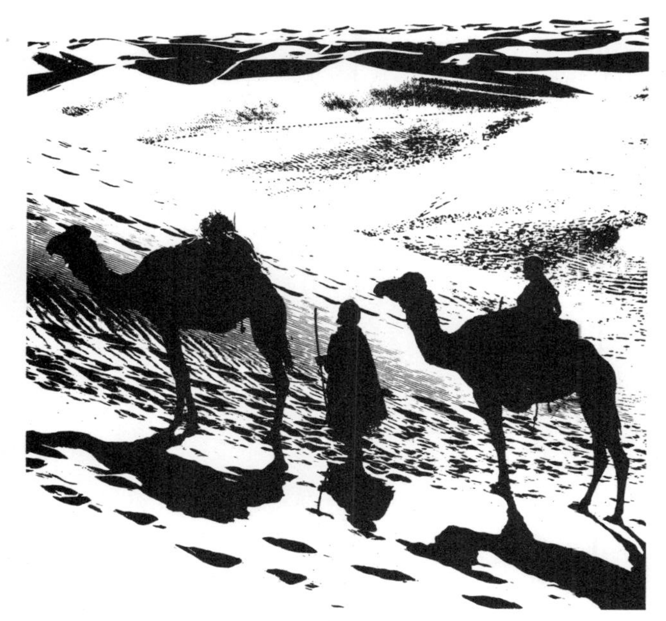

Deserts, drought and famine

A. H. Bunting
and
J. Elston

Desert and steppe regions have attracted travellers throughout history. Their records amply describe the extremes of heat and cold, the searing dry winds, and the bleak landscapes of flat sand, dunes and bare rock of the deserts themselves, and the vast plains of sparse grass and the arid hills of the surrounding steppe. Perhaps the most comprehensive view of deserts is that seen by the modern traveller by air. Flying south into the Sahara, he sees the dry southern slopes of the Atlas give place with dramatic suddenness to a flat terrain of rock, salt flats and sand, broken by great massifs of bare rock and arid mountains scored by the valleys and sand rivers eroded into them in the wetter periods of the remote past. For hundreds of miles the surface may be covered by loose material blown up into dunes from whose crests the wind lifts a haze of sand. Colours range from the near-black of sunbaked basaltic rock of ancient volcanoes and lava flows, through the bright reds to tawny and near-white. Apart from the blowing sand there is no movement. Even the oil wells with their perpetually burning flares of waste gas, or the isolated forts and airstrips seem deserted and alone in the hard and empty landscape. Here and there bright patches of green indicate an oasis. Onward to the south, small and scattered patches of cultivation begin to appear in the depressions, and slowly life returns. Scrub marks the valley bottoms, and at length, some 150 km north of Niamey and the Niger, cultivated land once again becomes characteristic of the landscape.

Perhaps the most striking feature of the Sahara is the great isolated massif of Tibesti in southern Libya and northern Chad, where in mountain terrain reaching up to nearly 3,000 metres there are cultivated fields and green woodlands, watered by mountain streams flowing down through the foothills only to evaporate in the burning sands of the surrounding desert.

The desert scene

There are ten major desert regions in the world. Four – the cold deserts – have hot summers and relatively cold winters; these are the deserts of western and south-western North America, Patagonia, Turkestan and the Gobi. The others, the Sahara, Namib-Kalahari, Arabian, Iranian (which includes the Thar), Atacama and Australian deserts, are hot, at least during the day, throughout the year. There are areas in Antarctica where little snow falls and the land surface is bare rock, but the primary reason why these valleys are deserted is because they are too cold for life, rather than that the water balance is unfavourable.

Deserts cover about five per cent of the land surface of the Earth. The largest of them, the Sahara of North Africa, is more than 5,000 km from east to west and up to 2,000 km north to south. It is about the size of the United States of America.

The map shows that deserts are distributed with a certain symmetry. Rain falls very unevenly over the Earth's surface, but all deserts lie in a band stretching from about five to forty-five degrees north and south of the equator. Close to the equator there is a region of heavy rainfall where some rain falls in every month and the mean precipitation is often two metres a year (sometimes very much more), which exceeds the total potential evaporation per year, so that many major rivers – the Amazon, Orinoco, Niger, Nile, Mekong and Salween – rise in or flow through these regions. This is the humid, tropic zone of evergreen forests. Then, often about ten degrees from the equator, comes a band of more moderate rainfall, often more than 1 m/y, with a distinct dry season. In this zone rainfall equals or exceeds evaporation during the rainy season, but during the dry season the total of potential evaporation is much greater than the quantity of excess water stored in the soil during the rains, so that the profile is dried by transpiration through the vegetation. This is the seasonally arid tropic zone of tree or scrub vegetation. Further from the equator the length of the season during which rainfall exceeds evaporation becomes shorter and shorter until, in the desert regions, evaporation exceeds rainfall throughout the year. Therefore as one moves away from the equator the vegetation is normally grass steppe, gradually becoming sparser until it grades into desert like the Sahara.

There is, of course, an underlying climatic mechanism for this more or less regular pattern of amount and distribution of rainfall – the so-called Hadley cell. At the equator the large receipt of solar radiation, much of it as bright sunshine and usually over the ocean, leads to a large rate of evaporation. Moist air is less dense than dry air and so it rises, forming an ascending column of humid air. As it rises the pressure becomes less and the air expands and cools. Consequently it becomes saturated with water vapour, so that clouds form leading to rain. These features determine the equatorial belt in which rainfall is large and fairly evenly distributed throughout the year.

The position of the sun relative to the Earth changes with the seasons. At the equinoxes it is directly overhead at noon on the equator. At the June solstice it is overhead at noon at the northern tropic, at the December solstice at the southern tropic. Thus the region of maximum receipt of solar radiation, the input of energy into this engine, moves north and south with the changing season. The equatorial belt of maximum rainfall is driven northwards as the sun 'moves' northwards and 'returns' to the south after the northern midsummer. This seasonal movement of the rain belt determines the seasonal distribution of rainfall, which in turn determines the climate and vegetation of the seasonally arid tropics.

The rising column of moist air at the meteorological equator does not continue to move away from the Earth's surface, for it is retained by gravity. Instead it divides into two streams which bend over and move towards the polar regions. Because water is lost by condensation from the thin cold air, it becomes drier and thus denser. Consequently the air descends in two regions of high barometric pressure to the north and south of the moving meteorological equator. The circulation cell is completed by a wind returning, closer to the surface of the Earth, to the region of low pressure at the meteorological equator. Because of the eastward rotation of the Earth these wind movements are not due north/south. Instead they trend westward so that the movement of air in the cell has a helical pattern. Moreover the pattern itself is complicated by numerous local rotating cells of high and low pressure, including large depressions as well as hurricanes and cyclones.

The regions of high pressure, with descending dry air, lie roughly between 15°–20° and 35° of latitude from the equator. These are not exact bands around the world because the simple Hadley pattern (which describes reasonably well the Sahara and the situation in northern

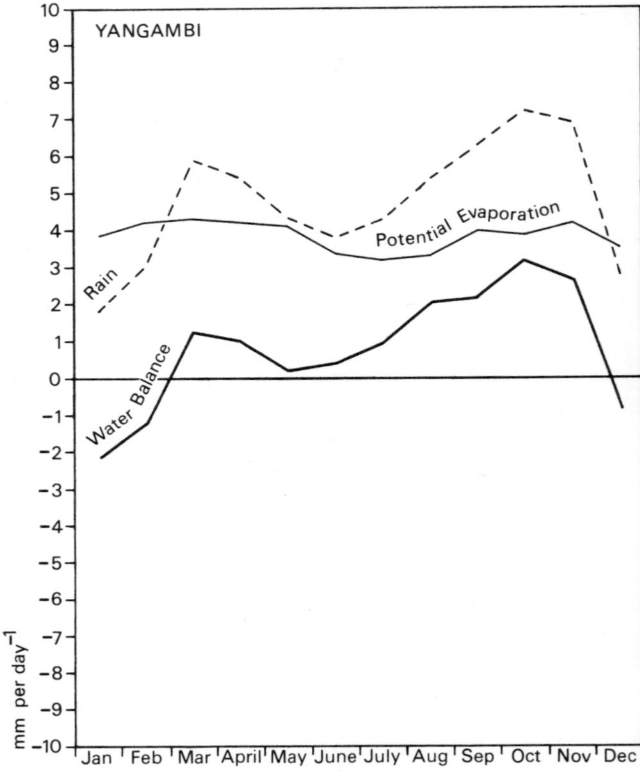

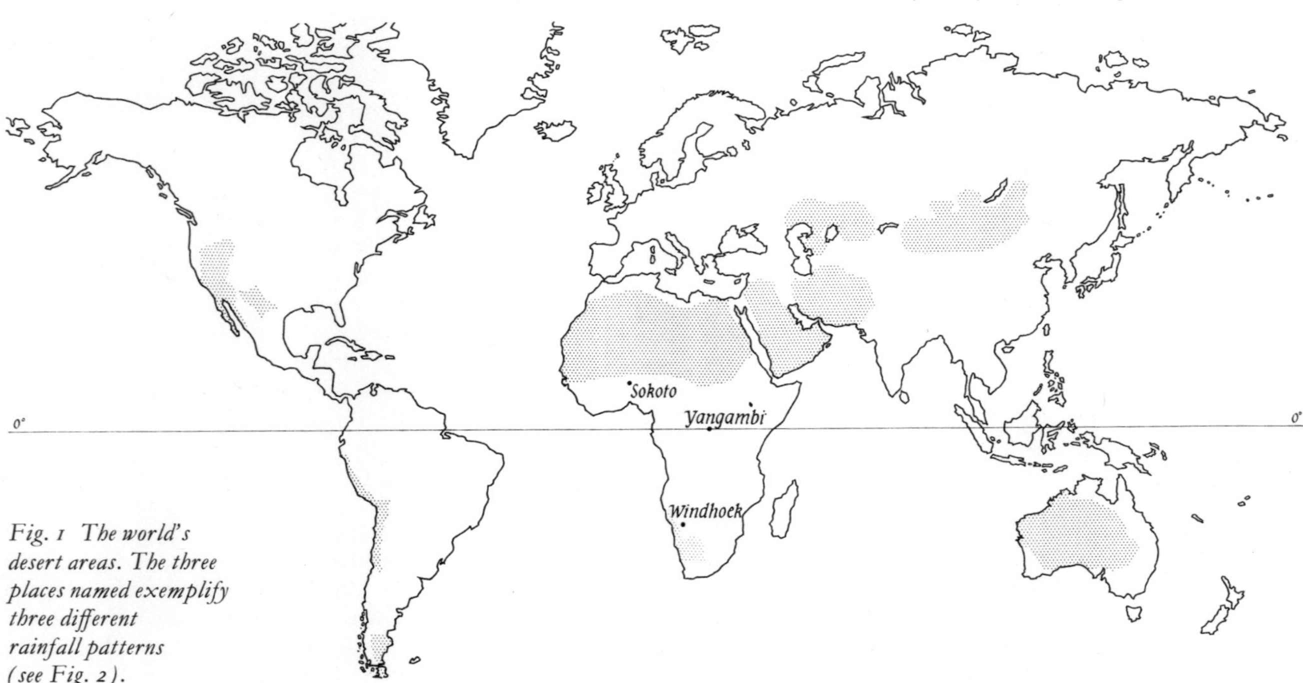

Fig. 1 The world's desert areas. The three places named exemplify three different rainfall patterns (see Fig. 2).

Fig. 2 The water balance, month by month, at Yangambi in Zaïre (humid in most months), Sokoto in Nigeria (seasonally dry), and Windhoek near the Namib desert.

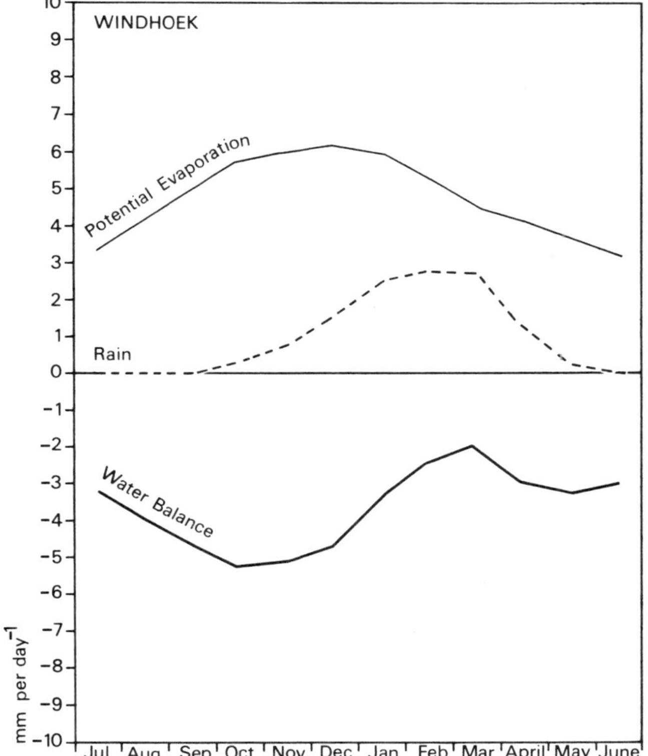

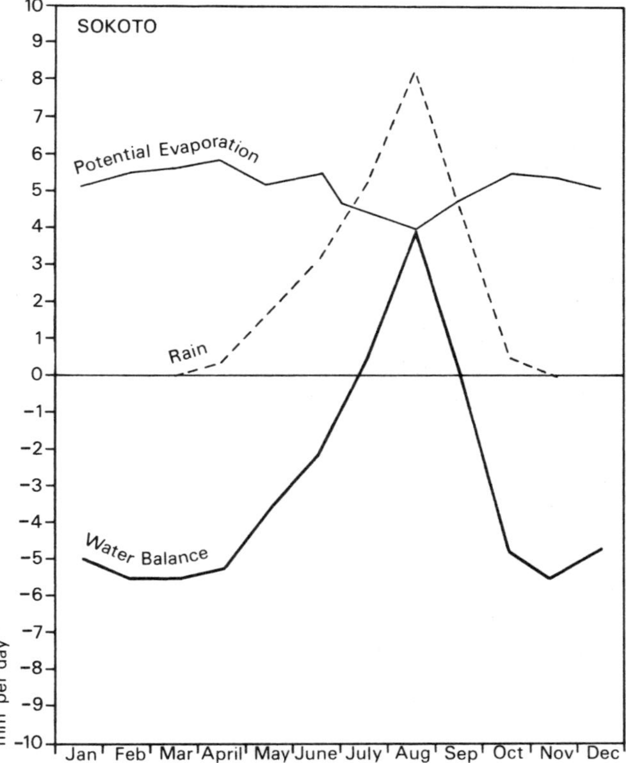

Africa and western Asia) is modified by the relative distribution of land and sea and by topography. In particular, regions far from the sea may be dry because initially moist air moving inland has lost as rainfall most of the water it contains before it reaches them – especially if a mountain range lies in the way. This 'rain shadow' effect helps to account for the dryness of parts of the Gobi desert, the Kalahari, and the dry parts of the United States east of the Rocky Mountains. The Patagonian desert along the western seaboard of South America extends further south than the comparable Kalahari desert on the west side of Africa because the warm current which moves towards Antarctica on the west side of the South Atlantic pushes the climatic zone southwards. Southern Africa is too broad to allow the corresponding Indian Ocean currents to affect the circulation of the atmosphere in the eastern part of the South Atlantic.

The desert of southern California and north-west Mexico is rather special. Here the air, caught between the sea and the mountains, is much moister than it is over other deserts, but the usual causes of rainfall are absent. Pressure is high, and so the air does not ascend and cool; it is relatively clean and there are no violent atmospheric disturbances. As a

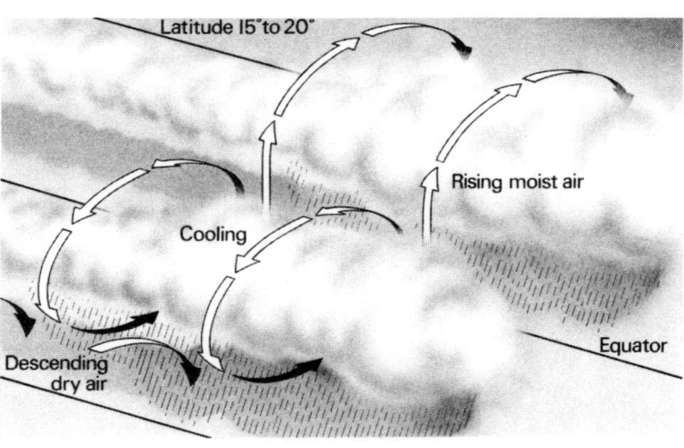

Fig. 3 The Hadley cell. This is a simplified diagram, taking no account of the complications introduced by the Earth's rotation.

Fig. 4 Artesian well, drilled into a sloping aquifer or water-bearing stratum.

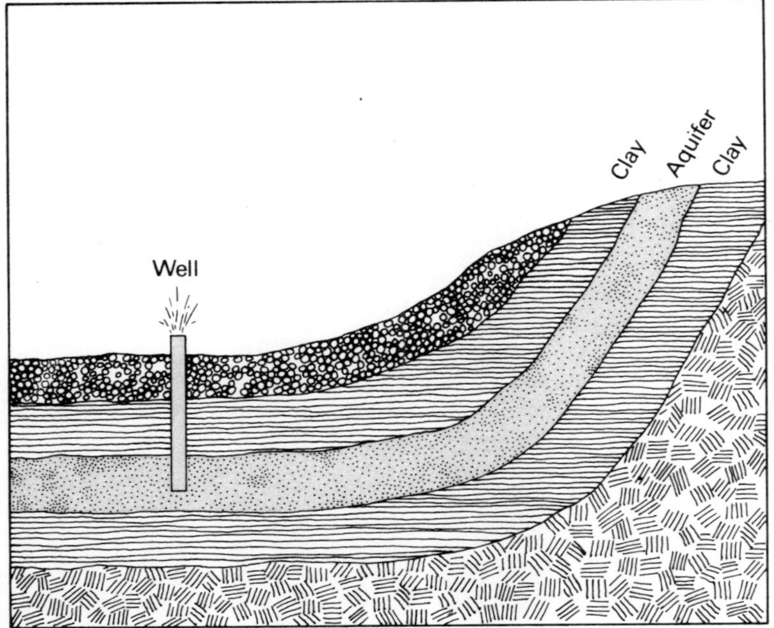

result much of the scanty precipitation is in the form of fog which is converted, in the more northerly industrial and urban areas, into smog by atmospheric pollutants.

We do not understand the reason why the desert valleys of Antarctica are so dry. It may be that the air flowing down them becomes compressed as it descends, and is consequently slightly warmer, evaporating the snow before it reaches the ground or perhaps preventing snow from falling by evaporating water from the clouds themselves.

The seasonally arid regions merge imperceptibly into the hot deserts. This means that the margins of deserts are difficult to define and so to map. Hence our map may differ a little from maps drawn by others – one man's desert may well be another's grass steppe.

Water – above and below ground

Few deserts are totally rainless, and around their margins rainfall may increase over relatively short distances. At Bilma, towards the centre of the Sahara, mean rainfall is only 2 cm a year, and for several years in succession there may be no rain at all; while the average annual rainfall at Khartoum, about 80 km south of the Bayuda desert, is 16 cm and some rain falls each year.

The pattern of rainfall is extremely erratic in both space and time. Much of the rain in desert climates falls in very localized thunderstorms, often of extreme violence, so that flash floods may occur in depressions and ancient water courses. This intense rainfall leads to considerable erosion and may move boulders together with great quantities of sand and stones. At Petra in Jordan, a sudden quite unexpected storm in 1963 killed twenty-three French visitors and their guide and driver as they went up a *wadi* to see the ancient town. Both the total rain per year, and its distribution within the year, become more and more variable as the mean rainfall decreases.

While the surface soils of deserts are usually dry, the subsoil may be seasonally moist, and there may even be a permanent water table quite near the surface. Where the roots of plants are able to reach this water, vegetation will grow vigorously in the brilliant light and warm air of a desert – such places are the oases. Beneath the Sahara there are immense quantities of underground water which is apparently flowing slowly outwards. Much of it is 'fossil water' laid down many thousands of years ago when the climate was very much wetter. Water 25,000 years old, accumulated in a pluvial period, has been found beneath the Western desert in Egypt. It is not a renewable source but that part of the underground store which is occasionally recharged from current rainfall is renewable, and can be freely used at the average rate of recharge. The houses of the ancient settlements, and the palms, vegetables and grass make many oases green islands in a grey-brown sea of sand and rock which are remarkably attractive, even though the water is often polluted and the flies numerous and persistent.

In places the ground water, new and old, flowing from higher ground through permeable strata, is confined by sloping beds of impermeable rocks above and below, so that it is under pressure at the lower levels. In such a situation artesian wells yield water without pumping. Artesian water is very important in Australia and parts of southern Africa, where it is often used to water grazing animals in the grasslands around the deserts. It is also used for irrigation schemes within deserts. However, unless artesian water is continuously recharged (which is usually possible only where a wetter region lies close to a desert margin) the pressure forcing it out falls as it is used. Even where more water can be obtained cheaply by pumping, fossil artesian water cannot last indefinitely. In some valleys of the Californian desert artesian ground water formerly used for irrigation has already been exhausted.

Water draining into deserts from wetter regions or from local rainfall often evaporates completely, depositing any salts dissolved in it. In large internal drainage basins like that of Lake Chad the water is often brackish; sometimes it is extremely saline, as in the Danakil portion of the East

African rift in Ethiopia and the Dead Sea depression in its northern extension in Israel and Jordan; both of these are below sea level.

Unlike the soils of more humid areas, those of desert regions are seldom or never leached by rain. Many therefore tend to be saline. The accumulation of salt is a particularly serious problem in irrigation schemes, and many medieval irrigation areas in the Euphrates basin and other parts of the Middle East had to be abandoned for this reason. Nearly half of the great modern irrigated tract in the deserts of Pakistani Punjab is already affected by salinity to some degree, and some of the land is now too salt for cultivation. It has been suggested that as much as 20,000 hectares of irrigated land in the Indian subcontinent are lost per year for this reason.

Extremes of heat and cold

After its dryness, the temperature regime is the next climatic feature that impresses a newcomer to the desert. Extreme heat during the day alternates with cold, often intense, at night. This is a consequence of the water regime.

In more humid regions clouds partly shield the Earth from the sun's rays, and vegetation reflects a substantial part of the energy which reaches the surface. Most of the retained energy is used to provide the latent heat of evaporation of water from liquid to gas in the leaves of plants. On the other hand, in deserts the skies are cloudless and most of the solar energy reaches the ground. Little radiation is reflected unless the surface is very light in colour, and little or no energy is absorbed as latent heat. Hence most of the energy is available to heat the surface and the air adjacent to it. As a result of all this the climates of the hot deserts are among the warmest in the world.

The hottest screen temperature recorded in the *Guinness Book of Records* is 58°C at al'Aziziyah in Libya on 13 September 1922. The surface of the ground, where the change from radiant energy to sensible heat occurs, becomes far warmer than the air. A surface temperature of 82.5°C was measured by Cloudsley-Thompson in the Red Sea Hills, Sudan, when the air temperature in the open was no more than about 42°C. However, the temperature of the soil decreases with depth so, for example, the temperatures in the underground burrows of animals are much cooler than those of the air and soil surface during the day.

At night both the surface and the air cool rapidly, losing heat through the cloudless skies by long-wave radiation to the intense cold of outer space. Thus nights are cold and frost is not uncommon. At Wadi Halfa the warmest temperature ever recorded in a meteorological screen was 52.5°C and the coldest −2.5°C. The contrast in temperature between night and day is greater than in many other parts of the world. Temperature falls very sharply at sunset, and warm clothes are necessary at night for the desert traveller.

The maximum amount of water vapour that air can hold depends upon temperature, and increases sharply as the temperature rises. The relative humidity is the ratio of the amount of water vapour actually present in the air to the maximum amount that the air could hold at the same temperature. Since day temperatures in desert climates are very warm, daytime relative humidities are very small, even though the absolute quantity of water in the atmosphere is often much the same as in more humid but cooler places. The combination of very warm temperatures and very small humidities leads to large rates of potential evaporation of any liquid which may be present in plants or animals, or received from sporadic rainfall. The effect is still further increased by the action of wind. But as the temperature falls after sunset, the air may become cool enough to be saturated by the water it contains and dew may fall, though seldom enough to have any significant effect on the life of living things.

The wind and the sand

The hot deserts are high-pressure regions, so winds blow from deserts outwards towards the poles and the equator. These winds are dry and often very dusty. The *harmattan*, the cold north winter wind from the Sahara, can clothe the country in dust and obscure the sun as far south as Ibadan or Lagos. When it blows, aircraft are often unable to land at Kano, and outbreaks of meningitis (a dust-borne disease) sometimes occur near Lake Chad. The *sirocco* of the African coast is a similar wind but extremely hot.

The intense heating of the ground, and the air in contact with it, often produces ascending and rotating columns of air in which dust may be dragged upwards in a vortex with a relatively quiet centre. Small columns of this sort are known as 'dust devils'. On a larger scale the vortices may not be so sharply defined, but the motion is no less violent; these form the *haboobs* of northern Sudan, in which great quantities of dust are carried high into the air. The heat, the powerful motion and the dust may be intensely frightening, even to the experienced desert traveller. Dust devils and *haboobs* commonly occur in the early afternoon when the ground is hottest.

Deserts form over a great variety of geological formations, and all exposed rocks are liable to be affected by wind erosion. The continuous and often very rapid motion of the air carrying particles of dust sculpts the exposed rock, and the resulting fantastic shapes, colours and patterns frequently give great beauty to desert landscapes.

Erosion may be aided by the action of temperature extremes between day and night, since extreme heating and cooling of rock surfaces leads to a more marked alternation of expansion and contraction in the outer than in the inner layers. Any liquid water present, if it freezes and therefore expands, adds to the mechanical effects of the temperature variations, and carbon dioxide dissolved in it may assist by chemical action. The resulting strains and stresses fracture all but the hardest rock, and a characteristic onion-like pattern of layers is often formed. Eventually these processes of mechanical erosion break down the softer rocks into sand. When the rock is very hard, or in the cooler deserts, erosion may be incomplete and the desert becomes covered by a stony surface. Indeed, surfaces covered by stone and rock debris are much commoner than loose sand and dunes.

In deserts the sand particles have a characteristic angular form, and though they vary in size from place to place they are often more or less uniform in one area. The wind sweeps the particles into dunes, those of a crescent shape (*barchans*) being formed where the sand does not cover all the ground and the wind is more or less constant in direction. These dunes lie with their gently sloping backs, which are usually not smooth but patterned into ripples, facing the wind and their leading edges swept forward in a curve with a steep forward slope. The whole dune advances slowly as the sand is moved by the wind up the back and over the edge. *Barchans* usually lie in belts along the prevailing wind; the largest examples may be 400 m long and 30 m high.

Dunes of a second type, *seif* dunes, are long ridges of sand, extending roughly parallel to the prevailing winds, sometimes narrow but often a few hundred metres wide; they may be of immense length and age. The biggest may be hundreds of kilometres long and 150 m high. Among the best-known systems are the fixed and often cultivated *qoz* dunes of Kordofan, at least some of which are continuous with bare *seif* dunes which extend far up into the desert to the north.

Where strong winds blow, sand is sucked into the air by frictional drag between the moving air and the sand surface. The grains ascend steeply, reaching speeds close to that of the wind, perhaps a few metres per second. They then follow a long, even, falling trajectory towards the ground. Small particles of dust remain longer in the air sustained by turbulence, but larger particles descend more rapidly. When they strike the ground they may bounce back or 'splash' up a few other grains so that the wind sweeps them along more easily. Thus there is a continual movement, dust held in the air, larger grains riding the wind for shorter or longer distances, and large grains creeping along the surface aided by the impact of those descending. These movements form an unstable flat bed of sand so that waves form naturally, varying from small ripples to larger transverse *barchans* of all sizes.

Where the wind rolls or twists helically about a horizontal axis parallel to its direction of movement it will tend to sweep up the loose sand into a ridge parallel to its own direction. Two parallel 'horizontal roll vortices' working together could form a *seif* dune. Such vortices have been observed, and they offer the most plausible explanation we have of these remarkable features.

Water and life

Virtually all life on earth depends on primary production by green plants and this, in turn, depends among other things on water. In terrestrial environments the movement of carbon dioxide into a green plant through the stomata, which is the starting point of primary production, is inevitably associated with the outward movement of water evaporated from the wet cell surfaces of the cavities below the stomata. Land plants have evolved a complex but precarious compromise which allows them to assimilate carbon dioxide as rapidly as they can without losing water faster than it can be replaced by inward movement from the soil or other parts of the environment, and so drying out. The life, growth and development of vegetation depend on this compromise. The more complete the security against water shortage, the smaller the potential rate of growth; the greater the potential rate of growth, the greater the risk of damage or death by dehydration. Only within very strict limits can land plants have it both ways.

Animals in dry regions have even more complex problems. As secondary producers they depend on green plants. They too have to exchange gases with the atmosphere in breathing, so also run the risk of dehydration. They depend on water to remove potentially harmful byproducts of metabolism from their bodies. Moreover, because they exchange heat energy less efficiently than plants can, they are generally far more sensitive to high external temperatures.

The essential features of water in plant communities, and in the animal communities which depend on them, can be represented in ecological terms as a series of flows and balances. In an assimilating plant community water is moving continuously. Over the year water enters the system as precipitation, sometimes as mist, fog or snow (which is particularly important in the continental USA and USSR), but mostly, in the warm desert climates, as rain. Some of this runs away over the surface into streams, rivers

Fig. 5 The water cycle: an endlessly circulating system in which all water returns eventually to the sea and re-enters the system from there.

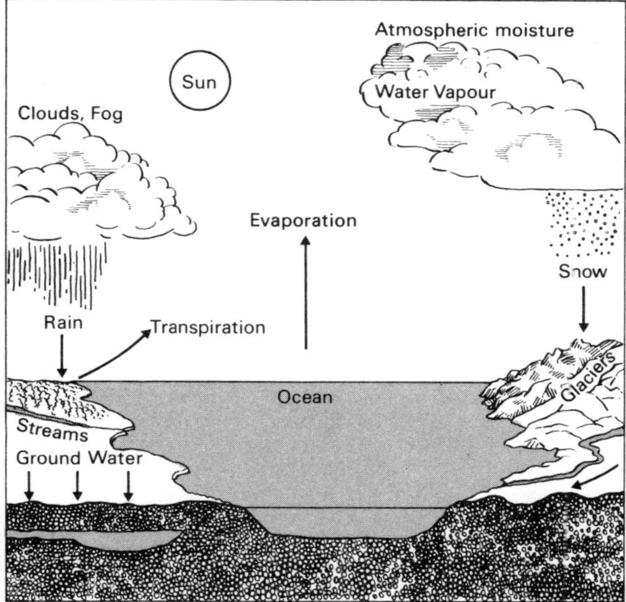

and lakes, and so ultimately to the sea, while some enters the soil. If the upper part of the soil, which contains the roots, is already wet, water drains through until it meets a water table or an impermeable layer. If it is not wet, water will be stored in the soil until it is wetted to its full capacity (which varies substantially from soil to soil, least in sands, most in clays and fen soils) to hold water against drainage. Only when this state has been reached will further receipts of water lead to drainage.

Water from the soil enters plants, and moves through them to the leaves and out into the atmosphere, by purely physical processes. Essentially we can think of vegetation as a sort of green wick through which more or less free water in the wet soil evaporates into the much drier air. The water evaporated from plants, animals, exposed water surfaces and wet soils moves away in the atmosphere, and eventually condenses somewhere as rain or snow.

The ultimate fate of much of the condensed water, and the ultimate source of much of the precipitation, are both in the sea. The exchanges of energy and water vapour at the surface of the oceans both charge and drive the hydrological cycle as a whole.

The potential rate at which water can evaporate from the leaves of a plant or from a vegetation-covered surface depends on, and can be estimated from, the temperature, the supply of energy available to provide the latent heat of evaporation, and the dryness and rate of movement of the ambient air. However, the soil and the vegetation offer a series of resistances to the flow of water, and these vary with the water content of the soil and plants. If ample water is available for evaporation, the total resistance is small. Then the rate of its use depends solely on the environment and approaches the potential rate. On the other hand, if water is in short supply, the resistances in the soil and the plants (whose stomata tend to close) may be sufficient to halt water loss. These water balances depend on the weather, and in desert regions they are unfavourable not only for growth but even for survival itself.

Adapting to life in the desert

In all but the most extreme arid areas various plants and animals are able to live and reproduce by means of special adaptations. In plants, which are stationary, three such adaptations are found – in life-history, in structure and in physiology. Animals, which can move, have a fourth possibility – adaptations in behaviour.

Most wild vegetation in the world is dominated by perennial plants. Many perennials grow larger than annuals and can form communities largely closed to annuals, which are then forced into a subordinate status. In desert regions, however, perennials are often at such a disadvantage that they cannot do this. Instead, many of the plants are ephemerals which pass the adverse periods as seeds. These germinate rapidly after a shower of rain, soon flower, set seed and die. Many travellers have recorded the amazingly rapid and brilliantly colourful blooming of the desert, during which some cover is produced in even the most unpropitious circumstances. Given water, and provided they are not saline, many desert soils are extremely fertile, because in the absence of leaching they do not become acid nor lose nitrogen and other nutrient elements through leaching.

While desert ephemerals evade drought by their short life cycle, such perennials as endure it do so by virtue of special physiological or morphological characters such as succulence, in which water loss is restricted and the plants maintain sufficient internal water to enable life to continue. Many such species, assigned to a very diverse array of unrelated families, have more or less cylindrical leaves, branches or stems, often with fluted sides. The thick outer layers are impermeable to water, and some species have spines that discourage grazing animals other than the camel, which appears to eat thorny shoots with relish. The stomata, those minute pores in the green surfaces through which water vapour and carbon dioxide move out and in respectively, are deeply sunk into the outermost layers. This lengthens the path along which water vapour has to diffuse from the interior of the plant into the dry external atmosphere, and so decreases the rate of loss.

Many people think of such typical desert plants as cacti, but in fact cacti in the botanical sense are restricted to the deserts of the New World. In the Old World their place in the ecology of deserts is taken by similar-looking members of the Euphorbiaceae (spurge family). Many of the shrubs and small trees of the drier parts of the scrub and grass steppe, such as *Acacia*, have finely divided leaves arranged in a very open canopy so that only part of the radiation falls on them; and they are often (as in the South African Karroo) widely and even seemingly regularly spaced. Yet other forms have no leaves. Instead they have developed flattened leaf stalks and stems or branches held vertically, which minimizes the radiation they receive. These adaptations decrease the rate at which water is lost per unit area of land, and enables the vegetation to grow for a longer time on a limited amount of water.

Among the most bizarre of desert plants is *Welwitschia mirabilis*, a long-lived (up to 100 years) flowering plant, which is relatively abundant in scattered sites among the sands of the Namib desert. It has a short stocky stem of perhaps 60 to 90 cm, at the top of which are borne two broad leaves, the only ones the plant ever has. These grow at their bases throughout the plant's life and are worn away at their older, outer ends by the hot sand. This living relic of a distant past survives and reproduces in one of the most adverse environments known to man.

Because work on the adaptive physiology of desert plants can only be done in the open in the heat of the desert day, we know less about their physiology than their morphology. In particular very little is known about their internal water relations, an aspect that must be of the greatest importance. However, we do know that in some succulent plants, the stonecrops and ice plants (Crassulaceae) the stomata open only at night. In most plants adapted to more humid places, the stomata open to take in carbon dioxide during the day when there is light to drive the photosynthetic processes. At night, when photosynthesis is not possible, they close. In the Crassulaceae the stomata are firmly closed during the day and normal assimilation cannot occur. Instead, carbon dioxide is taken in at night when the stomata are open, and combines with simple organic acids in the cells. Next day it becomes available, inside the plant, for photosynthesis. On the whole, however, the growth rates of such plants are small, for they have sacrificed ostentation for survival.

The green vegetation of the desert is easily seen – not so the animals, of which a surprising number are hidden in the inhospitable landscape, surviving for very long periods without drinking. They conserve water carefully (their solid excreta are extremely dry), and that which they cannot avoid losing, mainly in exhaled breath, is made good by the so-called metabolic water produced when carbohydrates are burnt for energy; 1 kg of carbohydrate yields more than 0.5 litre of water when completely oxidized. This is apparently sufficient to meet losses and to ensure the elimination of the potentially harmful products of metabolism.

There are many species of invertebrates in desert regions. Perhaps the scorpions are most symbolic, the beetles best adapted, and the locust most important to man. Practically all the desert invertebrates have thick skins which help to lessen the rate of water loss. When free water is available many can use it to regulate their temperature by evaporative cooling, using their wings as a fan. There are also common patterns of adaptive behaviour, with two special features. Thus many of them hide in the soil or under rocks, where temperatures are cooler and they are not exposed to the direct heat of the sun. Secondly, their pattern of activity has both annual and daily rhythms. They are inactive during the hottest part of the day, and active in the evening and at night. They also spend substantial parts of the year in a sort of suspended animation. These special forms of behaviour are the principal adaptations of desert invertebrates to the environment; for it seems that physiologically and morphologically they differ little from their relatives in humid regions, except in their reliance on metabolic water.

The locust has long been known as a pest: it was one of the biblical plagues of ancient Egypt. The adaptive behaviour of the desert locust in relation to environment is both curious and important. There are two distinct behavioural types, the solitary and gregarious phases. When the food supply is poor, as it is most of the time in deserts, locusts are no more than grasshoppers, each leading a more or less solitary life and foraging for itself; but if the food supply improves after a more humid period, the number of solitary locusts increases. When a critical population density is exceeded, the new locusts become gregarious and gather together in large numbers, at first as hoppers (immature individuals which do not fly) which develop into mature forms with clear black markings and, more important, are much more active than their solitary predecessors. When it is hot they tend to fly, moving rapidly downwind in large swarms which migrate out of the deserts into the surrounding more humid areas, where they are very destructive. Since these swarms cannot be effectively controlled, the art of locust control is to prevent the hoppers from developing into swarming locusts. This can only be done through close international co-operation transcending political boundaries. Such combined action was highly successful in the Middle East and north-east Africa during the late fifties and sixties, and no serious swarming has occurred for many years.

Apart from the ostrich, the vertebrates of the desert are mostly small and light-coloured. Most of the larger grazing animals of the steppe and savannah, like the antelopes and their predators the lion and cheetah, cannot survive in the desert. Nor can amphibians like the toad, for they have little control over water loss through their skins and would dry up in such an environment. But certain reptiles, like snakes and lizards, have become well adapted. Their skin is dry and covered by an impervious layer of horny scales which prevents water loss and is resistant to the abrasion of a stony habitat. Some of these, the spiny-tailed lizards, are nocturnal, only warming themselves in the sun in the morning before retreating below ground to avoid the heat of the day. The larger American Gila monsters, whose names *Heloderma horridum* and *Heloderma suspectum* record man's feelings about them, are sluggish, poisonous lizards up to 60 cm in length, but few fatalities have been reported. Some lizards 'swim' upon the sand rather than run upon it, and have pointed noses so that they can burrow quickly. Among the snakes there are a number of poisonous species, including the New World rattlesnake and the Old World asps (species of vipers).

Most birds depend absolutely on a regular supply of water, and few can live exclusively in deserts. Nevertheless, the number of visitors is often surprisingly large. They can and do fly substantial distances from their watering points in oases and elsewhere in search of food or safety from hunters, and they are of course more easily seen than other desert creatures. Like those of invertebrates and reptiles, most of the adaptations of resident birds concern behaviour rather than structure or physiology. For instance, the male sand-grouse is reported to take water to the young in the nest by soaking its breast feathers and allowing the chicks to 'comb' them.

The commonest wild mammals are small jumping rodents, including gerbils and jerboas. Even in the Australian desert there are ecologically equivalent marsupials that look similar and behave in the same ways. All are nocturnal, feed on plants or seeds, and spend most of the day in the cool of their burrows, though they can often be seen sunning themselves in the early morning. Many mammals, including the large desert antelopes like the oryx and addox, do not drink at all, relying on metabolic water and the water present in their forage. Unhappily the survival of these two classic desert species is at present endangered, not by the desert but by man, for they are being hunted out of existence by wealthy 'sportsmen'. Indeed the survival of the Arabian oryx probably now depends upon captive animals in a zoo in the United States, not on animals in the wild.

Besides relying on metabolic water, desert mammals have other special adaptive physiological features. They do not sweat, any fat they store tends to be in special 'depots' rather than as an insulating layer beneath the skin, and they often have light coats to shield them from the sun's rays. Some can drink large amounts of water very rapidly when opportunity offers. For instance, a dehydrated camel weighing 325 kg was observed to drink 103 kg of water, nearly one-third of its initial weight, in less than ten minutes.

Wild camels were not originally creatures of the true hot desert, but of the grassy desert margins. Their ability to store water throughout their tissues is a great advantage both to them and to man. Contrary to some popular beliefs, water is not stored in the humps of camels; they are fat 'depots' comparable to the humps of zebu cattle. Fat storage, water storage and an effective regulation of water use combine to make the camel the most important, indeed virtually the only, beast of burden in the desert. Bactrian (two-humped) camels still live wild in the Gobi desert, but the single-humped Arabian camel, or dromedary, is no longer found outside domestication.

Man and the desert

Man, in all his types, Australian aboriginal, Caucasian, Mongolian and American Indian and Negro, has colonized the deserts and desert margins. Such desert-dwellers tend to be tall and thin rather than short and fat. There are some special adaptations that we all develop quite quickly in deserts. Sweat soon becomes less salty, urine more concentrated. Like those of other animals, however, our greatest adaptations are in behaviour. Clothes are loose and voluminous, often light-coloured, shielding from the heat outside. Houses have very thick walls, with few and small windows, so that the sun cannot shine directly into them, forming as it were 'overground burrows'. Movement is largely by night and during the cool hours of the morning or late afternoon, from one rare watering point to the next.

Settlements can exist only near permanent water supplies, either natural or man-made, like the relatively large civil engineering works constructed to capture and store run-off water on which the ancient settlements of the Negev and many arid parts of Asia and Africa were based. Similarly, hills or sloping ground were terraced and shaped so that run-off flowed into surface reservoirs or underground cisterns, to be stored against times of drought.

Many desert people are nomad pastoralists with flocks of sheep and goats, rather than farmers. Indeed nomads are the only people who can put the meagre natural resources of the desert zone to some sort of economic use. To this day their migration routes take advantage of the ancient run-off systems which are systematically used so that grazing and movement can continue for as long as possible.

Many deserts, like the Sahara, the Arabian desert and the Gobi, have been traversed for thousands of years by trade routes. Silk, spices and China tea used to reach the eastern Mediterranean on the backs of camels. Morocco leather, in which the rich bound their books, came across the Sahara from the goats that lived in what is now northern Nigeria and other parts of the Sudanian zone. One of the alternative names, Cordovan (Kordofan) leather, is more indicative of its origin. Again, the salt eaten by people in the equatorial belt of West Africa once came across the Sahara. Herodotus evidently gathered much of his information about the geography of the ancient world from desert travellers. Gibbon records the long migration of an obscure Baltic tribe through France and Spain (as the Vandals), into North Africa where some remained (as the Berbers), and yet others, the Garamantes, moved on out of recorded history, across the desert to the south where, to this day, they offer the only possible basis for conjecture about the hundreds of stone circles which stand in Senegal and the Gambia, silent evidence of an ancient culture. The Romans brought great blocks of porphyry weighing tens of tons from the Red Sea hills of Egypt. But perhaps the most significant trade was in slaves, pictured in ancient Egyptian reliefs, who were brought to Nubia, and so to Egypt, along the Darb al Arba'in (the Road of Forty Days) from Darfur to Nubia. In modern times the desert retains a harsh, austere attraction for many who find in it a challenging but relaxing escape from the increasingly burdensome complexities of our civilization, into a life which deals directly with nature in one of her simplest forms.

The famous European desert travellers made their crossings against this background of existing settlement and trade. Marco Polo, one of the fathers of desert travel and of European trade missions, crossed the Iranian desert in about AD 1272. He went on to cross the Takla Makan, that extremely arid region which forms the south-western part of the Gobi complex. He continued along the southern edge of the Gobi and reached China, where he spent many years as a senior adviser to the court of Kublai Khan. His anecdotal, amusing and intensely interesting account of these travels, written in prison, was of course generally disbelieved at the time, but it is still one of the most accurate, as well as one of the best, travellers' tales.

The peoples of the desert, including the Arabs long before the rise of Islam in AD 622, traditionally valued learning. Present-day science and mathematics have descended in part from the astronomical observations of pastoralists of the deserts and desert margins. The Arabs preserved much of the learning of the ancient world through the Dark Ages, and Arab travellers and geographers, including the redoubtable Ibn Battutah (1304–68), perhaps the greatest of Muslim travellers, described the Arabian and Iranian deserts and the Sahara. After Islam had reached the Atlantic along both the Mediterranean and the Sudan routes, the fabulous city of Tombouctou on the banks of the Niger, where it flows through the southern Sahara, became the centre of a local Islamic culture. Then Sokoto and Kano, the twin cross-roads of the pilgrimage routes to Mecca and the north-south trade route from the Mediterranean, became the most important cities of West Africa.

Is the climate changing?

All climates fluctuate. We take for granted the short-term irregular fluctuations which we call weather, and we understand and expect the regular diurnal and seasonal changes which distinguish night from day and summer from winter. Everywhere men adapt their ways of life to variations of these kinds. We are also well accustomed to seemingly random year-to-year variations, wet and dry summers, failure of the monsoon, exceptional rains and early snow melt leading to flooding, whether in the Po Valley or Bangladesh.

There are other longer-term variations. Cycles of around eleven, eighty, and two hundred years can be demonstrated in historical records of weather and of population distribution in northern Europe. On a much longer time scale the evidence of former colder periods, the ice ages in high latitudes, and of wetter and drier periods in lower ones, is unquestionable. But because the short-term variations are superimposed on the long-term ones the resulting patterns of actual climate are not easy to disentangle.

The sequence of dry years in the Sahelian zone of West Africa from 1968 to 1973, and the widespread suffering to which it led among the nomadic herds and herdsmen of the southern fringe of the Sahara, evoked pity and a degree of anxiety in western Europe and North Africa. In some of these years there were short periods of drought in Ethiopia and Rajasthan, disappointing monsoons in the Indian subcontinent, and floods in Bengal. Then in 1974, when the drought was broken by satisfactory rains in much of the Sahel, parts of the United States experienced unexpected drought, in a year when the yield of the North American grain crop was critical for world food supplies. All this led to suggestions that the world's climate is about to change, with potentially disastrous consequences for mankind.

Much professional opinion regards these suggestions as exaggerated, even alarmist, but in relation to the drier (and colder) inhabited areas of the Earth it has been necessary to examine them with great care. In a marginal region changes which are small on a global scale, and could be accommodated without difficulty elsewhere, lead all too easily to substantial effects on the life of plants, animals and man. It is said that during the last twenty-five years the average growing period in Britain has decreased by two weeks. Yet this has apparently been offset almost automatically by the continuous production of appropriately adapted crop varieties, as well as by changes and improvements in husbandry and management. So the average yield of our cereals has increased steadily and substantially during this period. But a decrease of a fortnight in the already marginal crop or grazing seasons of the Sahel, where both the technical and the logistic support of agriculture and stock raising are very weak, can easily move the effective northern limit of these activities two hundred kilometres to the south – a small distance relative to the global size of the Hadley cell, but devastating for the people who live in it.

This is essentially what happened in the Sahel, with much local variation, between 1968 and 1973. The first point to recognize is that it had happened before. Fig. 7 represents the five-year running averages of rainfall from 1906 to 1969 as a percentage of the long-term mean, from five stations in the West African climatic region. Severe regional droughts occurred in the drier parts of West Africa in 1912–15, 1940–44 and 1947–49. Each of these was accompanied by a spate of writings about climatic change and the advance of the desert, usually linked with doom-laden prophecies about the consequences of man's agricultural and environmental sins. The latest period was more prolonged but not more intense than any of the others.

The second point is that the drought of 1968–73 aroused far more concern outside West Africa than any of the earlier ones. Because of the growth of human population it directly affected a larger number of people, and because of improved communications, international organizations, the changed nature of the political relations between France and her overseas territories, and the growth of humanitarian interest, it became known to virtually everyone in western Europe and North America.

The third point is that it could have been foreseen. By 1968, when the running averages could be plotted to 1965, the situation on the ground and the trend of the curve could evidently have given sufficient cause for alarm. At that time governments could have seen to water supplies, reserve food stocks, roads, airfields, trucks and aircraft. Had they done these things they could have prevented the impending drought from leading to disaster and death.

Fig. 5 The Sahel on the southern fringe of the Sahara.

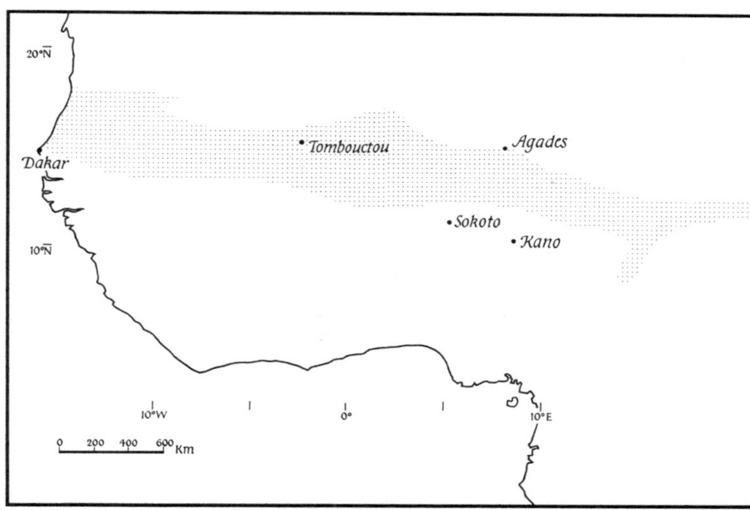

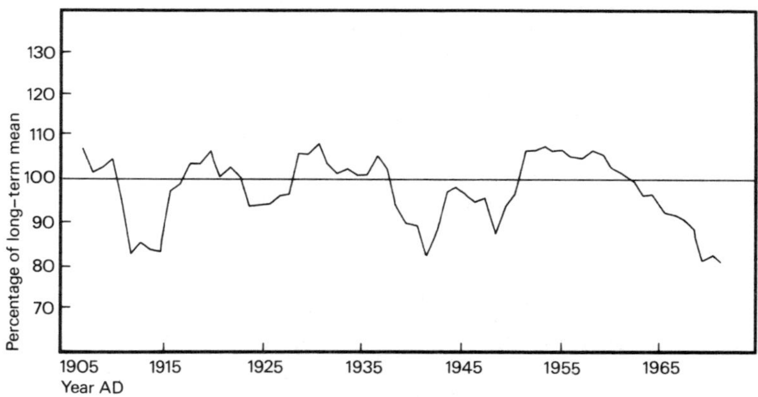

Fig. 6 Five-year running averages of rainfall in the Sahel, 1906 to 1969. This method uses the averages of overlapping five-year periods (1905 to 1909, 1906 to 1910, 1907 to 1911, etc.) to smooth out short-term fluctuations and make long-term trends more evident.

The fourth point is that it will happen again; drought will return to the Sahel. No one knows when, but the rainfall curves can warn governments in time about the main longer-term fluctuations. As to the annual fluctuations, we have recently substantiated statistically what most agronomists in the seasonally arid parts of West Africa have learnt from experience, that individual seasons differ characteristically in weather from one another. We have suggested that it is possible to predict from the early-season rainfall the general character of the coming season as a whole in seventeen years out of twenty. So although there is much more research and testing to do, and much to learn about the underlying mechanisms, we already have some prospect that an agricultural weather watch could provide a useful early warning system for both annual and medium-term hazards.

The fifth point is that even if they are warned, individual governments can do little in isolation. None of the Sahelian states (with the possible exception of Chad) is large enough, or suitably located geographically, to offset or handle the consequences of climatic fluctuation on this scale within its own frontiers. Nigeria, which extends from the Sahel zone through the savannahs to the tropical forest zone, weathered the long drought without difficulty. Roads and railways, and a common administration, made it possible to exploit the complementary ecologies of different regions. Thus grain could be moved from wetter to drier areas, and animals and humans in the reverse direction. Nor were any unusual problems reported from the Sudan. The governments and peoples of the western nations and of the countries of the wetter parts of West Africa, wishing to avert future disaster in the Sahel, will no doubt give appropriate support in good time to the regional agencies and instruments which the governments of the Sahel themselves are establishing for this purpose.

The sixth point is a more general extension of the fifth. In virtually all other arid parts of the world, unlike the Sahel, the desert and the cultivated areas grade into each other within the boundaries of individual states. Rajasthan is a dry extension of the Indian Punjab; the Danakil country is less than 300 km from the Ethiopian plateau. So long as people continue to live in marginal and desert areas, it is the duty of those who accept (or seize) the responsibilities of governme[illegible] to safeguard the lives of those they govern by organizing reciprocal support between the marginal and the more favoured parts of the national domain.

The seventh point is that there are few places in the developing world where it is inevitable that people must live in perpetuity in the desert or on its margins. They do so now because they have always done so and wish to go on doing so, or because they have no choice. But the old ways are changing. In a world in which the transistor radio hangs round the camel's neck, and the economies of developing countries are growing and diversifying, the young are less eager than they were to follow in the old ways as new ones become possible. Oil, irrigation, industry, communications and tourism are altering patterns of life, and sovereign independent governments may well see greater advantages for their nations in using their investment resources for purposes other than developing the desert. To this point we shall return.

The eighth point relates to long-term changes in climate. These too have happened before and we may confidently expect them to happen again. Crocodiles, hippopotami and cattle may yet again live in what is now the central Sahara, as they did about 20,000 years ago. Conversely, the fixed dunes of southern Kordofan and Darfur, now covered by vegetation, may once again be free to ripple and move in the wind. In the present state of knowledge we can neither predict nor control these changes. Man's wisdom and technique, or his agricultural sins, may hasten or delay the processes of change. So far as we can foresee they cannot hope to arrest them. On a smaller scale the factual evidence does not suggest that the Sahara or other deserts have been advancing continuously during the past seventy-five years. Yet it is possible to discern in the records, though hardly to prove, that the fifties marked the end of a period of increasing rainfall and ushered in one of increasing aridity. Even if they are real, these changes are far smaller (plus or minus five per cent of the long-term mean) than the year-to-year variations and the irregular short- and medium-term fluctuations (plus or minus fifteen per cent of the long-term mean) which do the most serious damage.

A look to the future

The human population of the world, and its needs and effective demand for agricultural products, including food, are likely to continue to increase for a century and more to come. Many people see in the deserts and desert margins a large untapped agricultural resource which could help to meet these needs. They are aware that agriculture probably began in semi-arid regions in both the Old World and the New, that it spread into even drier regions as irrigation developed, and that in many countries today irrigated farming in desert regions adds substantially to national incomes.

Deserts have several inherent advantages for agriculture – more or less predictable weather, clear skies, warmth, fewer diseases, unleached soils often well supplied with plant nutrients. But they usually have three important disadvantages – there are no farmers, no markets or associated roads and other infrastructure, and no water. To set up a desert for profitable crop production is an extremely expensive business, and it carries substantial risks. Neither governments nor entrepreneurs are likely to give priority in investment to farming the desert or desert margins unless the prospects of profit are encouraging (as in California), there is an established farming population which cannot be helped to advance in any other way (as in India and Pakistan), or there are few development alternatives (as in Israel). They will be even less inclined to invest in deserts if they believe that the arid parts of the world are becoming drier and that the deserts are spreading.

Nor is it possible to argue that desert farming is essential, despite its cost, because of the world's increasing demand for food. Such extra food as is required will be (and indeed is being) far less expensively produced by improving farming where it is, on existing farms and by existing farming societies. These include most of the world's poor and hungry, who are themselves the great majority of the people development is about. Advances of this sort have been most prominent in the developed world, particularly in North America and eastern Europe. In the developing world they have been widespread in irrigated areas, but in the next phase they are likely to become important also in the seasonally arid agricultural areas of the tropics.

To an extent they will depend on more water – from rivers, from more effective 'harvesting' of run-off water, ground water and dew (in special circumstances), and perhaps from the sea – although getting rid of the salt is a costly business with present technology and at the present free-market price of energy. They will also depend on improved farming systems, including shorter-season varieties less sensitive to dry conditions, and appropriate methods of soil management. But as one near the desert margin these methods become increasingly unreliable in practice. In these regions, where crops give way to stock, extra water (particularly when provided by government) all too easily helps cattle numbers to exceed the capacity of even the extended nomad territory to support them. The conflict between private ownership of the stock and public ownership of all the resources necessary to maintain them must either damage the resources or alter the social relations of stock raising, particularly as the markets for animal products become more and more attractive (as they have in West Africa, Kenya, Botswana and other countries).

Unlike some of our colleagues, we are on balance positive and hopeful in our conclusions about the dry regions of the tropical and subtropical world. We know well that some of the difficulties are insuperable at reasonable cost, and that the others are substantial. But the opportuniies are substantial too, and we believe that mankind will learn how to grasp them. For the rest, we expect that large areas of the deserts and other dry regions will remain as they are, and that their unique physical and biological features are consequently likely to be conserved on a large scale throughout the foreseeable future.

Suggestions for further reading

G. W. Brown (ed.): *Desert Biology*, 2 vols. Academic Press, London, 1969 and 1974.

J. L. Cloudesley-Thompson and M. K. Chadwick: *Life in Deserts*. Foulis, London, and Dufour, Chester Springs, PA, 1964.

Herodotus: *The Histories of Herodotus of Halicarnassus*. Translated and introduced by Harry Carter. Oxford University Press, London.

E. S. Hills (ed.): *Arid Lands*. Methuen, London, and Barnes & Noble, New York, 1966.

Ibn Battuta: *Travels in Asia and Africa*. Translated and selected by H. A. R. Gibb. Routledge, London, 1929.

Marco Polo: *The Travels of Marco Polo*. Penguin Books, Harmondsworth and New York, 1965.

W. G. McGinnies and B. J. Goldman (eds.): *Arid Lands in Perspective*. American Association for the Advancement of Science, Washington, D.C., 1969.

G. Mountfort: *Portrait of a Desert*. Collins, London, 1965.

W. Thesiger: *Arabian Sands* (paperback edition). Longmans, London, 1974.

Desolate and barren, waterless and treeless – the dictionary definition of a desert truly sums it up. Man and beast and a few dry sticks of shrubs, in a million square miles of rock and of sand moulded by the wind and all lit by a searing sun; it seems incredible that anyone or anything can live there. But live they do, and in places even make a living. Deserts cover one-twentieth of the Earth's surface. The Sahara (*opposite*) alone is nearly as big as the United States – and during the recent drought and famine its southern edge has tended to advance, eating up marginal farming and grazing land. Yet there is hope that the worst effects of these changes can be stemmed, with wise and timely action, and even to some extent reversed.

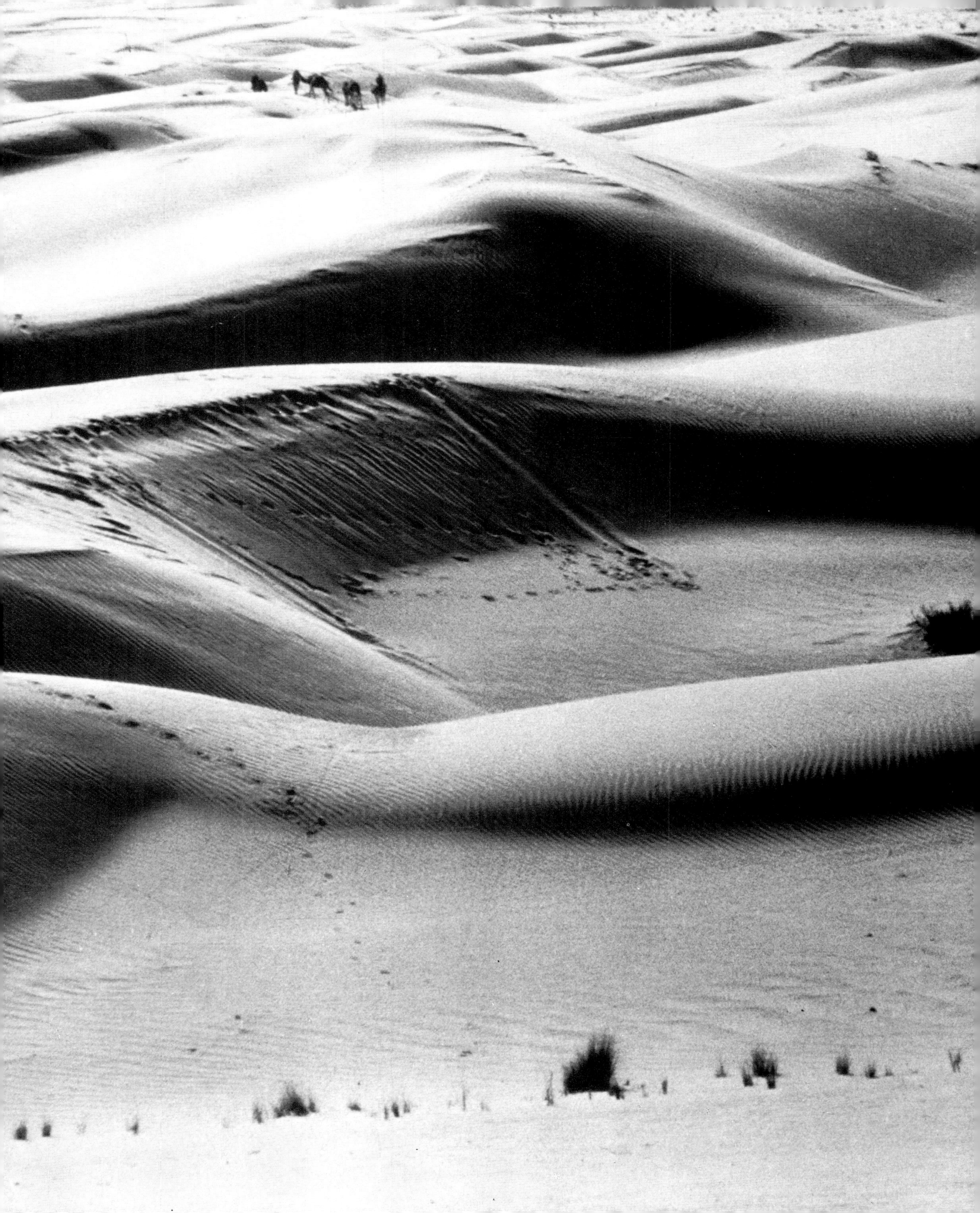

2

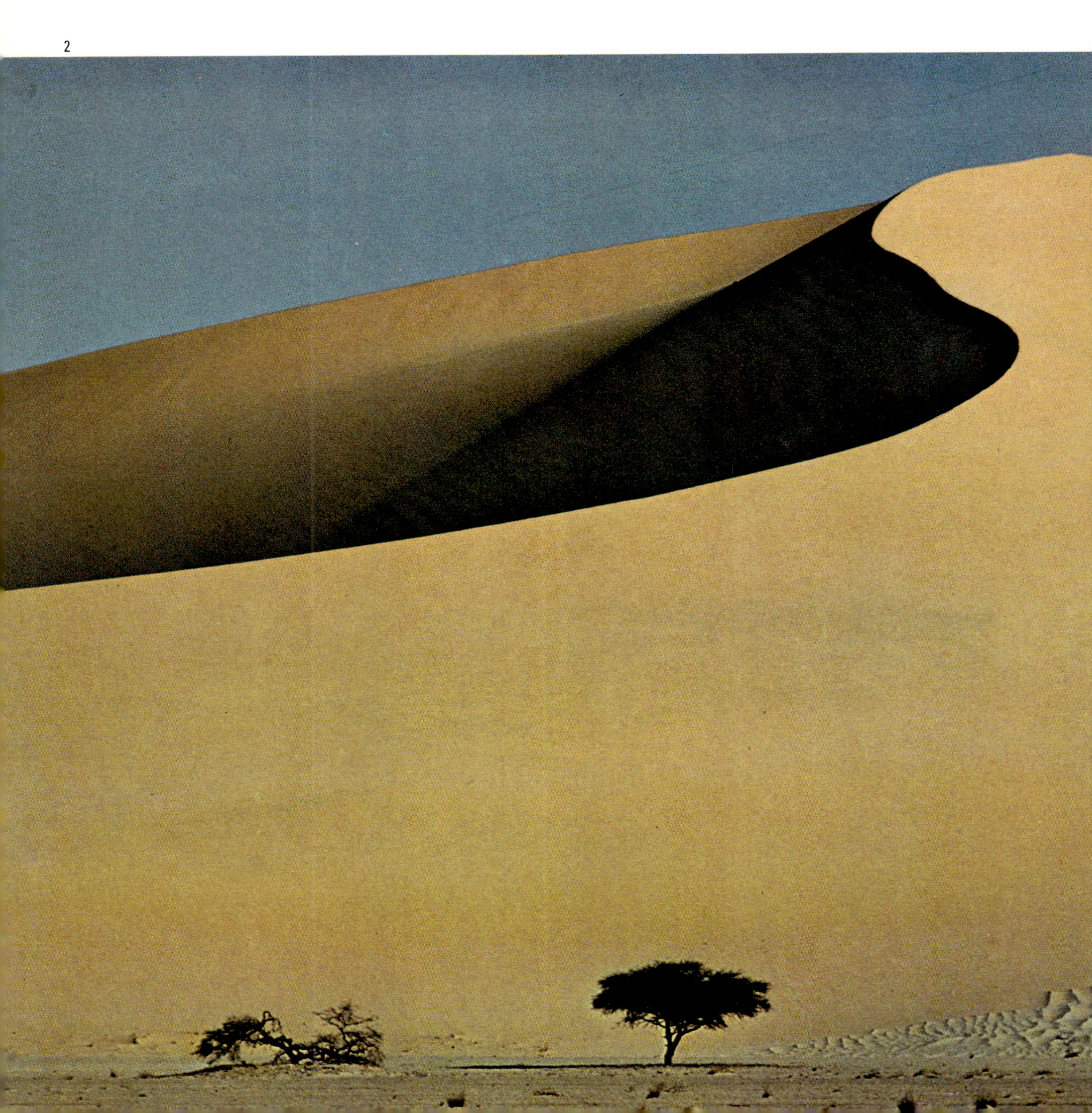

The harsh beauty of the world's deserts has been described by travellers ever since Marco Polo crossed the Gobi desert in the thirteenth century. Above all, deserts have an extraordinary range of colours: nearly black in ancient lava flows, tawny in the Eastern Air mountains of Niger (2), brick-red in Australia's Northern Territory (3, Mount Olga, with Ayers Rock in the distance), delicately pink in the Atacama desert, Chile (4).

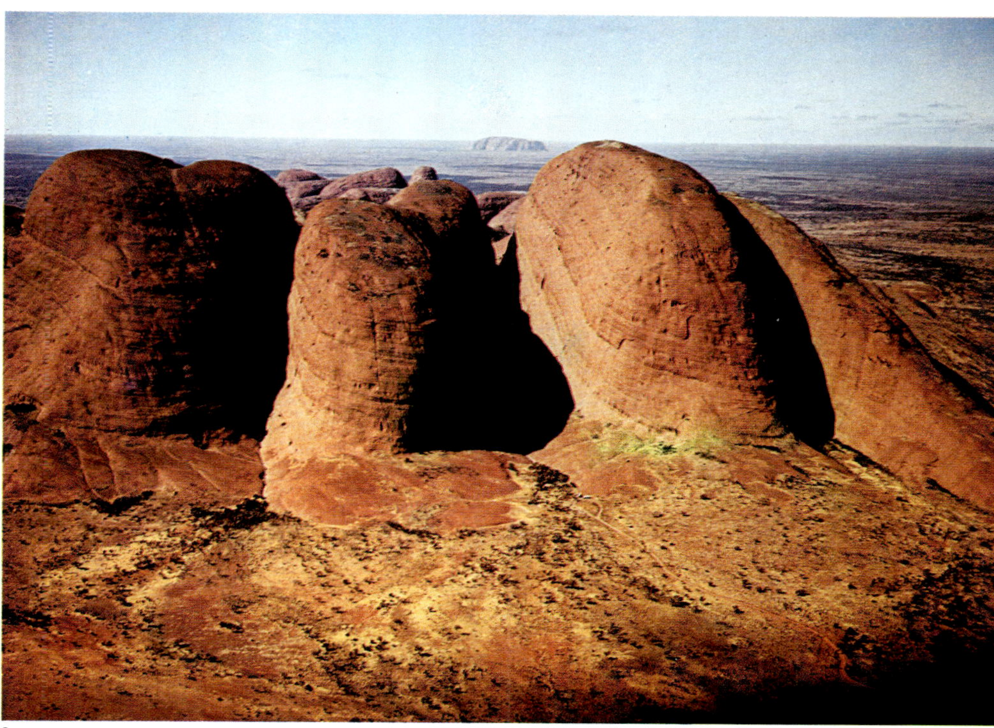

3

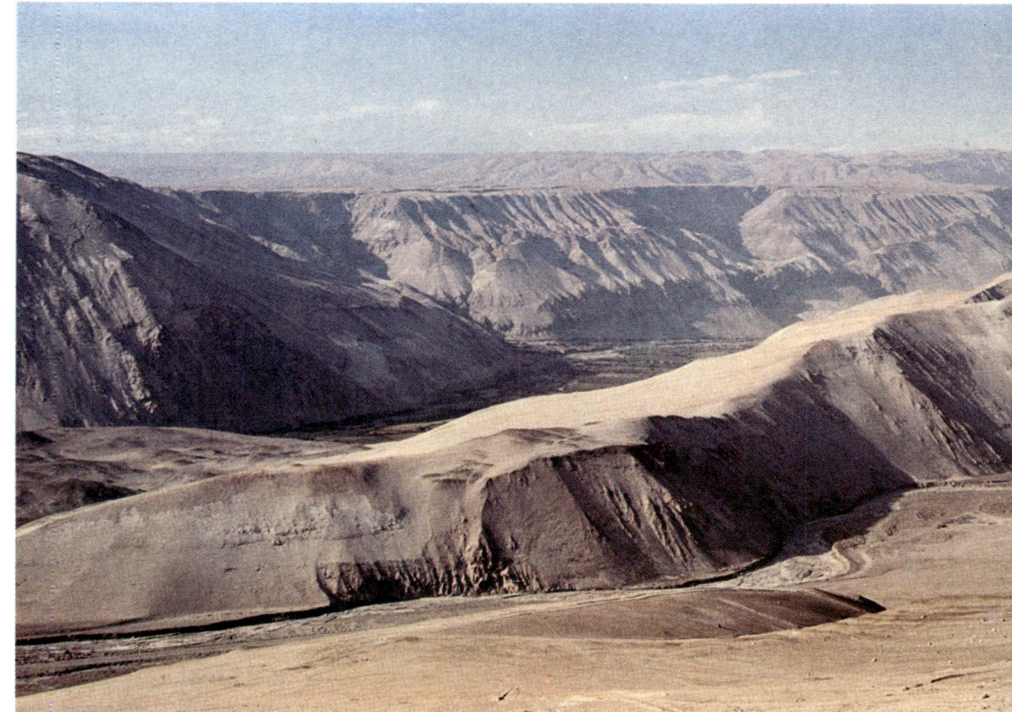

4

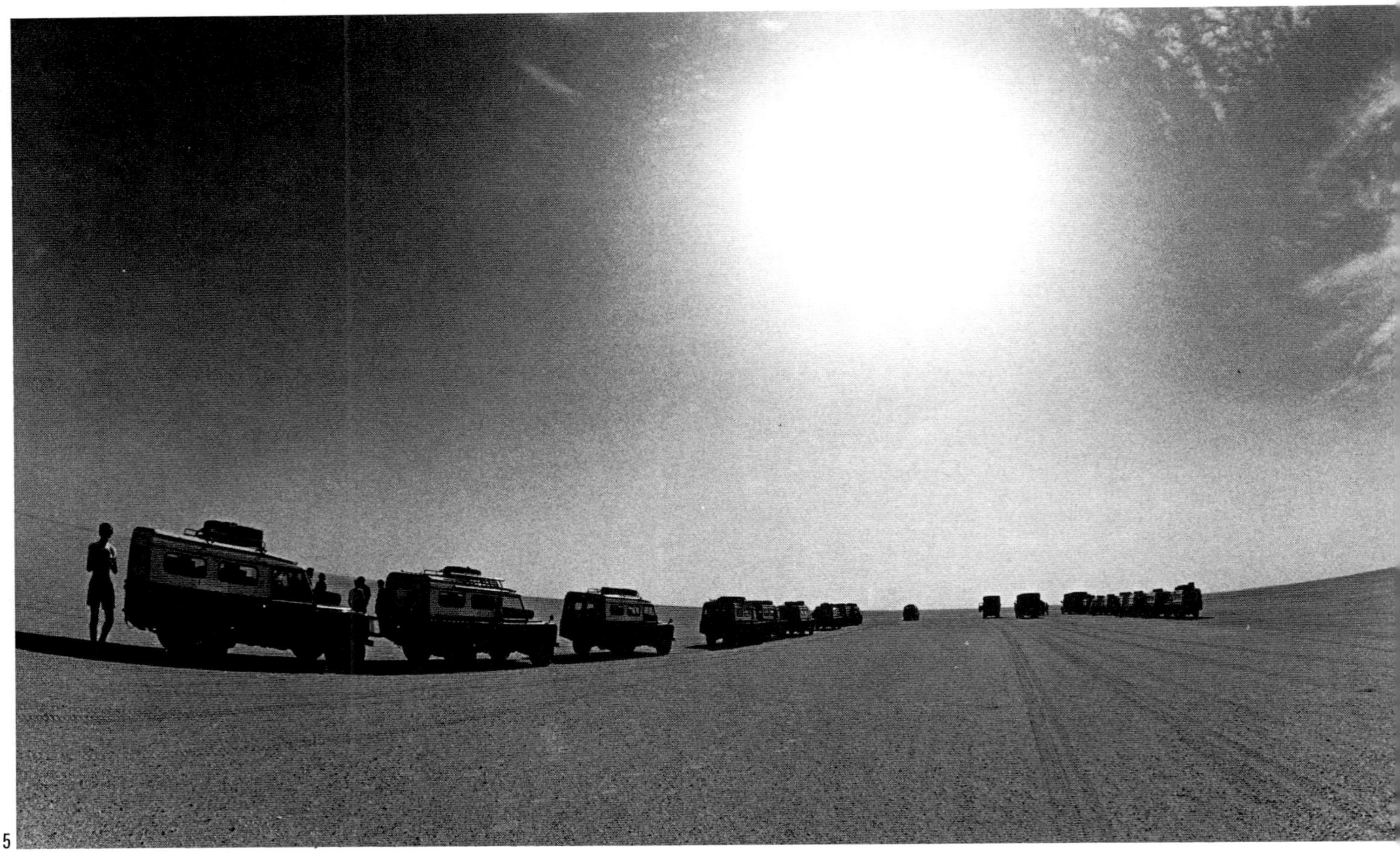

5

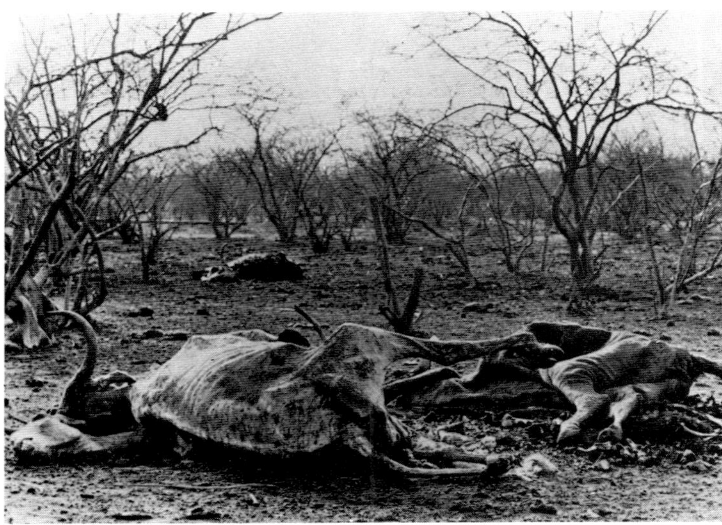

6

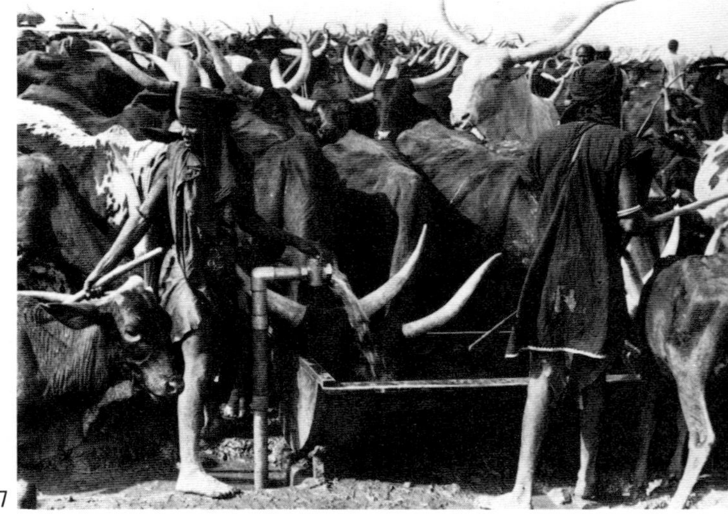

7

Under a blazing sun, a convoy of trucks ferries in supplies to the drought-stricken Sahel (5). In 1973 this marginal belt of semi-desert country stretching across West Africa, south of the Sahara, was dotted with starved, dehydrated corpses of cattle (6) as the native herdsmen and farmers, after five years without rain, saw the desert spreading south. But even in the Sahel there is subterranean water; tools, drilling equipment and pipes, brought in by international aid schemes, can tap these reserves so that thirsty cattle can be watered (7) and they and their owners can have a chance to survive until the rains come. Through a parched and drought-cracked river bed (8) the water begins to flow again. This is in Kenya's Northern Frontier Province, many hundreds of miles east of the Sahelian zone but still part of the drought belt that runs right across Africa, from Mali to the Danakil desert in Ethiopia.

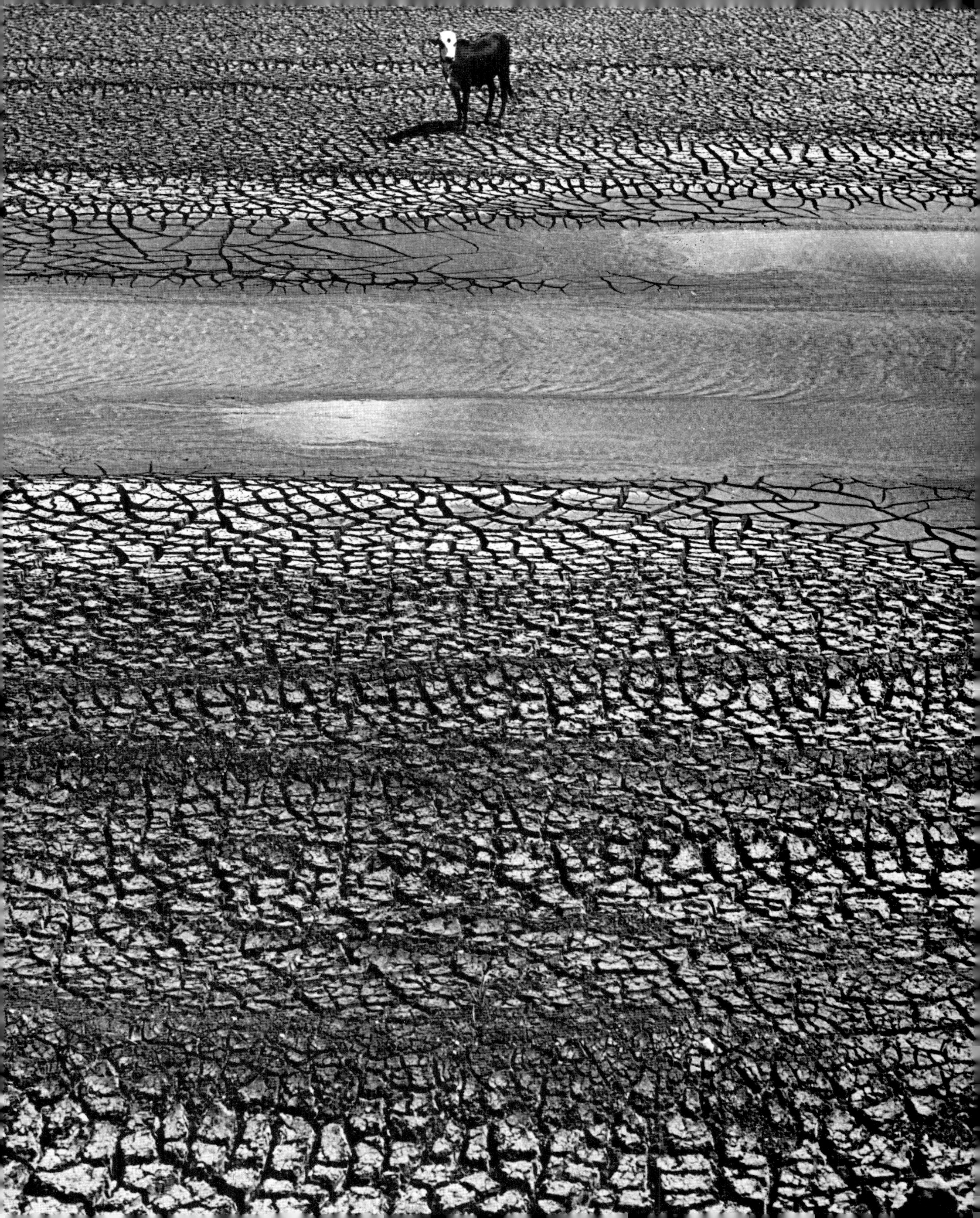

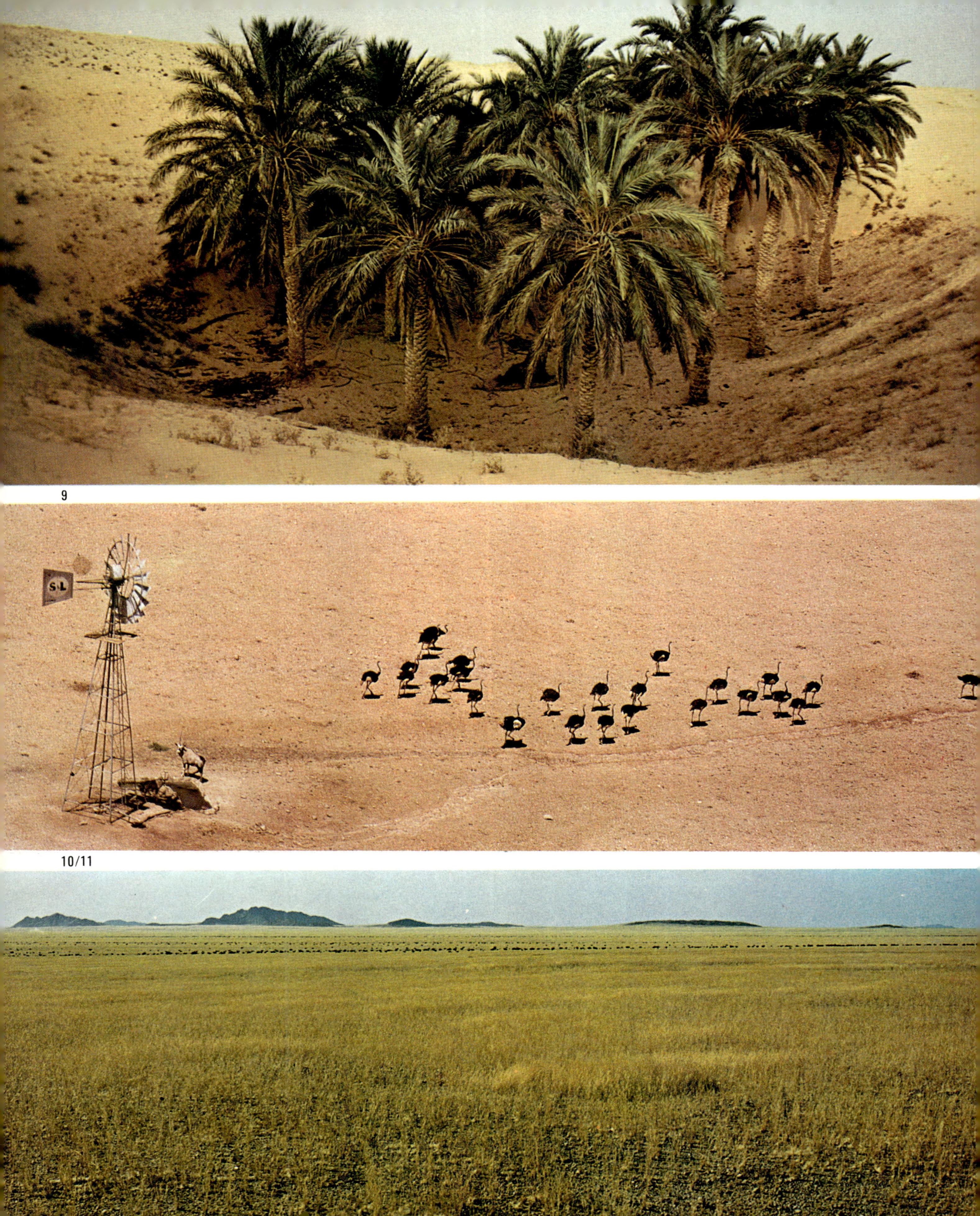

9

10/11

The everlasting search for vater is the prime fact of lesert life for man and beast ınd plant alike. Where subsoil vater is near enough to the urface, plants can flourish, ike these date palms (9) in an Algerian oasis. In the Namib lesert of S.W. Africa nfrequent boreholes (10) aise water by wind-driven ›umps. On the rare occasions vhen rain falls, the bare ›rown soil becomes a sheet of olour (11) as dormant seeds, n a matter of days, germinate, blossom and die. Here and there, standing ›ools, silt-laden and brackish 12), will only yield drinkable vater in spoonfuls, scraped rom the soil around them ınd allowed to settle.

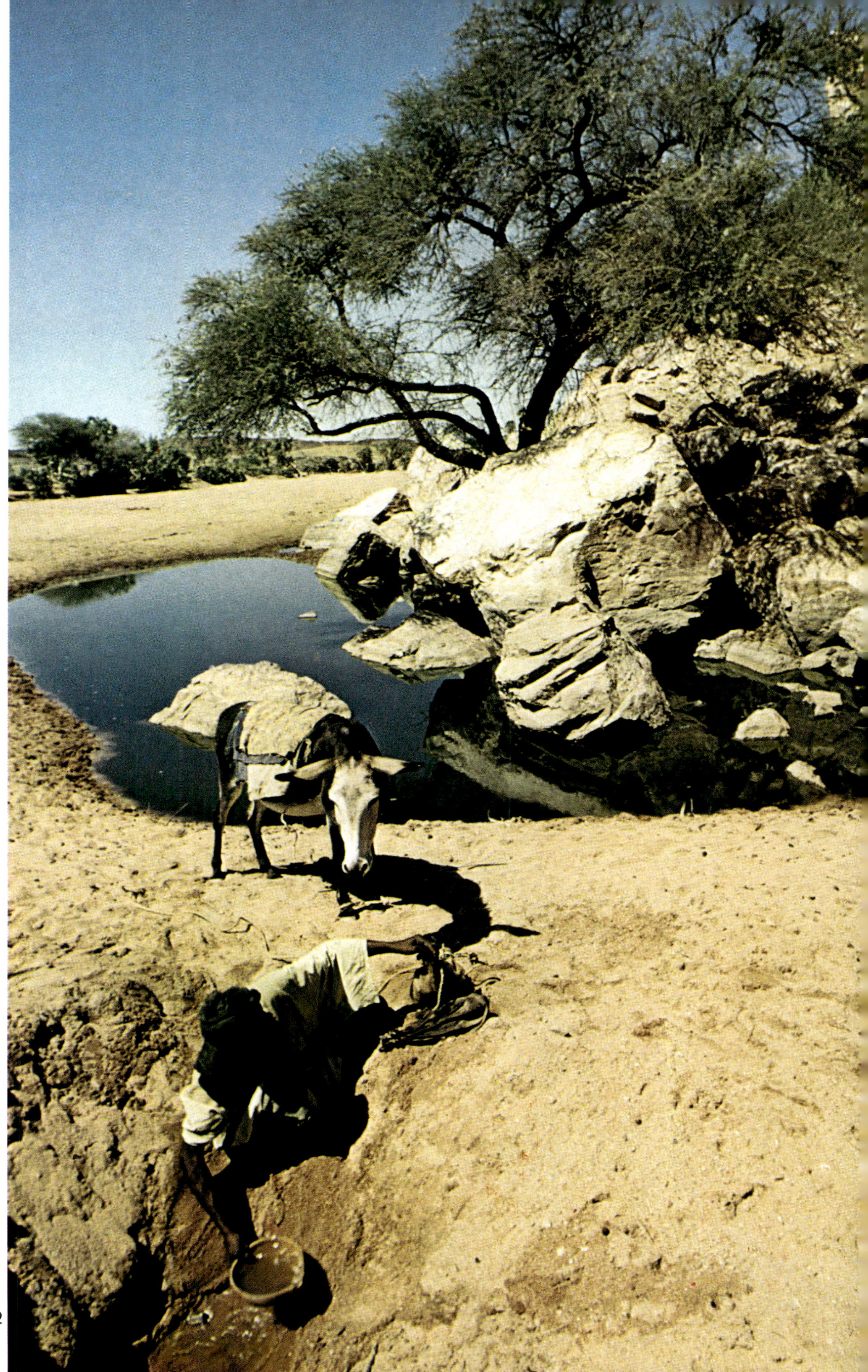

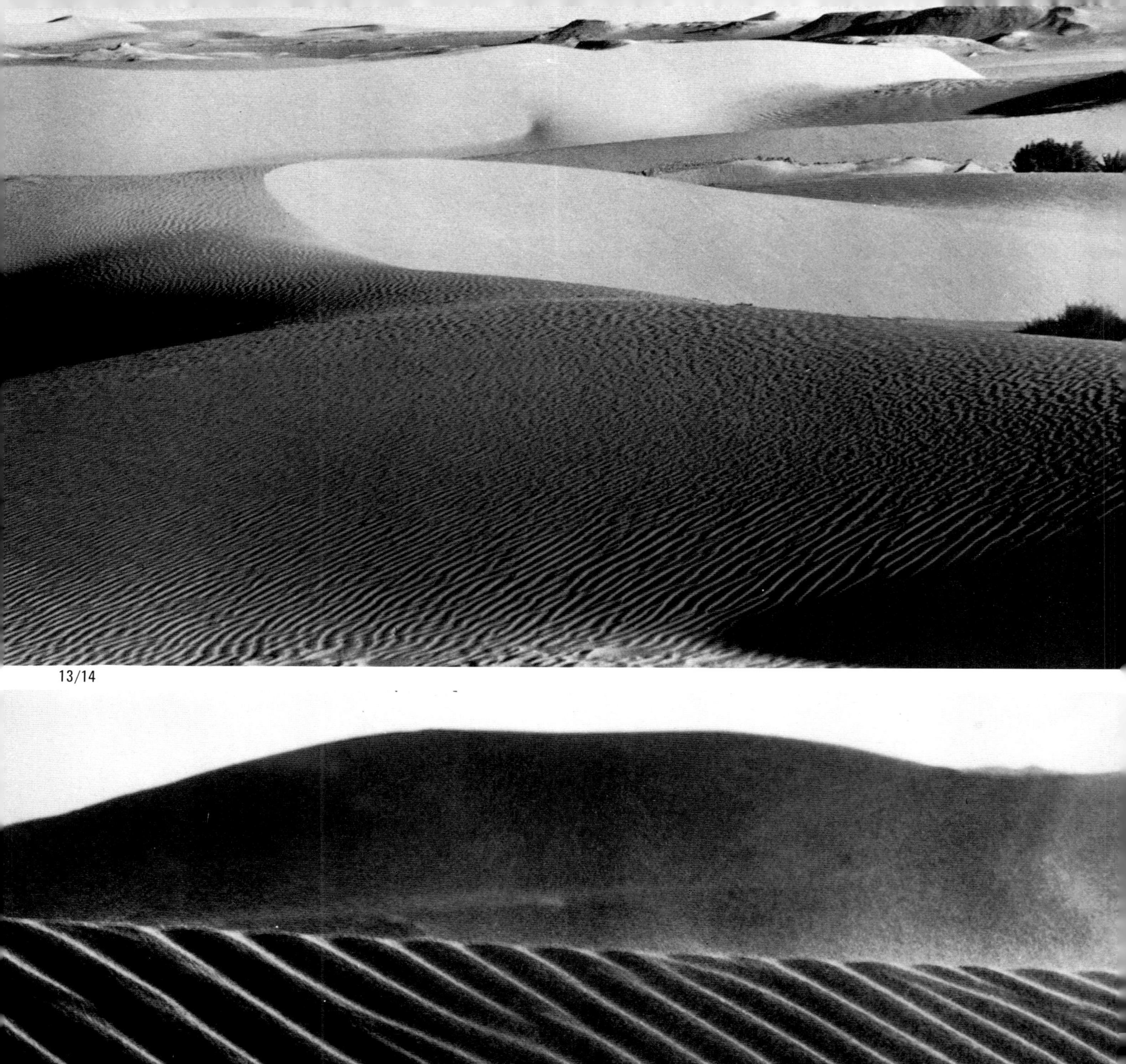

13/14

Sculptured by the wind, the world's deserts are often covered with shapes of abstract beauty. The creeping, crescent-shaped dunes of the Sahara, called *barchans* (13), are formed where the wind blows constantly from one direction and the sand does not cover all the ground. As the sand is blown up the gentle, rippled rearward slope and down the steep leading slope, the whole dune moves slowly forwards. Where the sand is deeper, long parallel ridges, or *seifs*, may be formed (14), sometimes half a mile wide and hundreds of miles long, in the direction of the wind, probably where winds have a rolling twist to their forward motion. The lacy edges of Red Bluff, Western Australia (15) show the scouring, grinding effect of millennia of wind-blown sand.

15

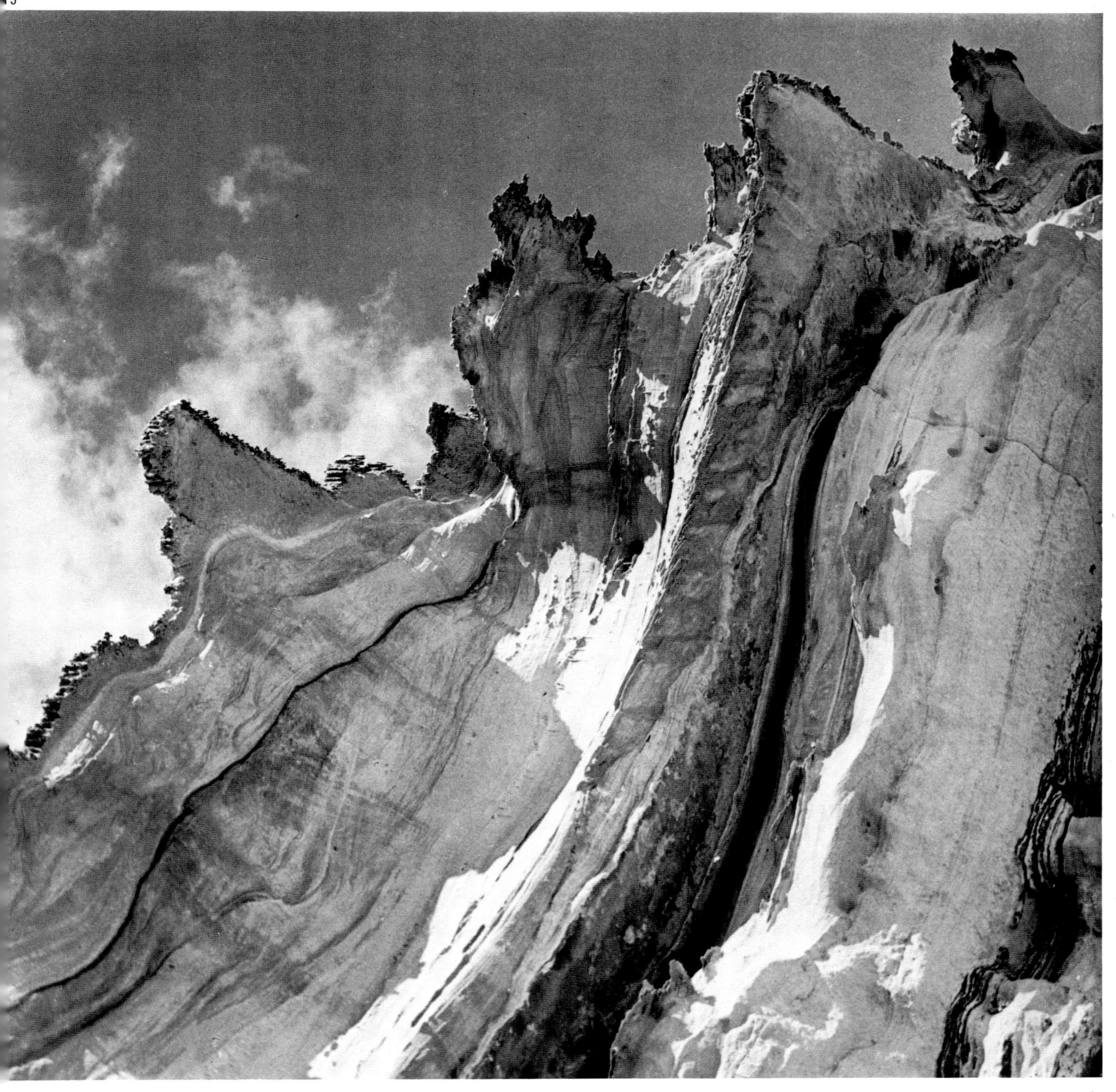

Plants fight for survival in the desert with bizarre and varied adaptations. The leaves of some acacias have thick, impervious outer layers; others (16) have stout thorns to discourage grazers. The near-cylindrical surface of the gemsbok cucumber (17) presents the minimum area of evaporation. Living relic of a distant past, *Welwitschia mirabilis* (18) has just two leaves, strap-like and up to two yards long; as their tips are worn away by wind and sand they grow out from the base. The cactus, that typical desert plant, is a native of the New World; the picture opposite shows prickly pear (*Opuntia*) in the Galapagos Islands (19).

16

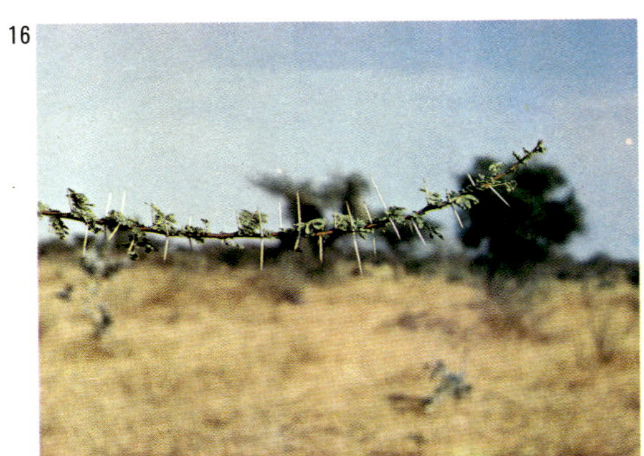

17

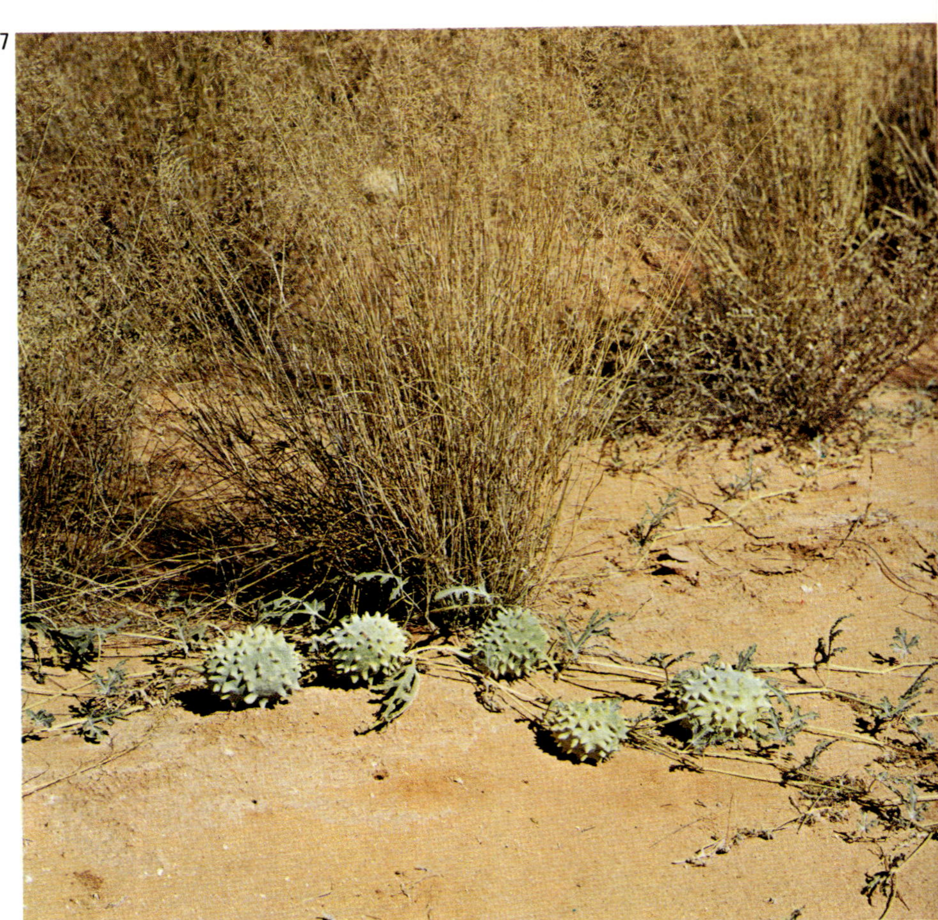

18

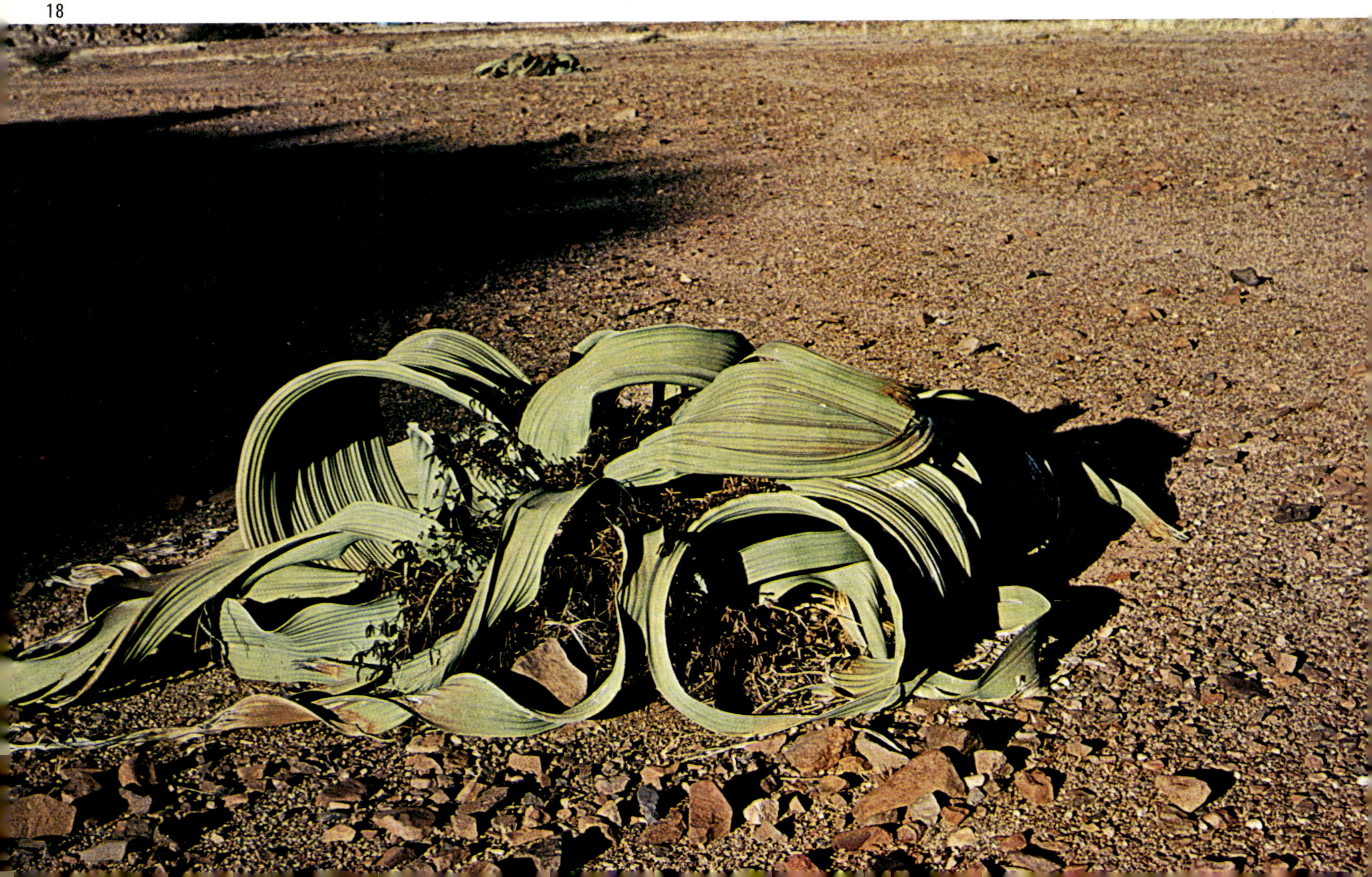

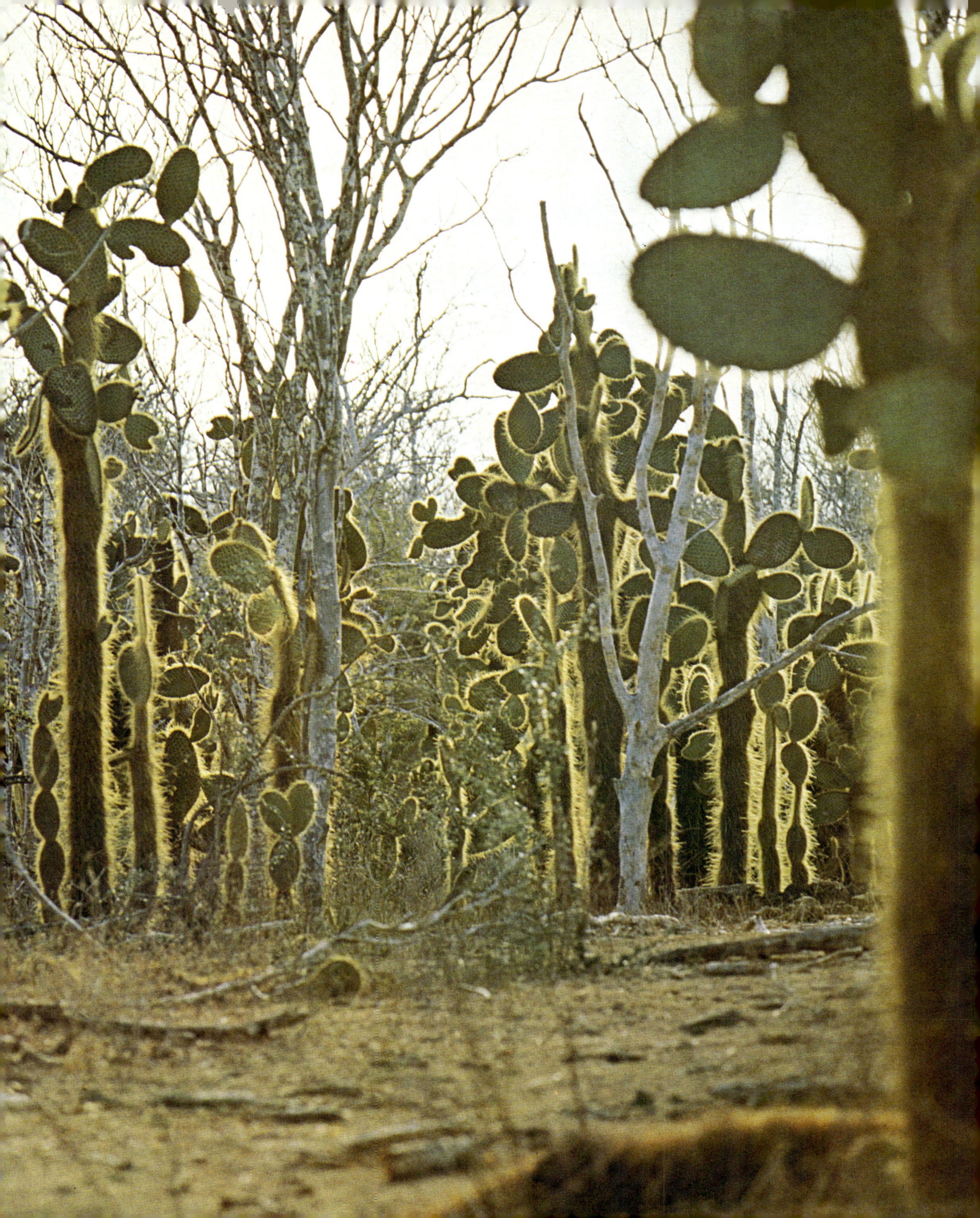

Animals too have adapted in different ways to lessen evaporation and escape the heat of the sun. The sand goanna, an Australian lizard (20), scuttles over the sand with a 'swimming' motion, and its pointed snout enables it to disappear quickly by burrowing. The Arabian oryx (21) can survive long waterless periods, partly by using the water produced by its own metabolism – the ultimate in desert economy. One kilogram of carbohydrate, completely burnt up for energy, can yield half a litre of water. The locust, that biblical plague of Egypt (22), prevents drying out with a horny shell or, properly, an external skeleton.

21

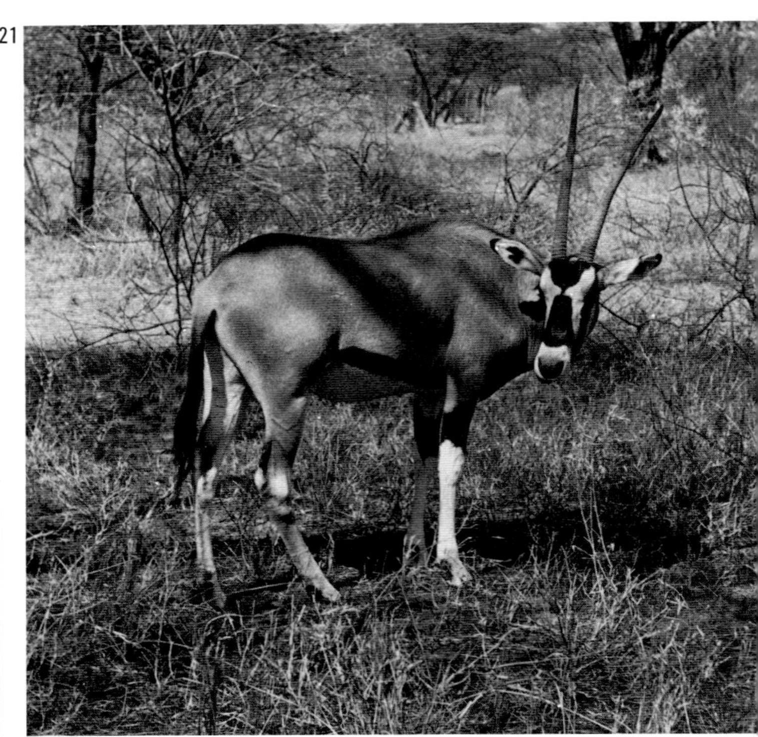

20

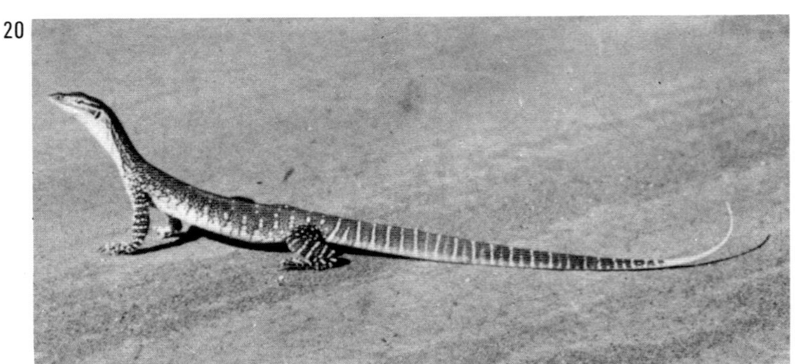

22

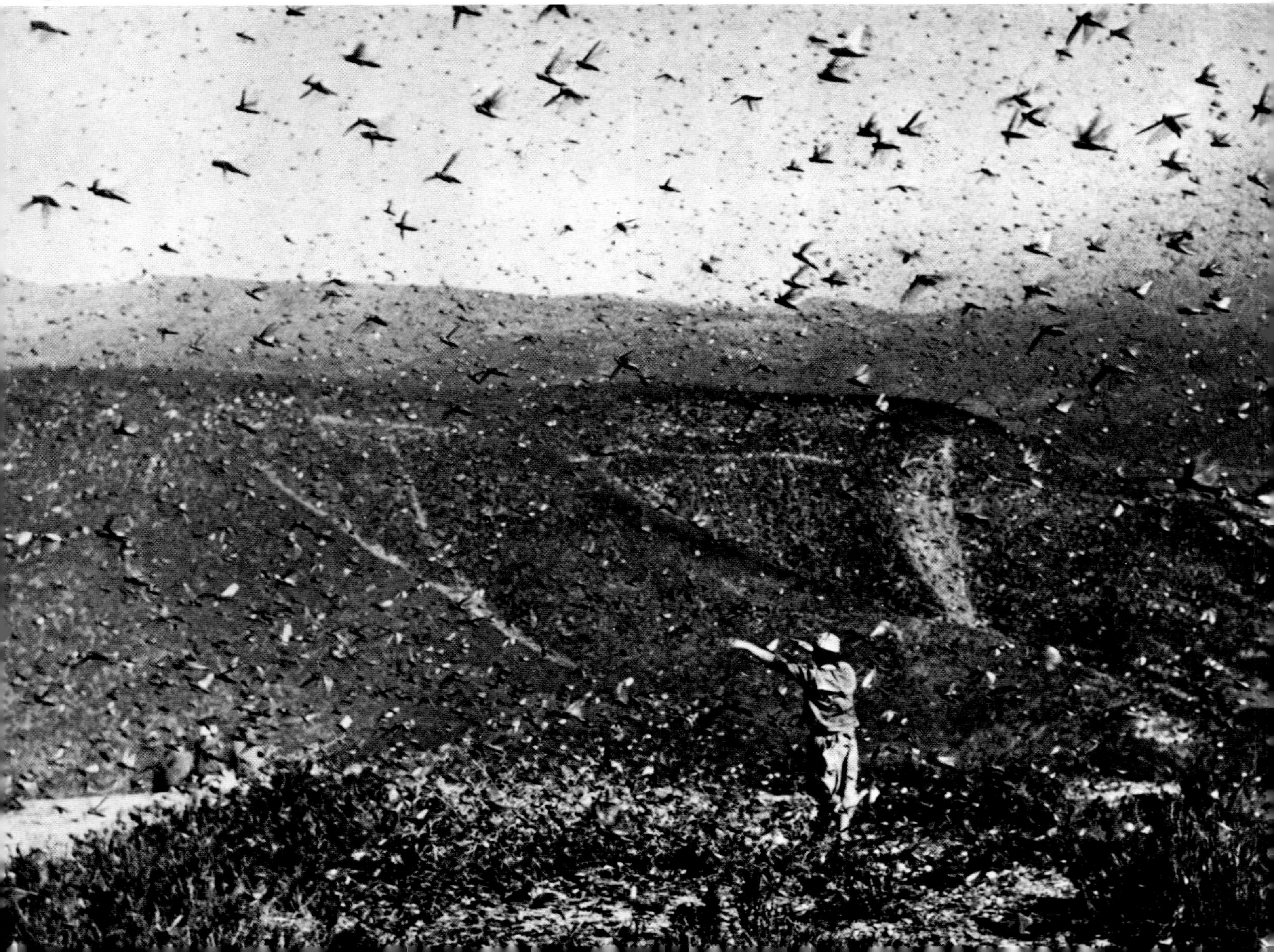

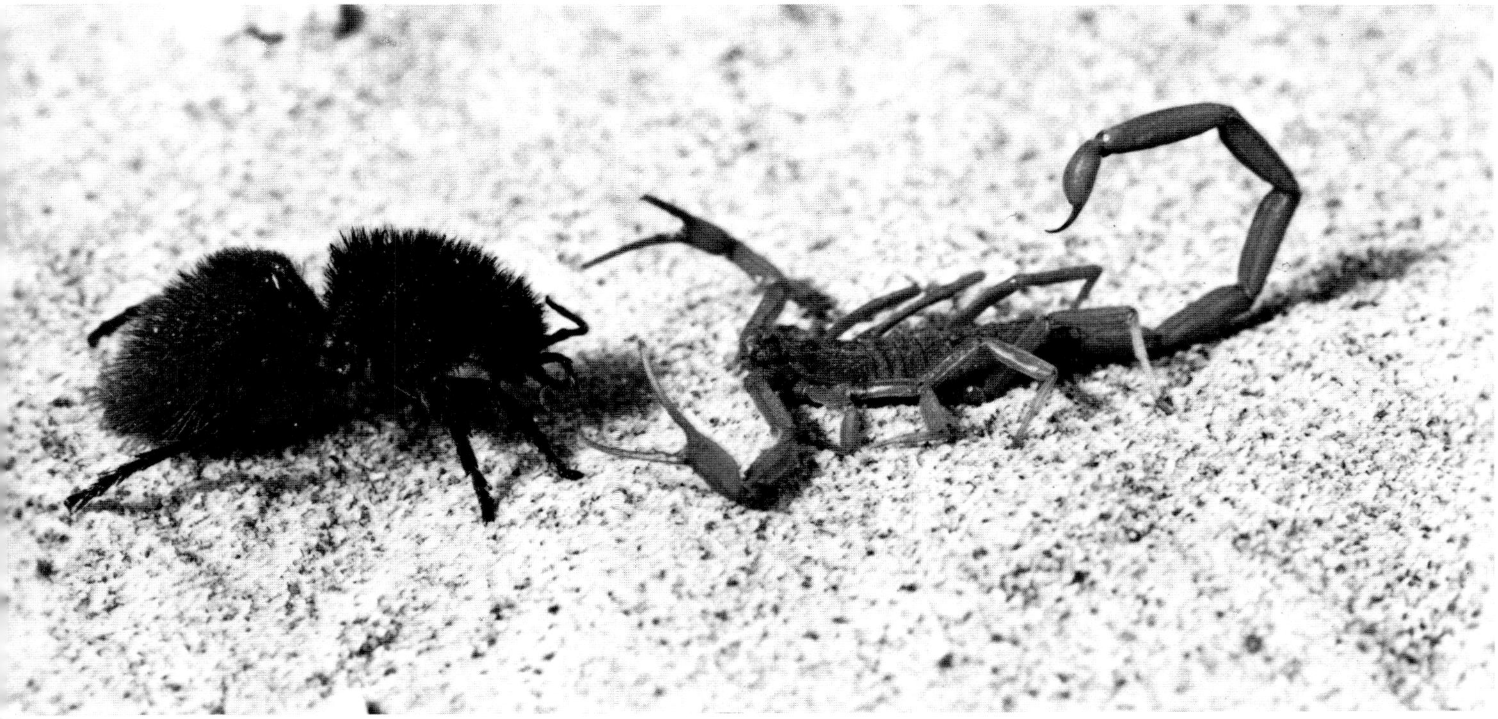

23

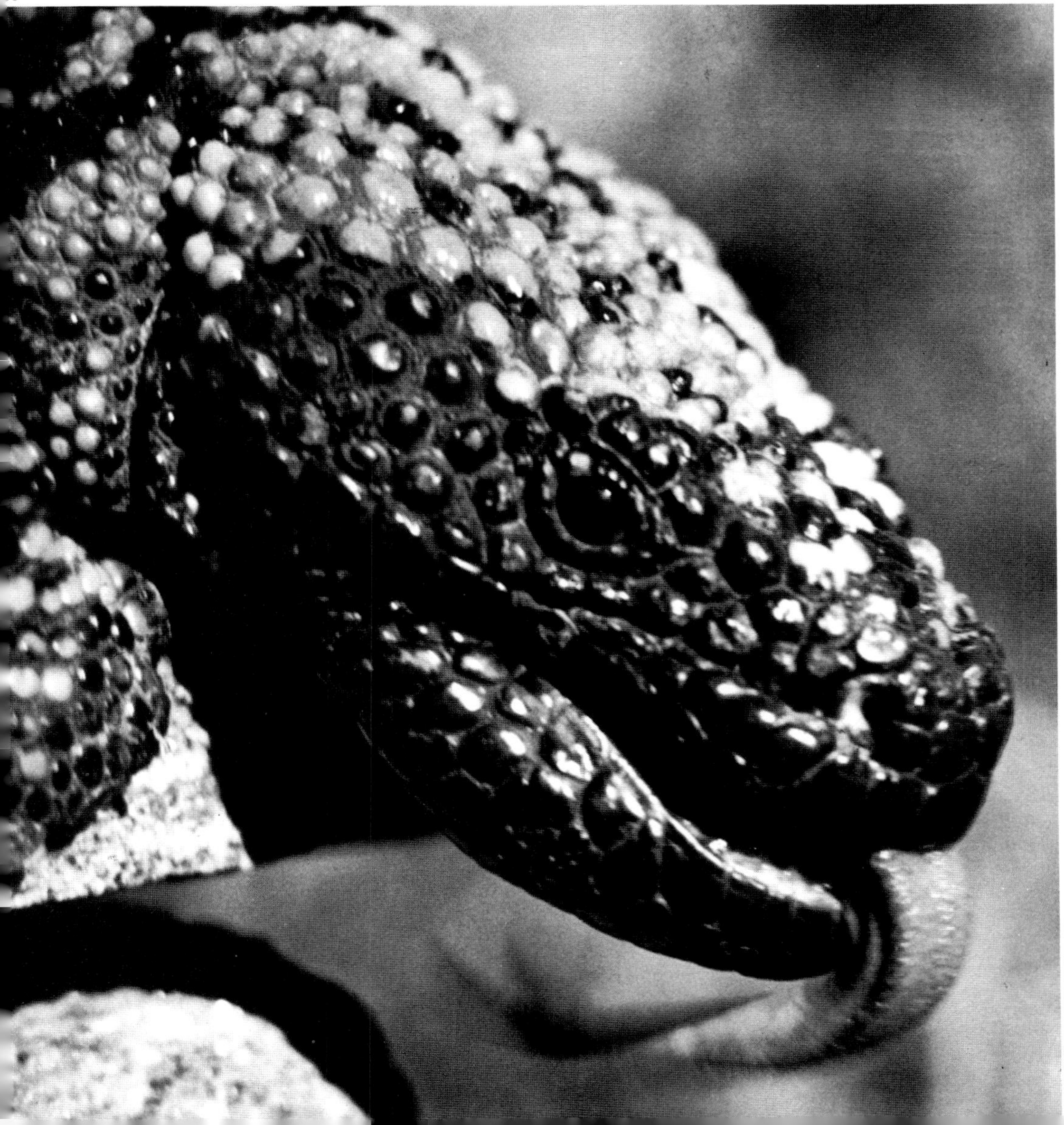

The vicious sting of the scorpion (23), here seen attacking a velvet ant in the Colorado desert, California, is an effective weapon against enemies of all sizes. For survival in desert conditions, however, it relies like the locust on its horny exoskeleton. The gila monster too, a large New World lizard, has a thick, warty skin to protect it against dehydration (24).

24

Man, like other animals, adapts in various ways to desert living, either consciously or by evolution. A tall, lanky physique, as in these Dinka tribesmen of Southern Sudan (26), is more favourable than a short, stout one. Nomadic Tuaregs (25 and 27) protect themselves from the fierce heat in loose, voluminous robes, and houses (28) tend to be white – to reflect the light – and thick-walled for coolness, like a kind of above-ground burrow.

25

26

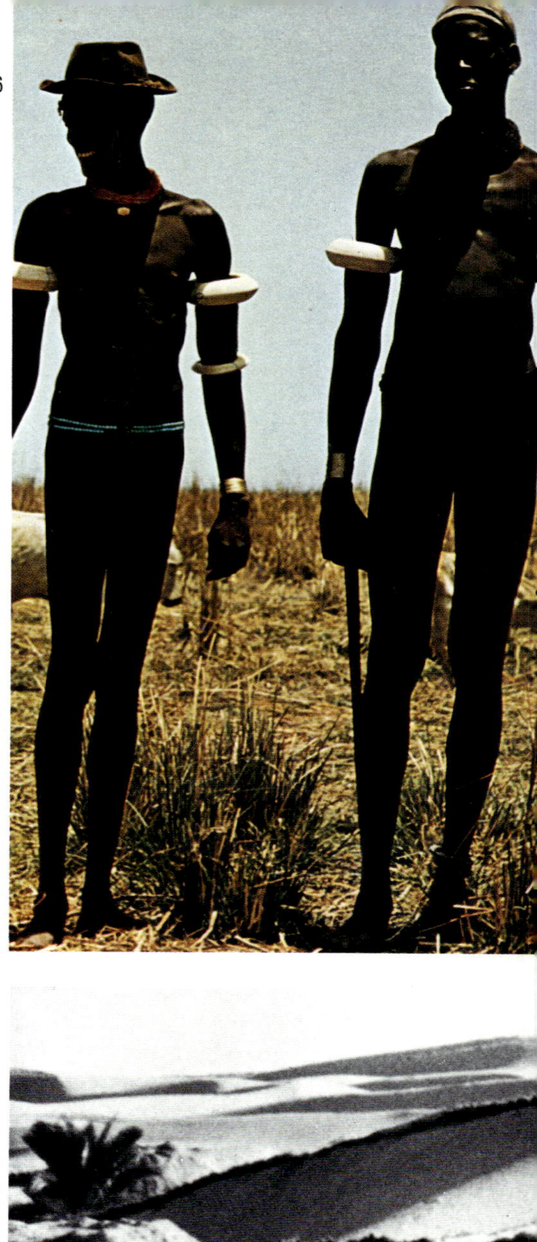

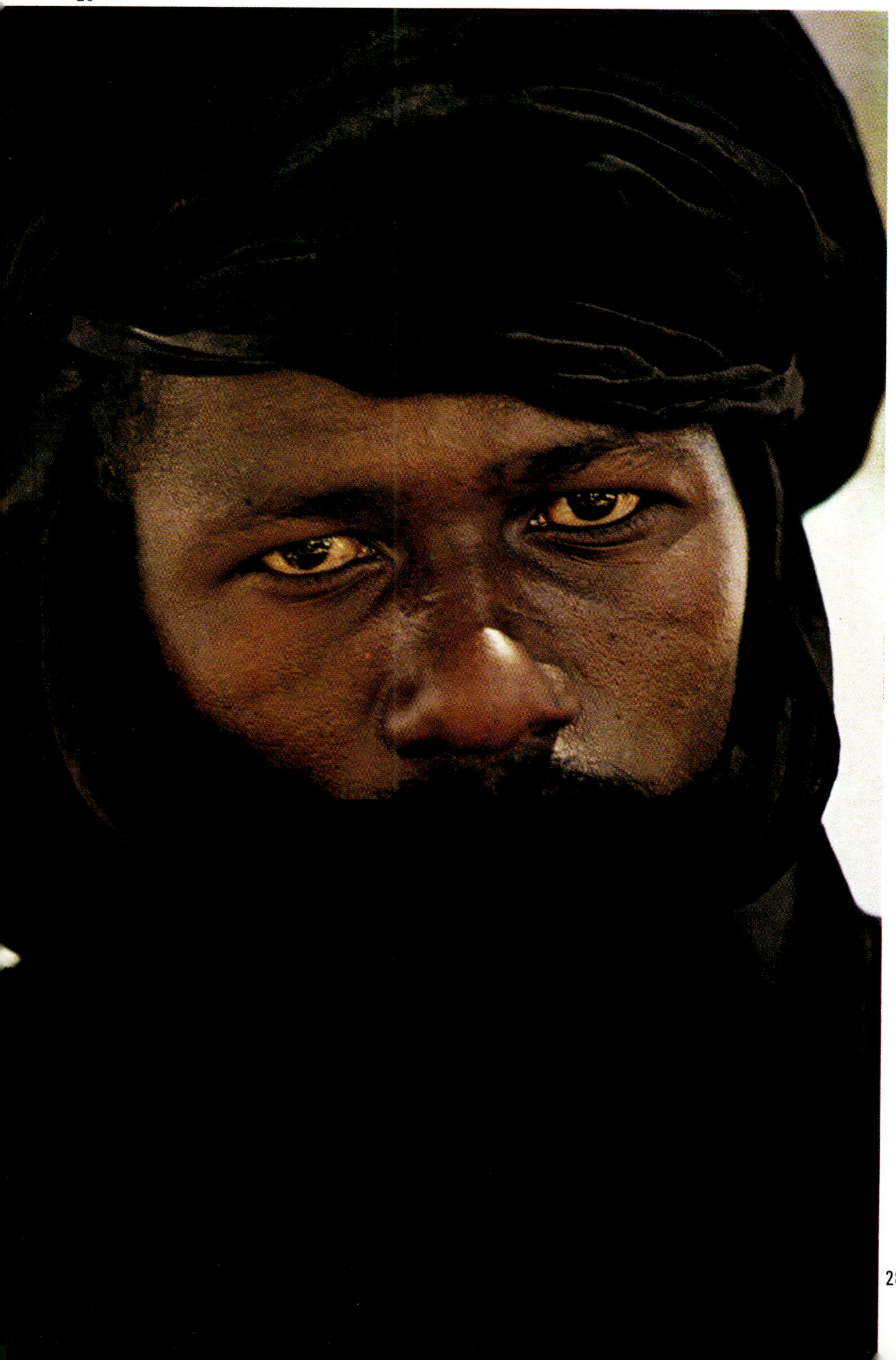

28

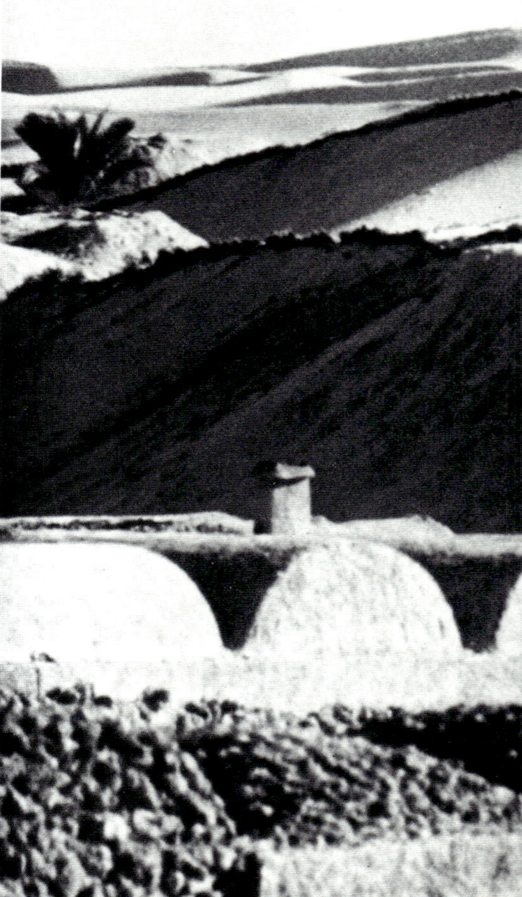

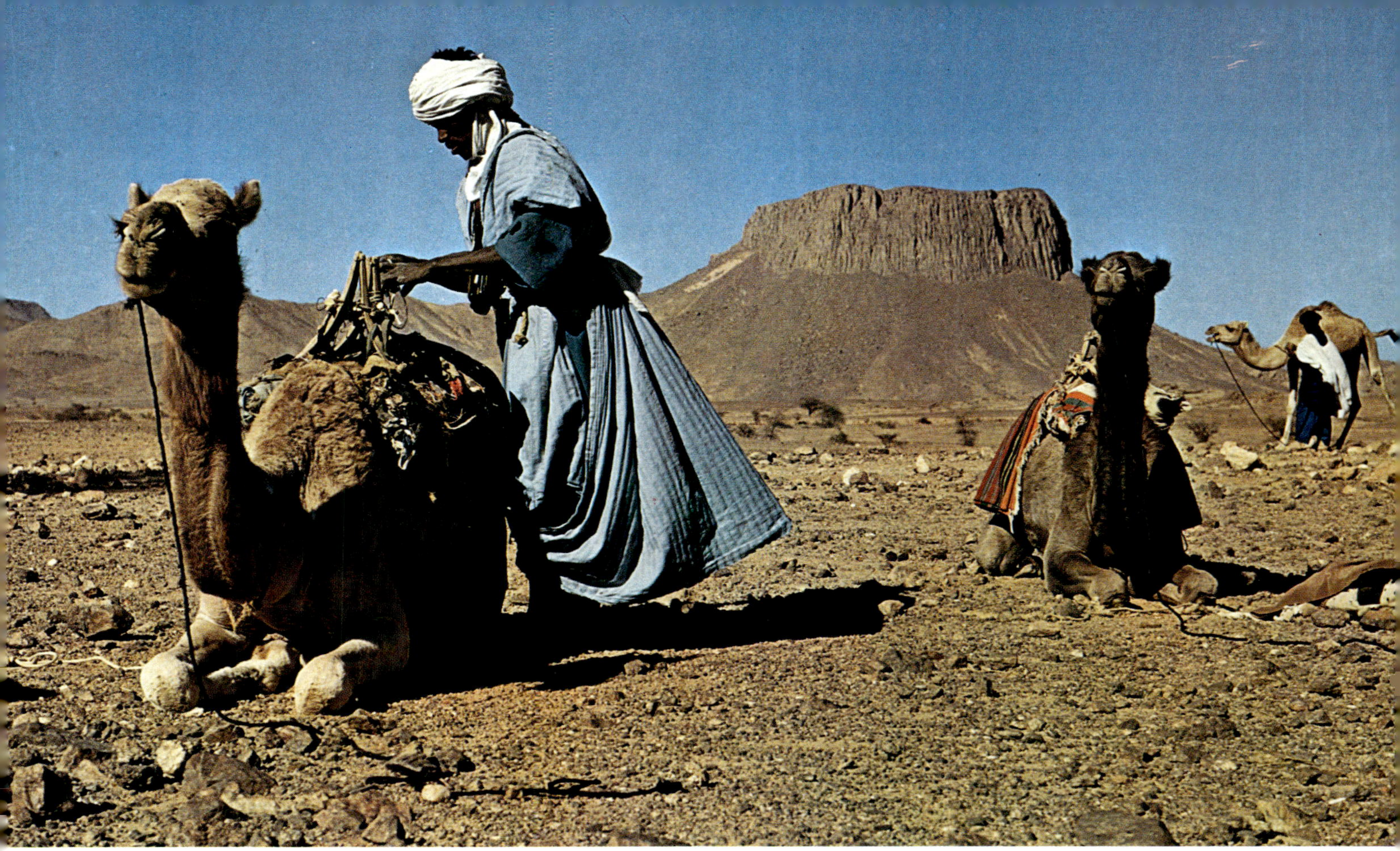

27

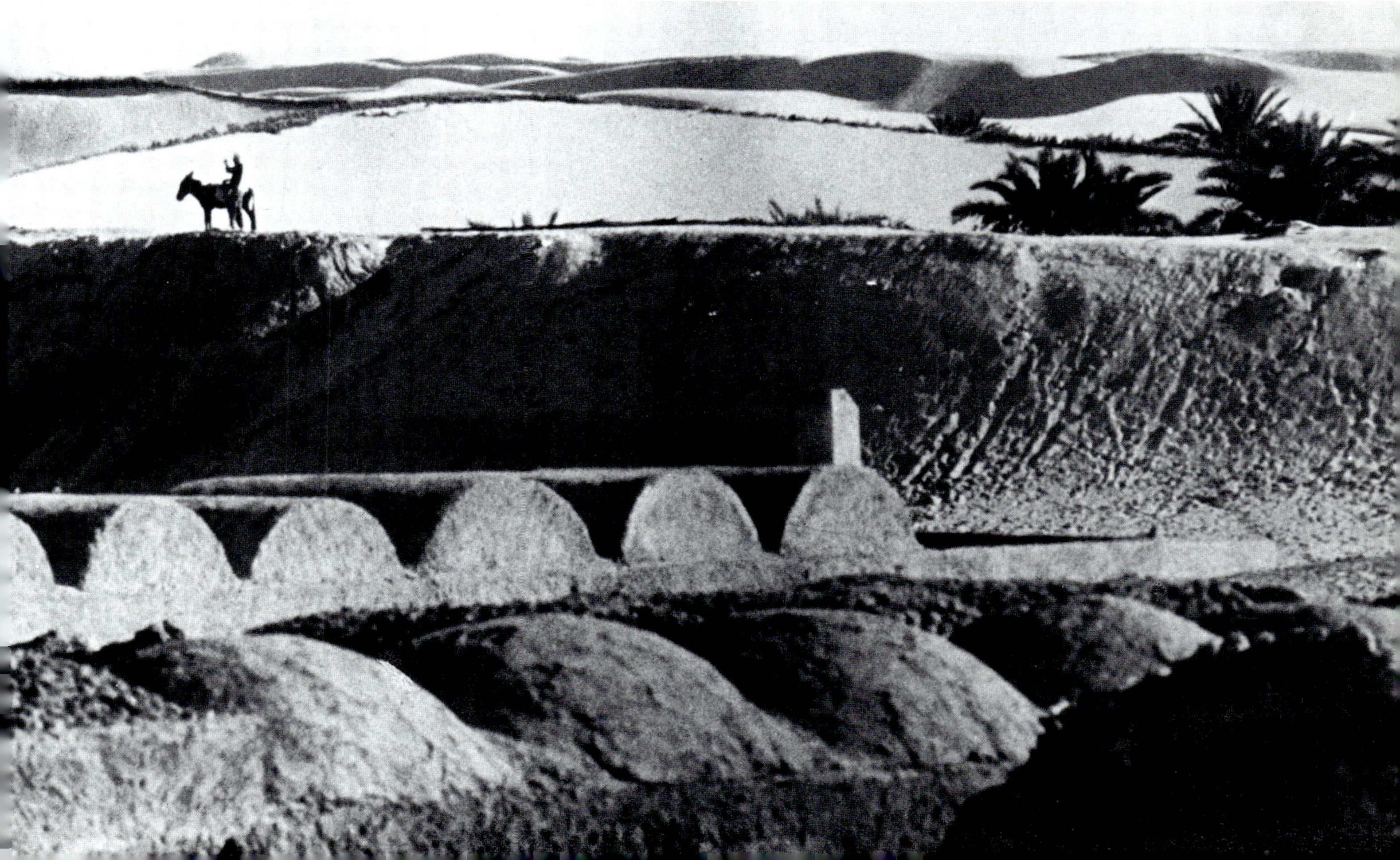

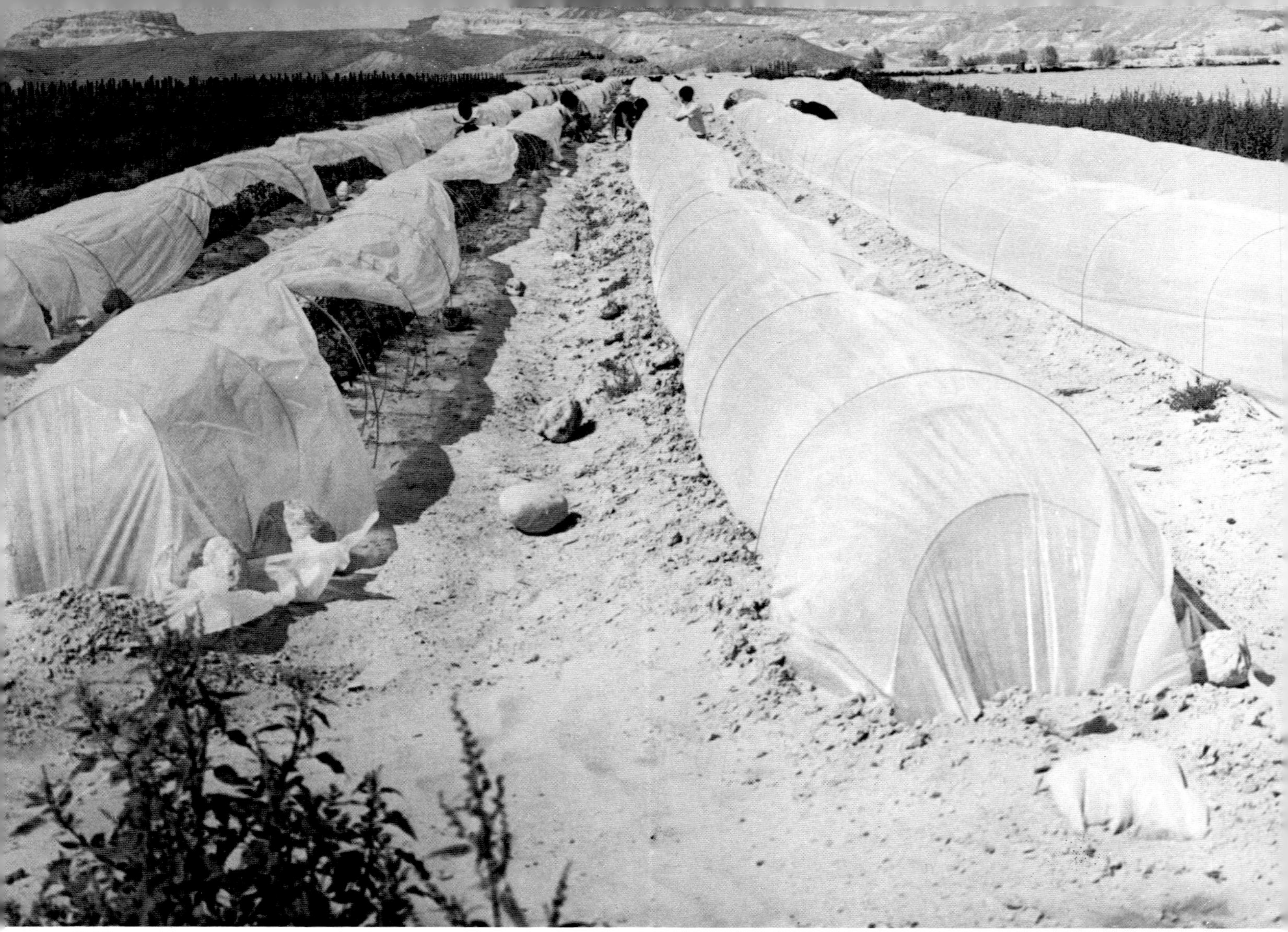

29/30

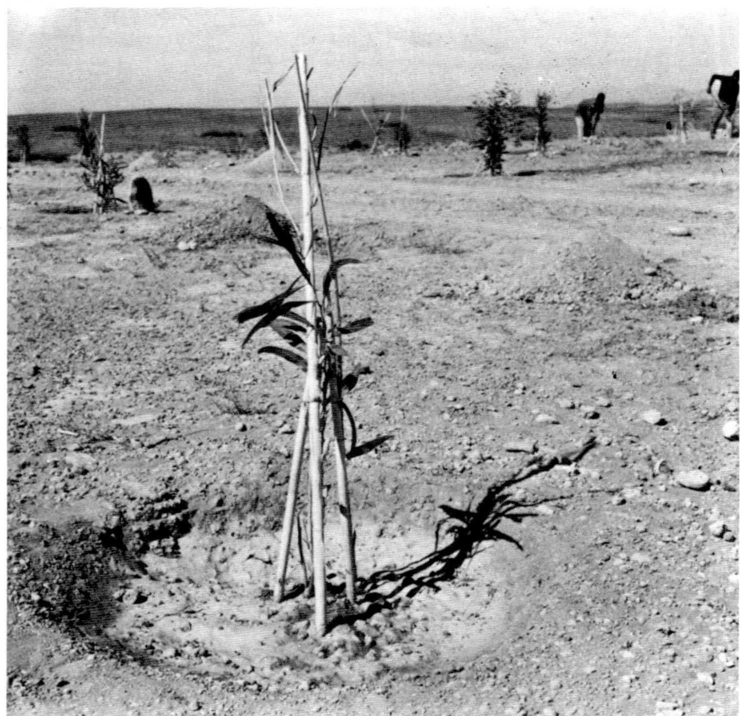

To tame the desert, to make it 'blossom like the rose', has been man's dream for centuries. Even in the grimmest conditions the desert can, to some extent, be reclaimed and made to bear fruit. The Negev, in Israel, is a prime example of the application of modern science and technology to desert farming (29); here a crop of green peppers is being grown under polythene cloches, which conserve water that would otherwise go to waste. In the Moroccan Sahara (30) reclamation starts with tree-planting to shade and protect the soil.

7

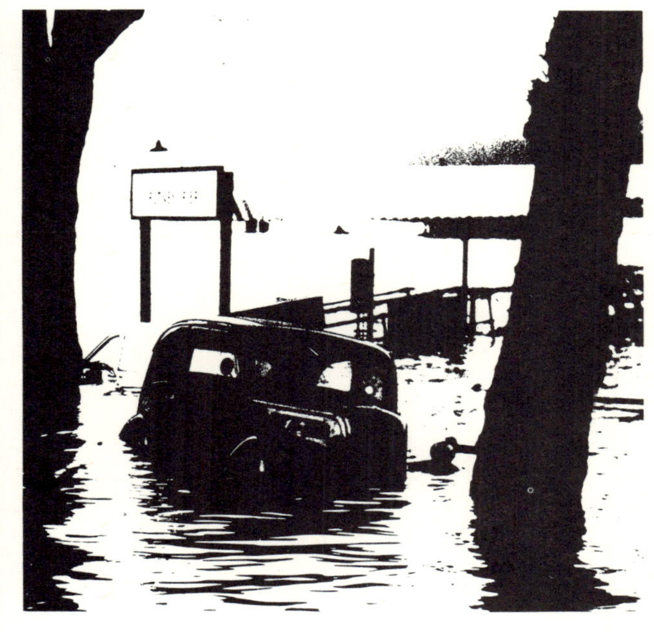

The flood of waters upon the earth

Sir Norman Rowntree

THE BIBLE DESCRIBES what is doubtless the best-known flood in the history of man:

> The rain was upon the earth forty days and forty nights. And the flood was forty days upon the earth; and the waters prevailed exceedingly upon the earth; and all the high mountains that were under the whole heaven were covered . . . And all flesh died that moved upon the earth . . .

The story of Noah attributes the disaster to human wickedness (a view which persisted in many parts of the world until modern times), and it may have been intended as a moral tale. The folklore of peoples in every continent teems with accounts of flood disasters, and at one time it was suggested that a single world event gave rise to these stories. It is now generally considered, however, that they merely point to the ubiquitous nature of flooding.

When nature produces a catastrophic flood it may be likened to a brilliant general engaged in a military operation who achieves maximum effect through surprise. If the timing and magnitude of every flood could be predicted, it is unlikely that there would be many disasters affecting human life. A flood achieves its surprise by the unexpected volume of the rainfall, snow, wind, tide or earthquake which initiates it and by the suddenness of its onset. The time between its likelihood and its actual occurrence is rarely more than a few hours or days, and even this is often reduced by uncertainty as to precisely where the flood will occur.

Man himself has often contributed to the danger by ignoring the possibility of flooding and establishing communities in places liable to be submerged at irregular intervals. Similarly, his own construction works have induced disasters when they have failed, or have at least greatly enhanced the danger of events which, in natural conditions, might have been comparatively mild.

There are many types of floods, varying in magnitude and frequency. Their effect on man depends on both the climate and the geography of the area where they occur. In places where great floods are unlikely to occur more often than once in 1,000 or even 10,000 years, there can be little precise information; they form a part of folklore and there is no accurate record.

Throughout geological time there have been enormous variations in sea level, and the earth's surface shows evidence of inundations and subsequent drying-out of huge areas of land. These changes are long-term effects of the forces of nature about which scientists speculate on the past and 'doom watchers' on the future. Precise records relate only to the comparatively recent past when, for instance, the Mississippi, the Indus and the great rivers of China have produced classical disasters. But such events seem important to us only when they affect our own communities; many happen in remote areas and may even pass unnoticed.

Disaster strikes

A number of the great flood disasters in history seem to have arisen from the invasion of coastal areas by the sea, in conjunction with river flooding. In recent years there have been a number of instances, one of which was in January 1953 when there was a surge of the North Sea due to the combination of very low atmospheric pressure with violent north winds. This led to a rise in sea level, and the water could not escape through the narrow Straits of Dover. The storm water piled up to nearly 3 metres above the predicted tide level in the Thames estuary, and to more than 3 metres along the Netherlands coast, where 1,835 people were drowned. Almost all south-west Holland was submerged, and the dykes were breached at many points. Vessels of every description – rowing-boats, tank landing craft, rubber dinghies, amphibious vehicles and the entire Dutch fishing fleet – were pressed into service to rescue thousands of marooned people. Helicopters snatched villagers from rooftops, trees and the tops of windmills, and altogether 68,000 survivors were evacuated from the flooded areas.

In Britain the sea broke through to a distance of two to three miles inland, and to a depth of twenty feet. Sweeping over the protective walls of seaside resorts, it carried away bungalows, caravans and people, and in only a few hours there were great changes in the coast line.

The year before, on 15 August 1952, a flood due entirely to exceptional rainfall destroyed part of the small English town of Lynmouth and its tiny harbour at the height of the holiday season. During the preceding 24 hours there had been an average rainfall of 143 mm (5.7 inches) over the whole catchment area of 102 square kilometres, and more than 200 mm (8 inches) over 44 square kilometres. There were two periods of intense rainfall at about 3 p.m. and 9 p.m. GMT, and these produced peak flows during the night, when holidaymakers were asleep in the many hotels along the banks of the narrow watercourse. The resulting flood brought down trees and rocks which temporarily blocked the narrow, steep valley through which the River Lyn reaches the sea. As these blockages broke down, the flood effects were greatly increased and caused tremendous devastation in an area where equable conditions normally prevail. Thirty-four people lost their lives, many buildings were demolished along with parts of the harbour, and cars were washed into the sea. The element of surprise was complete. Damage, including the values placed on lives, amounted to over £9 million.

In many parts of the world 100 mm of rain in a single storm is not unusual, and this, spread over an area of 100 square kilometres, represents 10 million cubic metres of water or, more dramatically, one million tonnes. If the catchment area is already wet, then a large part of it will concentrate to flow down a river in a few hours, and it is this concentration which leads to flooding. Even in moderate climates very much higher rates of rainfall have occurred. In 1911, for example, 1,170 mm fell in 24 hours at Baguio in the Philippines, and in 1955 there were 280 mm of rain in one day at Dorchester, England.

The catchment area

The maximum rate at which a river flows after heavy rain is related to the nature of the catchment area; it may be circular or long and narrow, it may be flat land leading to a slow run-off or mountainous, causing the rain to concentrate rapidly in the streams. The rate of concentration is affected by the nature of the vegetation, which itself varies according to the time of year. Then there are natural obstructions in the course of a river, sometimes augmented by fallen trees or ice barriers, all of which control the flow. There have been notable flood disasters resulting from the breakdown of such temporary natural obstructions, or of man-made dams if they are breached by an abnormal volume of water.

If the precipitation upon a catchment area is in the form of snow, it may remain stored there for many days or months, awaiting warmer weather before appearing in the rivers as water; then the rate at which the snow melts determines the maximum flow that will occur. Occasionally the melt can be extremely rapid, and the snowfall of many months suddenly appears in the river system, leading to a major disaster.

Heavy snow-melt floods constitute a much greater problem in mountainous regions with regular snowfalls and summer melts. Large quantities of soil, previously frozen, may be removed and carried down the rivers. In California the volume of a flood has been known to be increased by 10 per cent owing to the volume of solid matter contained in it.

When the land sinks

Floods are not always a consequence of rain or snow, for they may occur as the result of the insidious depression of land areas in relation to adjacent sea levels. Some parts of the world are particularly notable for this situation, which is often caused by man's own drainage methods. London has become lower by about half a metre over the last 150 years and, since it is close to a tidal river, extensive and costly embankment and tidal-barrier works are now being constructed to prevent the city from being dangerously flooded. Even more serious is the danger threatening Venice, where the abstraction of underground water has also caused the ground level to sink, and the frequent inundation of this wonderful city has become a matter of world-wide concern.

In California the Sacramento River system is elaborately controlled to mitigate flooding over an important agricultural area, where drainage and agricultural development have led to the shrinkage and substantial lowering of the land, and a consequential increased liability to flooding. This danger in areas which have sunk in relation to the sea can be greatly aggravated by nature's wilder events, as happened in the North Sea in 1953. Similar emergencies of frightening suddenness can occur in low-lying areas with the arrival of a tsunami, or 'tidal wave', induced by an earthquake or volcanic eruption, perhaps many hundreds of kilometres away. When Krakatoa erupted in 1883 (see p. 211) the town of Telok Betong in Sumatra, some 40 km distant across the Sunda Strait, took the brunt of a colossal tsunami which arrived one hour after the eruption. Situated on a flat coastal plain at the head of the funnelling shores of Lampong Bay, it was in the worst possible place, and never stood a chance. The engineer of a ship in the harbour described the disaster:

> The ship made a formidable leap, and immediately afterwards we felt as though we had plunged into the abyss. . . . Like a high mountain, the monstrous wave precipitated its journey towards the land. Immediately afterwards another three waves of colossal size appeared. And before our eyes this terrifying upheaval of the sea, in a sweeping transit, consumed in one instant the ruin of the town; the lighthouse fell in one piece, and all the houses of the town were swept away in one blow like a castle of cards. All was finished. There, where a few moments ago lived the town of Telok Betong, was nothing but the open sea.

From devastation on the low hills behind the town, it was afterwards calculated that the wave, when it crossed the shoreline, was 27 metres high, or about 87 feet.

Fig. 1 The bursting of Dale Dykes dam in 1864: an artist's impression of the disaster.

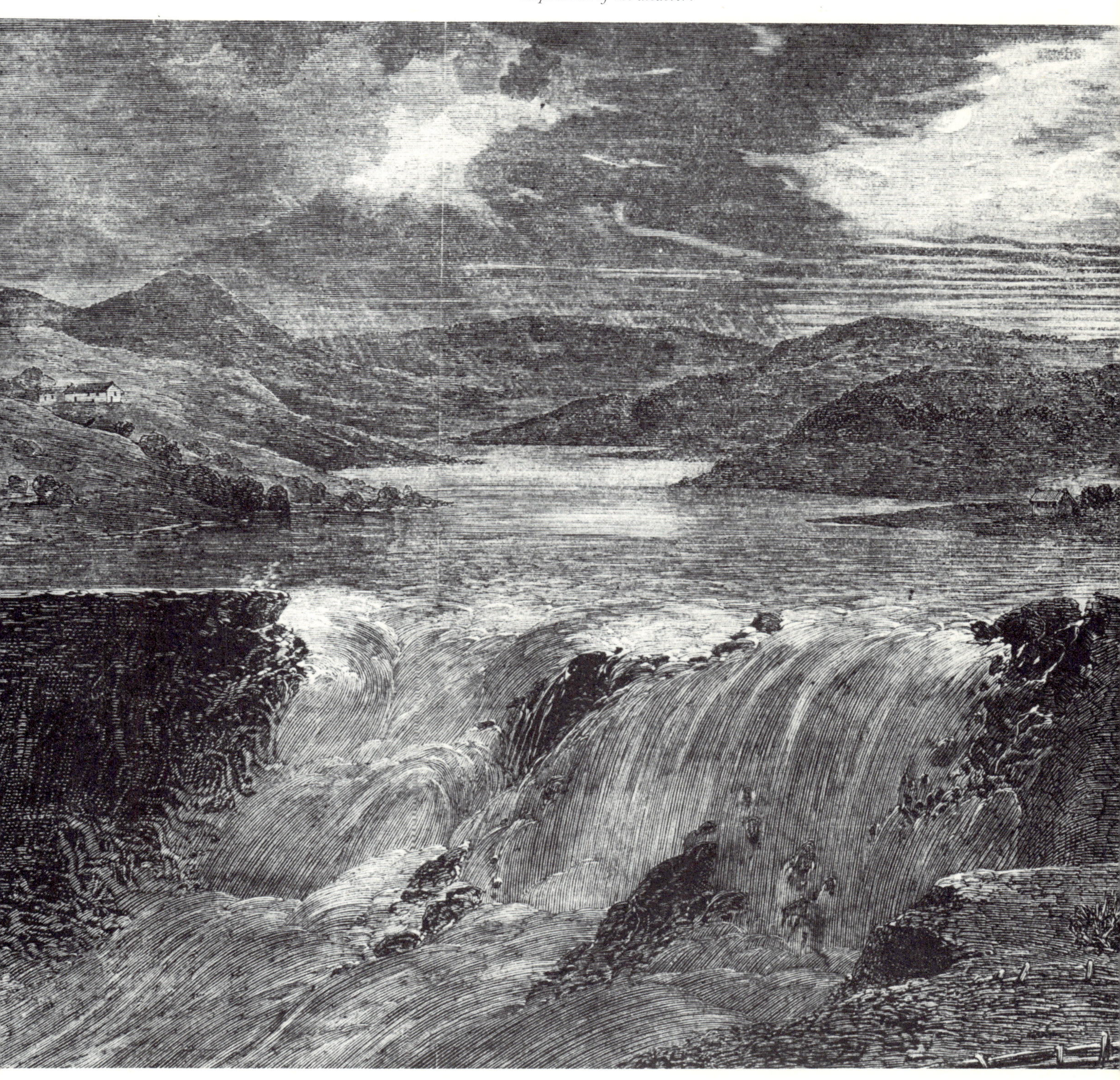

Fig. 2 The pattern of erosion and deposition in a meandering river. The cross-section shows the river-bed at A – B or at any point one or more wavelengths upstream or downstream.

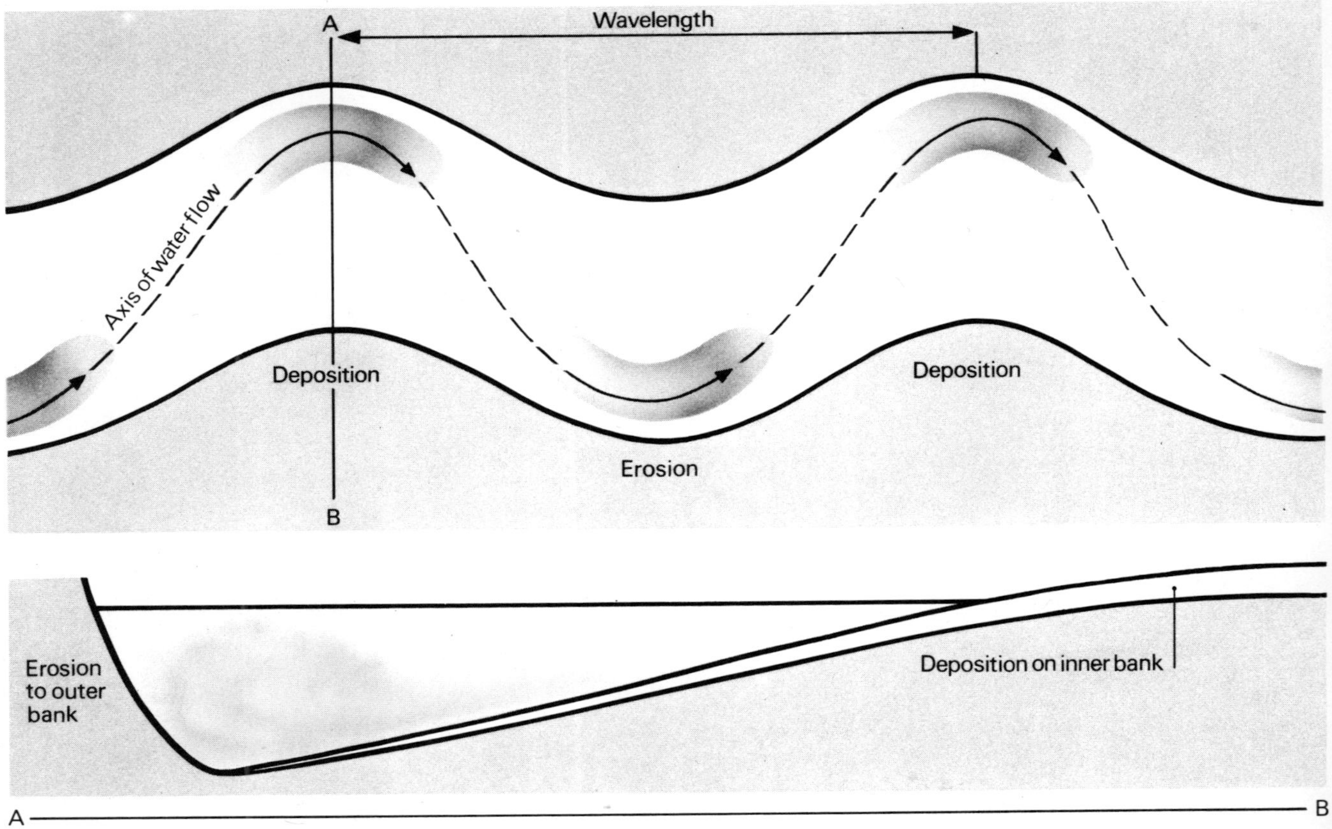

Man-made floods

Finally, there are those floods which are dangerous and severe not necessarily because of their magnitude, but because they should never have occurred and are therefore unexpected. These are man-induced floods arising from the sudden failure of constructions such as dams. The water they hold back, often in the form of huge lakes, is inevitably a threat to the narrow downstream areas; but fortunately failures are rare. If such a dam does break, everything in the water's path is destroyed until it can disperse in the wider lower reaches. In England, one of the worst disasters occurred in Sheffield in 1864 with the failure of the Dale Dykes dam, when nearly 250 people died. The terrible disaster at Johnstown, Pennsylvania, in 1889, when 10,000 people lost their lives, was described in these words by an eyewitness:

> When the dam broke the water seemed to leap, scarcely touching the ground, and bounding down the valley. Its front was like a solid wall, twenty feet high, crashing,

roaring, and carrying everything before it. The torrent in front looked dusty; that must have been the spray. The houses went down before it, tottered for a moment, and then rose, crushing against each other like eggshells.

Another shocking catastrophe was the failure of the Malpasset dam in southern France in 1959, when 396 people were drowned. On the night of 3 December the dam, 58 metres high and located a few kilometres north of Fréjus, suddenly collapsed. About 50 million cubic metres of water poured down the valley in a vast tidal wave, wiping out the town in a few minutes. Some people were swept right out to sea, while others were buried under the thick mud which covered the entire area. The only building to survive was the already ruined Roman arena. 'The Romans built better than we did,' an onlooker remarked sadly. However, there was nothing wrong with the design of the dam itself, but an unnoticed stratum of clay at one end weakened the arch structure. In contrast, the Vaiont dam disaster in northern Italy, which occurred in 1963 and led to the loss of over two thousand lives, although involving a dam of similar design, ironically demonstrated the inherent safety of such a dam. In this case the dam itself, 265 metres high and one of the largest in the world, was barely damaged although water rose to a height of 200 metres above it when a whole mountainside collapsed into the reservoir (as had been feared by the locals for some time) and displaced huge quantities of water.

Scars on the face of the earth

If we consider the results of flooding, it is clear that it has a marked effect on the appearance of the earth's surface, and the more rapid and concentrated the movement of the water, the greater the effect. The steady flow of streams has a slow, insidious effect, but the major pattern of river beds is governed by the periods of exceptional flow. The characteristics of a river channel can be related to those flows which fill the natural river channel – what are called 'bank-full' discharges – but serious floods spreading beyond the natural banks cause major changes in the watercourse. The consequent erosion of the soil and rock, its conveyance in the fast-flowing water and its deposition are all part of the process by which the earth's surface is shaped.

In this process the effects of flooding are different in the steep rapidly running rivers of mountainous or hilly regions from the slow meandering flows typical of the lower reaches of mature rivers coursing through flat lands to the sea. The pattern of flow in a steep upland river is determined not only by the natural tendency of the moving water to oscillate, but by the geological characteristics of the rocks over which it flows. It will constantly tend to cut its way through the softer material and along the lines of faults in the rock, but in times of rapid flow the volume of water carries large quantities of coarse material downstream. The size of the rocks and the distance they are moved depend on the amount of energy in the water. Even in steep mountainous valleys, flood plains can be formed through which the stream will tend to wander from side to side.

As a river proceeds to the lower, flatter lands, the pattern of erosion and deposition becomes more formalized and predictable in shape. Water flowing along a channel sets up oscillations in three dimensions, with amplitudes extending vertically and horizontally in the cross-section of the river, and a wavelength in the direction of flow. The effect of these movements is to create meanders in which the cross-section changes so that the deeper parts of the stream are on the outside of the bends. As time goes on, the bends move downstream and tend to become more convoluted. This pattern of development corresponds to periods of medium flooding when the water does not quite overflow the river banks.

In severe floods more drastic changes occur, for the river may take short cuts, straightening out some sections, and elsewhere removing large quantities of material from the outer banks of bends. At the same time the flood plain itself will be submerged and the water, flowing at a slower rate, will deposit silt on adjacent land. Man's attempts to control this process by designed embankments can be only partially successful and some change due to erosion is inevitable.

When the sea floods the land a similar, though limited, effect takes place in extreme conditions. The erosion of material from cliffs to form beaches, from which it may again be eroded later and deposited elsewhere, is a continuing process. In times of abnormal flood surges this may suddenly be speeded up, with occasionally disastrous results (Pl. 3).

Although the changes in land surface can be rapid, and on a large scale during extreme flood conditions, they are rarely in themselves disastrous but need to be considered in relation to the social effects that result from the movement and the inundation. It is through man's failure to recognize the inevitability and scale of floods that extreme damage usually develops.

In rural areas, agricultural and residential development tends to be adapted to cope with floods that can be remembered. It is only the major storms, which occur perhaps once in a hundred years or more, that are likely to surprise the inhabitants and cause major damage to property. Consequently, flooding in country districts is more likely to affect the yield of crops than to damage property.

Many surveys have been made with a view to discovering how much people realize the flood risks they run, and what value they place upon protection. In general it seems that unless there has been a recent major inundation there is little concern, or willingness to insure against flood damage, or pressure for flood-protection schemes. When serious floods do occur they make news headlines, but the majority of the population are remote from the subject except in very rare cases. Local action will be taken, however, when floods recur at intervals of only a few years.

However, there are major exceptions to this where tidal surges are concerned. The 1953 North Sea flood, which inundated 1,600 square kilometres in the Netherlands, and in England killed 300 people, flooded 24,000 houses and 200 industrial buildings, led to the construction of new sea defences and warning systems costing many millions of pounds.

The value of these protective measures was demonstrated in 1976, when an even higher tide occurred as the result of north-east winds gusting to 100 mph which prevented the ebb of one tide and drove the next above the normal level. On this occasion many people were evacuated in time, and the 20 lives lost were not the result of flooding. However, the sea defences were breached in a few places, causing the washing away of a railway line, but only 400 houses were flooded. The Storm Tide Warning System itself was certainly successful, for each of the five sections into which the east coast of England is now divided received successive preliminary and full warnings as the rising tide moved southward along the coast.

These events, separated by 23 years, show that defensive measures are worth while, but that there can always be a greater threat than that which has gone before. It is this which makes it so difficult to decide just how much money and effort should be committed to protection against an unknown future. One of the major problems is to maintain readiness and effective warning measures when such long periods of time elapse between situations of potential disaster. The more effective the physical defences the longer the time is likely to be between disaster situations.

The deltas of the large rivers such as the Ganges are also particularly vulnerable. The July–August 1974 floods in Bangladesh covered 800,000 square kilometres (an area almost equal to that of Texas and Louisiana combined) and caused the loss of 1,323 lives, the whole catastrophe being enhanced by its remoteness and the poor communications in the region. Where inundations occur on such a scale the lives of the inhabitants who survive remain at risk from the spread of water-born disease, particularly when the safe wells and springs have been flooded by grossly polluted water. In remote areas the time needed to bring in safe new supplies is almost certain to be too long to prevent the drinking of unsafe water, and often there is no fuel for boiling water.

Counting the cost of protection

Apart from the loss of life in major flood disasters, the effects of repeated inundation on the agricultural economy have to be borne in mind. Such considerations must take into account the types of crops to be grown and the profitability of the land, before it can be decided how much protection should be provided.

Very different factors apply when considering the problems of floods affecting urban areas. It is often thought remarkable that urban communities should have developed in situations where floods can occur, but the explanation is simple. Most of them originated hundreds of years ago, and it was not until the industrial revolution started having its effect in the nineteenth century that it was physically possible for such communities to develop remote from rivers. In earlier years water could not be carried long distances and, if industrial activity was required, water power was needed and it had to be obtained from rivers. Moreover, the transport of heavy goods had to be by boat, and even the canal system tended to follow the routes of the principal water courses except when crossing between catchments.

In these circumstances it was natural for towns to be built alongside rivers. However, modern communities do not readily accept such risks, and the damage which can occur may justify extensive flood-protection measures. Urban flooding is more notable for inconvenience than for large-scale tragedy. Lives can be saved by evacuation if the warning system is efficient, but the damage to property cannot easily be mitigated. Purely on the basis of lives saved, money spent on flood-protection schemes might be better spent on road safety, but the protection of property and the fear of sudden disaster to a community encourages proportionately greater expenditure on flood protection.

The impact of flood damage on life and property can be reduced to approximate economic terms, but when a large enough disaster occurs, the social consequences lead to a public demand for protection beyond that which can be economically justified. In such cases intangible factors, such as the desire for security, come into play and involve political decisions.

One of the most famous water planning and management authorities in the world is the Tennessee Valley Authority

Fig. 3 If, in any particular set of conditions of climate and territory, a number of floods are plotted, peak flow against catchment area, a group of points like this will result. A curve can then be drawn, to cover all normally expected flood maxima – the first thing the designer of dams and reservoirs needs to know. It is not possible, nor economic, to cater for the occasional freak storm. In August 1917, in the Redaven valley north of Dartmoor, after a violent rainstorm, maximum run-off was measured at 9.9 cm an hour; this was three times the limit shown by the design curve.

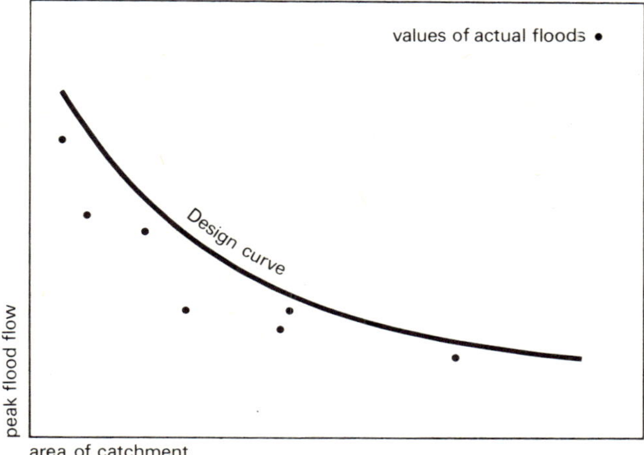

in the USA. The TVA Act of 1933 authorized the construction of 'dams and reservoirs in the Tennessee River and its tributaries' to 'control destructive flood waters in the Tennessee and Mississippi River drainage basins'. Originally set up in the depression years to provide work, the TVA has developed techniques of economic appraisal of flood-protection schemes which in themselves spectacularly justify the many major works carried out. Technical Report No. 26, *Floods and Flood Control* (1961), forms an authoritative compendium of hydrological and engineering knowledge based on extensive practical experience and success. It includes interesting assessments of economic advantages gained. In Chapter 12, the assessment of flood damage is studied and the concept of estimating 'preventable damage' and its value is set out. In the fifteen years 1945 to 1960, flood damage valued at more than $24.5 million was averted on the lower Ohio and Mississippi rivers, and the total damage preventable by the TVA reservoir system amounted in the one year 1960 to $8,788,000. If increased land values are taken into account this figure becomes $13,288,000. These cold figures represent only part of the advantages gained, both because it is difficult to estimate the enormous gain in human happiness and security and also because other great advantages, such as hydro-electric power generation and water recreation, should be entered on the credit side of the activities of the Tennessee Valley Authority.

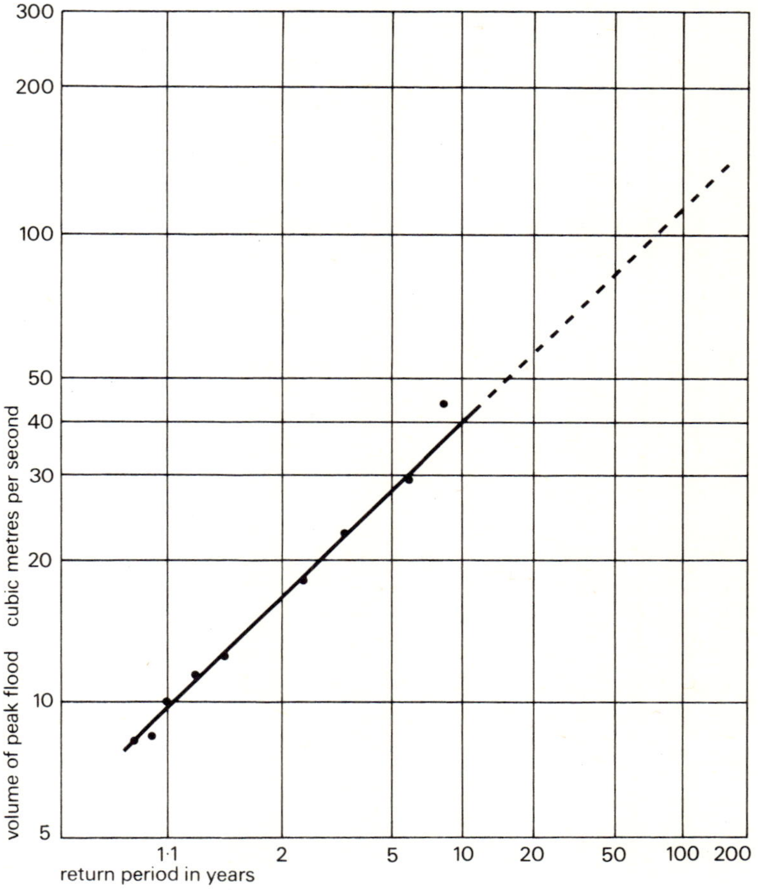

Fig. 4 The bigger the flood the longer the interval of time before it is likely to recur. This is to state the obvious, but it is still useful for the water engineer to be able to quantify the obvious. If values of maximum annual flood flows are listed in order of magnitude and their return periods calculated, the results plotted on a logarithmic scale will approximate to a straight-line relationship for the particular flow gauging site at which the river flows were measured. A limited extrapolation of the straight line enables the magnitude of less frequent floods to be estimated, but the accuracy of estimate decreases rapidly as the line is extended into longer return periods (broken line).

Fig. 5 A given unit of 'effective' rainfall (discounting evaporation, percolation etc.) running off into a river in a given time T will give a shape of flood flow which can be worked out for any specific river flow measuring station from the record of previous flood flows. This is that station's 'unit hydrograph' – an essential device in forecasting the course of any flood.

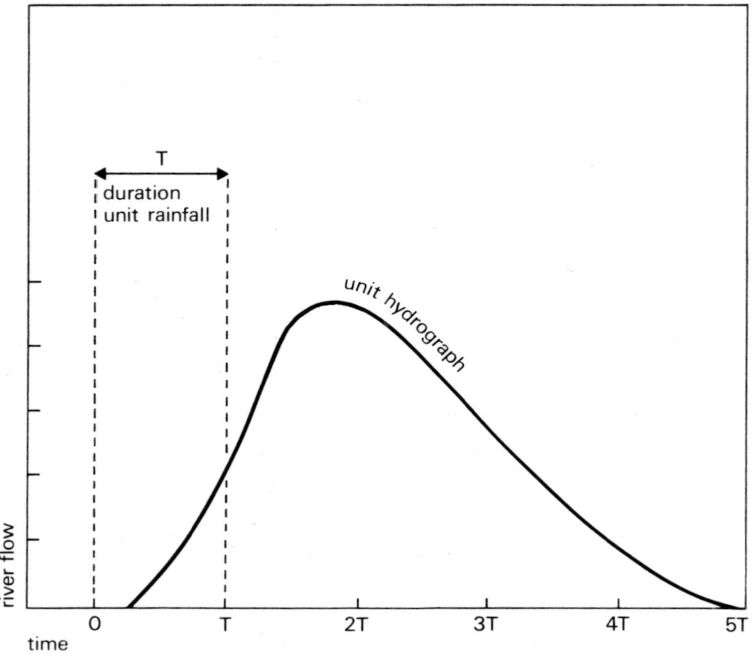

Problems and solutions

Hydrology is the science which deals with the waters of the earth. Flood hydrology, as the name implies, is concerned with the forecasting, assessment and prevention of flooding, and is therefore required to provide information for many purposes. Works on rivers or in areas subject to flooding, and works for the purpose of flood control, are designed to withstand floods of some stipulated probability. The effects of changes in land use, flood plain development, and engineering works affecting the river, are evaluated to assess the acceptability of proposals and to determine what steps should be taken to deal with adverse secondary effects. For example, it is possible for a reservoir to reduce floods in the river valley immediately downstream, but to increase the magnitude of flood peaks still further downstream by delaying the flood and causing it to coincide with the peaks from other tributaries with which it was formerly out of phase. The operation and management of warning systems require forecasts regarding the size and timing of approaching flood events. They therefore call for the collection and immediate analysis of data on the causative factors such as rainfall, and the flood flow upstream.

For design purposes, there are several possible approaches to the estimation of floods. In some, such as works for river channel improvement and flood bank design, we need only consider the maximum flood level related to the peak flood discharge, the duration of the flood being of no great concern. On the other hand, problems involving flood storage, or the extent of inundation, must be based on the flood volume, and in many cases its duration and the expected interval before a further flood may be expected. Duration and timing become even more important when surges and tidal problems are involved.

The Roda gauge on the Nile at Cairo has been in operation for some 2,500 years, but the systematic collection of data on high river flows is, generally speaking, a recent development. In some places, flood peak levels have been recorded in some way for a long time; but there is no record of changes affecting the relationship between the recorded level and the real flood magnitude. Data from the place for which information is required are often not available, even when other points on the same river may have records. The hydrologist is therefore usually working with little or no reliable information.

In the early days simple studies of an area were made by taking into account any recorded major floods and the size of the catchment. Then formulae were evolved to calculate somewhat greater floods than those already experienced. Gradually, these calculations became more complex as factors like rainfall intensity and the slope of the catchment

Fig. 6 Composite hydrograph from successive rainfalls. The three small hydrographs enclosing the areas Q_1, Q_2 and Q_3 following rainfalls R_1, R_2 and R_3 combine to form the total hydrograph representing the actual resulting river flow.

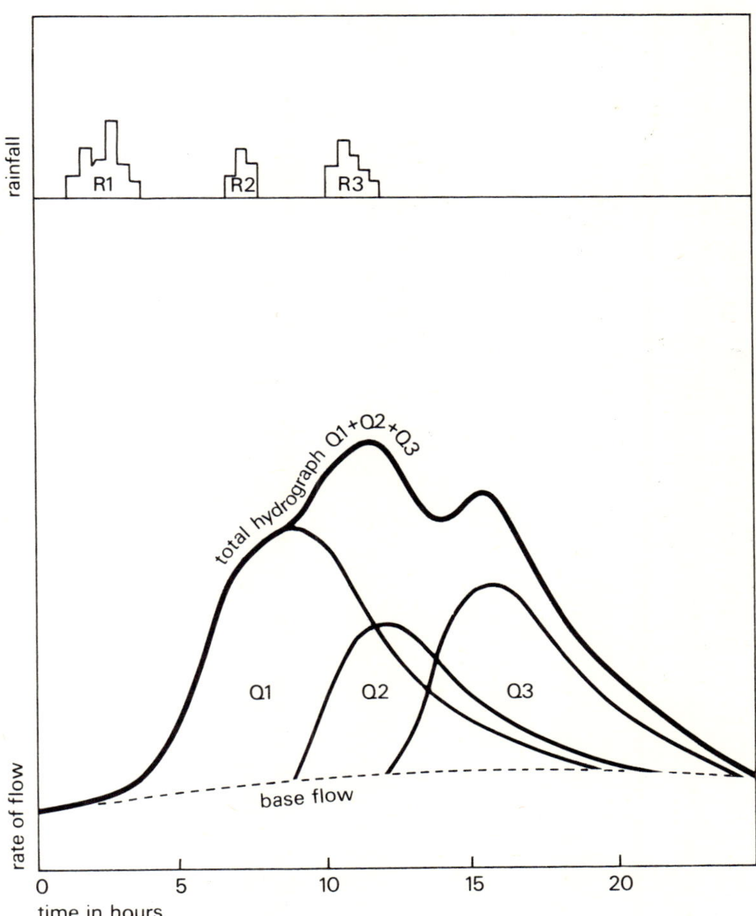

were introduced, but there was still no attempt to estimate the frequency at which floods might occur. As protection schemes became more complex, ways were found to express potential floods of any chosen probability as multiples of the known mean annual flood. Because there is often more information available about rainfall than river flow, it proved valuable to establish a unit of effective rainfall, called the 'unit hydrograph'. This is arrived at by dividing the total rainfall between evaporation, soil wetness, percolation into deep rocks and the effective rainfall – the latter being the amount which will contribute to a flood. The unit hydrograph represents the effective rainfall during a selected period of time, and can therefore be used to calculate the total water for a storm of any duration or intensity. Furthermore, it can be used with estimates of rainfall to produce estimates of extreme floods.

Today mathematical models make it possible to calculate the floods which may be produced in a wide catchment area from a variety of storms, taking into account a large number of geographical and climatic variables, and to evaluate the effects of reservoirs and flood control works. This is a powerful aid in planning, in the operation of control measures, and in flood forecasting. But there are three separate zones in the world – temperate, tropical and arid – where different meteorological factors lead to heavy rainfall. Although similar methods of analysis may be used in all these, the results are very different and cannot usually be transposed from one zone to another. Arid-zone hydrology presents particular difficulties for, by the very nature of the country, population is sparse and information on past events limited. Therefore collection of rainfall data has been extremely difficult; but new methods, such as measurement by radar and monitoring from satellites, offer great new possibilities. In such countries watercourses are formed over the years by rare or occasional floods, particularly on steeper slopes. The stream beds tend to peter out on flat land where flood waters spread out and are absorbed by the ground or lost by evaporation. In such cases, occasional floods are likely to be, on balance, beneficial, for in some places they recharge the ground water or provide sweet water areas in otherwise brackish water-bearing strata.

Floods in these arid areas are very sudden and usually of short duration. The very speed of events can constitute a danger to unwary travellers who may be crossing or following the dry bed of such a watercourse. Although an approaching flood wave can sometimes be heard, it has not always been recognized in time.

In most countries there is an excessive confidence that floods can be avoided by the application of good engineering design and construction, or by good catchment

Fig. 7 Generalized plan and section of a typical flood embankment system. Such a system would incorporate a fairly complex land drainage scheme in order to preserve agricultural use of the land.

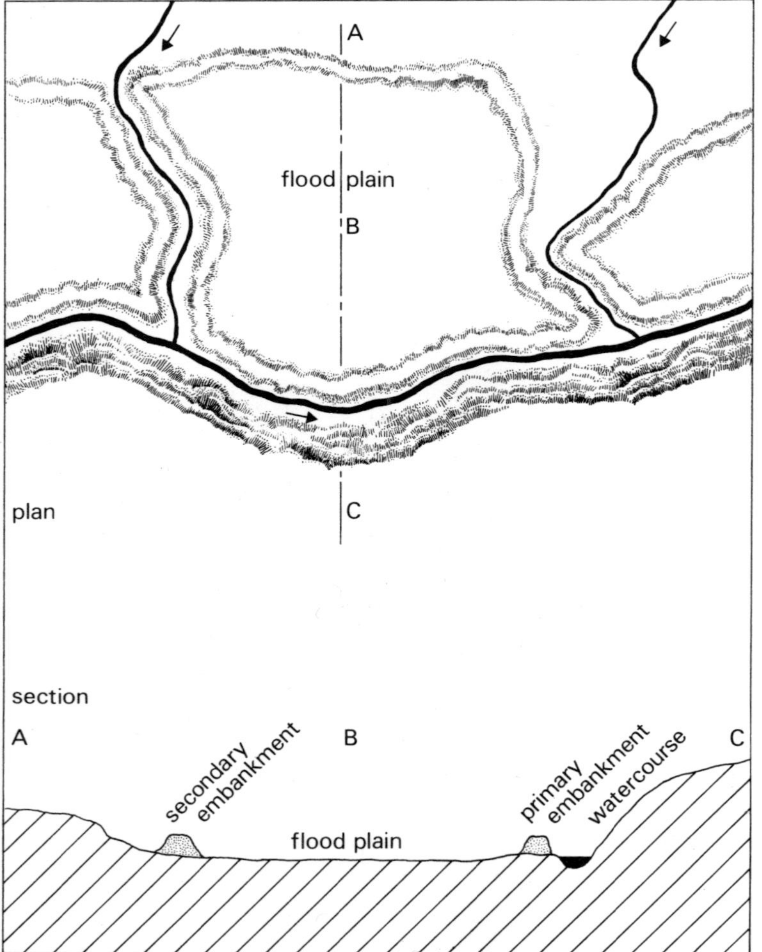

management or strong sea defences. It is therefore politically difficult to provide money and resources to carry out extensive protection works, and even more difficult to prevent the encroachment of building in flood-plain areas. Even in the United Kingdom, with its well-developed planning system, there are still industrial and housing developments on land naturally liable to flooding.

Clearly there must be a balance between the advantages of development and the risks that are being taken, but unhappily when the works have been completed and safely occupied for many years, the risks are forgotten. In these circumstances planning legislation is difficult to apply in practice except in the immediate aftermath of disaster.

More recently the need has arisen to assess the magnitude of flooding against which it is worth while providing protection. When existing protection works are overtopped by an exceptional flood, the disaster comes as an unpleasant surprise and the dangers to an unsuspecting population are increased. Consequently the design and extent of flood protection involves finely balanced decisions on the basis of good engineering designs.

The simplest remedy is to ascertain the areas liable to be inundated by the 'design flood', and to prevent development within these zones. But as we have seen, in a highly populated country this is unlikely to be accepted as a practicable safeguard against the biggest floods of low probability, say once in 1,000 years. Furthermore, extensive tracts of the best agricultural land, with its associated dwellings and village communities, lie in areas subject to flooding unless protection works are constructed and maintained.

Historically the primary method has been to provide river embankments to keep flood waters within the natural channel (Fig. 7, section B–C). Such methods, which are generally cheap and involve little change of land use, can probably provide protection in about nine cases out of ten, even in the more difficult situations. Such banks have often been created gradually by the excavation of material from the bed when the removal of flood debris is necessary to maintain the discharge capacity of a river.

Gradually areas of semi-protected land are extended behind the banks, forming traps for flood water when, as is almost inevitable, the banks are overtopped. The call then arises for further protection and a second line of banks may be constructed at a distance from the river (Fig. 7, section A–B). In this way a limited flood plain is created along which surplus water can flow during the more severe events. The demarcation of the zone by a second line of banks is an added advantage, but this is rarely possible in urban districts.

Fig. 8 Modification of flood hydrograph by storage. The total curve is the natural hydrograph, the flow that would be experienced in the absence of flood control. The existence of a storage reservoir means that the flood waters cannot rise above the line a–b. The volume of water released after the peak has passed (B) is equal to the volume of water stored (A), and the heavy line marks the modified hydrograph.

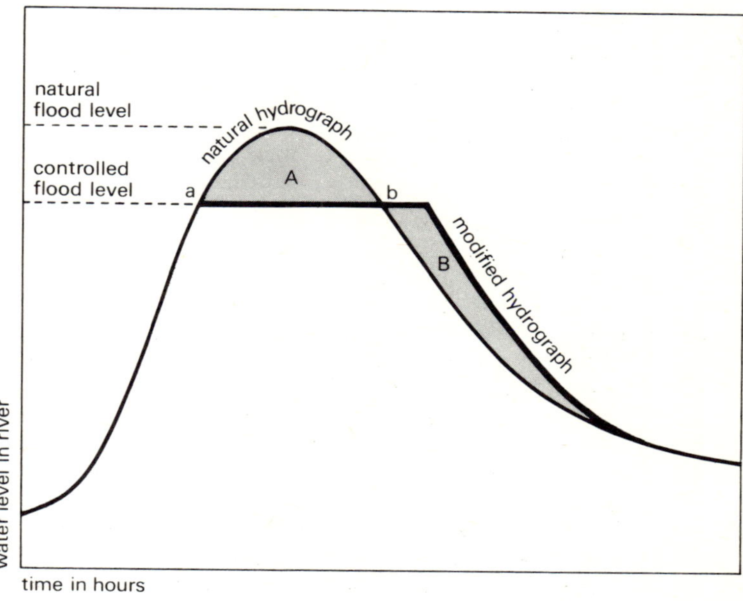

Restriction of an area over which water can spread will inevitably mean that the river channel must carry a greater volume. As a consequence the average level of the river itself will be higher, adjacent land will be flooded more frequently, and there will be further demands for protection. The construction of banks along a river adjacent to the estuary often involves either more protracted flooding of nearby areas, or the need to install large low-lift pumps to keep low-lying land free of water. The fenlands of East Anglia are an excellent example of such complex drainage, where the valuable agricultural produce and the associated villages and towns justify the expense of the system. Here the protective methods against river flooding have been remarkably successful and have produced a real sense of local security. This very fact greatly enhanced the shock when the unexpected and far less likely invasion by the sea took place in 1953.

Control of flooding by the sea is a very different problem, but must still form part of an over-all scheme. In England and Wales the responsibilities for river and sea flood management are vested in a single administration. This is as it should be, for good engineering is useless if it is not supported by sensible and efficient over-all planning and administration.

When flooding occurs, the water level at a point in a river rises fairly steeply and then falls more slowly as the peak passes downstream (Fig. 8). The line *ab* represents the level above which flooding occurs at that point, and the area A above the line shows the volume of water which would overflow the river banks. It is a remarkably small proportion of the total volume of the increased flow, and clearly the removal of volume A would prevent flooding. For a very long time dams have been built to form reservoirs of river water for towns. More recently reservoirs have been used to retain the peak flows of the larger floods so that the water can be discharged hours or days later, when the river can safely carry it (Fig. 8, B). The water levels at that point would then follow the thickened line and the danger of a flood would be averted.

The simplest method is to construct a reservoir for the single purpose of flood management and normally to keep it empty, but it is more usual for it to be used for a number of purposes. For instance, many of the large reservoirs in California were originally designed to store water for hydro-electric power generation, but now a large part of their capacity is allocated for flood control. Perhaps the most difficult problem in the safe management of such water storage is posed by weather forecasting, upon which so much of the control must be based.

Throughout the world there have been rapid advances in the science of hydrology during the last 20 years, and many countries are now capable of multi-purpose water storage, but unless the various agencies for water supply, river management, power generation, and recreational use are well co-ordinated, the complex operations become difficult. It is apparent that a good, broadly based water administration is needed to operate and justify such a complex process. In any country the problems are considerable but where a river crosses the boundaries of a number of countries they are greatly magnified.

If a number of reservoirs are located in the same river system the hydrology of the system has to be well understood, not only in order to get maximum advantage from the storage available, but to ensure that when a reservoir is used to delay the peak flow in its controlled tributary, the time at which the flood peak is allowed to arrive at the main river does not coincide with the maximum flow from the system as a whole. Moreover, as far as possible, the onset of later rainfall downstream needs to be anticipated, otherwise peak flows in lower reaches may be increased rather than decreased.

In order to maintain control in such complex situations, which will inevitably differ on each occasion, it is usual to provide a centre to which the readings of rainfall and river flow in various parts of the system are relayed. Recently two new techniques have been introduced which should help this process: radar to measure the amount and precise location of rainfall as it is occurring, and mini-computers to handle the complicated calculations needed. Mathematical modelling techniques enable the information to be translated into river-flow predictions on which the expert in charge of the control centre can base his decisions – which reservoir to use to store the flood, and which to discharge in readiness for further rain. Unlike other control systems, flood management involves only intermittent manning, consequently the maintenance of equipment and provision of skilled staff is both difficult and expensive. On the other hand, where major floods arise from melting snows the time when this will occur is more predictable. But even there problems arise from the difficulty, if not impossibility, of measuring the volume and water content of snow lying ready to melt. Thus the measurement of precipitation can only be a means of making early predictions; the actual measurement of river flow will remain the only means of providing accurate information about the timing and volume of a flood to come.

Where there are such uncertainties in the management of rare events in random locations, it is difficult to justify large expenditure in providing a high degree of safety. In some regions subject to recurrent floods the countries cannot afford the necessary work nor provide the skilled manpower for control, and in such extreme cases there will continue to be horrifying disasters. Similarly, catastrophes which follow the overflow or bursting of dams – events which have been sufficiently frequent to force many countries to apply strict conditions to design, construction and inspection – have a special horror of their own. The panic and defenceless condition of people suddenly overwhelmed, perhaps in the peace of the night, have been all too graphically described by those who have survived.

Whenever the mitigation of floods is considered, or the results of a disaster are examined, the dominant theme is devastation, sometimes with loss of life, always with the loss of property. So it might seem easy to justify expenditure on preventive schemes by the savings which would arise. Yet attempts to calculate the benefit/cost ratio in terms of money are not always easy to make and to justify owing to the unpredictability and rarity of the events. The real justification for the world-wide effort to reduce the scale of flood risk is relief from the horrors of a sudden large-scale tragedy and the impact made on communities lying in the path of a flood. Such disasters and the tragic situations they leave behind are too soon forgotten, and they can never all be avoided.

There is no doubt that throughout the world people will become more and more intolerant of catastrophe. Some disasters such as earthquakes will always be impossible to prevent and cannot even be much ameliorated. Similarly there are some floods, such as tidal surges in remote but populated areas, which will continue to be disastrous, but gradually scientific and engineering knowledge, applied where money and administrative ability are available, should be capable of limiting the effects and amounts of flood damage. Only in the last 20 years have there been big advances in understanding the hydrology of floods; with the development of the computer and its application to mathematical simulation of river-flow behaviour much better prediction can now be made of flood levels.

Similarly, the engineering of flood-protection methods has progressed to the point where the limitations on effectiveness are no longer technical but simply financial and political. Radar measurement of the amount, location and timing of rainfall, coupled with efficient telecommunication systems to and from control centres, should enable more sophisticated flood storage schemes to be operated in conjunction with conventional protective embankment works. The tidal sluice now being constructed in the Thames estuary for the protection of London is an example, as it is linked with a complex downstream flood embankment development which will at last make south-east England safe from future combinations of large river flows and unusually high tides.

Nevertheless the forces released by flood water can be

such that by their unexpected timing and location there will be danger of disaster from time to time, particularly as precautions make such events less frequent and communities are lulled into false feelings of security.

Suggestions for further reading

Johan van Veen: *Drain, Dredge, Reclaim – the art of a nation.* Martinus Nijhoff, The Hague, 1962. An account of the history of the polder projects and Delta barrage schemes associated with coastal protection in the Netherlands.

Floods and Flood Control. Tennessee Valley Authority Technical Report No. 26, 1961. A largely technical description of the methods used to protect the Tennessee Valley against the ravages of floods. The introductory chapters describe the effects of historic floods before and after protective works, such as large reservoirs and embankments, were constructed.

Robert Raikes: *Water, Weather and Prehistory.* John Baker, London, 1967. An unusual description of the possible archaeological effects produced by some aspects of climate.

Arthur Holmes: *Principles of Physical Geology* (chapters 17-19). Nelson, London, 2nd ed. 1922. This is one of the best standard textbooks in this subject, and in these three chapters the geomorphology of rivers is clearly described.

Flash floods engulf a township near Brisbane, Australia, while a traffic sign, like King Canute, vainly orders the waters to give way. Surprise is the element which enables floods to achieve the status of catastrophes, and in arid zones like the Australian outback, where stream beds peter out in flat country and rainfall is normally very slight, there is virtually no warning. Fortunately the duration of such floods tends to be brief, and some long-term effects, e.g. the recharging of ground water, may even prove ultimately beneficial.

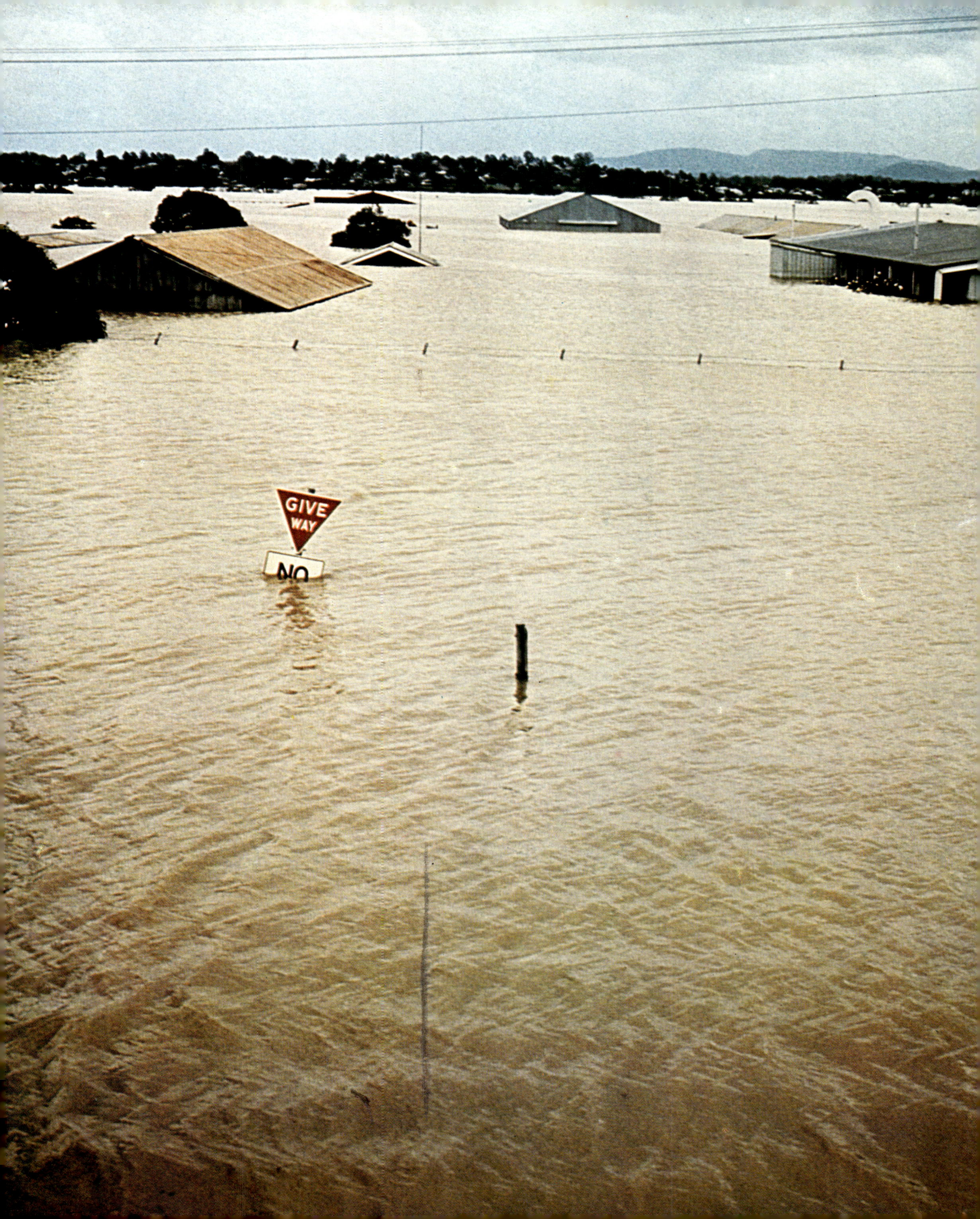
GIVE
WAY
NO

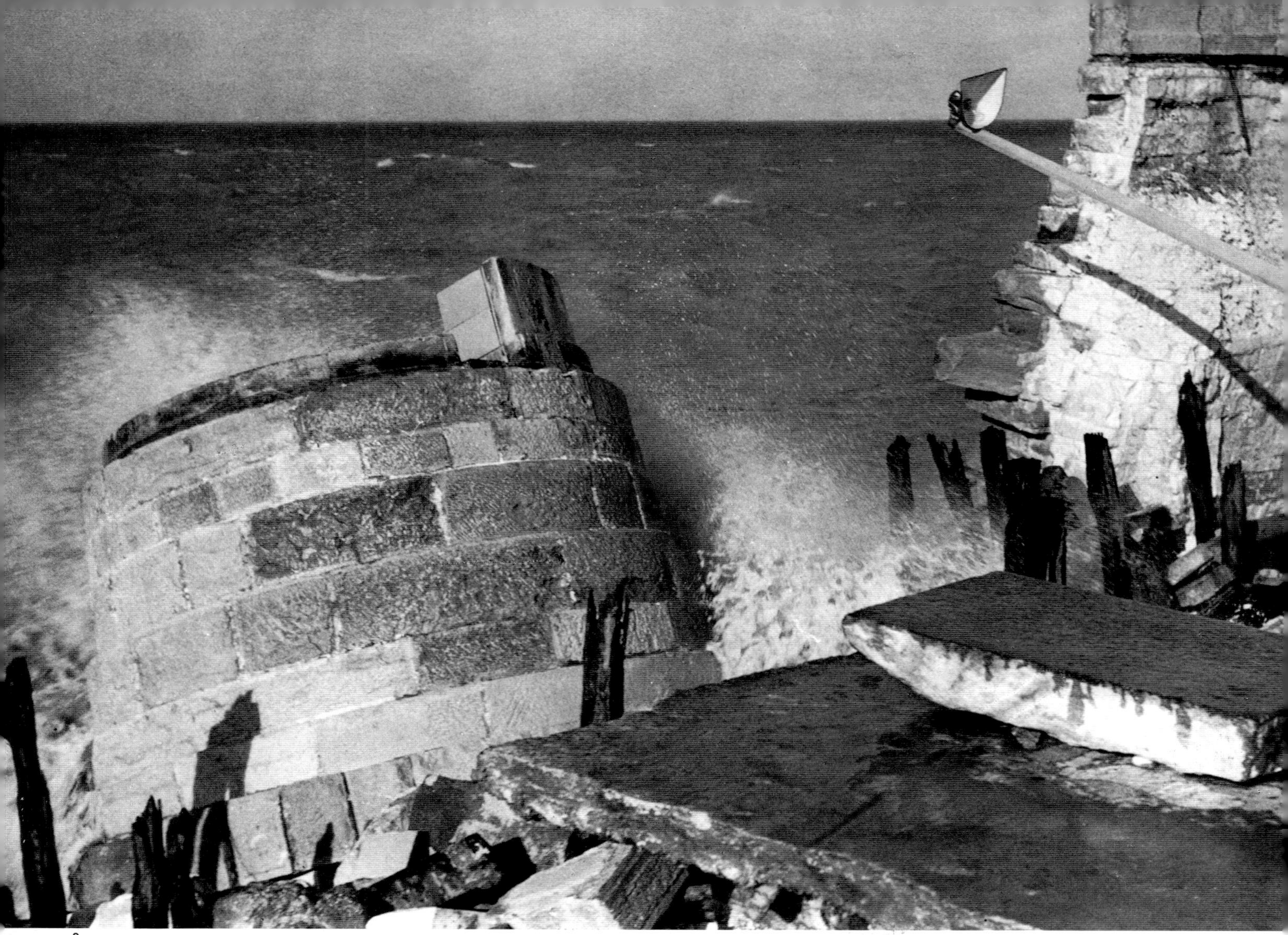

2

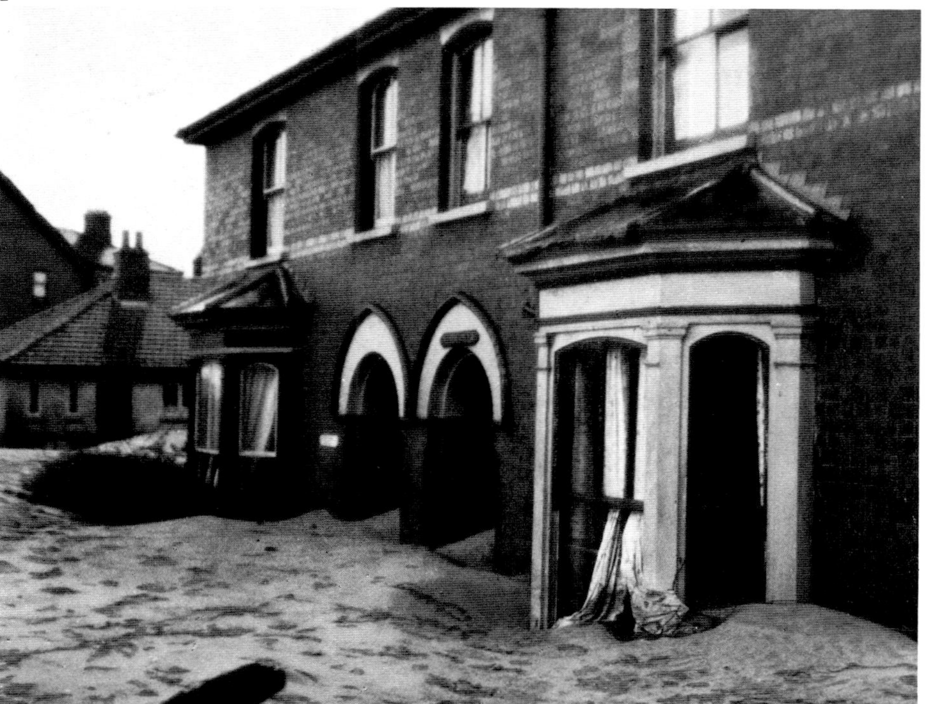

3

Shattering the coastal defences of England and the Netherlands, the tidal surge of 1953 swallowed up 2000 lives and a vast expanse of territory on both sides of the North sea. At Margate (2) the lighthouse was thrown into the sea and the jetty reduced to débris; sand to a depth of four feet formed a temporary beach in the streets of Sutton-on-Sea, Lincolnshire (3). In the Netherlands (4) the devastation was even more extensive, with floodwaters rampaging through broken dykes and sweeping away houses, roads and railways.

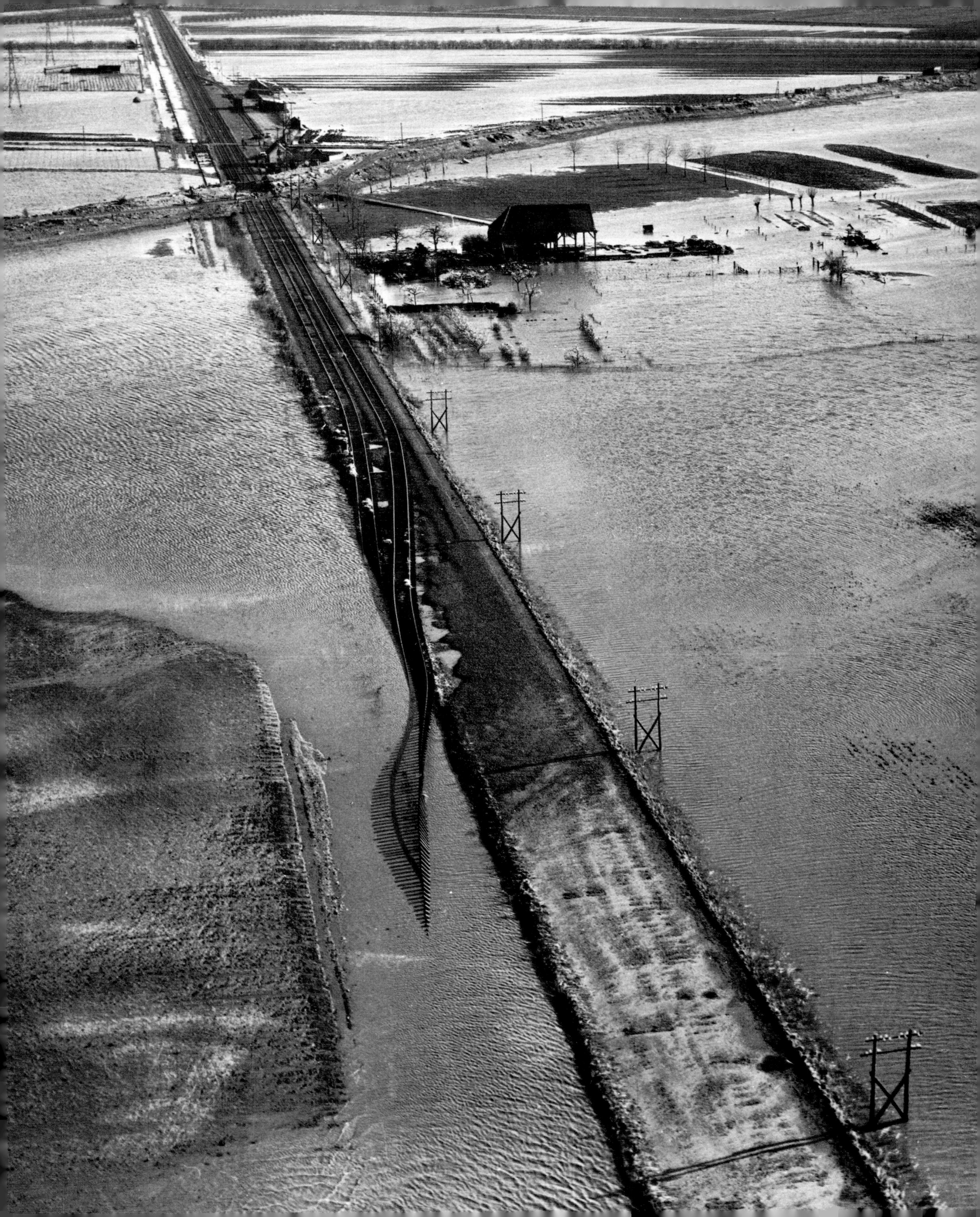

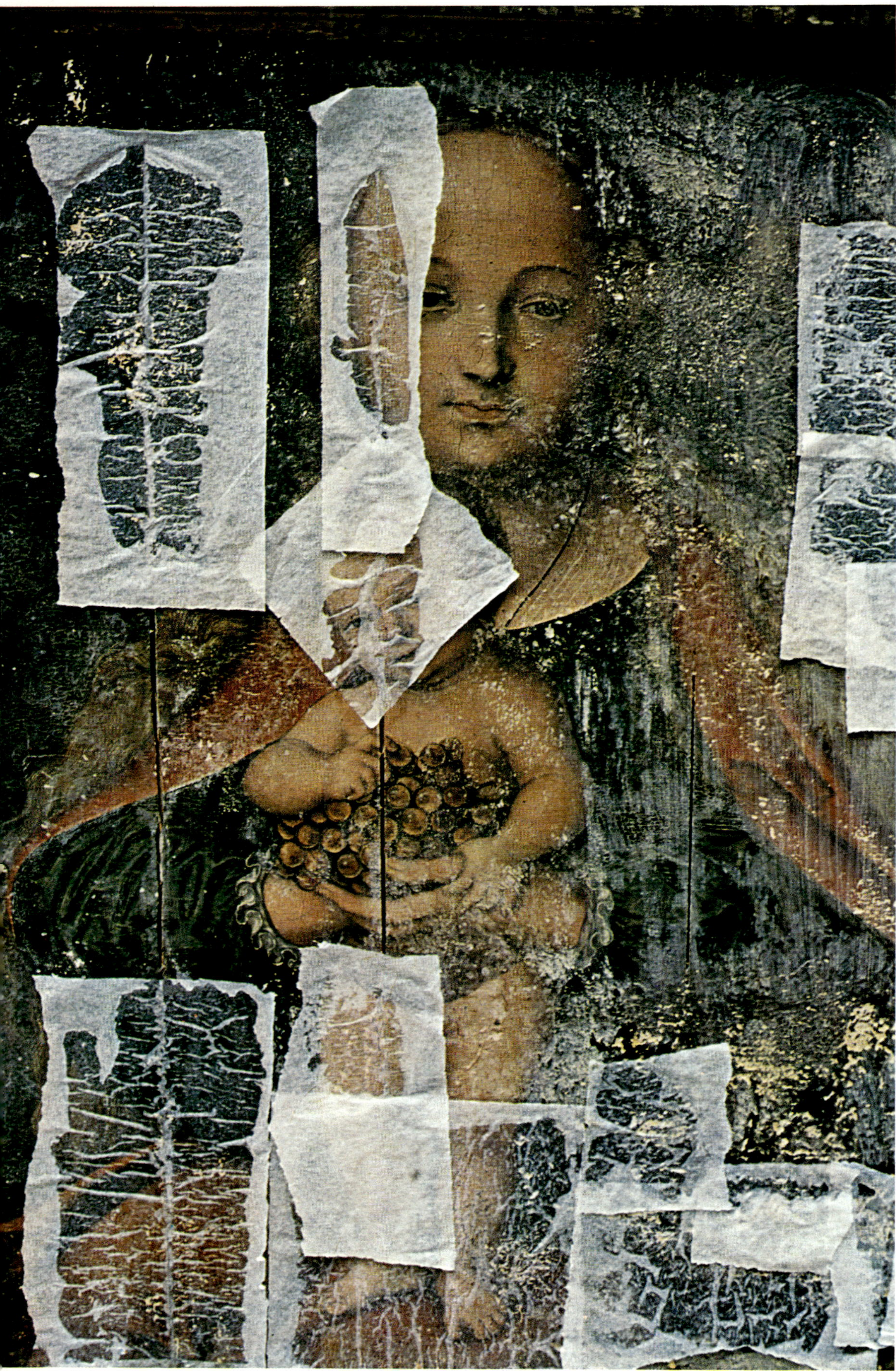

5

Madonna in blotting-paper (5) symbolizes one aspect of the ravaged city of Florence after the floods of November 1966, when one of Europe's greatest cultural treasure-houses was overwhelmed. Tons of muddy water, hurled down by the swollen Arno and its tributaries, all but swept away the Ponte Vecchio, seen here at the height of the flood (6) and after the waters had receded (8). The slime-filled streets (7) and shattered buildings were painstakingly cleaned and restored, but many irreplaceable works of art, not to mention lives and property, were lost beyond recall.

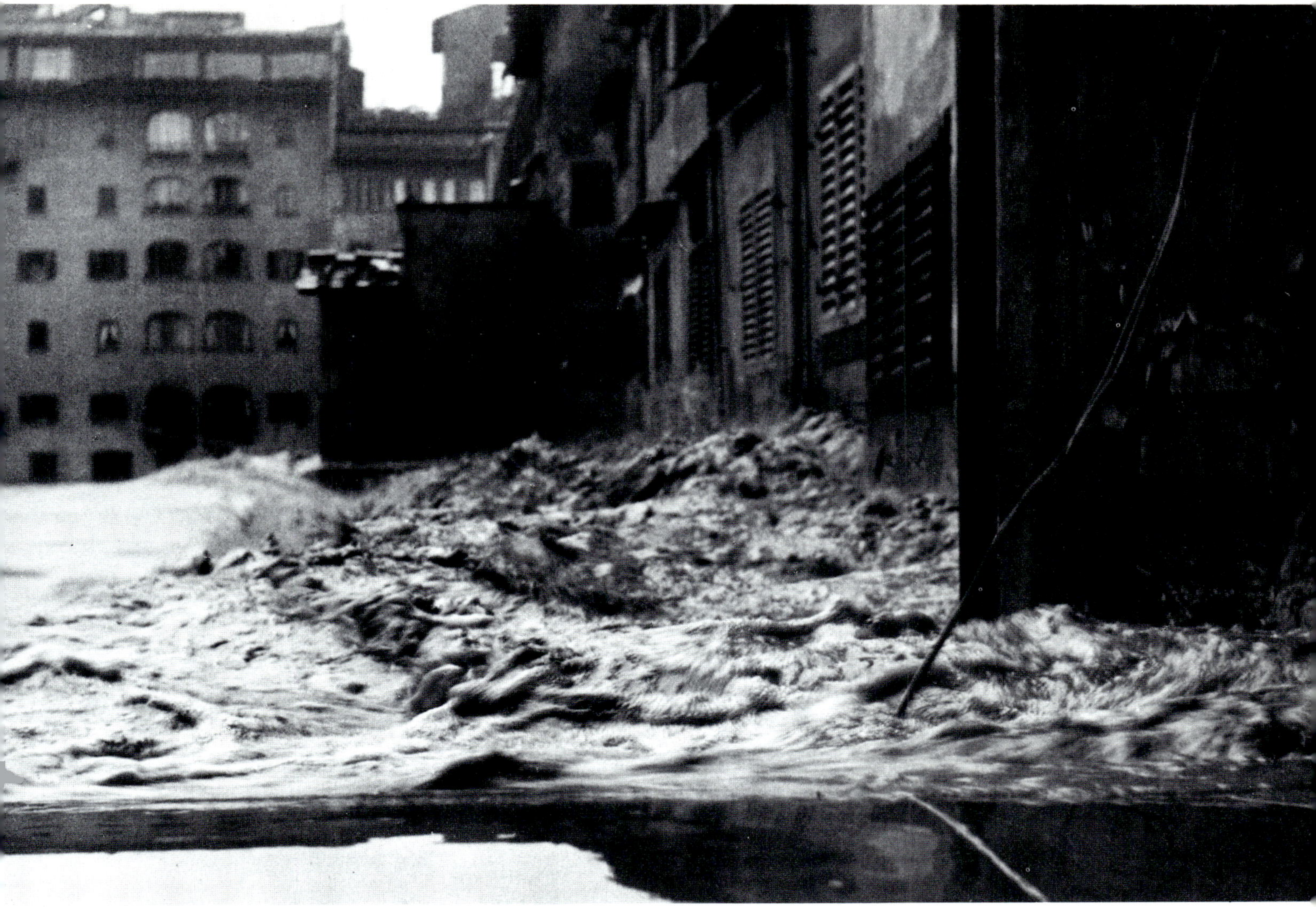

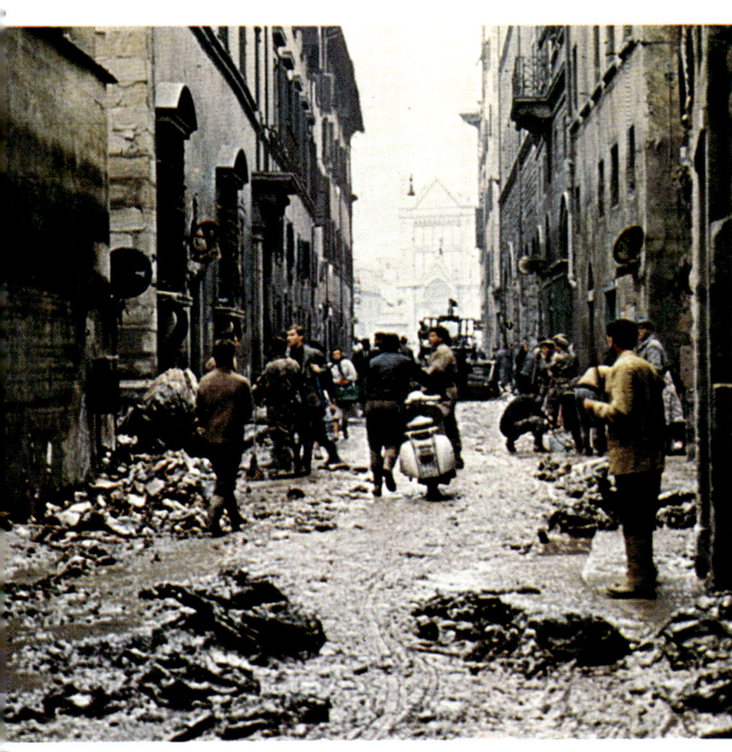

7

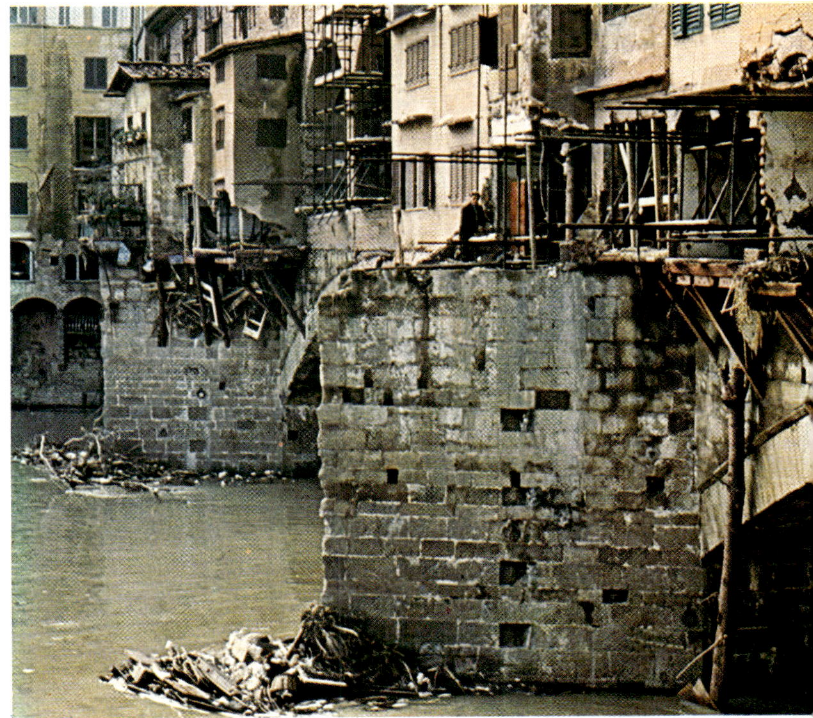

8

Rescue comes at the eleventh hour as a helicopter and motorboat 'swim' a herd of cattle (9) to safety across a flooded plain in Australia's Northern Territory during the flash floods of 1974. Out of 4000 head of valuable Santa Gertrudis cattle, only 30 were lost in one of the best-organized rescue operations ever mounted in that country. In Romania (10) a helicopter again plays a key role in bringing to safety men stranded on the bridge over the River Mures

9

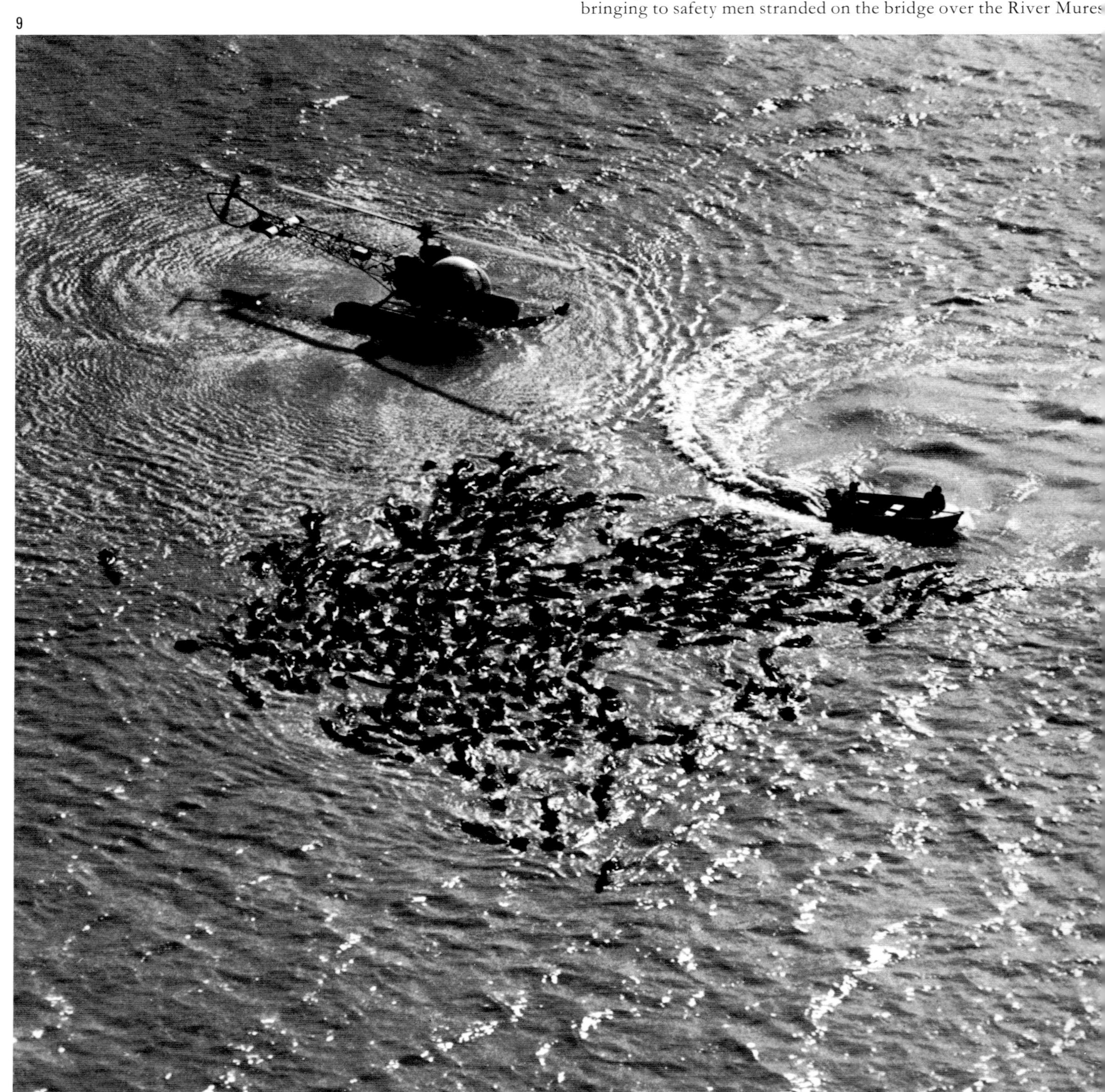

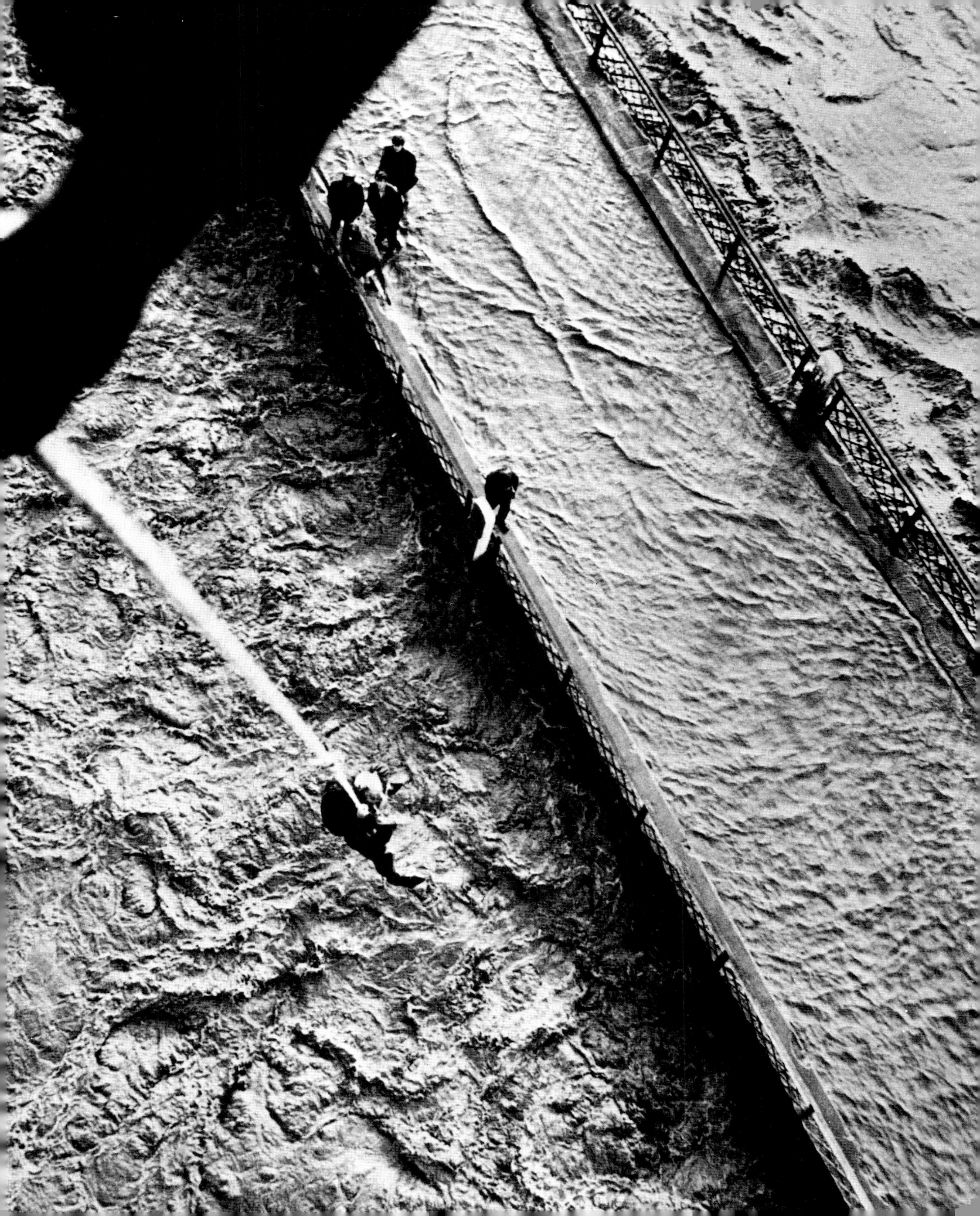

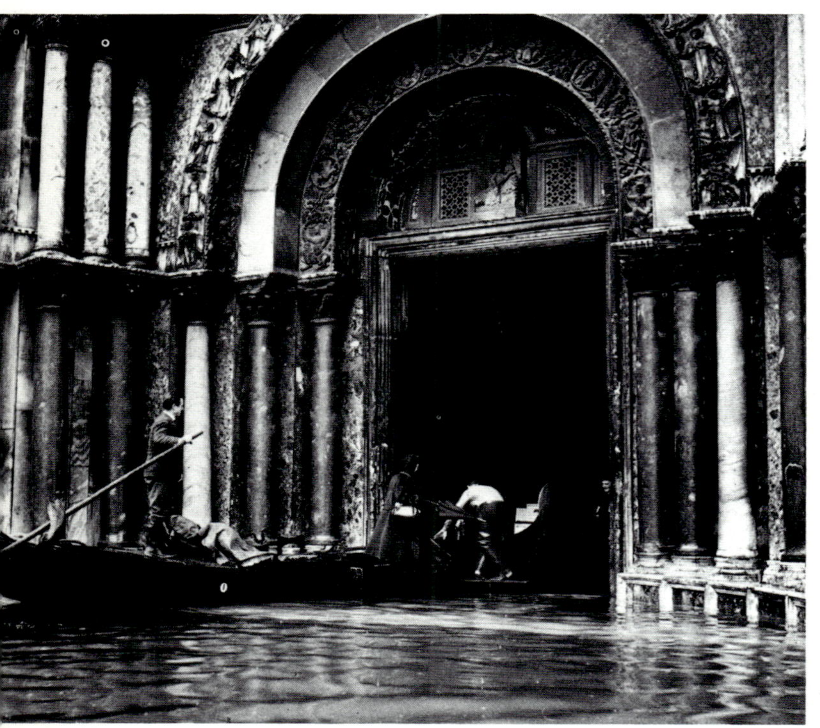

11

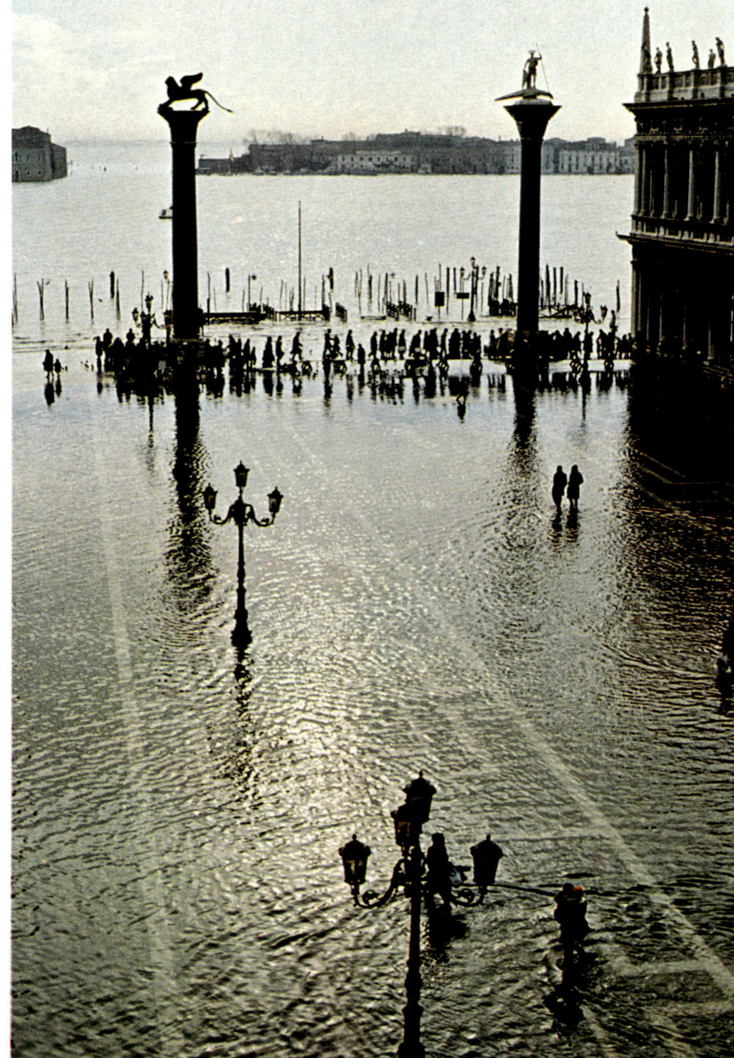

12/13

Venice, submerged, continues to function, even when piazzas become waterways. A gondola (11) conveys worshippers across St Mark's Square to mass at the Cathedral, while elsewhere the Venetians go matter-of-factly to work on duckboards (14). Sinking ground level, caused by the abstraction of underground water, has resulted in frequent flooding of this wonderful city.

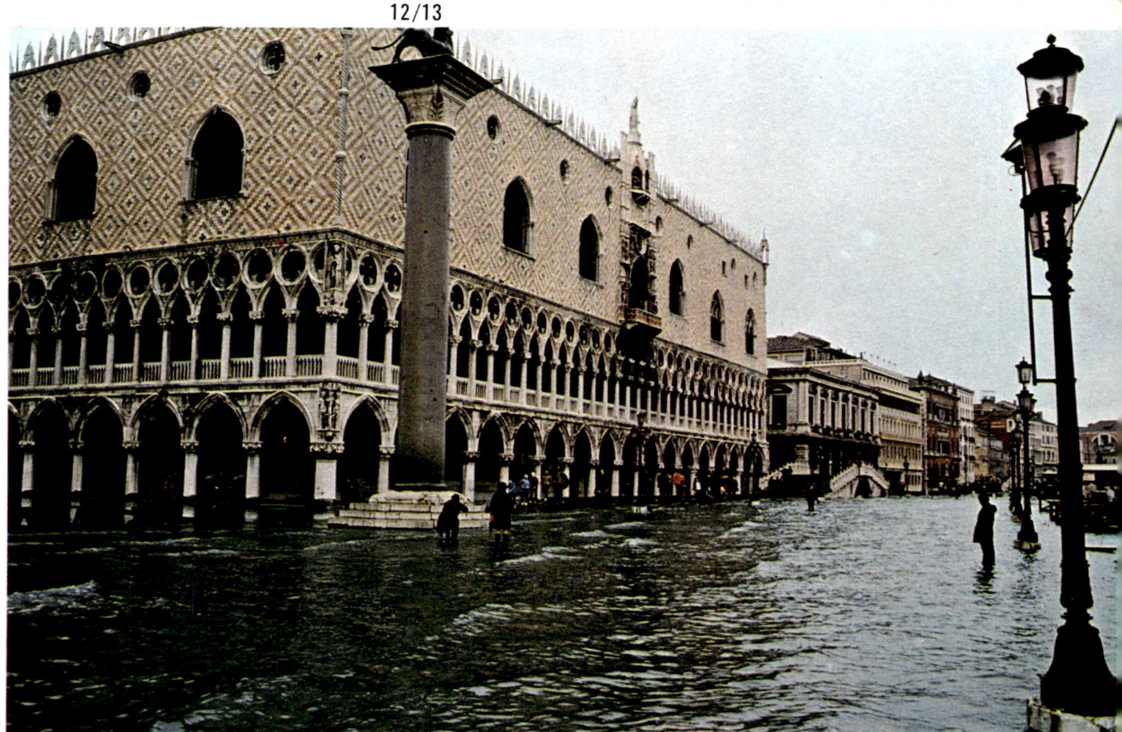

14

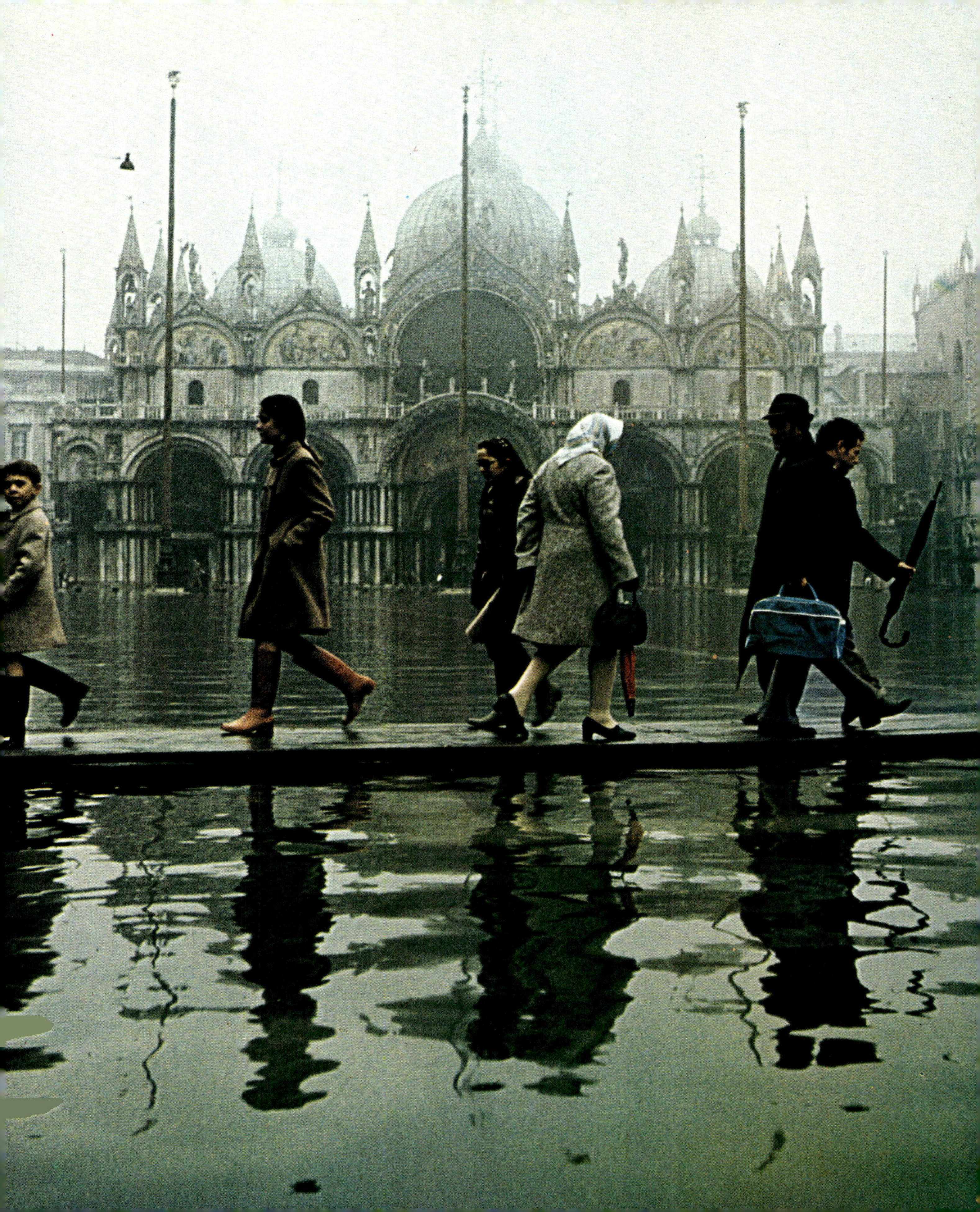

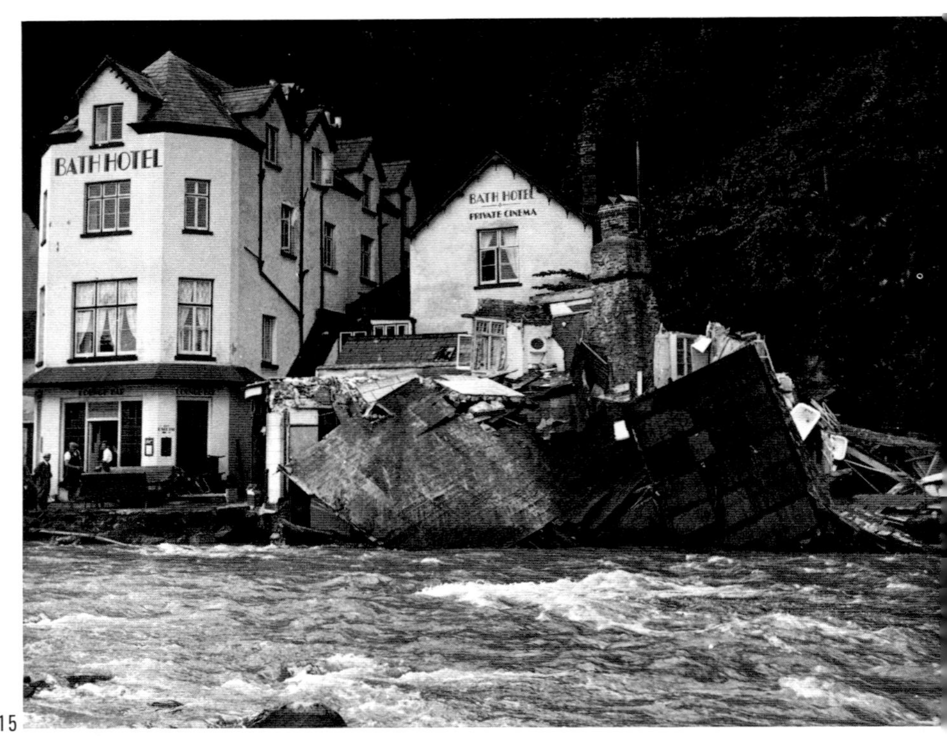

15

16

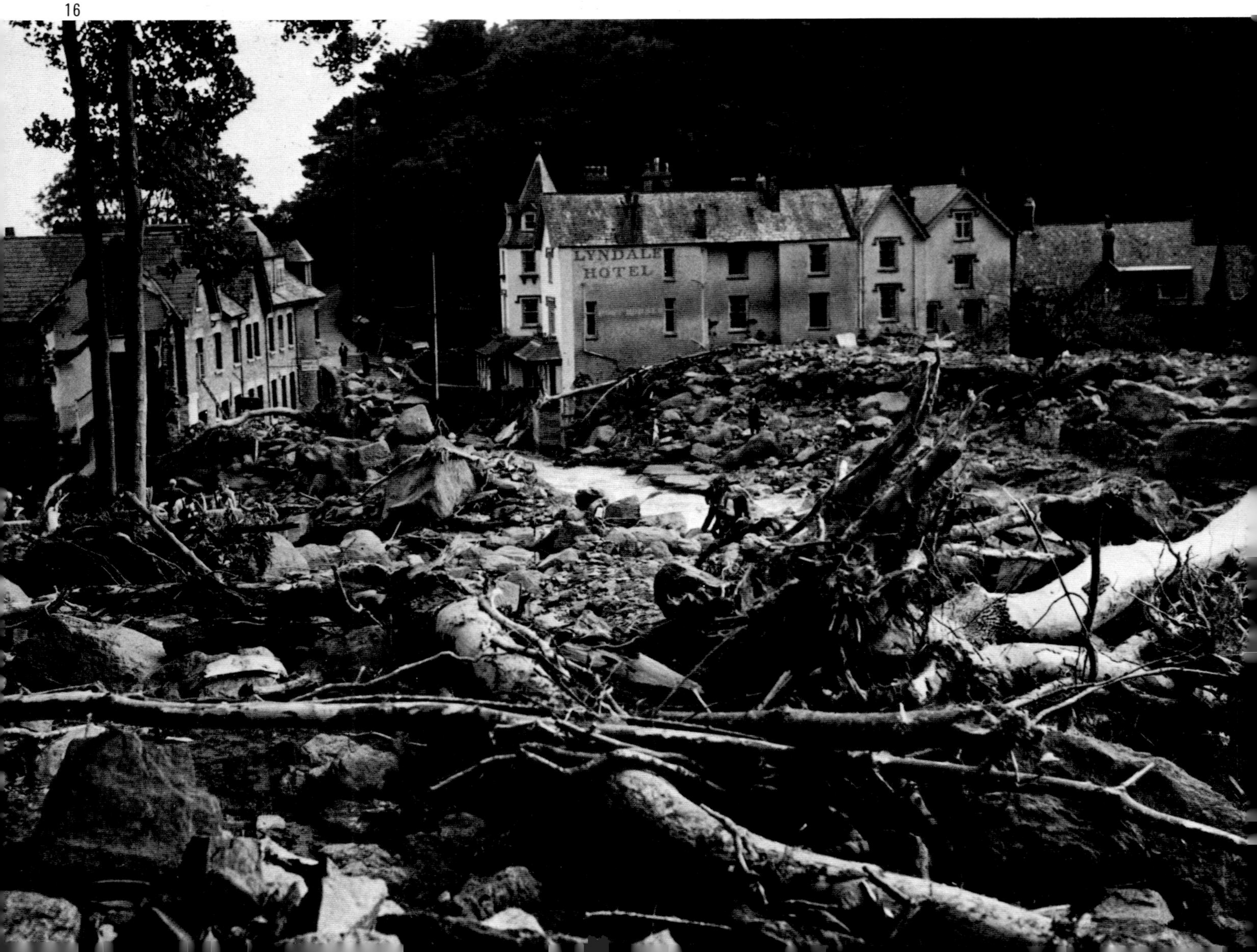

17

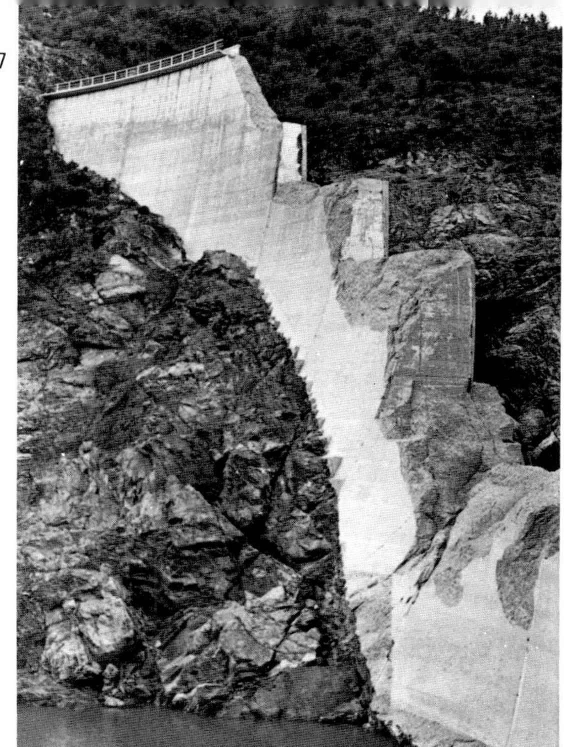

Smashed, shattered and annihilated, man-made constructions collapse before the destructive power of water. At Lynmouth, in Devon, 1952, the main street (15) became a rushing torrent overnight in which 34 people lost their lives. The stream brought down huge boulders, pine trees and tons of mud (16) which, trapped by the town's first few houses, turned Lynmouth into a seething cauldron of débris-filled water. At Fréjus (17) in 1959 a huge breach was made in the dam wall, releasing a crushing mass of water into the valley below. At Putnam, Connecticut, in 1955 (18) a wall of water three stories high is seen at the actual moment of overleaping the river bank and crashing down on one of the city's main streets.

18

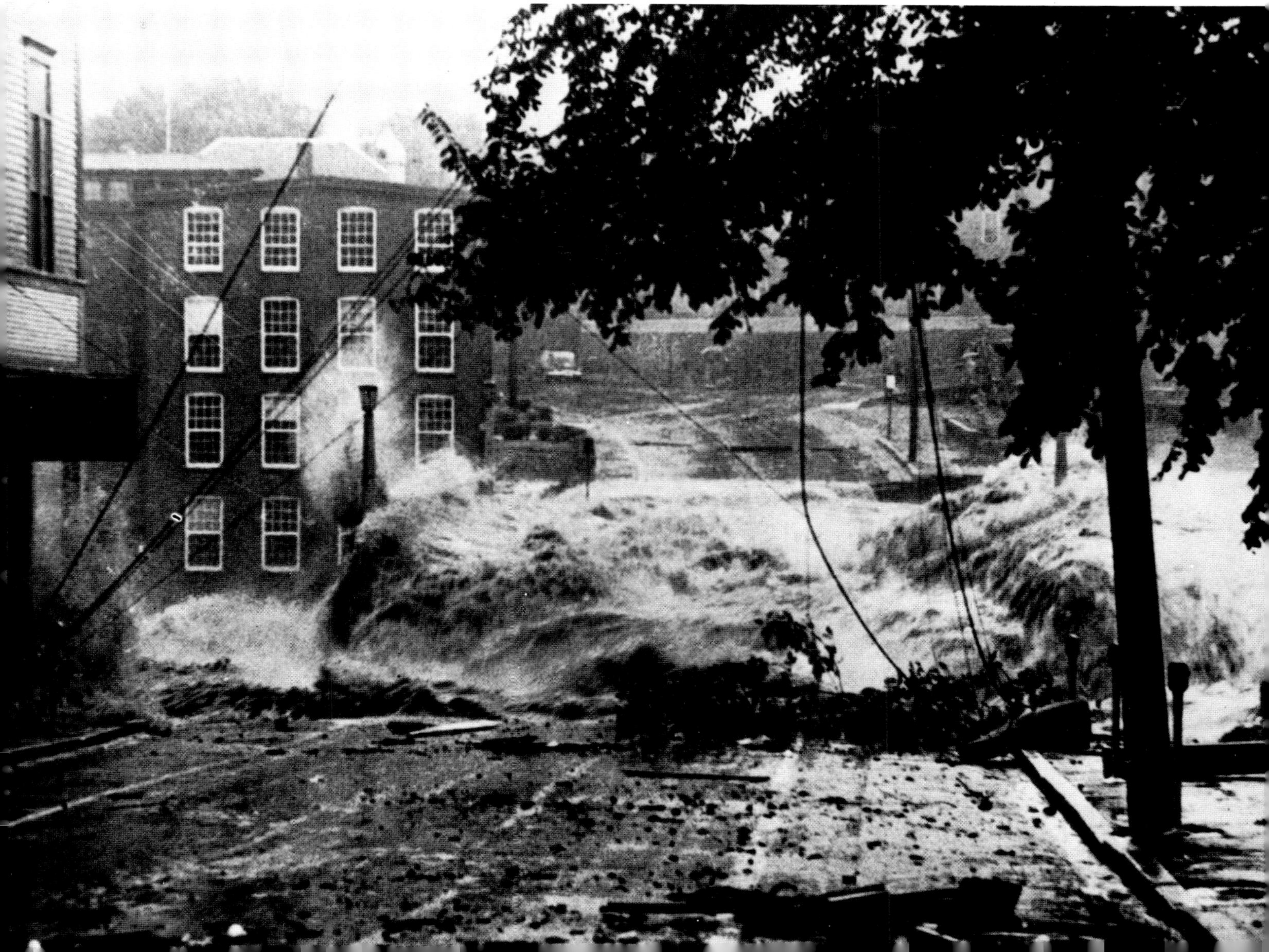

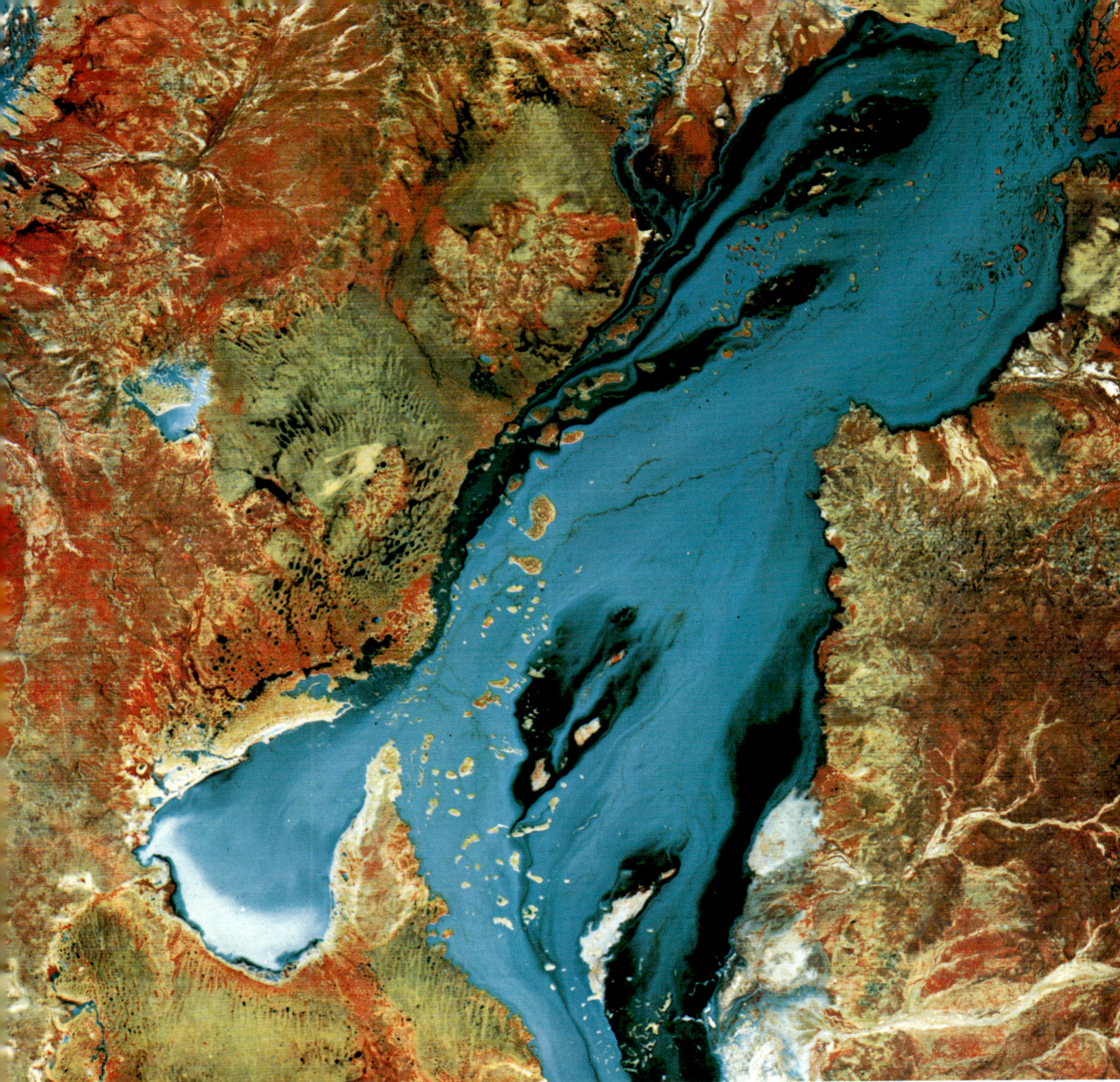

19

Floods on a cosmic scale are shown in satellite images of (19) the inundation of Central Australia, which covered an area of 11,000 square kilometres, and (20) the flooding of the Mississippi River at St Louis, contrasted with the normal situation. On the left the river system is seen at normal levels, where A indicates the Missouri's and B the Illinois's confluence with the Mississippi. The right-hand image accurately shows the two major areas of inundation (C). The white dots are fair-weather cumulus clouds. The colours, of course, are not the true colours that would be seen by the human eye at that altitude. They are made up of thousands of lines measured by an optical scanner registering in four separate regions of the spectrum (see p. 272); vegetation shows up red, water in various shades of blue.

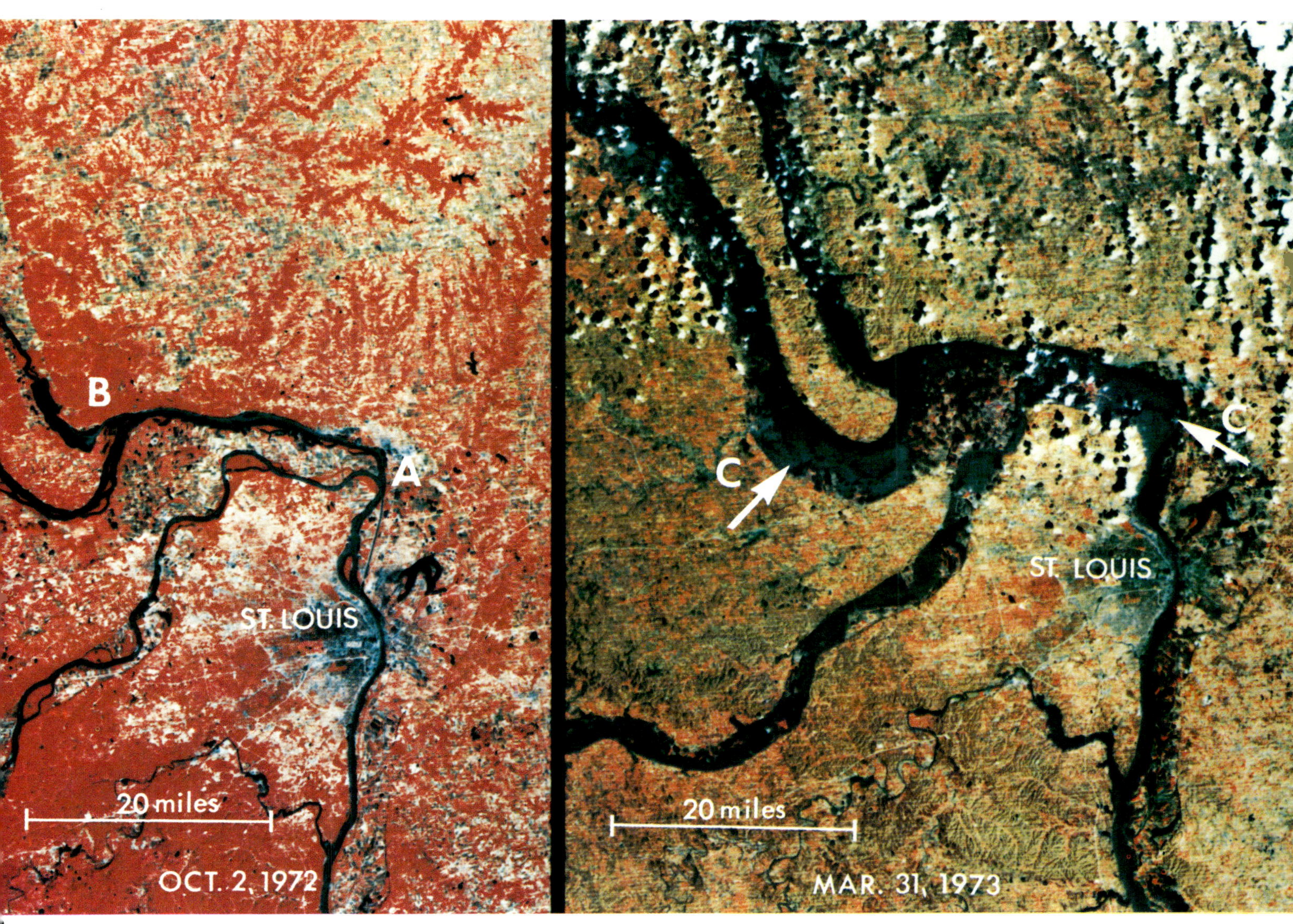

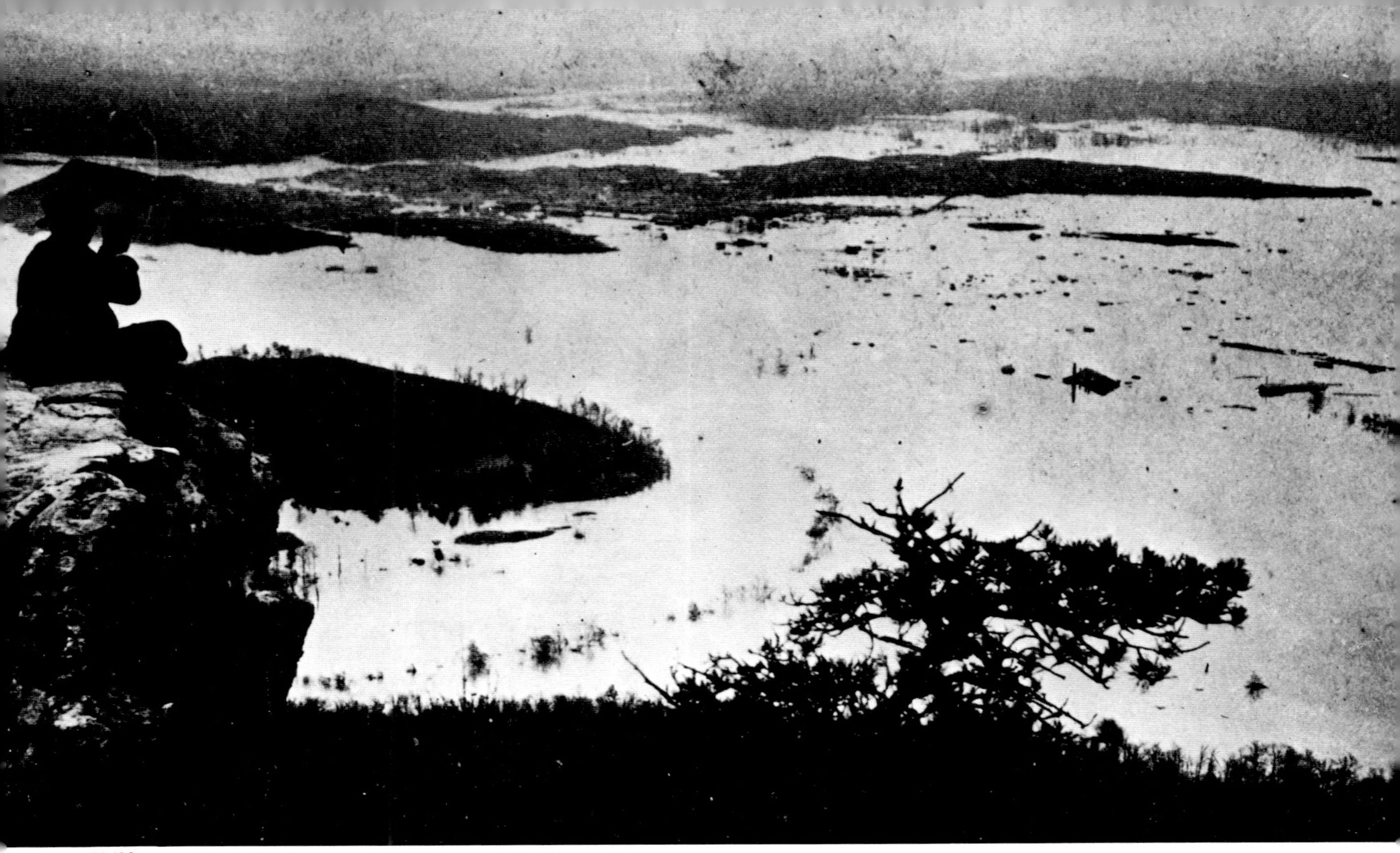

21/22

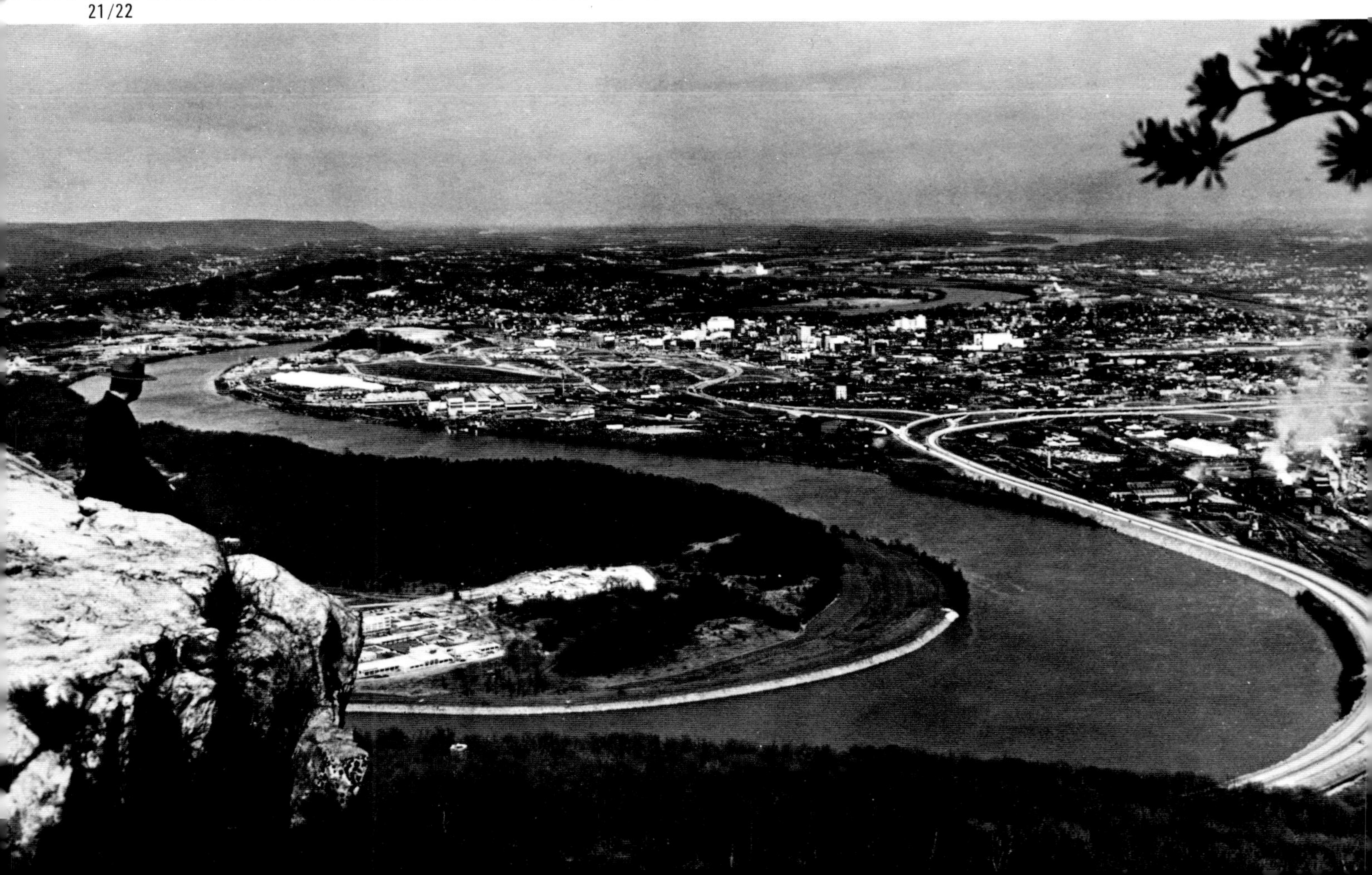

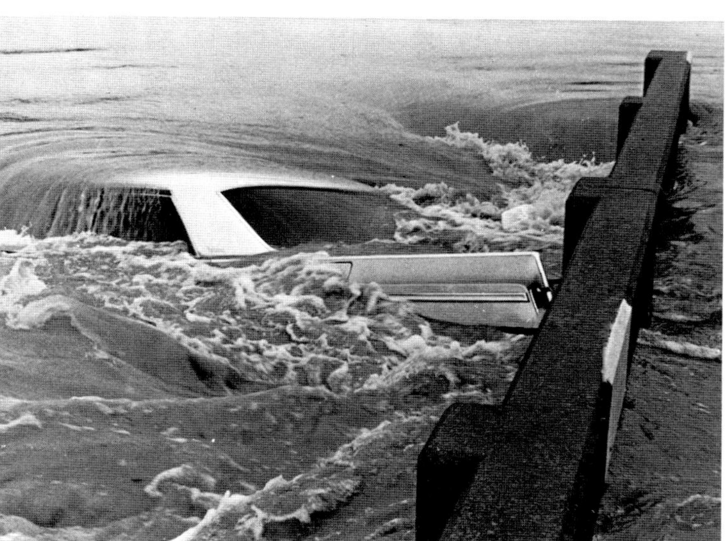

3/24

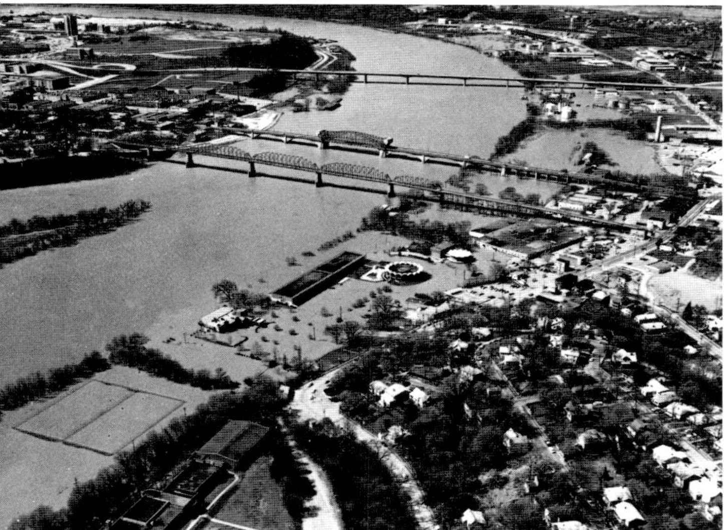

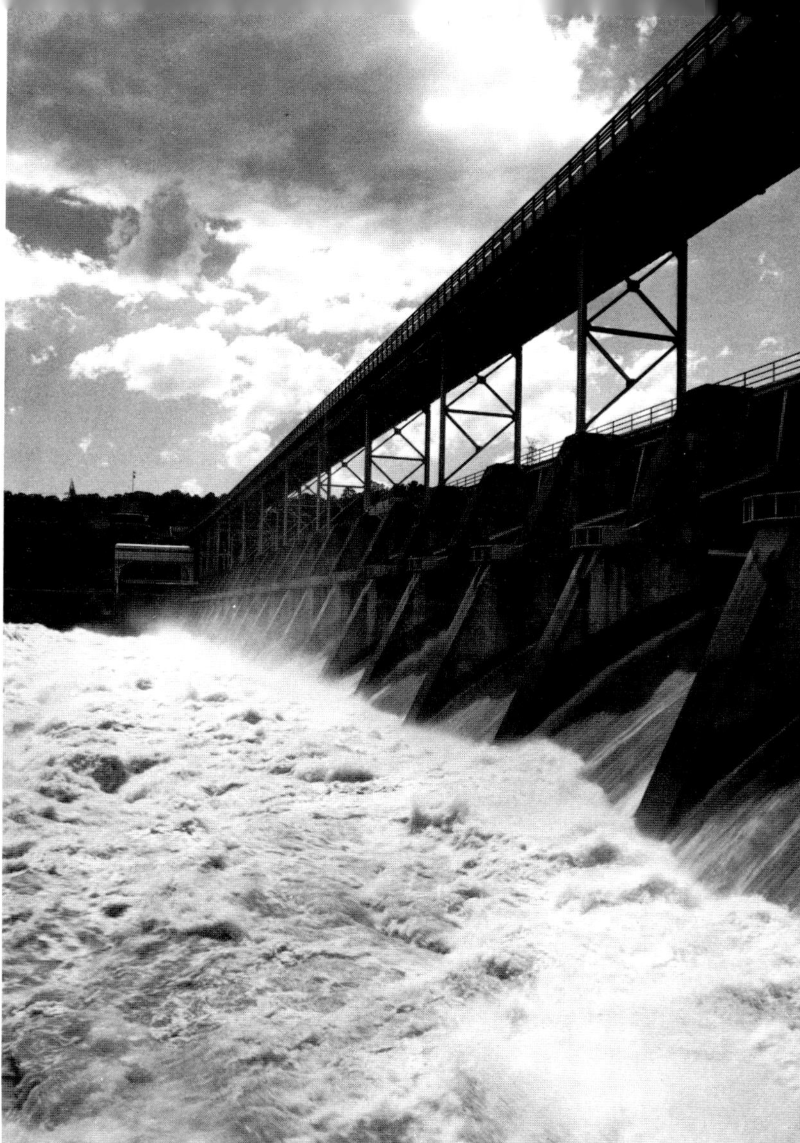

25

Flood-control efforts and achievements by the TVA on the Tennessee River at Chattanooga in 1933 are illustrated by comparison of the same view in 1867 and 1967 (21/22). In 1867 only the highest ground escaped, whereas comparable floods in March 1973 (23/24), though dangerous and potentially deadly, occasioned only minor damage. Without regulation the river would have been 5 metres higher. A TVA dam (25) is shown at the height of the floods, as millions of tons of water thunder through the sluices.

A drowned world surrounds this Bengali farmer who has lost everything in the 1974 flood except what he carries on his head. Geographically vulnerable to flooding, and unable to afford elaborate flood control schemes, Bangladesh typifies the predicament of Third World countries in spite of an age of technological expansion.
26

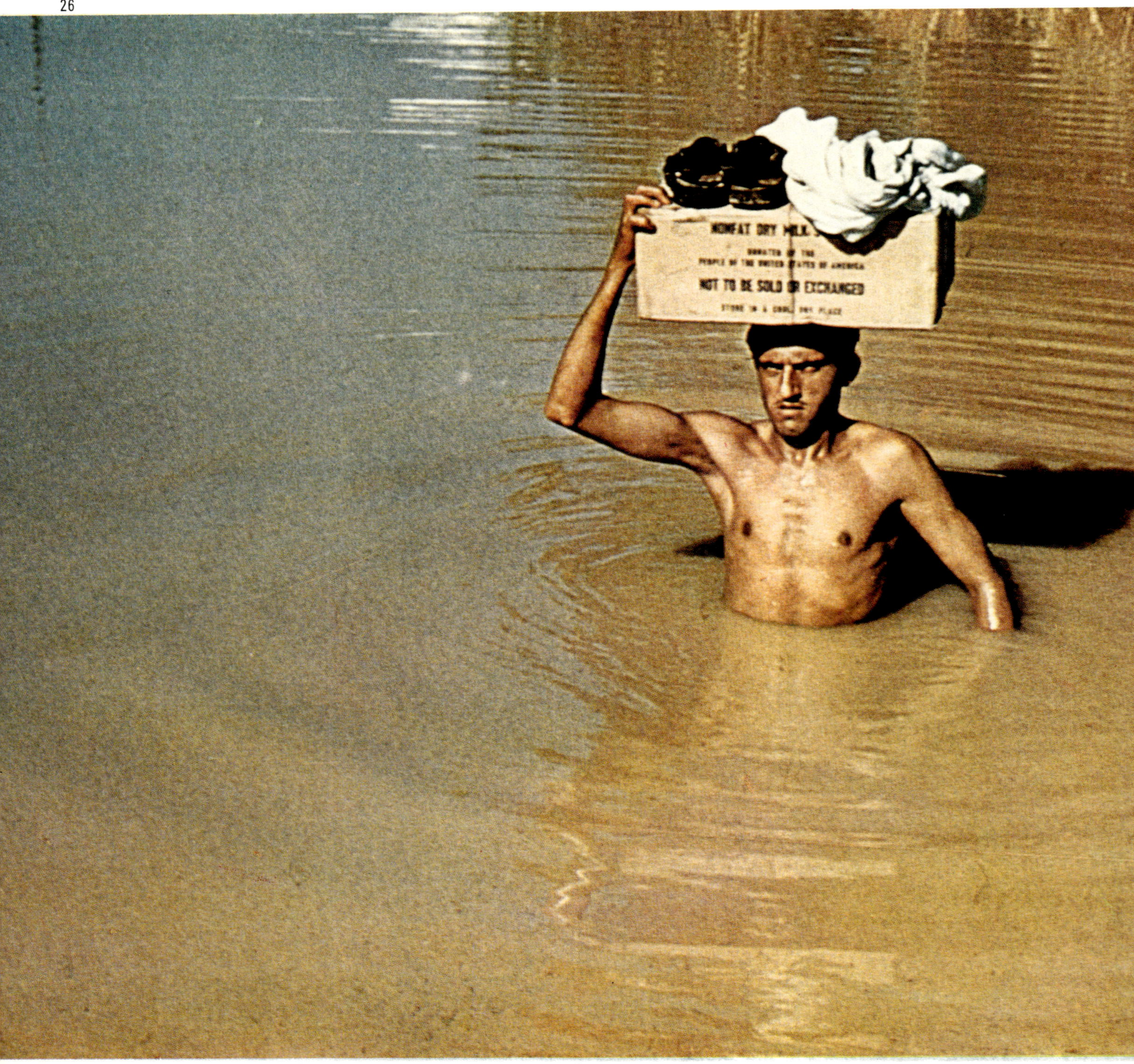

8

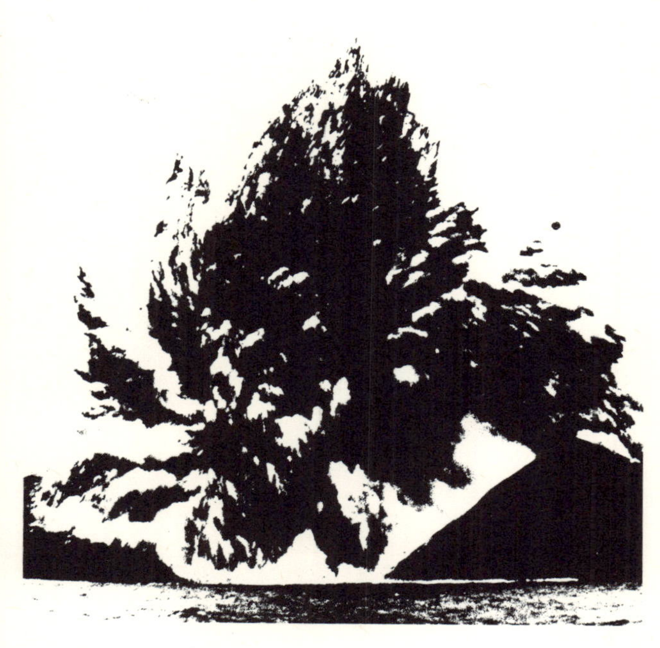

Volcanoes

E. A. Vincent

Seen at close quarters, a volcanic eruption is an impressively energetic phenomenon, but being narrowly localized in space and time, it is rather superficial on the scale of the whole Earth. As my professor of geology once remarked to the class of first-year students of which I was a member: 'Would you conclude from the presence of a boil on the back of your neck that your whole body was filled with pus?'

Man has always feared volcanic manifestations as forces beyond his control, bringing death and destruction. But he has also gradually learned that they may bring some compensating benefits: rich volcanic soils; deposits of minerals and ores; and more recently, potential sources of usable heat and energy. The very existence of volcanoes, as of the earthquakes almost invariably associated with them, indicates that the planet Earth is not a static body but a dynamic organism in a constant state of change and evolution.

The Earth, as we go from surface to centre, is divided into three well-defined concentric zones: at the outside a superficial crust varying in thickness but averaging perhaps 30 to 40 kilometres, underlain by a mantle composed of silicate rocks on the whole more dense than those encountered in the crust, and extending to some 2,900 kilometres from the surface, in turn underlain by a nickel-iron core extending to the centre of the Earth at a depth of 6,400 kilometres. The raw materials of volcanoes, the molten silicate mixtures called *magmas*, are chiefly generated within the upper portions of the mantle by partial melting of rocks at depths not exceeding a few hundreds of kilometres.

Converging lines of geophysical and geological research have led during the past 15 years to the development of the concept of *plate tectonics*, a model which provides for the first time a satisfying and no doubt essentially correct framework for understanding the dynamic behaviour of the outer parts of the Earth. The distribution pattern of present and recent volcanic activity is one of the Earth's major features, well-explained in terms of the new theory.

In many regions of the globe the study of the behaviour of earthquake waves strongly suggests that there is a zone about 70 km down where the dense rocks of the mantle may carry a very small proportion of molten material. The mantle rocks above this zone, together with the crust, behave as a series of rigid plates which can move relatively to one another by sliding on the lubricating, partially melted, mantle layer, driven by large-scale convective circulation within the mantle.

The margins of these plates are of two main types. First there are 'constructive' margins where magma from deeper in the mantle rises at the crest of the mid-oceanic ridge systems and slowly adds basaltic material to the oceanic crustal plates, which are separating symmetrically at a rate of a few centimetres per year either side of the ridge. Most of this basalt (estimated to add about 4 cubic kilometres of new rock to the ocean floors every year) is erupted quietly into deeper water, but occasionally volcanoes emerge above the ocean, for example in Iceland, the Azores, St Helena and Tristan da Cunha, spaced along the mid-Atlantic ridge.

Unless the Earth is expanding in diameter, which does not appear to be the case, the continuous addition of new material to the ocean floor must be compensated by the return of a corresponding amount of material to the mantle; this happens at 'destructive' plate margins, of which the most conspicuous border the Pacific Ocean. There, the rigid plates plunge downwards at about 45° in so-called subduction zones characterized by earthquakes having focal depths up to 300 kilometres or more; behind these subduction zones, towards the continental masses, are located the volcanoes of the Pacific island arcs and the western seaboard of the American continent. The striking island arc system of the western Pacific extends from Alaska and the Aleutians, through Kamchatka to Japan, the Philippines, Indonesia, to Tonga and New Zealand.

The thermal energy required for convective circulation of materials within the mantle, and for causing the local partial melting of these materials that gives rise to magmas, is mainly due to the disintegration of small amounts of the radioactive elements uranium, thorium and potassium contained within the Earth. In the case of the island arc systems it has been calculated that frictional energy developed between the descending plate and the continental crust and mantle above it could also be a significant source of energy for remelting these rocks and producing the chemically rather distinctive island arc magmas.

There is a fuller account of plate tectonics in the next chapter (p. 238). The development of the concept probably constitutes the single most important advance ever made in our understanding of the Earth and the way its internal forces work. The interested reader is referred to the excellent account by E. R. Oxburgh listed in the references at the end of the chapter.

The physics and chemistry of eruptions

The silicate melt produced by partial fusion of mantle material and emitted at the majority of volcanoes gives rise on cooling to rocks called *basalt*. Several varieties of basalt are recognized on a world-wide scale, with subtle

Fig. 1 Map locating the known active volcanoes of the world. The tinted area delineates the major earthquake belts, and makes clear the connection between volcanoes and earthquakes. Compare also the map of the main tectonic plates of the Earth's crust, on pp. 250–251.

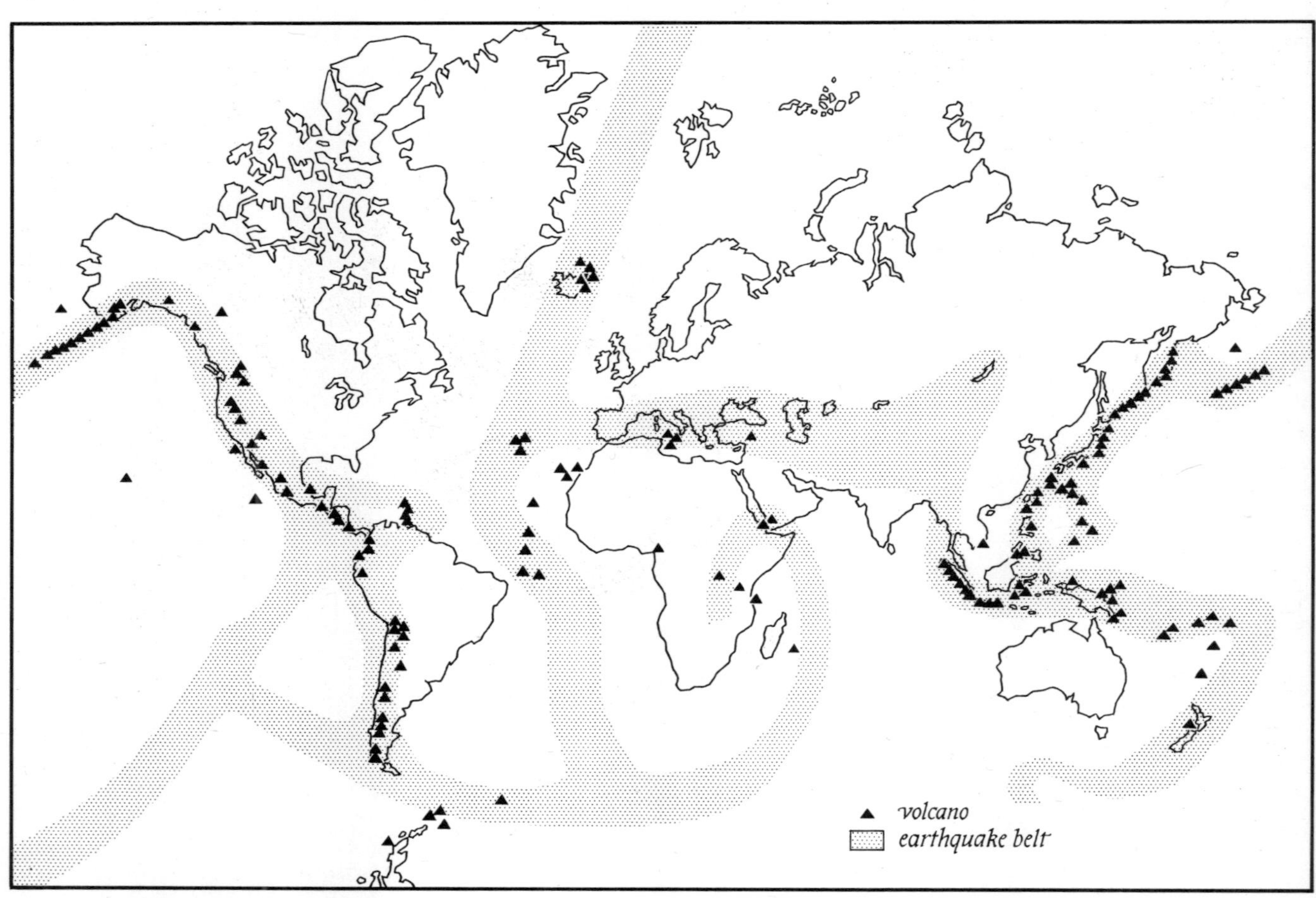

Approximate chemical compositions of four important types of volcanic rock
(Percentages by weight of the elements)

	('Basic' →	'Intermediate' →	'Acid')	
	Basalt	*Andesite*	*Trachyte*	*Rhyolite*
Oxygen	43.8	45.9	45.8	49.1
Silicon	23.0	25.3	27.3	34.7
Titanium	1.4	0.8	0.4	0.1
Aluminium	7.6	9.1	9.6	6.9
Iron	8.9	6.7	3.3	1.6
Manganese	0.2	0.1	0.1	0.03
Magnesium	4.8	2.7	1.3	0.1
Calcium	7.6	5.6	3.1	0.6
Sodium	1.8	2.7	2.9	2.6
Potassium	0.7	0.9	6.1	4.2
Phosphorus	0.2	0.2	0.1	0.04

yet definite chemical differences. While basalt and its near relatives greatly predominate over all other types in space and time, the magmas directly emitted at the world's volcanoes nonetheless exhibit a wide range in chemical composition and hence in physical properties. Typical chemical compositions of basalt, andesite, trachyte and rhyolite (a compositional range from 'basic' through 'intermediate' to 'acid' in the geologist's rough and ready nomenclature) are given in the table. These analyses are of solid, cold rocks, often collected long after the eruption that produced them, and do not reflect exactly the total composition of the original melt or magma, mainly because the latter always contained a few per cent by weight of dissolved volatile substances, such as water and carbon dioxide. These volatile constituents remain in solution in the hot silicate melt as long as the latter is under pressure within the Earth, but as the magma ascends close towards the surface a point is reached where their internal vapour tension exceeds the hydrostatic pressure on the magma and the volatiles separate in an independent gaseous phase. It is essentially this phase separation, this gas loss, which provides the energy for a volcanic eruption near the surface, and the manner of the separation which mostly determines the mechanism and general type of eruption.

All things are relative, and although from time to time there are dangers and spectacular disasters associated with the eruption of basaltic magmas, these eruptions are usually fairly quiet. Basalt lavas have temperatures at the surface up to 1100°C and their composition is such that their viscosity at this temperature is quite low, perhaps comparable with that of a heavy oil. Under these conditions the separation of silicate melt and gas proceeds easily, and although explosive phenomena do occur they are usually much less violent than those associated with the eruption of andesitic, trachytic and rhyolitic materials where the melt may have a viscosity several orders of magnitude higher than basalt at a comparable temperature.

Whatever the magma composition involved, the principal products of a volcanic eruption will be coherent, solidifying *lavas*; explosively fragmented materials called *pyroclasts*; and *gases*. Most land volcanoes emit all three in varying proportions at various times.

Island of ice and fire

Iceland sits astride the mid-Atlantic ridge and appears to have done so for about 50 or 60 million years, since early Tertiary times. Thus we have preserved for us in one small area a record of the north Atlantic volcanicity during much of the period during which that ocean was being formed by the separation of Europe and Africa from the Americas by continental drift. Present-day volcanicity in Iceland is restricted to a tectonic depression, or *graben*, bounded by tensional faults, which is the surface expression of the crest of the mid-Atlantic ridge in south-central Iceland. Parallel with the ridge and the edges of the graben, volcanic activity tends to occur along tensional fissures, often with the quiet emission of enormous volumes of lava, as in the famous eruption of Laki in 1783.

Preceded by a week of local earthquake shocks, the eruption lasted from early June 1783 until February 1784, beginning violently with enormous lava fountains bursting from a row of small craters which quickly grew along a fissure 30 kilometres long. Huge volumes of fluid basalt flowed through the valley of the Skaftá River, filling it and overflowing on to the plains above and, during a later phase of the eruption, following a second valley to the south-east. In the eight months during which the eruption lasted, basaltic lavas flooded an area of 565 square kilometres, a total volume estimated at 12.3 cubic kilometres being emitted. While the Laki eruption was certainly smaller than many prehistoric and Tertiary fissure eruptions, the average production of lava from the fissure during its earlier stages was about 2,200 cubic metres per second – about double the discharge of the Rhine near its mouth.

Fig. 2 Part of southern Iceland, showing the row of craters along the eruptive fissure of the great Laki eruption of 1783. The shaded area shows where the lava flowed and solidified – to an average depth of over 20 metres.

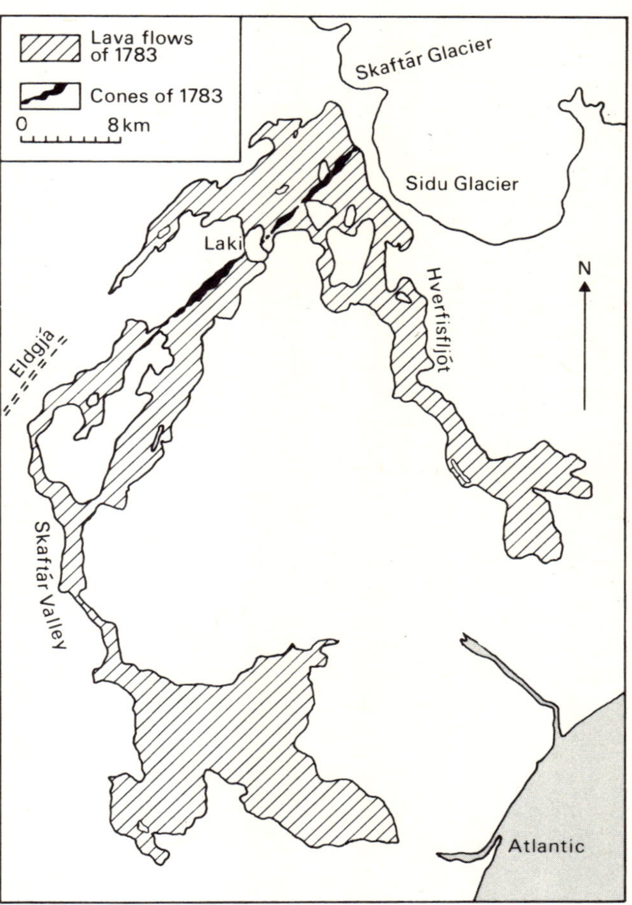

The Laki eruption was the greatest catastrophe Iceland has known. Significantly, this relatively gentle, but inexorable outpouring of lava caused no direct loss of life, though many farmsteads were overrun or severely damaged. It was the indirect effects which proved catastrophic. Mainly owing to pollution of the atmosphere by enormous amounts of volcanic gases, especially sulphur dioxide (of which the Icelandic volcanologist Professor Thorarinsson estimates that 130 million tons were produced), the growth of grass over the whole of Iceland during the summer of

1783 was disastrously stunted. Half the cattle and three-quarters of all the sheep and horses in the country perished, in turn causing a famine in which nearly one-quarter of Iceland's then total population of just under 50,000 died. The bluish, acid, sulphurous haze from the great eruption further reduced visibility to the point where the Icelandic fishermen could no longer put to sea and another prime source of food was denied the country during the 'Great Haze Famine'. The haze from the Laki eruption was observed all over Europe and into Asia and Africa during the summer and autumn of 1783.

A more or less parallel rift fault line passes through south-central Iceland at a distance of about 5 kilometres from Laki, and this controlled the smaller prehistoric fissure eruption of Eldgjá and in more recent times the volcanoes of Katla and Surtsey. The latter is of interest as a small volcano whose birth and development could be continuously observed. Activity began on 14 November 1963 with a shallow submarine eruption producing steam clouds and jets of black pyroclastic material at three places along half a kilometre of the Eldgjá–Katla fissure system and 10 kilometres to the south-west of the Vestmann Islands. The ejected rock fragments piled up around the vents and by 16 November an island had appeared which, three days later, measured 600 metres long and 60 metres high with a central fissure open to the sea. By April 1964 the edifice had grown to the point where the sea no longer had direct access to the vent and the lavas, instead of being explosively fragmented on contact with cold water, began to form fountains in the crater. It also emitted coherent fluid basaltic flows which formed a protective carapace over the southern part of the new island. These solid lavas have enabled Surtsey to resist complete destruction by marine erosion, which has been the fate of two other but ephemeral islands of pyroclasts in its immediate neighbourhood. Surtsey was sporadically active for three or four years and has been the subject of much detailed study; the pattern of its colonization by plants and animals has proved particularly interesting.

Further evidence that the south-central Icelandic rift system is by no means quiet volcanologically was provided by the eruption at Heimaey in the Vestmann Islands in 1973. There it was the earlier, explosive phase of the activity which caused so much damage to property, the greater part of the fishing port of Vestmannaeyjar being buried beneath pyroclastic deposits – 'ash' and 'cinders'. A lava flow later entered the harbour and it was feared that it would block the entrance to the most important fishing port in Iceland. In the event, it is said that the resultant shallowing of the harbour bar has actually improved the anchorage!

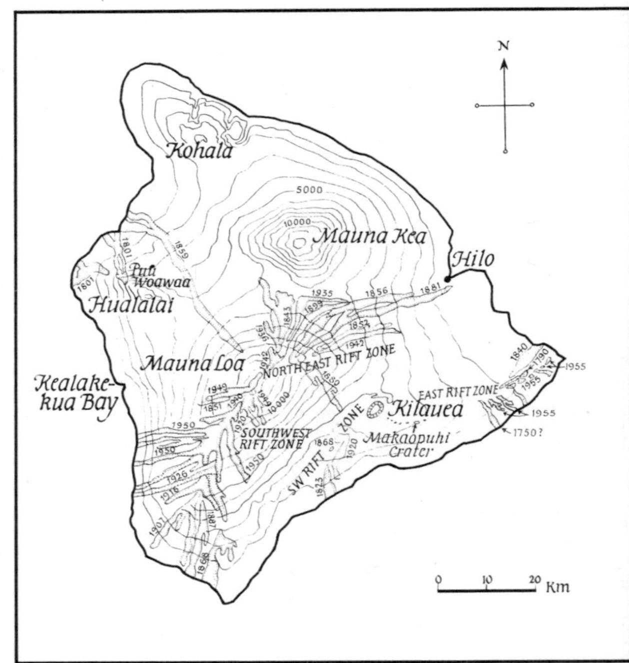

Fig. 3 Hawaii and its volcanoes. The dates of some of the major eruptions are shown.

The giant volcanoes of Hawaii

The active volcanoes of the Hawaiian islands provide certain contrasts with those of Iceland. Again the magmas are basaltic and eruptions, though spectacular, are generally not very dangerous.

Their tectonic setting is unusual, since they are situated neither on a spreading ridge system nor at a destructive plate margin, but in the middle of the oceanic crust of the Pacific plate itself. The islands lie in a line about 600 kilometres long extending west-north-west to east-south-east, the north-westerly islands and seamounts being about 18 million years old and no longer active, while Hawaii itself at the south-eastern end of the chain began activity about 6 million years ago and still continues. This striking linear arrangement, with the regular diminution in age along the chain, has led to the interesting if controversial suggestion that the Hawaiian volcanoes are fed from a local pipe-like channel of upsurging magma originating very deep indeed within the Earth, at the core-mantle boundary. So-called *mantle plumes* of this kind remain more or less fixed for quite long periods of time, so the Hawaiian chain could be explained in terms of the Pacific plate moving steadily in a west-north-west direction above a fixed 'hot spot' where the plume impinges upon it.

The Hawaiian volcanoes are classified, because of their

form, as *shield volcanoes* and represent the largest single volcanic edifices upon the Earth. Hawaii itself consists of a complex of five volcanoes, only the smaller part of which projects above the Pacific Ocean. The largest volcano, Mauna Loa, has a total height of about 10 kilometres and a diameter of around 400 kilometres at its base. The angle of slope of this vast shield is only 4°–6° and the present summit of Mauna Loa, occupied by a circular collapse caldera, is about 4 kilometres above sea level: thus despite its gentle slopes, it is a very large mountain indeed.

The frequently erupted basalt lavas are highly mobile and the active craters within the summit caldera of Mauna Loa, and the neighbouring volcano of Kilauea, are frequently filled with lakes of incandescent lava at temperatures up to 1100°C or higher. Escaping gases often throw the lava upwards in spectacular fountains tens or hundreds of metres in height. Most Hawaiian eruptions, however, do not occur at the summit regions but lower down on the flanks of the volcanoes, which are traversed by a system of rifts, thus bearing some resemblances to the Icelandic fissure type of source.

Beyond occasionally destroying plantations, crops and forests, the lava flows of Hawaii seldom produce great hazards to life and property. Sometimes they do, and there have been times when the port of Hilo, lying at the mouth of a depression between ancient lava flows of Mauna Loa and Mauna Kea, has been threatened. One such occasion was during an eruption from the rift zone on the northern flank of Mauna Loa which began on 21 November 1935. After becoming ponded up in a saddle between Mauna Loa and Mauna Kea, the lava broke out and turned towards Hilo on 22 December, and by the 26th had covered a quarter of the distance to the port. At the instigation of the then Director of the Hawaiian Volcano Observatory, Dr T. A. Jaggar, the United States Air Corps dropped high explosive bombs on two carefully selected target areas from a height of 3,500 ft above the lava on 27 December. The bombs ruptured the solidifying crust of the lava and breached the marginal levees so that, making use of the local topography, the lava was made to flow out laterally in a relatively harmless direction, instead of following its original course. Jaggar's experiment was brilliantly successful; the rate of progress of the lava towards Hilo diminished rapidly and within 30 hours of the bombing it had stopped completely.

Yet Jaggar's was not the first attempt of its kind. During the greatest historical eruption of Etna, in Sicily, in 1669, the lavas reached the walls of Catania where they were held up for a time before penetrating into the city. Under the leadership of Diego Pappalardo, half a hundred men turned out, protecting themselves against the heat with wet hides, and with picks and axes hacked a breach through the lateral moraine of the lava above the town so that the molten river could flow harmlessly away to one side. They were too late for their attempt to have had much chance of success, and when the people of the neighbouring village of Paterno heard that the flow had indeed been breached and the lava diverted, they sent out 500 heavily armed men with trumpets and drums and put Pappalardo and his helpers to flight, fearing that the diverted flow would now threaten *their* village!

Despite the impression of inexorable creeping progress given by the slowly advancing front of a blocky lava flow, it is often possible, by making intelligent use of local irregularities in the terrain, to deflect it by artificially erected barriers. In this way considerable areas of plantation were saved in Hawaii in 1955 by low walls of earth and brushwood hurriedly pushed up by bulldozers.

Three Italian volcanoes

The active and recently active volcanoes of the Mediterranean have been the subject of observation by man for longer than any others. In scale they are many times smaller than the Icelandic and Hawaiian examples but show more variety of magma type and structure. In terms of plate tectonic theory, the Mediterranean is a complex region; perhaps the most we should say here is that the volcanicity appears related to the collision of the African and Eurasian plates which, since Tertiary times, has resulted in the uplift of the Alps and Himalayas.

Within the province basic and acid magmas exist side by side and many Italian geologists believe that the former are, as usual, mantle-derived though often subsequently modified chemically in various ways, while the latter are produced by remelting of siliceous rocks of continental crustal type. These acid magmas with their enclosed gases are potentially very explosive; even the basic magmas sometimes have compositions sufficiently different from those of Iceland or Hawaii to be more viscous, so that the proportion of explosively ejected rock materials may be higher.

Vesuvius, although quiescent now for 30 years, is of course the best-known volcano in the whole region. Prior to the greatest known eruption of Vesuvius, in AD 79, the volcano had apparently been regarded as extinct. The mountain and surrounding countryside were heavily settled and cultivated by the Romans, who foresaw no particular danger even though mild earthquake tremors had been felt over the previous 16 years. These reached a climax on 24 August 79 and the volcano erupted, with the

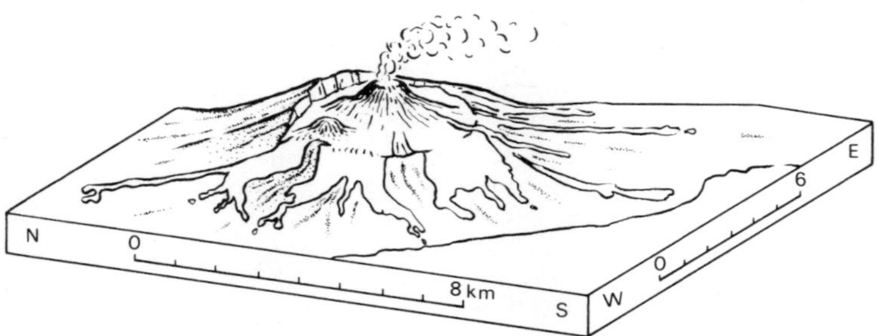

Fig. 4 Block-diagram of Vesuvius, showing the modern volcanic cone within the wall of Monte Somma, left after the ancient volcano was blown away in the eruption of AD 79 (after Rittmann).

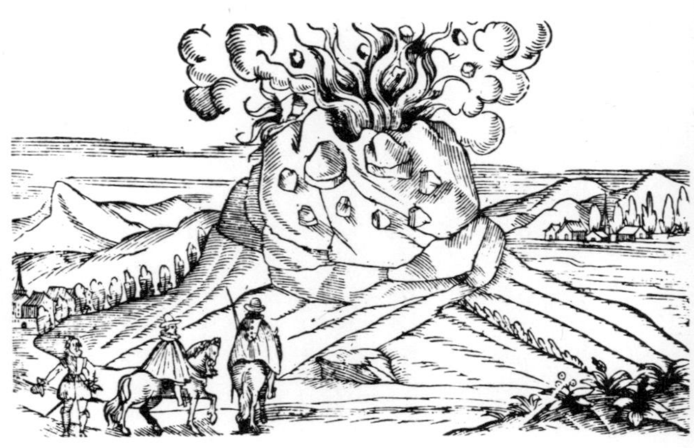

Fig. 5 An eruption of Etna: engraving from Sebastian Münster's 'Cosmographia Universalis', 1628.

emission of enormous volumes of gases which cleared the blocked vent and carried a dense cloud of ashes and blocks high into the air, distributing them widely over the surrounding country. Pompeii, to the south-east, was buried beneath the ash fall and the smaller city of Herculaneum to the west overwhelmed by flows of hot mud formed by the condensing steam from the volcano mixing with the ash. The great blast of gases, pumice and finely comminuted ash rising vertically from the crater and spreading out in the form of a gigantic Mediterranean pine tree was described in one of the two famous letters written by Pliny the Younger to Tacitus (lib. vi; 16, 20) sometimes referred to as the earliest surviving volcanological documents. I am indebted to my colleague Dr E. R. Oxburgh for this translation:

> A cloud rose up (to distant onlookers it was not clear from which mountain it came, but it was subsequently established to have been Vesuvius). In general appearance and shape it resembled nothing so much as a pine tree: for it poured forth and was carried upwards into the sky like a very tall trunk with side branches here and there, rising I suppose under the first force of the blast; then when that was spent, or even because its own weight became too much for it, it spread out sideways, sometimes dazzling white, sometimes patchy grey, depending upon its content of earth or ash.

Pliny's uncle commanded the Roman fleet off Cape Misenum at the time of the eruption and the nephew's account of his uncle's experiences on the mainland below Vesuvius, and of his death, apparently by asphyxiation, is vivid. Unfortunately, his account does not extend to the fate of Pompeii and Herculaneum.

When the activity diminished somewhat it was seen that the whole original summit region of the volcano had disappeared, leaving an immense crater inside an annular wall – the wall of Monte Somma. The modern Vesuvius has grown up over the centuries within the old Somma crater which it now overtops. The event of AD 79 began a new phase of activity for the long dormant volcano, for having cleared its throat during that eruption, Vesuvius has remained intermittently active for nearly 2000 years and many accounts of its eruptions exist. Some of the best, dealing with events not only at Vesuvius but in the whole of the region during the later eighteenth century, were written in a series of letters to the Royal Society in London by Sir William Hamilton (husband of the Lady Hamilton of Nelson fame), then British Ambassador at the Court of Naples.

In more recent times a major eruption occurred during 1906, during which the villages of Ottaiano and San Giuseppe were overwhelmed by ashes and lava fragments, with considerable loss of life. This culminated in a huge gas blast from the main crater, lasting 18 hours. The gases are estimated to have been ejected with a velocity of 500 metres per second and the ash-laden cloud to have reached a height of 13 kilometres. The most recent eruption occurred in March 1944, producing both major lava flows and pyroclastic activity; although a sizeable eruption, it was much smaller than the 1906 event.

Since 1944 the volcano has remained dormant, with no obvious signs of life beyond one or two small steam vents in the empty crater, but its history shows that it will erupt again one day. The Italian Government and the University of Naples maintain a well-equipped, modern observatory at a relatively safe spot on the flanks of the volcano. There a continuous watch is maintained on such phenomena as the temperatures and volumes of steam produced in and around the crater, and local seismic activity, so that as much warning as possible may be given of an impending resumption of activity. At present the geophysicists at the Vesuvius observatory are inclined to think that increased seismic activity in parts of the Phlegraean Fields during recent years may well presage an eruption in that region before Vesuvius is again active. The last eruption in the Phlegraean Fields built the pyroclastic cone of Monte Nuovo in 1538. But a few years ago minor earthquakes and appreciable relative movements of fault blocks around Pozzuoli gave some cause for alarm, and parts of the town were temporarily evacuated.

Etna, in Sicily, is Europe's largest volcano. Again, it produces basaltic lavas and pyroclasts, though different in composition from those of Vesuvius. A recent estimate suggests that Etna has been persistently active for the past 66,000 years or so. Its earliest products are submarine 'pillow lavas' exposed at Acicastello on the east coast of Sicily, and the present-day volcano is over 3,000 metres in height and 35 kilometres in diameter at the base. Seldom entirely inactive, Etna has erupted both from the summit crater and, during its long history, from hundreds of small parasitic vents and cinder cones dotted about its slopes: clearly Etna's plumbing is complex, or even haphazard. The uppermost parts of the mountain are frequently showered with ashes and cinders, while lava flows may attain lengths of a few kilometres. Habitation and cultivation stop about halfway up Etna, which is an inhospitable and exposed mountain, where even quite major eruptions seldom do very much damage or greatly endanger life. As at Vesuvius, a small observatory was set up in the early years of this century, but in April–June 1971 this was overwhelmed by lavas issuing from vents which opened in the flanks of the volcano two hundred metres below the summit crater. During the later phase of this eruption the sites of lava emission migrated north-eastwards to lower levels on the mountain, one flow reaching the village of Fornazzo, cutting a road and destroying several houses as well as devastating crops, forests and cultivation. But during historic times there have occasionally been more serious eruptions, probably the biggest being a flank eruption in 1669 when the lavas reached the town of Catania and poured into the sea. No volcano is safe and although great gas blasts or 'Plinian' eruptions like the AD 79 event at Vesuvius are not recorded at Etna, the danger of a major outbreak low on the flanks, as in 1669, always remains.

Stromboli, in the Aeolian Islands just north of Sicily, is another basaltic volcano which is almost continuously in a state of mild eruption from its ever-open vent set a little below the summit. It is a huge volcano like Etna, but only the topmost part of the edifice projects above the waters of the Mediterranean. Occasionally even Stromboli may produce without warning a violent eruption, as on 11 September 1930. The vent must have been mostly blocked for at 8 a.m. on that day a dense cloud of ashes burst suddenly from the crater and rose eddying into the air for about ten minutes. Then all was quiet until two hours later when two incredibly violent explosions occurred, which were heard 60 km away. A mushroom-shaped cloud 2½ kilometres in height rose from the crater, while blocks of rock weighing up to 30 tons were hurled on to the village of Ginostra, 3 kilometres away. An instant before the explosions the whole island was heaved bodily upwards about a metre, and then fell back again, causing a sea wave, or tsunami, 2 metres in height around the coasts of the island. The explosions, which cleared the vent plug, were followed by a dense shower of incandescent lava fragments lasting 40 minutes, to be followed in turn by the copious emission of ashes. All this loose material accumulated on the uppermost slopes of the volcano in a bed almost a metre thick which became unstable and began to slide downwards. The movement pulverized the brittle material and released the occluded gases to form an emulsion of ashes in hot gas, in a mass 10 metres high which rushed down to the sea through a narrow gully at a speed of 15–20 metres per second. The avalanche must have contained 75,000 cubic metres of material at a temperature of at least 700°C. Three people perished in the avalanche, while a fourth died of his injuries when scalded in the boiling sea near the point where it reached the coast. For 12 hours or so several lava streams poured down the slopes of Stromboli into the sea, but the whole violent eruption lasted barely 15 hours.

Island-arc volcanoes

While mobile basaltic magmas are encountered at island-arc volcanoes, the geological setting leads more easily than at other types of plate margin to the development of magmas of intermediate and acid compositions, such as andesite, trachyte and rhyolite. Such magmas are indeed represented among the Italian volcanoes as well – the island of Lipari is famous for its acid rhyolitic lavas, one flow of which was so viscous and cooled so quickly that it could not crystallize at all but was supercooled to a black, lustrous glass called obsidian. Sometimes similar viscous lavas do not cool quickly enough for the rock to retain most or all of the volatile components of the original magma. Thus the gases, separating from the melt and expanding at the surface as a result of reduced pressure, froth up the viscous mass into a light aerated *pumice*. If the vapour tension of the gases were sufficient and the temperature high enough, the gas bubbles in the rock melt could go on expanding until only a thin membrane separated bubble from bubble. Eventually the membranes would rupture and very suddenly a dispersion of hot gas bubbles in a continuous phase of rock melt would change to a dispersion of rock melt in a continuous phase of hot gases – a dense emulsion without confining walls, having a very low over-all viscosity and behaving as an exceedingly mobile, very hot fluid.

It was such an emulsion formed by the extrusion of hot viscous lava at Montagne Pelée on the island of Martinique

Fig. 6 Mont Pelée, Martinique. The arrows show the track of the nuée ardente of 8 May 1902. (After Macdonald.)

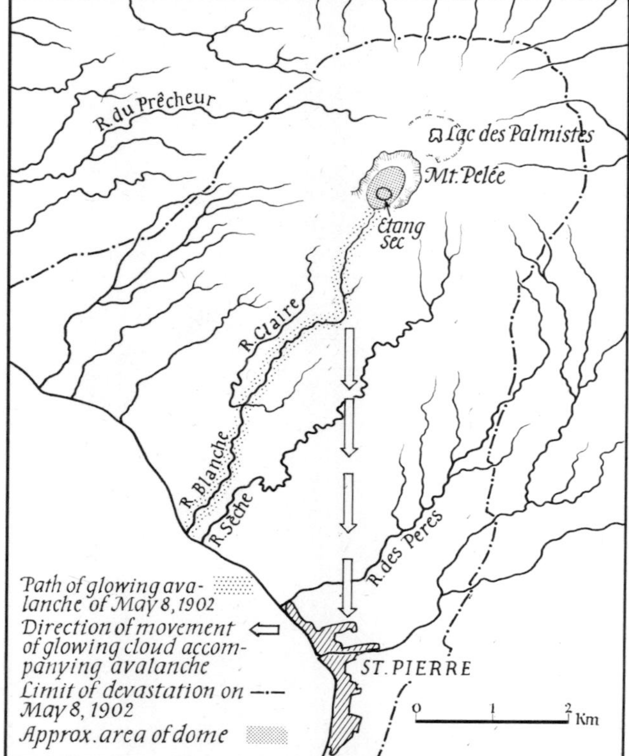

in the West Indies that caused the utter destruction of the city of St Pierre on 8 May 1902. Only two inhabitants survived the disaster, one being a prisoner in a windowless underground cell of the local prison.

Early in April new fumaroles (steam vents) had been observed in the upper parts of the canyon of Rivière Blanche, running south-west from the summit of Pelée towards St Pierre. On 23 April minor earth tremors were felt, while slight falls of ash and sulphurous fumes were noticed in the streets of the town. During the succeeding fortnight explosions occurred at the summit and the falls of ash intensified, blocking some streets, obscuring the sun and causing the death of birds and animals by smothering or asphyxiation. Gradually panic built up in the population, but a commission sent by the Governor of the island from Fort de France reported that there was no real danger and that evacuation was unnecessary: it is alleged that the administration wished to keep the people in St Pierre for an important political election on 10 May.

On 5 May a torrent of boiling mud destroyed the sugar mill at the mouth of Rivière Blanche, entombing at least 30 workmen; by 6 May violent eruptions were occurring at the summit of the volcano, with massive explosions. An exodus from the town began but troops were ordered to stop the flight.

On the morning of 8 May an immense column of vapour was rising from the crater. At 7.50 a.m. four huge explosions occurred, ejecting upwards a black cloud pierced with lightning flashes. Another cloud was simultaneously ejected laterally from the crater and rolled down the mountainside. A reconstruction of events shows that this avalanche overflowed the crater into the canyon of Rivière Blanche, which deflected it westwards away from the direction of St Pierre. The river valley was filled with the welded, compacted rock materials falling out of the emulsion, while the hurricane-like surge of hot gas and finer suspended ashy materials in front of the avalanche was not deflected, and travelled straight down to annihilate the town. The clock on the Military Hospital stopped at 7.52: the whole catastrophe was over in two minutes. Thirty thousand people perished almost instantaneously; the blast, travelling at least 150 kilometres per hour, unroofed all the houses, tearing down thick stone and concrete walls and causing widespread fire. Ships in the harbour capsized, with heavy loss of life, but it is to a handful of survivors from these vessels that we are indebted for first-hand accounts of the disaster.

Most loss of life seems to have been due to contact with the hot gases, for the blast left only a thin layer of ash over the city. Glass and porcelain objects were fused and metal articles twisted into fantastic shapes, while the wooden decks of ships in the harbour were set on fire. The temperature of the gases must have been between 800° and 1,000°C even at a distance of 8 kilometres from their source at the summit of Pelée. The great French geologist Alfred Lacroix, who visited Martinique shortly after the disaster, witnessed several later, less destructive examples of incandescent avalanches, and described them as *nuées ardentes*, glowing clouds, a term that has been widely adopted.

The eruption of Pelée in 1902 ranks among the most catastrophic of modern times, the peculiar formation and behaviour of the nuées ardentes resulting from the acid composition and high viscosity of the magma involved. Eruptions of this kind have been mercifully rare during historic times; yet by far the biggest was not Pelée, but the eruption of Katmai, in an uninhabited region of Alaska, in 1912.

The Katmai eruption was preceded by earthquake tremors, at which the few Indians living in the region fled, so that no first-hand account exists. It seems that it probably resembled in some respects a fissure eruption of the Laki type, but emitting an incandescent gas-rock emulsion instead of coherent fluid lava. The emulsion *(ash flow*) travelled 20 kilometres along a valley, filling it and leaving a flat plain 4 kilometres across consisting of a layer of welded rock fragments (called *ignimbrite*) having an average thickness of some 30 metres. For years after the eruption, multitudes of fumaroles – small vents emitting gas and steam – arose in the ignimbrite sheet, and the locality was dubbed the 'Valley of Ten Thousand Smokes'. Had the Katmai eruption occurred in a densely inhabited region, it would have constituted a natural disaster far greater than that of Pelée.

Such ash flows as that of Katmai may form coherent masses of rhyolitic rock as the hot silicate melt fragments settle out from the suspending gases and weld together as they cool. Unlike basalts, silicate melts of this kind of composition do not crystallize very readily and fragments of supercooled glass generally make up a notable proportion of most ignimbrites, giving the rocks characteristic textural features which can be recognized in the field and in thin sections under the microscope. Careful study of many supposedly vast rhyolitic lava fields, from geologically ancient as well as from geologically recent volcanoes, has shown them to be ignimbrites, with the implication that they have been formed by the same type of eruption as at Katmai. There are considerable tracts of recent ignimbrite in New Zealand, Italy, Hungary and the United States, to name but a few examples, and devastating eruptions could occur again. Pelée showed how destructive they can be, and that was a small event compared with Katmai, itself small in comparison with some 'fossil' ignimbrite fields.

Krakatoa, an island arc volcano in the Sunda Strait between Sumatra and Java, produces andesitic and basaltic materials and the enormous eruption of 1883 was in fact of the same general type as that of Vesuvius in AD 79. Intermittently active during historic times, the volcano by 1883 consisted of a large island with three overlapping volcanic edifices, and two smaller islands probably representing the remains of an earlier structure. In May, pumice and ash were first ejected and the eruption climax came on 26–27 August, with violent explosions that threw columns of ash and rock fragments to heights of up to 80 kilometres, showering back over an area of 750,000 square kilometres; the explosions were heard as far away as Alice Springs in Australia and Rodriguez Island in the Indian Ocean – distances approaching 5,000 kilometres. The ash caused total darkness for 24 hours at places 200 kilometres away, and fine dust from Krakatoa circulated in the upper atmosphere all around the world for years, optically scattering sunlight and causing spectacular sunsets. A ten per cent reduction in the average intensity of solar radiation was recorded at the observatory at Montpellier in France for a period of 4 years after the eruption.

Fig. 7 The islands of the Krakatoa group before the eruption (A), immediately afterwards (B), and in 1960 (C). The broken line shows the approximate area of the collapse caldera or hollow in the sea floor after the ejection of the magma. It would be about 30 km across. (After MacDonald.)

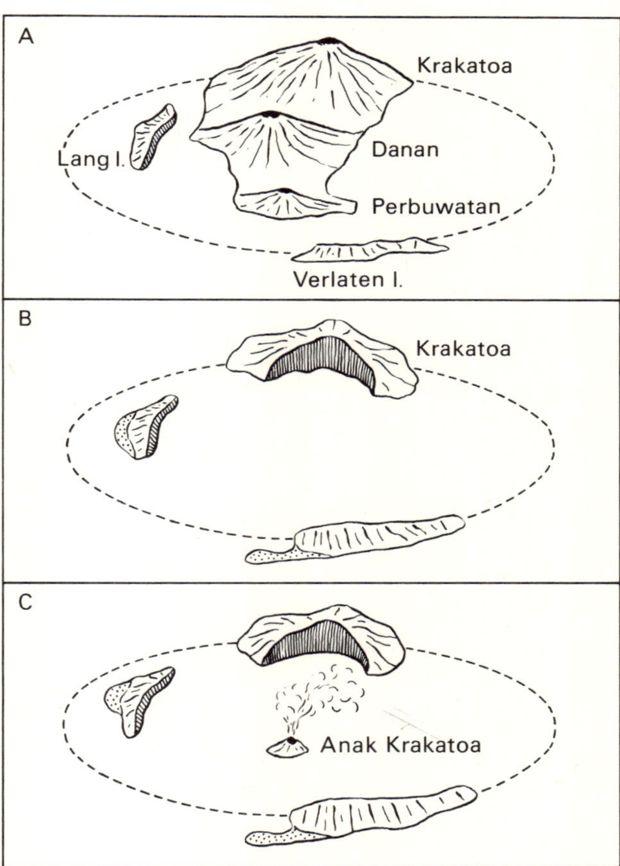

When Krakatoa reappeared to view, two-thirds of the island had vanished. The explosions, estimated to be equivalent to about ten atomic bombs, or 2,000,000 tons of TNT, fragmented and dispersed about 20 cubic kilometres of rock material. Later geological investigations showed that this was all new, magmatic material; the missing part of the island had not itself been blown away but had apparently subsided into the void left by the magmatic material ejected from below. In this collapse caldera, the later small island of Anak Krakatoa has grown and has been intermittently active ever since.

As in the case of the Laki eruption in Iceland a century earlier, the enormous death toll from the great eruption of Krakatoa – some 36,000 people – was due almost entirely to phenomena consequent upon the eruption, and not to the eruption itself. In this case, tsunami waves, which arrived at the shores of Java and Sumatra about half an hour after the cataclysmic explosions which caused them, attained heights of some 40 metres and inundated all the low-lying coastal areas, with the destruction of nearly 300 towns and villages.

A rather different kind of volcanic hazard is posed by the neighbouring volcano of Kelut, in Java. This has a standing lake in its crater, which is periodically ejected during eruptions, the water mixed with the volcanic ash forming a hot mud flow, or *lahar*, not unlike that which overwhelmed Herculaneum in AD 79. This rushes down the flanks of the volcano with annihilating force. In a severe occurrence in 1919, the lahars of Kelut took some 5,000 lives and destroyed 130 square kilometres of farmland. After this, Dutch engineers drove a system of tunnels through the summit slopes of the volcano in order to keep the crater lake drained and so reduce the lahar hazard. By this means they succeeded in reducing the volume of water in the lake by 80 per cent, and during a violent eruption in 1951 no large lahars were formed. However, this eruption destroyed the tunnel system and at the same time greatly deepened the crater. Further attempts were made to drain the lake, but without complete success and the eruption of Kelut in 1966 again produced lahars which killed hundreds of people. Happily, after this eruption, it proved possible to construct a new drainage tunnel at a lower level and once again to drain the crater lake.

Forecasting volcanic eruptions

Volcanoes are both potentially hazardous and beneficial to man. Basaltic volcanoes, in particular, produce lavas rich in iron, calcium, magnesium and other nutrient elements, which on weathering quickly produce very fertile soils. Despite the dangers from periodic eruptions, the slopes of such volcanoes are often intensively cultivated and quite densely settled. Vesuvius, for example, is said to have been cultivated right up to the summit before the great eruption of AD 79. The benefits of exploiting the rich volcanic soils are not lightly foregone; neither are well-established settlements in the vicinity of quiescent or only occasionally active volcanoes willingly abandoned. Thus there is a need for steady growth in man's ability to forecast volcanic activity and to take necessary precautions as soon as warning signs are recognized. But the systematic study of volcanoes is a relatively new branch of science and although knowledge increases rapidly, the art of volcano forecasting is very much in its infancy. Volcanic phenomena are so variable, their occurrence in time so apparently haphazard, that such forecasting is a daunting task.

From the distribution pattern of present-day volcanicity, and that of geologically recent times as deduced from the record of the rocks, it is a truism that the vast majority, if not all eruptions in the geologically near future will occur within the regions that are active today. About 80 per cent of the world's active volcanoes occur in subduction zones, and about 16 per cent are associated with rift zones such as the oceanic ridge systems, Iceland, and the East African rift. The remaining 4 per cent include volcanoes associated with colliding plate margins (as in the Mediterranean), or within plates (such as the Hawaiian islands).

Little has been said in this chapter about the detailed geological structure of volcanoes. In contrast to the great fissure volcanoes of Iceland, and the shield volcanoes of Hawaii, where the outpouring of fluid lavas generally exceeds in volume the production of explosive, fragmentary materials, most volcanoes of small to moderate size are composed of a mixture of lavas and pyroclastic materials in which the latter predominate: the more viscous the magma, the greater the tendency towards explosive behaviour. Detailed geological study of the products of such a mixed volcano throughout its history as exposed in the field, backed with laboratory studies of petrology and chemistry, can sometimes allow quite a detailed reconstruction to be made of the eruptive pattern and its variation with time, thus materially aiding in forecasting future behaviour. For instance, many volcanoes started life emitting the products of a basaltic magma, but over long periods of time the magma composition can be seen to have changed towards more explosive intermediate and acid types. R. W. Decker, for example, states that 'in hindsight, the small to moderate eruptions of highly siliceous pumice at Krakatoa in Indonesia during the early summer of 1883 was a warning of the giant blast that occurred there in August of the same year.'

The time-span over which reliable observations have been made by man is very short in comparison with the life-time of a major volcano, and it seems that some of the most violent outbreaks in historic times have occurred at volcanoes previously regarded as extinct. Vesuvius, prior to AD 79, had long been in repose; Tambora in Indonesia erupted for the first time in history in 1815, killing 10,000 people and causing a further 50,000 deaths from starvation; Santa Maria in Guatemala erupted in 1902 with a heavy death toll; and the eruption of Katmai in 1912 was, as we have seen, the biggest volcanic eruption of the present century. Events of this kind are virtually unpredictable from geological evidence alone.

During the past 20–30 years, geological observations at active and potentially active volcanoes have been increasingly supplemented by the application of geophysical methods. The intimate association of over three-quarters of the world's active volcanoes with earthquake zones at destructive plate margins suggests that seismology could be applied to eruption forecasting. As the Soviet volcanologist G. S. Gorshkov remarks, nearly every eruption or increase of volcanic activity is preceded by a swarm of earthquakes, so that no fairly large eruption, at least, should come as a surprise in volcanic regions where there is constant seismological surveillance. Volcanoes, however, behave as individuals, no two showing quite the same pattern of connection between the earthquakes and eruptions, so that quantitative prediction is still not possible. Not merely is the number of premonitory earth tremors recorded important, but also their total energy, and the depth and spatial distribution of their foci. A major paroxysmal eruption of the volcano Bezymianny in the Kamchatka arc, in 1956, for example, occurred during a period of decrease in the total energy of recorded earthquakes. Pinpointing the earthquake foci will indicate whether they are within or close to the volcanic structure itself, or well beyond it, in which latter case any danger is likely to be less imminent. The sources of the shallow, local microearthquakes that can be recorded at all active volcanoes, whether or not they are actually erupting, are probably several, and in general connected with movements of magma and separation of gases immediately beneath and within the volcanic structure itself. Some connection has been observed, however, between the number and magnitude of deep-focus earthquakes (with foci more than 70 km deep) in subduction zones and the frequency of volcanic eruptions, for example in the SW Pacific.

While we think of volcanic rocks as brittle materials on the scale of a hand-specimen at ordinary temperatures, on a larger scale mixed structures of solid lavas and looser pyroclastics behave differently and yield considerably in response to applied stress without shattering. Thus before an eruption magma may rise into local chambers, fissures and channels in the volcanic structure, causing actual changes in the volcano's shape, which are detectable. The patterns and exact locations upon the volcano of regions of swelling and subsidence may be of use in forecasting an eruption, and are monitored by various means. As in Hawaii, triangulation survey networks can be established using high-frequency radio waves or optical laser beams which enable distance measurements to be made with a precision of about 5 parts in a million, and the lengthening and shortening of survey lines in the network can be translated into a physical picture of the changes in shape of the volcanic edifice. Another, simpler method also practised in Hawaii and at many other volcanoes is to instal 'tiltmeters' (usually based upon movements of water in a long tube, or of a small pool of mercury) which continuously record minute changes in the angle of slope of the ground into which they are set. Tiltmeter observations (which may be accurate to one twenty-fifth of a second of arc) show that the summit regions of the Hawaiian volcanoes definitely inflate before an eruption, increasing the tilt of the ground, and deflate after an eruption. Similar phenomena are observed at some of the active Japanese volcanoes, and tiltmeter observations form a valuable supplement to seismometer monitoring.

The subterranean movements of magma to higher levels in a volcano before eruption cause small but measurable changes in the local gravitational and magnetic fields, and systematic monitoring of these may also be of value in eruption forecasting. Another interesting way of following the underground movements of bodies of magma is to record photographically, from the ground or from the air, the increased infra-red radiation from local 'hot spots' which are usually difficult or impossible to detect by ordinary temperature measurements on the ground.

As at Vesuvius, a close watch can be kept of temperature variations of fumarole gases or local hot springs in and around a quiescent volcano. Sir William Hamilton wrote of Vesuvius in 1772: 'It is certain that, by constant attention to the smoak that issues from the crater, a very good guess may be given as to the degree of fermentation within the Volcano. By this alone I foretold the two last eruptions.' But again, volcanoes behave individually, and a rise in fumarole temperatures may precede an eruption at some but not at others. Likewise, variations in the chemical composition of the gases may be significant: while the vapour emitted from most fumaroles consists almost entirely of re-heated rainwater from the surface, there is nearly always some admixture of gases which were originally dissolved in the magma itself, and sharp increases in the contents of hydrogen chloride and sulphur dioxide have been observed before an eruption.

Great progress has been made in recent years with the methods of observation outlined above, and in general the recording of premonitory earth tremors, together with observations of tilt and deformation of the volcanic edifice, so far promise the best means of forecasting an eruption. Where continuous, systematic geophysical monitoring is carried out – as in Hawaii and at some Japanese volcanoes, but regrettably at few others – entirely unexpected eruptions cannot occur. However, it is usually easier to predict with some confidence *where* an eruption will happen than *when* it will happen. What is badly needed is a greatly increased provision of well-equipped volcanological observatories in all the potentially hazardous regions of the world. Eruptions are so sporadic in general that governments become complacent about the dangers; yet the cost

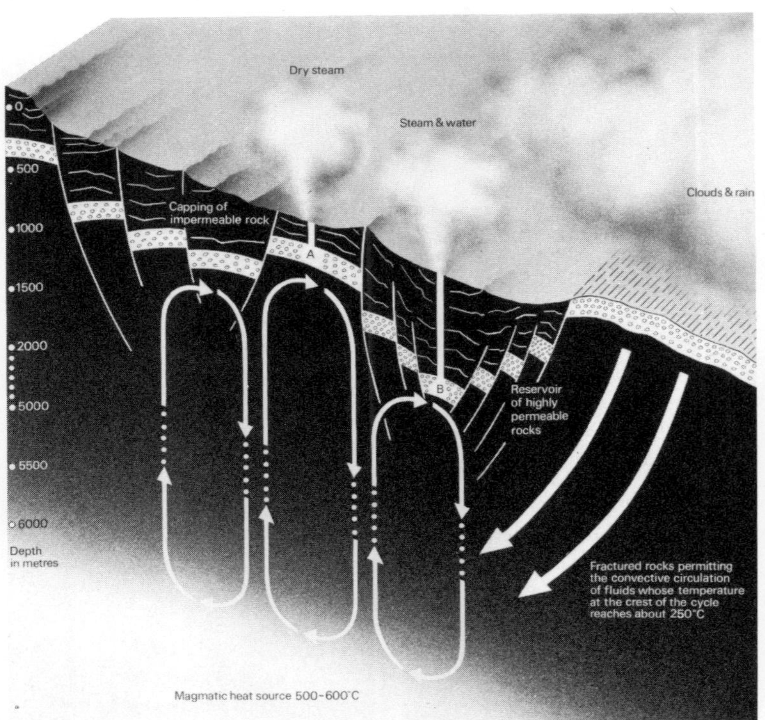

Fig. 8 Schematic model of a geothermal field (after Marinelli). To the right of the diagram, permeable rocks reach the surface and the system is replenished by surface waters. Reservoir A, at a depth of 400 metres, is subjected to a hydraulic pressure of 40 kg/cm², at which the boiling point of water is about 250°C. In this reservoir there will therefore be both liquid water and water vapour, and a borehole will deliver dry steam at the surface which can be fed directly to turbines to generate electricity. Reservoir B, at a depth of 1300 metres, is subjected to a hydraulic pressure of 130 kg/cm². The boiling point of water at this pressure is 330°C, while the geothermally heated water in the reservoir at B is, as in the case of A, at a temperature of only 250°C (see diagram). In B, therefore, only liquid water exists, which will boil as it rises up the borehole, so that the steam arriving at surface will entrain droplets of liquid water which must be removed before passing the steam to the turbines.

of providing forecasting facilities would be trivial in terms of any national budget.

Harnessing the Earth's heat

During the waning stages of activity one often observes in volcanic districts such phenomena as steam and gas vents (fumaroles and solfataras), geysers and hot springs. Most of these emit ordinary ground water heated by volcanic sources and sometimes mixed with a certain proportion of original gaseous constituents of magmatic origin. Naturally occurring hot waters of this kind are locally exploited as sources of energy: in Iceland, for example, extensive use is made of them for domestic and industrial space heating.

Bodies of magma – hence sources of heat – exist at no very great depths in active volcanic regions. Not all magmas ascending from the mantle and lower crust break cover to be extruded at volcanoes, and many such materials migrate upwards only to stop, cool and crystallize very slowly at various depths within the crust, up to a kilometre or two from the surface. Such intrusive masses of magma are often found in the geological record closely associated with volcanoes, but not invariably.

Observations in deep mines and boreholes show a general increase in temperature with depth, the average thermal gradient being around 30°C per 1,000 metres, though the value varies widely from place to place. The average outward-directed heat flow at the Earth's surface is about 1.3 microcalories per square centimetre per second. This heat flux, integrated over the whole globe, would correspond to an energy source of 30,000 million kilowatts – five thousand times less than the solar energy received by the Earth – but nonetheless the total heat content of the outermost 2 kilometres of the crust is about two thousand times as much as that contained in our total known reserves of fossil fuels. If only this energy could easily be harnessed! As it is, the extraction of crustal heat energy in regions of near average heat flow and gradient would require the input into the process of more energy than would be recovered, and it is only in regions of exceptionally high heat flow and gradient that profitable recovery of geothermal energy is thermodynamically feasible. Such regions correspond more or less with the volcanically active (or recently active) regions of the globe, where still-hot masses of magma approach the surface: it is important to remember, however, that high heat flow may locally be observed in regions remote from recent volcanicity, and due to altogether different local causes.

The pioneer attempt to harness geothermal energy for the generation of electric power – a very successful attempt – was the well-known Larderello enterprise in Tuscany. Although the surface rocks around Larderello are not volcanic at all, but sediments, gas-charged fumaroles had long been known in the district and in 1817 a Frenchman, François Larderel, started to exploit these industrially as a source of boric acid. Towards the end of the nineteenth century, he began to drill wells to augment the production of the boron-rich vapours, and these wells produced superheated steam at such temperatures and pressures that the idea developed of using the steam to generate electric power. Beginning in 1913, the installations steadily grew, and by 1951 Larderello was producing 257 megawatts of cheap electricity, a figure that had risen by 1973 to 365 megawatts, representing about 7 per cent of all Italy's power production. As well as the geothermal field of Larderello and the much smaller neighbouring field around Monte Amiata, natural steam is used to generate electricity on a lesser scale at The Geysers, California, and Wairakei on the North Island of New Zealand (where the present output is around 200 megawatts). The latter areas are capable of more extensive exploitation, and the Californian field plans to more than double its electricity generation by 1980. The Larderello field is now at about the limit of exploitation, and a programme of exploration for possible new geothermal fields is going on in Italy. Smaller geothermal power installations are in operation or planned in Japan, Mexico, the Soviet Union, Iceland, and elsewhere.

The first condition for exploitable geothermal energy is a heat source, possibly a buried magmatic source, at a depth between, say, 3 and 10 kilometres and a temperature about 500°–600°C. This will provide a suitably enhanced local geothermal gradient but, since the thermal conductivity of rock is so low, this is useless unless the source is overlain by porous and permeable rocks in which ground water can transfer the heat energy to the surface by convective circulation. The available water must be sufficient to yield large quantities of steam, but not so much that the heat source is only able to raise its temperature slightly (as happens in Hawaii). The circulation rate, largely governed by the mechanical characteristics of the reservoir rocks, must lie in the optimum range where convection is fast enough to transfer heat effectively from the source upwards, but not so fast that the upper surface of the heat source is cooled more rapidly than heat is being transferred to it by conduction from below. Then, the porous and permeable reservoir must be overlain by a capping of impermeable rocks – conditions analogous to those required for the accumulation of petroleum. At Larderello, the heat source is thought to be a cooling magmatic intrusion, possibly related to the exposed granite of the island of Elba which is not far away. The reservoir rocks are cavernous dolomitic limestones, and the cap rocks mostly dense impermeable clayey sediments. At Wairakei, the steam rises from sandstones and along fault-zones, while the cap-rock is mainly provided by silica and calcium carbonate deposited in the course of time by the natural vapours themselves.

In favourable conditions the circulating water may become considerably superheated under pressure in the reservoir, and when tapped by drilling may emerge as dry steam which can be fed directly to the generator turbines. At Larderello the natural steam pressure may reach 25 atmospheres and its temperature 230°C. Under different conditions, as at Wairakei, the steam contains water droplets, which must be removed before passing it to the turbines.

Natural vapours of this kind invariably contain other gases and chemical compounds which cause corrosion of the machinery in the power plants and can be a considerable problem. The development of newer, resistant materials for turbine blades, valves and steam pipes has greatly alleviated this difficulty in recent years.

It seems surprising in many ways that so little has hitherto been done in other countries to follow the success of the Larderello experiment. However, the present energy crisis is leading at last to an intensification of interest in the possibilities of geothermal energy and several countries have initiated exploration programmes. It would cost relatively little to measure the terrestrial heat flux in the many boreholes drilled throughout the world every year, and the data collected would quickly enable a much more detailed picture to be built up revealing regions of enhanced heat flux. Following this, the recognition of possibly favourable geological structures in the vicinity for the accumulation of natural steam presents no very great difficulties. It is clear that the more recently active volcanic districts of the world will become targets of increased exploration for sources of natural steam and hot waters in the years to come.

Suggestions for further reading

GENERAL TEXTS

Ch. Krüger (ed.): *Vulkane*. Anton Schroll, Vienna, 1970.

G. A. Macdonald: *Volcanoes*. Prentice-Hall, Hemel Hempstead and Englewood Cliffs, N.J., 1972.

H. W. Menard: *Geology, Resources and Society*. W. H. Freeman, Reading and San Francisco, 1974.

A. Rittmann: *Volcanoes and their Activity* (translated from the German by E. A. Vincent). Wiley-Interscience, New York and London, 1962.

PLATE TECTONICS

E. R. Oxburgh: 'The Plain Man's Guide to Plate Tectonics' in *Proceedings of the Geological Association*, London, vol. 85 (1974), pp. 299–357.

INDIVIDUAL ERUPTIONS

Sir William Hamilton: *Observations on Mount Vesuvius, Mount Etna and other volcanoes in a Series of Letters addressed to the Royal Society*. London, 1772.

A. Lacroix: *La Montagne Pelée et ses Eruptions*. Paris, 1904.

F. A. Perret: *The Vesuvius Eruption of 1906*. Washington, D.C., 1924.

The Royal Society Krakatoa Committee: *The Eruption of Krakatoa and Subsequent Phenomena*. London, 1888.

S. Thorarinsson: 'The Lakagígar Eruption of 1783' in *Bulletin Volcanologique*, Brussels, vol. 33 (1970), pp. 910–29.

ERUPTION FORECASTING

R. W. Decker: 'State-of-the-Art in Volcano Forecasting' in *Bulletin Volcanologique*, Brussels, vol. 37 (1973), pp. 372–93.

Various authors: *The Surveillance and Prediction of Volcanic Activity*. Earth Science Publication No. 8, UNESCO, Paris, 1971.

GEOTHERMAL ENERGY

G. Marinelli: 'L'Energie géothermique' in *La Recherche*, Paris, vol. 5, no. 49 (1974), pp. 827–36.

The most spectacular show on Earth is a volcano in full eruption, though earthquakes and floods may cause more casualties and greater damage. Stromboli (*opposite*), off the north coast of Sicily, has been continuously active since prehistoric times; in spite of that incandescent fountain of gas and lava, it is considered one of the milder types of volcano. Below the 20 to 25 miles of the Earth's crust lies the mantle, within certain zones of which primitive rock materials locally become molten, and may rise to the surface. Volcanoes can be regarded, in a sense, as Earth's safety valves. In the case of Stromboli the valve functions efficiently; but sometimes the outlet is blocked, the pressure inexorably rises, and cataclysm results. Krakatoa, in 1883, blew its top with the mightiest explosion in the history of man, heard over 3,000 miles away; the resulting tsunami waves killed 36,000 people.

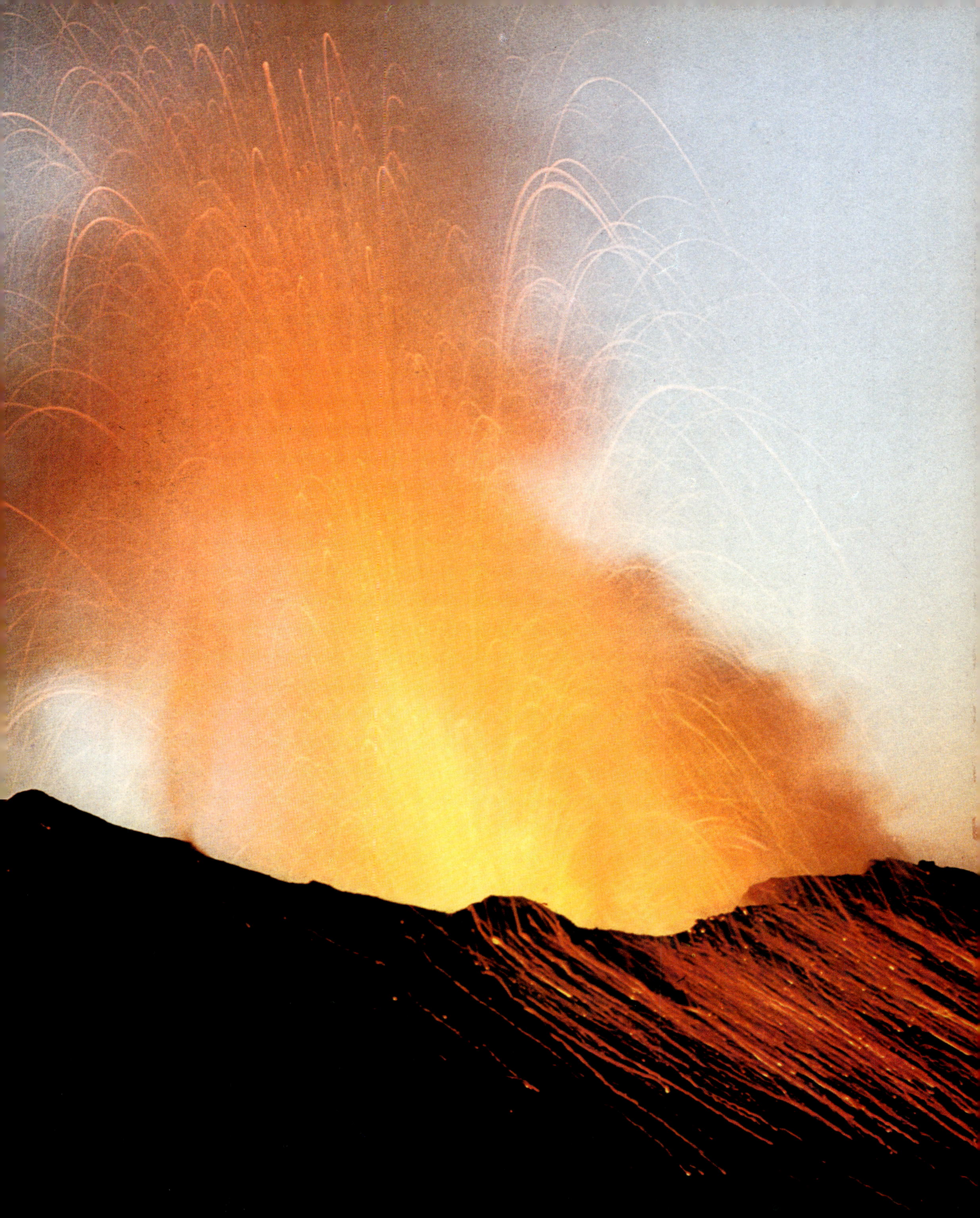

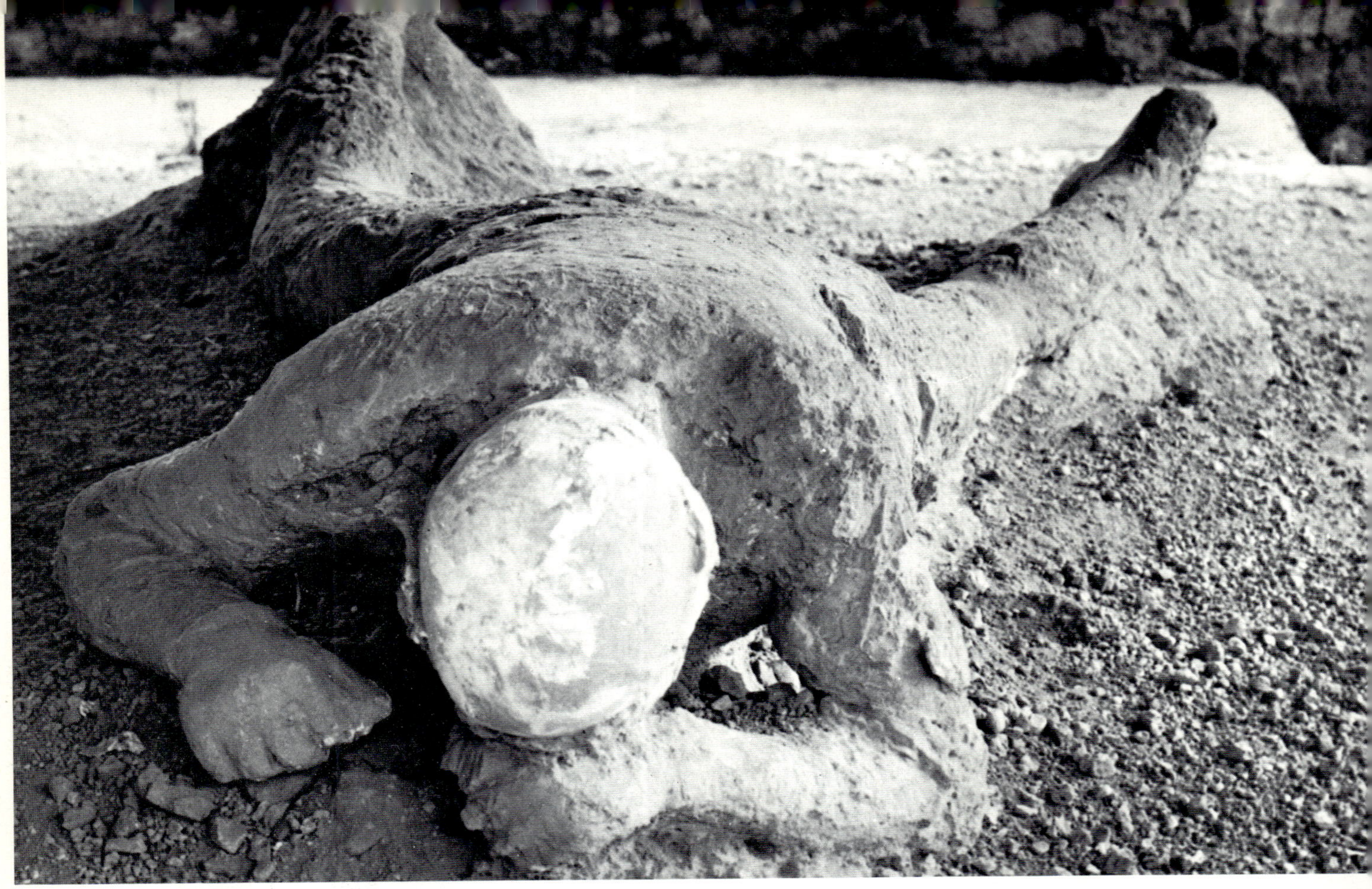

2

Throughout recorded history volcanic outbursts have killed thousands in some of the most dramatic expressions of nature's power. When Vesuvius destroyed Pompeii in AD 79, burying the town under a dense rain of hot ash, hundreds died where they stood – or ran. Their completely calcined bodies crumbled to dust; plaster casts of the empty spaces left in the cooled ash make museum exhibits of harrowing realism (2). Another eruption of Vesuvius in the late eighteenth century (3) was sketched by Sir William Hamilton, British Ambassador to Naples and husband of Nelson's mistress, in a vivid and accurately observed account which he sent to the Royal Society in London. Santorin, in the Aegean, had a major eruption in 1866; a contemporary engraving (4) shows rocks being shot from the cone, one of which sank a ship. The Royal Society also published a 500-page report on the cataclysmic explosion of Krakatoa in 1883. An illustration in this (5) shows a huge column of ash and dust rising from the crater, shedding rock fragments on the surrounding land. When Mont Pelée erupted in 1902, a hurricane-like surge of hot gas and fine ash, travelling at 90 miles an hour, killed 30,000 people in a matter of seconds. This was the dreaded *nuée ardente*, or 'glowing cloud', so named by the French geologist Alfred Lacroix, who photographed this later, much smaller example of the same phenomenon (6).

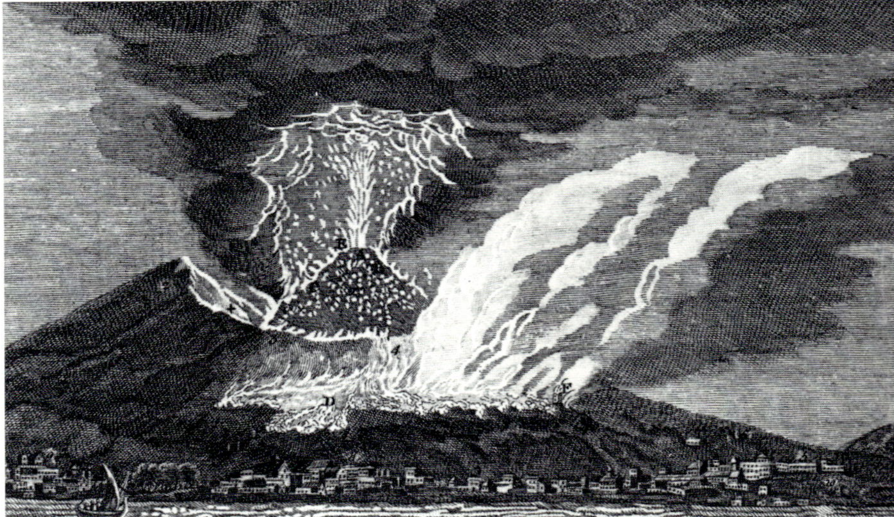

3

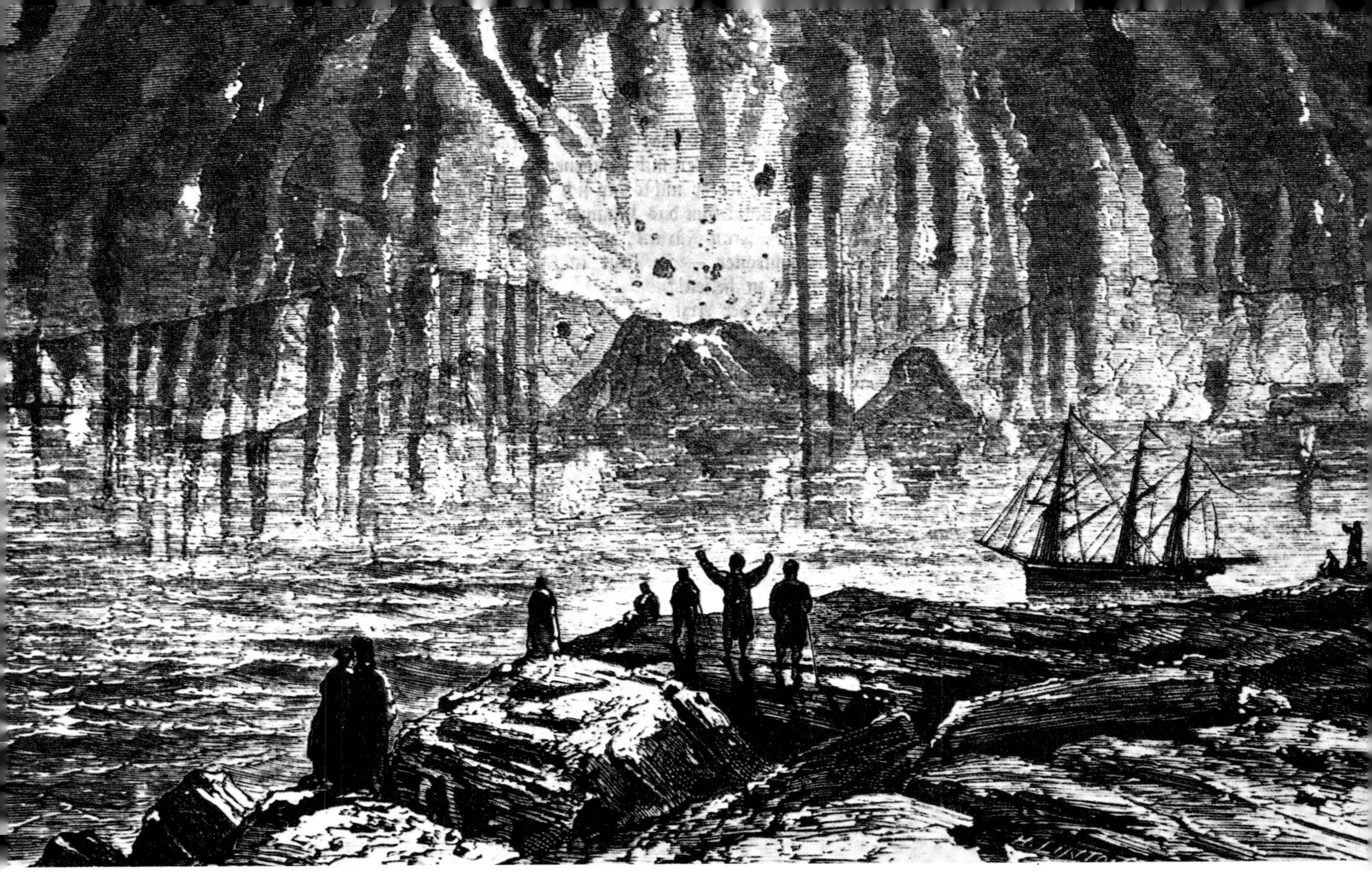

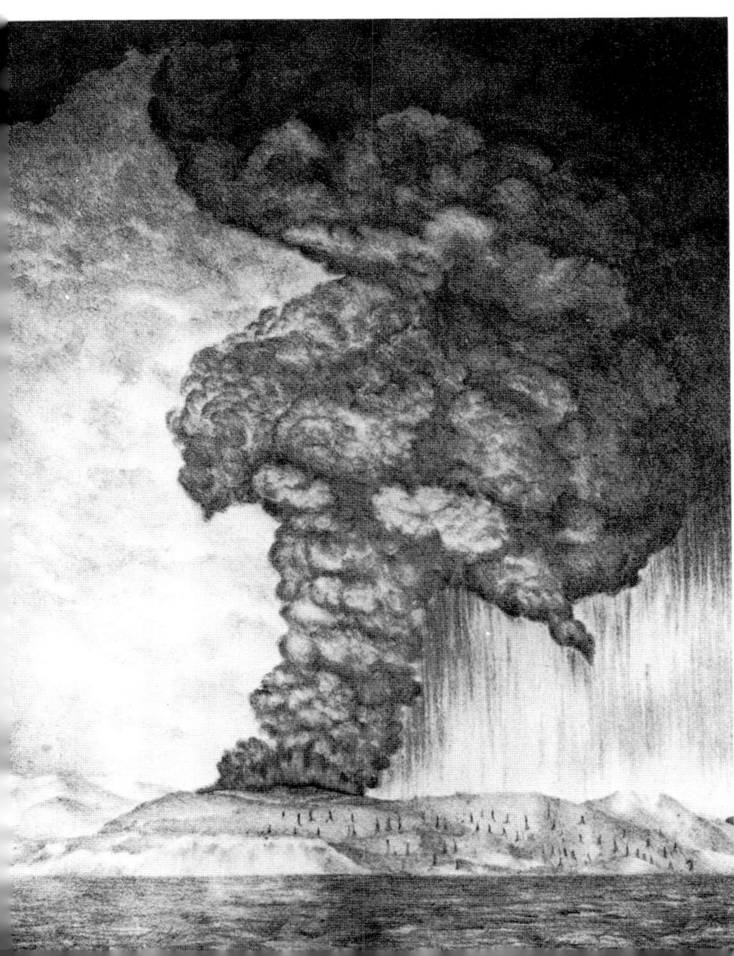

5

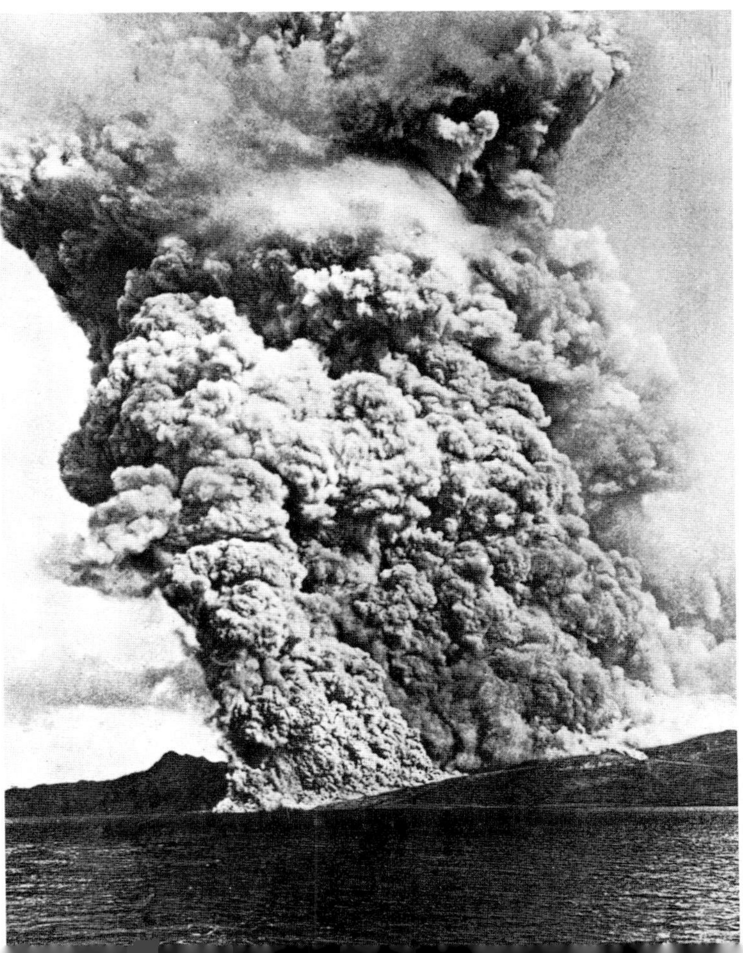

6

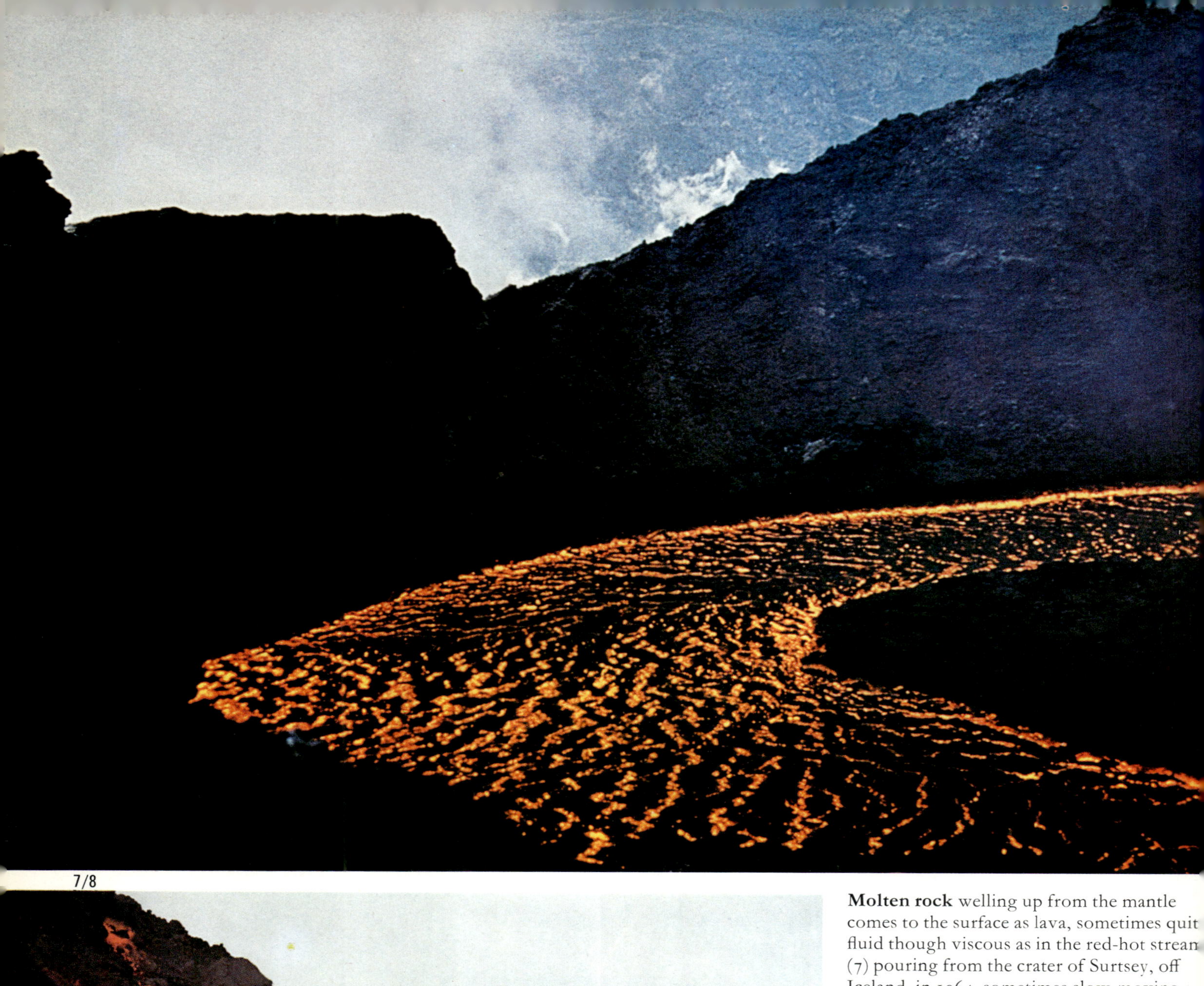

7/8

Molten rock welling up from the mantle comes to the surface as lava, sometimes quit fluid though viscous as in the red-hot strean (7) pouring from the crater of Surtsey, off Iceland, in 1964, sometimes slow-moving, thick as new-mixed concrete, like this inexorably advancing flow from Etna (8). With its wide range of chemical composition, lava can cool to the smooth, ropy form called *pahoehoe* (15) or to the roug blocky *aa* form (16); the names are from Hawaii, where both kinds are found.

Strange and beautiful shapes and colours are revealed when sections of volcanic rock 0.03 mm thick are seen under a microscope, by ordinary or polarized light. Basalt from East Greenland of Tertiary age – perhaps 6o million years old – shows, in ordinary light (9, × 20), pale greyish to brownish pyroxene, colourless plagioclase feldspar, and granules of black opaque iron-titanium

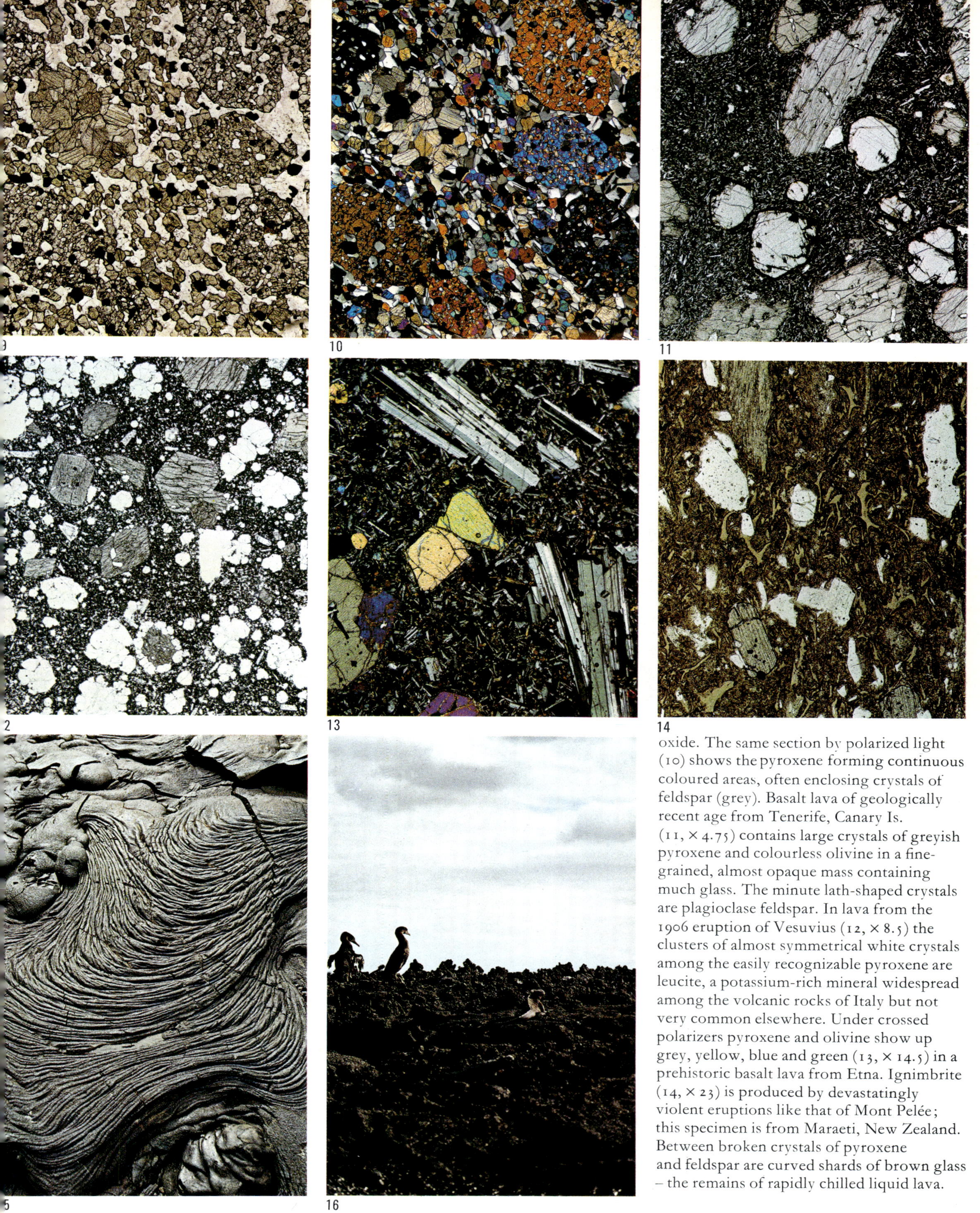

9

10

11

12

13

14

15

16

oxide. The same section by polarized light (10) shows the pyroxene forming continuous coloured areas, often enclosing crystals of feldspar (grey). Basalt lava of geologically recent age from Tenerife, Canary Is. (11, × 4.75) contains large crystals of greyish pyroxene and colourless olivine in a fine-grained, almost opaque mass containing much glass. The minute lath-shaped crystals are plagioclase feldspar. In lava from the 1906 eruption of Vesuvius (12, × 8.5) the clusters of almost symmetrical white crystals among the easily recognizable pyroxene are leucite, a potassium-rich mineral widespread among the volcanic rocks of Italy but not very common elsewhere. Under crossed polarizers pyroxene and olivine show up grey, yellow, blue and green (13, × 14.5) in a prehistoric basalt lava from Etna. Ignimbrite (14, × 23) is produced by devastatingly violent eruptions like that of Mont Pelée; this specimen is from Maraeti, New Zealand. Between broken crystals of pyroxene and feldspar are curved shards of brown glass – the remains of rapidly chilled liquid lava.

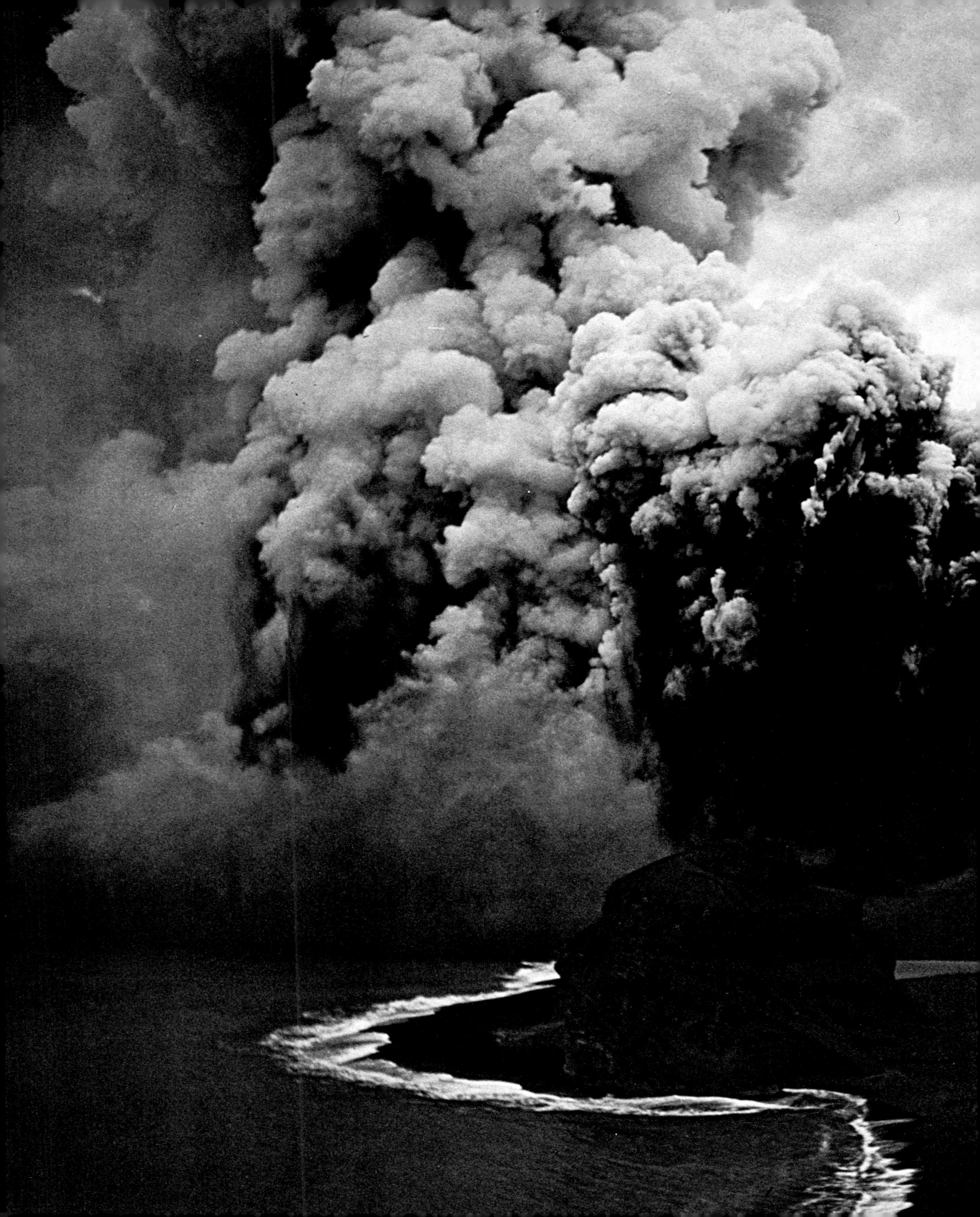

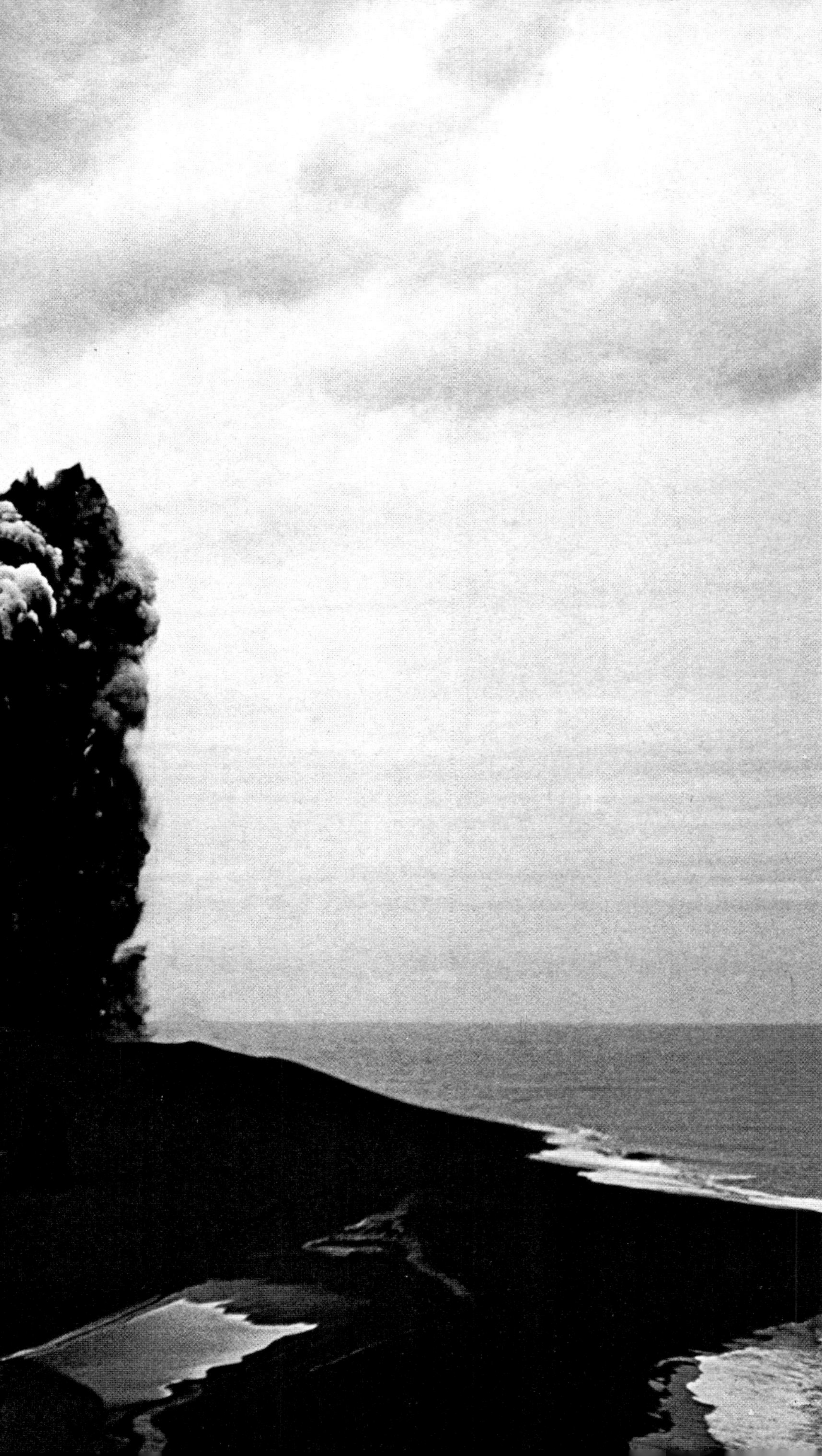

Out of the depths of the ocean a cloud of smoke and steam, 500 yards high, towers above Capelinhos in the Azores, marking one place on the submarine split where two of the Earth's crustal plates are slowly drifting apart. Along the length of the mid-Atlantic ridge, extending from north of Iceland almost to Antarctica, molten basalt is constantly welling up from the mantle layer to add about four cubic kilometres to the ocean floor each year. Mostly this pours out quietly into deep water, but occasional surface eruptions indicate the enormous forces at work on the drifting, jostling plates of the Earth's crust.

A river of liquid fire pours into the sea from the new-born island of Surtsey, off Iceland (18). The hot basalt (1100°C or more) has risen quite slowly from the depths, the volcanic gases have had time to escape, and the lava flows freely, with about the same viscosity as a heavy motor oil. By contrast, from the crater of Kilauea in Hawaii (19), molten basalt and gases burst out together in a frothing, explosive fountain 500 yards high.

18

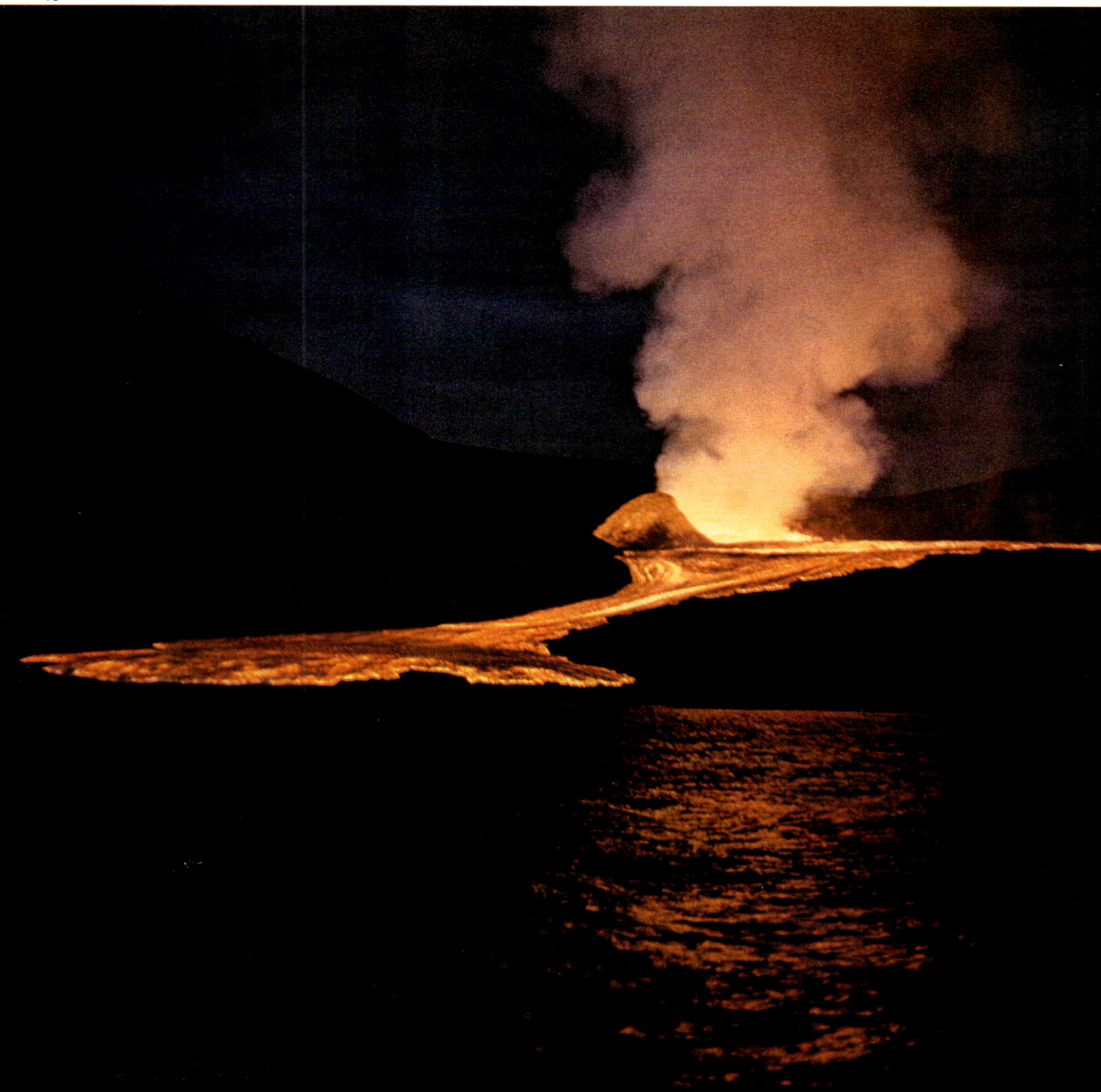

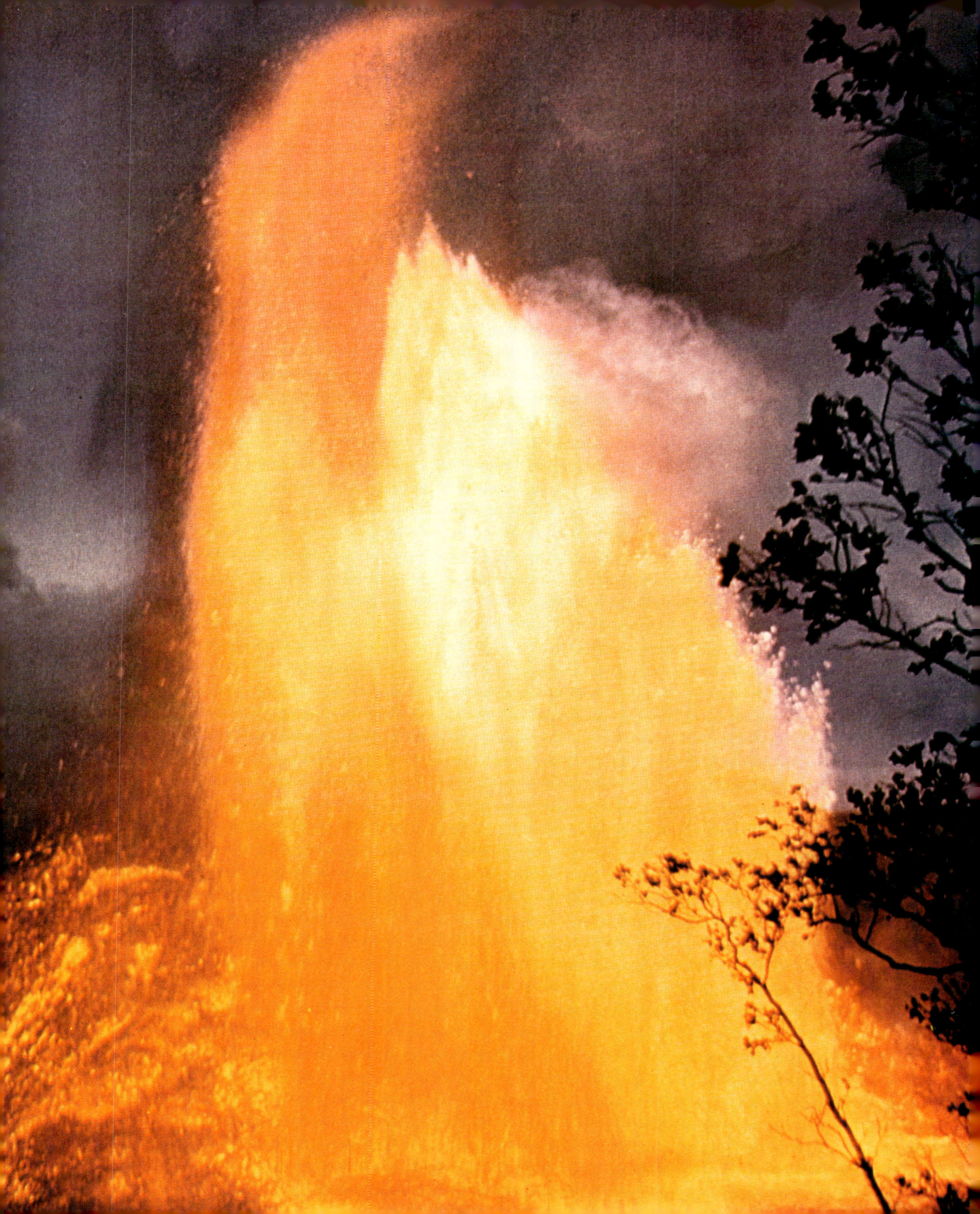

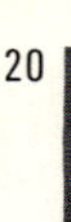

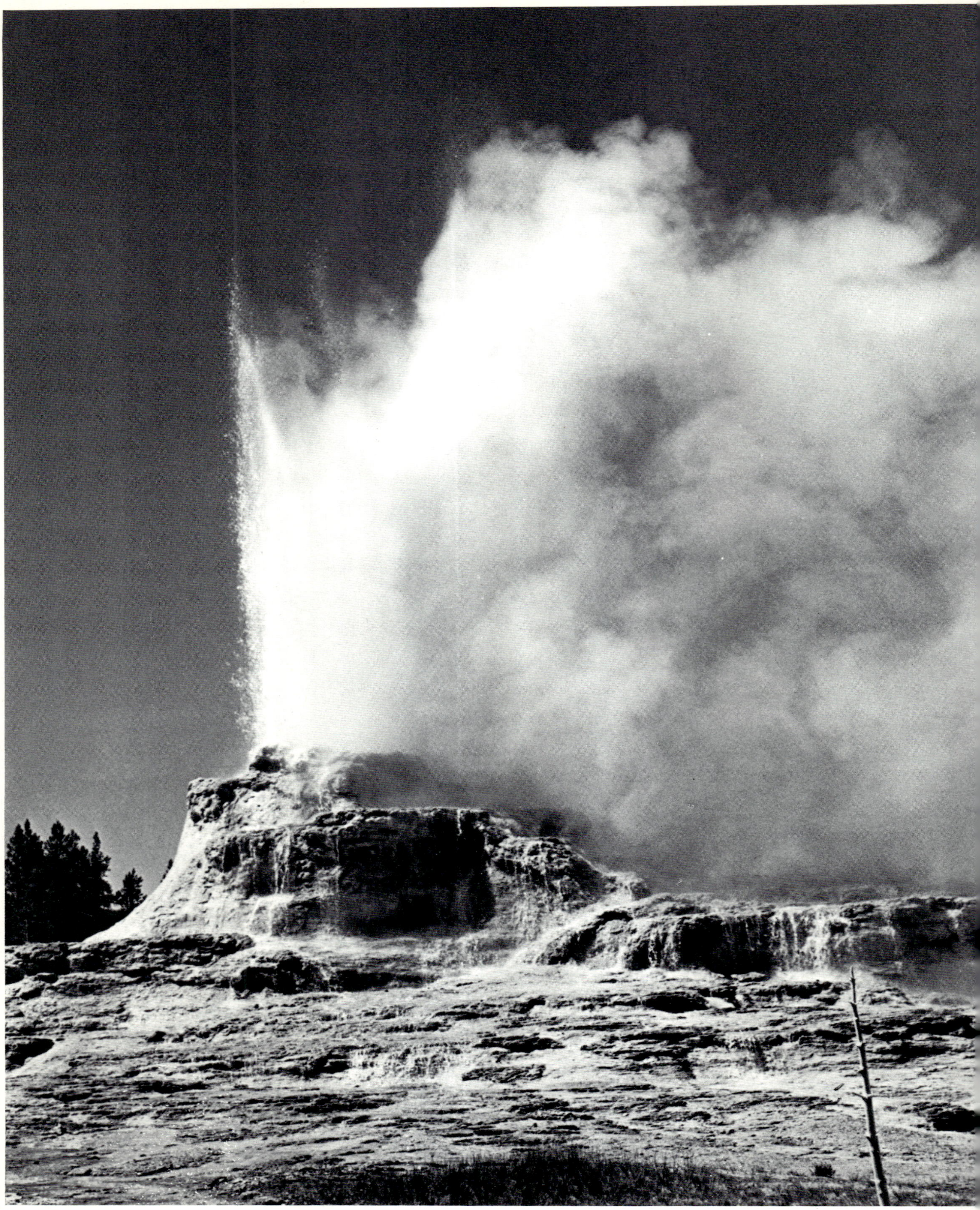

A plume of steam shoots out from Castle Geyser in the Yellowstone National Park (20). Geysers, steam vents nd hot springs are often the effects of waning volcanic ctivity, caused by bodies of hot magma, not far from he surface, heating the ground water. Residual volcanic eat, long-lasting and at shallow depths, is also esponsible for pools of boiling mud at Pozzuoli, near Naples (21) and for the scattered plumes of steam, nown as fumaroles (22); these are on the Galapagos slands, where volcanic activity has been dormant for enturies.

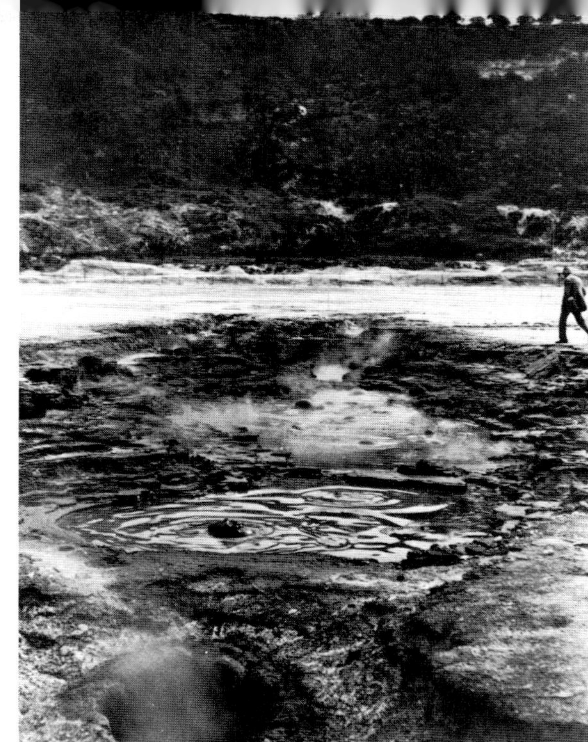

21

2

Here a volcano was born. On the hillside above the harbour of Vestmannaeyjar, Iceland's prime fishing port (23), on a January night in 1973, a 30-yard split opened up in the ground (24). Swiftly it lengthened and widened, pouring out flaming lava – the newest addition to the volcanic activity of the mid-Atlantic. Before the next day dawned, women, children and the old were mustered at the harbour (25) and ferried across to the mainland by fishing boat, as the skies flamed red behind them and the lava and ashes engulfed their homes (26).

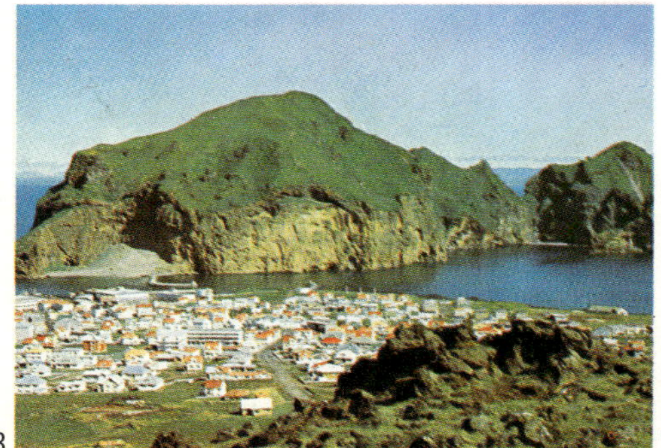

23

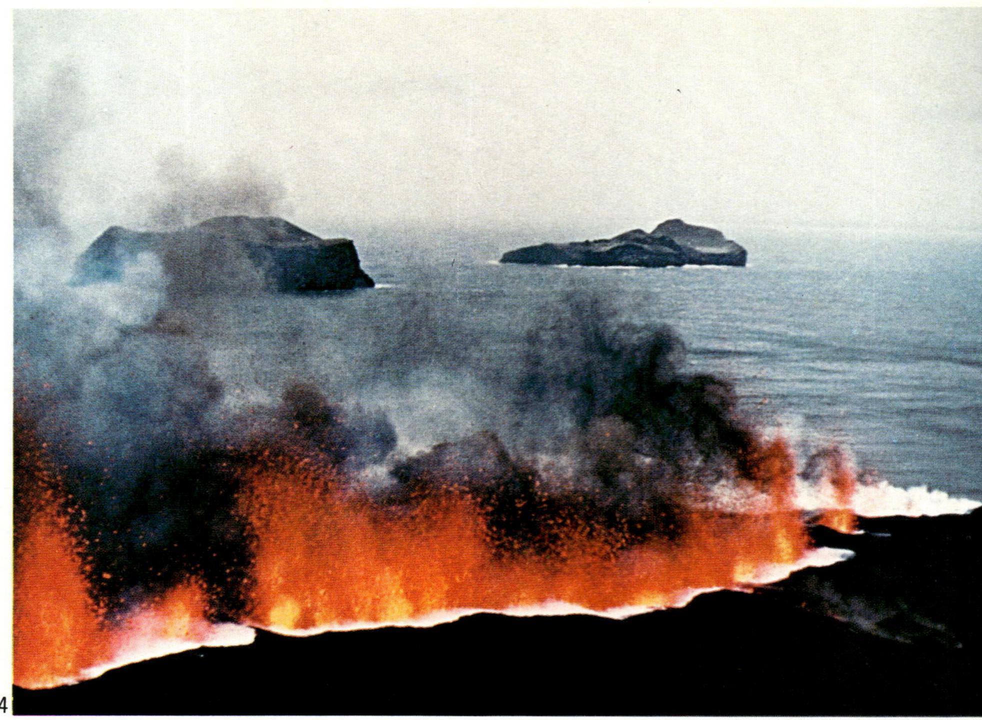

24

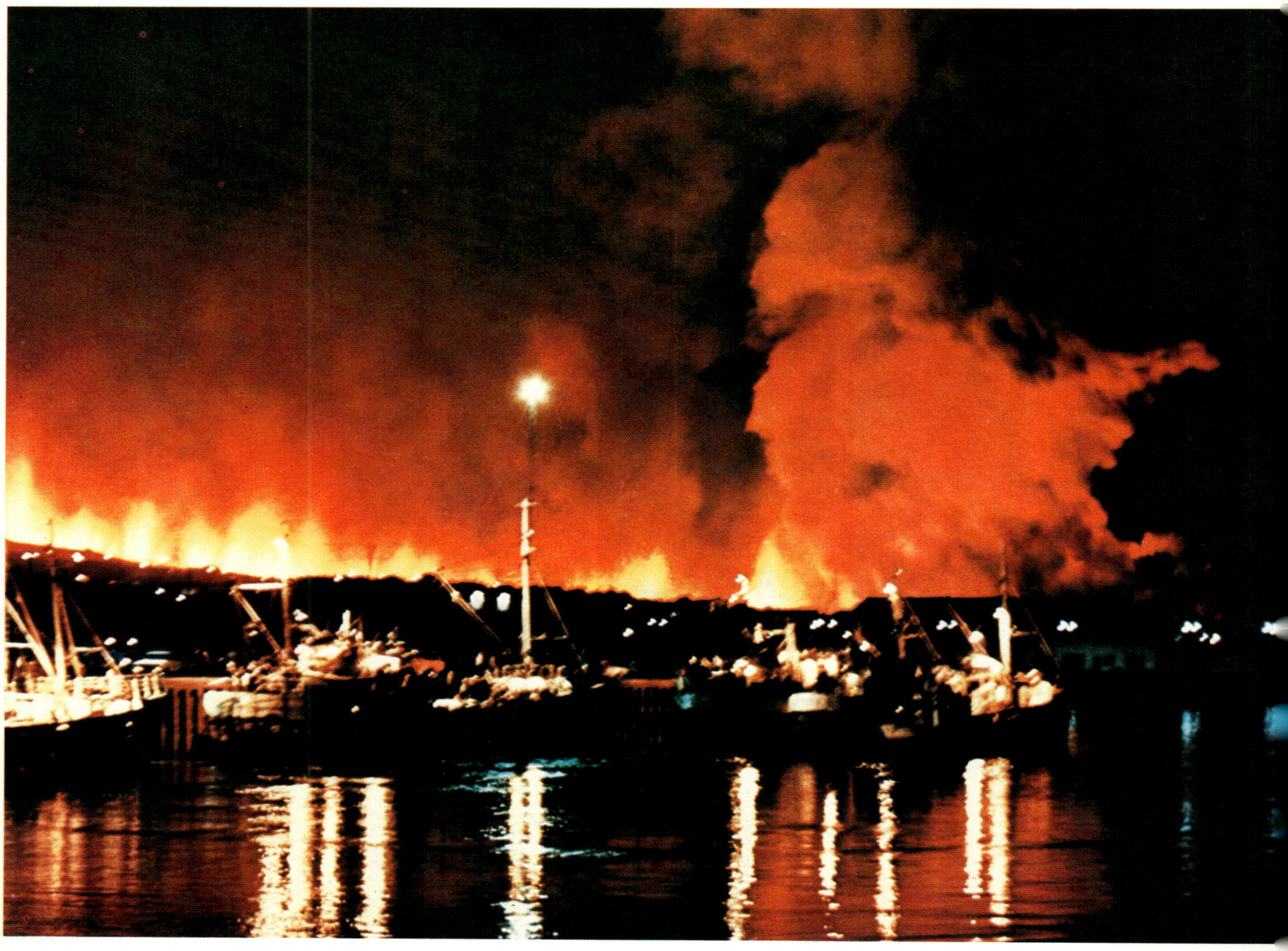

25

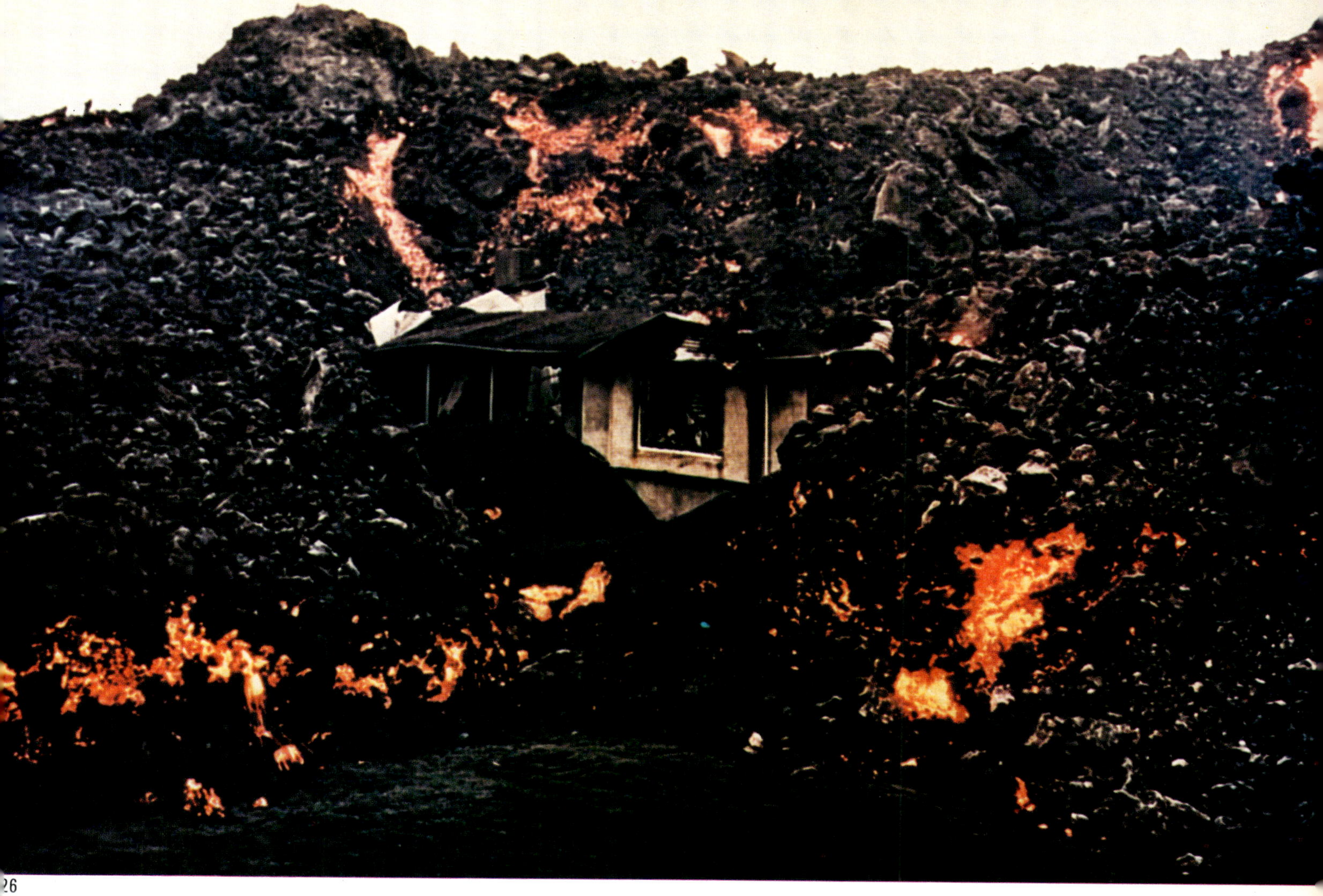

26

To cool the flowing lava, sea water was umped on to the advancing front, when the ruption was a fortnight old, in an attempt to ave the harbour (27). This was partly uccessful; though many experts doubted whether it would have any effect, boreholes rilled into the seaward end of the lava sheet, weeks later, showed temperatures of 1,000°C t 15 yards where the fire hoses had not layed, but where the sea water had been umped on, it was 700°. The harbour was aved (28) – even improved – but the town tself was little better than a smoking heap of inders (29). However, volcanoes are othing new to Iceland: the town is being ebuilt, and its life has started up again.

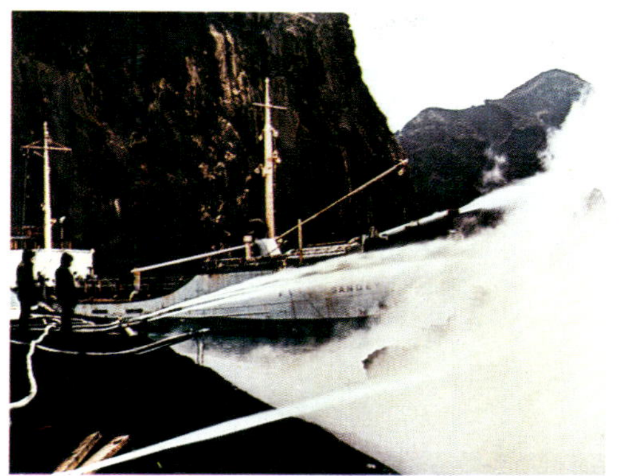

27

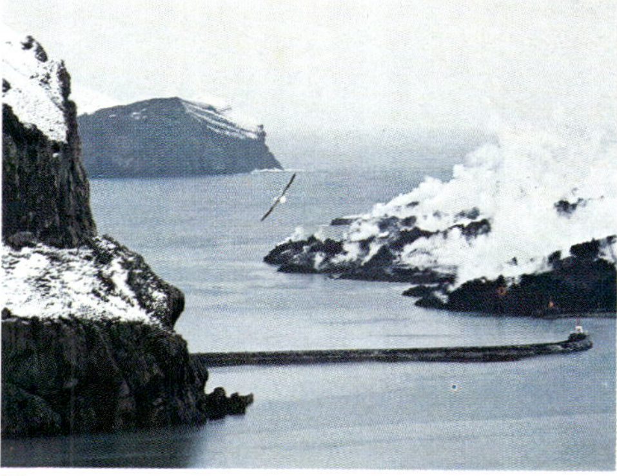

28

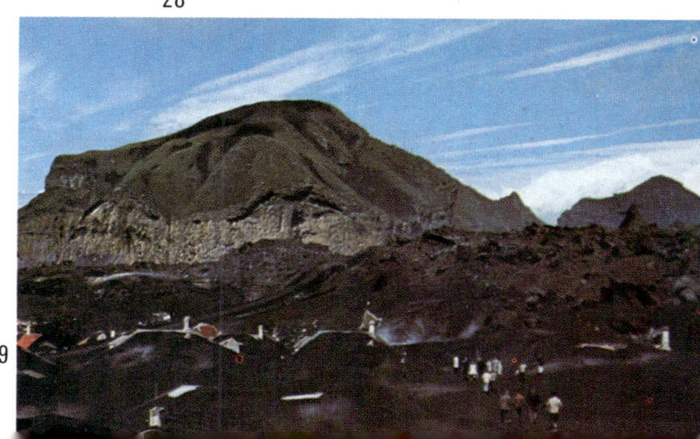

29

Volcanoes in the service of man. In Iceland, springs heated by reservoirs of magma are used to warm greenhouses (30) in which tropical fruit is grown, and Reykjavik's houses enjoy volcanic space-heating. At Wairakei, in New Zealand's North Island (31), steam heated in the same way provides the means to generate about 200 megawatts of electricity.

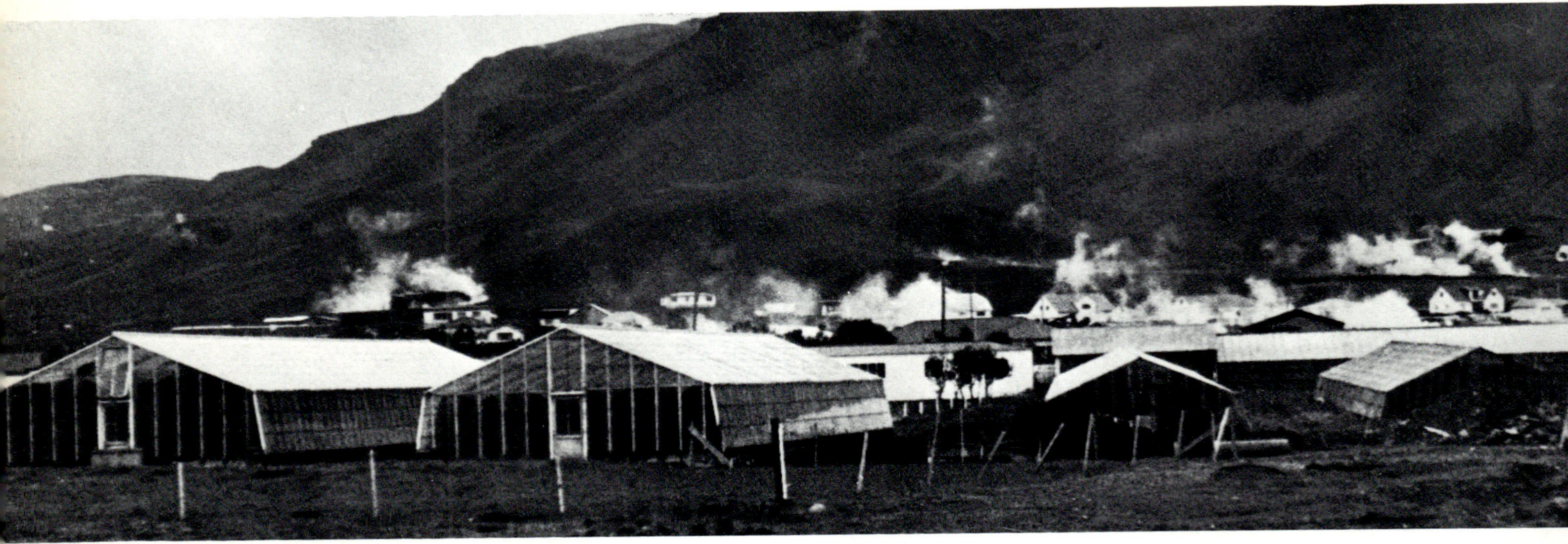

30/31

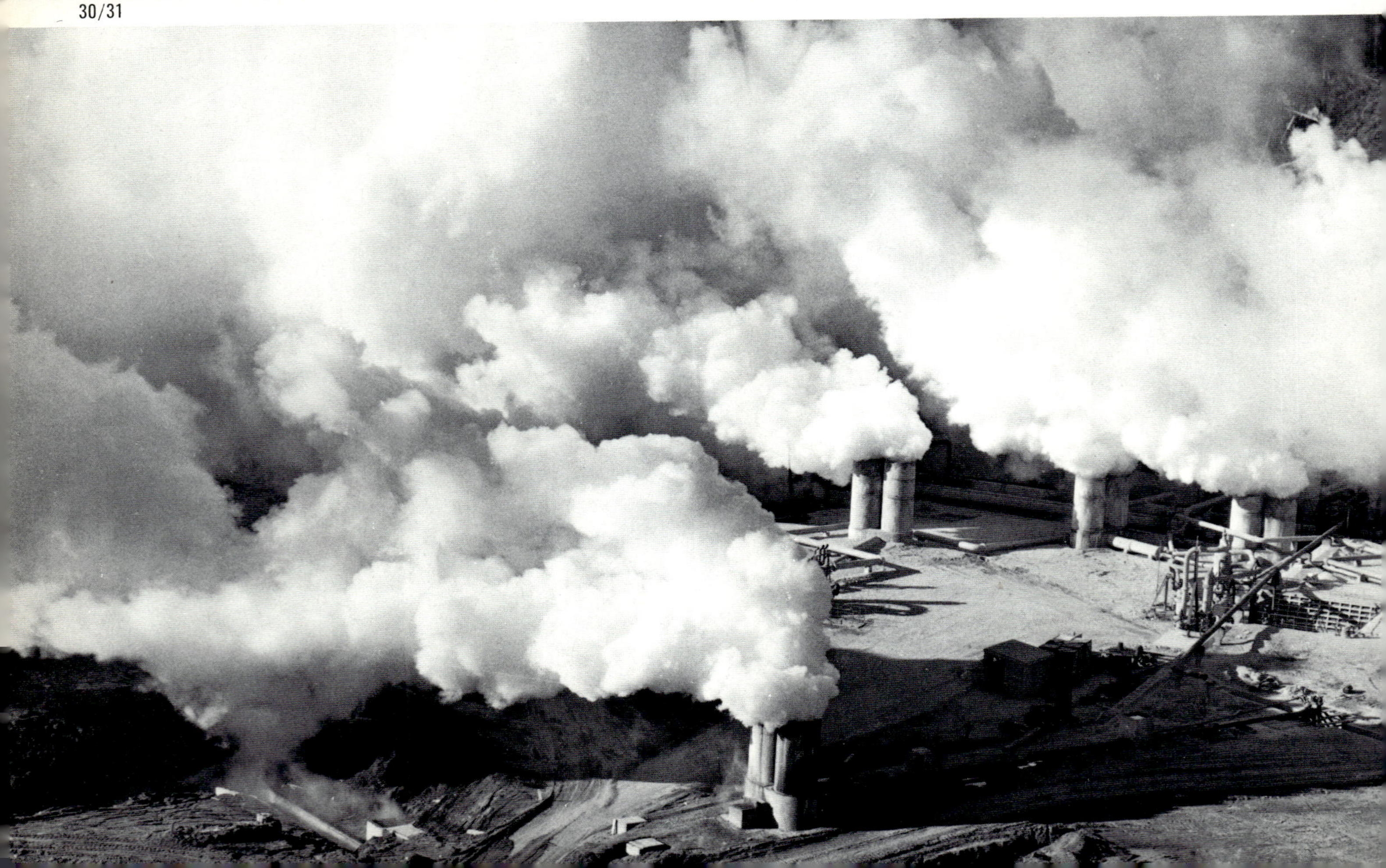

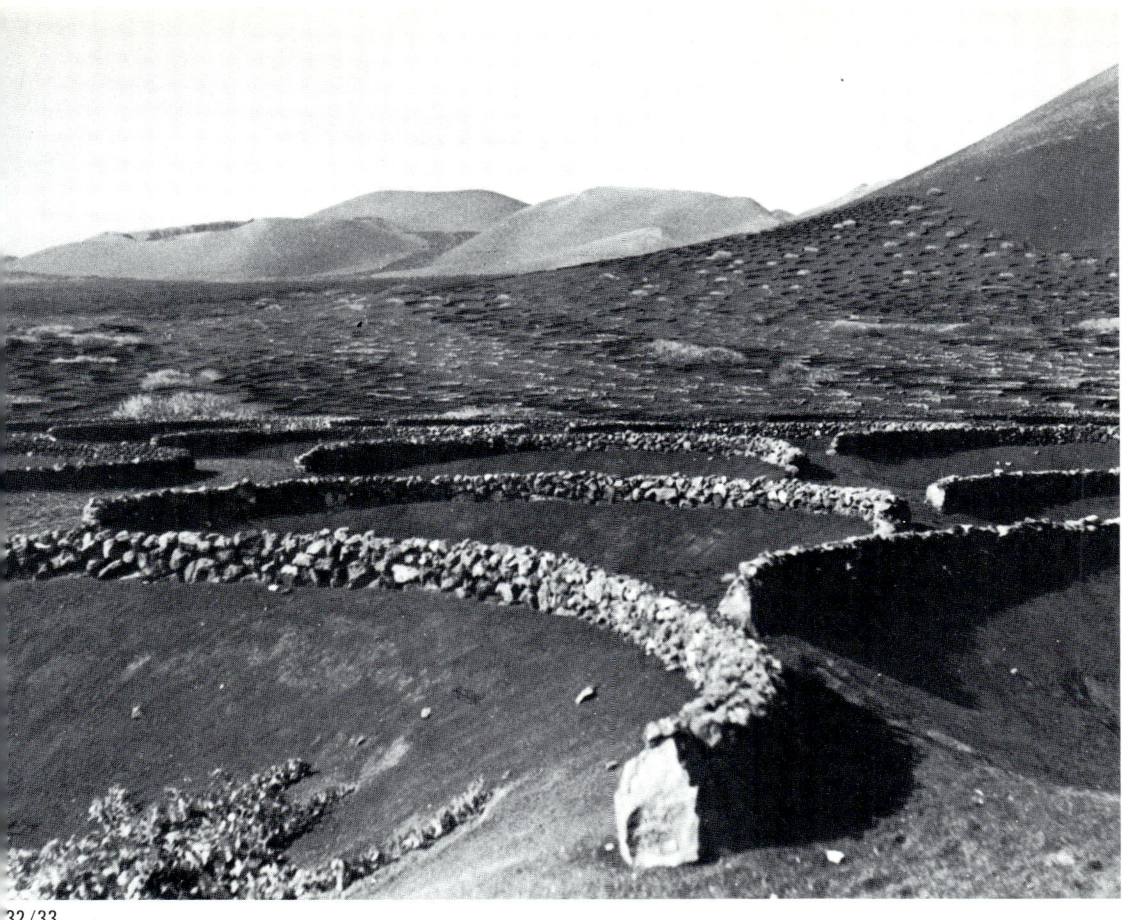

32/33

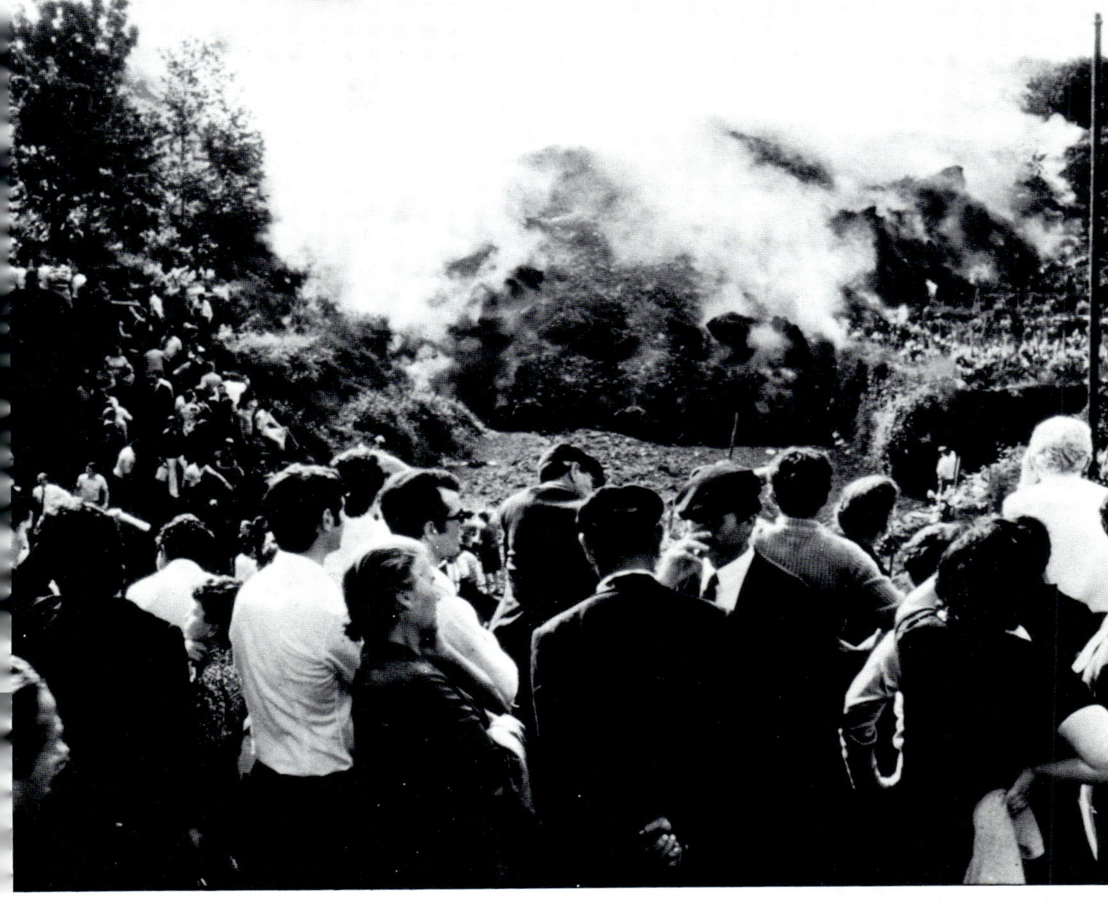

Difficult and hazardous is the life of the agriculturist who lives near a volcano. On the lava fields of Lanzarote in the Canaries (32) a thin, poor-quality soil supports vines; the growers spread fragments of porous, cindery lava round the roots to catch and condense the atmospheric moisture. Often, as here, the vines are planted in shallow pits, screened from the perpetual trade winds by walls of basalt lava blocks. On the slopes of Etna, too, vineyards and orchards are planted, but every so often an eruption destroys them. Villagers watch helplessly (33) as lava from the eruption of 1971 moves relentlessly down through their fields and vineyards. Blocky, viscous lava like this, still glowing red behind the solidifying front, would be moving at less than 20 yards an hour, giving time to stand and watch, or to save movable goods.

Volcanologists at work. The need to investigate at the actual point of eruption, in the search for better understanding of these forces, better warning techniques, perhaps even, in the end, some degree of control, takes precedence over physical danger. A scientist wearing protective clothing, silvered to reflect the heat, analyses the gases given off by Etna's lava (34). Another tests the volcano's temperature (35) at the edge of the crater; temperature variations are an important clue to imminent activity.

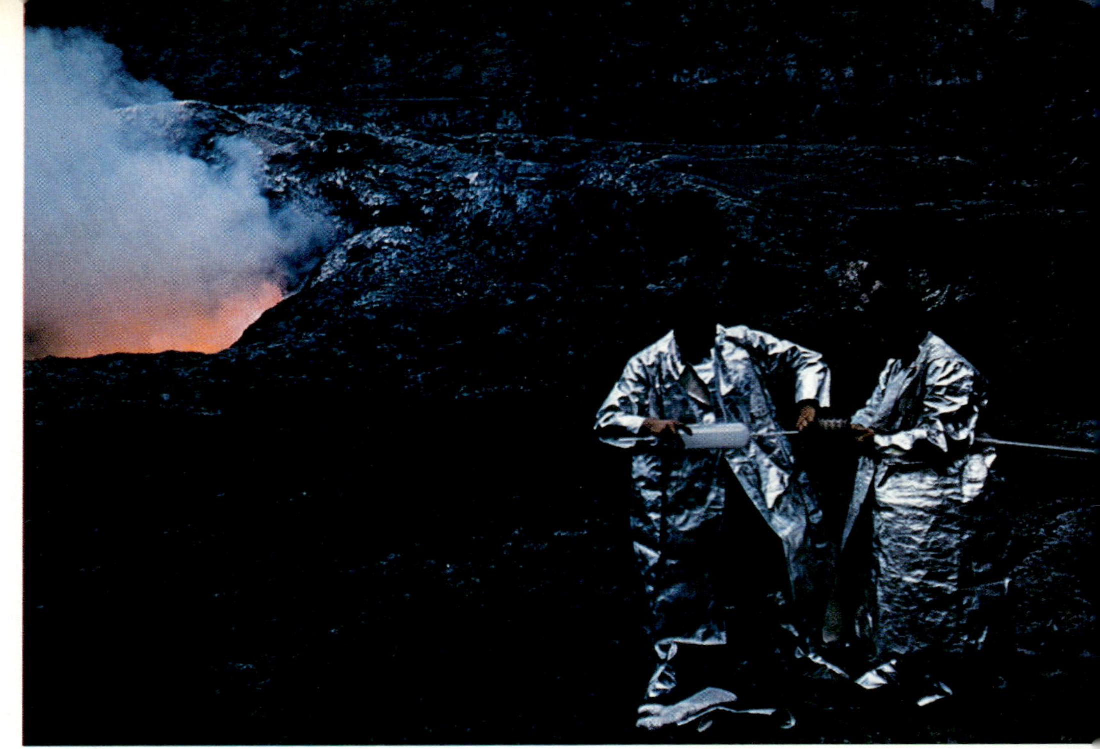

34

35

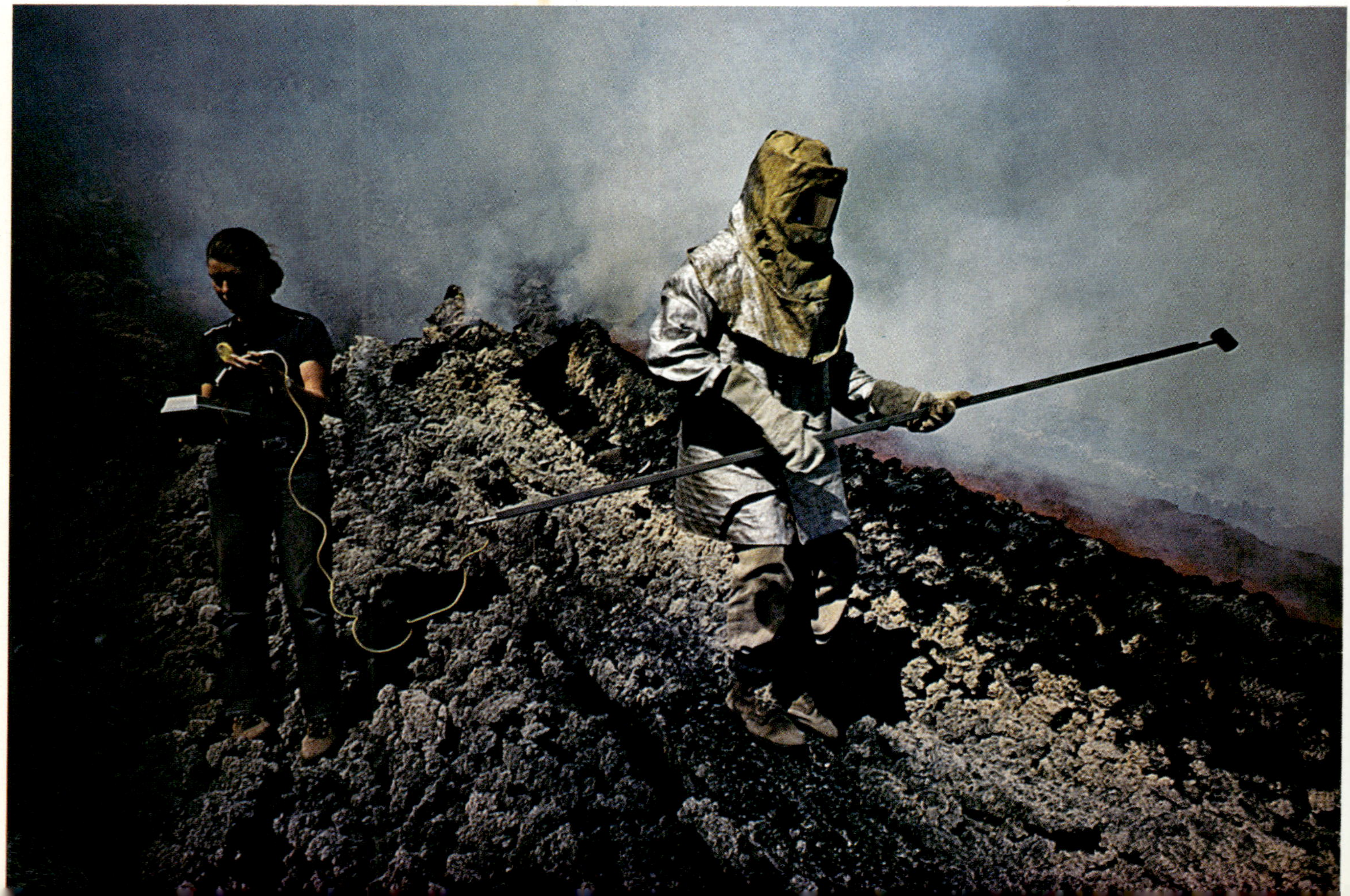

9

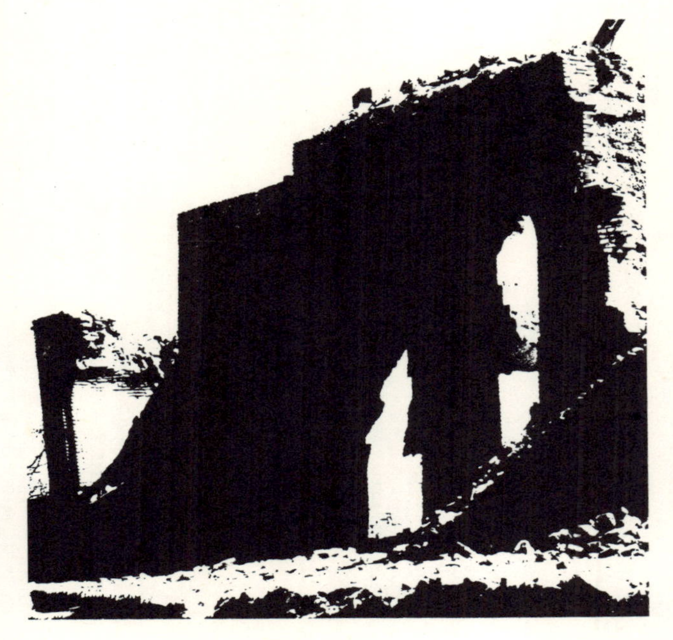

Earthquakes and drifting continents

N. N. Ambraseys

Since the beginning of the eighteenth century earthquakes have caused a death-toll throughout the world of about three million. More reliable statistics relating to fatalities during the present century show that more than 850,000 people have been killed and that the immediate loss of property has amounted to more than $30,000 million. The damage estimated for the State of California alone over 100 years is $6.75 billion; for a single San Francisco earthquake similar to that of 1906 the damage is estimated today at $1.25 billion. With the spread of urban settlements and the investment in large projects in hitherto sparsely populated parts of the world the toll taken by earthquakes, and particularly the damage caused, has been steadily increasing. Today more than 550 million of the world's population live in earthquake regions.

Earthquakes are one of the most destructive natural hazards, if not to human life itself, most certainly to the works of man and to his social and economic structures. The total number of people killed annually, about 15,000, is certainly less than the number of persons killed by motor cars every year in the United States alone, or by the anopheline mosquito during the last pre-DDT decade. Snakebites alone kill annually more than half of the average number of people killed by earthquakes, while preventable diseases such as tetanus, to say nothing of drugs, kill more per year than earthquakes. Yet, although an earthquake may be no more horrifying than road accidents, the impact of its destructiveness is more traumatic because it involves wholesale rather than piecemeal catastrophe, just as a massacre appears more horrifying than a series of murders. Indeed, the fact that road accidents can be avoided makes the number of its victims infuriating, rather than terrible.

The fear of the gods and the beginning of wisdom

All the early writers on this subject were undoubtedly deeply impressed with the nature of the tremendous forces at work in the production of earthquakes. Yet, of those we know, few indulged in speculations concerning their origin. The ancient Greeks, like many others, recognized divine displeasure, particularly of Poseidon, as the cause of earthquakes and of the associated geological and volcanic interference. However, this ceased to give universal satisfaction even as early as the time of Thales and Anaximenes and in the sixth and fifth centuries BC philosophers such as Anaxagoras, Democritus and others suggested different physical explanations for their occurrence. Notwithstanding a dissident minority, however, the old doctrine still continued to be generally accepted. Diodorus, in describing the terrible earthquake of 373 BC by which Helice and Bura in Achaea were destroyed, noticed those philosophers who substituted physical causes and laws in place of the divine agency, but rejected their view and ranked himself with the religious public who traced earthquakes to the wrath of Poseidon. Herodotus in the fifth century BC admitted Poseidon's responsibility for earthquakes, but only incidentally; what chiefly strikes him is not the phenomenon of the earthquake as an individual event, but the event as part of a system of habitual occurrences. It was, however, in the fourth century BC, with Aristotle, that the generic cause of earthquakes began to lose its divine origin and an attempt was made to establish the characteristic causes and effects of the phenomenon. Aristotle felt that earthquakes, as other natural phenomena, were the result of the 'air element', or 'vapours' produced by exhalation. The main interest in Aristotle's work on earthquakes lies not so much in any particular conclusion that he reached about the generic cause of the phenomenon, as in the fact that, looking back, we can see that this was the start of a slow development in the separation of natural science from the formerly all-embracing natural philosophy. Aristotle noticed correctly that earthquakes are relatively local phenomena and most severe in soft ground, sometimes being associated with hot springs and seismic sea-waves (tsunami). He pointed out that earthquakes are usually followed by aftershocks and subterranean noises and he described possible connections between earthquakes and eclipses.

After the time of Aristotle there are very few writers among the Greeks and the Romans who contributed anything worthy of notice, the exception being Strabo. Strabo wrote early in the first century BC, and his ideas contain the germ of almost everything that has been advanced in modern times. Although he accepted Aristotle's view on the origin of earthquakes, he noticed that earthquakes are responsible for causing significant changes in the ground level, not only sub-aerial but also submarine, as a result of which the earth is rent, affecting the flow of rivers and creating new lakes. Referring to the earthquake of the fourth century BC in Iran which devastated Rhagae, or Shahr-Ray, now a suburb of Teheran, he said that 'the earth was so grievously rent that numerous cities and villages were destroyed, and rivers underwent changes of various kinds.' Strabo attributed seismic sea-waves to sudden changes in the level of the submarine floor caused by earthquakes which in other places such as in the region of the Dead Sea are also associated with volcanic eruptions. In his writings he gave accounts of many important earthquakes that occurred during and before his time in

Fig. 1 Bas-relief found in Pompeii showing the temple of Jupiter in the forum falling in the earthquake of AD 63. This was above a domestic votive altar dedicated to the household gods in memory of this earthquake.

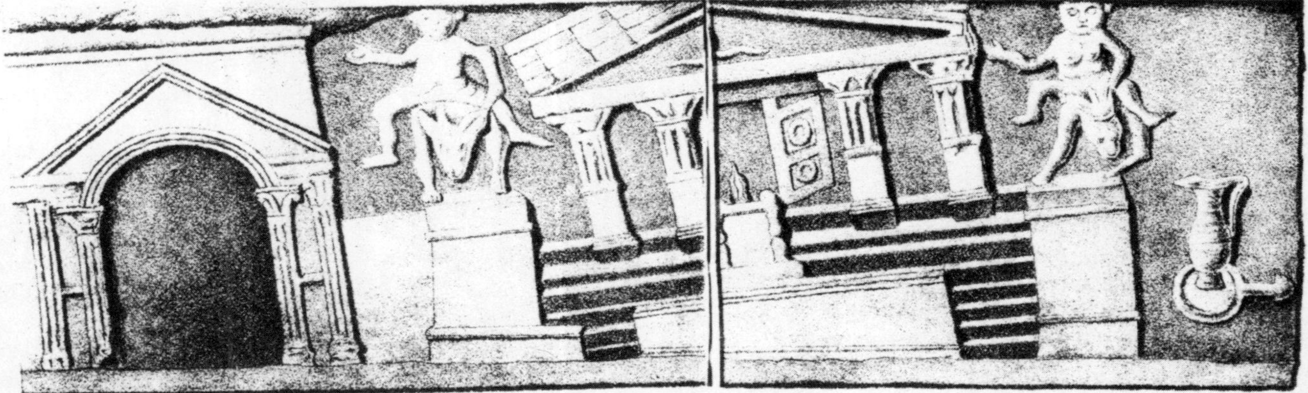

many parts of the then known world as far as the upper reaches of the Indus river, presumably at Taxila, and drew rational conclusions about the seismicity of the world. According to the nineteenth-century geologist Sir Charles Lyell, Strabo's views on earthquakes express ideas 'the profoundness of which modern geologists are only beginning to appreciate'. About a century after Strabo, the Chinese astronomer Tchang Heng designed and built an instrument for judging the direction of earthquake motions; it is said that the instrument was capable of detecting events at distances of 600 kilometres.

Up to the middle of the eighteenth century, many pamphlets and books were written on earthquake phenomena, but they contain very little on the origin of earthquakes that is of more than ordinary interest. Their authors drew their illustrations most from Aristotle, Pliny and Seneca, all of them insisting upon the cavernous and perforated interior of the earth and the presence of combustible vapours, and above all on the anger of Heaven. Mustawfi, in the fourteenth century AD, relating the aftermath of the Tabriz earthquake of 4 November 1042 in which 40,000 people were killed, points out that after this earthquake there was a long spell of only minor activity which caused no damage to the city. This, he says, was attributed to the network of underground water conduits, *qanats*, and deep wells beneath Tabriz, which acted as ventilators and escape routes for the powerful vapours and pressures that build up in the earth and cause earthquakes. Leonardo da Vinci, in his description of the seismic seawave associated with the earthquake of 1481 near Antalya off the southern coast of Turkey, implies a cavernous interior of the earth, a view which reflects the complete lack of development of the ideas proposed by Aristotle, which by the end of the seventeenth century had solidified into dogma.

From antiquity to the present day men have felt much the same about an earthquake. For the ordinary people the special horror of the event was, and to some extent still is, the awful belief that an earthquake was a deliberate sign from a wrathful God. Even today, in many parts of the world no attempt at a scientific explanation has as yet made an earthquake a generally understandable happening, like war or famine. Up to the middle of the eighteenth century, both occidental and oriental writings suggesting that earthquakes are natural happenings are few in number. To advocate this view openly was a bold act likely to shock most devout people and anger their religious instructors.

Science takes a hand

Two events, or series of events, led to the birth of seismology in the middle of the eighteenth century, when those who studied earthquakes began to draw their illustrations from contemporary records and no longer from the writings of Aristotle, Seneca or Pliny. The first event was the remarkable series of earthquakes in England during the year 1750, the second the destructive earthquake of Lisbon in 1755. The birth of seismology had a slow and gradual labour, the clergy quarrelling with philosophers, not scientists. The scientists in their own right already had a considerable public in the learned world accustomed to their views. In 1738 Ephraim Chambers's *Cyclopaedia* had defined the word 'earthquake' as 'in natural history a vehement shake – of the earth; from natural causes'. John Michell (*c.* 1724–93), at one time Woodwardian professor of geology at Cambridge, must in these terms be considered the first true seismologist. He differed from his predecessors in freeing himself entirely from the shackles of the old classical writers and his work relied only on the

Fig. 2 Tchang Heng's seismoscope, the first successful attempt to detect a distant earthquake, made in AD 132 during the post-Han dynasty. Nothing showing the internal arrangement has come down to us but, judging from a description of its mechanism, it may have consisted of an inverted pendulum; eight dragon-heads were placed at equal distances around its upper circumference, each with a ball in its mouth. Around the lower circumference were eight frogs, each directly under a dragon's head, and each with its open mouth so placed that it would receive the ball if it should be dropped from the dragon's mouth. According to the description, this instrument indicated not only the occurrence of an earthquake, but also the direction of the shock.

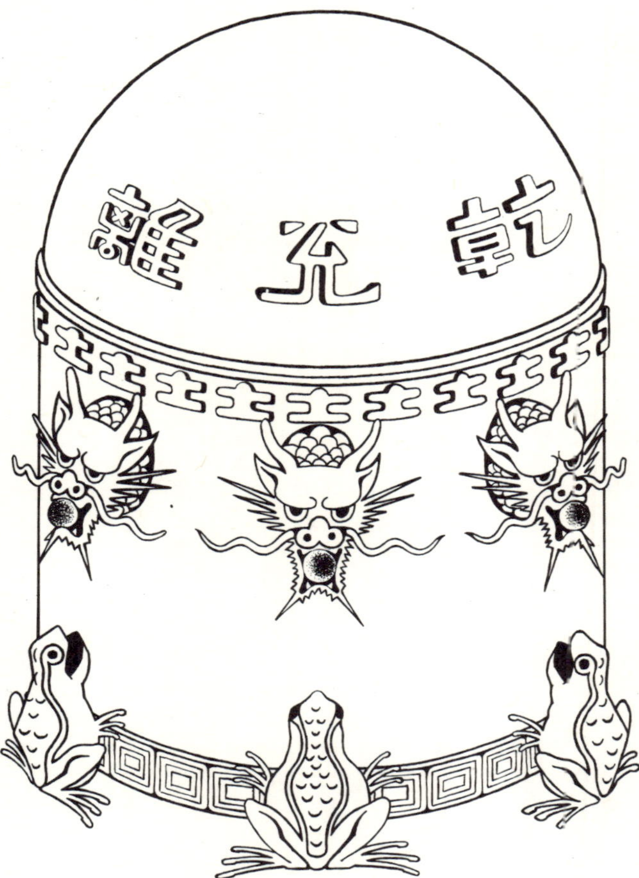

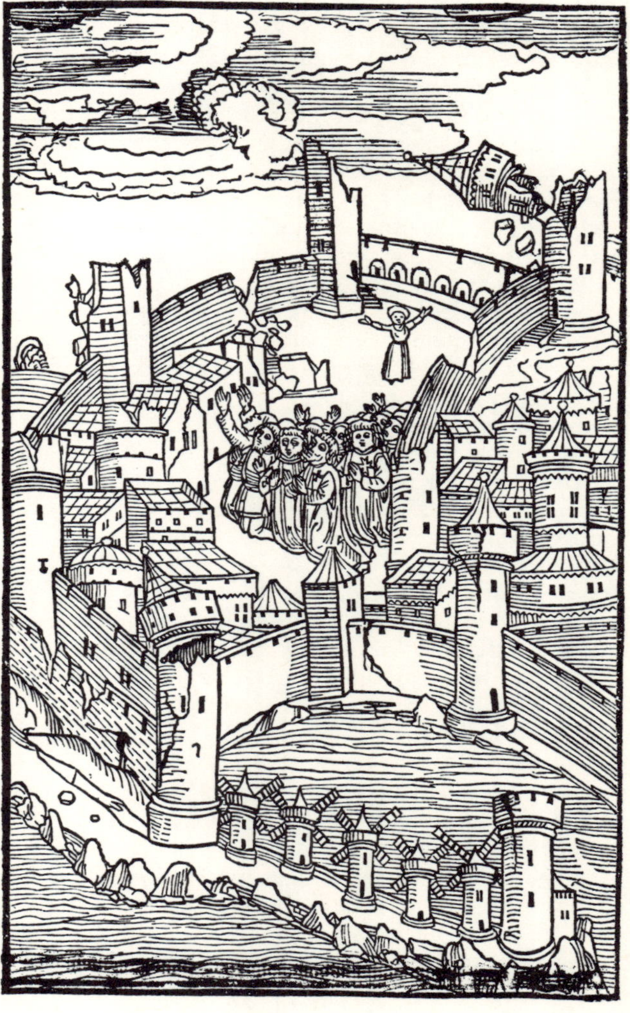

Fig. 3 A late fifteenth-century print showing the effects on the city of Rhodes of the earthquakes of 1481. It is very probable that this is the earthquake described by Leonardo.

evidence of modern observers. He distinguished the principal difference between those phenomena which are essential to, and others which have no connection with, the origin of earthquakes. Thus, he distinguished between the occurrence of aftershocks and the recurrence of large earthquakes in seismically active regions. He also noticed that the ground motion during earthquakes is partly propagated by waves which travel with varying velocities, and he devised two methods for determining the position of the epicentre, that is the point from which the shock emanated. Both were afterwards overlooked, and both have been re-invented. Michell's 'random guess' as to the depth from which the earthquake originated, the focal depth, like Newton's guess with regard to the density of the earth, is one of those intuitions which only occur to the ablest minds.

His work was followed by many pioneering ideas, and advance, though slow, was considerable. Sir William Hamilton (1730–1803), British envoy at the court of Naples in 1764, noticed how the amount of damage caused by the Calabrian earthquake of 1783 depended on the nature of the site, how buildings situated on rock suffered much less than those founded on alluvium in the plains. David Milne (1805–90) invented the word 'seismometer', our oldest seismological term, and also determined the position of an earthquake epicentre from two or more lines of direction. Robert Mallet (1810–81) an engineer and bridge builder in Ireland, was one of the first to experiment with the propagation velocity of earth-waves caused by the detonation of gunpowder and by earthquakes. Michele Stefano de Rossi (1834–98) and Giuseppe Mercalli (1850–(1914) devised the first rational scale of earthquake intensity. Montessus de Ballore (1851–1923), a graduate of the Ecole Polytechnique, produced one of the most complete earthquake catalogues, containing 171,434 events. The results that he obtained from the study of these data contributed significantly to the understanding of global seismicity. John Milne (1817–90), a mining engineer from the Royal School of Mines and the founder of the Seismological Society of Japan, was a pioneer not only in the development and construction of instruments capable of recording distant earthquakes, but also in organizing a network of seismic stations throughout the world.

Thus, by the turn of the century, seismology was already an established branch of science and slowly growing. The earthquakes of San Francisco of 1906, Messina of 1908, Tokyo of 1923, like the earthquakes of London and Lisbon of the mid-1700s, stimulated a general interest in earthquakes and their effects, and particularly in the possibility of minimizing the hazards of these natural phenomena.

One of the most important advances during that period and in recent years has been the development of instruments of increasing sophistication, capable of recording all types of earth movements, and of magnifying these movements millions of times. One reason for this rapid development in instruments and research was the need to provide a data base for studying how to discriminate between nuclear tests and natural earthquakes in order to make feasible a nuclear test ban treaty. Oil exploration, and the search for mineral resources, assisted by modern technological advances in instrumentation, added impetus. Never before had seismology received so much support for research and development; this allowed a minute study of the waves set up by earthquakes and nuclear explosions which travel through the whole interior of the Earth, providing clues not only to the region they traverse but also to the way in which they were generated at their source. It is not surprising, therefore, that in the mid-1960s there was an almost explosive growth of research in seismology related to earth sciences and to earthquake engineering.

The Earth's drifting crust

Another important recent advance in understanding the cause of earthquakes has been the recognition, not so much of an orderly global distribution of earthquake activity, which was already known and commonly accepted since Robert Mallet's time, 100 years ago, but of its relation with an equally orderly system of tectonics. Alfred Wegener in 1912 had argued that if the Earth's crust could flow vertically in response to vertical forces, it could also flow laterally. He envisaged the continents as moving like shallow rafts through a sea of basalt and upper mantle (outer core) material. This idea of continental drift was inspired by observation of the remarkable fit of the present profiles of the east coast of South America and west coast of Africa. It met with opposition and for many decades numbers of earth scientists were – and some of them still are – reluctant to accept Wegener's hypothesis.

Interest in continental drift was revived forty years later when paleomagnetic data, that is records of the changes of the earth's magnetic field embodied in ancient rocks, indicated that they had subsequently shifted, allowing the calculation that drift between North America and Europe had occurred during the last 300 million years. In recent years evidence for continental drift has become stronger and stronger; it has been found, for instance, that the contact between rocks formed about two billion years ago and about 500 million years ago, on both the African and South American coastlines, is offset by just the amount required by the geographical fit. The similarity of older fossils on the two continents and their age, gave an approximate date for the separation of Africa from South America. Also the evidence that new oceanic crust was being generated at the mid-oceanic rises made the idea of continental drift acceptable to more scientists; indeed many now believe that the idea has attained the status of a theory. The implications of this for seismology and geology are far greater than the question of whether the continents were once a single mass, for it marks the emergence of the concept that the Earth has a mobile crust.

Today, it is commonly accepted by the majority of earth scientists that the Earth's surface consists of relatively thin blocks or plates, some of enormous size, which as a result of their relative movement and interaction spread apart at the rifts, slide past one another at large wrench faults, collide head-on to form mountain ranges or are underthrust at island arcs. These lithospheric plates, which constitute part or the whole of individual continents and oceans, are the most rigid part of the Earth, about 100 kilometres thick. They are driven by convection

Fig. 4 Fit of South America and Africa with the mid-Atlantic ridge, as defined by earthquake epicentres, in between.

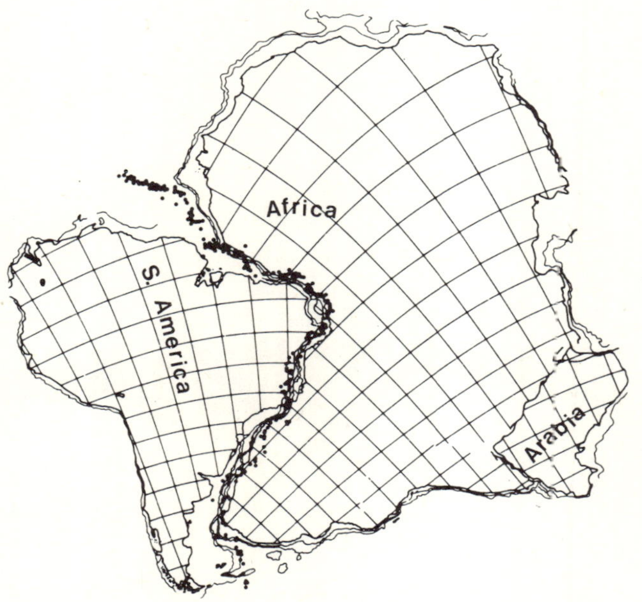

Fig. 5 The mechanism of the oceanic rift.

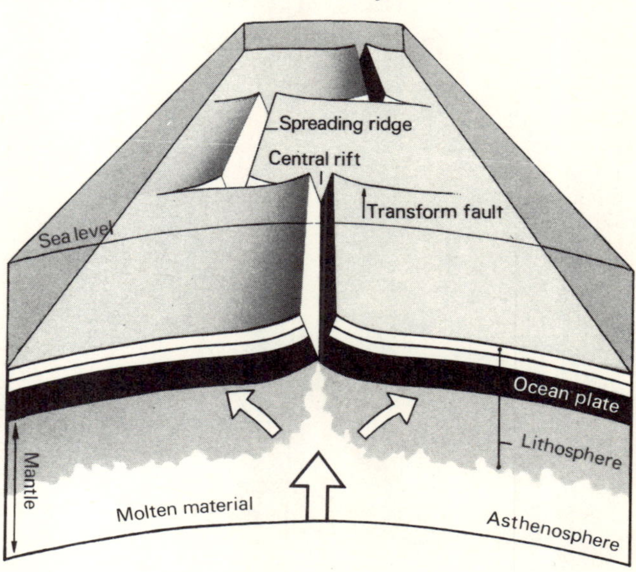

currents in the underlying asthenosphere, a layer several hundred kilometres thick which has no effective strength, but the actual driving mechanism of the plates is still purely conjectural.

Continental rifts are due to the extension or spreading of the crust; they are many tens or hundreds of kilometres long, 10 to 50 kilometres wide with a central strip of crust downthrown by one to five kilometres. Examples of such rifts are those of Baikal in the Soviet Union, the Rhine Graben, the Gregory Rift in Africa, the Ethiopian Rift, and the Dead Sea. They have undergone a gradual extension of a few kilometres during the last 10 to 30 million years, being occupied today by lakes and rivers, and they may be considered to be incipient plate boundaries.

Oceanic rifts, such as the Mid-Atlantic and other oceanic ridges, have been created on the margins of thin oceanic plates, slowly driven apart by the asthenosphere which circulates in underlying convection cells. This process allows new, hot material to be extruded to the surface and fill the gap between diverging plates, thus creating new oceanic crust, or rather causing the diverging plates to grow as they move away from each other, healing the gap.

The mode of plate interaction opposite to extrusion, that is of oceanic plates moving against each other, known as subduction, is responsible for the creation of deep-sea trenches such as those bordering the Pacific; the Tonga–Kermadec trench, the Mindanao and Marianas, and those of Japan, of the Kuriles and of the Alaska–Aleutian arc. These features are caused by the convergence of lithospheric plates, which have carried the Earth's surface down to oceanic deeps of more than 10 kilometres. Subduction may be brought about by two equally thin converging plates, one of which on collision is forced to dip under the other and in so doing sinks into the underlying hot asthenosphere where at great depths it is ultimately consumed. Thus, extrusion and subduction are processes that slowly cycle material between a cold lithosphere and a hot asthenosphere, in turn generating and consuming crustal material.

With converging continental plates, however, the model of plate interaction is different. Continental plates are lighter than oceanic ones and on slow collision they cannot easily sink through the heavier upper asthenosphere. Instead, their slow convergence produces folding and the building of mountains with deep roots.

The interaction between oceanic and continental plates is also responsible for building up mountains. In this case the oceanic plate dips under the continental one, and the latter begins to grow at the expense of the former.

Mountain ranges such as the Himalayas, rising to an average height of 5 kilometres, were built up in stages during the past 200 million years and are still growing. There old ocean-floor sediments, many kilometres thick, have been squeezed and uplifted as the Indian subcontinent has drifted northward to become a relatively recent

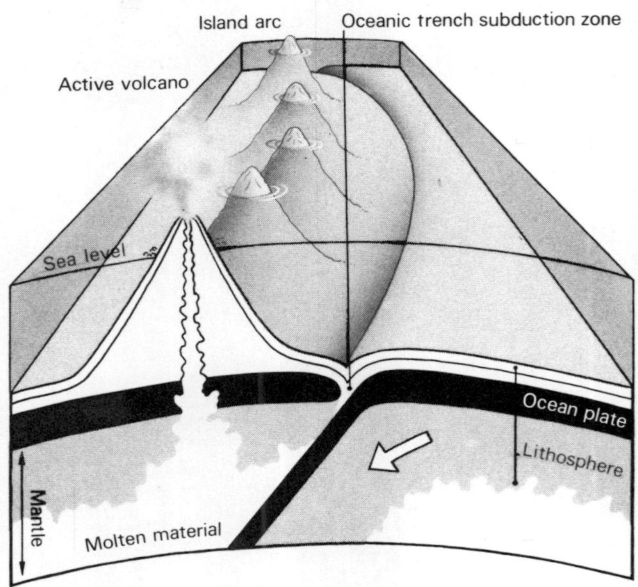

Fig. 6 The opposite of the oceanic rift: subduction.

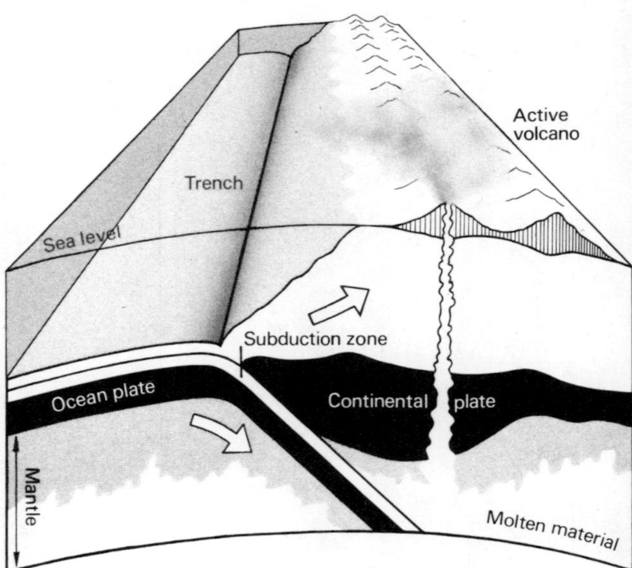

Fig. 7 Interaction of continental and oceanic plates.

feature of Asian geology. The Zagros mountains in Iran, rising to heights of 3 kilometres, have been created by the contraction of the crust between the Arabian and Persian plates. Shearing and thrusting along 1,000 kilometres of contact between these two plates has resulted in contraction of the Earth's crust by 1,000 kilometres, and the building of a major mountain range.

Where two plates are moving at a tangent to each other, neither creating nor consuming lithospheric material, we have a transform fault. This type of dislocation in the Earth's crust is nearly vertical, and along it the separated segments have slid in a horizontal or nearly horizontal manner. The San Andreas fault in California, the Anatolian fault in Turkey, and other wrench faults in New Zealand, the Philippines and South America are typical examples of this type of discontinuity. They may extend for over 1,000 kilometres, separating major portions of the crust that move slowly in relation to each other at a rate which may be as much as 3 centimetres per year.

The surface of the Earth is therefore covered with a relatively small number of plates, all slowly jostling one another in a complex way, in the process being compressed, pulled apart or sheared, and by so doing causing earthquakes. Hence, the edges or boundaries of the plates as well as incipient plate boundaries are delineated by the occurrence of earthquakes. Consequently, a map of earthquake epicentres provides a map of the outlines of the plates and of their present-day activity. The recognition of this relationship between zones of earthquake activity and the margins of converging or diverging continental and

Fig. 8 Transform fault. When the strain is released, resulting in an earthquake, the two segments move past each other horizontally, perhaps with some degree of vertical displacement as well.

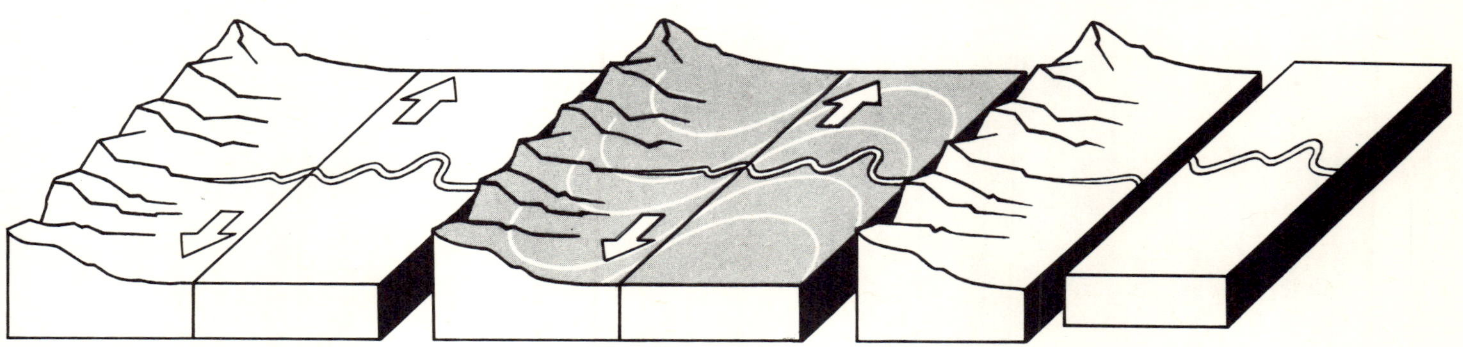

oceanic plates has itself contributed to the concept of the new global tectonics. Combined with information from geomagnetism and other branches of science, the evidence provided by seismology gives us a basis for learning more about the processes that may lead to the generation of an earthquake.

Measuring earthquakes

The majority of hypotheses for the generic cause of earthquakes are based on the sudden release of strain energy caused by a fracture of the rocks in the Earth's crust or by a slip along existing faults. There are a number of different mechanisms which either together or separately can produce such movements. Fracture may be brought about either by increasing stresses in the lithosphere or by a decrease in strength of the crustal material, or by a combination of the two. Thus, material under stress becomes increasingly weak, unstable and prone to fail. At the moment of fracture part of the stored strain energy will suddenly be released and will radiate in the form of elastic waves, causing the lithosphere to vibrate at great distances from the site of the fracture. It is precisely these waves that are responsible for the damage caused by earthquakes.

Stress changes that may lead to fracture of rock masses in the upper crust can be brought about naturally by such means as the rapid accumulation of thick deposits in river deltas, or through human intervention by the impounding of reservoirs, deep tunnelling and mining works. Stress changes in the crust can also be caused by tectonic forces such as those produced by the impeded motion of plates or by rock expansion caused by alteration. The weakening of rock masses by constant stress leading to fracture is also possible through the increase of pore water pressure in the rocks, or through weathering and chemical changes at greater depths and temperatures.

It is obvious, therefore, that the amount of strain energy that can be accumulated before an earthquake depends on the maximum stress that can be supported by the Earth's crust and the volume of rock involved. Fracture of the crust, or slip on an existing fault, will release an amount of strain energy which will be some fraction of the total stored in the mass at breaking point. It is this fraction of the total energy stored in the rocks that determines the size of an earthquake, commonly measured on a Magnitude scale. If it be assumed for the sake of simplicity that the strain energy per unit volume of the mass from which the major part of the earthquake energy is released is approximately constant, then the Magnitude or size of an earthquake reflects the volume of crustal material that participates in the fracture.

The most common measure of the size of an earthquake is its Magnitude, which, as defined by Charles Richter, may be computed from the amplitude of the surface waves produced by the earthquake at a seismic station. Magnitude is a measure of the amount of energy released by the shock in the form of earthquake waves. Other things being equal, earthquakes of small magnitude do not affect so large an area on the Earth's surface as do earthquakes of

Fig. 9 Worldwide distribution of earthquake locations, 1961 to 1967. Note how the pattern corresponds to the map of plate boundaries on pages 250–1.

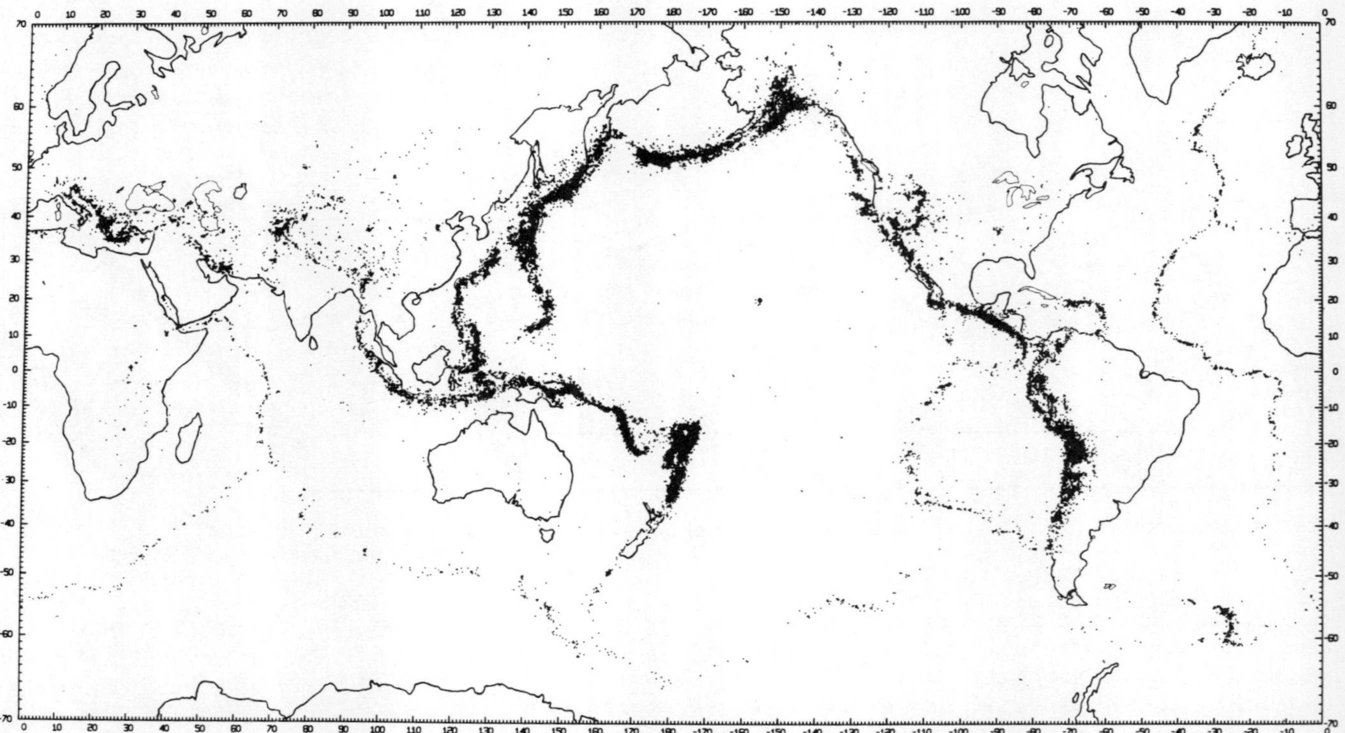

larger magnitude, nor do they cause the ground to shake for as long a time. The duration of shaking and the size of the area affected are therefore a measure of the Magnitude of an earthquake. For instance the large earthquake in Mongolia of 1905 was felt within a radius of nearly 2,000 kilometres; the Alaska earthquake of 1964 was felt almost 800 kilometres away from the epicentre and the shaking lasted more than one minute. In contrast, the much smaller but equally destructive earthquake of 1963 in Skopje was not felt more than 200 kilometres from the epicentre and lasted just under 5 seconds.

During the sixty years of instrumental record, no earthquake Magnitude has been larger than 8.9. And since earthquake magnitudes are limited by the competency of the region involved to store strain energy, it is very likely that each earthquake region would have a characteristic maximum Magnitude. Both theoretical and observational considerations point to a maximum possible earthquake Magnitude not in excess of 9.

Nuclear blasts release amounts of energy comparable to those of medium earthquakes. Thus, a Hiroshima-type bomb of 20 kilotons, usually called a nominal bomb, if detonated underground in solid rock at a depth of a few kilometres, will produce an earthquake equivalent to a magnitude of 5.2, or slightly smaller than the Tashkent earthquake of 1966. A bomb of 50 times greater yield, one megaton, releases energy equivalent to an earthquake of about magnitude 6. However, only a small fraction of this energy is converted into seismic waves, much depending, among other factors, on the confinement of the explosion, that is on the depth and strength of the rocks in which it is detonated. It takes a nuclear explosion of a yield equivalent to about 10 megatons, that is 500 Hiroshima-type bombs, deeply buried in solid rock to produce seismic energy equivalent to that of an earthquake of magnitude 7. During the period 1961 to 1970, more than 300 underground nuclear explosions were carried out in the Nevada testing site alone. These tests were performed within an area of 4,500 square kilometres, at depths varying from a few hundred metres to 2.5 kilometres, and they released a total amount of energy corresponding to about 18 megatons. This is a colossal amount of energy, equal to that which nature can produce through large earthquakes. It makes one wonder how far human intervention in natural processes on such an unprecedented scale can go before we begin to affect the environment irreversibly.

Chemical explosions also release energy comparable to that of small earthquakes. An explosion in the North Sea of 10 tons of TNT, carried out at a depth of 200 metres on 20 July 1971, registered a magnitude of 4.3; a strip mine explosion in British Columbia on 5 April 1972 showed a magnitude of 4.7.

Rock bursts too are likely to release strain energy that compares with that of medium-size earthquakes. Rock bursts are caused by a sudden and often violent failure of rock masses in deep quarries, tunnels and mines. They involve the fracture and collapse of tens of thousands of cubic metres of highly strained rocks at depths from a few hundred metres to two kilometres. Rock bursts in the Ruhr and Essen districts in Germany, at Thionville in France, in Pennsylvania, Virginia, Missouri and Arizona in the United States, in India, Czechoslovakia, Canada and South Africa, have released seismic energy corresponding to magnitudes between 4 and 5. In Wales, spurious earthquakes are usually due to rock bursts; and the same applies for numerous events in Canada and South Africa. Since the locations of nuclear or chemical explosions and rock bursts are known, these events have afforded opportunities for special seismological investigations and valuable data for the location of earthquakes have been obtained in this manner. In other words, these events have been used to 'calibrate' instruments and techniques for the location of real earthquakes.

The most destructive earthquakes are usually shallow, involving the fracture of rock masses to depths of a few kilometres or a few tens of kilometres. At the moment of fracture, the distorted rocks break away towards equilibrium, and by doing so they create a fracture zone along which displacement occurs of the two sides relative to one another. This displacement may be a few centimetres or many tens of metres. Strain energy is drawn from a wide zone on both sides of the actual fracture, part of which is converted into seismic waves and part into heat, which at sufficient depth may be high enough to melt the rocks. The velocity with which the two sides of the fracture break away is very high and in hard rocks it may reach values of one or two metres per second. This fracture, or faulting, may extend along the surface for a few kilometres or a few hundred kilometres, predominantly in zones along plate boundaries but also within plates. Faulting generally occurs along the existing faults in the Earth's crust, which are the flaws associated with earlier earthquakes and therefore the most likely site for a large strain energy release. Of course, there are many instances where earthquakes are not known to be associated with faulting, either because fracture did not extend to the surface or because the earthquake area was not surveyed adequately.

The Magnitude of an earthquake is the product of the length of rupture, the depth of faulting, the rigidity of the rocks and the displacement of the two sides of the fault relative to one another. Thus, other things being equal, a Magnitude 5 earthquake occurring at 10 kilometres' depth is likely to be associated with the rupture of a volume of material of 85 km^3, or with a rupture zone on the Earth's surface, say, 4 kilometres long and 2 kilometres wide. A Magnitude 7 earthquake will be associated with a zone 60 kilometres long and 12 kilometres wide, while a Magnitude 8 earthquake may cause a rupture in excess of 300 kilometres in length.

An earthquake may be described by several different parameters: by the latitude and longitude of its epicentre (the vertical projection of its focus on the Earth's surface); by the depth of the focus below the epicentre; by its magnitude, which is a measure of the energy released in seismic waves; by its epicentral intensity, which is a measure of the maximum destructiveness of the shock; by its radius of perceptibility, in other words the area over which the shock was felt; and by the mechanism which produced the event. The geographical co-ordinates, the magnitude and the focal depth can be worked out from information supplied by seismographs; thus the Turkish earthquake of September 1975, which cost over 1,900 lives, was of magnitude 6.7, the epicentre was at 38.6°N, 41.0°E, and the focus was at a depth of 20 km. On the other hand the epicentral intensity, the perceptibility radius, the distribution of the intensity (i.e. the isoseismal lines) and the amount of surface faulting all need investigation in the field.

Before the advent of modern seismological instruments, as early as the middle of the eighteenth century, investigators of earthquakes realized the usefulness of some kind of scale for the measurement of the effects of an earthquake at a particular locality, i.e. the need for a measure of the earthquake's destructiveness. Since then, more than forty different scales have been devised, either to express the relative Intensity of different earthquakes or to trace the variation of intensity of a single earthquake through its disturbed area. Like other semi-empirical measures, Intensity, when assessed at a large number of points, may show regular distribution patterns which can help seismologists to assess the depth from which earthquakes originate, the rate at which seismic energy is absorbed with distance from the focus and other seismic parameters. Intensity is a useful means of conveying in a single rating of the scale a measure of the effect of ground motion on man-made structures and on the ground itself. The assessment of Intensity depends on surface conditions rather than on the actual magnitude of the earthquake. For instance, an earthquake will appear catastrophic if it destroys a large number of poorly built houses, but might have had no great effect on better-built constructions; equally, in an uninhabited area the earthquake will not be described as destructive at all. Thus assessment of intensity is related to man-made structures and to subjective field reports, and is therefore only of definite value when the factors involved, determining the intensity, are common to different earthquakes.

It is very common for newspaper reports appearing a few hours after an earthquake to quote an Intensity for the event, before a field team has had an opportunity to assess the effects of the earthquake. More often than not this is the result of reporters confusing the Magnitude of the shock, which can be calculated as soon as it has been recorded in some part of the world, with Intensity.

The results: fire, flood and famine

Early and modern history shows that the lasting effects of major earthquakes during the past twenty-five centuries would not seem to have been very significant for a developed and stable community. Soon after a large earthquake, vested interests have invariably led people to act once again with disregard for the prospect of more such calamities in the future. Yet modern writers have attempted to use earthquakes to account for gaps in the sequence of civilizations and for large movements of peoples, hypotheses for which there is little historical justification. Earthquakes in the past have had little, if any, serious influence on major or global historical developments. They did often account for the premature decline of a local economy or for a crisis in local human affairs. But they have never caused the ruin of a culturally advanced state, far less the end of a civilization. In contrast with wars, epidemics and other long-lasting calamities which have serious and prolonged effects, earthquakes, no matter how large, seem to have had little long-term impact on man. It may be that men react to the inevitable hazard in a special way, distinct from the preventable hazard. Personal, political, religious and economic interests seem to overshadow, and in some cases suppress, the lessons to be learnt from earthquakes. For example, villages ruined by earthquakes are often rebuilt on different sites, whereas cities, where significant economic and political interests are involved, have been rebuilt, enlarged and embellished, invariably on the same site with the same materials and methods of construction, even when it was known that the site was unsuitable and that it had contributed to the magnitude of the disaster. A typical example is the city of Antioch, modern Antakya in Turkey. Since its foundation the city, built partly on an island of the Orontes river and partly on solid ground, had suffered from earthquakes. On 13 December AD 115 it was almost totally destroyed, but because of its strategic importance was rebuilt by the Emperor Trajan, who issued an edict which restricted the height of buildings to 60 feet, but there is good historical evidence to show that this restriction was never enforced. On 14 September 458 the city, particularly the part built on the island, was almost totally destroyed together with the buildings of the new city, and the Emperor Leo rebuilt the city although it was pointed out to those concerned with the reconstruction that building on the island was likely to be unwise. The part of the city on the island, being settled by merchants, was of course rebuilt, only to be totally destroyed on 29 May 526 by another earthquake which caused the death of more than 200,000 people. Once again it was rebuilt on the same site, by the Emperor Justin. This is not unlike the history of many towns and cities in Japan, Alaska, South America and Europe in the present century.

In a developing country of limited resources and with investments concentrated in single major projects, such as large dams, mines, oilfields and refineries, it is the consequences that should be feared rather than the earthquake phenomenon itself. An earthquake, for instance, may cause heavy loss of life, which is, of course, lamentable; but it may also cause the collapse of, say, a large dam, which can have far more disastrous consequences. Apart from the total loss of the structure, which may set back the economy by hundreds of millions of pounds, flooding will add to the death-toll taken by the earthquake. The silting up of downstream valleys and erosion will destroy cultivation for many years to come; communications will be disrupted and industry depending on hydropower will suffer. In an unstable economy these effects may lead to famine and a denudation of the country with far-reaching consequences. Fire following an earthquake can also have disastrous effects on the dense population of a city, and the failure of a nuclear power plant is unthinkable.

Earthquakes have been unnecessarily destructive because man has made them so by investing his wealth with disregard for, or by miscalculating the risk of, the hazards that Nature may have in store for him. This disregard stems from a variety of causes, the most important being the mere lack of awareness and of technical knowledge to alleviate such hazards. Investigations of earthquakes have shown more than once that houses built with local materials and methods of construction, using traditional techniques that were developed through the ages for building against earthquakes, suffer far less damage than modern types of rural or urban houses. This is mainly due to the fact that modern materials and methods of construction are advancing far too fast for the rural and urban small builder to adapt them to local conditions. Moreover, modern materials need greater care and skill in handling. Mixing water and cement with aggregates, unless in the right proportions, will not produce concrete; nor will the mere addition of steel bars produce reinforced concrete. The extreme situation is found among the former nomads in Central Asia, Iran and Africa who are totally incapable of building proper permanent dwellings of any kind, and they represent a considerable percentage of the total population of the earth. Another cause for this disregard for earthquake hazards is the apathy of the populace, which is founded in ignorance. It is not uncommon today for people to accept earthquakes and their effects as Acts of God about which very little can be done. It is usually forgotten that today's Acts of God are often tomorrow's acts of criminal negligence. Obviously the only antidote to this attitude of mind is education.

Relief and restoration

Ideally, to design and build engineering structures against earthquakes in different parts of the world, it is necessary to have a seismic zoning map showing areas of probable maximum earthquake activity carefully delineated. Although we cannot, at the present time, accurately predict the time of occurrence of future earthquakes, it is possible to indicate with some degree of accuracy zones where earthquakes of a certain size or magnitude may occur. The construction of such a map requires basic seismological and geological data: the location of earthquake foci or epicentres, the Magnitude of the earthquakes and the way the region fits into the global system of tectonics, or continental drift.

The location of past earthquakes can be obtained from the records of seismographs throughout the world, and local seismic networks, but it is essential, especially in countries where instrumental data are not available or scarce, that all the available historical information be compiled, analysed and studied. In many cases the location of earthquakes determined prior to 1955 may be in error by as much as 50 to 100 kilometres and these should be recalculated using modern techniques and methods of analysis. Also, if there have been too few earthquakes during the period of observation, data obtained from instrumental records may be insufficient or incomplete for seismic zoning. In such cases one can turn to the tectonics of the region. The reason is that if a certain fault zone is characterized by some peculiarity in its tectonic history and structure, and if earthquakes of a certain nature are registered somewhere in this zone, it may be assumed that earthquakes of the same nature may arise in the future further along its whole length. The argument here is that the few centuries for which earthquake data are available is a negligibly short period when compared with the time-scale involved in the generation of a causative fault zone. Given sufficient data, therefore, the time when earthquakes of different magnitude will recur, and their location with respect to a particular site, may be assessed.

The results from such a zoning study will provide the planner and engineer with useful information for the selection of the most favourable sites for development, or reconstruction, as well as with the appropriate criteria for designing engineering structures to resist future earthquakes with minimum damage and loss of life.

The problem of reducing earthquake damage and of restoring housing after an earthquake may be divided into two stages: planning before an earthquake, and emergency action after the event. Both stages should be studied in advance by a local authority.

After an earthquake it is usually difficult to establish an effective central agency for the direction and control of rehabilitation and reconstruction in the affected area, and much effort and funds are diffused in disparate activities. There is always the difficulty of deciding, on the spur of the moment, how local and foreign aid should best be used and what priority should be given to the innumerable needs of the area. Invariably, this problem is left to the local authorities to resolve or to an *ad hoc* committee without much deliberation. Often a large proportion of the aid is misused. The lack of regional development plans and the absence of any planning policy may result either in regrettable reconstruction errors, or in long delays which can have detrimental repercussions on the efforts to restore the affected area.

To facilitate the establishment and effective operation of such an agency, a country should have an act or ordinance passed by the central legislature, empowering the agency to carry out research, make building regulations, prepare seismic zoning maps, and to apply any or all of them in any desired area. In addition, the agency should be kept informed and up-to-date on town and country planning developments, should participate in the country's economic policy in the event of a disaster, and should direct emergency and permanent housing.

Planning before an earthquake is extremely important in reducing earthquake damage and in minimizing earthquake after-effects. Such planning, no matter how well it may apply in one part of the world, may prove completely insufficient or even detrimental in another. It should be intended as a starting point, it should be studied, and amended as need be by the agency's professional men who are familiar with the local problems involved. There is no way of producing rules-of-thumb which will be generally applicable, or effective, without adapting them to local conditions.

The most important item in the planning stage is education. The relief and restoration of a country crippled by an earthquake is largely based on the efforts of its inhabitants. Superstitions, misinterpretation of well-known natural phenomena and ignorance, often lead to additional disasters. The population must be educated about natural phenomena and their effects. It should be explained that improperly built houses are death-traps, and that the owners should be responsible and aware of what might happen during an earthquake.

The economic effects that an earthquake may have on a developing country or on a poor community can lead to serious and in some cases uncontrollable local disasters, far more important than the immediate effects of an earthquake. The damage and sudden crippling of the unstable economy of such a country could lead to population movements, to a latent emigration, increase in taxation and to unpleasant, though necessary, loans from foreign countries and consequent economic and social concessions. Such hazards have long been associated with crises in local human affairs, the extent of the crisis being inversely proportional to the financial resources available and stability in the affected country or community. These are really historical effects and could lead to a major but local historical change. For instance, as early as the fifth century BC an earthquake in Sparta gave the opportunity to the helots to shake off their yoke. On 17 June AD 978 an earthquake marked the end of Siraf, a declining trading port on the Persian Gulf and one of the centres of trade with China. As a result of the earthquake the harbour of Siraf, near modern Tahiri, sank below the sea and then ships went instead to Ra's Naband, on the eastern point of the cape opposite Siraf. On 21 June 1139, Gandja, the former Elizavetpol, now Kirovabad, was destroyed by an earthquake in which more than 100,000 people perished. This gave the opportunity for the Georgians to sack the ruined city. The earthquakes of 1157 in Syria caused great damage, killing thousands of people. They brought about a temporary peace between Moslems and Crusaders, who were too busy repairing shattered fortresses to think of serious aggressive expeditions for some time to come, but these earthquakes caused little change to the final outcome of the crusade. The earthquake of 1320 completely destroyed Ani, the capital of the Armenian province of Airarat, causing its inhabitants to disperse into various parts of the world, even as far as Poland, Romania and Iran, but the real cause for the desertion of the ruined city was the decadence of the Mongol dynasty in Armenia. The Lisbon earthquake of 1 November 1755, on the other hand, provided an opportunity for the rebuilding of the city on a grand scale and also for reducing the trading privileges of the British and Dutch, thus embittering their relations with Portugal. More recently, the earthquake of 26 July 1963 almost totally destroyed Skopje, capital of the slowly developing republic of Macedonia in Jugoslavia. Although only 1,000 people were killed, the earthquake caused property damage in excess of £120 million; the replacement costs and loss of income amounted to £450 million, a crippling loss for the underdeveloped economy of the republic. Like Lisbon, however, Skopje was rebuilt, emerging after the earthquake, although with considerable sacrifices, as a modern city bringing to the country an unprecedented rate of development. Both the people and their leaders realized that the disaster presented them with a rare opportunity not only to rebuild a better city but also to reorganize their local economic and social structure. Lisbon, Skopje and a very few other cases are the exception rather than the rule. Elsewhere, after a short period of enthusiasm for ambitious plans of restoration, the interest of the few concerned with reconstruction begins to die down, as the available funds are found to be insufficient and the problems posed become more involved and less exciting; apart from those affected by the disaster, few in the country are directly concerned and soon the whole question is forgotten. Clearly man tends to ignore the lessons taught by earthquakes and carries on as before.

Can we predict earthquakes?

At the present level of technology, earthquakes cannot be prevented. Nor for some years to come can such events be economically predicted in the detail required to safeguard the national economy of a developing country. Even so, subject only to minimal economic and budgetary restraints their disastrous effects can be prevented. Experience with earthquakes demonstrates the direct relationship between good-quality construction and minimum damage. This relationship is of great significance, because much greater and more definite progress in over-all protection from earthquakes can be achieved by improving building materials, methods of construction and design techniques, and by enforcing these methods, than by attempting prematurely to predict earthquakes or to seek out seismically safer sites in which unsound dwellings and other engineering works will continue to be erected. Naturally an intelligent use of development in both prediction and construction comes nearest to economic practicability.

Earthquake prediction was a continuous preoccupation for the early soothsayer, astrologer or prophet, and there are many recorded instances of forecasting destructive earthquakes. Earthquake prediction is also increasingly practised by the modern seismologist, particularly in recent years since the need to discriminate between nuclear explosions and earthquakes, and because funds provided for research have drastically decreased. Neither class of prophet is particularly effective, even when accurate, as they are invariably greeted with scepticism by the people, who seem strangely reluctant to believe that an earthquake will occur whether it is forecast by a credited astrologer or a seismologist. For instance, the earthquake of 1042 in Tabriz was predicted by the astrologer Abu Tahir Shirazi, who tried in vain to persuade the people to leave. Earthquakes had happened in Tabriz sufficiently frequently to be likely to occur again, yet the main reaction to the prediction was one of apathy, and when it occurred more than 40,000 people were killed.

The earthquake of February 1549 in the district of Qayin in Iran was also predicted by the Qadi of that place who tried unsuccessfully to convince his people to stay out in the open that particular night; they refused to listen and the Qadi stayed out alone but finding the night very cold returned to his house where he soon perished with 3,000 people in the district. Apparently, the Qadi himself was not too sure about his prediction.

There are of course cases, particularly in the less earthquake-prone parts of the world, where after a small earthquake the prediction of a bigger one to come has caused panic. This was the case with the London earthquakes of 1750. Two shocks on 8 February and 8 March caused slight damage but much greater concern in the city, and started a real panic. The tidiness of an interval of exactly four weeks between the two shocks gave the opportunity for a prophecy to circulate that at a future interval of four weeks, London would be destroyed by a third and devastating earthquake. On the eve of the prophesied disaster Horace Walpole said, 'within these three days 730 coaches have been counted passing Hyde Park Corner with whole parties removing into the country'. Those who did not go right out of town camped in nearby fields and women made 'earthquake gowns' for a vigil in the open. And when nothing happened, many stayed away for a few more days, and on their return the lifeguardsman who had prophesied the event was sent to the madhouse.

Today, earthquake prediction on a scientific basis is making slow but steady progress. At this time, however, there is little to predict the timing of earthquakes with any significant degree of certainty, and it is a point of contention among scientists as to whether an earthquake prediction and warning system can be developed. The question is not only whether the accurate place, time and magnitude of an event can be predicted, but whether warning the people is likely to be effective. The time problem when giving a warning is vastly different for different parts of the world. The colossal loss of life in recent years in Bangladesh was not due to a failure of the far more advanced system of warning against hurricanes and cyclones, but to the fact that this warning did not reach the inhabitants of the danger zone because of a total lack of communications in these areas. With earthquakes it is not only the prediction and warning problems that are important but also the social and economic implications of forecasting. False alarms and inaccurate timing could create more problems than already exist. Recent attempts to forecast earthquakes in Japan have resulted in great tension and damage to the local economy. Such prediction would be welcomed by scientists and engineers, but for the general public it is uncertain whether this would solve more problems than the social, economic and even political ones that it must create.

Suggestions for further reading

M. de Ballore: *Ethnographie sismique et volcanique*. Honoré Champion, Paris, 1923.

Committee on the Alaska Earthquake: *The Great Alaska Earthquake of 1964: Human Ecology*. National Academy of Sciences, Washington D.C., 1970.

A. Cox: *Plate Tectonics and Geomagnetic Reversals*. W. H. Freeman, San Francisco and Reading, 1973.

C. Davison: *The Founders of Seismology*. Cambridge University Press and Macmillan, New York, 1927.

T. D. Kendrick: *The Lisbon Earthquake*. Methuen, London, 1956; Lippincott, Philadelphia, 1957.

X. Le Pichon, J. Francheteau and J. Bonnin: *Plate Tectonics*. Elsevier Science Publishing Co., Amsterdam and New York, 1973.

N. Newmark and E. Rosenblueth: *Fundamentals of Earthquake Engineering*. Prentice-Hall, Englewood Cliffs, N.J. and Hemel Hempstead, 1971.

C. Richter: *Elementary Seismology*. W. H. Freeman, San Francisco and Reading, 1958.

All the tragedy and horror of an earthquake are summed up and symbolized by a bereft, weeping little girl who stands among the ruins of Kakhk, in Persia. In the afternoon of 31 August 1968 this medium-sized town in the Khorasan mountains was hit by an earthquake that registered 7.1 on the Richter scale of magnitude; 12,100 people were killed, and damage was estimated at $25,000,000. As such things go, this was a fairly severe shock, about equivalent to a 10-megaton bomb: over 80 have been registered, in this century alone, as strong or stronger. Since the beginning of the century, nearly 900,000 people have been killed in earthquakes; direct damage has been calculated as about £30,000 million. Small wonder that strenuous efforts are being made to find out more about this most horrifying and destructive of nature's forces – why and where earthquakes happen, what can be done to modify their effects, and even whether there is any possibility of predicting them.

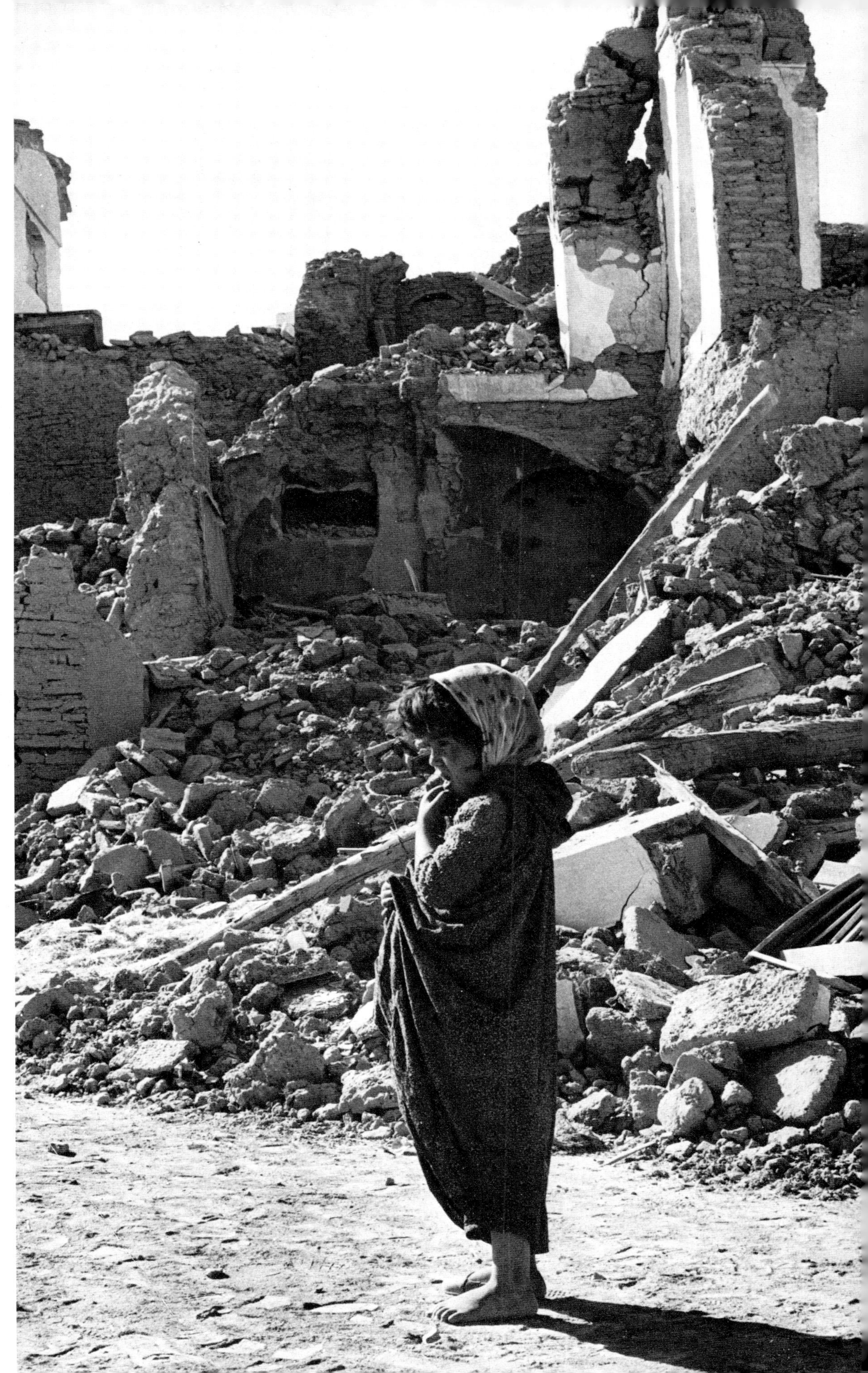

2

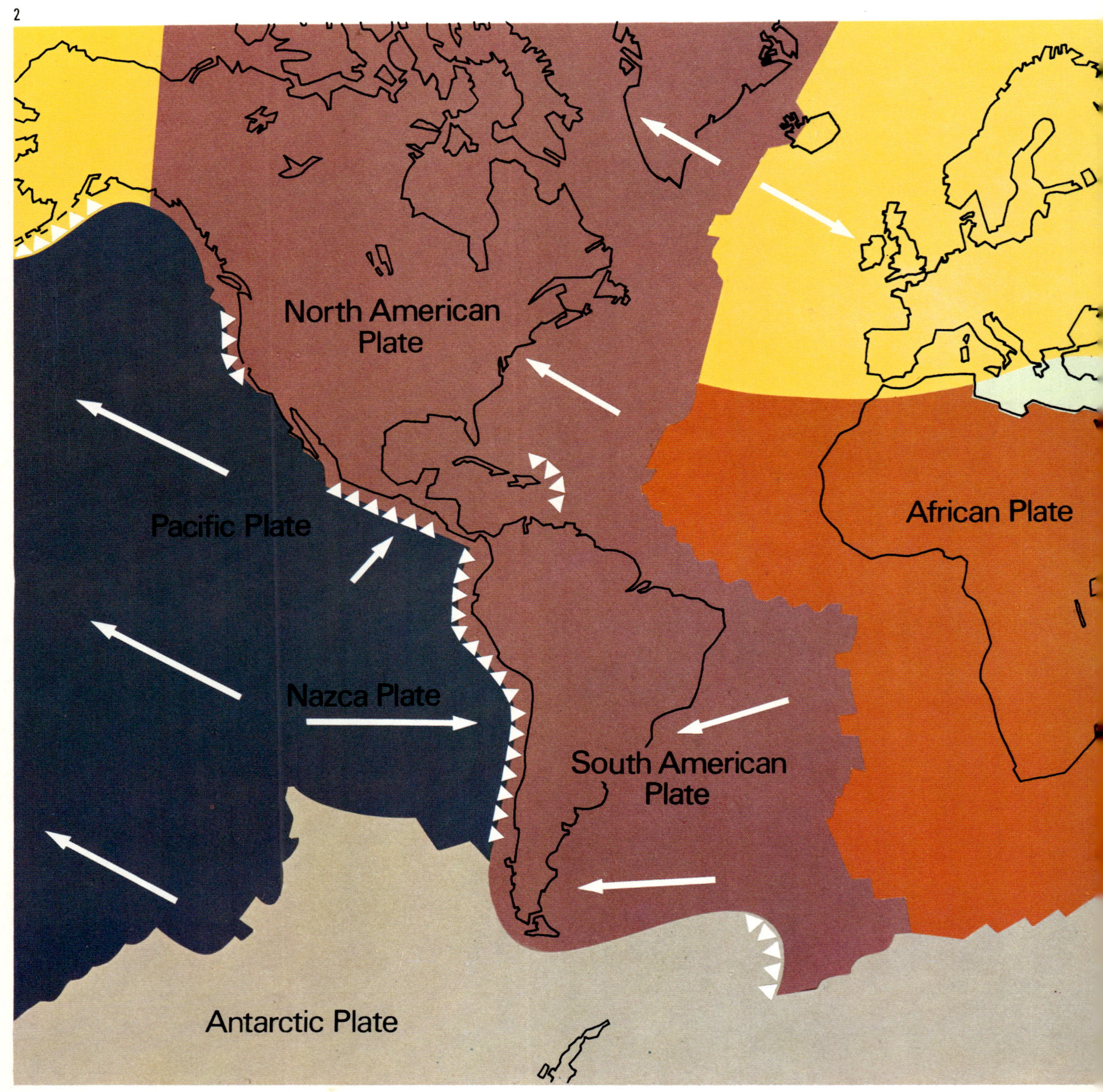
North American Plate
Pacific Plate
African Plate
Nazca Plate
South American Plate
Antarctic Plate

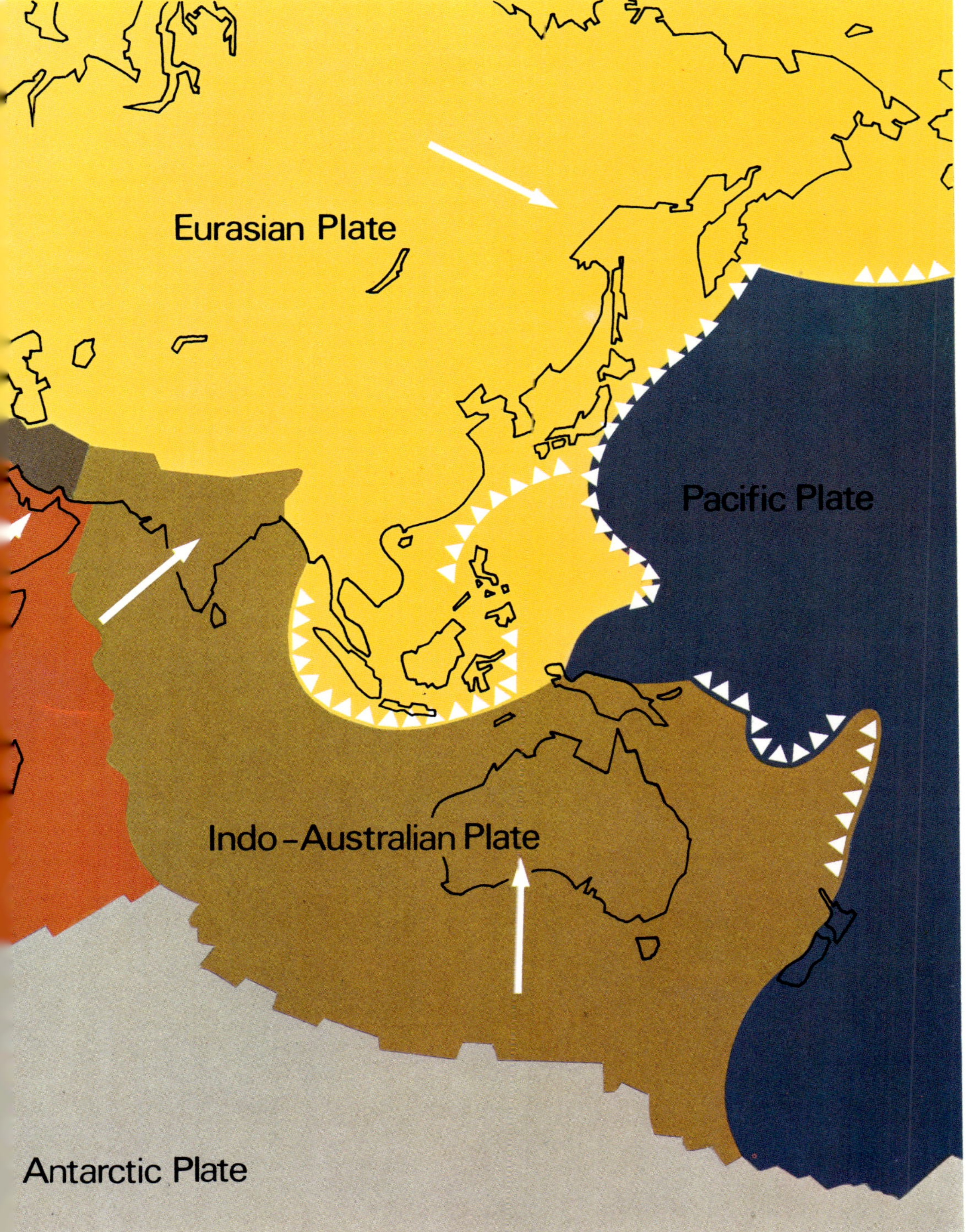

The drifting jigsaw puzzle of the seas and continents makes up a picture that has helped earth scientists to understand the cause of earthquakes. Six huge crustal plates, some 60 miles thick, and a number of smaller ones (not all shown here) move over the underlying hot asthenosphere ('sphere of no strength') in a complex way – colliding head-on, drifting apart, sliding past each other. The arrows show the directions in which the plates are moving, and the rows of triangles show lines of pressure, where one plate is being forced against another. Where this happens, the thinner sub-oceanic crust is forced under the thicker but lighter continental mass, and it is here, in these regions of stress, that most earthquakes occur.

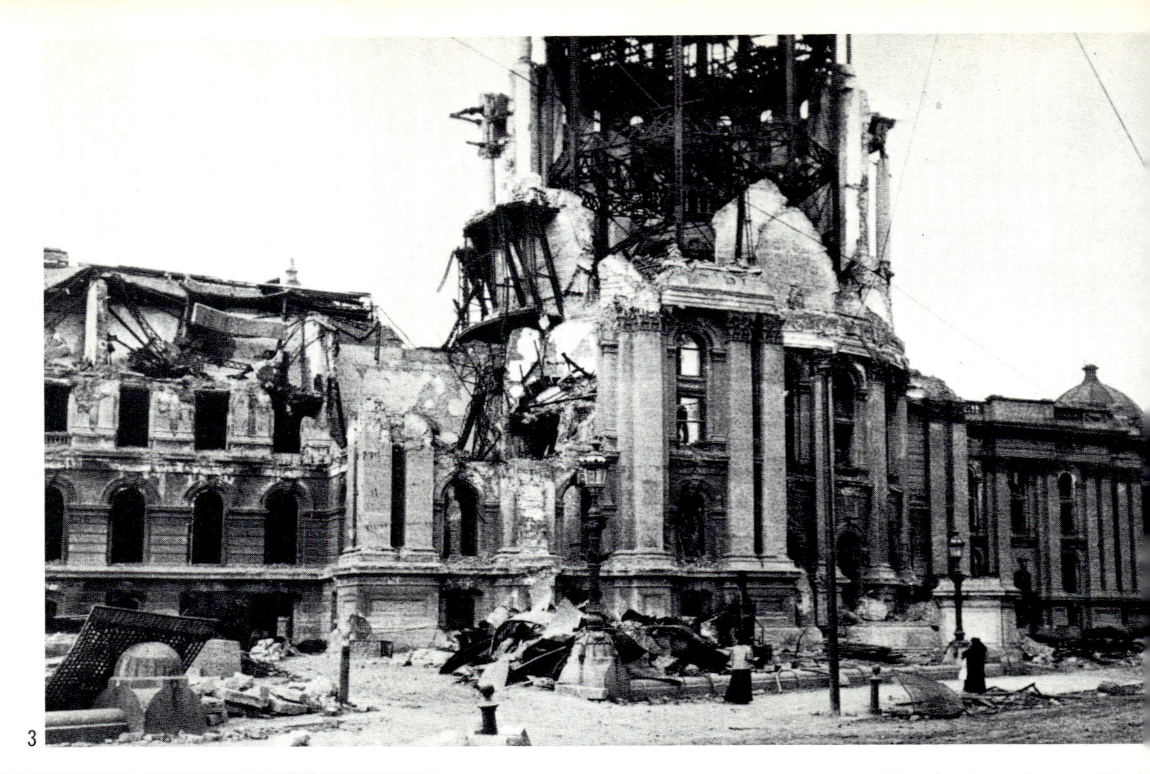
3

4

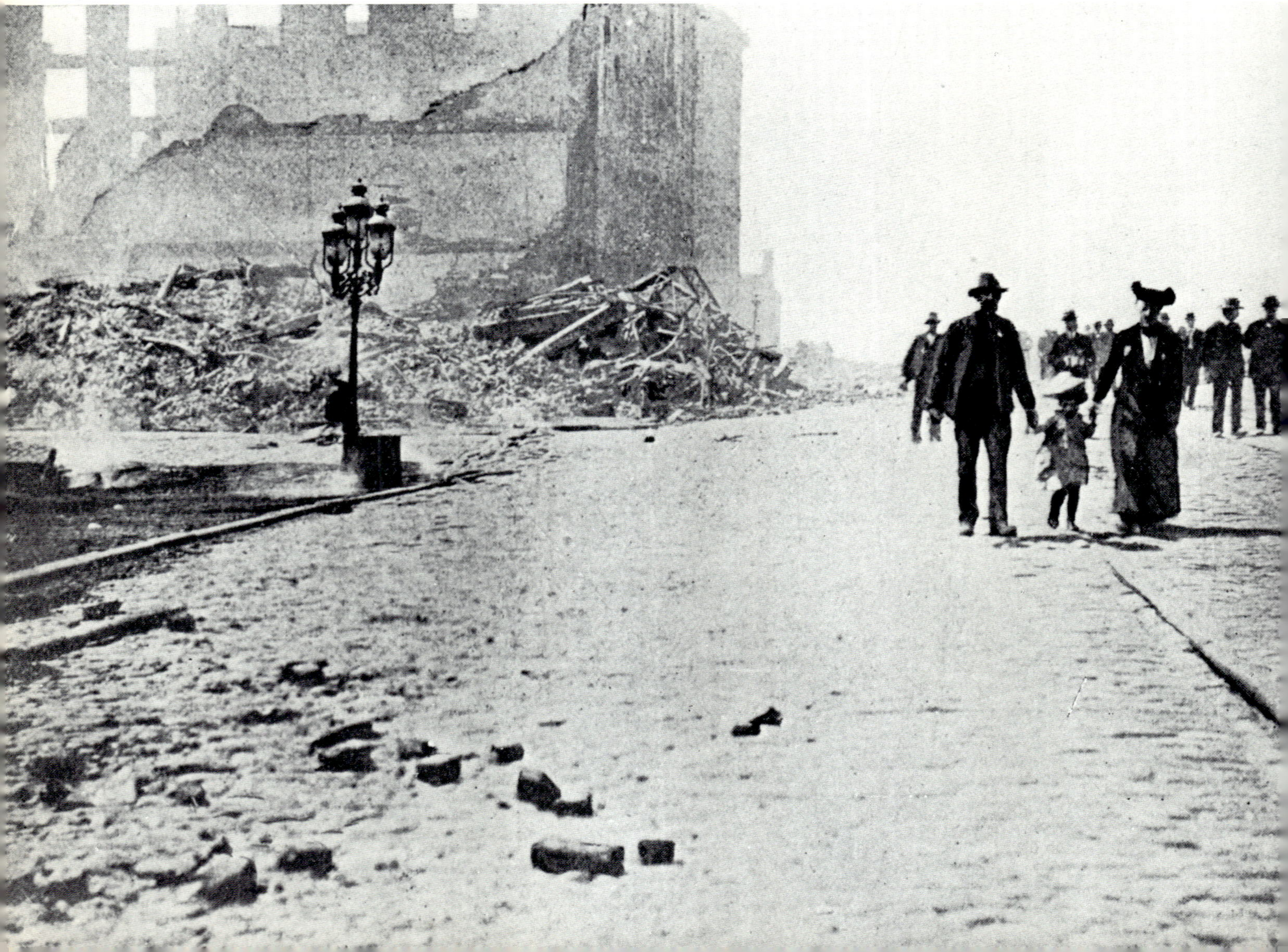

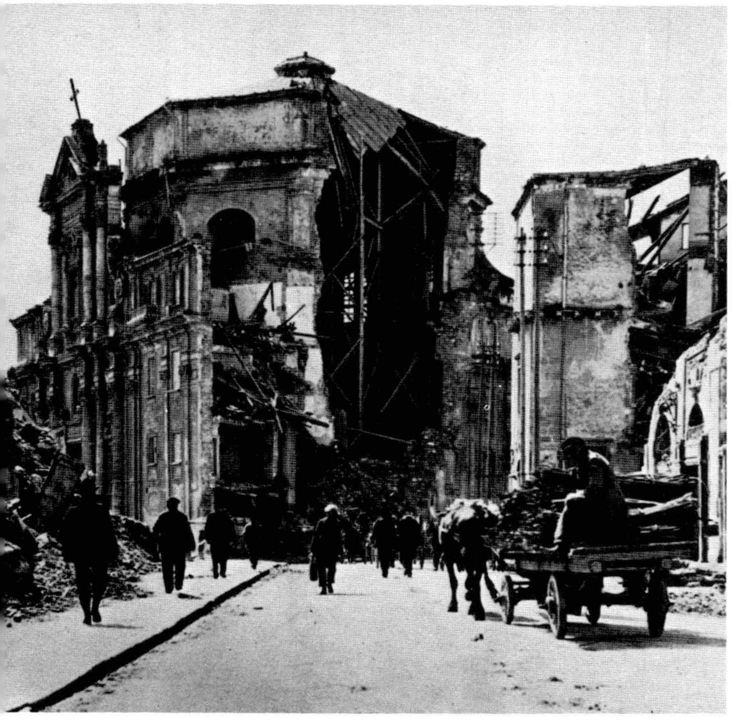

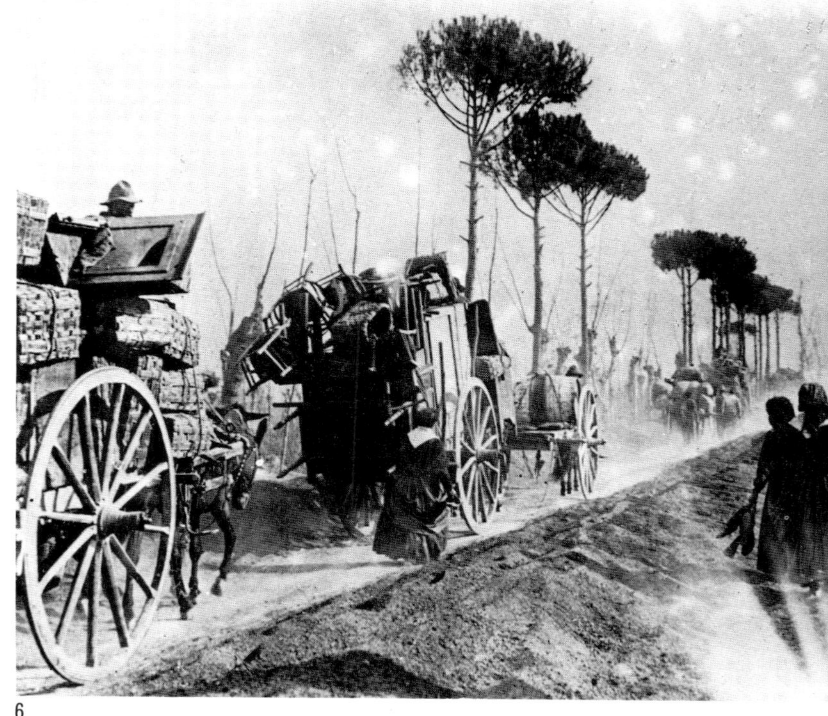

6

Vhen disaster struck San 'rancisco in 1906, with a Iagnitude 8.3 shock, estruction was immense and videspread. The City Hall (3) vas reduced to a gutted shell, 10ugh the tower girders held. 'ire was added to the horror; a hapeless pile of smoking rubble 4) was all that was left of the ffice block at the corner of South Iarket Street and Main Street. 'he death toll, at 750, was elatively light. Two years later Iessina in Sicily (5) suffered an arthquake measuring 7.5 on the .ichter scale, which killed 7,000. As much as 60 miles own the coast severe shocks 'ere felt, and panic-stricken efugees filled the roads leading ut of Catania (6). Probably the entury's worst earthquake was 1 1923 (7); reaching Magnitude .3, it caused 99,000 deaths in 'okyo and the surrounding ountry. The resulting *tsunami* evastated Kobe harbour (8).

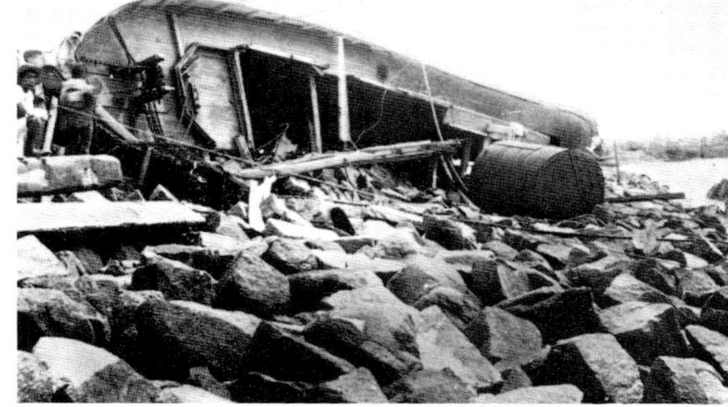

7/8

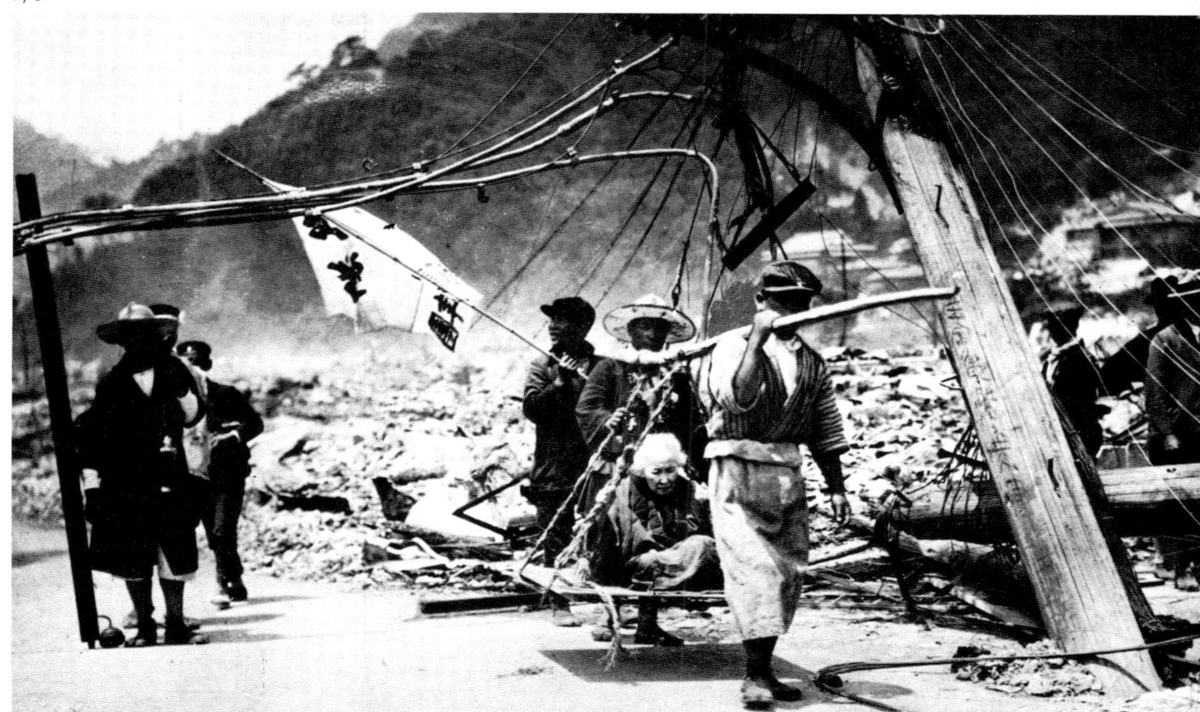

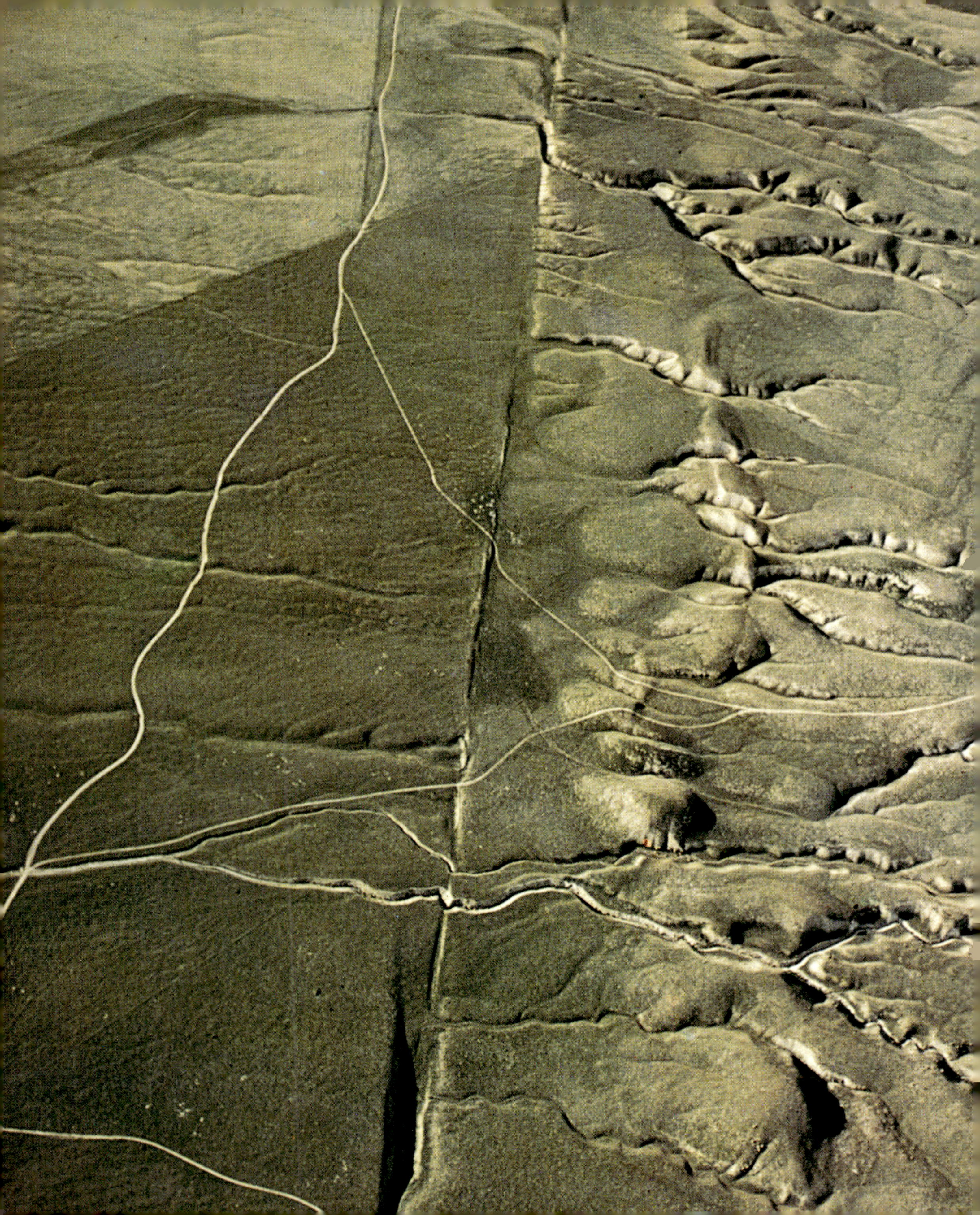

One of the most closely watched regions of the world is the San Andreas fault, a crack in the Earth's crust which runs nearly half the length of California (9). Here two tectonic plates are moving past each other, slowly, inexorably and with enormous force (see Pl. 2). As the shearing strain builds up, every now and then it becomes more than the rocks can bear, the two plates move once more, and the release of tension, the jerk as they move, causes an earthquake. Sometimes this is quite a minor shock, sometimes, as in 1906, a major disaster. The resultant off-setting of roads, streams and other features can be seen from the air along the fault line – most clearly in the neatly planted rows of an orange grove (10).

0

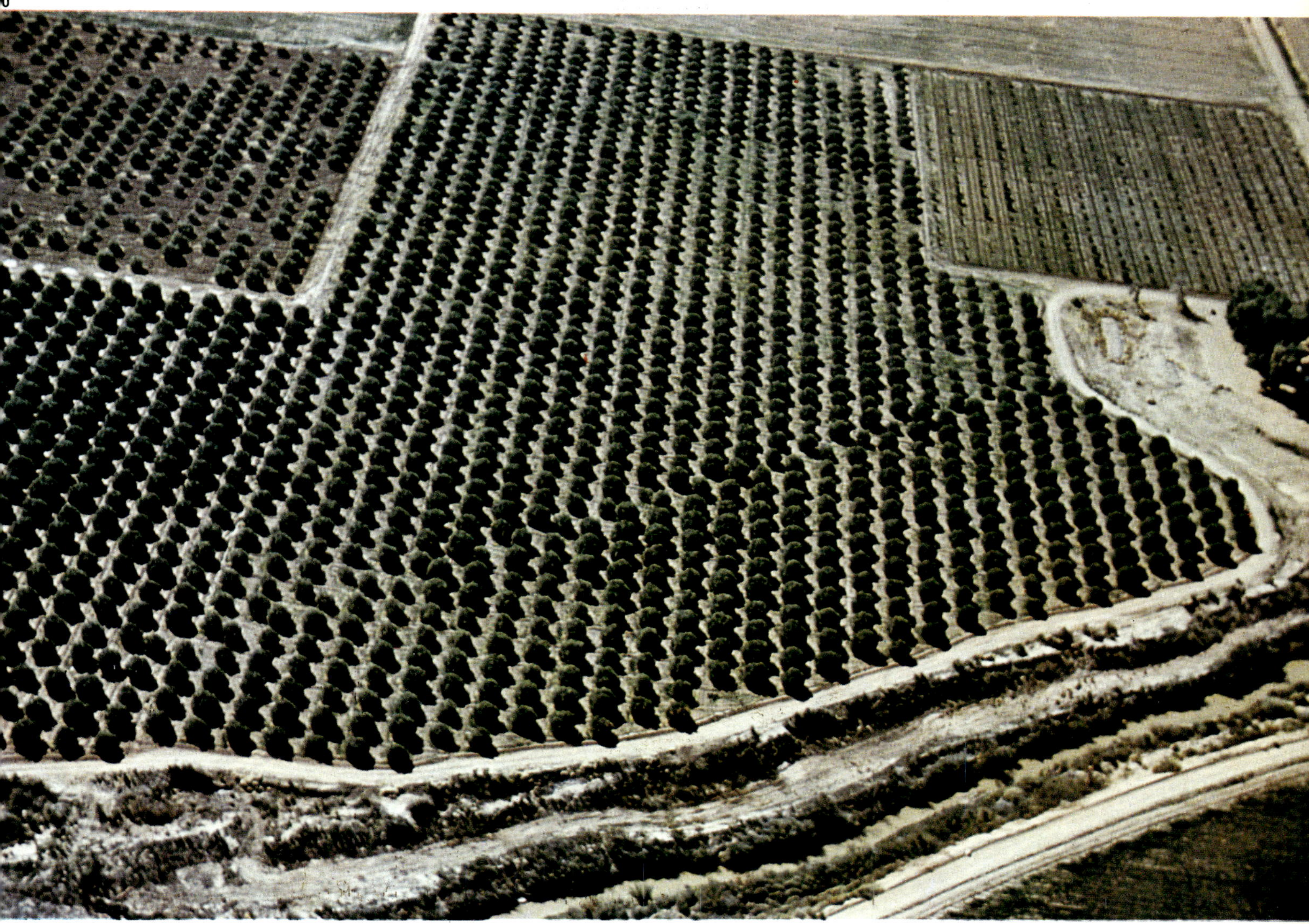

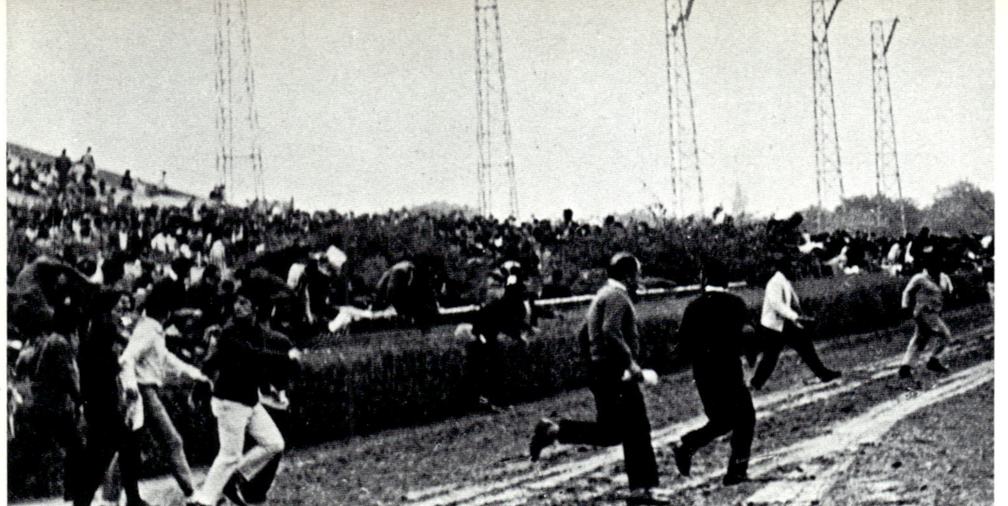

Panic-stricken spectators at a Lima racetrack (11) scattered on to the grass as the first tremors were felt, on 31 May 1970, of what was to be one of the worst disasters ever to strike the earthquake-troubled Andean coast. Seconds later the town of Huaraz, 180 miles to the north, was in ruins (12, 13), nine-tenths of its houses disembowelled shells. Huge rock falls from the surrounding mountains added to the chaos (14), and cracked, shattered roads (15) showing vividly how the earth had moved, slowed aid convoys to a nervous crawl.

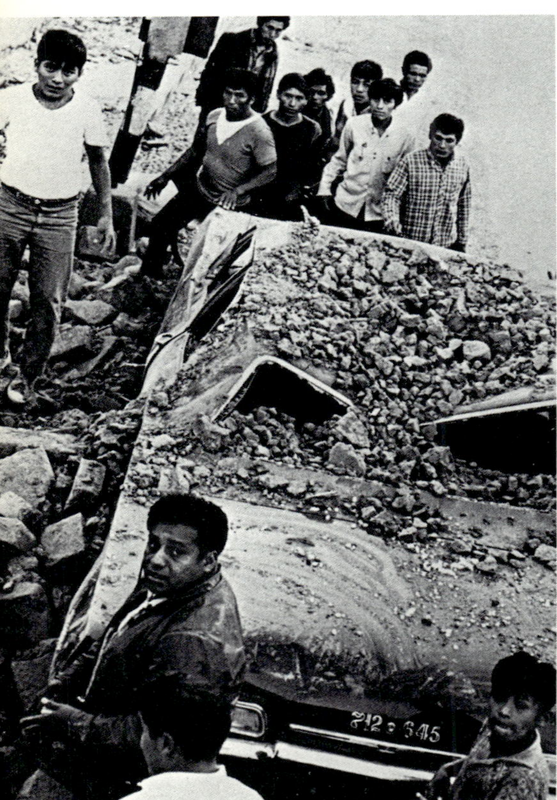

12

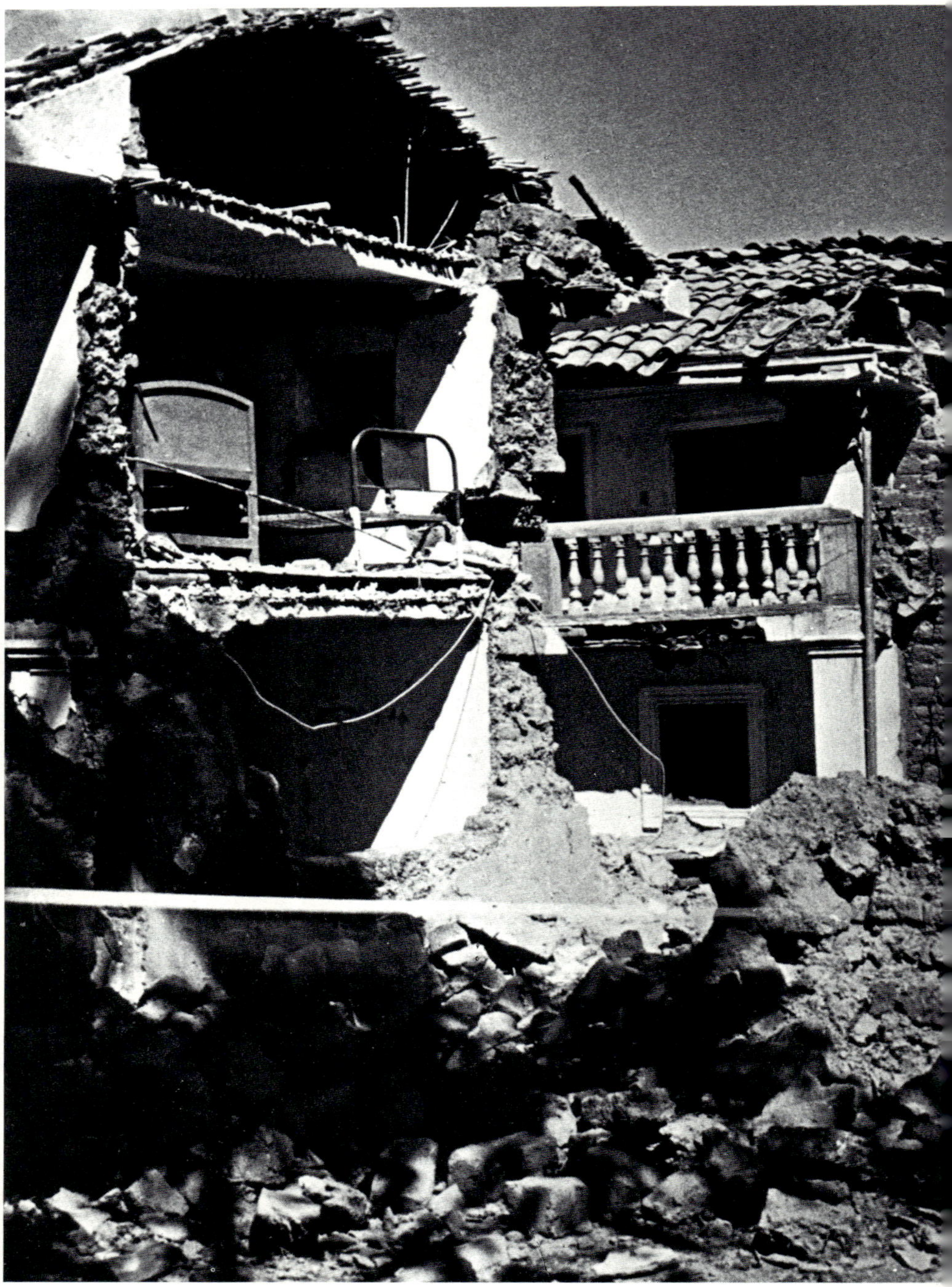

13

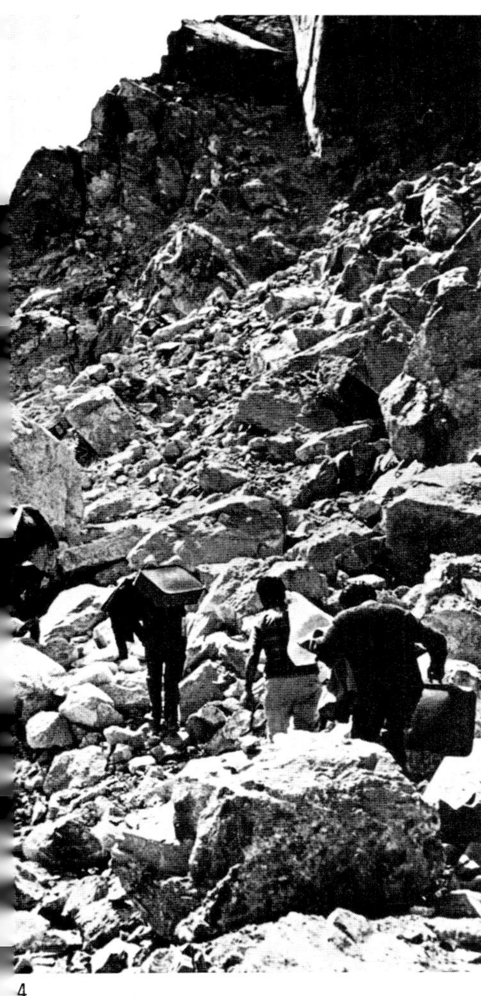

4

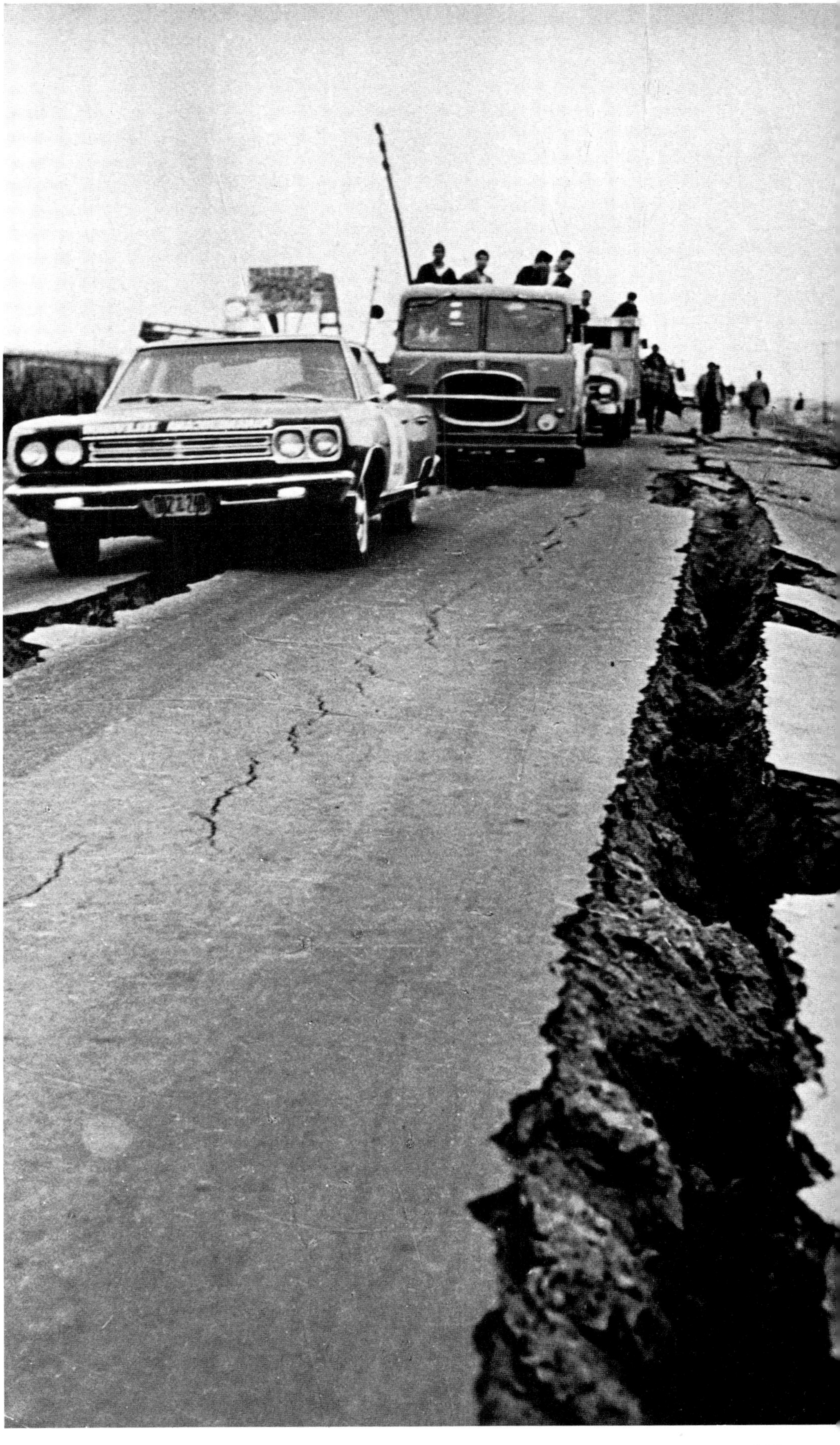

15

A gigantic rock slide in the mountains 30 miles north of Huaraz blotted out the town of Yungay. The rock face had been known to be unstable, and liable to fall at any time; the shock of the earthquake merely gave it the fatal nudge. The photographer who took this awe-inspiring sequence of pictures described how, as the ground moved 'two foot forward, two foot to the side, up and down eighteen inches', first a tremendous snow avalanche was shaken loose (16); then the rock, more resistant, began to fall (17); clouds of red dust rose (18, 19) as the rocks, some as big as houses, rolled down the mountainside. The town was buried in rock and mud ten metres deep, and out of 20,000 inhabitants only 2,500 survived.

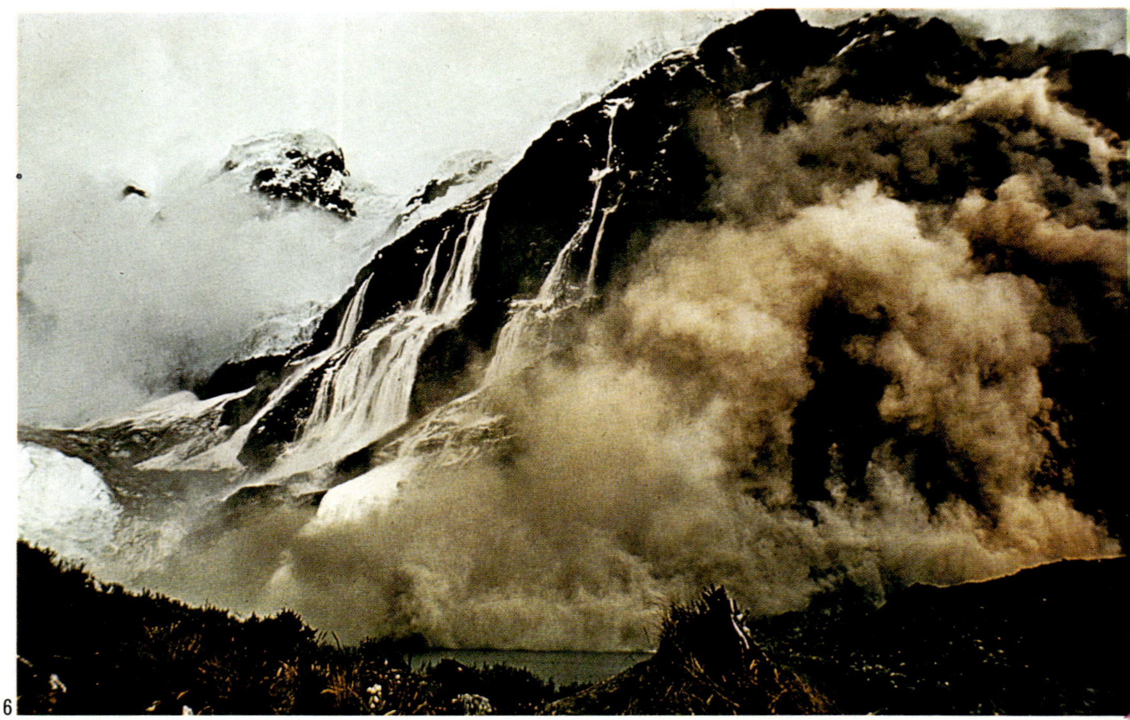

16

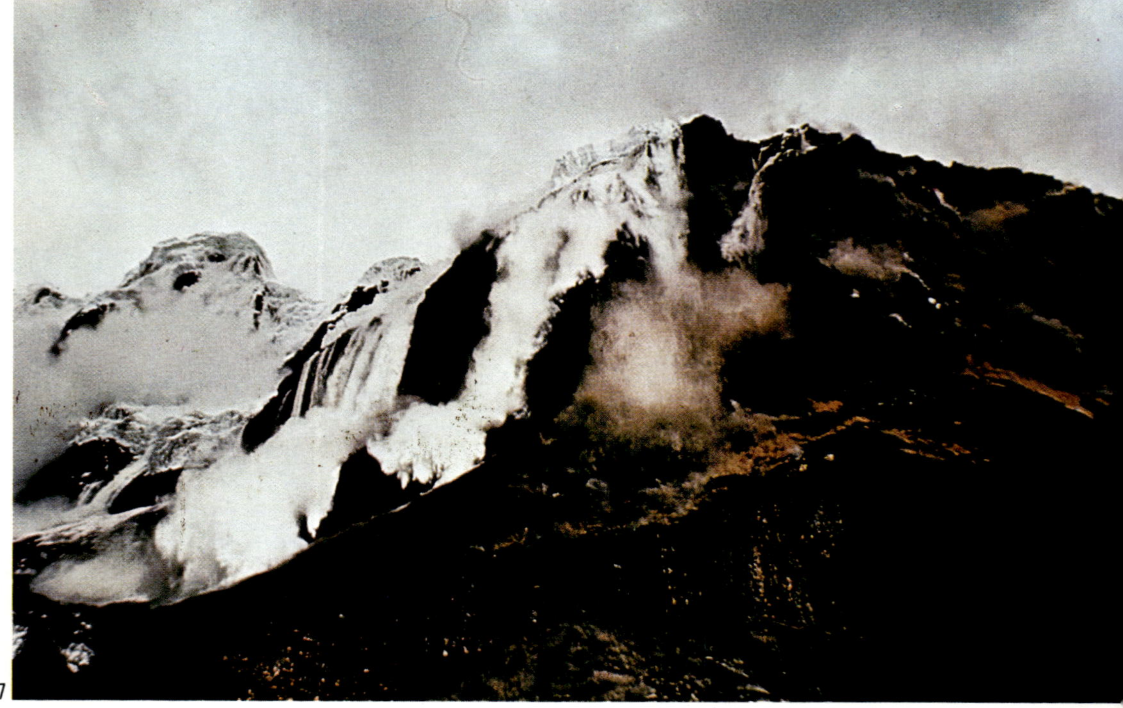

17

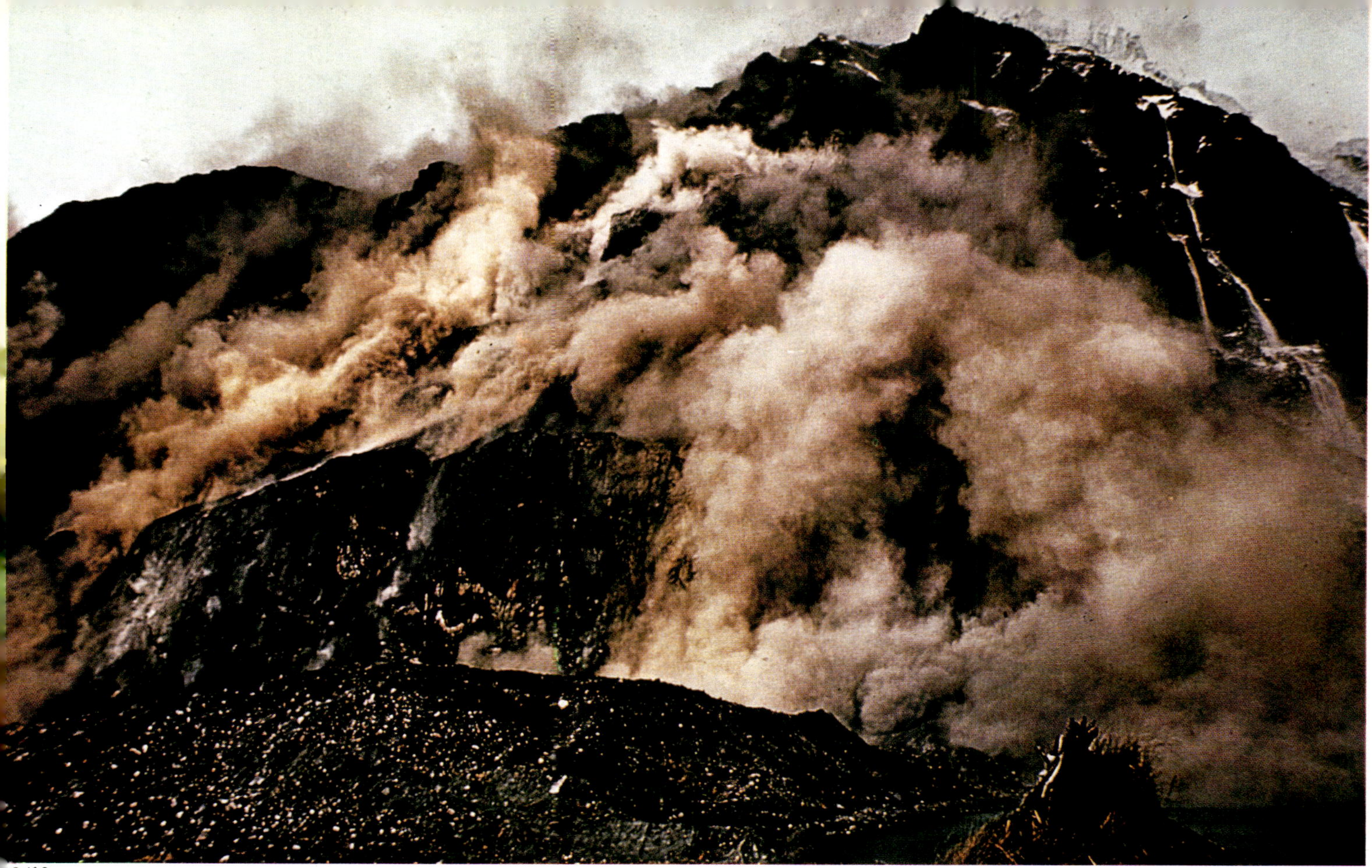

8/19

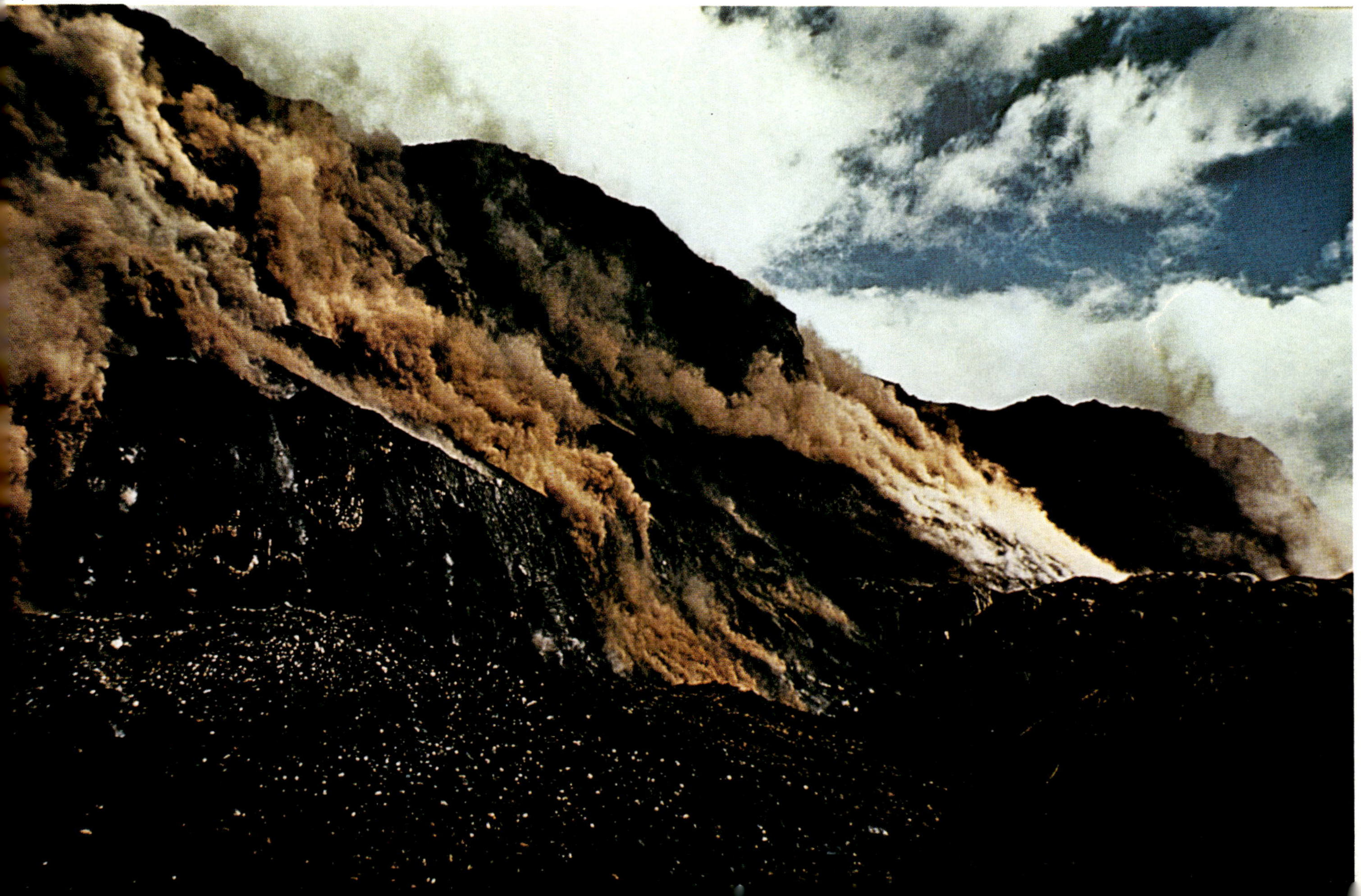

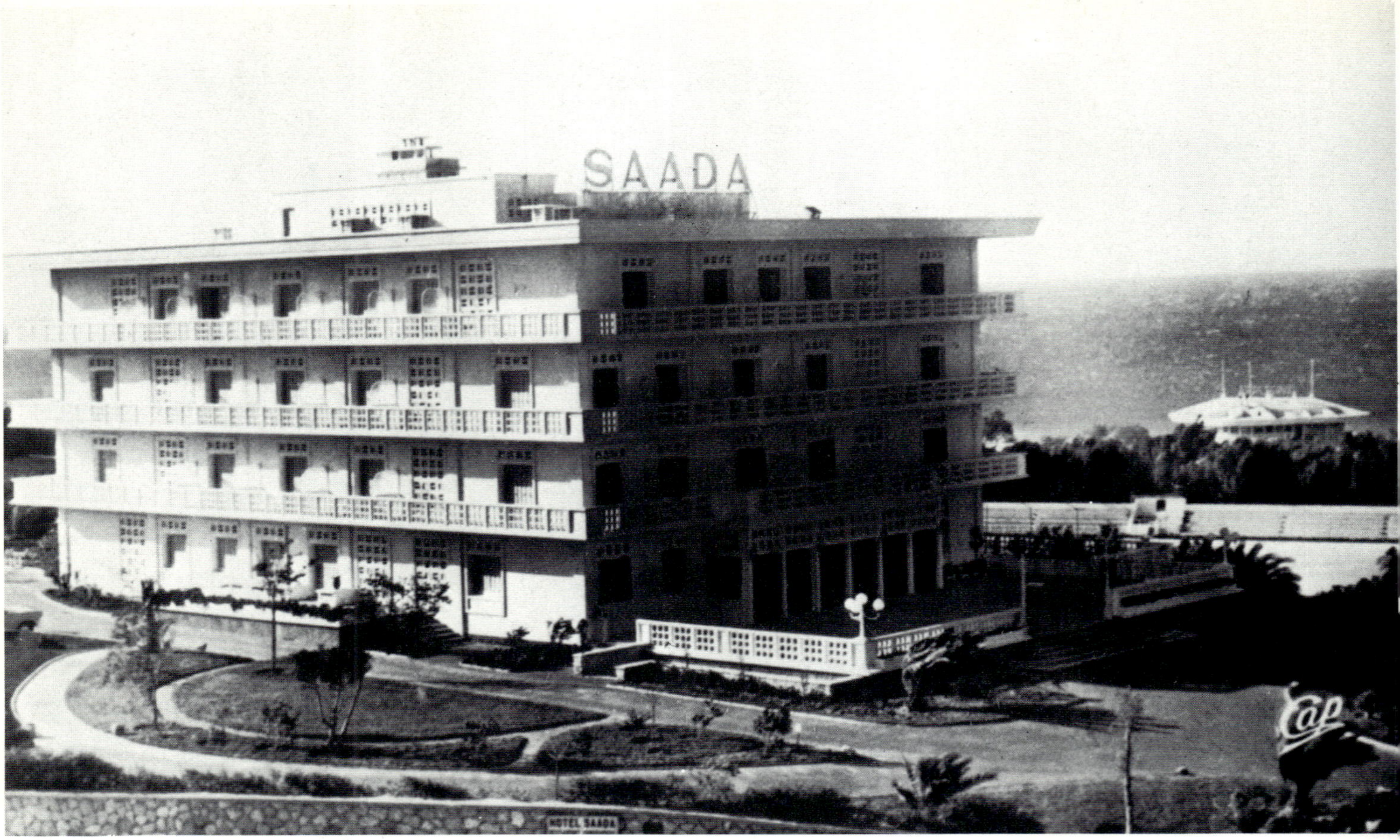

20/21

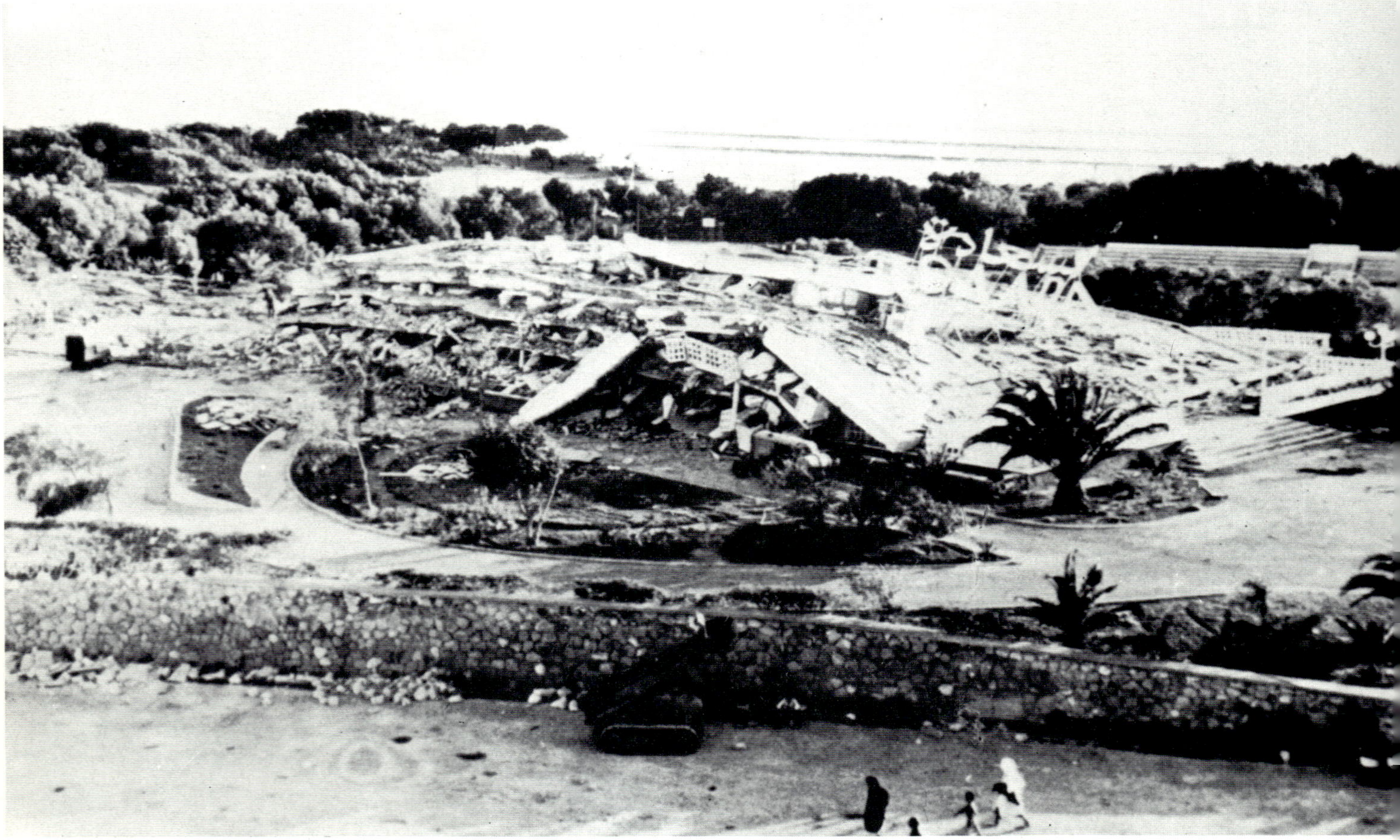

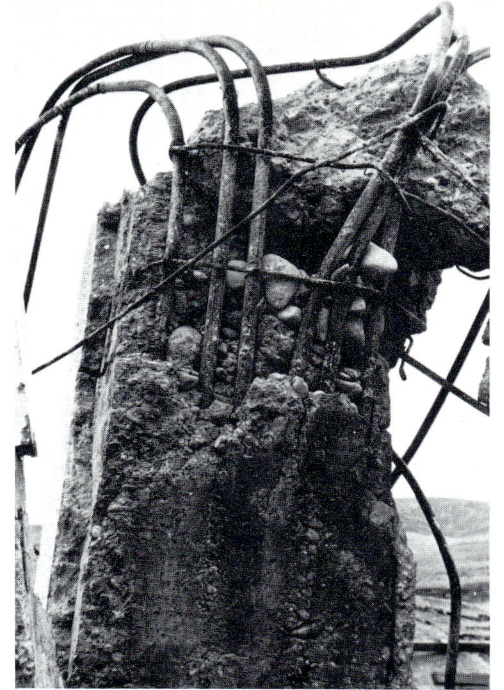

22

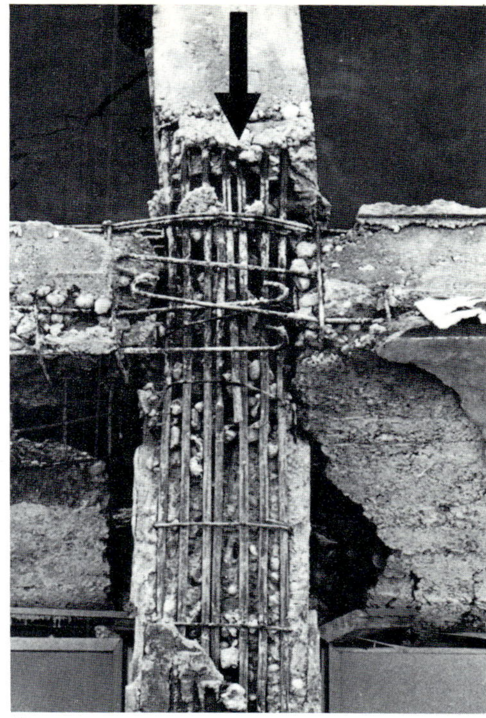

23

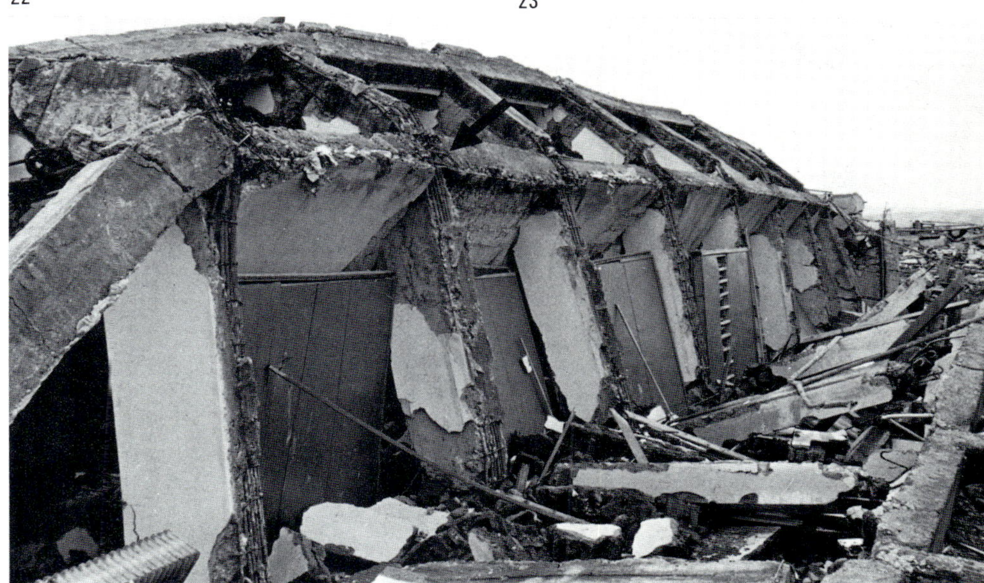

24

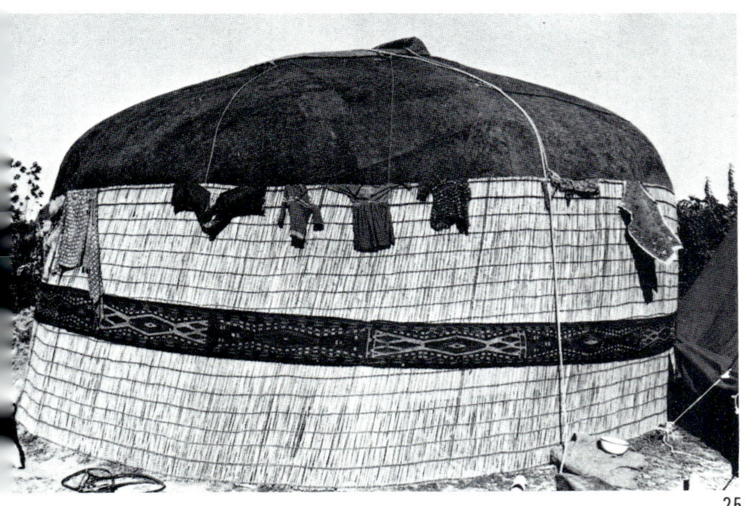

25

Why do buildings collapse so completely? How could such a modern, solid-seeming structure as the Saada Hotel, Agadir (20), fold up like a pack of cards (21) when a Magnitude 5.9 shock hit Morocco in 1960? To an architect or engineer, earthquake ruins often tell a clear tale of skimped materials and lethally bad workmanship. A reinforced concrete structure designed, but not built, to resist earthquake forces shows poor-quality concrete (22), empty joints (23, arrowed), and failure of connections between columns and beams (24). But the traditional, indestructible Turcoman *yurt* (25) stands up without difficulty to the earthquakes of Iran and central Asia.

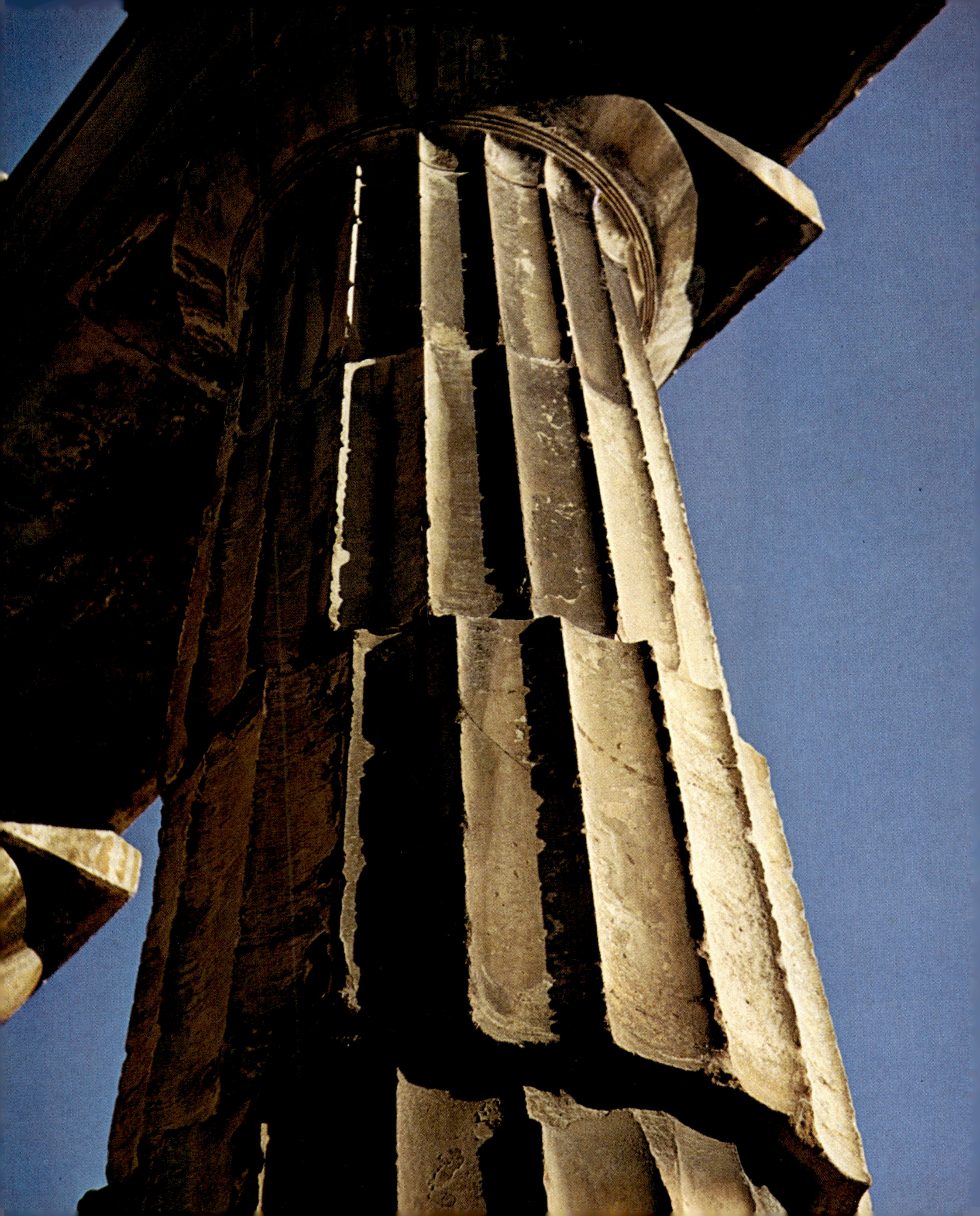

26

Visible sign of an earthquake in time past, the displaced drum of a column in the temple of Hephaistos (26), in Athens, suggests that the city may not be as free from earthquakes as is generally believed. Only a few hundred miles to the east, after all, major shocks are still frequent, and this is reflected in the architecture. A two-storey timber-framed house in western Turkey (27) is an example of traditional earthquake-resistant design, developed with local materials and methods of construction that have saved thousands of lives. This house, damaged but still standing, stood 50 yards from the fault-break associated with the Gediz earthquake of 1970. The simple timber-framed bungalow (28) is one of three remaining in Leucas (Ionian Islands), designed and built by British navy carpenters in 1825 after a destructive earthquake; timber cross-bracing, worked out by rule of thumb and common sense, enabled these houses to resist at least five serious earthquakes, but they are now being replaced by modern – and far more dangerous – buildings. This picture was taken after the damaging earthquake of 1973.

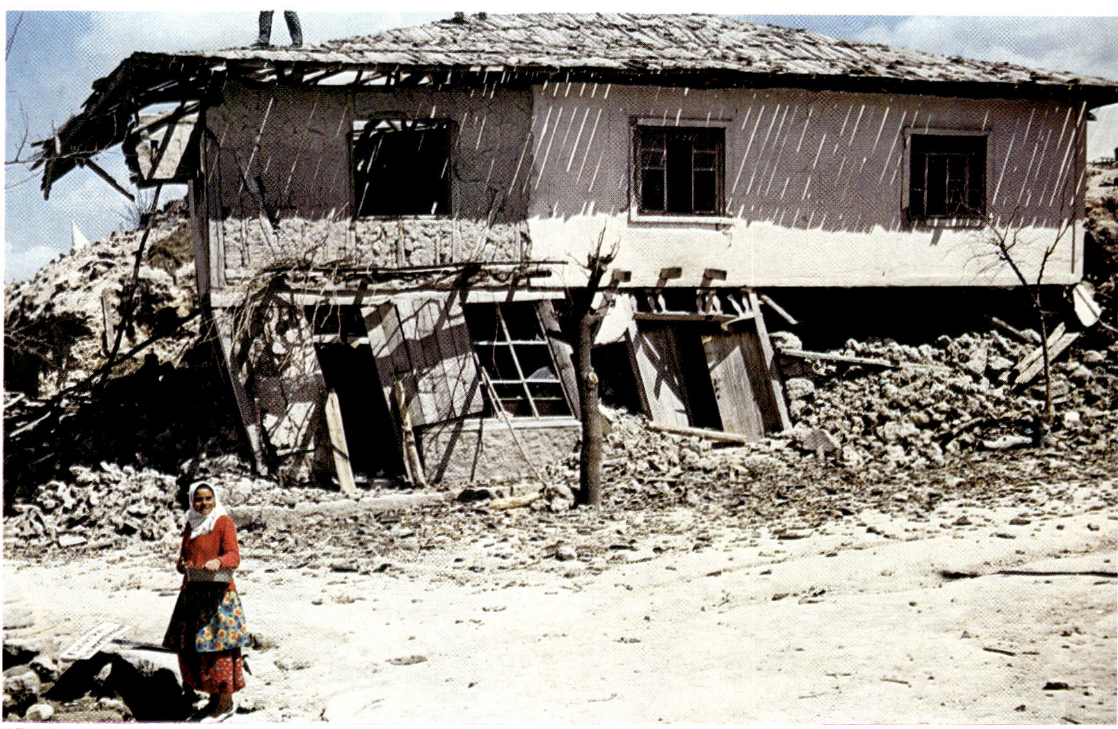

27/28

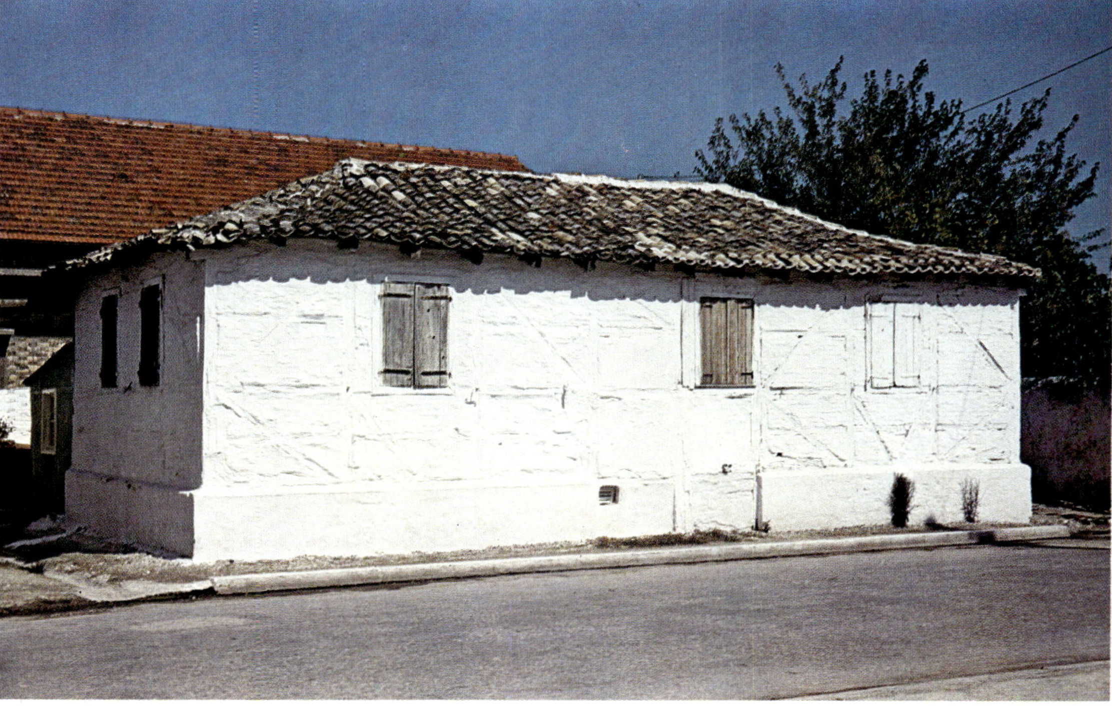

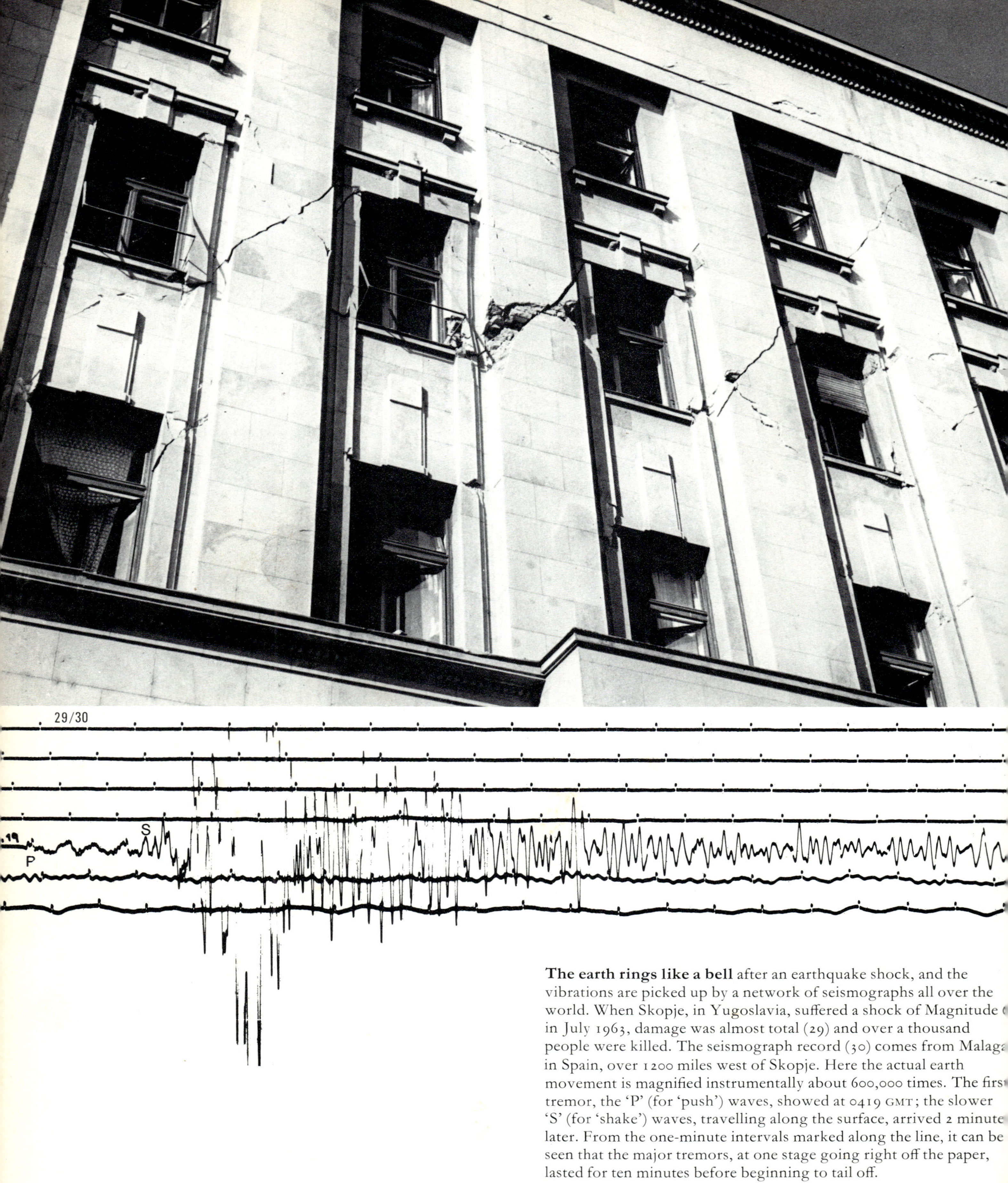

The earth rings like a bell after an earthquake shock, and the vibrations are picked up by a network of seismographs all over the world. When Skopje, in Yugoslavia, suffered a shock of Magnitude 6 in July 1963, damage was almost total (29) and over a thousand people were killed. The seismograph record (30) comes from Malaga in Spain, over 1200 miles west of Skopje. Here the actual earth movement is magnified instrumentally about 600,000 times. The first tremor, the 'P' (for 'push') waves, showed at 0419 GMT; the slower 'S' (for 'shake') waves, travelling along the surface, arrived 2 minutes later. From the one-minute intervals marked along the line, it can be seen that the major tremors, at one stage going right off the paper, lasted for ten minutes before beginning to tail off.

10

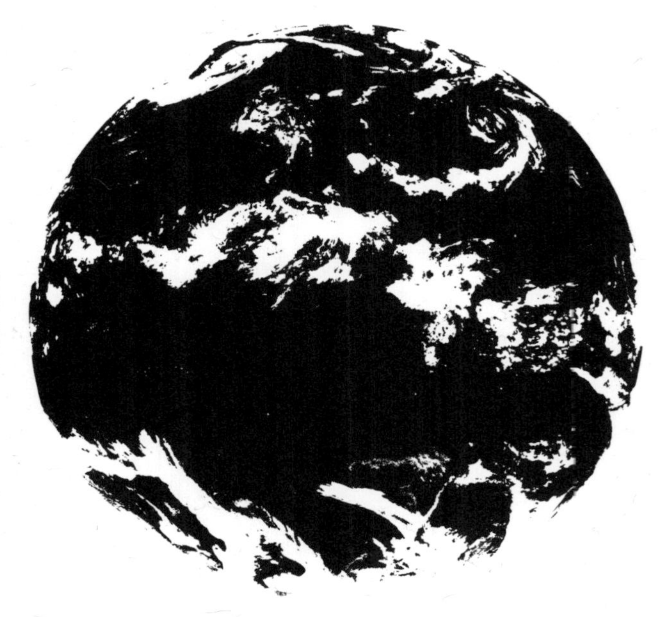

Satellites: a new look at nature

W. J. Campbell

W. J. Campbell

'I AM THE EYE through which the Earth beholds itself', proclaimed Shelley's Apollo as he gazed down out of a Greek sky from his winged chariot. Within a hundred and fifty years of the writing of this line the Apollo satellite programme gave a number of men, going to or returning from the moon at fairly regular intervals, the chance to be the 'eye' by which the earth became capable of beholding itself. These men were both preceded and followed by a wide variety of inanimate electronic eyes which have given and will continue to give mankind so many new looks at his world that he will for ever think differently about it than he did before he created the tools called satellites. With them we have quickly and greatly expanded the breadth and depth of our vision, and we know that because of them we and our relationship with the forces of nature will permanently change.

This chapter is about a revolution and, like most revolutions that have had the greatest impact on man, it is a quiet one. Very little about it is secretive, yet few people seem to know that it is happening. Its potential for altering man's interaction with all other forms of life travelling on Spaceship Earth is utterly immense. Its potential for giving man a better understanding, and therefore closer spiritual contact with nature, is even greater. What began it all was the essentially simultaneous creation of two tools which, had they been created separately, would not have started a revolution – the computer and the satellite. The revolution may be called Understanding Spaceship Earth.

I believe that the creation of these tools will alter man's relationship to his planet more than his invention of the wheel or the internal combustion engine. This could be so for many reasons, the most profound of which is that the computer and satellite do not allow us to shape nature to our anthropocentric ends, but are rather the means by which we shall take several jumps forward in our understanding of nature. Our earlier tools were basically those that allowed us to make a declaration of independence from nature; the two new ones are part of the new revolution based upon a declaration of interdependence *with* nature.

Without the computer, satellites could not be launched; and satellites collect data at an astonishing rate – one hundred billion bits of information in twenty-four hours for the latest ones – and without the computer this information explosion would inundate us with largely useless and expensive data. But even more important than controlling satellites, and collecting, storing, sorting, analysing and distributing the information they transmit, the computer enables us to put it to ultimate use in solving a wide variety of numerical models of physical, chemical, social, ecological and biological phenomena that we need in order better to understand Spaceship Earth.

Without satellites we could never accumulate the facts we urgently need to properly interpret the forces of nature. We would continue seeing only parts of important processes and never the whole. Our data would continue to be fragmented and piecemeal, our concepts incomplete, and our understanding limited. This revolution is fortuitously timely. Man's geometrically explosive growth, coupled with his exploitation of natural resources, has brought him to the brink of doing irreparable harm not only to himself but to all life. The computer and the satellite give him the chance for a change of direction. He now has the means of establishing a worldwide data base to prevent inadvertent ecological disaster, of global monitoring to prevent deliberate environmental degradation, of developing increasingly complex and accurate numerical models to predict the consequence of his actions, the behaviour of the forces of nature, and their mutual interaction.

Towards an expanded vision

The year 1975 marked the fifteenth anniversary of the use of meteorological satellites, which began on 1 April 1960, when the experimental TIROS-1 was launched. Within a few days of its ascent into a near-Earth orbit (the television pictures it transmitted often being oblique and poorly illuminated views which, compared with the images of today, look appallingly primitive) the new data were being put into operational use in weather forecasting. Poor as the images were, they allowed us to see whole weather systems for the first time. For centuries man had plotted surface measurements in an effort to develop concepts about the complex processes going on in the fluid overhead, and in this century he had succeeded in sending instruments on balloons up through the fluid to get more data. The weather he sought to understand was mostly associated with cyclonic storms with wavelengths greater than 1,000 kilometres, therefore his view of these waves was always fragmented, even though he increased the density of his meteorological stations to alarmingly expensive levels. Not only were the basic elements of weather very large but they changed very fast – that is, large-scale spatial changes occur at small time scales.

Before the launch of TIROS-1 there were a few meteorologists who dreamed about the possibilities of getting a large view of the Earth and its complex fluid processes from satellites. After that first launch the dreamers abounded, and within a decade a long series of meteorological satellites were launched, carrying increasingly complex arrays of instruments – improved camera systems, infra-red radiometers, solar ultra-violet radiometers, data collection and

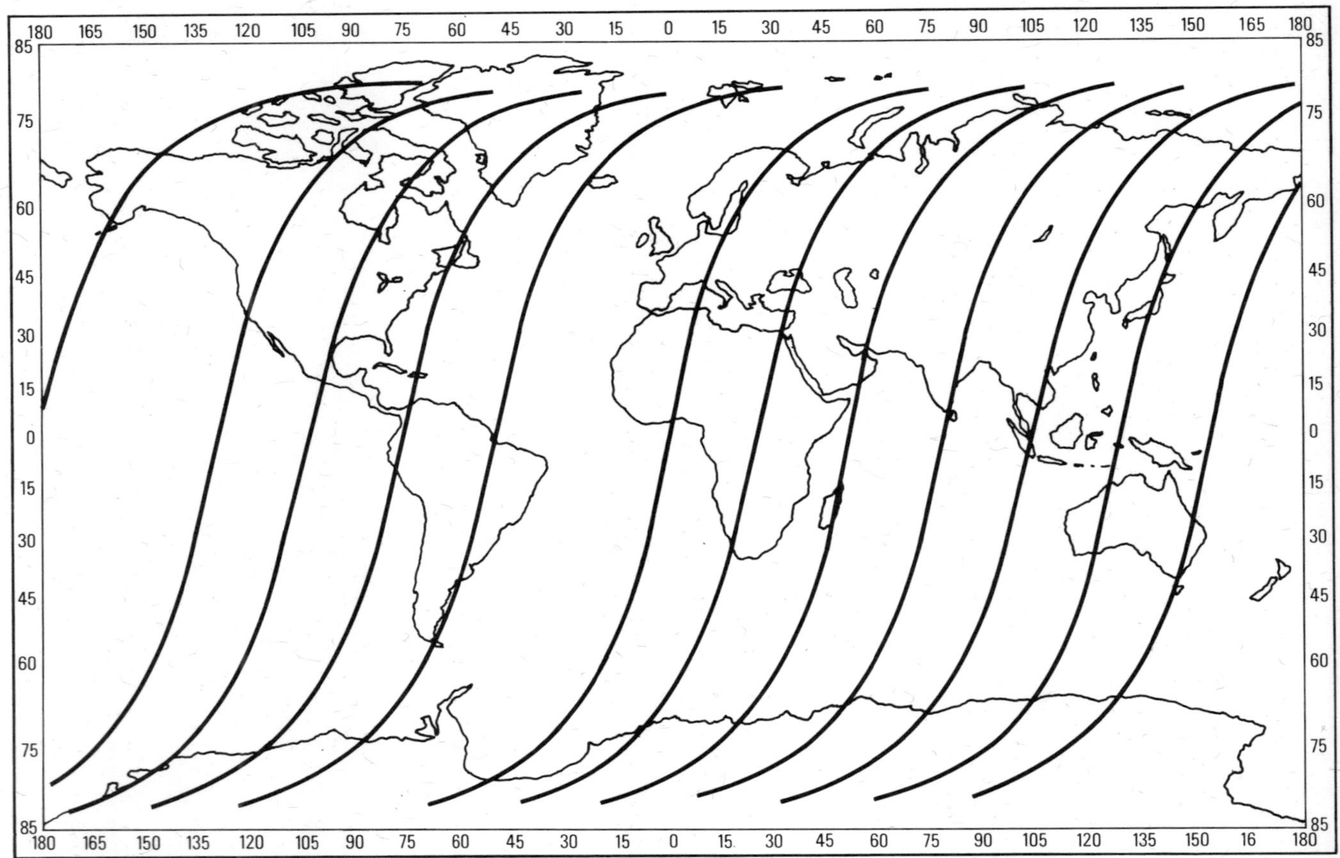

Fig. 1 A typical day's coverage by a polar-orbiting satellite. As the Earth rotates, the satellite's true path relative to the ground forms a helix, trending from east to west. The apparent change of direction at the north and south reflects the distortion introduced by this particular form of projection.

relay systems, and instruments to measure solar proton and electron fluxes. Two basic types of orbit emerged – polar orbits in which the satellites travel close to the Earth at altitudes of several hundred kilometres, with typical globe-circling periods of 90 minutes; and geostationary orbits in which the satellites orbit at great altitudes (35,800 kilometres) above the equator, their speed matching the rotational speed of the Earth. Thus to an observer on the ground the satellite appears to be always in the same spot. Images from satellites in both kinds of orbit will be shown in this chapter. The use of remote sensing by meteorological groups throughout the world has been so intensive, and going on for so long, that most people do not associate the familiar phenomenon of the weather satellite with the term.

At about the same time that TIROS-1 was launched, meteorologists had succeeded in creating numerical models of the atmosphere for the entire planet. The physics necessary for these models had been known for many decades. The set of equations which must be solved – energy, momentum, and mass conservation – are among the most complex and difficult to handle that man has ever produced, and it was not until the advent of the high-speed large-memory computer that attempts could be made to do so for the whole world. After the early solutions had been achieved, it quickly became obvious that the limitation of accurate forecasting was neither physics nor numerics, but the lack of detailed input data over most of the globe. Since no nation or group of nations could afford to cover the oceans with observing ships nor the vast inaccessible land areas with weather stations, the satellite quickly became the prime tool for acquiring large-scale data within small time scales.

The photographs of the Earth taken from Apollo spacecraft showed the cloud structure of half the globe in reasonable detail (Pl. 1). Of course astronauts going from or returning to the home spacecraft could only obtain pictures of it for a few days each way, and computer models need a continuous input to generate reasonably accurate forecasts. This is where the geostationary satellites came to the fore. They are far enough away to see the entire planet, and they orbit with a fixed Earth reference point, thus observing the same weather system sequences at time scales as short as 20 minutes. The Applied Technology Satellite (ATS) series has been providing this kind of data for a number of years. A pair of simultaneous visible and infra-red images of earth taken by ATS-6 on 14 July 1974 (Pls. 2, 3) show how the wave structure associated with the mid-latitude cyclones stands out, how the infra-red images delineate ocean temperature structure (warmer water is darker, cooler water lighter), how the clouds are affected by large mountain ranges. By combining a number of sequential images like these a motion picture can be made which shows the majestic flow of weather systems half a continent in size, the birth and death of frontal systems, the whipping motion of jet streams, and the incubation of hurricanes.

For a more detailed look at weather systems and ocean temperature structure the polar orbiting satellite moving at altitudes of several hundred kilometres fills the bill. In the fifteen years since the start of the TIROS series three more American series have arrived. TIROS-X ended in 1966, to be followed by the ESSA (Environmental Science Services Administration) series, which was followed by two series still in existence, NIMBUS and NOAA (National Oceanographic and Atmospheric Administration, which is the new name of ESSA). Let us examine some of the forces of nature viewed from these marvellous eyes.

The single meteorological phenomenon which has received greatest attention from satellites is the cyclone, for the simple reason that it generates most of the rain and snow falling on earth. Nearly all the weather problems we have to cope with are associated with cyclones (and with hurricanes, which are small, intense cyclones). Twin tropical cyclones as seen by NIMBUS-4 (Pl. 6) reveal details of the cloud structure and how similar the cyclones are. A 'textbook' cyclone imaged by the same satellite is so detailed that various cloud types can be identified (Pl. 4).

NIMBUS-5 carries not only a mapping radiometer operating at visible and infra-red wavelengths, but another operating in the microwave region with a wavelength of 1.55 centimetres. (This instrument, the Electronically Scanned Microwave Radiometer (ESMR), and its unique applications will be discussed later.) By studying such cyclones and fronts at various wavelengths – visible, infra-red and microwave, which have different degrees of cloud penetration – we are becoming more aware of the large, complex energy and momentum transfer occurring in cyclones.

The meteorological satellites also acquire vast amounts of data on the oceans: one of the most interesting ocean images was obtained (Pl. 7) by the infra-red radiometer on NIMBUS-5, in which the start of the Gulf Stream is visible as the result of a colour-enhancing process which brings out considerably more detail than would be seen in the original black-and-white image. The state of Florida is in the centre in yellow and green, while the warmest (red) area is Cuba seen in the southern part of the image. The bright yellow patch north of Florida is a storm, while the dappled red, green and yellow area in the Gulf of Mexico relates to a layer of stratocumulus cloud. The Gulf Stream waters are coloured purple to the north of Cuba and east of Florida. Such colour-enhanced infra-red images of oceans are the best means we have yet had to study the gross behaviour of ocean currents.

Because of the high contrast between water and sea ice, meteorological satellites give excellent data on sea-ice dynamics and structure that could not have been acquired in any other way. Consider the NIMBUS-4 image (Pl. 8) of Scandinavia on 13 April 1970. The sea ice, especially in the Gulf of Bothnia, shows up brighter and crisper than the clouds. A much larger area of sea ice is shown in the NOAA-4 images of the Bering Sea and the eastern Arctic Ocean for 9 April 1975 (Pl. 10). Many of the ice features in this mosaic of three images can be seen through the clouds. Notice the interesting wave eddies formed in the clouds as they are carried southward over the Aleutian Islands. Proceeding north, the sea ice in the Bering Sea can be seen to have recently moved south because the large openings on the south sides of St Lawrence and Nunivak Islands do not have thick ice present. In the Bering Strait the ice is blocked up off the northwest coast of Alaska, a recently re-frozen shore lead is evident, and the ice cover over the Beaufort Sea is very fractured. Sequential sets of such

Fig. 2 Artist's conception of one of the first Nimbus weather satellites in Earth orbit. A photosensitive cell (A), trained on the horizon, keeps the satellite stabilized with the aid of gas jets (B) so that it always points vertically downwards. Two banks of three high-resolution television cameras (C) photograph the cloud cover; infra-red scanners (D) do the same thing when the clouds are in darkness. E is the memory store, which records all these data and releases them, on command, to Earth through the antenna (G). A television camera (F) transmits continuously a picture of the clouds immediately underneath.

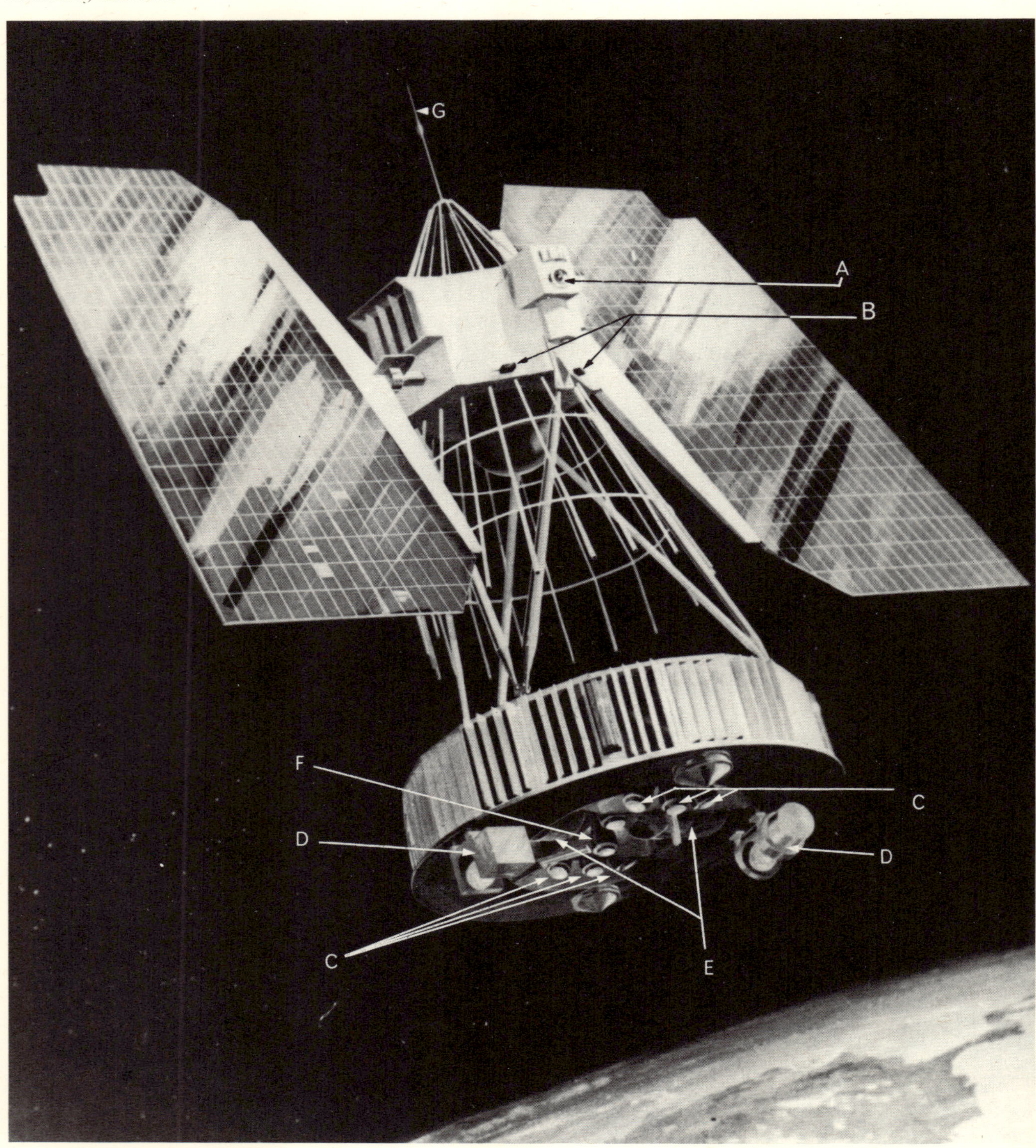

images have been used to study the complex dynamics of sea ice, and we are just starting to use the data in numerical models of ice-covered oceans which will eventually be coupled to numerical weather prediction models.

Meteorological satellites have played, and will continue to play, a very important role in man's future remote-sensing activities. But they are not capable of giving us much of the data urgently needed to understand the working of Spaceship Earth.

A high-resolution look at the Earth

The great success of the meteorological satellites in obtaining large-scale, low-resolution, synoptic images of large-scale phenomena in the atmosphere quickly made scientists in other disciplines aware that for many problems, especially environmental ones, man needed a more detailed high-resolution look at his planet. During the 1960s the increasing social and political focus on environmental degradation resulted in a significant number of people seeing for the first time our species as a crew, whose size is doubling about every thirty-five years, living on a spaceship whose life-support system is showing signs of stress and even failure. Man came to see his planet not as a celestial, orbiting rock, but as an ineffably complex living entity. Thus he finally lost his anthropocentric view of nature, to find himself confronted with the sublime but unsettling realization that he is only a small part of a complex web of life in which an alteration to any part is ultimately felt by all.

Interdependence superseded independence in his new awareness. With sudden clarity he saw that his rampant tool-building growth was endangering not only his own existence but also that of myriad other species as well. His science daily enlarged on the tragedy as the evidence came in, and man realized that he did not even have a means of diagnosing the anthropogenic and natural diseases that were affecting his world. The scope, extent and dynamics of environmental pollution caused by 'popullution', and the complex natural feedback processes occurring because of it were largely undefined.

These were the thoughts that gave birth to LANDSAT-1, the first high-resolution imaging satellite. Since its launch on 23 July 1972 we have indeed learned a new way to see. What do I mean by this? Well, if anything can be said to be common to all space experiments it is that they teach us the same lesson – the results will be unpredictable. When LANDSAT-1 (originally called ERTS-1 for Earth Resources Technology Satellite) was being developed the decision was made to fly a high-resolution imager called a multispectral scanner (MSS). This operated in four spectral bands, and was capable of delineating from space objects as small as 100 metres. To the complete surprise of all who have worked with the imagery, many objects having linear forms smaller than this can easily be seen, and numerous earth features appear that cannot be seen on the surface. Perhaps even more useful, the images are showing us that the shape of remotely sensed objects may be less important than their spectral signatures, those unseen radiations by which many significant surface phenomena can be identified and studied. The range and extent of the application of this imagery in the short time since the launch of LANDSAT-1 is unprecedented – floods, earthquakes, forest fires, volcanic eruptions, sediment transport, strip mining, lake and estuary pollution, urban development, crop census, surging glaciers, snowfall variations, and watershed forecasts, to name but a few. The illustrations used to demonstrate these capabilities are not photographs, but are made up of thousands of lines measured by an optical scanner. Unless otherwise stated, each image covers 34,000 square kilometres of the earth's surface, and each is area-correct – that is, it is not only an image but actually an accurate map of the area. All of them can be used to correct existing maps.

Consider the comparison of a 1:1,000,000 scale map of southeast Texas with a LANDSAT-1 image (Pl. 12) at the same scale. The existing map did not have a large lake shown on it (note white circle). Maps of areas all over the world are daily being corrected with the use of LANDSAT imagery. In places like Antarctica LANDSAT is giving the first accurate maps of the region. Simply said, LANDSAT-1 is the best mapping tool ever created.

Although high-resolution satellite imagery is only a few years old, there are very few who doubt that it is the best way to observe man's impact on his planet. His cities and farmlands, showing up clearly in the images, appear as geometric fungi growing over an amorphously shaped landscape, and can now be measured and quantitatively assessed in relation to the natural forces that nurture and sustain them. The satellite allows us to see vast processes moving as a whole and not in small disparate elements. Many people had assumed that aerial photography was a sufficient tool for man to take a wider look at his activities, and believed that a great number of aircraft flying parallel legs could produce as large a picture of any area as one wished; but such is not the case. Even if one had unlimited aircraft and funds to operate them, the resulting mosaic would not provide the synoptic view (an over-all view at one instant) needed to see rapidly changing phenomena. Neither would such a photograph have the spectral information so necessary to observe most of the phenomena we need to record. Indeed, our experience with aerial photography has shown that it is impossible to make an

Fig. 3 The electromagnetic spectrum. From the ultra-short waves (one Angström unit is one ten-millionth of a millimetre) to the very long radio waves, all are simply different forms of one phenomenon. Satellites 'see' in various bands of this spectrum, such as visible light, infra-red, and the 1.55 cm in the microwave region (approximately over the 'C' in 'Centimetres') used by ESMR.

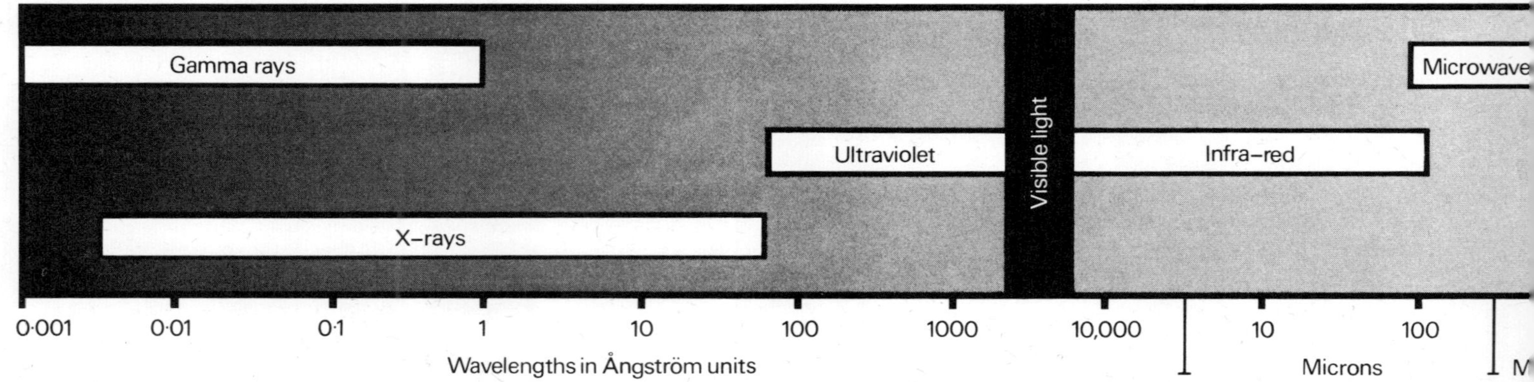

accurate mosaic photograph in even one colour of a large area, since lighting is constantly changing during the time needed to fly over it.

The MSS carried on LANDSAT-1 scans in four discrete regions of the spectrum – green, red, near infra-red, and infra-red. Certain features show up better at one or other of these frequencies. For example, all water bodies are clearer in the infra-red images, whereas geological structures are best in the green. When all four images are combined electronically into one, live vegetation shows up red, has a red signature we say, as in the image of Texas. The various shades of red are the signatures of different kinds of vegetation, and the information content of an image is greatest when all MSS frequencies are used.

The varying signatures from different vegetation make it a very useful tool for studying crops and forests. At present the prime use for LANDSAT data is for the International World Crop Survey Programme which monitors crops worldwide to measure acreage, forecast yield, and look for plant diseases. In the image of the San Joaquin Valley of California (Pl. 13), farm land appears as geometric fingers advancing on the Sierra Nevada Mountains to the east and the Coast Range to the west. Analyses of such images of farmland have shown that growing crops, wet planted fields, ploughed fields, harvested fields etc. can be detected in areas as small as 10 acres, and that the crop identification ability approached or exceeded an accuracy of 90 per cent. A normal crop inventory of an area taking many thousands of man hours can be produced from LANDSAT imagery in less than a hundred hours.

This potential of LANDSAT for land-use classification is immense. Analysis of the image of the San Francisco Bay region (Pl. 14) showed that seventeen distinct use classes could be delineated and mapped. The bright white band in the northeast section is low-level cloud. The white-blue area in San Francisco Bay is a sediment plume caused by fill

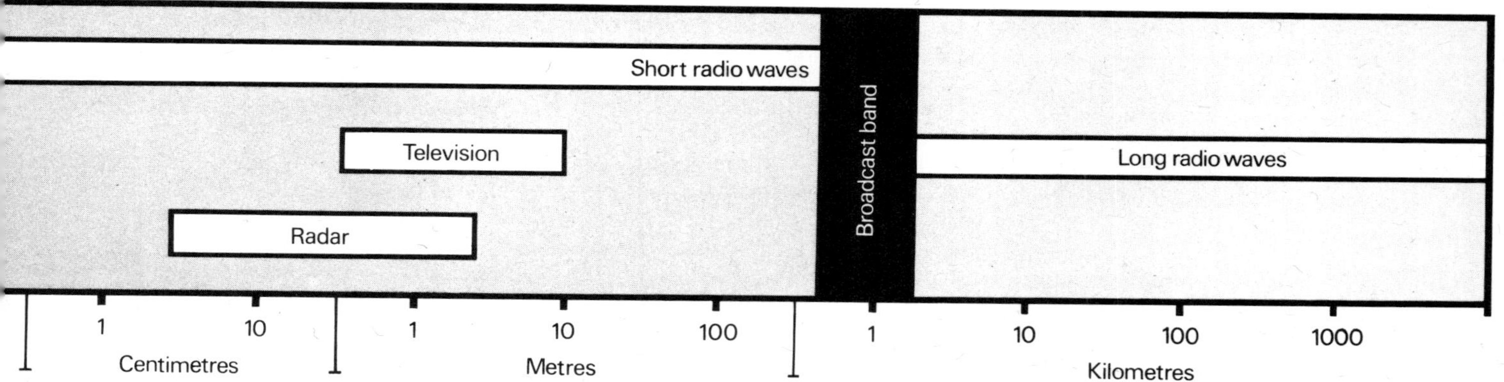

operations, and shows that LANDSAT can be used to monitor both natural and man-made sediment pollution. Less dramatic sediment plumes can be seen at both the north and south ends of San Francisco Bay, and the lineal feature of Golden Gate Bridge is also visible, even though it is only 40 metres wide. Likewise the turbidity variations of lakes, estuaries, and coastal waters can be studied by analysis of sequential LANDSAT images in a far more complete way than is possible by ship and aircraft observations, and at a fraction of the cost.

LANDSAT can also detect forest fires, which are a source of nuclei on which cloud droplets can form. Numerous burnt areas have been observed and occasionally an actual fire is spotted. One of these is shown in an image of part of the Northwest Territories of Canada. A very large tundra fire is seen along the eastern edge with the burn scar plainly visible (Pl. 19). The smoke plume extends northwestward for hundreds of kilometres. The dark areas in the image are tundra lakes; the small white patches are cumulus clouds.

An interesting case of strange objects appearing on images is illustrated in an enlarged picture of an area of southwestern Washington State (Pl. 15), approximately 100 km across. Mount St Helens appears in the northeast part of the image and the Columbia River at the southeast corner. The numerous white polygons covering the western half of the image did not have the 'signatures' of farms, and investigators could not at first identify them. A field trip to the area revealed that all the polygons were areas of recent clearcutting. By recent I mean less than a few years, since new growth would appear with a red signature. This showed that the timber companies were cutting forest at a prodigious rate, no doubt in anticipation of the hopefully soon-to-come day when clearcutting will be outlawed in the United States, as it is in countries with more enlightened environmental laws.

Few scientists have been as thrilled with LANDSAT images of Spaceship Earth as geologists. New or improved small-scale geological maps of many areas are being made from images showing regional landforms, Quaternary deposits, sediment patterns, and the distribution of distinctive features. Existing maps are being checked to correct mislocated or omitted rock-unit contacts, fold axes, lava flows etc. This work is leading directly into various geological applications such as the study of landform structures and dynamic surface processes. Most types of geomorphic units are exceptionally well displayed in the images. An image of part of Central Australia shows the complex structure of the folds with remarkable clarity. No existing geological map of the area revealed the folds in anything like the detail in the image. Another example shows part of Central China, giving the dendritic drainage pattern in extraordinary detail (Pls. 16, 17).

Geological mapping of the Wind River Range, Wyoming, during a five-year period succeeded in locating the major fractures of only 10–15 per cent of the range. Yet one scientist using one LANDSAT image mapped the fracture patterns of the remaining 85 per cent at a comparable level of intensity and accuracy in three hours. It has been estimated that air photography of this area would cost $200,000, and would yield less information than the one image. LANDSAT can also monitor the effects of earthquakes, and since images of essentially all landmasses have been obtained under cloud-free conditions, before-and-after analyses of future earthquake fracture patterns will be possible.

Occasionally volcanoes are actually caught erupting, such as one in the Kurile Islands north of Japan (Pl. 18). The northern half of the image shows an area of white stratocumulus cloud with an interesting vortex pattern around the north end of the island in the centre of the picture. Notice the wave patterns induced in the cloud layer as it flows between the two islands. The most striking feature is the plume of dark smoke emanating from the recently active volcano near the north end of the central island.

Perhaps the most important use that has been made of LANDSAT imagery has been in research associated with water. Recent numerical models relating man and his population-doubling time of 35 years to the resources necessary to sustain him, predict that over much of the Earth water supplies will become critical at about the same time as food supplies. Without an adequate understanding of how water behaves within the complex heat engine called Earth, man will suffer greatly as his numbers expand geometrically. Even with an understanding of water he will undoubtedly suffer unless population growth is checked. We can only hope that along with an increasing understanding of the intense fragility and complexity of our environment we will find a way of making each person realize that he has only the right to replace himself biologically, and no more. Can we create a worldwide ethic that equates the act of a couple having more than two children with murder? But I stray. The reader must excuse me for it is easy to wax philosophical when we consider how fundamental water is to us, and how very little we understand its behaviour.

The problem is that we usually have either too much or too little water, or at best we think we do when it is related to our varying and increasing needs. As far as floods are concerned, we are sure they are too much. The mapping of Mississippi River floods, and records of flash floods in Central Australia have shown the remarkable hydrological applications of LANDSAT. Since most floods move too fast to be sequentially photographed by aircraft, only LANDSAT can in such cases provide the required data on the dynamics of flooding.

Only 2.7 per cent of the water on earth is salt-free, and about 85 per cent of that exists in the form of snow and ice, 90 per cent of it being contained in the Antarctic and Greenland icecaps. Therefore, increased research on snow and ice is essential to our future, and LANDSAT is providing unique data for this work. Only a start has been made, but already the results provide a wonderful contribution. Although snow is a major source of water to mankind, we were unable to delineate its rapidly changing areas on any large scale until the satellite came. Since snow cover can vary rapidly, it has been difficult to study its cause and effect in any way. Now LANDSAT images reveal the complex way in which winter snow melts during spring and summer. Coupled with stream-flow information these provide a more complete understanding of an area's water system and allow run-off forecasts of greater accuracy. Such images can also reveal how thicker and more extensive vegetation occurs on slopes and in valleys where the snow cover is not so great. Likewise as the snow melts, the areas of intense run-off are revealed by a darker signature, due to absorption of moisture by the ground.

An excellent image of western Scotland shows how the winter snow cover can be accurately delineated (Pl. 21). The northeastern part of the image shows stratocumulus cloud cover, but the white areas in the remainder of the picture are either snow or ice. Moray Firth is visible just south of the cloud layer in the north-central part of the image, and Loch Ness can be seen extending southward. Numerous lochs of western Scotland can be seen and Ben Nevis is clearly visible together with numerous other mountains.

Because snow and ice have relatively high reflectance and LANDSAT gives worldwide coverage, such measurements of the global extent of snow and ice cover and its seasonal variations can be made. These observations can develop much insight into the world's freshwater supply and global climatic trends. The monitoring of glaciers as well as snowfields can yield vital information concerning lakes and streams fed by glacier melt, and the movement of glaciers and their mass balance variations can be very sensitive indicators of climatic change. LANDSAT is therefore a new and exciting tool for glaciological studies, providing data on a scale which could not be accumulated by the world's glaciologists in centuries. Not only does it offer wide observations over inaccessible regions, which is where most glaciers are, but its multispectral repetitive coverage yields observations of moraines, movements, snowlines and other more subtle features. A particular example of such capability is the recording of glacier surges, those sudden unusually rapid advances of glaciers which can cause devastating floods by blocking, then releasing large volumes of melt water.

One, perhaps symbolic, LANDSAT image is of a single place on our spaceship that has all known climate zones and vegetation types in its domain, and is therefore a microcosm containing the complex processes that shape our existence – Kilimanjaro (Pl. 20). A white cloud cap sits above and slightly to the south of the peak. Beneath and just north of this the snow-covered summit is visible. Downslope from the snow is a dark region of minimal vegetation, followed by concentric bands of increasingly dense growth until the brightest red shows tropical growth on the lower slopes. The snow melt does not go far, because we can see that beyond the lush growth the mountain is almost surrounded by a dark area indicating sparse vegetation into which the streams with their heavier growth penetrate and disappear.

Yes, LANDSAT has taught man a new way to see Spaceship Earth.

The day-or-night, clear-or-cloudy sensors

All the foregoing satellite sensors operate in either the visible or infra-red regions of the electromagnetic spectrum, say in wavelengths ranging from 0.4 to 8.0 micrometres. There were two reasons for carrying these sensors on the first generation of scientific satellites. First, the level of sensor technology and the means of handling the data were far more advanced in these frequencies than in the far infra-red and microwave regions, a much broader spectral range spanning wavelengths of about ten micrometres to tens of metres – in other words from just beyond visible wavelengths all the way to short radio waves. Secondly, those of the scientific community who first seized on the remote-sensing satellite as a research tool were the meteorologists, who were primarily interested in obtaining synoptic images of clouds which could best be done by using visible and infra-red sensors. No other group of scientists reacted so rapidly and so positively to the possibilities of remote sensing. As a result of their great zeal and work they succeeded in getting the first weather satellite launched as early as 1960. It took more than a decade longer to launch LANDSAT-1, while the largely oceanographic satellite, SEASAT-A, is still on the drawing boards. Nevertheless the TIROS, NIMBUS, and NOAA series, primarily designed for meteorological applications, afforded a great deal of data needed by a variety of geophysical disciplines.

Nothing succeeds like success, and it did not take long for other investigators to climb aboard the remote-sensing band wagon. One great problem quickly manifested itself – the phenomenon of most interest to the meteorologists, the clouds, obscured the areas of interest to most other scientists, the surface of the oceans and continents. At a given time clouds cover approximately one-half of the surface of the earth, and infra-red as well as visible radiation emitted or reflected by its surface is absorbed and diffused by cloud droplets and crystals. We have seen how high-resolution imagery of limited areas obtained by LANDSAT-1 during cloud-free conditions provides very useful data for a wide variety of investigations; however, giving full, large-scale coverage of the surface was not possible using infra-red and visible light sensors. Any scientific investigation of phenomena involving variations over large areas in a short time – such as sea ice, tsunamis, ocean-wave spectra, rainfall and snowfall – were hampered by lack of data, while at the same time the meteorologists suffered from a surfeit. Furthermore, visible and infra-red radiation emanating from any surface gives information only about the state of the surface and nothing about what is going on beneath it. This is because radiation of such short wavelengths is lacking in penetration.

With these considerations in mind, renewed attention was given in the mid-1960s to the possibility of mounting microwave sensors on satellites. Since cloud particles are small, it was possible to select a microwave sensor with a wavelength of several centimetres that could look through clouds. Because all surfaces emit microwave radiation, it was also possible to observe surfaces in the dark. These possibilities had been known for a long time, but the technology needed to realize them did not exist until quite recently. Very rapid advances during the last decade in antenna and oscillator design have opened an exciting new chapter in man's view of his planet because his 'eye' can now be equipped with a day-or-night, clear-or-cloudy sensor.

There are basically two ways to use microwave radiation – active and passive. Active microwave radiometers are those that emit the energy which is received. The most generally known type of this kind is radar, an acronym created from Radio Detection And Ranging, since its early use was for detecting military targets. Modern remote-sensing radars are substantially different from their predecessors in that they scan in a vertical plane rather than a horizontal one. Side-looking airborne radar (SLAR) scans through the angle from vertical to horizontal on both sides of an aircraft, and the scanning rate is synchronized with the aircraft speed to produce area-correct images. A recent image (Pl. 22) of the sea ice off the north coast of Alaska at Point Barrow was obtained through a solid overcast which totally obscured the surface. Each band looks almost like a photograph, and is marked with white fiducial lines five kilometres apart. This image shows the structure of the ice in great detail, with leads (open water areas appearing dark), first-year ice and multi-year ice floes clearly visible. When a layman sees one of these SLAR images taken through cloud and in the dark, the first question he asks is, 'Why don't you have one of these radars in a satellite?' The answer is simple – radars, because they are active systems, demand a great deal of energy, and no observational satellite yet made has had sufficient to run one. A secondary, though almost equally important, consideration is that conventional radars need large antennae, and to achieve a sufficiently high resolution from satellite altitudes the antennae would have to be immense, in the order of tens of metres. Recent advances in synthetic aperture radars (SAR) now make it possible to mount radars on satellites and NASA plans to fly one on SEASAT-A, scheduled to be launched in early 1978.

Passive microwave radiometry is another matter entirely. A passive sensor measures the amount of energy naturally emanating from a scene, and the signal received by the

Fig. 4 Arctic ice cover, as shown by ESMR's microwave scanning, and by a naval atlas. The latter's delineation, based on long-term averages of ship and aircraft reports, is often quite erroneous.

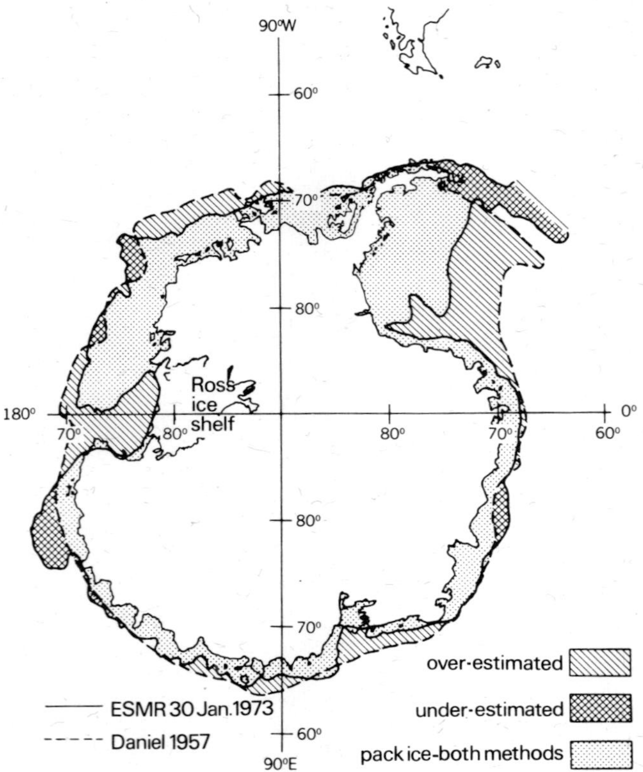

antenna includes several components – an emittance component which is related to the surface temperature, a transmitted component having a subsurface origin, and a reflected component. For the shorter microwave wavelengths, say from a millimetre to several centimetres, the opacity and temperature of the intervening atmosphere also contribute to the received signal. The composite signal is called the brightness temperature. Because of the complexity of the physics of emissions at these wavelengths the interpretation of the signal is difficult, so difficult indeed that we do not yet know how to interpret the signatures (received brightness temperature) of many substances on earth. But these complexities are well worth working with because of the penetration capabilities of microwaves. Information about subsurface conditions is, for many scientific problems, more important than information about the surface itself – for example, synoptic measurements of soil moisture.

Passive microwave sensors have been flown on research aircraft since the early 1960s. The first one flown on a satellite is the electronically scanned microwave radiometer (ESMR) on board NIMBUS-5 which was launched in December 1972. For a number of years my colleagues and I have been flying two special NASA research aircraft, Galileo I and Galileo II, over various parts of the earth, getting passive microwave images to help us interpret the satellite ESMR images. The amount of data in each ESMR image is staggering, covering a very wide range of physical effects, but much remains to be done before we can gather the harvest.

The ESMR on NIMBUS-5 sees only one wavelength, 1.55 centimetres. This particular one was chosen for a variety of tasks including the remote sensing of tropical storms with large droplets. Therefore the images, except those of polar regions where such droplets do not exist, will have areas in which the signatures are the result of storms. For future ESMRS with wavelengths greater than about three centimetres the images will give signatures only of the surface – land, water, ice.

The first ESMR image of the entire earth was constructed from data acquired between 12 and 16 January 1973. Each data cell covers an area approximately 25 kilometres across, and a specific colour is assigned to given ranges of brightness temperatures with the values for each in degrees Kelvin (°K)* given at the lower edge of the image (Pl. 23).

The most striking feature is the strong contrast between land and water, with an average difference of brightness temperature of nearly 160°K. Central South America, central Australia and south and central Africa show the

* 0°C = 273°K: 100°C = 373°K.

Fig. 5 *The same kind of scan, for the Antarctic. Old-style ice-mapping methods will certainly be superseded by the quicker and more accurate ESMR method.*

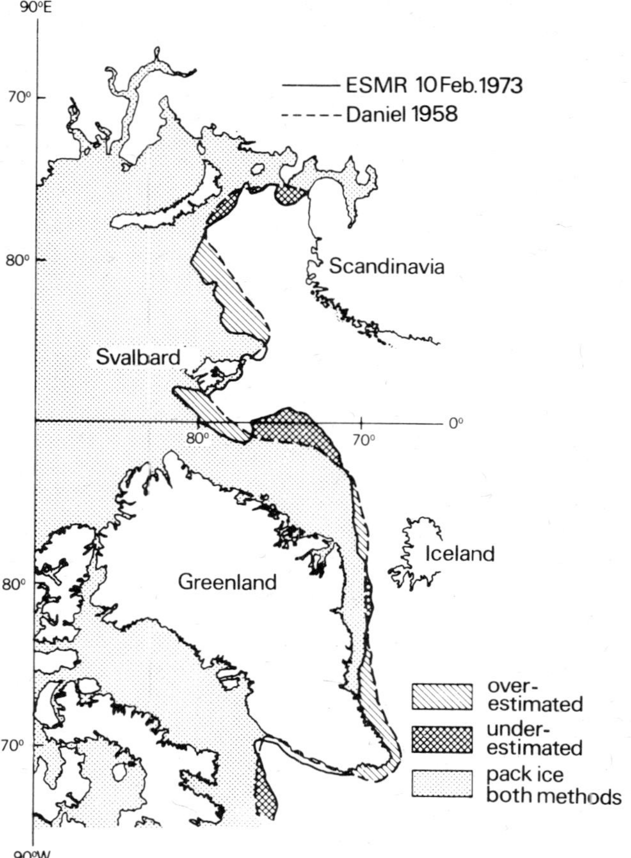

highest brightness temperatures, owing to two effects: land with vegetation has a warmer signature than desert, and hot land has a warm signature. The lowest brightness temperatures occur over the oceans in the temperate regions. Soil moisture effects can be seen in the St Lawrence and Mississippi valleys, where the relatively damp ground partially covered with dead vegetation has a lower brightness temperature than its surroundings. The sharp boundaries between the Sahara and central Africa, and between the South American coastal desert and the Andes plateau, reflect soil moisture and also soil fertility through the resulting vegetation cover.

The low brightness temperature over the oceans is strongly increased by the rain and large cloud droplets in the intervening atmosphere. The band circling the globe at the equator, having a dark-green or bright-blue signature (170°K to 189°K), is associated with the intertropical convergence zone, a region of strong vertical motion in the atmosphere which forms extensive large cumulo-nimbus clouds. Other bands extending towards the higher latitudes correspond to extratropical weather fronts. The series of bands extending from Japan to the west coast of the United States represents the sequential positions of a fast-moving storm system which migrated rapidly eastward during the five days over which the image was formed.

In a more detailed ESMR of Europe (Pl. 24) the combined soil moisture and vegetation brightness temperature is seen to increase gradually from north to south. Sequential images of this kind will enable us to study the variability of soil moisture supply and its relation to crop productivity.

Perhaps the most exciting ESMR images have been those of polar regions because real advances in our understanding of the dynamics and morphology of sea ice have resulted from them. Sea ice covers approximately 13 per cent of the world's oceans at any given time, but its influence on world climate and weather is a most significant part of the air–ocean interface because it acts like a massive heat transfer valve between a very cold atmosphere (mean temperature −30°C) and the much warmer oceans (mean surface water temperature −1.5°C). Our knowledge about the polar sea ice canopies has always been meagre because of the logistic difficulties involved. We know from observations by ships and ice drifting stations that sea ice can move very fast – velocities of 40 kilometres per day are not uncommon – but man has had no means of observing its gross behaviour before the advent of ESMR. The early meteorological satellites sensing in the visible and infra-red were unable to give the needed data since these ice canopies are in the dark for half the year, and when they are sunlit they are cloud-covered 80 per cent of the time. Now ESMR images of the Arctic have shown that great differences can exist between the actual ice cover and the long-term average boundaries given in atlases, which have been compiled from ship and aircraft reports. They also reveal the different areas of young first-year ice and multi-year ice. Similar differences can be seen in the Antarctic, where the variation from atlas presentation is even greater. Clearly the seasonal changes of both polar ice canopies can be seen on ESMR imagery with an accuracy not even dreamed of a decade ago.

These early images show us that science has been woefully informed about much of our planet, and we may be sure that in the future ESMR will help us to develop a clearer understanding of the complex atmosphere–ocean–ice–land interaction that determines the well-being of Spaceship Earth.

Whither the scientific satellite?

With the inventions of the wheel and the internal-combustion engine mankind was not given the option to turn back and forgo their use. Man and the tools he creates become locked into an ongoing relationship in which the tools can both improve and degrade his quality of life, with good and bad possibilities abounding. So it is with the scientific satellite. We of this century know too well the profound social and environmental decay induced by misuse of tools which were optimistically conceived of in the last century as the means of creating Utopia. When I consider the development of the automobile and aeroplane, guided by the absurd philosophy that to make them bigger and faster was to make them more beneficial to society, I am reminded of Thoreau's accurately presaged fear of a world in which 'men become the tools of their tools'.

The scientific satellite is not only here to stay but will undoubtedly be increasingly used in the foreseeable future. Whether or not they become increasingly beneficial to society is up to us. I hope I have convinced the reader that the potential for great benefit to mankind is real. Satellite observations of the environment may well become the most effective means by which we are able to assess and eventually control ecological degradation. They are capable of providing the kind of sequential, synoptic data needed for a clearer understanding of the basic geophysical and biological workings of our planet.

The advantages are easy to see, but can the same be said of the disadvantages? All kinds of readjustments must be made by man when a powerful new tool is put to use. The grim landscape of technological history is strewn with cases in which the desire to exploit the opportunities cancel out concern for the side effects; DDT is a good example. What are some of the problems?

I believe that the foremost is fair sharing of information. In the food-and-resource-short world we are rapidly approaching, it is imperative that all people, and not just the technologically advanced few, have access to satellite data relevant to their needs. Consider the political and social effects if one or several nations with the aid of secret satellite data discovered untapped critical minerals, found out how to track large schools of pelagic fish, developed improved techniques for worldwide crop forecasts, and did not share this knowledge. The case for international co-operation in the use of scientific satellites is absolute; there is no alternative. All peoples are interdependent, especially concerning the state of Spaceship Earth. In this regard, the record gives some cause for optimism. The World Crop Survey using LANDSAT data has been a success. The Apollo-Soyuz rendezvous has shown that international co-operation in manned as well as unmanned spaceflight is possible.

Another problem in the use of scientific satellites involves their immense cost. The greater part of the burden of designing, launching and guiding them, and retrieving and distributing the data, has been borne by the United States. With the increasing number and complexity of satellites, that country has been forced to spend more and more of its resources on social needs, therefore many voices are asking that the burden of providing the satellite information to other nations be partly borne by them. They point out that roughly $100 billion has been spent on space since 1961, and that such a rate of expenditure cannot be maintained. Certainly some international means of sharing both the data and the burden must be found.

What will the future satellite be like? The platforms are unlikely to evolve as fast as the sensors, since they are now capable of doing essentially everything demanded of them. They fly at altitudes ranging from near-earth orbits with periods of rotation of 1½ hours, to geosynchronous orbits of six earth radii. They carry fuel cells and solar panels enabling them to operate for several years with only minor steering corrections dictated from earth.

On the other hand, the evolution of the sensors is happening so fast that even those of us involved in the space programme have a difficult time keeping up with the progress. One could say that this evolution is constantly aimed at achieving three basic things. First, increased resolution. The LANDSAT imagery with its 100-metre resolution was a landmark, but the need for higher-resolution data studies has become obvious for such things as crop surveys, and infra-red sensing for many tasks such as delineating ocean currents.

The second evolutionary aim is directed at achieving an all-weather, day-or-night microwave sensor with high resolution. The ESMR imagery was a great advance, providing new understanding of many natural phenomena, especially polar ice; but its footprint of 25 kilometres drastically limits its use. The proposed launching of a synthetic-aperture radar in 1978 may be expected to provide yet another landmark.

The third evolutionary aim is increased spectral resolution. The four spectral bands on LANDSAT are most useful, but certain crop types could be better classified using two more bands. There is no way of predicting precisely which visible spectral bands will prove most suitable for which task, therefore as new needs appear and new techniques are created, more varied and sharper spectral bands will be employed.

Undoubtedly there will be problems, as there are with all new tools, but I believe that the risks are well worth the potential rewards. For a scientist involved in this work these are very exciting times, and I know that I shall never again do such thrilling research. For the non-scientist the excitement is also there. Even the most disinterested and casual peruser of the pictures and images of the earth must be aroused to a new understanding and perception of his planet. Being able to see our lands and oceans, to watch their seasons and motions, to note the grand feedback mechanisms that determine their climates, and to perceive the effects of pollution, is to become closer to Earth. The new views simultaneously show us nature's grandeur and intense fragility, and we can go forward not only with a clearer understanding, but also with a thrill. Would not Shelley's Apollo have been thrilled to behold the earth through such eyes as these?

Acknowledgement

This chapter could never have been written without the generous help of six scientists of the Goddard Space Flight Center, NASA. The one person who deserves the most credit for the success of Landsat and other sensor systems discussed is Dr William Nordberg, who is in charge of the Applications Directorate, and it was he who made it possible for me to obtain most of the images shown. His assistant Mr Charles Bohn succeeded in finding the most beautiful Landsat images from among the tens of thousands stored in the data center. Dr Per Gloersen, who is a leader in the field of microwave remote sensing, provided the ESMR images. Drs Fritz Hassler and John Theon kindly contributed the meteorological images, and Dr Warren Hovis is responsible for the magnificent colour-enhanced view of the Gulf Stream.

Suggestions for further reading

E. C. Barrett: *Climatology from Satellites*. Methuen, London, 1974.

Louis J. Battan: *Radar Observation of the Atmosphere*. Chicago University Press, 1973.

Desmond King-Hele: *Observing Earth Satellites*. Macmillan, London, 1966.

Howard Miles (ed.): *Artificial Satellite Observing*. Faber & Faber, London, 1974.

A new look at Spaceship Earth is given by satellites, manned and unmanned. The picture opposite, photographed from an Apollo spacecraft, shows the entire African continent in reasonable detail, and much of the Antarctic ice cap. Madagascar and Arabia are clearly visible, and the cloudless expanse of the Sahara. Photographs like this show the cloud patterns of nearly half the globe: note the equatorial cloud belt over Africa, northern Madagascar and the Indian Ocean, also the swirling spiral of a high-pressure area (lower right). This is an example of what the wavelengths of visible light can show. Other, unseen forms of radiation can be received by satellites – microwaves, infra-red, or a combination of infra-red with other colours in multi-spectral scanning – to give a wide range of information in extraordinary detail. Satellites are not only a new way of viewing natural and man-made phenomena: they have radically changed our view of our crowded, ineffably complex planet.

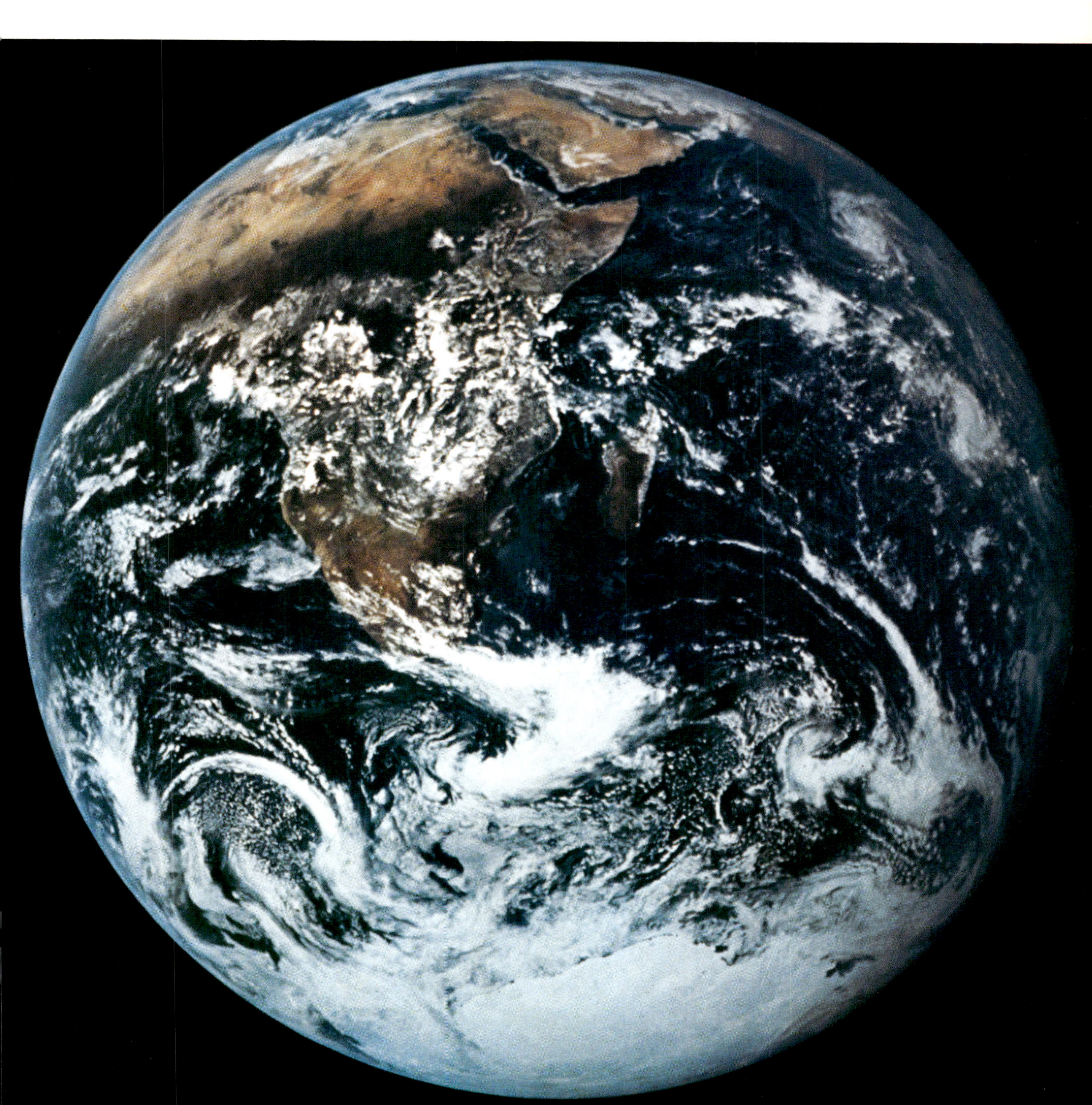

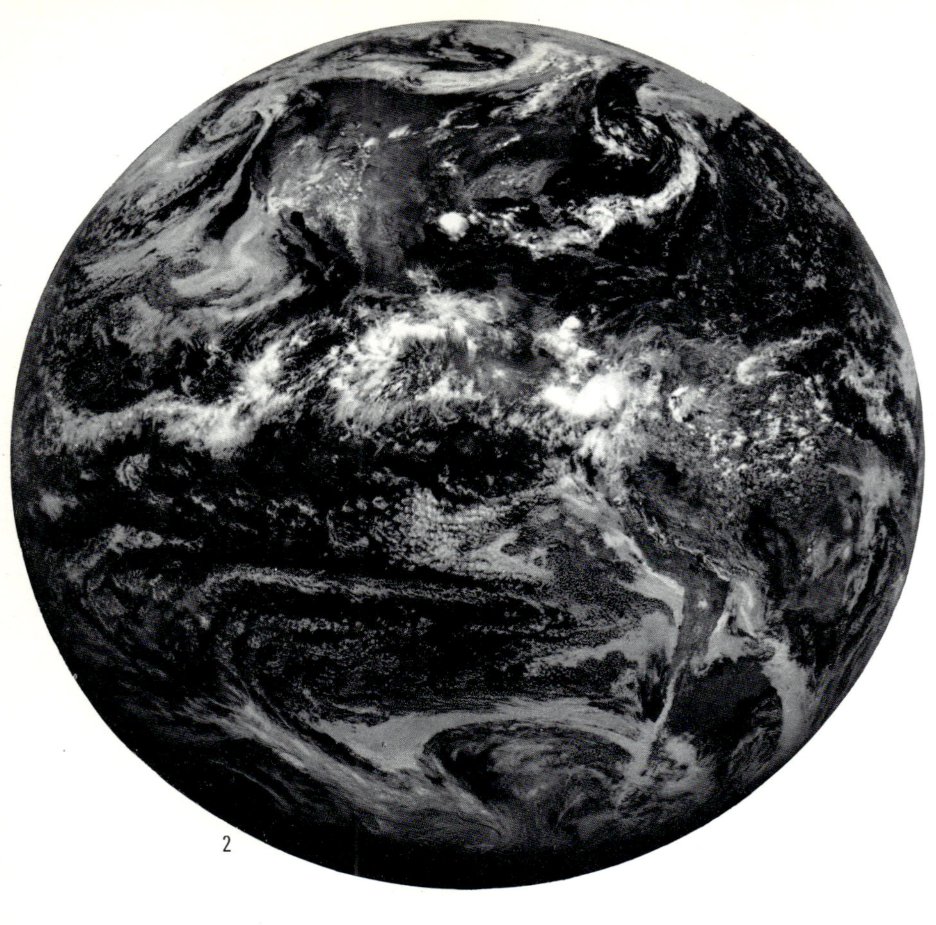

2

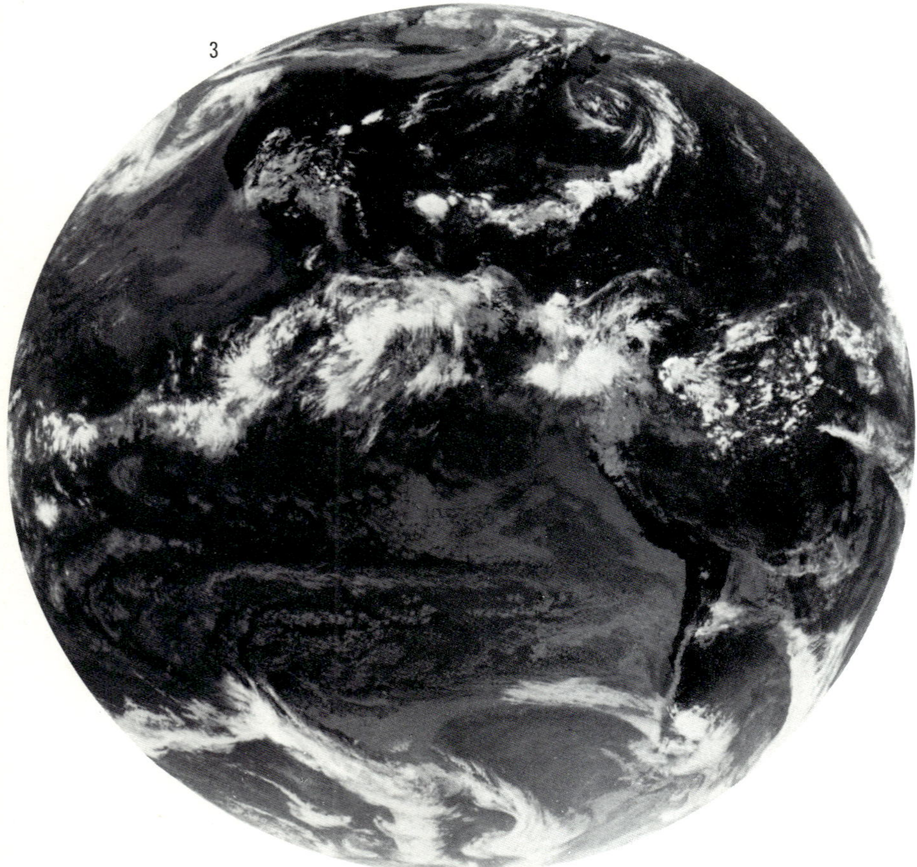

3

A satellite's view of the Americas. The Applied Technology satellite (ATS) took these simultaneous pictures in visible light (2) and infra-red (3) over the Pacific, showing the west coast of North and Sout America through almost its entire length. The infra-red image makes things stand o more clearly, such as the cloud patterns of the mid-latitude cyclones, one off northerr California (top left), one to the south of Nova Scotia (top right). It also indicates ocean temperatures, showing the warmer areas darker and the cooler water lighter.

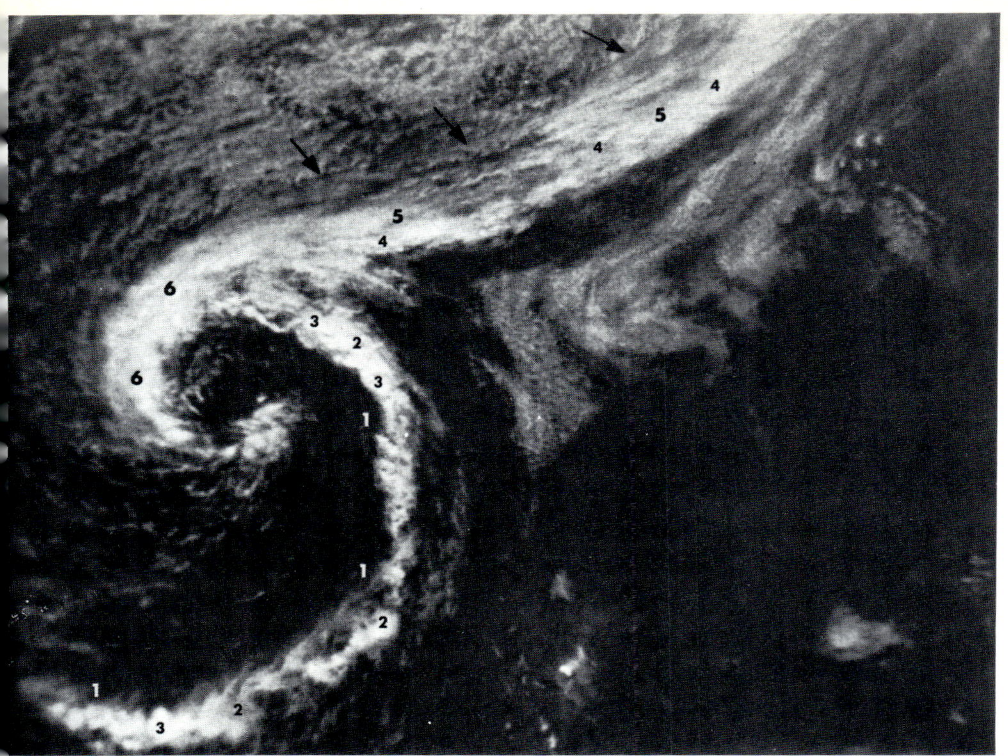

Weather in the making is shown by this 'textbook' example of a low-pressure area in mid-Atlantic (4), photographed by Nimbus-4. The surface analysis (5) shows the meteorologist's interpretation of what the camera sees. The numbers on the photograph pick out the cold front *1*, marked by cumulus clouds *2*, some of considerable height *3*. Bands of cirrus cloud *4* can be seen along the warm front *5* and in the occlusion *6*, the area where the cold front has caught up the warm front and is advancing underneath it. Note the abrupt end of the cirrus band (arrows); this marks the course of the jet stream north of the warm front.

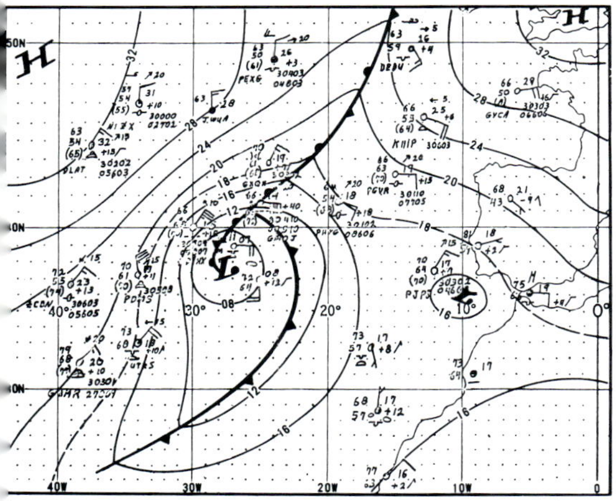

Twin tropical cyclones south of India, each the mirror image of the other, make clear the Coriolis effect: cyclones move anti-clockwise north of the equator, clockwise in the southern hemisphere (6).

4

6

Relative Temperature

Cold Cool Warm

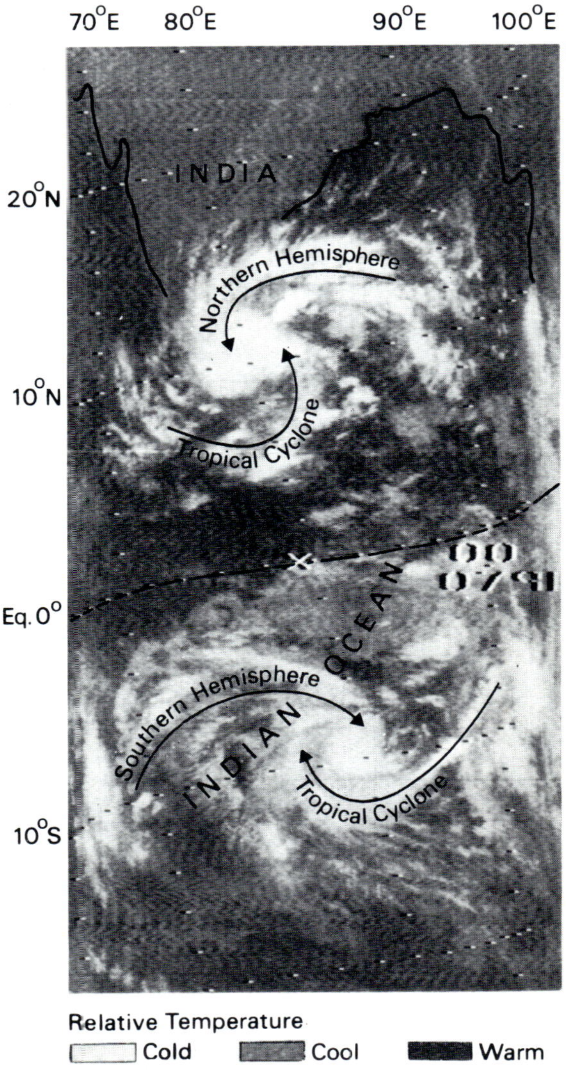

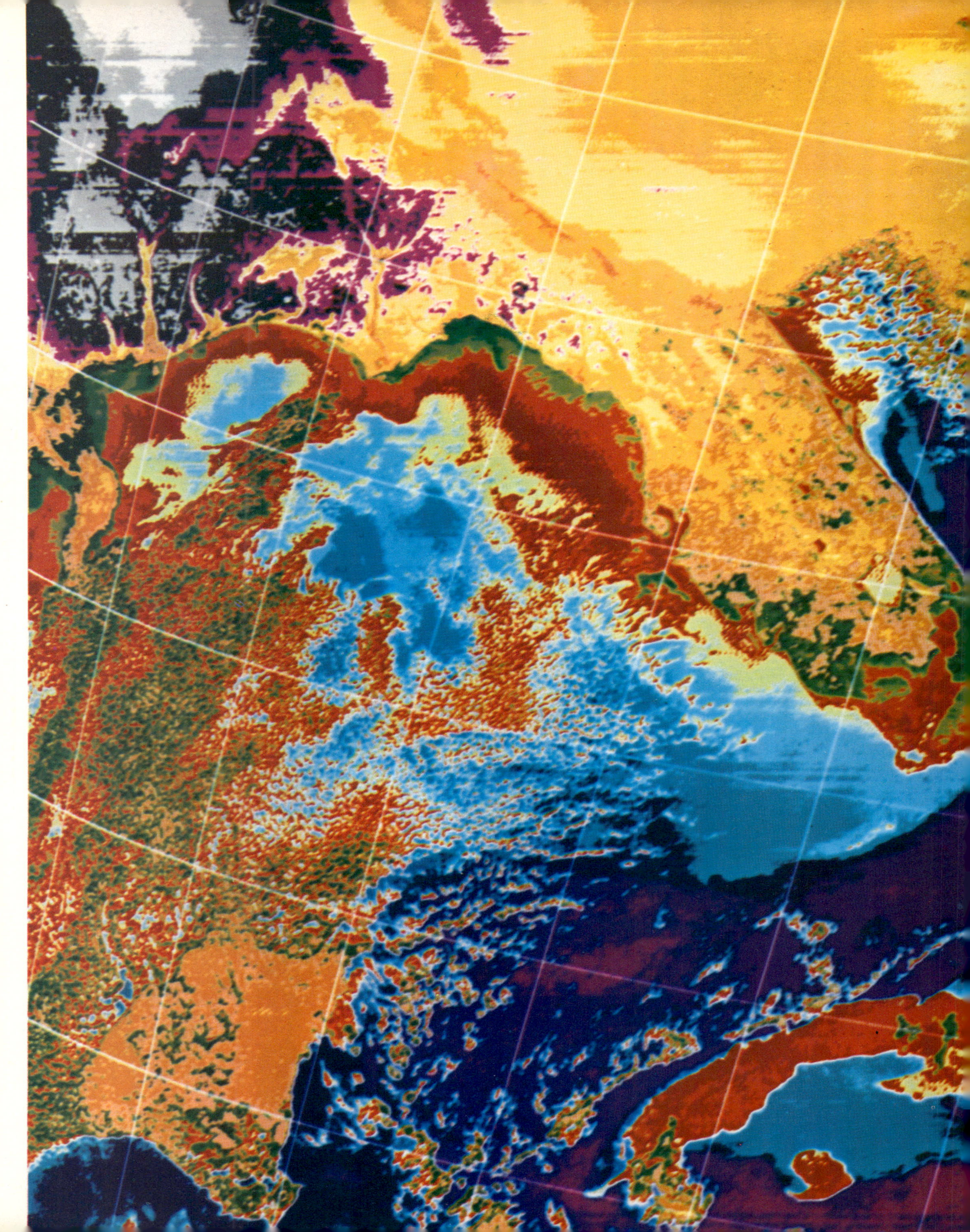

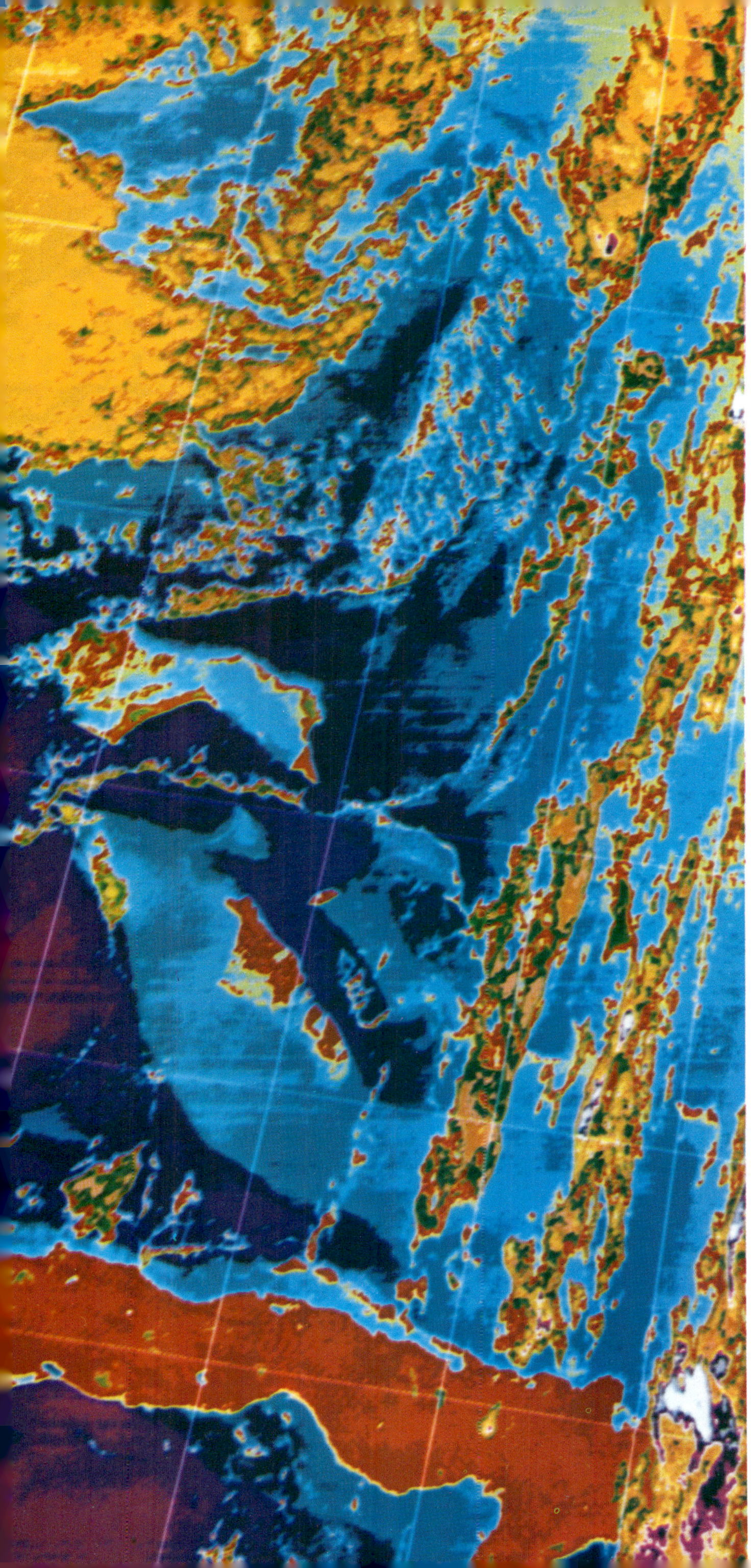

7

Temperature translated into colour by a process which enhances the monochrome infra-red picture to bring out hidden detail makes ocean currents strikingly visible. The red-orange strip at the bottom is Cuba, and the Florida peninsula can be seen to the north of it. Between them is the purple (warm) water of the Gulf Stream. The yellow (cool) patch north of Florida is a storm area, and the dappling of green and red over the Gulf of Mexico is a layer of cloud.

8

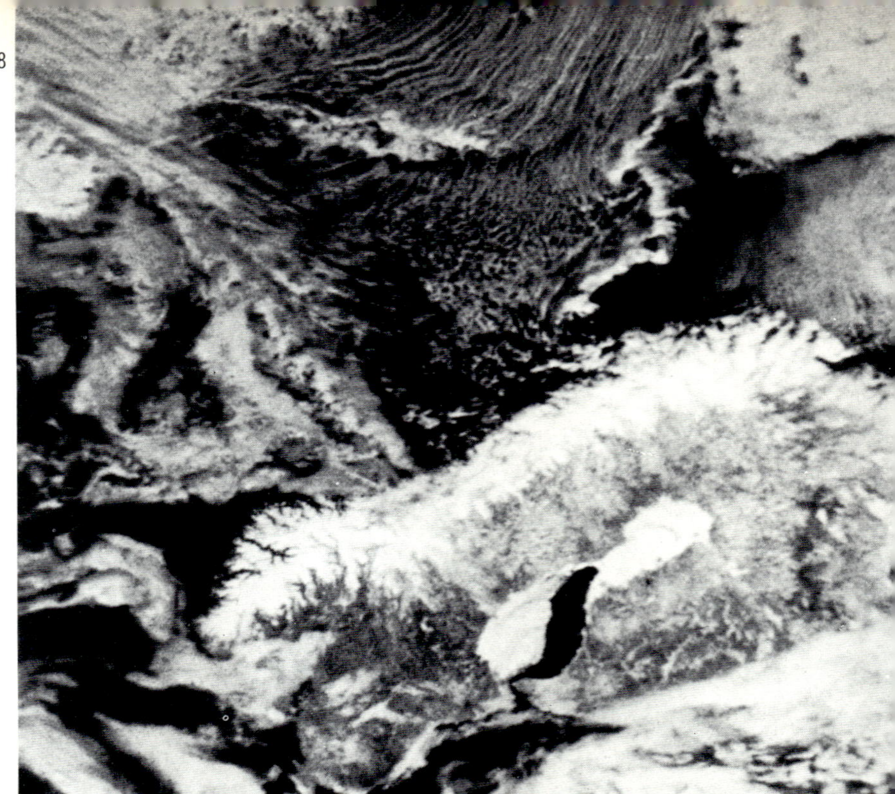

10

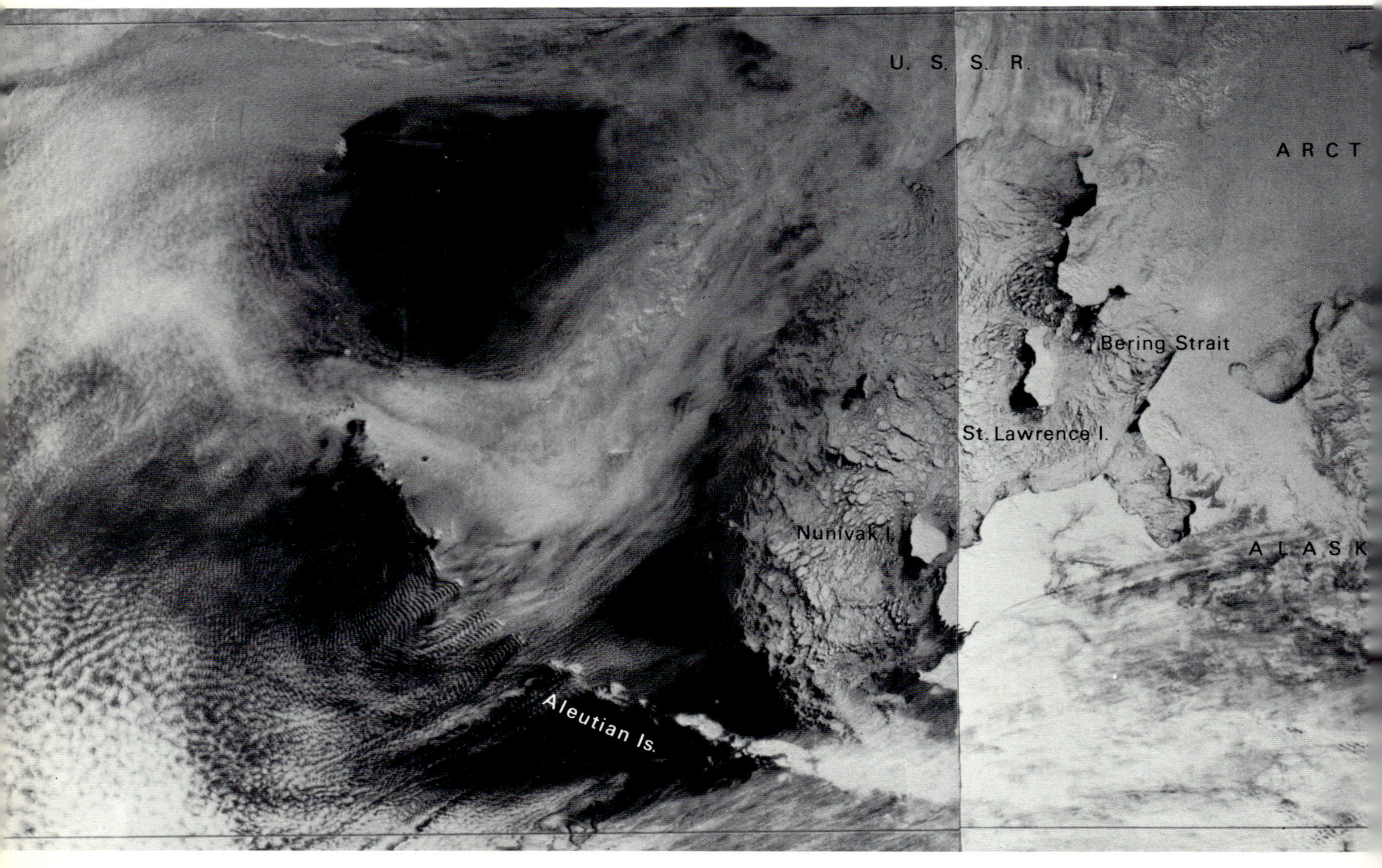

U. S. S. R.

A R C T

Bering Strait

St. Lawrence I.

Nunivak I.

A L A S K

Aleutian Is.

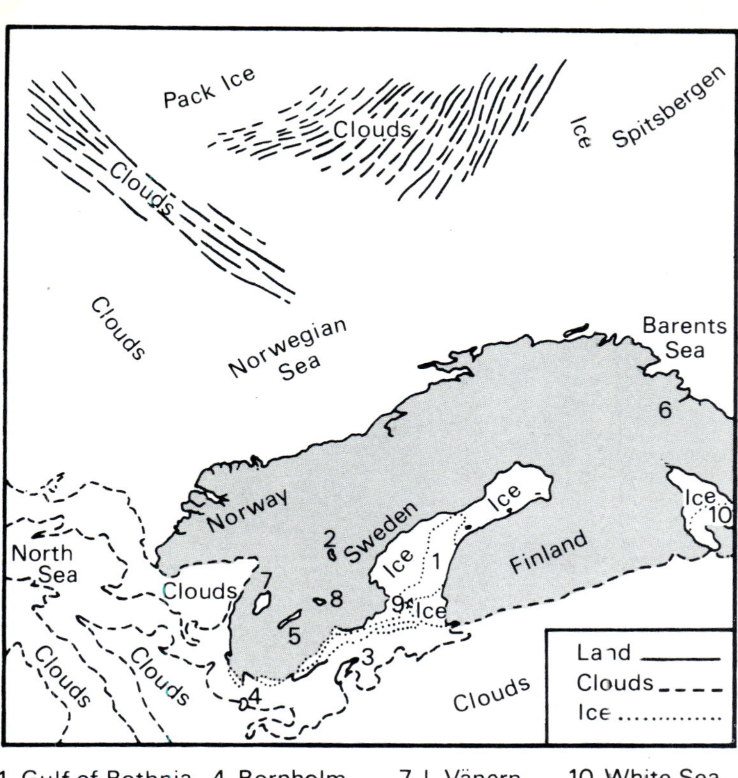

Snow, ice and cloud over and around Scandinavia (8) were picked out with beautiful clarity by Nimbus-4 in April 1970, when the Gulf of Bothnia was still partly ice-covered. The key (9) shows the salient features, from the Arctic pack ice to a layer of cloud over northern Russia. A mosaic of three satellite pictures (10) taken over the Bering Strait and the eastern Arctic shows a much larger area of sea ice; sequences of such photographs give a new understanding of the large-scale dynamics of ice movement. Dark patches south of St Lawrence and Nunivak Islands indicate that the ice has recently moved south, and the clear water has not completely refrozen. Ice on the Beaufort Sea, too, is much broken up.

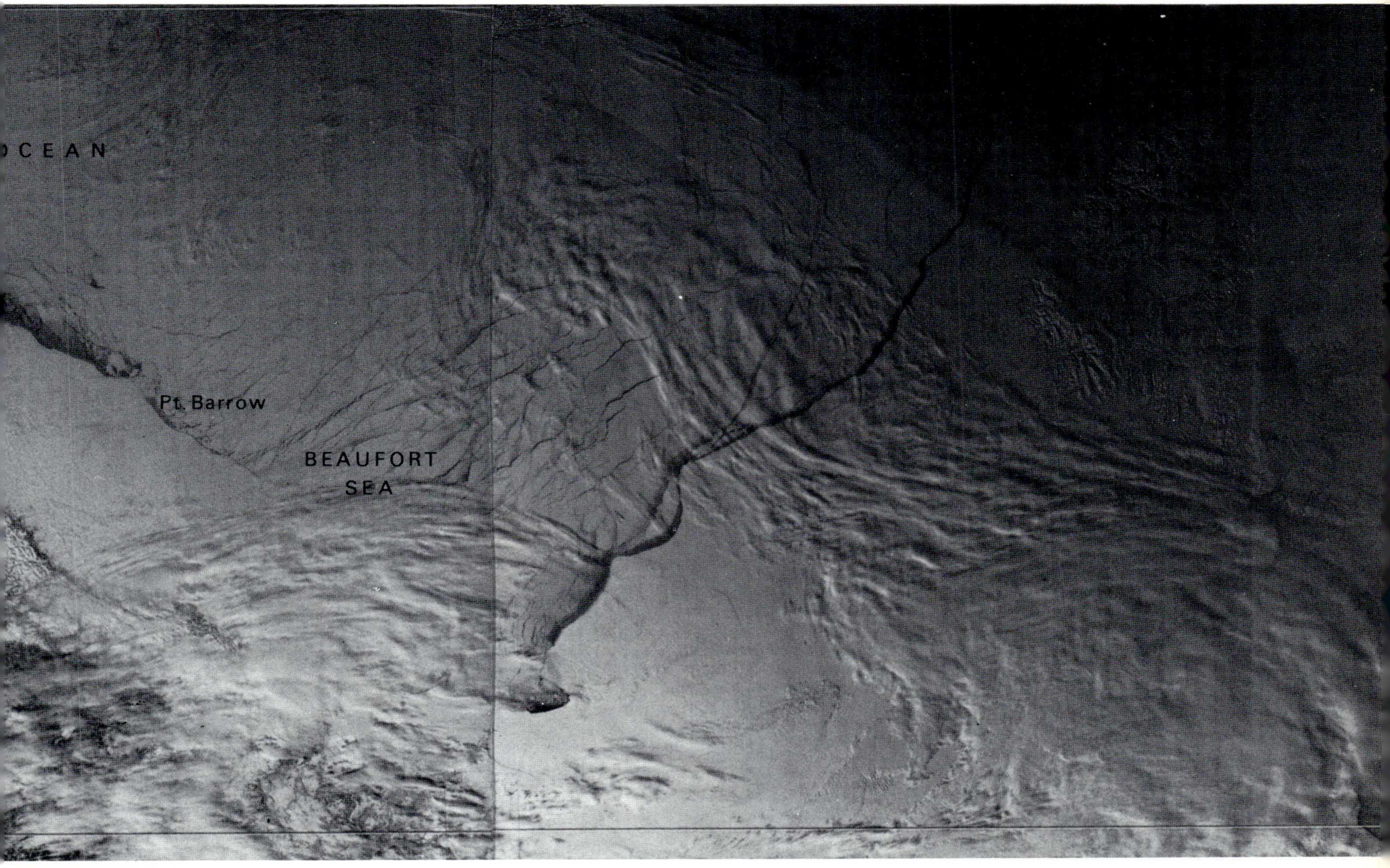

OCEAN

Pt. Barrow

BEAUFORT SEA

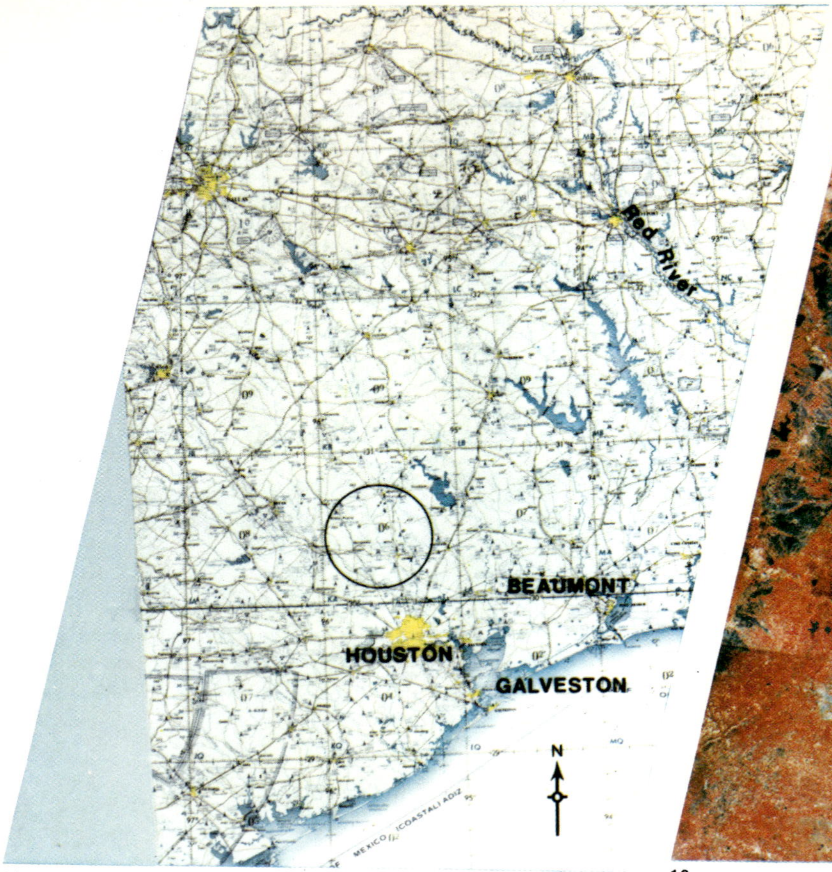

11

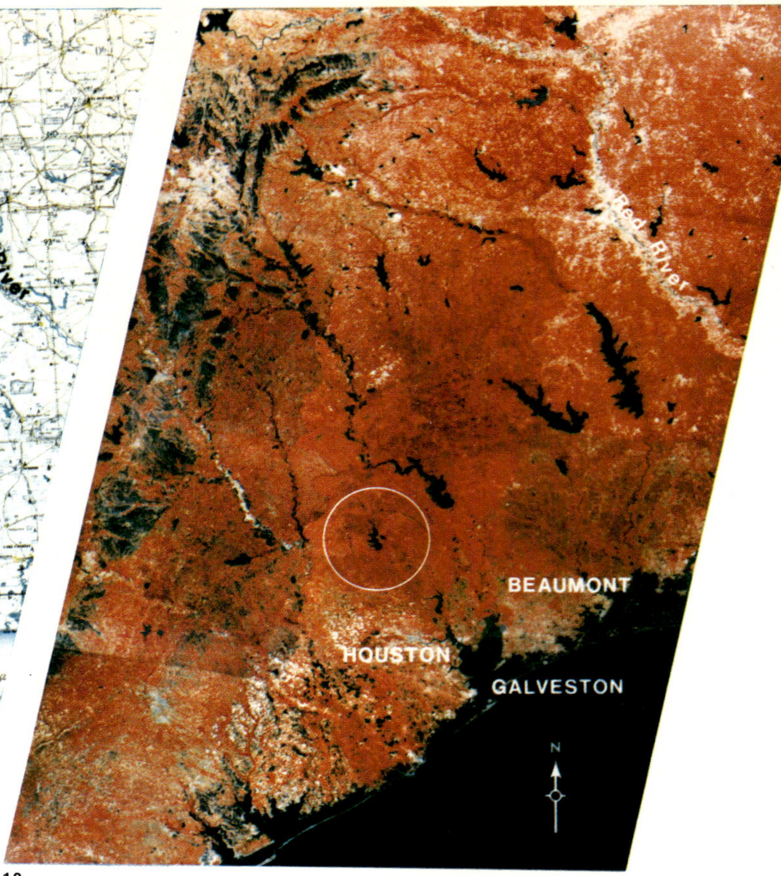

12

14

For a really high-resolution view of the planet, the LANDSAT series of satellites was devised, using not conventional photography but a multi-spectral scanner producing images made up of thousands of lines measured by an optical scanner. The detail, resolution and accuracy of these images are such that the they can even be used to correct maps. Compare the map of south-east Texas (11) with the LANDSAT image of the same area to the same scale (12): the latter shows (in the white circle) a lake which is missing from the map. LANDSAT scans in four different regions of the spectrum, and when these are combined in one print, vegetation shows up in varying shades of red. Crop surveys can be carried out in a fraction of the time needed by other methods. In the San Joaquin valley. California (13), farmland can be seen advancing from the valley towards the Coast range on the left and the Sierra Nevada on the right. Even the Golden Gate bridge, 130 feet wide, can just be seen in a LANDSAT image of the San Francisco Bay region (14). The blue-white plume of sediment, caused by fill operations, shows how these images can be used to monitor pollution, among their many other uses.

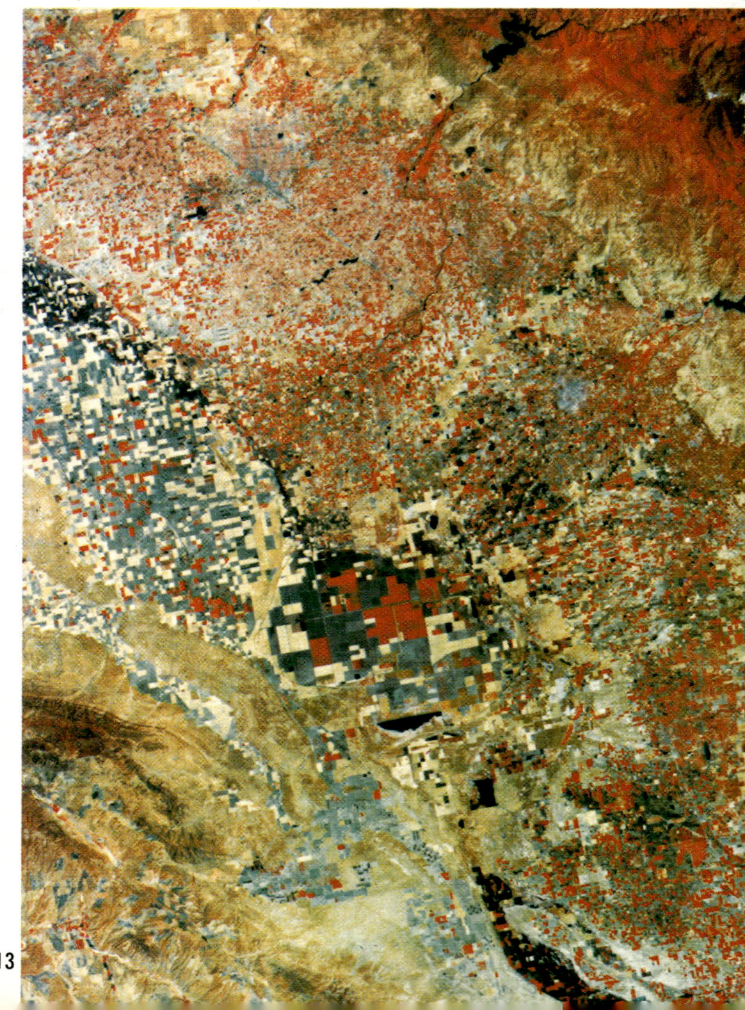

13

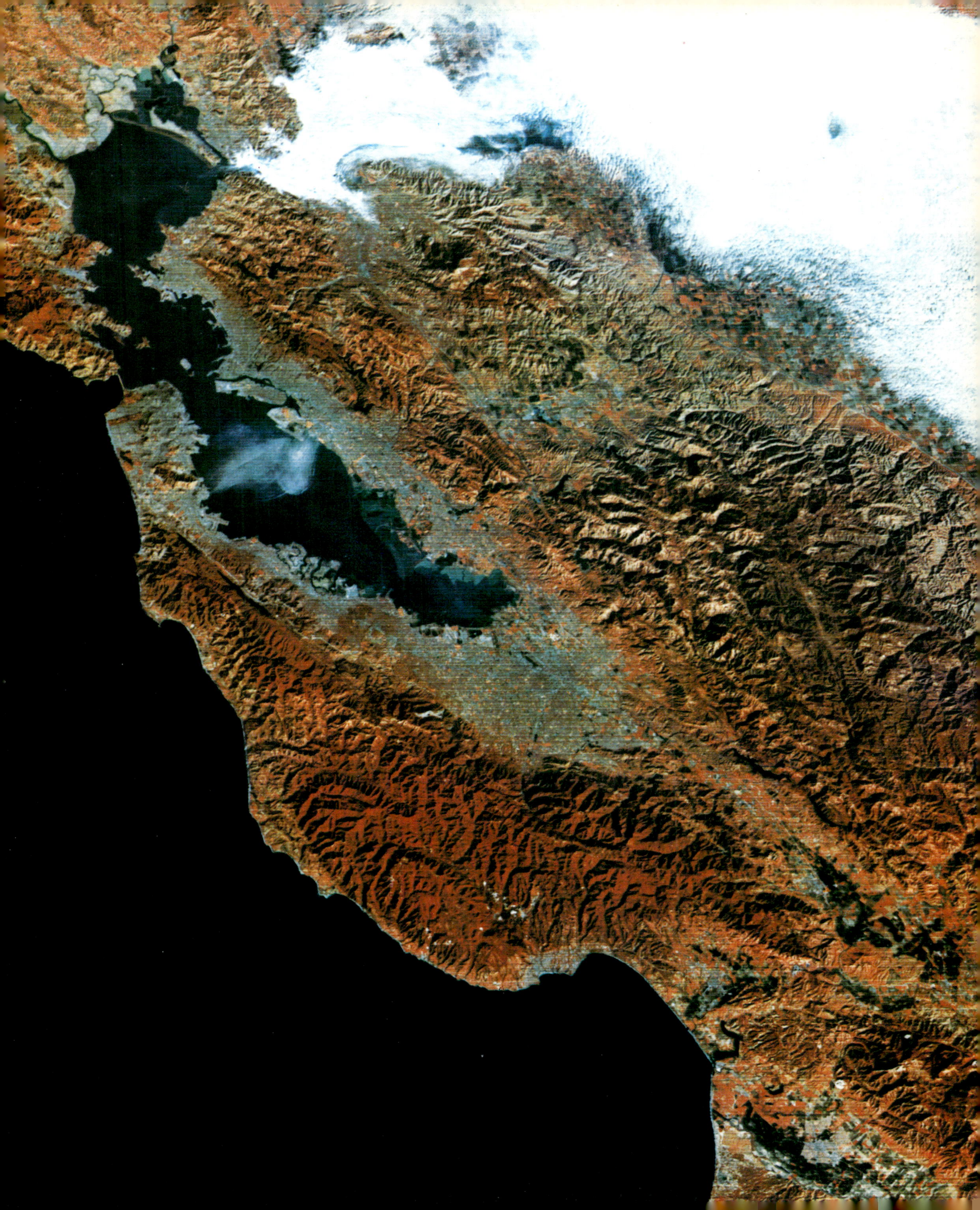

An inexplicable rash of irregular marks on a LANDSAT image (15) called for some detective work on the ground. This is an area of Washington state, between the Columbia River (bottom left) and Mount St Helens. The patches could not be vegetation, which would appear red; closer investigation showed that they were areas of recent 'clearcutting', where all the timber had been felled wholesale – a form of gross over-exploitation that only the satellite can monitor satisfactorily.

15

The Earth's bone structure is revealed by LANDSAT imagery in a way no other method can approach. From Central Australia comes this picture of a complex series of folds (16); the vegetation in the stream beds shows up red, and in the upper centre a large meteorite crater is revealed. A tracery of rivers and tributaries in Central China (17) makes a pattern like the veining of a leaf.

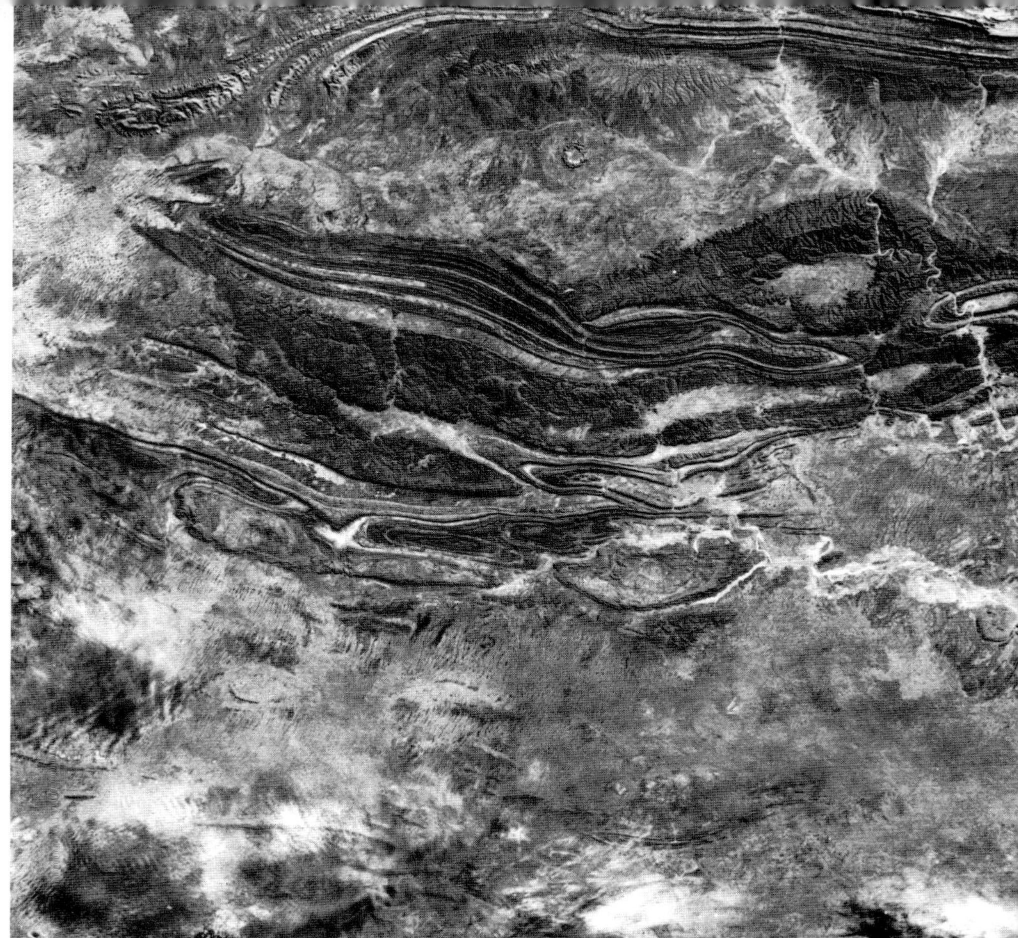

16/17

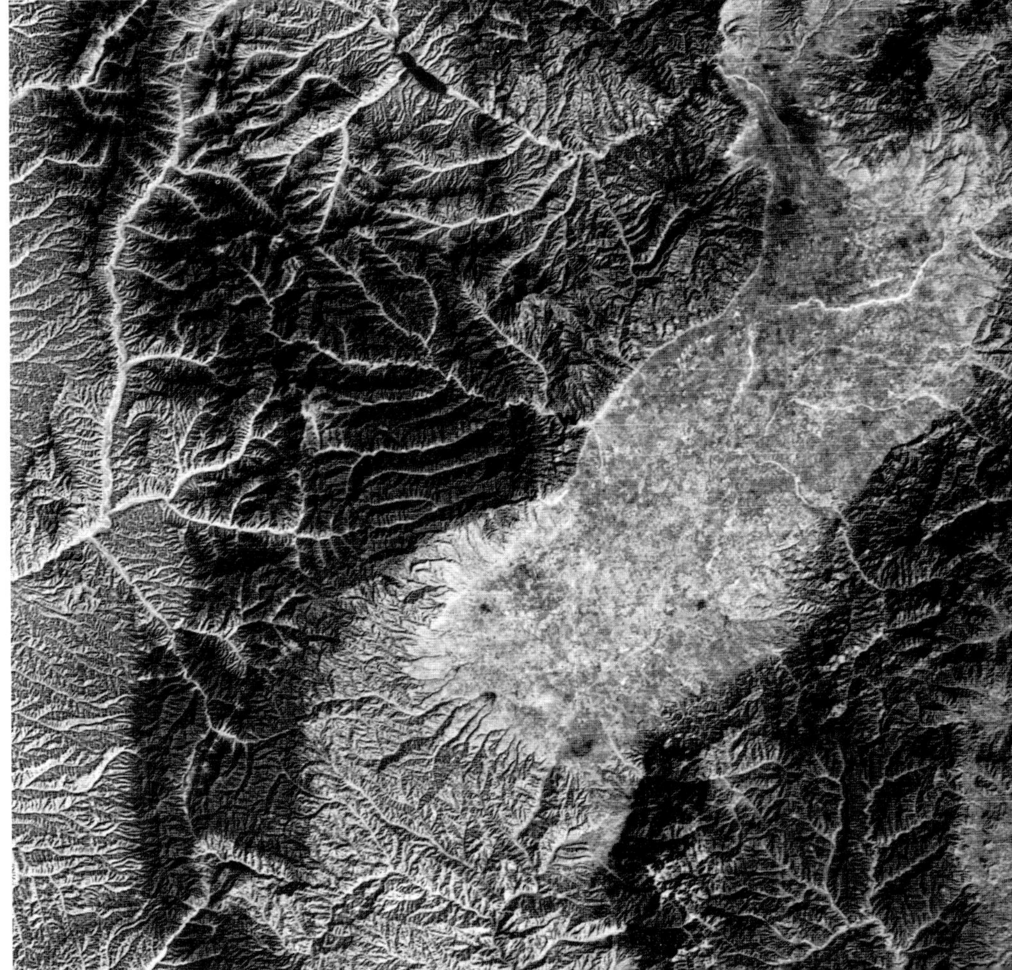

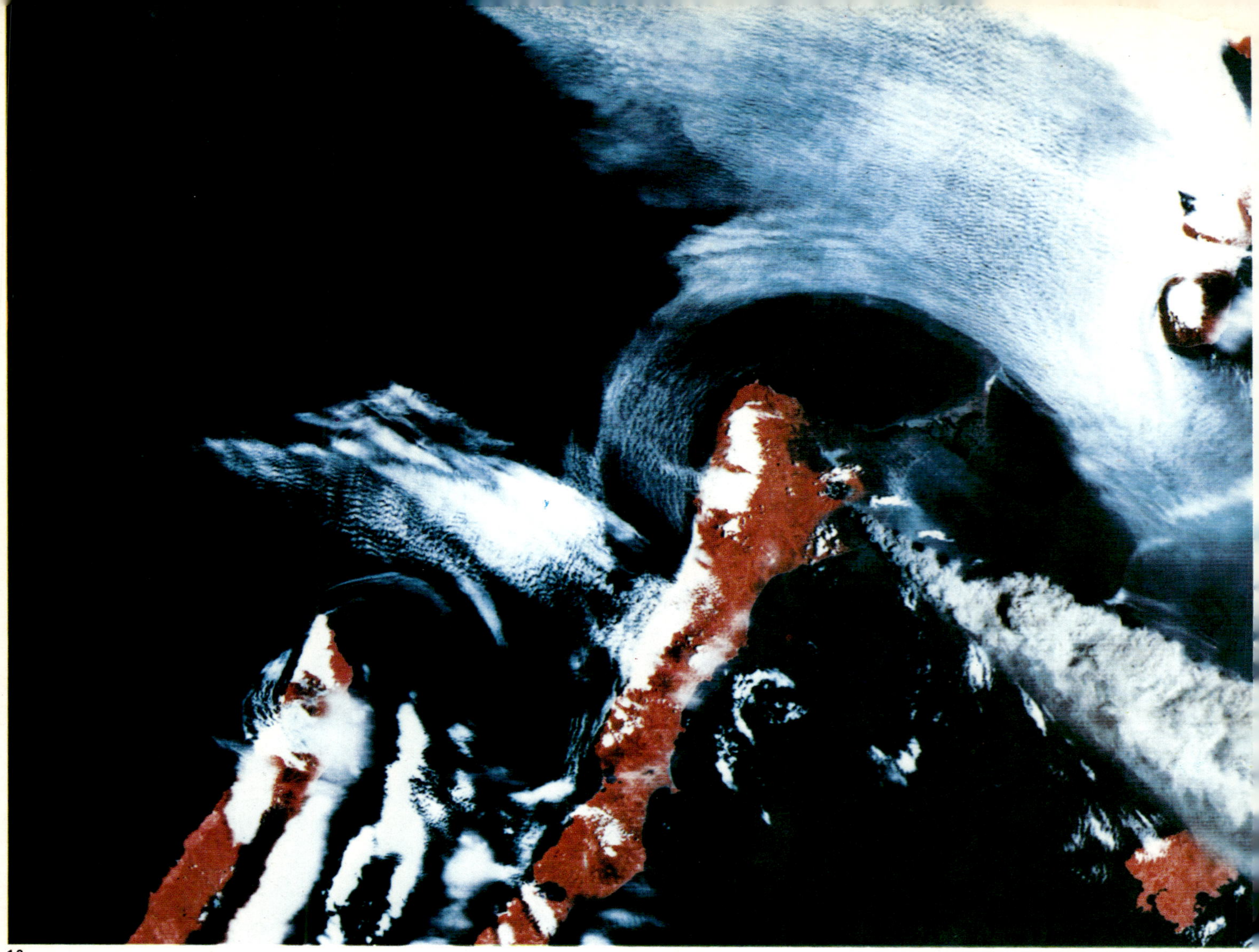

18

Volcanoes, forest fires and other manifestations of the forces of nature can often be observed in satellite images. Passing over the Kurile Islands, for instance, on 16 July 1973, an ERTS (Earth Resources Technology Satellite) caught a volcano in mid-eruption (18). A thin layer of cirrus forms a vortex round the cone. A very large tundra fire in the North-West Territories of Canada (19) can be seen sending a stream of smoke for 125 miles towards Great Bear Lake, an arm of which can just be seen at the top of the picture.

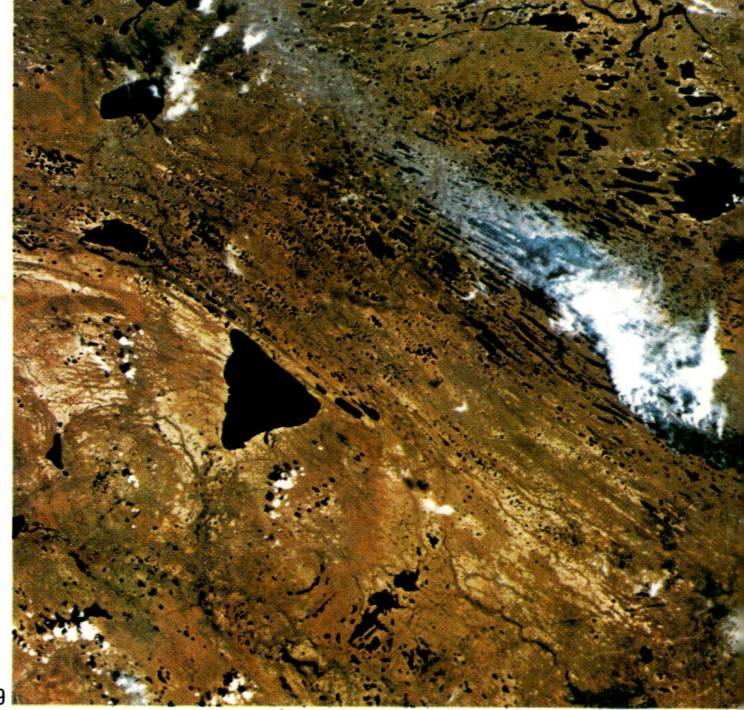

19

The full range of LANDSAT'S information-carrying capacity is shown in this astonishing view of the summit of Kilimanjaro, 'Old Man of the Snows'. Through the white of the cloud cap can be seen the permanent snow of the summit (grey) and a dark zone of minimum vegetation. Below this, concentric bands of dark and light red show zones of increasingly dense tropical growth, shading into a dark area of sparse growth in which snowmelt streams, with heavier growth (red threads), gradually peter out.

20

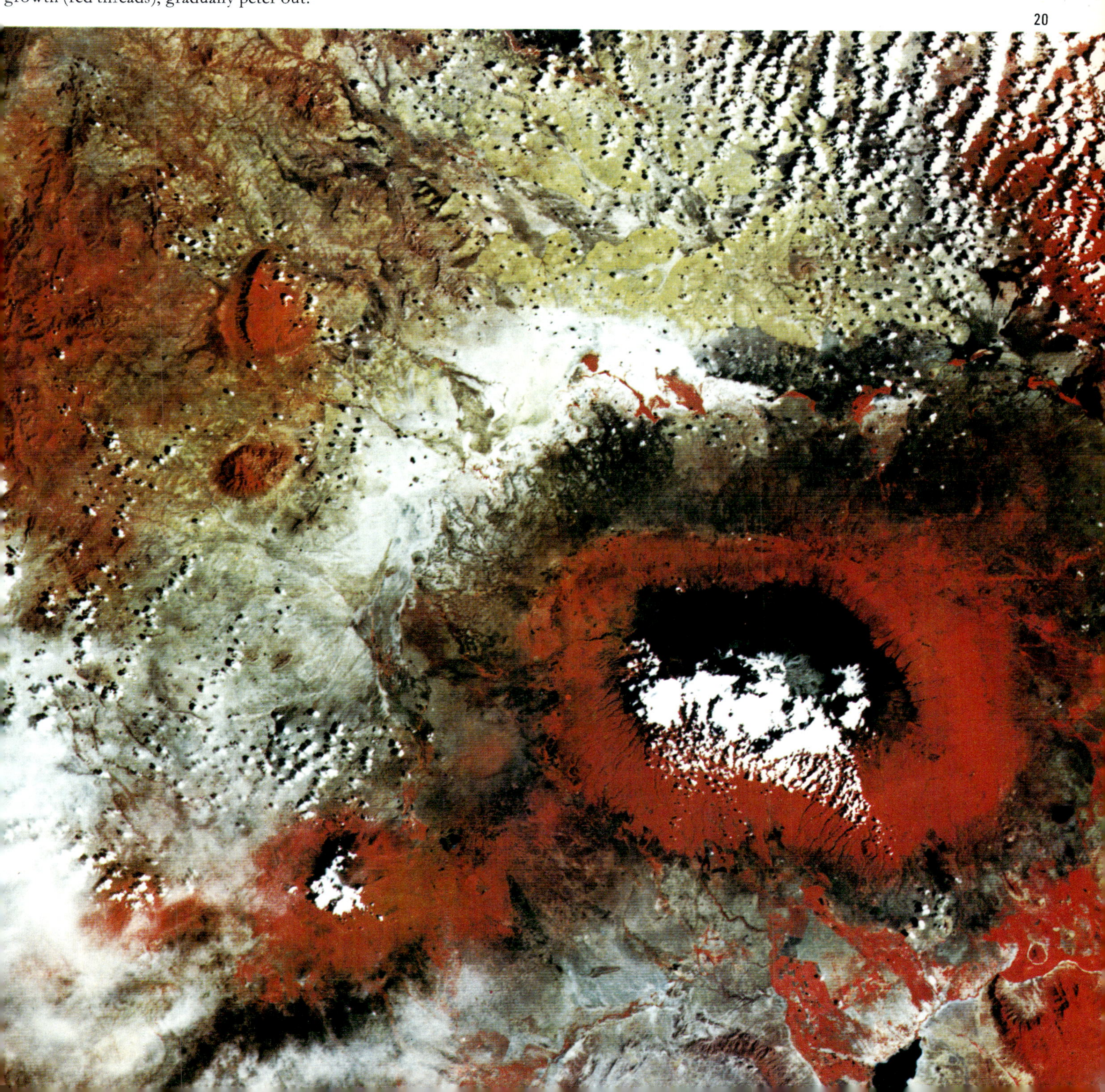

In the Highlands of Scotland the winter snow cover can be accurately delineated by LANDSAT. At the top of the picture the Moray Firth just shows below stratocumulus cloud, with the unmistakable long shape of Loch Ness to the south.

21

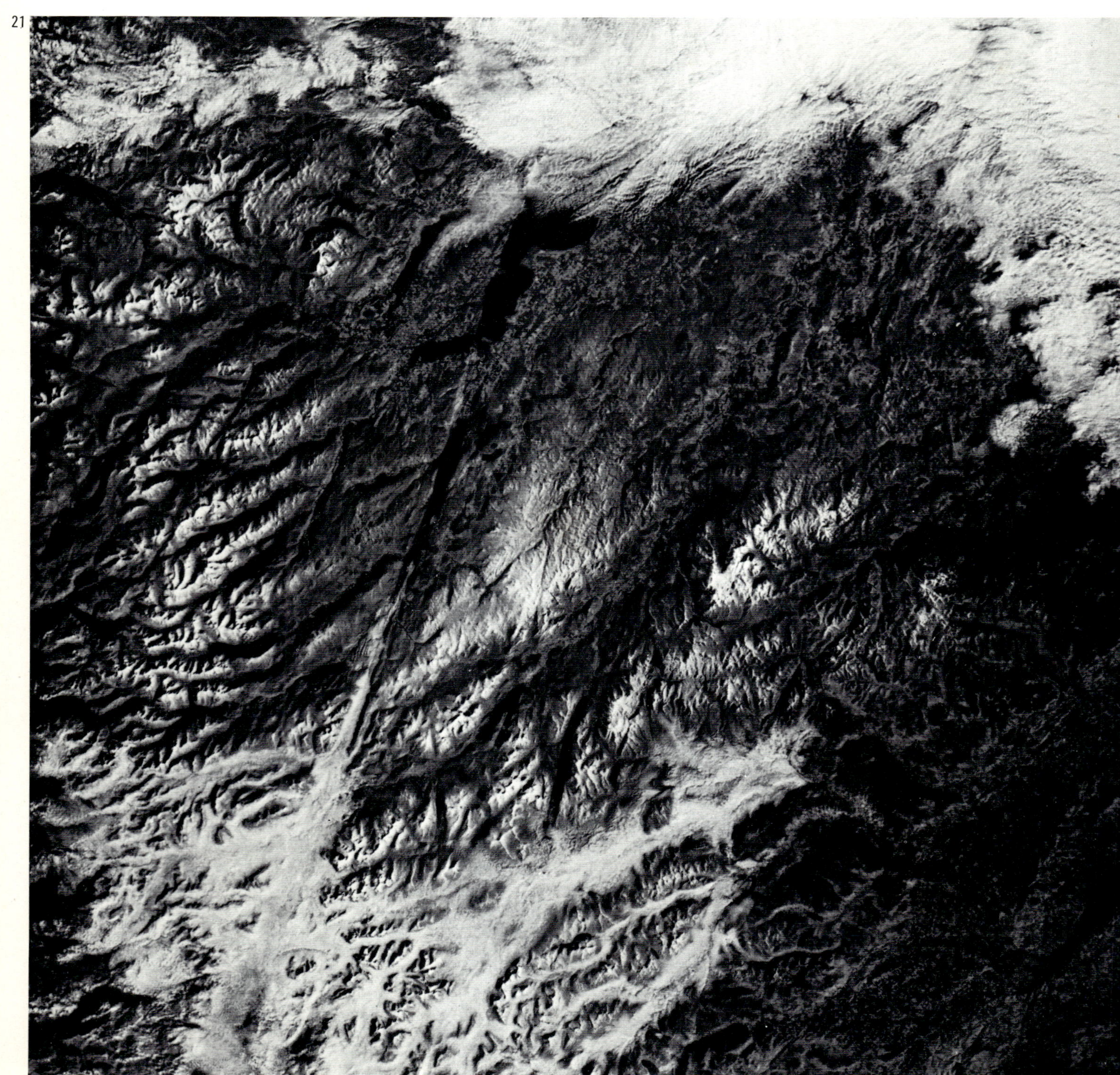

Photographed through cloud, this picture of sea ice off Point Barrow, Alaska, was taken by airborne radar, not by satellite, for radar's wavelength of several centimetres enables it to 'see' through cloud or darkness. The thin white lines mark intervals of five kilometres; the broad band is the area vertically below the aircraft, which the sensor cannot reach. Point Barrow is at the bottom of the picture, with open leads on either side of it appearing dark. The upper part of the picture shows cracked and fissured sea ice.

22

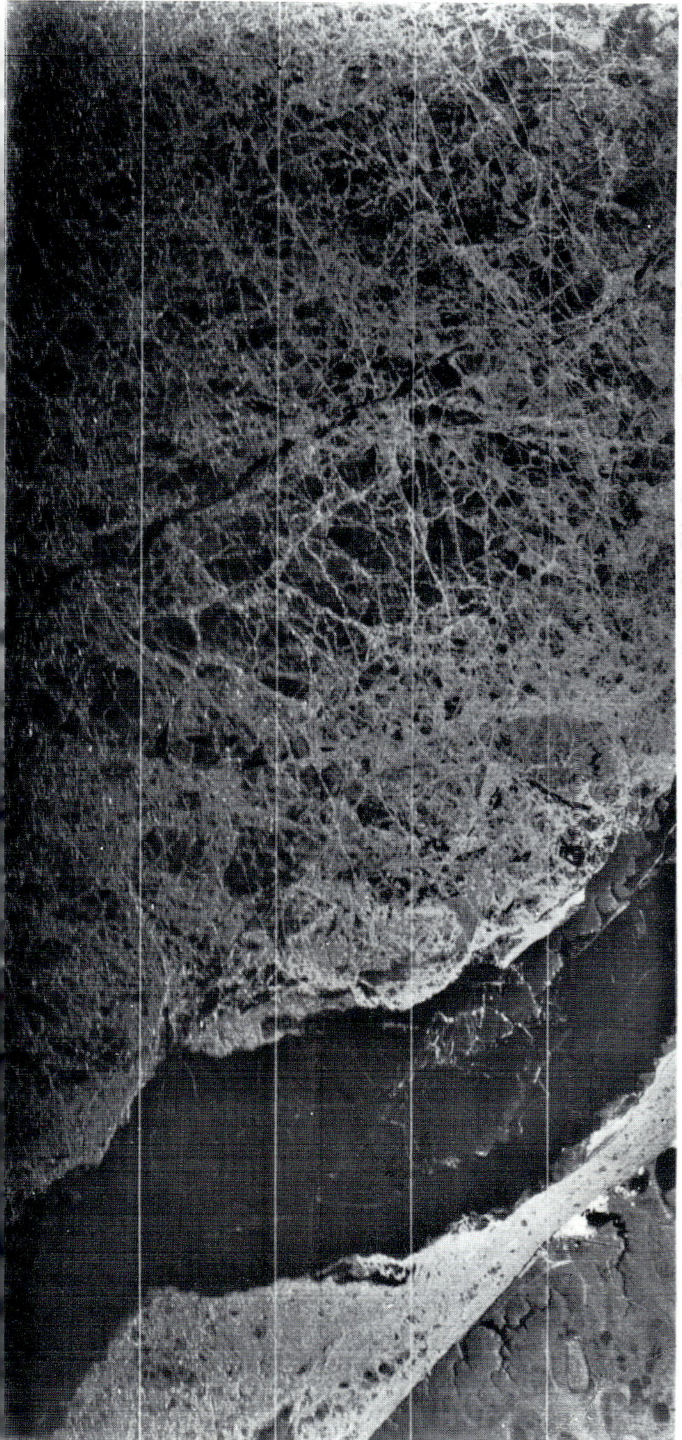

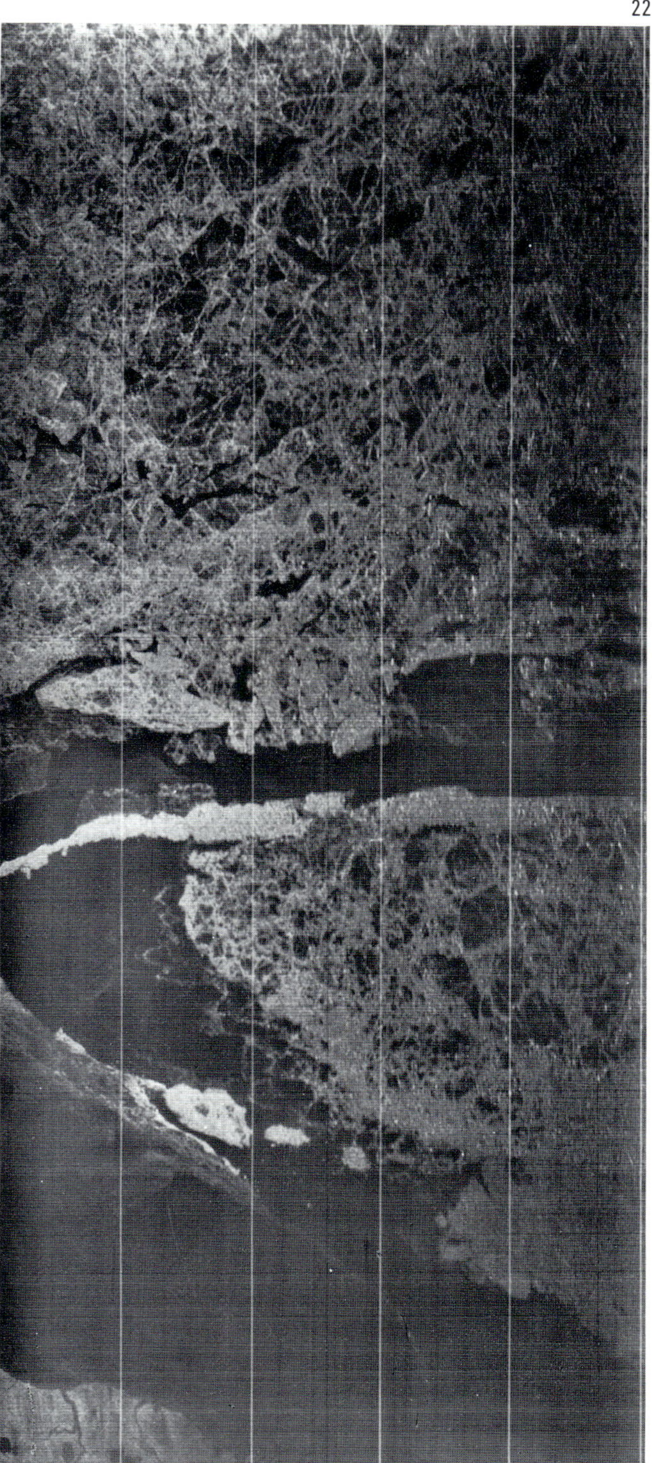

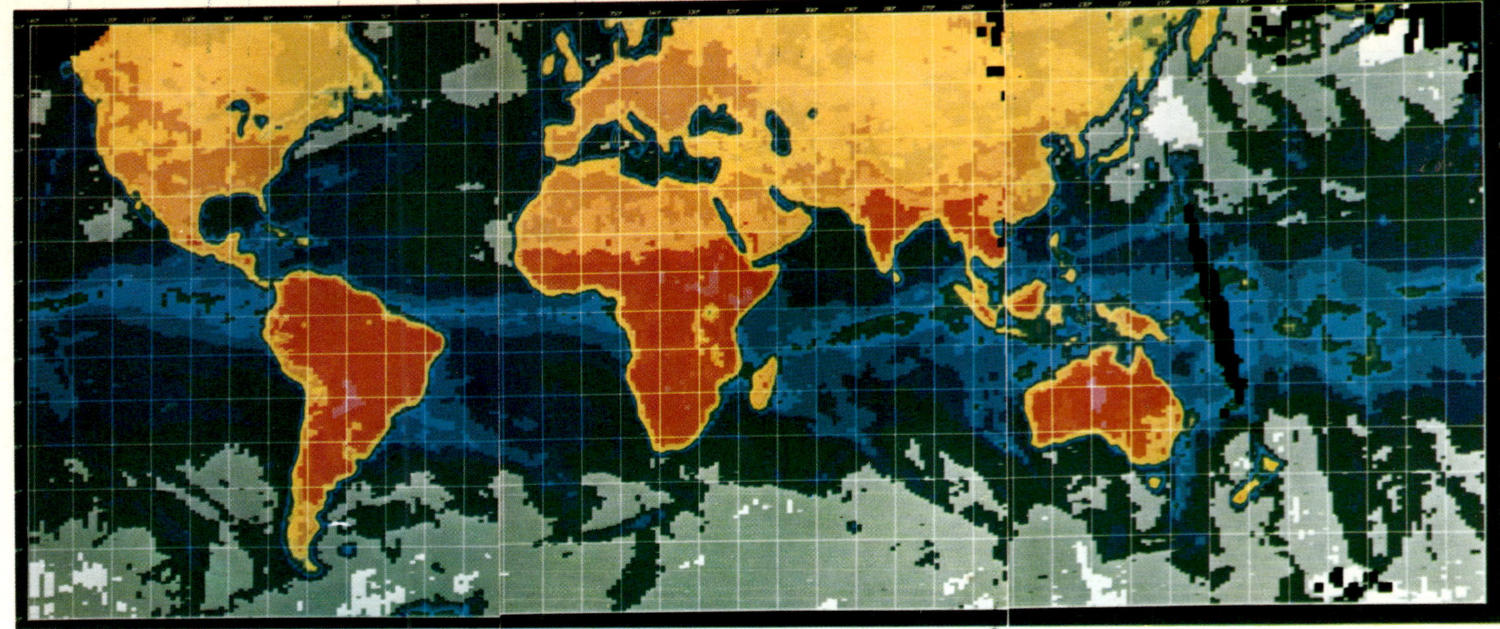
23

An intricate mosaic of coloured squares builds up into a picture packed with information but sometimes difficult to interpret. Microwaves of 1.55 cm wavelength are received by a satellite-borne sensor, which measures the energy of the received signal and translates it into one of a chosen range of colours (see key). This signal is made up of a number of ingredients – surface temperature, soil moisture, reflected temperature and others – and the total effect, the 'brightness temperature', is measured in degrees Kelvin. The first microwave image of the whole world (23) was built up over five days' orbits. Note the sharp line between the Sahara and Central Africa, where soil moisture and vegetation cover raise the brightness temperature. A similar map of Europe (24) shows soil moisture and vegetation brightness temperature rising from north to south. The coloured squares on both these maps are 25 km across.

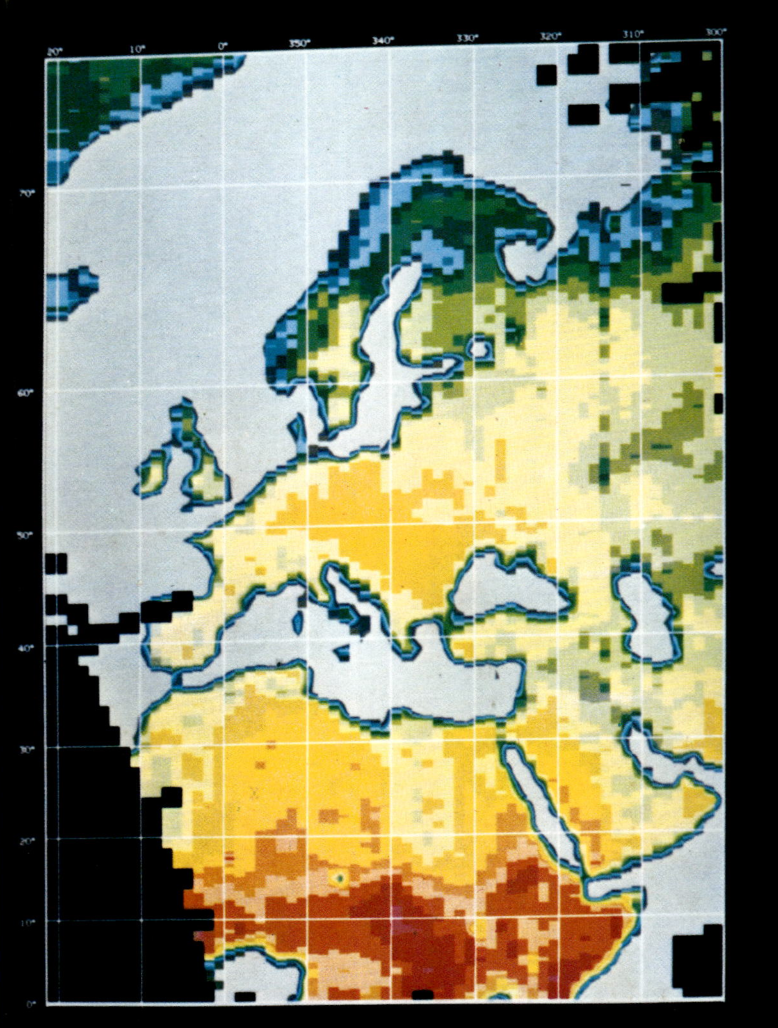

24

Acknowledgments

The illustration sections have been the responsibility of the publishers, who would like to thank all the authors for their unfailing help and advice in the choice of pictures and wording of the captions. Individual acknowledgments are due as follows:

1 Life and the forces of nature

Chapter symbol: Department of Biochemistry, New York University School of Medicine.
1 High Altitude Observatory, Boulder, Colorado.
2 Stanley L. Miller.
3 Professor Sydney W. Fox.
4 Natural History Photographic Agency (photo M. Savonius).
5,6 E. S. Barghoorn.
7,8 M. I. Walker.
9 Heather Angel.
10 Eric Hosking.
11 National Aeronautics and Space Administration.
12 J. M. Terhune/Biofotos.
13 Ianthe Ruthven.

2 The air around us

Chapter symbol: US Department of Commerce, Weather Bureau.
1 National Oceanographic and Atmospheric Administration.
2 National Aeronautics and Space Administration; by courtesy of the Director-General of the Meteorological Office.
3 From the Diana Wyllie filmstrip/slide set *Cloud Forms*.
4 Wayne C. Carlson/Frank W. Lane.
5 US Navy.
6 US Department of Commerce, Weather Bureau.
7 Dewey Bergquist/Frank W. Lane.
8 Paul Huffman/Frank W. Lane.
9,10 From the Diana Wyllie filmstrip/slide set *Cloud Forms*.
11,12 From the Diana Wyllie filmstrip/slide set *Air Pollution*.
13 Parker PR Associates Ltd.

3 Thunder and lightning

Chapter symbol: K. Berger/Frank W. Lane.
1 Maurice Nimmo/Frank W. Lane.
2 Dr W. P. Winn.
3–7 General Electric Co./Frank W. Lane.
8 Professor John Latham.
9 C. B. Moore/Frank W. Lane.
10 T. L. Morgan/Frank W. Lane.
11 Agfa Colour/Frank W. Lane.
12,13 Picturepoint.
14 From the Lockyer Collection in the National Meteorological Library; by courtesy of the Director-General of the Meteorological Office.

4 Snow and avalanches

Chapter symbol: Scientific archives of Carl Zeiss, Oberkochen.
1 Bradford Washburn.
2 Professor Valter Schytt.
3 J. Allan Cash (photo C. de Jaeger).
4 Eidgenössische Institut für Schnee- und Lawinenforschung (Swiss Federal Institute for Snow and Avalanche Research: EISL), Davos (photo Edi Wengi).
5 EISL (photo M. de Quervain).
6 Photograph Collection of the International Glaciological Society.
7 EISL (photo Edi Wengi).
8–11 Photograph Collection of the International Glaciological Society.
12 EISL (photo M. Schild).
13 EISL (photo Air-Zermatt).
14,15 EISL (photo Edi Wengi).
16 EISL (photo M. Schild).
17–20 EISL (photo Edi Wengi).

5 Glaciers and ice ages

Chapter symbol: Bradford Washburn.
1 Photograph Collection of the International Glaciological Society.
2 Charles Swithinbank.
3 W. M. Swithinbank.
4 Charles Swithinbank.
5 Bradford Washburn.
6 Photograph Collection of the International Glaciological Society (photo E. Lachapelle).
7 Photograph Collection of the International Glaciological Society.
8 Professor Valter Schytt.
9 Goddard Space Flight Center, National Aeronautics and Space Administration.
10 Photograph Collection of the International Glaciological Society (photo Austin Post).
11 Photograph Collection of the International Glaciological Society.
12–13 NERC copyright. Reproduced by permission of the Director, Institute of Geological Sciences.
14 Cambridge University Collection: copyright reserved.
15–17 Professor Valter Schytt.
18 J. Allan Cash (photo Robert Sinclair).
19 J. Allan Cash.
20–21 Photograph Collection of the International Glaciological Society.
22 Camera Press.
23 Australian Information Service, London.
24 Professor Valter Schytt.
25,26 Steve McCutcheon/Frank W. Lane.
27 Australian Information Service, London.
28 Charles Swithinbank.
29 US Navy; by courtesy of Charles Swithinbank.

6 Deserts, drought and famine

Chapter symbol: Popperfoto.
1 Camera Press (photo M. Desjardins).
2 Robert Harding Associates (photo Jon Gardey).

3 Australian Information Service, London.
4 Roger Perry.
5–6 Christian Aid.
8 Frants Hartmann/Frank W. Lane.
9 Robert Harding Associates (photo J. Edwardes).
10 Gert Behrens/Ardea.
11 Clem Haagner/Ardea.
12 Robert Harding Associates (photo Jon Gardey).
13,14 Camera Press (photo Josephine Nelson).
15 Camera Press (photo Ered Combs).
16 Jeremy Elston.
17 Clem Haagner/Ardea.
18 Gert Behrens/Ardea.
19 Heather Angel.
20 W. R. Taylor/Ardea.
21 John Karmali/Frank W. Lane.
22 Centre for Overseas Pest Research.
23 Pence/Frank W. Lane.
24 Günter Senfft/Frank W. Lane.
25 Robert Harding Associates (photo Jon Gardey).
26 P. Blasdale/Ardea.
27 Robert Harding Associates (photo D. W. Atkins).
28 Camera Press (photo M. Desjardins).
29 Camera Press (photo Moshe Millner).
20 Su Gooders/Ardea.

7 The flood of waters upon the earth

Chapter symbol: Popperfoto.
1 Australian Information Service, London.
2 Fox Photos.
3 Frank W. Lane.
4 By courtesy of the Royal Netherlands Embassy, London.
5 Gianni Tortoli/Colorific!
6 Foto Locchi, Florence.
7,8 Sunday Times.
9 Australian Information Service, London.
10 Camera Press (photo Ager).
11 Camera Press.
12,13 Alexis N. Vorontzoff.
14 Gianni Tortoli/Colorific!
15 Fox Photos.
16 Frank W. Lane.
17 Keystone Press Agency.
18 American Red Cross/Frank W. Lane.
19,20 Goddard Space Flight Center, National Aeronautics and Space Administration.
21–5 Tennessee Valley Authority.
26 Christian Aid.

8 Volcanoes

Chapter symbol: S. Jónasson/Frank W. Lane.
1 Micek/Frank W. Lane.
2 Edwin Smith.
3 Thames and Hudson archive.
4 Archive of the Austrian National Library, Vienna.
5 Thames and Hudson archive.
6 Thames and Hudson archive.
7 S. Jónasson/Frank W. Lane.
8 Daily Telegraph Colour Library.
9–14 Professor E. A. Vincent.
15,16 Heather Angel.
17 Haroun Tazieff.
18 S. Jónasson/Frank W. Lane.
19,20 US Department of the Interior, National Park Service.
21 Professor E. A. Vincent.
22 Heather Angel.
23 S. Jónasson/Frank W. Lane.
24–7 Sólarfilma, Reykjavik.
28,29 S. Jónasson/Frank W. Lane.
30 High Commissioner for New Zealand.
31 Christoph Krüger.
32 Professor E. A. Vincent.
33 Daily Telegraph Colour Library.
34 Haroun Tazieff.
35 Daily Telegraph Colour Library.

9 Earthquakes and drifting continents

Chapter symbol: Professor N. N. Ambraseys.
1 Camera Press (photo Delaney/Hacker).
2 Adrian Ball Associates.
3 Popperfoto.
4–8 Radio Times Hulton Picture Library.
9,10 John S. Shelton.
11–15 Camera Press.
16–19 John Stanton and John Glasgow.
20,21 American Iron and Steel Institute.
22–8 Professor N. N. Ambraseys.
29 Keystone Press Agency.
30 Professor N. N. Ambraseys.

10 Satellites: a new look at nature

All illustrations by courtesy of Goddard Space Flight Center, National Aeronautics and Space Administration.

For the illustration on p. 173, acknowledgments are due to the Sheffield City Libraries.

Maps by Hanni Bailey.

Diagrams by Peter Bridgewater, John Messenger, T. D. Odle, Mike Ricketts, and Creative Force/London.

Index

Page numbers in italics refer to illustrations